standard catalog of ® AMERICAN MUSCLE CARS
1960-1972

John Gunnell

©2006 Krause Publications
Published by

krause publications
A subsidiary of F+W Media, Inc.

700 East State Street • Iola, WI 54990-0001
715-445-2214 • 888-457-2873
www.krausebooks.com

Our toll-free number to place an order or obtain
a free catalog is (800) 258-0929.

Library of Congress Control Number: 2006931393

ISBN 13: 978-0-89689-433-4
ISBN 10: 0-89689-433-9

Designed by Paul Birling
Edited by Brian Earnest

Printed in the United States of America

DEDICATION

*This book is dedicated to Lightening McQueen, Sally Carrera, Tow Mater and
the other Disney-Pixar Cars movie characters who are creating a new generation of
auto enthusiasts. We need them! Rock on!*

FOREWORD

The Standard Catalog of American Muscle Cars 1960-1972 is the latest book in our "Standard Catalog" series. It combines our successful "standardized database" approach to automotive history with a unique focus on the hottest models and model-options made during the classic muscle car era. Each listing gives you what you expect in a Standard Catalog (styling, features, model codes, price, weight, production total, engine info and options), but the descriptions are targeted to specific cars with special packages and all the wildest performance engines.

In other words, we are not going to lump all Super Sports, Mustangs or Coronets together as if they are equal. Instead, we are going to focus on the most awesome versions of these street prowlers such as the SS 454 with the LS6, the Mustang Boss 429 and the Hemi Super Bee. To the extent that research is available — and it varies by car — we are giving you the real nitty-gritty in this book. In most cases, you'll be able to pinpoint exactly what your muscle car should have and how many just like it were built. And you won't have to wade through all the "small-blocks" that shared the same body, but weren't really muscle cars in the purest sense.

Putting all the genuine muscle cars in the spotlight wasn't an easy task, because the automakers that built these cars didn't always break down the information about them the way we would like to have it today. For example, it is not always clear what factories certain cars were built in or what options were available because of the way that factory options were listed in our sources. A fat white-lettered tire may have been available as an option on every Firebird or the option may have been limited to only Formulas and Trans Ams or even to

only Trans Ams. Don't get me wrong, we have gone through the options list and edited them as best we could to fit only the muscle cars, but here again, we are open to hearing from you about clarification on option applications. Another important thing to note is that when tire and engine options are listed, the prices given are the amounts added when upgrades were made to standard equipment. In other words, adding those F60-15 white letter tires may have cost $50, but that was really $50 over the cost of the standard G78-15 black sidewall tires.

It is also important to note that there is some degree of controversey in the hobby about things like Hemi production or how many Super-Duty Pontiac were built with aluminum front end sheet metal and "Swiss cheese" frames. We didn't "make up" any of the numbers used in this catalog, but there may be some collectors who use and rely on different numbers.

Be all the above as it may, we feel this first edition of *The Standard Catalog of American Muscle Cars 1960-1972* does an excetional job of creating a standardized database for muscle car collectors. And, as always, we're committed to "building" this book as time goes on. Our other big catalogs on prewar car, postwar cars, late-model cars, imported cars and light-duty trucks started off the same way and have become essential reference books for millions of collectors. *The Standard Catalog of American Muscle Cars 1960-1972* is your book. We hope you'll use it and enjoy it when you're "playing with your toys" and we invite your input and comments on how we can improve this dynamite database as time goes on.

John Gunnell

May 5, 2006

CONTENTS

standard catalog of® AMERICAN
MUSCLE CARS
1960-1972

CONTENTS

JERRY HEASLEY

INTRODUCTION

In some people's minds, Hudson, Oldsmobile and Chrysler got the muscle-car ball rolling. In Hudson's case, it hopped up its big flathead six with "Twin-H" power and started winning early stock car races. Then Olds took the step of stuffing a big "mill" into its "little" 88 body and created the first "super car." Chrysler's awesome 300 Letter Car was different than the trim-size Rocket 88 — but the basic formula was the same: lots of horsepower per pound. With dual carbs on the brutal "Firepower Hemi," the 300 could move like the Cannonball Express on a downhill run from on top of Old Smokey.

By the early '60s the "Yank Tank" Ford Galaxies and Chevy Impalas were being issued in high-performance packages with alpha-numerical names like SS and 500 XL. By that time Chrysler's "Beautiful Brute" was up to letters F and G. Pontiac joined in the name game with its straightforward "Super Duty" designator.

Pontiac, by the way, gets the nod as originator of the muscle-car niche for turning its "curved-dash Tempest" into the GTO. The three-letter option included what became the uniform of muscle cars — bucket seats, a floor shifter, a scooped hood, and fat red-lined tires. The Bonneville engine was stuffed under the hood and the hot setup — memorialized in song — was "three deuces and a four-speed and a 389." Maverick exec John DeLorean snuck the car to market as an extra-cost option. Breaking the rules paid off in big-time sales numbers.

Before the decade ended, Gee-Tee-O clones were rolling out of GM, Ford and Chrysler factories from coast to coast. With the factories building ready-made street performance cars, no one needed a subscription to *Hot Rod* magazine to enjoy going fast in a car that you could "build" to your personal taste. Instead of visiting Honest Charlie's Speed Shop, all you had to do was go to the nearest car dealer and sign on the dotted line.

Pretty soon the trend towards street-and-strip performance that began with big-engined mid-size cars began to show up in additional formats. There were muscular compacts, muscular Corvettes, muscular versions of the Mustang-inspired pony cars, muscular full-size cars and even a couple of muscle station wagons. (Some wagons, in fact, had weight-distribution characteristics that made them great drag racers.) Another change in the muscle car was its move from the budget-priced bracket into more of the luxury niche. Then, there was a backlash reaction that inspired the Road Runner, Super Bee, GTO Judge and other "stripper" models.

Although muscle-car sales were never a really big chunk of the total market, they were significant. In fact, the company's performance image pushed Pontiac into third place in industry sales throughout the '60s. When you added its muscle car deliveries to its other business, it made Pontiac a giant for 10 years. Muscle cars also made headlines, projected a specialty image and attracted younger customers who tended to remain brand loyal as they outgrew their muscle-car years.

The classic muscle-car era didn't last very long. It was at its peak from the early '60s to the early '70s and lasted no more than a decade and a half from its start to its close. Today, we are seeing prices for rare muscle cars surpass those being paid for the classical cars of the Great Gatsby era. *The Standard Catalog of American Muscle Cars 1960-1972* is your personal guide to the burning hot muscle-car marketplace.

AMC MUSCLE 1965-72

AMC

American Motors Corp. (AMC) was formed when Nash-Kelvinator and Hudson merged in 1954. Just before the start of 1958, AMC decided to discontinue Nash and Hudson. Instead, it would concentrate on selling a revised series of cars, including a new version of the original Rambler compact. AMC was the only major U.S. automaker to increase sales in the recession year of 1958. The consumer trend was to smaller cars and the Rambler was the only U.S. compact car around. AMC was at the right place at the right time. Rambler registrations doubled for 1959.

The first true AMC/Rambler V-8 appeared in 1956 as the 250-cid engine. This was a lightweight engine that tipped the scales at around 600 lbs. in most configurations. From the start, it was designed to be the stepping-off point for a whole new family of V-8 engines originally known as Rambler V-8s and later thought of as AMC V-8s. Large 4.75-in. bore spacing allowed for subsequent increases in displacement. The bore size varied from 3 1/2 inches in the original 250-cid version to four inches in a 327-cid version that bowed in 1957 and lasted through 1966 to 3 3/4 inches in the 287-cid version that bowed in 1963 and lasted through 1966.

The 327-powered Rambler Rebel of 1957 was the first AMC product to hint that muscle cars would be part of the company's future. The fastback-styled 1965 Marlin was the first AMC car to take off after the muscle car pack. It was inspired by cars like the Galaxie "fastroof," the Barracuda, the Mustang 2 + 2 and GM's full-size '65 fastbacks. With two V-8s available, the Marlin offered some snappy driving to go with its streamlined look.

In 1966, AMC upped the ante in the power department. A carefully designed intake system promoted a high volumetric efficiency of 77 percent and uniform mixture distribution to all cylinders. Starting with the Special Edition 1966-1/2 Rambler American Rogue, a totally new "thinwall casting" engine family starting at 290 cid was introduced. This new engine series was lighter than the previous 250- through 327-cid engine family was and made the Rouge suitable for the Stoplight Grand Prix. The old-style 287/327 cid V-8s were still used in the Classic and Ambassador until the end of the 1966 model run. In 1967, the continued Rouge and the hotter-engined Marlin represented AMC's muscle car contenders.

JERRY HEASLEY

The AMC 290 was made available in a four-barrel version with 10.0:1 compression and a thirst for premium fuel. In 1968, Kaplan Engineering bored this motor up to 302 cid to get the most out of it without breaking the Sports Car Club of America's (SCCA) Trans-Am rules. A new AMC two-seat sports car dubbed the AMX came out for performance fans. Even with the 290 it was fast, but a pair of larger V-8s was optional.

Also in 1968 1/2, a new 390-cid V-8 was released. Like the other AMC "mills," it was a 90-degree overhead valve engine with "premium" high nickel-content Cast-iron block and heads (as all AMC V-8s were since 1956). It had a 4.17 x 3.57-in. Bore and stroke and a 10.2:1 compression ratio, generated 315 hp and an incredible 435 lbs.-ft. of torque at only 3,200 rpm. The horsepower rating would later climb to as high as 340 hp in cars like the Rebel Machine.

In 1970, the 290-cid engine was stroked to get 304 cid and the 343 was similarly modified to get 360 cid. AMC released its largest displacement ever 401-cid V-8 in Javelins, Matadors and Ambassadors in 1971 and made it available through 1974 except for approximately 84 401s installed in Matador fleet and police sedans in 1975. It is thought that five 401s were installed in 1975 Matador coupes. The 401 was basically a stroked 390. AMC's Marketing Department wanted an over-400-cid motor to compete with the "Big Three's" big block V-8s. "401" sounded like a big block, though it was not. It should be noted that all the 290, 304, 343, 360, 401 V-8s were "medium-block"-sized engines and not small or big blocks in size and weight.

From 1955 to 1972, all optional four-barrel engines required premium leaded (ethyl) fuel due to the higher compression ratios. AMC V-8s were used in certain AMC/Jeep and Chrysler/Jeep products from 1970 through circa 1992.

1965 MARLIN

1965 Marlin

The 1965 Marlin was introduced in February 1965 as a midyear addition to the line. It was basically a Rambler Classic with special fastback roof styling. Different taillights were used, but the grille was of the Classic type with the vertical division bars removed. A special Marlin hood ornament was used. The Marlin was American Motors Corp.'s answer to the Ford Mustang, but could accommodate six passengers, as opposed to only four in the Mustang.

Series Number	Body/Style Number	Body Type & Seating	Factory Price	Shipping Weight	Production Total
MARLIN — SERIES 50 — V-8					
50	6559-7	2d FsBk-6P	$2,931	3,367 lbs.	8,322

NOTE: Price and weight for base V-8. Production total for all V-8.

ENGINES

BASE V-8: Overhead valves. Cast-iron block. Displacement: 287 cid. Bore and stroke: 3 3/4 x 3 1/4 inches. Compression ratio: 8.7:1. Advertised hp: 198 at 4700 rpm. Advertised torque: 280 at 2600 rpm. Recommended idle speed: 475 rpm. Five main bearings. Hydraulic valve lifters (non-adjustable). Carburetor: Carburetor: Holley two-barrel model 2290-2699. Cooling system capacity: 18 qts. without heater, 19 qts. with heater. Crankcase capacity less filter: 4 qt. Single exhaust. Standard V-8.

OPTIONAL V-8: Overhead valves. Cast-iron block. Displacement: 327 cid. Bore and stroke: 4 x 3 1/4 inches. Compression ratio: 9.7:1. Advertised hp: 270 at 4700 rpm. Advertised torque: 360 at 2600 rpm. Recommended idle speed: 475 rpm. Five main bearings. Hydraulic valve lifters (non-adjustable). Carburetor: Holley four-barrel model 4150-3044 Single exhaust system. Optional V-8.

OPTIONS

Air conditioner adaptor group with heavy-duty radiator and seven-amp battery ($19). All-Season air conditioner ($312.05). Power-saver fan required with V-8 ($321). 40-amp alternator ($8.95). Appearance Group A includes rocker panel moldings, wheel opening moldings and spinner wheel discs ($60.30). Appearance Group B, includes same as above except wire wheelcovers for Marlin ($94.90). Back-up lights ($10.70). Heavy-duty battery ($6.50). Front disc brakes, includes power assist ($79.95). Slim bucket seats with front armrest and cushion ($99.50). Wide bucket seats without con¬sole, 440/770 reclining seats required ($59.50). Slim front bucket seats with armrest and console, requires reclining seats ($119.50. Front bumper guards ($11.50). Front and rear bumper guards ($23). Electric clock ($15.95). Two-tone paint ($19.95). Special paint color application ($29.50). Dowgard coolant ($5). Heavy-duty cooling system ($14.95). California crankcase ventilation ($5.05). 327-cid V-8 four-barrel engine ($81.95). Rear foam seat cushion ($9.95). Individually adjustable front seats ($20). Reclining front seat ($25.50). Tinted glass ($45.50). Tinted windshield only, ($19.95). Headrest ($12). Light Group ($19.60). Inside tilt mirror ($4.95). Outside mirror, either side ($5.30). Outside rearview mirror with remote-control ($11.95). Oil-bath air cleaner with L-head ($7.15). Padded panel and visors ($19.95). Padded visors ($4.50). Power brakes ($42.95). Power Saver fan ($19.60). Power steering ($85.95). Power tailgate window ($31.95). Front power windows ($59.50). Power front and rear windows ($102.25). Push-button radio and antenna in ($58.50). Push-button AM/FM radio ($129.30). DuoCoustic rear speaker ($12.60). VibraTone rear speaker ($40.50). Heavy-duty radiator in American ($3.35). Heavy-duty radiator ($5.35). Airliner reclining seats ($25.50). Front seat belt deletion ($11 credit). Retractable front seat belts ($7.50). Retractable front and non-retractable rear seat belts ($26.70). Retractable seat belts front and rear ($45.80). Heavy-duty front and rear shocks ($3.85). Heavy-duty front and rear springs, in American ($5.15 cars/$6.55 wagons). Heavy-duty front and rear shocks and rear springs ($5.05). Heavy-duty front and rear extended springs ($7.30). Adjustable steering wheel, requires automatic transmission ($43). Flash-O-Matic transmission ($193.65). Flash-O-Matic Shift Command transmission, requires slim bucket seats ($208.65). Twin Stick transmission ($134.50-$147.50). Twin-Grip differential ($37.55-$42.70). Undercoating ($17.20). Wheel discs ($20.55). Wheel discs with spinners ($14.05-$34.55). Wire wheelcovers with spinners ($48.70-$69.15). Windshield washer ($11.95). Electric wipers ($10.95). Vinyl upholstery ($15.00-$24.50). Credit for Weather-Eye heater deletion ($72-$79). Various tire options.

AMC

1966 ROGUE

"Do Rogues really come with rally stripes?"

"No, but with the new engine
they drive that way."

'66 Rambler American Rogue

1966 Rogue

The Rambler Rogue Typhoon V-8 arrived on April 7, 1966. It came standard with an anemic 199-cid/128-hp six-cylinder engine, but the big news was that a brand-new V-8 was optional equipment. The new, thinwall AMC 290-cid V-8 was introduced in a limited number of 1966 Rogue hardtops. Most, but not all, of these Rogues were either Sun Gold with black roof and trunk lid or Solar Yellow with a black roof and trunk lid. This engine was brought out in the small American line to try to somewhat compete with the highly successful Ford Mustang. The two-barrel 290 spewed out 200 hp, which was good for grocery getting. A four-barrel version with 225 hp was aimed at the high-performance set. With the 225-hp "Typhoon 290" V-8, the '66 Rogue was a definite "break-the-mold" machine for AMC. You got a choice of Shift Command automatic or the American's first four-speed manual gearbox — a Borg-Warner unit. Also included were spinner wheel covers, a blacked-out grille, V-8 badges on the rear fenders, power steering and power brakes.

Series Number	Body/Style Number	Body Type & Seating	Factory Price	Shipping Weight	Production Total
ROGUE — SERIES 10 — V-8					
10	6609-7	2d HT-5P	$2,668	2,926 lbs.	2,353

ENGINE

OPTIONAL V-8: Overhead valves. Cast-iron block. Displacement: 290 cid. Bore and stroke: 3.75 x 3.28 inches. Compression ratio: 10.0:1. Advertised hp: 225 at 4700 rpm. Advertised torque: 300 at 3200 rpm. Recommended idle speed: 600 rpm. Five main bearings. Hydraulic valve lifters (non-adjustable). Carburetor: Carter AFB four-barrel. Exhaust: Single exhaust with crossover. (Duals not available).

OPTIONS

Power brakes ($42). Power steering ($84). Air conditioning ($303). Front disc brakes ($91). Two-tone paint. Turbo-cast wheelcovers. Wire wheelcovers with spinners. Slim band whitewall tires. Bumper guards with rubber facings. Black vinyl-covered hardtop roof. Safety headrests. Tachometer. Rear seat foam cushions. Cruise Command speed control, automatic transmis¬sion mandatory. Special black two-tone paint, for Rogue with vinyl roof. AM all-transistor radio. Air-Guard exhaust emissions control system. Four-Way hazard warning signals. Remote control left-hand outside rearview mirror. Automatic transmission ($187). Four-speed manual floor shift transmission. American six-cylinder Positive Traction rear axle.

1966 MARLIN

1966 Marlin

The "fish car" was back for another season, but it didn't even "net" as many buyers as the original had. It was a great idea, but even an AMC lover has to admit that a clean sheet of paper approach would have worked better than grafting a helldriver's ramp on the top of the Rambler Classic. The important thing, though, was AMC's growing focus on the youth-car market.

The 1966 Marlin received few changes. A new grille was used and many features, formerly standard, were now optional. This included power steering and brakes. The price dropped by nearly $500. And the Rambler nameplate was deleted from the rear of the car.

Series Number	Body/Style Number	Body Type & Seating	Factory Price	Shipping Weight	Production Total
MARLIN — SERIES 50 — V-8					
50	6659-7	2d Fsbk-6P	$2,707	3,331 lbs.	3374

NOTE: Price and weight for base V-8. Production total for all V-8.

ENGINES

BASE V-8: Overhead valves. Cast-iron block. Displacement: 287 cid. Bore and stroke: 3 3/4 x 3 1/4 inches. Compression ratio: 8.7:1. Advertised hp: 198 at 4700 rpm. Advertised torque: 280 at 2600 rpm. Recommended idle speed: 550 rpm. Five main bearings. Hydraulic valve lifters (non-adjustable). Carburetor: Carburetor: Holley two-barrel model 2209-3305. Single exhaust.

OPTIONAL V-8: Overhead valves. Cast-iron block. Displacement: 327 cid. Bore and stroke: 4 x 3 1/4 inches. Compression ratio: 8.7:1. Advertised hp: 250 at 4700 rpm. Advertised torque: 340 at 2600 rpm. Recommended idle speed: 550 rpm. Five main bearings. Hydraulic valve lifters (non-adjustable). Carburetor: Carburetor: Holley two-barrel model 2209-3305. Single exhaust system.

OPTIONAL V-8: Overhead valves. Cast-iron block. Displacement: 327 cid. Bore and stroke: 4 x 3 1/4 inches. Compression ratio: 9.7:1. Advertised hp: 270 at 4700 rpm. Advertised torque: 360 at 2600 rpm. Recommended idle speed: 475 rpm. Five main bearings. Hydraulic valve lifters (non-adjustable). Carburetor: Holley four-barrel model 4160-3201. Single exhaust system.

OPTIONS

Power brakes ($42). Power steering ($84). Air conditioning ($319). Power steering ($95). Front disc brakes ($91). Two-tone paint. Turbo-cast wheelcovers. Wire wheelcovers with spinners. Slim band whitewall tires. Bumper guards with rubber facings. Black vinyl-covered hardtop roof. Reclining seats, bucket-type. Safety headrests. Tachometer. Appearance group with wheel discs, rocker and wheelhouse moldings. Cruise Command speed control, automatic transmission mandatory. Air-Guard, exhaust emissions control system. Four-Way hazard warning signals. Remote control left-hand outside rearview mirror. AM/FM all transistor radio. Automatic transmission ($187). Four-speed manual floor shift transmission. 327-cid/250-hp two-barrel V-8 ($32). 327-cid/270-hp four-barrel V-8 ($65). Positive traction rear axle was optional.

AMC

1967 ROGUE

JERRY HEASLEY

1967 Rogue

The 1967 Rambler American models used the same body styling as the previous year's models, with only minor changes. New taillamps were of the same, rectangular shape, but were shorter and higher. The Rouge was based on the American and this year cameas both a two-door hardtop and a convertible. A new side molding decorated Rogues. It was positioned lower on the beltline. Once again, an inline six was the standard engine, but the Rouge didn't become a real muscle car until you added an optional V-8. A 343-cid V-8 with four-barrel carburetion was also available as optional equipment.

A total of 2,196 Rouges were put together this year and less than 300 — make that less than 290 — were ragtops. Too bad AMC didn't have the resources to give this pint-sized performance package the promotional push that the Chevy Nova and Dodge Dart were getting. With more sales on the charts, AMC might have dropped in a bigger engine and had itself a "scrambler" a couple of years earlier. If you're into rare muscle, go for a Rouge ragtop.

Series Number	Body/Style Number	Body Type & Seating	Factory Price	Shipping Weight	Production Total
ROGUE — SERIES 01 — V-8					
01	6709-7	2d HT-5P	$2,379	2,896 lbs.	1,908
01	6707-7	2d Conv-6P	$2,555	3,054 lbs.	288

NOTE: Price and weight for base V-8. Production total for all V-8.

ENGINES

OPTIONAL V-8: Overhead valves. Cast-iron block. Displacement: 290 cid. Bore and stroke: 3.75 x 3.28 inches. Compression ratio: 10.0:1. Advertised hp: 225 at 4700 rpm. Advertised torque: 300 at 3200 rpm. Recommended idle speed: 600 rpm. Five main bearings. Hydraulic valve lifters (non-adjustable). Carburetor: Carter AFB four-barrel. Single exhaust with crossover. (Duals not available.)

OPTIONAL V-8: Overhead valves. Cast-iron block. Displacement: 343 cid. Bore and stroke: 4.08 x 3.28 inches. Compression ratio: 10.2:1. Advertised hp: 280 at 4800 rpm. Advertised torque: 365 at 3000 rpm. Recommended idle speed: 600 rpm. Five main bearings. Hydraulic valve lifters (non-adjustable). Carburetor: Carter AFB four-barrel. Exhaust system: Single with crossover, standard, duals optional on all but American.

(Note: the 343 four-barrel V-8 was available half-year in the 1967 model run in the American two-door sedan, hardtop and, rumored, the convertible. Any American model ordered with this motor was called a "Super American" at dealers and on the street, but not officially by AMC. Only an unknown handful of these cars were ordered and sold by dealers as it was well known that the 1967 American body was not designed to take this powerful of a motor and body integrity was a major problem, especially in the hardtop and very much so in the convertible. No four-door sedans or wagons are known to have received a 343 four-barrel engine, though it is possible an "insider" or special dealer might have gotten one.)

OPTIONS

All-transistor manual radio ($49). All-transistor push-button radio ($57). Tachometer. All-Season air conditioning ($311). Twin-Grip differential ($37). Electric washer/wipers, electric wipers mandatory with V-8 ($18). Power steering ($34). Power brakes ($42). Power tailgate window ($31). Exterior appearance group, includes rocker moldings and wheelcovers ($77). Full wheel discs, standard on Rogue ($21). Turbo-cast wheelcovers ($61). Reclining bucket seats with center armrest and cushion, for Rogue convertible, standard on Rogue hardtop ($96). Safety headrests ($15). V-8 handling package. Sports steering wheel, 440 and Rogue only ($11). Black or white vinyl roof for hardtops ($75). Three-speed manual transmission with overdrive ($115). Automatic transmission ($174). Four-speed manual transmission, with V-8 engines only ($184). Shift-Command automatic transmission with thumb-button operated floor shift, in Rogue with buckets and console ($192). V-8 290-cid/200-hp two-barrel ($119). V-8 290-cid/225-hp four-barrel engine ($32). V-8 343-cid/280-hp four-barrel ($91). Air Guard exhaust emissions control system for V-8s ($45). Closed crankcase ventilation system, mandatory in California ($50). Heavy-duty clutch for V-8 with manual transmission ($5). Dual exhaust ($26).

1967 MARLIN

1967 Marlin

The 1967 Marlin was longer, lower and wider and had a two-inch increase in wheelbase. The sporty AMC entry retained its distinctive fastback roof styling and semi-elliptical side window openings. It was basically an Ambassador with a fastback roof, instead of being a streamlined Rambler Classic. American Motors hoped to increase Marlin sales by upgrading the car in this manner. It was also quite a distinctive product: a large, six-passenger sports car aimed at the family man with a "Walter Mitty" complex. There were smoother bodysides, a new rectangular gas filler door and Rally lights incorporated into the grille. Side marker lights could be seen on the trailing edge of the rear fenders, just ahead of the wraparound rear bumper ends. A full-length lower body molding helped create a slim appearance and followed the pattern seen on Rebels, arching over both wheel-housings. The rear deck area was cleaned-up a bit by removal of the large, round medallion. Marlins (as well as Ramblers) with V-8 power had V-shaped emblems at the forward edge of the front fenders. Unfortunately, the Marlin again had problems in the marketplace, as sales dropped to even lower levels than the previous year's drop-off.

Once again, the Marlin probably would have sold better at the Fulton Fish Market than it did at AMC dealerships. Nevertheless, as a collector car, the AMC fastback does have a following and this is definitely the year to follow up on. The '67 is more like the Dodge Charger than the earlier Marlins and will be an even more desirable "catch of the day" as time goes by.

ENGINES

OPTIONAL V-8: Overhead valves. Cast-iron block. Displacement: 290 cid. Bore and stroke: 3.75 x 3.28 inches. Compression ratio: 9.0:1. Advertised hp: 200 at 4600 rpm. Advertised torque: 285 at 2800 rpm. Recommended idle speed: 600 rpm. Five main bearings. Hydraulic valve lifters (non-adjustable). Carburetor: Holley two-barrel model 2209-3308-1. Single exhaust with crossover.

OPTIONAL V-8: V-8. Overhead valves. Cast-iron block. Displacement: 343 cid. Bore and stroke: 4.08 x 3.28 inches. Compression ratio: 9.0:1. Advertised hp: 235 at 4400 rpm. Advertised torque: 345 at 2600 rpm. Recommended idle speed: 600 rpm. Five main bearings. Hydraulic valve lifters (non-adjustable). Carburetor: Holley two-barrel 2209. Exhaust system: Single standard, duals optional.

OPTIONAL V-8: Overhead valves. Cast-iron block. Displacement: 343 cid. Bore and stroke: 4.08 x 3.28 inches. Compression ratio: 10.2:1. Advertised hp: 280 at 4800 rpm. Advertised torque: 365 at 3000 rpm. Recommended idle speed: 600 rpm. Five main bearings. Hydraulic valve lifters (non-adjustable). Carburetor: Carter AFB four-barrel. Exhaust system: Single with crossover, standard, duals optional.

OPTIONS

Adjust-O-Tilt steering wheel ($42). Cruise-Command automatic speed control ($44). Power disc brakes ($91). All-Season air conditioning ($350). Stereo system with 8-track tape ($133). Black or white vinyl roof ($75). Two-tone paint ($19). Reclining bucket seats ($142). Individually adjustable reclining seats ($45). Center console, with bucket seats and console shift options only ($113). Electric clock ($16). Tachometer ($48). Sports steering wheel ($16). Safety headrests ($45). AM/FM all-transistor radio ($134). Vinyl upholstery ($25). Turbo-cast wheelcovers ($40). Light Group ($16). Three-speed manual transmission was standard. Three-speed manual transmission with overdrive ($115). Automatic transmission ($217). Four-speed manual transmission, with V-8 engines only ($184). Shift-Command automatic transmission with thumb-button operated floor shift ($217). V-8 290-cid/200-hp two-barrel engine ($119). V-8 343-cid/235-hp two-barrel engine ($58). V-8 343-cid/280-hp four-barrel engine ($91). Air Guard exhaust emissions control system for V-8s ($45). Closed crankcase ventilation system, mandatory in California ($50). Heavy-duty clutch for V-8 with manual transmission ($5). Dual exhaust ($26).

Series Number	Body/Style Number	Body Type & Seating	Factory Price	Shipping Weight	Production Total
MARLIN — SERIES 50 — V-8					
50	6759-7	2d Fsbk-6P	$2,963	3,342 lbs.	2,190

NOTE: Price and weight for base V-8. Production total for all V-8.

AMC

1968 JAVELIN SST

1968 Javelin SST

The new Javelin filled the slot vacated by the unsuccessful Marlin. It was American Motors Corporation's entry into the pony car market that Ford created with the Mustang in 1964. Styling characteristics included a split grille with black-out treatment and form-fitting bumper, single, square head¬light housings integrated into fenders, round parking lamps integrated into the bumper (below the headlights), a clean-lined body with smooth-flowing lines and a semi-fastback roof line with wide, flat sail panels. The profile exhibited a "venturi" silhouette. A full-width rear bumper, horizontal rectangular tail lights and a black-out rear panel treatment characterized the rear. Javelin chrome signature scripts were seen in the left-hand grille insert, on the front fenders behind the wheel opening and in the center of the deck latch panel. Standard equipment included a heater, Flo-Thru ventilation, dual paint stripes along the upper belt line, dual horns, wide profile tires and, for V-8s, a performance suspension with sway bar. The SST came with all these standard Javelin features, plus reclining front bucket seats with front foam cushions, a wood-look Sports steering wheel, wood-look door panel trim, full wheel discs, rocker panel moldings, side window moldingss and a hood scoop molding.

The Javelin went on sale September 26, 1967. By January, a total of 12,390 had been sold — a great number for AMC. The company took the Javelin to Daytona Beach and other racetracks to show that it could really go. Later, the car showed promise in the new Trans-American racing series and, with full factory backing, narrowly missed unseating the championship Ford Mustang factory team. The SST name stood for "super-sonic transport" and the "Jay 390" — as drag racer Doug Thorley described it — was one of the fastest AMC products ever (at least until the AMX bowed at midyear.)

ENGINES

STANDARD V-8: Overhead valves. Cast-iron block. Displacement: 290 cid. Bore and stroke: 3.75 x 3.28 inches. Compression ratio: 9.0:1. Advertised hp: 200 at 4600 rpm. Advertised torque: 285 at 2800 rpm. Recommended idle speed: 650 rpm. Five main bearings. Hydraulic valve lifters (non-adjustable). Carburetor: Motorcraft 8HM2. Single exhaust with crossover, duals optional on all but American and all wagons.

OPTIONAL V-8: Overhead valves. Cast-iron block. Displacement: 343 cid. Bore and stroke: 4.08 x 3.28 inches. Compression ratio: 10.2:1. Advertised hp: 280 at 4800 rpm. Advertised torque: 365 at 3000 rpm. Recommended idle speed: 650 rpm. Five main bearings. Hydraulic valve lifters (non-adjustable). Carburetor: Carter AFB four-barrel. Exhaust system: Single with crossover standard, duals optional except wagons.

OPTIONAL V-8: Overhead valves. Cast-iron block. Displacement: 390 cid. Bore and stroke: 4.17 x 3.57 inches. Compression ratio: 10.2:1. Advertised hp: 315 at 4600 rpm. Advertised torque: 425 at 3200 rpm. Recommended idle speed: 650 rpm. Forged crank and rods. Hydraulic valve lifters (non-adjustable). Carburetor: Carter AFB four-barrel. Exhaust system: Duals standard on all 390 V-8 engines.

(Note: This engine, when introduced in February of 1968 was advertised as the "AMX 390".)

OPTIONS

Power brakes ($42). Power steering ($85). Air conditioning ($356). Dual exhaust V-8 ($21). Solex glass, all windows ($31), windshield only ($21). Headrest, with bench seat ($35), with buckets ($49). Power disc brakes, V-8 ($97). Power steering ($84). Stereo 8-track player ($195). Individually adjusting seat ($49). White vinyl seat upholstery ($20). Adjust-O-Tilt steering ($42). Shift-Command automatic transmission with floor shift and console ($269). Twin-Grip differential ($42). Vinyl roof ($85). Turbo-cast wheelcovers, SST ($51. Handling package ($17). GO Pack performance package includes: 343-cid V-8, dual exhaust, power disc brakes, E-70 wide profile tires, Handling package and Rally stripes ($266). Visibility group package ($27). FM push-button radio and antenna ($61). AM/FM push-button radio and antenna ($134). Quick-ratio manual steering ($16). Four-speed manual transmission with floor shift ($184). Wire wheelcovers ($51). Three-speed manual transmission was standard. Automatic transmission was optional on all with floor control on specific models. Four-speed manual floor shift transmission with V-8 only. Four-barrel carburetor. Positive traction rear axle. Heavy-duty clutch.

Series Number	Body/Style Number	Body Type & Seating	Factory Price	Shipping Weight	Production Total
JAVELIN SST — SERIES 70 — V-8					
70	6879-7	2d HT-4P	$2,692	3,099 lbs.	23,599

NOTE: Price for Javelin SST with base V-8. Production for all Javelin SST V-8s.

1968 AMX

1968 AMX

Round number two in the AMC revitalization program officially kicked off on February 24, 1968, with the midyear introduction of the AMX two-seat sports car at the Chicago Automobile Show. Actually, the car had made its initial public appearance about a week earlier, when it was press previewed at Daytona International Speedway in Daytona Beach, Florida. The model designation stood for "American Motors Experimental" and it was the first American two-passenger, steel-bodied production-type sports car to be seen since the 1955-1957 Ford Thunderbird. A kid brother to the Javelin, the AMX was built off the same platform. Features included thin-shell reclining bucket seats, a carpeted interior, woodgrained steering wheel and door panel trim, a 290-cid/225-hp V-8, a four-speed manual transmission, a special suspension, glass-belted Goodyear tires and a four-barrel carburetor. Power options included the 343-cid V-8 and a 390-cid engine with 315 hp that turned the little sportster into a real speed demon. It looked like a short Javelin with louvered hood bulges and a non-divided grille treatment. It carried special model identification within a large ring of chrome on the sail panels.

The AMX appeared in dealer showrooms during March 1968. Each AMX built in 1968 earned a metal dashboard plate bearing a special number (numbers 000001 to 006175 were used). This was intended to designate its rather special nature. However, the first 550 units, assembled in calendar year 1967, did not have this feature. Craig Breedlove established 106 world speed records with a 1968 AMX at Goodyear's Texas test track in February 1968. A number of replica Craig Breedlove model AMXs with red, white and blue paint jobs and the 290-cid V-8 and four-speed transmission were sold. The number of Craig Breedlove Special AMXs made is believed to

have been 50 cars. "This is no Rambler," said *Car and Driver*. "It is — to quote a sensitive and eloquent artist friend from the Left Coast — "one son-of-a-bitch motorcar."

Model Number	Body/Style Number	Body Type & Seating	Factory Price	Shipping Weight	Production Total
AMX — SERIES 30 — V-8					
30	6839-7	2d HT-2P	$3,245	3,097 lbs.	6,725

NOTE 1: Price for base V-8. Production for all V-8s.

ENGINES

BASE V-8: Overhead valves. Cast-iron block. Displacement: 290 cid. Bore and stroke: 3.75 x 3.28 inches. Compression ratio: 10.0:1. Advertised hp: 225 at 4700 rpm. Advertised torque: 300 at 3200 rpm. Recommended idle speed: 650 rpm. Five main bearings. Hydraulic valve lifters (non-adjustable). Carburetor: Carter AFB four-barrel. Exhaust system: Duals.

OPTIONAL V-8: Overhead valves. Cast-iron block. Displacement: 343 cid. Bore and stroke: 4.08 x 3.28 inches. Compression ratio: 10.2:1. Advertised hp: 280 at 4800 rpm. Advertised torque: 365 at 3000 rpm. Recommended idle speed: 650 rpm. Five main bearings. Hydraulic valve lifters (non-adjustable). Carburetor: Carter AFB four-barrel. Exhaust system: Single with crossover standard, duals optional.

OPTIONAL V-8: Overhead valves. Cast-iron block. Displacement: 390 cid. Bore and stroke: 4.17 x 3.57 inches. Compression ratio: 10.2:1. Advertised hp: 315 at 4600 rpm. Advertised torque: 425 at 3200 rpm. Recommended idle speed: 650 rpm. Five main bearings. Forged crank and rods. Hydraulic valve lifters (non-adjustable). Carburetor: Carter AFB four-barrel. Exhaust system: Duals standard on all 390 V-8 engines. (Note: this engine, when introduced in February of 1968, was advertised as the "AMX 390".)

OPTIONS

Specific prices for AMX options are not available. The options list was about the same as for Javelin (at about the same prices) plus, over-the-top striping, chrome steel mag wheels and dealer accessory Rally Pak gauge cluster. Automatic transmission was optional on all with floor control on specific models. Four-speed manual floor shift transmission standard AMX, optional, with V-8 only, on other models. Four-barrel carburetor. Positive traction rear axle. Heavy-duty clutch.

1969 SC/RAMBLER

JERRY HEASLEY

1969 SC/Rambler

This was the final season that the Rambler nameplate would appear. The SC/Rambler was based on it. A total of 4,204,925 Ramblers were sold from 1950-1969 and the SC/Rambler was, without a doubt, the hottest one ever made. Formerly the Rambler American, the 1969 base model got a shortened name. The Rambler retained its compact dimensions and overall styling in line with AMC's new policy of maintaining design continuity from year to year for its low-priced models. American nameplates were gone from the grille and a new chrome side molding was used. Some of the mechanical improvements earmarked for the more expensive AMC products were incorporated in the Rambler. They included a new accelerator cable linkage, suspended accelerator pedal, Clear Power 24 battery and parking lamps that remained on with headlamps.

With the help of Hurst Products Corp., a special Rogue offering was built exclusively during 1969. It was called the Hurst SC/Rambler and. Original programming called for a limited run of just 500 units, but supply was far outstripped by demand. Ultimately, three runs of this model were made. They are known as A, B and A' (version 2) cars. Standard equipment on the Group A SC/Rambler included: AMX 390-cid V-8 four-speed all-synchromesh close-ratio transmission, special Hurst shift linkage with T-handle, Sun tech mounted on steering column, dual exhaust system with special mufflers and chrome extensions, functional hood scoop for cold-air induction, Twin-Grip differential, 10 1/2-inch-diameter clutch, 3.54:1 axle ratio, front power disc brakes, rear axle torque links, handling package with heavy-duty sway bar, springs and shocks, heavy-duty radiator and cooling system, 20.0:1 manual steering ratio, and special application red, white and blue exterior finish. The other groups

were similar with the paint and graphics differences. The A Group, had the major portion of the bodysides painted red, with a blue racing stripe traveling down the middle of the body and across the roof and deck. There was also a large blue arrow, pointing towards the hood scoop. The second, or B Group of Hurst SC/Ramblers were finished more conservatively. They had a largely white exterior, with narrow red and blue stripes. The third group reverted to the original, or A, style.

Series Number	Body/Style Number	Body Type & Seating	Factory Price	Shipping Weight	Production Total
SC/RAMBLER — SERIES 01 — V-8					
01	6909-7	2d HT-6P	$2,998	2,988 lbs.	1,512

NOTE: The SC/Rambler came only with V-8 power. A total of 1,012 A-Group editions were built. A total of 500 B-Group editions were built.

ENGINE

BASE V-8: Overhead valves. Cast-iron block. Displacement: 390 cid. Bore and stroke: 4.17 x 3.57 inches. Compression ratio: 10.2:1. Advertised hp: 315 at 4600 rpm. Advertised torque: 425 at 3200 rpm. Recommended idle speed: 650 rpm. Five main bearings. Forged crank and rods. Forged crank and rods. Hydraulic valve lifters (non-adjustable). Carburetor: Carter AFB four-barrel. Exhaust system: duals standard on all models with 390 engine.

OPTIONS

Automatic transmission. Heavy-duty 70-amp battery ($8). Heavy-duty battery and 55-amp generator ($26). Heavy-duty cooling system ($53). Positive traction rear axle ($42). Available rear axle gear ratios ($5). Power steering ($90). Front and rear bumper guards ($25). Tinted glass, all windows ($32), windshield only ($23). Push-button radio and antenna ($61). Undercoating and underhood insulation pad ($21). Electric windshield wipers, required in V-8 Ramblers ($15). Code 56-4 Appearance group with sill moldings and wheel discs ($39). Code 70-1 Handling package with heavy-duty sway bar, shocks and springs ($17). Light group, includes door switches, trunk, courtesy, glovebox and other lamps ($23). Visibility Group with outside rearview remote control mirror, electric window/washer etc. ($29). (NOTE: Some options may have been standard in the SC/Rambler.)

1969 AMX

AMC

JERRY HEASLEY

1969 AMX

The 1969 AMC was described as being "more racy look-ing than ever," but was really little changed. Its introduction as a late-1968 entry precluded major revisions for its second year. There was a new 140-mph speedometer and a tachometer with a larger face. Many minor running changes evolved as the year progressed, the most obvious being the addition of a hooded dash panel cover in most '69s. New convenience items included a passenger grab handle above the glovebox and a between-the-seats package tray. Leather upholstery trims were a new option. Standard equipment included all safety items, front and rear ashtrays and armrests, cigarette lighter, collapsable spare tire, Sports steering wheel, courtesy lights, dual exhaust, carpets, Flo-Thru ventilation, glovebox lock, dual horns, instrument panel gauge cluster with tachometer, rear traction bars, front head restraints, reclining bucket seats, front foam seat cushions, wheel discs, heavy-duty suspension, E70 x 14 fiberglass-belted blackwall tires, four-speed manual transmission with floor shift, and 225-hp four-barrel V-8.

Introduced as a midyear entry was the Big Bad AMX. This option-created-model came in three colors and had the bumpers painted the same shade as the body. A total of 284 orange-col-ored Big Bad AMXs were built as well as 195 similar models finished in blue and 283 additional cars done in green. A limited number of 52 or 53 Super Stock AMXs were made by the Hurst Corp. for AMC as special turn-key NHRA drag racing cars.

ENGINES

BASE V-8: Overhead valves. Cast-iron block. Displacement: 290 cid. Bore and stroke: 3.75 x 3.28 inches. Compression ratio: 10.0:1. Advertised hp: 225 at 4700 rpm. Advertised torque: 300 at 3200 rpm. Five main bearings. Hydraulic valve lifters. Carburetor: Carter AFB four-barrel. Exhaust system: Single with crossover standard on Javelin, duals optional on Javelin, duals standard on AMX .

OPTIONAL V-8: Overhead valves. Cast-iron block. Displacement: 343 cid. Bore and stroke: 4.08 x 3.28 inches. Compression ratio: 10.2:1. Advertised hp: 280 at 4800 rpm. Advertised torque: 365 at 3000 rpm. (Automatic transmission) 550 rpm. Five main bearings. Hydraulic valve lifters (non-adjustable). Carburetor: Carter AFB four-barrel. Exhaust system: Single with crossover standard except AMX (duals standard on AMX) optional all others.

OPTIONAL V-8: Overhead valves. Cast-iron block. Displacement: 390 cid. Bore and stroke: 4.17 x 3.57 inches. Compression ratio: 10.2:1. Advertised hp: 315 at 4600 rpm. Advertised torque: 425 at 3200 rpm. Five main bear-ings. Forged crank and rods. Hydraulic valve lifters (non-adjustable). Carbu-retor: Carter AFB four-barrel. Exhaust system: duals standard on all models with 390 engine.

OPTIONS

Power brakes ($42). Power steering ($95). Air conditioning ($369). Rear bumper guards only ($13). Special application paint colors ($39). Automatic transmission oil cooler ($18). Stereo 8-track tape player, with manual radio ($195). All except Ramblers, AM/FM push-button radio and antenna ($134). Center armrest seat with cushion, bucket seats mandatory, in AMX, with four-speed ($35). Leather, upholstery trim ($79). Quick ratio manual steering ($16). Air-Command ventilation, not available with air conditioning ($41). Wire wheelcovers, ($51). Turbo-cast wheel covers ($46). Six-inch extra-wide wheel rims ($72). Handling Package group ($19). Higher-rate front and rear springs. Heavy-duty shocks ($19). Light group ($20). Electric clock plus, visibility pack-age group ($43). E70-14 red line tires ($34). Go Package (Code 39-1), which retailed for $233.15 on cars with the 343-cid V-8 and $310.85 on cars with the 390-cid engine. It included power disc brakes, E70 red line tires, 6-inch-wide wheel rims, handling package, Twin-Grip heavy-duty cooling system and black white, red, blue or silver over-the-top racing stripe.

Series Number	Body/Style Number	Body Type & Seating	Factory Price	Shipping Weight	Production Total
AMX — SERIES 30 — V-8					
30	6939-7	2d HT-2P	$3,297	3,097 lbs.	8,293

AMC

1969 JAVELIN SST

Javelin SST in Matador Red.

1969 Javeline SST

The 1969 Javelin had a new twin-venturi grille with a round, bull's-eye emblem on the left-hand side. Otherwise, it was largely unchanged. The side stripes were redesigned. There had formerly been two narrow parallel stripes running full-length along the beltline. Now there was a larger C stripe traveling down the mid-side of the car and turning downward at the trailing edge of the front wheelhousing. This change was put into effect on January 9, 1969, so both designs appeared on 1969 cars. Another Javelin revision was a new trim treatment for the instrument panel in standard-level cars and extensive use of woodgrained paneling in the SST interior.

Introduced as a midyear addition was the Mod Javelin, which came in the same colors as the Big Bad AMX. Many Mod Javelins were marketed with the Craig Breedlove options package. It included a rooftop spoiler and simulated exhaust rocker mountings. A limited number of Javelins and some Rambler 440s were built in Germany, by Karmann Standard equipment.

Series Number	Body/Style Number	Body Type & Seating	Factory Price	Shipping Weight	Production Total
JAVELIN SST — SERIES 70 — V-8					
70	6879-7	2d Fsbk-4P	$2,633	2,836 lbs.	23,286

ENGINES

BASE V-8: Overhead valves. Cast-iron block. Displacement: 290 cid. Bore and stroke: 3.75 x 3.28 inches. Compression ratio: 10.0:1. Advertised hp: 225 at 4700 rpm. Advertised torque: 300 at 3200 rpm. Five main bearings. Hydraulic valve lifters. Carburetor: Carter AFB four-barrel. Exhaust system: Single with crossover standard on Javelin, duals optional on Javelin, duals standard on AMX .

OPTIONAL V-8: Overhead valves. Cast-iron block. Displacement: 290 cid. Bore and stroke: 3.75 x 3.28 inches. Compression ratio: 9.0:1. Advertised hp: 200 at 4600 rpm. Advertised torque: 285 at 2800 rpm. Five main bearings. Hydraulic valve lifters. Carburetor: Motorcraft 6200. Exhaust system: single exhaust with crossover.

OPTIONAL V-8: Overhead valves. Cast-iron block. Displacement: 343 cid. Bore and stroke: 4.08 x 3.28 inches. Compression ratio: 9.0:1. Advertised hp: 235 at 4400 rpm. Advertised torque: 345 at 2600 rpm. Five main bearings. Hy-

draulic valve lifters. Carburetor: Motocraft 6200. Exhaust system: Single with crossover (no duals available with this engine).

OPTIONAL V-8: Overhead valves. Cast-iron block. Displacement: 343 cid. Bore and stroke: 4.08 x 3.28 inches. Compression ratio: 10.2:1. Advertised hp: 280 at 4800 rpm. Advertised torque: 365 at 3000 rpm. Five main bearings. Hydraulic valve lifters (non-adjustable). Carburetor: Carter AFB four-barrel. Exhaust system: Single with crossover standard except AMX (duals standard on AMX) optional all others.

OPTIONAL V-8: Overhead valves. Cast-iron block. Displacement: 390 cid. Bore and stroke: 4.17 x 3.57 inches. Compression ratio: 10.2:1. Advertised hp: 315 at 4600 rpm. Advertised torque: 425 at 3200 rpm. Five main bearings. Forged crank and rods. Forged crank and rods. Hydraulic valve lifters (non-adjustable). Carburetor: Carter AFB four-barrel. Exhaust system: duals standard on all models with 390 engine.

OPTIONS

Three-speed manual transmission was standard in most models. Automatic transmission ($171-$223). Close-ratio four-speed manual transmission with floor shift ($205). 290-cid/225-hp four-barrel V-8 ($45). 343-cid/280-hp four-barrel V-8 ($91). 390-cid/315-hp four-barrel V-8 ($168). Heavy-duty 70-amp battery ($8). Heavy-duty battery and 55-amp generator ($26). Heavy-duty cooling system ($53). Dual exhaust as separate V-8 option ($31). Positive traction rear axle ($42). Heavy-duty clutch in Javelin with 200-hp V-8 ($11). Available rear axle gear ratios ($5). Power brakes ($42). Power steering ($95). Air conditioning ($369). Rear bumper guards only ($13). Special application paint colors ($39). Console with Shift-Command/column shift ($53). Instrument cluster with tachometer and 140-mph speedometer ($50). Automatic transmission oil cooler ($18). Rally Side paint stripes, replacing pin stripes ($27). Stereo 8-track tape player, with manual radio ($195). AM/FM push-button radio and antenna ($134). Center armrest seat with cushion ($35). Leather, upholstery trim AMX only ($79). Quick-ratio manual steering ($16). Shift-Command, column control, in Javelins except SST with 343 V-8 ($223). Shift-Command, floor control, in Javelins with 200/280 hp V-8s ($287). Four-speed close-ratio manual floor shift, except with 200 hp V-8 ($205). Twin-Grip differential ($42). Air-Command ventilation, not available with air conditioning ($41). Wire wheelcovers, 14-inch, base Javelin ($72), Javelin SST ($51). Black, white or blue vinyl roof ($100). Turbo-cast wheelcovers, Javelin ($67), Javelin SST ($46). Six-inch extra-wide wheel rims ($72). Full wheel discs ($21). Handling Package group ($19). Heavy-duty shocks ($19). Light Group ($23). Electric clock plus, visibility package group ($43). E70-14 red line tires ($75). Go Package (Code 39-1), retailed for $233.15 on cars with the 343-cid V-8 and $310.85 on cars with the 390-cid engine. It included power disc brakes, E70 red line tires, six-inch wide wheel rims, handling package, Twin-Grip heavy-duty cooling system and black white, red, blue or silver over-the-top racing stripe. The Javelin Go Package (code 39 1/2), retailed for $265.50 when the 343-cid V-8 was ordered and $343.25 when the 390-cid

engine was specified. It included the V-8, dual exhaust, power disc brakes, E70 wide profile red line tires, 6-inch-wide wheel rims, handling package, and black fiberglass hood scoops.

1970 AMX

PHIL KUNZ

1970 AMX

AMC said the '70 AMX was made tougher because it was a tough year. Unfortunately, the killer kammback had tough sledding in the marketplace. That's what makes it hard to find and especially collectible today. With a 6.56-second 0-to-60 time, this too-rare two-seater can rip off 14.68-second quarter-miles at 92 mph. It's just not your Uncle Roscoe's Rambler!

The 1970 AMX got new tail lights and a completely restyled front end that was shared with Javelin performance models. The frontal treatment featured a grille that was flush with the hood and redesigned bumper housing squarish parking lights. A horizontally divided, cross-hatched grille insert, with prominent bright vertical moldings, was used and incorporated circular rally lights. The restyled hood had a large Ram-Air induction scoop that took in cold air for the engine. Height was reduced about one inch, while overall length grew. Standard equipment included all items used with Javelin SSTs, plus a heavy-duty 60-amp battery, courtesy lights, rear traction bars, a Space-Saver spare tire, a tachometer, a 140-mph speedometer, 14 x 6-inch styled steel wheels, E78-14 black sidewall tires, a four-speed manual floor shift transmission and a 360-cid-290-hp four-barrel V-8 with a dual exhaust system. The metal dashboard plates affixed to 1970 models were numbered 14469 to 18584. This was the final year for the original type AMX, although the model name would be used again on performance image Javelin and Hornet-based models.

Series Number	Body/Style Number	Body Type & Seating	Factory Price	Shipping Weight	Production Total
AMX — SERIES 30 — V-8					
30	7039-7	2d HT-2P	$3,395	3,126 lbs.	4,116

ENGINES

BASE V-8: Overhead valves. Cast-iron block. Displacement: 360 cid. Bore and stroke: 4.08 x 3.44 inches. Compression ratio: 10.0:1. Advertised hp: 290 at 4800 rpm. Advertised torque: 395 at 3200 rpm. Five main bearings. Hydraulic valve lifters. Carburetor: Motorcraft 4300 Series four-barrel. Exhaust system: Single standard, duals optional, duals standard on AMX.

OPTIONAL V-8: Overhead valves. Cast-iron block. Displacement: 390 cid. Bore and stroke: 4.17 x 3.57 inches. Compression ratio: 10.0:1. Advertised hp: 325 at 5000 rpm. Advertised torque: 420 at 3200 rpm. Five main bearings. Forged crank and rods. Hydraulic valve lifters. Carburetor: Motorcraft 4300 Series four-barrel. Exhaust system: Duals standard on all models with 390 engine.

OPTIONS

Shift-Command automatic transmission. Close-ratio four-speed manual transmission with floor shift. AMX V-8 390-cid/325-hp four-barrel engine ($11). Heavy-duty 70-amp battery ($13). Axle ratios, all optional ($10). Heavy-duty cooling, standard with air ($16). Dual exhaust, as separate option ($31). Twin-Grip positive traction rear axle ($43). Power brakes ($43). Power steering ($102). Air conditioning ($380). Rear bumper guards ($13). Command Air ventilation system, without air ($41). Tinted glass. Two-tone finish with "black shadow" treatment ($52). Rally side stripes, solid color ($32). Power front disc brakes ($84). Eight-track stereo tape with manual radio/twin rear speakers ($195). Leather-trimmed bucket seats ($34). Quick-ratio manual steering, for racing ($16). Tachometer and 140 mph speedometer with V-8 ($50). Shift-Command, floor control AMX with "390" V-8 ($118). The Code 39 1/2 Go-Package retailed for $298.85 on the "360" AMX and $383.90 on the "390" AMX. It included one of these engines, power front disc brakes, F70-14 blackwall tires with raised white letters, Handling Package, heavy-duty cooling system, and functional Ram-Air induction scoop.

AMC

1970 JAVELIN SST

JERRY HEASLEY

1970 Javelin SST

The new Javelin shared its basic styling features with the AMC, but retained its own twin venturi-type grille without the previous bull's-eye badge. The headlights were better integrated into the nose, sharing a common upper border molding with the main grille. The car had the same front bumper, front parking lights and hood as the AMX and like the AMX was an inch lower and 2 inches longer.

Two limited-production Javelin SSTs were offered. The Javelin Trans Am had all SST equipment (minus sill moldings and paint stripes), plus front lower and rear deck spoilers, a black vinyl interior, the "390" Go Package, F70-14 glass-belted tires with raised white letters, 14 x 6-inch mag-style wheels, a Space-Saver spare tire with a regular spare wheel, an AM push-button radio, a tachometer, a 140-mph speedometer, a Visibility Group, a Light Group, power steering, a Twin-Grip differential, a 3.91:1 rear axle ratio, a four-speed gearbox with Hurst floor shifter and a 390-cid four-barrel V-8 with heavy-duty cooling system. These cars were replicas of the Ronnie Kaplan Trans-Am Racing Team's competition machines and were finished in a three-segment red, white and blue paint scheme created by industrial designer Brooks Stevens. Only 100 cars were built.

Series Number	Body/Style Number	Body Type & Seating	Factory Price	Shipping Weight	Production Total
JAVELIN SST — SERIES 70 — V-8 SST					
70	7070-7	2d HT-4P	$2,848	2,863 lbs.	17,113
TRANS AM					
70	7079-7	2d HT-4P	$3,995	3,340 lbs.	(100)*
MARK DONOHUE					
70	7079-7	2d HT-4P	—	—	(2,501)*

NOTE: *The total of 19,714 Javelin SSTs includes both the Trans-Am and Mark Donohue Javelin models, as these were package models based on the Javelin SST.

ENGINES

BASE V-8: Overhead valves. Cast-iron block. Displacement: 304 cid. Bore and stroke: 3.75 x 3.44 inches. Compression ratio: 9.0:1. Advertised hp: 210 at 4400 rpm. Advertised torque: 305 at 2800 rpm. Five main bearings. Hydraulic valve lifters. Carburetor: Motorcraft 2100 Series two-barrel. Exhaust system: Single with crossover.

OPTIONAL V-8: Overhead valves. Cast-iron block. Displacement: 360 cid. Bore and stroke: 4.08 x 3.44 inches. Compression ratio: 9.0:1. Advertised hp: 245 at 4500 rpm. Advertised torque: 365 at 2400 rpm. Five main bearings. Hydraulic valve lifters. Carburetor: Motorcraft 2100 Series two-barrel. Exhaust system: Single with crossover.

"MARK DONOHUE" V-8: Overhead valves. Cast-iron block. Displacement: 360 cid. Bore and stroke: 4.08 x 3.44 inches. Compression ratio: 10.0:1. Advertised hp: 290 at 4800 rpm. Advertised torque: 395 at 3200 rpm. Five main bearings. Hydraulic valve lifters. Carburetor: Motorcraft 4300 Series four-barrel. Exhaust system: Single standard, duals optional, duals standard on AMX.

"TRANS AM" V-8: Overhead valves. Cast-iron block. Displacement: 390 cid. Bore and stroke: 4.17 x 3.57 inches. Compression ratio: 10.0:1. Advertised hp: 325 at 5000 rpm. Advertised torque: 420 at 3200 rpm. Five main bearings. Forged crank and rods. Hydraulic valve lifters. Carburetor: Motorcraft 4300 Series four-barrel. Exhaust system: Duals standard on all models with 390 engine.

OPTIONS

Shift-Command automatic transmission. Four-speed manual floor shift transmission in Javelin "360" and "390" V-8s. 360-cid/245-hp two- barrel V-8 ($41). 360-cid/290-hp four-barrel V-8 ($86). 390-cid/325-hp four-barrel V-8 ($168). Heavy-duty 70-amp battery ($13). Axle ratios, all optional ($10). Heavy-duty cooling, standard with air ($16). Dual exhaust, as separate option ($31). Twin-Grip positive traction rear axle ($43). Power brakes ($43). Power steering ($102). Air conditioning ($380). Rear bumper guards ($13). Command Air ventilation system, without air ($41). Center console, with column automatic shift only ($53). Tinted glass. Simulated exhaust-type rocker panel moldings ($32). Rally side stripes, solid color Javelin. Power front disc brakes, V-8 engine required ($84). Eight-track stereo tape with manual radio/twin rear speakers ($195). Leather trimmed bucket seats ($127). Quick-ratio manual steering, for racing ($16). Javelin Code 533 spoiler roof, not available with vinyl top ($33). Tachometer and 140 mph speedometer with V-8 ($50). Shift-Command, column control, Javelin with "304" V-8 ($200). Shift-Command, column control, Javelin with "360" V-8 ($233). Shift-Command, column control Javelin six ($195). Shift-Command floor control Javelin with "304" V-8 ($264). Shift-Command, floor control, Javelin with "360" V-8 ($287). Four-speed floor shift, Javelins with 290/325-hp V-8 ($205). Black, white or blue vinyl roof, Javelin only ($84). Turbo-cast wheelcovers for Javelin SST ($49). Wire wheelcovers for Javelin SST ($49). Styled steel wheels, 14 x 6 inch, for Javelin SST ($72). The Code 39 1/2 "Go Package" retailed for $298.85 on the "360" AMX and $383.90 on the "390" AMX. It included one of these engines, power front disc brakes, F70-14 blackwall tires with raised white letters, Handling Package, heavy-duty cooling system and functional Ram-Air induction scoop.

The Code 39 1/2 Go Package retailed for $321.65 on the "360" Javelin and $409.75 on the "390" Javelin.

1970 REBEL MACHINE "390"

JERRY HEASLEY

1970 Rebel Machine "390"

The 1970 Rebel Machine "390" was the highest horsepower V-8 AMC ever built in a stock street car. AMC sales VP Bill Pickett said that the Rebel Machine was another youth-oriented car introduced in recognition of the important marketing axiom "Youth must be served." It's too bad that AMC didn't paint a Confederate flag on this baby and get them to use it in the "Dukes of Hazard." They would have sold a bunch more of them then — why the production company alone would have bouht a couple of dozen to smash up while outrunning Boss Hawg.

The 1970 Rebel received new rear quarter panel styling and a more massive rear bumper. There were two large, horizontal, rectangular tail lights with Rebel spelled out between them. There was a new vertically split and horizontally segmented grille. The Rebel SST had a bright metal molding on the front fenders, between the door handle and side marker lights. Model identification lettering was placed behind the front wheel opening and, on SST, below the rear roof pillar. There was similar Rebel lettering on the left lip of the hood.

The Rebel Machine was introduced at the National Hot Rod Association's World Championship Drag Race, in Dallas, Texas, during October 1969. Standard on this model were all Rebel SST features (except rear armrests and ashtrays), high-back bucket seats, Space-Saver spare tire, power front disc brakes, Ram-Air hood scoop, Handling Package, heavy-duty cooling system with Power-Flex fan, carpeting, 15 x 7-inch styled steel wheel, E60-15 fiberglass-belted tires with raised white letters, four-speed manual floor shift transmission and a 390 cid/340 hp four- barrel V-8 with dual exhaust. The Machine had the highest-output engine ever used in an American Motors product offered for public sale.

Of a total of 2,326 cars run, approximately the first 1,000 units were finished in white, with the lower beltline and hood done in blue. A red stripe traveled down the front fender and along the car to the deckside region. From there, the stripe crossed over the trunk and came back along the opposite bodyside. There were also blue and white stripes over the trunk, behind the red one and integrated into it. Later editions of the model were finished in a choice of solid colors and featured a black-out hood treatment with silver pinstriping, plus optional red, white and blue graphics that could be added on the grille and body.

Series Number	Body/Style Number	Body Type & Seating	Factory Price	Shipping Weight	Production Total
REBEL MACHINE — SERIES 10 — V-8					
10	7019-7	2d HT-6P	$3,475	3,650 lbs.	1,936

ENGINE

BASE V-8: Overhead valves. Cast-iron block. Displacement: 390 cid. Bore and stroke: 4.17 x 3.57 inches. Compression ratio: 10.0:1. Advertised hp: 340 at 5100 rpm. Advertised torque: 430 at 3600 rpm. Five main bearings. Forged crank and rods. Hydraulic valve lifters. Carburetor: Motorcraft 4300 Series four-barrel. Exhaust system: Duals standard on all models with 390 engine. (NOTE: This engine's additional horsepower and torque over the standard 1970 AMC 390 engine were gained with special cast-iron "hi-flow" intake manifold and slightly larger exhaust manifolds and exhaust system.)

OPTIONS

Heavy-duty 70-amp battery ($13). Axle ratios, all optional ($10). Heavy-duty cooling, standard with air ($16). Dual exhaust, as separate option ($31). Twin-Grip positive traction rear axle ($43). Power brakes ($43). Power steering ($105). Air conditioning ($380). Cruise control, with automatic ($60). Front and rear bumper guards ($32). Tinted glass, all windowsel ($37). Tinted windshield ($30). AM push-button radio ($62). AM/FM push-button radio, all AMC except Hornets ($134). Tilt-O-Just steering wheel ($45). Shift-Command, with floor shift, Rebel "Machine" with "390" V-8 ($188).

AMC

1971 HORNET SC "360"

JERRY HEASLEY

1971 Hornet SC "360"

When finished in red, white and blue, the SC "360" looked kind of like a postal delivery car, even though it was really a SpeeDee Delivery rig! Unfortunately, back in '71, priority mail was about as good as things got and the hot hornet didn't buzz up many buyers.

The Hornet received no major styling changes for 1971. The Hornet SST models had color-keyed carpets, cigarette lighter, Command-Air ventilation, glovebox, full width package tray, Custom steering wheel, and movable rear quarter windows. The Sportabout added a carpeted cargo area, rear liftgate, cargo compartment lock, and Space-Saver spare tire. The SC/360 sports sedan had the same equipment as Hornet SST passenger models plus front sway bar, slot style wheels, Space-Saver spare tire, D70-14 raised white letter tires, and a 360-cid/245-hp two-barrel V-8. Springtime changes included price increases for all Hornet SST V-8s. In addition, free sunroofs were provided as part of several Hornet packages.

The SC/360 was designed as a low-priced performance car that could pass as a compact and, thus, side-step rising insurance rates affecting the owners and buyers of such vehicles. Its trim included special around-the-beltline decals with SC/360 callouts at the trailing edge of rear fenders. Optional, at $199, was a Go Package that consisted of four-barrel carburetor, Ram-Air induction system, dual exhaust, Handling Package, tachometer, and Polyglas white letter tires. It included a wide hood scoop with black-out paint treatment. American Motors had programmed the model for 10,000 sales, but only 784 buyers were interested. The Hornet SC/360 was sold only in 1971.

Series Number	Body/Style Number	Body Type & Seating	Factory Price	Shipping Weight	Production Total
HORNET SC 360 — SERIES 01 — V-8					
01	7106-1	2d Sed-6P	$2,663	3,300 lbs.	784

ENGINES

BASE V-8: Overhead valves. Cast-iron block. Displacement: 360 cid. Bore and stroke: 4.08 x 3.44 inches. Compression ratio: 8.5:1. Advertised hp: 245 at 4800 rpm. Advertised torque: 365 at 2600 rpm. Five main bearings. Hydraulic valve lifters. Carburetor: Motorcraft 2100 Series two-barrel. Exhaust system: Single with crossover. (NOTE: Standard engine in the SC/360 and Javelin AMX.)

OPTIONAL V-8: Overhead valves. Cast-iron block. Displacement: 360 cid. Bore and stroke: 4.08 x 3.44 inches. Compression ratio: 8.5:1. Advertised hp: 285 at 4800 rpm. Advertised torque: 330 at 5000 rpm. Five main bearings. Hydraulic valve lifters. Carburetor: Motorcraft 4300 Series four-barrel. Exhaust system: Single with crossover standard, duals optional, (duals standard on SC/360 four-barrel).

(NOTE: In 1971, the early production-run 360-cids four-barrel V-8s had a 9.5:1 compression ratio and were stickered under the hood as "high-compression." Later engines received a drop in compression to 9.0:1. The reason the horsepower and torque figures did not drop from the 1970 engines with 10.0:1 compression was that a newly designed Cast-iron "Free-flo" exhaust manifold was used on all 1971 AMC V-8s. This manifold dramatically improved the flow characteristics of the "dog-leg" heads introduced in 1970. The dog-leg heads — coupled with the free-flo exhaust manifolds — created a match made in heaven and gave all AMC V-8 cars a major edge on performance compared to "Big Three" cars, even though compression ratios of the AMC engines were lower due to smog laws. All four-barrel engines required "premium" 98 to 100 octane leaded gasoline.)

OPTIONS

Shift-Command with column shift ($238). Four-barrel 360 cid/285 hp V-8 ($49). Optional axle ratios ($12-$14). Heavy-duty 70-amp battery ($14-$15). Twin-Grip differential ($47). Dual exhaust, in all with '360' four-barrel V-8 ($31). Engine block heater ($12). Cooling system including heavy-duty radiator, Power flex fan and fan shroud ($16). Cold Start package ($18-$19). Power brakes

($45-$49). Power steering ($100-$111). Air conditioning ($399). Heavy-duty cooling system ($16-$18). Tinted glass, all windows($40). Tinted windshield ($30), Headlight delay system ($23). Bodyside scuff molding ($27). Two-tone paint ($28). Power front disc brakes ($84). AM push-button radio ($67). Cus-

tom steering wheel ($14). Rim-blow Sports steering wheel ($37). Tachometer ($50). Undercoating ($18). Undercoating and hood insulation ($22). Standard wheelcovers ($27-$30). Custom wheelcovers ($25-$54). Turbo-cast or wire wheelcovers ($52-$75). Styled steel wheels ($46).

1971 JAVELIN-AMX

1971 Javelin AMX

The 1971 Javelin was completely restyled. There were highly sculptured raised fenders, a twin-canopy roof with air spoiler-type rear window lip, and new full-width tail lamps. The interior was completely redesigned and upgraded. It featured a curved cockpit-type instrument panel inspired by aircraft motifs. Three levels of trim were provided in one two-door hardtop style: base Javelin, Javelin SST and Javelin AMX.

The new AMX was a four-place automobile, replacing the former two-seater. A rear-facing cowl induction hood, flush wire mesh grille and optional front and rear spoilers were claimed as the design work of race driver Mark Donohue, who raced Javelins successfully in SCCA Trans-Am competition. Standard equipment on the Javelin-AMX included full wheelcovers, a center console (without armrest), a rear-deck mounted spoiler, slot-style wheels, E70-14 glass-belted tires and a 360-cid/245-hp two-barrel V-8.

Series Number	Body/Style Number	Body Type & Seating	Factory Price	Shipping Weight	Production Total
JAVELIN-AMX — SERIES 70 — V-8					
70	7179-8	2d HT-4P	$3,432	3,244 lbs.	2,054

ENGINES

BASE V-8: Overhead valves. Cast-iron block. Displacement: 360 cid. Bore and stroke: 4.08 x 3.44 inches. Compression ratio: 8.5:1. Advertised hp: 245 at 4800 rpm. Advertised torque: 365 at 2600 rpm. Recommended idle speed: (Manual transmission) 750 rpm; (Automatic transmission) 650 rpm. Five main bearings. Hydraulic valve lifters. Carburetor: Motorcraft 2100 Series two-barrel. Exhaust system: Single with crossover.

OPTIONAL V-8: Overhead valves. Cast-iron block. Displacement: 360 cid. Bore and stroke: 4.08 x 3.44 inches. Compression ratio: 8.5:1. Advertised hp: 285 at 4800 rpm. Advertised torque: 330 at 5000 rpm. Five main bearings. Hy-

draulic valve lifters. Carburetor: Motorcraft: 4300 Series four-barrel. Exhaust system: Single with crossover standard, duals optional.

OPTIONAL V-8: Overhead valves. Cast-iron block. Displacement: 401 cid. Bore and stroke: 4.17 x 3.57 inches. Compression ratio: 9.5:1. Advertised hp: 330 at 5000 rpm. Advertised torque: 430 at 3400 rpm. Five main bearings. Forged crank and rods. Hydraulic valve lifters. Carburetor: Motorcraft 4300 Series four-barrel. Exhaust system: Duals mandatory on all 401-equipped cars.

OPTIONS

Three-speed manual transmission with floor shift was standard in the Javelin Group. Shift-Command with floor shift and console, in AMX with "360" V-8 ($246), in AMX with "401" V-8 ($256). Four-speed manual transmission with floor shift, available in Javelin Group with 285/330-hp V-8s ($209). Optional axle ratios ($12-$14). Heavy-duty 70-amp battery ($14-$15). Twin-Grip differential ($47). Dual exhaust, in all with "360" four-barrel V-8 ($31). Dual exhaust were standard with the 401 V-8. Engine block heater ($12). Cooling system including heavy-duty radiator, Power flex fan and fan shroud ($16). Cold Start package ($18-$19). Power brakes ($45-$49). Power steering ($100-$111). Air conditioning ($399). Front and rear bumper guards ($32). Electric rear defogger ($52). Front manual disc brakes ($40). Engine block heaterl ($12). Heavy-duty cooling system ($16-$18). Tinted glass, all windows ($44). Tinted windshield ($32). Headlight delay system ($23). Deck luggage rack ($35). Bodyside scuff molding ($31). Power side windows ($120). AM push-button radio ($72). AM/FM Multiplex stereo ($224). AM/radio with 8-track and two speakers ($207). Leather bucket seats ($84). Corduroy fabric bucket seats ($52). Adjust-O-Tilt steering ($49). Standard wheelcovers ($27-$30). Custom wheelcovers ($25-$54). Turbo-cast or wire wheelcovers ($52-$75). Styled steel wheels ($99-$108). Electric wiper/washers ($22). Black, white, blue or green vinyl roof ($89). Handling Package, including power disc brakes, E60-15 Polyglas raised white-letter tires, 15 x 7-inch styled steel wheels and Space-Saver spare tire. Javelin/AMX "Go Package" including specified engine, four-barrel carburetor, dual exhaust, hood "T" stripe decal, Rally-Pac instrumentation, Handling Package, Cowl-Air carburetor induction system, heavy-duty cooling components, Twin-Grip differential, power disc brakes, E60-15 Polyglas raised white letter tires, 15 x 7-inch styled steel wheels and Space-Saver sp ($410.90 on Javelin/AMX with 360 V-8 and $498.95 on Javelin/AMX with 401 V-8).

AMC

1972 JAVELIN-AMX

1972 Javelin-AMX

Small styling changes were the order of the year on Javelins. New grille and tail light treatments were seen. The Javelin-AMX grille design matched the center-bulge horizontal blade pattern of 1971. At the rear, there was full-width cross-hatch type decorative patterning in two rows. Performance, too, was part of 1972 Javelin-AMX history, as George Follmer won a second SCCA Trans-Am title for AMC this year. Standard equipment on the Javelin-AMX included a custom steering wheel, color-keyed carpets, a glovebox lock, dual horns, high-back bucket seats, a three-speed manual transmission with floor shift, a cigar lighter, an automatic transmission oil cooler, a rear ashtray, a rim-blow Sports steering wheel, a rubber trunk mat, full wheelcovers, an electric clock, a center console (without armrest), a rear-deck mounted spoiler, slot-style wheels, E70-14 glass-belted tires and a 304-cid two-barrel V-8.

Series Number	Body/Style Number	Body Type & Seating	Factory Price	Shipping Weight	Production Total
JAVELIN — AMX — SERIES 70 — V-8					
70	7279-8	2dHT-4P	$3,109	3,149 lbs.	3,220

ENGINES

BASE V-8: Overhead valves. Cast-iron block. Displacement: 304 cid. Bore and stroke: 3.75 x 3.44 inches. Compression ratio: 8.4:1. Net hp: 150 at 4200 rpm. Net torque: 245 at 2500 rpm. Five main bearings. Hydraulic valve lifters. Carburetor: Motorcraft 2100 Series two-barrel. Exhaust system: Single with crossover. Code H.

OPTIONAL V-8: Overhead valves. Cast-iron block. Displacement: 360 cid. Bore and stroke: 4.08 x 3.44 inches. Compression ratio: 8.5:1. Net hp: 195 at 4400 rpm. Net torque: 295 at 2900 rpm. Five main bearings. Hydraulic valve lifters. Carburetor: Motorcraft 2100 Series two-barrel. Exhaust system: Single with crossover. Code P.

OPTIONAL V-8: Overhead valves. Cast-iron block. Displacement: 360 cid. Bore and stroke: 4.08 x 3.44 inches. Compression ratio: 8.5:1. Net hp: 220 at 4400 rpm. Net torque: 315 at 3100 rpm. Five main bearings. Hydraulic valve lifters. Carburetor: Motorcraft 4300 Series four-barrel. Exhaust system: Duals. Code P.

OPTIONAL V-8: Overhead valves. Cast-iron block. Displacement: 401 cid. Bore and stroke: 4.17 x 3.68 inches. Compression ratio: 8.5:1. Net hp: 255 at 4600 rpm. Net torque: 345 at 3300 rpm. Five main bearings. Forged crank and rods. Hydraulic valve lifters. Carburetor: Motorcraft 4300 Series four-barrel. Exhaust system: Single with crossover. Code Z.

OPTIONS

Torque-Command with floor shift was optional in Javelins, with the 304-cid V-8 ($282), with the 360-cid V-8 ($293) and with the 401-cid V-8 ($305). Four-speed manual transmission was optional in Javelins only in combination with the four-barrel 360-cid V-8 or 401-cid V-8 ($188). 360-cid two-barrel V-8 ($42). The 360-cid four-barrel V-8 ($85). 401-cid four-barrel V-8 ($162). Optional axle ratios ($12-$14). Heavy-duty 70-amp battery ($14-$15). Twin-Grip differential ($43-$46). Dual exhaust with 360-cid V-8 and four-barrel ($28-$31). Heavy-duty cooling system ($16). A cowl-air induction system was included in "Go-Package" option groups. All-Season air conditioning ($377). Front and rear bumper guards ($29). Center armrest cushion, without console ($54). Rear window defogger ($45). Front manual disc brakes ($47). Engine block heater ($14). Tinted glass, all windows ($40), Tinted windshield only ($30). Headlights-off delay ($21). Rear deck luggage rack ($32). Hood "T" stripe ($39). Power brakes ($44). Power front disc brakes ($77). Power steering ($106). AM push-button radio ($66). AM/FM Multiplex stereo with two rear speakers ($196). Stereo tape player with manual radio ($190). Functional lower front spoiler, with disc brakes only ($31). Quick-ratio manual steering, 16:1 ratio ($15). Adjust-O- Tilt steering wheel ($46). Three-spoke Sports steering wheel ($19). Black, white, blue, green or brown vinyl roof ($88). Custom wheelcovers ($50-$53). Turbo-Disc wheelcovers ($75-$78). Spoke-style wheels, including Space-Saver spare, for cars with options packages that include special spoke wheel prices ($34-$50), on others ($99-$104). Code 391 Javelin-AMX 360 Go-Package including specified engine, dual exhaust, hood 'T' stripe decal, black-out rear panel, Rally-Pack instrumentation, Handling Package, Cowl-Air induction, heavy-duty cooling, Twin-Grip differential, power disc brakes, E60-15 Polyglas raised white letter tires, 15 x 7-inch styled steel wheels, and Space-Saver spare with regular 14-inch wheels ($428). Code 392 Javelin-AMX 401 Go-Package, includes all above with 401-cid V-8 ($505).

BUICK MUSCLE 1965-72

Until the '60s, Buick was famous mostly for its large, powerful full-size automobiles. The marque, considered a cornerstone of the General Motors empire, had made some light cars in its early years, but it was the big Roadmaster (a.k.a. "Roadblaster") and Limited models that eventually cast the Buick image as higher-performance machines evolved. Also carrying the Buick banner was the Century, named for its original top speed and legendary for breaking the ice as the first "factory hot rod." Though big by muscle car standards, it was thought of as a "small" model with an oversized Roadmaster engine.

In 1961, Buicks suddenly looked lighter and cleaner. The new Special compact was introduced and would soon be joined by a fancier Skylark sport coupe version. Though not a true muscle car, it came with an aluminum V-8. There was little real news for 1962, but the season's offerings were attractive and well-executed. A styling tour de force arrived in 1963 when the Riviera sports-luxury car was introduced. It was a four-passenger sports coupe with timeless beauty.

The Skylark, which had grown into a mid-size car in 1964, came wrapped in a new supercar persona with the initials GS starting the following year. Since the muscle car movement was in full swing, Buick decided to offer the Riviera in GS guise as well. When a new Riviera — with some of the smoothest lines ever rendered by GM stylists — came along in 1966, a GS equipment option was continued. It would be a rare Riviera option for the rest of the decade.

In 1966 only, the GS monogram could be added to the Wildcat, a larger car that had a high-performance image, though not a real following in muscle car ranks. About 1,200 were made before Buick pulled the plug on that idea and decided to limit use of the GS tag to the models that it originaated on. In the case of the mid-size Special/Skylark series,

the GS designation was now applied to an indivual Gran Sport series featuring coupe, sport coupe and convertible models. A 401-cid V-8 with 325 hp was used in all three, while the Riviera GS used a 425-cid V-8 with 340- and 360-hp options. The "360" version carried double four-barrel carburetors for extra excitement.

As American car makers love to do, Buick heavily restyled the mid-sized Buick in 1968 to make it look more like a junior version of the hot-selling Riviera. With a S-shaped "swirl" down the sides of the body, it was a car that caught many admiring looks.

By the end of the 1960s, Buick had a strong following in the muscle car segment of the market. A 1970-1971 GSX option for the GS 455 coupe featured special paint colors, wild stripes and performance touches. The GSX would become one of the most sought-after Buicks from the 1970s.

Buick shocked the automotive world in 1971 with a new tapered-deck "boat tail" Riviera. This design was built through 1973 and will always stand out on the road. Skylark/GS models continued with little change from 1970-1972, although the potent GS 455s, with their Stage I engine option topping most performance cars in sheer acceleration, were de-tuned for 1971 to run on regular gas and decrease emissions.

As the United States government tightened fuel economy and safety standards, high-performance cars grew harder to find and sporty body styles began to change. By the mid-1970s, the GS and GSX would disappear entirely. (Note: Because of the way that factory options were listed in our sources, it is not always clear if certain options were avaiable only on specific models. Where tire and engine options are listed, the prices given are the amounts added when upgrades were made to the standard tire equipment.)

TOM GLATCH

BUICK

1965 SKYLARK GRAN SPORT

PHIL KUNZ

1965 Skylark Gran Sport

The Skylark Gran Sport was advertised as a Howitzer with windshield wipers. *Motor Trend* said, "It seems to us Buick has another winner in the Skylark Gran Sport. The point is better cars are being built and Buick is building them." As for Buick, it described its mighty new mid-sized muscle machine as "almost like having your own, personal-type nuclear deterrent." This was not your old man's Oldsmobile or your Pappy's Pontiac — it was like the destroyer escort version of your Big Bro's battleship!

This was Buick's intermediate-size Special in its plushest passenger-car form. All Skylarks included specific full wheel-covers, bright rocker moldings, bright wheelhouse moldings, a unique cove treatment with full-width tail lights and emblems centered in the front and rear. The Skylark badge appeared on the front fenders, the rear deck lid and the roof quarters (as well as on the rear fenders of the convertible). The interiors were trimmed plusher cloth-and-vinyl upholstery or in leather-grained all-vinyl upholstery. Front bucket seats were optional (but a mandatory option inside the Skylark Gran Sport).

The heart of the Gran Sport was a 400-cid/325-hp V-8. Also included were a heavy-duty crossflow radiator, a low-back-pressure dual-exhaust system, a beefed-up "convertible" frame, heavy-duty front and rear springs, specially-valved front and rear shock absorbers, a stiffer and thicker-than-stock front anti-roll bar, a four-control-arm rear suspension, a heavy-duty rear axle (3.36 gears with stick shift and 3.08 gears with automatic transmission), standard 9.5-inch diameter brakes with tougher linings and larger wheel cylinders, oversize 7.75 x 14 tires and heavy-duty 6-inch-wide wheels.

Series Number	Body/Style Number	Body Type & Seating	Factory Price	Shipping Weight	Production Total
SKYLARK GRAN SPORT — SERIES 44400 — V-8					
With Three-Speed Transmission					
44400	27	2d Sed-6P	2,805	3,394 lbs.	485
44400	37	2d HT-6P	2,945	3,407 lbs.	684
44400	67	2d Conv 6P	3,095	3,449 lbs.	123
With Four-Speed Transmission					
44400	27	2d Sed-6P	2,972	—	614
44400	37	2d HT-6P	3,112	—	3,677
44400	67	2d Conv 6P	3,262	—	598
With Automatic Transmission					
44400	27	2d Sed-6P	3,009	—	1,263
44400	37	2d HT-6P	3,149	—	7,678
44400	67	2d Conv 6P	3,299	—	1,426

ENGINE

BASE V-8: Overhead valves. Cast-iron block and heads. Bore and stroke: 4.188 x 3.641 inches. Displacement: 401 cid. Compression ratio: 10.25:1. Brake hp: 325 at 4400 rpm. Taxable hp: 56.1. Torque: 445 at 2800. Hydraulic valve lifters. Five main bearings. Carburetor: Rochester 4GC or Carter AFB four-barrel. Engine identification code LT. Called "400" V-8 in Skylark Gran Sport.

OPTIONS

F1 Convenience group includes glareproof inside rearview mirror, electric clock , ash tray light and glove box light ($22.92). Protection group on two-door models including door guards and fuel filler guard ($6.35). N7 air conditioner ($351). N8 air conditioner modification ($15.60). Carpet Savers ($6.89). Carpet Savers and Handi Mats ($12.40). Non-operating center console, with bucket seats ($48.42). Rear window defroster for coupe($21.52). Door guards ($3.77). All tinted glass ($31.20). Tinted windshield ($19.91). Heater and defroster delete ($73 credit). H1 back-up lights ($10.65). S7 remote-control outside rearview mirror on all closed models ($11.73). S7 remote-control outside rearview mirror on convertible ($7.27). Special order paint ($77.90). Two-tone paint, except convertibles ($16.46). L5 power brakes, requires automatic transmission ($42.50). C6 power steering ($96.84). U7 power windows ($102.22). Four-way tilt power seat adjuster with bucket seats ($66.71). D1 radio with manual antenna ($65.64). Rear seat speaker, except in convertibles ($17). Custom front seat belts with retractors ($7.53). Deluxe front seat belts as a delete option ($11 credit). Rear seat belts ($10.76). Rear trailer springs ($3.77). Tilt steering wheel, power steering required ($43.04). Custom fabric top on Skylark coupe and sport coupe ($75.32). Super automatic transmission ($209.63). A7 four-speed manual transmission ($188.30). Custom trim vinyl bucket seats in Syylark coupes and convertibles ($69.94). Custom trim vinyl bucket seats and tuxedo carpets in Skylark convertibles ($100.07). Wire wheel covers on Skylark ($64.56). G7 dual-speed windshield wipers with washers ($17.65).

1966 SKYLARK GS

1966 Skylark Gran Sport

The '66 Skylark GS was about as soft as Kevlar and hard not to love. Buick turned out a total of 13,816 Skylark GS packages for the 1966 model year. The Skylark GS could do 0-to-60 mph in 7.6 seconds and cover the quarter-mile in 14.13 seconds at 95.13 mph.

The regular Skylark was the basis for the GS version. It was Buick's plushest intermediate-size car and featured added exterior bright trim. The extra "gingerbread" included a full-length lower body molding with wheelhouse kick-ups, simulated vent grids on the front fenders, a Skylark script and emblems on the rear fenders and a specific rear cove panel. All Skylarks had Custom-padded seat cushions, specific Deluxe wheelcovers, ashtray and glove compartment lights and front interior courtesy lamps. Gran Sports included the Skylark features, plus a black matte-finish rear cove panel, Skylark GS emblems on the rear quarter panels and instrument panel, Gran Sport nameplates on the grille and deck and 7.75 x 14 whitewall or red line tires.

Bright simulated air scoops, body side paint stripes and a blacked-out grille added to the muscle car's flashier identity.

There was no hood ornament. GS interiors were trimmed all in vinyl, with a notchback front seat as standard equipment and front bucket seats optional. The Skylark had a 401-cid V-8 as standard equipment. However, this engine was listed as a 400-cid engine to get around a GM restriction against using engines with over 400 cubic inches in mid-size cars.

ENGINE

BASE V-8: Overhead valves. Cast-iron block and heads. Bore and stroke: 4.188 x 3.641 inches. Displacement: 401 cid. Compression ratio: 10.25:1. Brake hp: 325 at 4400 rpm. Taxable hp: 56.1. Torque: 445 at 2800. Hydraulic valve lifters. Five main bearings. Carburetor: Carter AFB-4054 four-barrel. Engine identification code MR.

OPTIONS

F1 Convenience group includes glareproof inside rearview mirror, electric clock, ashtray light and glove box light ($22.92). Protection group on including door guards and fuel filler guard ($6.35). N7 air conditioner ($351). N8 air conditioner modification ($15.60). Carpet Savers ($6.89). Carpet Savers and Handi Mats ($12.40). Non-operating center console, with bucket seats ($48.42). Rear window defroster for coupe ($21.52). Door guards ($3.77). Dual exhausts ($21.52). All tinted glass ($31.20). Tinted windshield ($19.91). Heater and defroster delete ($73 credit). H1 back-up lights ($10.65). S7 remote-control outside rearview mirror on all closed models ($11.73). S7 remote-control outside rearview mirror on convertible ($7.27). Special order paint ($77.90). Two-tone paint, except convertibles ($16.46). L5 power brakes, requires automatic transmission ($42.50). C6 power steering ($96.84). U7 power windows ($102.22). Four-way tilt power seat adjuster with bucket seats ($66.71). D1 radio with manual antenna ($65.64). Rear seat speaker, except in convertible ($17). Custom front seat belts with retractors ($7.53). Deluxe front seat belts as a delete option ($11 credit). Rear seat belts ($10.76). Rear trailer springs ($3.77). Heavy-duty susspension with heavy-duty front and rear springs, heavy-duty shock absorbers and heavy-duty stabilizer bar ($10.76). Tilt steering wheel, power steering required ($43.04). Custom fabric top on Skylark coupe and sport coupe ($75.32). Super automatic transmission with V-8 ($209.63). A7 four-speed manual transmission, V-8 required ($188.30). Custom trim vinyl bucket seats in coupes ($69.94). Custom trim vinyl bucket seats in convertibles ($100.07). Wire wheel covers ($58). G7 dual-speed windshield wipers with washers ($17.65).

Series Number	Body/Style Number	Body Type & Seating	Factory Price	Shipping Weight	Production Total
SKYLARK GS — SERIES 44600 — V-8					
44600	44607	2d Sed-6P	2,956	3,388 lbs.	1,835
44600	44617	2d HT-6P	3,019	3,428 lbs.	9,934
44600	44667	2d Conv 6P	3,167	3,289 lbs.	2,047

NOTE 1: 44607 production includes 178 with three-speed manual, 308 with four-speed manual and 1,349 with THM-300.

NOTE 2: 44617 production includes 450 with three-speed manual, 2,199 with four-speed manual and 7,285 with THM-300.

NOTE 3: 44667 production includes 136 with three-speed manual, 431 with four-speed manual and 1,480 with THM-300.

BUICK

1967 SKYLARK GS 340

Buick GS-340.
What the car enthusiasts are enthusiastic about.

We started out to build a car that would cost less than our fabled GS-400. We ended up with a very sporting machine in its own right: a 340-cu-bic-inch V-8, pumping out 260 horsepower. A whole new distinctive look, with hood scoops painted to contrast with the hood, broad striping on the rocker panel, special emblems. Inside, a clean, simple, black interior. And you know what? It still costs less than our fabled GS-400. A lot less.

No wonder the enthusiasts are enthusiastic.

1967 Skylark Gran Sport 340

Series Number	Body/Style Number	Body Type & Seating	Factory Price	Shipping Weight	Production Total
SKYLARK GS 340 — SERIES 43400 — V-8					
43400	43417	2d HT-6P	$2,845	3,271 lbs.	3,692

ENGINE

BASE V-8: Overhead valves. Cast-iron block and heads. Bore and stroke: 3.75 x 3.85 inches. Displacement: 340 cid. Compression ratio: 10.25:1. Brake hp: 260 at 4000 rpm. Taxable hp: 45.0. Torque: 365 at 2800. Hydraulic valve lifters. Five main bearings. Carburetor: Carter AFB-4055 four-barrel. Engine identification code NB.

OPTIONS

L6 air conditioner, heater required ($343.20). P2 carpet savers, all ($6.77). P1 carpet savers and Handi mats ($12.19). U3 electric clock and trunk light ($17.90). 17 heavy-duty cooling package ($42.13). X3 non-operating floor console ($31.60). B4 operating floor console, with Super Turbine automatic transmission and bucket seats required ($57.93). S5 automatic cruise control, not available with manual transmission ($44.23). M7 rear window defroster ($21.06). 04 door guards ($3.64). G5 economy rear axle ratio (no charge). L1 all tinted glass ($30.54). L2 tinted glass, windshield only ($21.06). 1C driver and passenger headrests with bench seats ($41.60). 1D driver and passenger headrest, with bucket seats ($51.93). 18 heater and defroster delete ($71.50 credit). O5 left-hand outside remote-control mirror ($7.10). W2 belt reveal and wheel opening moldings for hardtop ($31.60). Special order paint ($76.25). Two-tone paint ($26.33). G1 performance axle with positive-traction differential ($42.13). C1 power disc brakes all, but not available with wheel covers or chrome wheels ($147.45). R1 power brakes ($100.03). C7 power brakes ($41.60). Q5 4-way tilt-adjustable power seat ($69.51). C6 power steering ($94.79). D1 Sonomatic radio with manual antenna ($64.25). D5 AM/FM radio with manual antenna ($133.76). H2 Ride & Handling package, including special front and rear shocks, larger springs and a stabilizer bar ($5.27). J1 Custom front and rear seat belts ($6.32) J6 Custom front and rear seat belts, Custom belts and shoulder harness required ($7.90). 1B reclining driver and passenger seat with headrest, Strato bucket seat required ($83.10). Vinyl-trimmed Custom notchback seat ($36.86). J3 front driver and passenger shoulder harness and Custom seat belts. J4 front driver and passenger shoulder belt ($23.17). K3 speed alert ($8.43). S7 tilt steering wheel, except with column-shifted three-speed manual transmission ($42.13). U5 tachometer, console required ($47.39). F1 7.75 x 14 white sidewall tires ($31.60). F8 Wide-Oval red line tires on GS 400 (no charge). Custom vinyl top covering with rear quarter belt molding on coupe and hardtop ($84.26). B1 Super Turbine automatic transmission ($205.24). H1 trailer towing package, all without Ride & Handling or Automatic Level Control ($3.69). V1 deluxe wheel covers ($21.06). V2 chrome-plated wheels. U3 Convenience group, includes electric clock and trunk light ($17.90). GS ornamentation package, includes rear deck molding, rear deck molding extension, GS monograms, rear deck molding, rear quarter molding, grille molding, hood top center molding and front fender side ornaments for base Special coupe ($42.13). 07.

The GS 340 gets a bad rap because the GS 400 looks better on paper, but for the majority of "Joe Lunchbox" weekend muscle-car junkies, the 260-hp 340 and the GS-style body trim made this a fine everyman's muscle car. For collectors, the GS 340 offers plenty in the looks department and a bonus in the rarity department.

The GS 340 model was introduced at midyear, during the Chicago Automobile Show. A hybrid, it was technically part of the base Special V-8 series, but it was trimmed as a fancier GS model. Wide Red rally stripes and Red hood scoops were seen, as was a Red lower deck molding. Two body colors, white or platinum mist, were offered. An optional "Sport Pac" included specific front and rear shocks, heavy-duty springs and a large diameter-tabilizer bar. Standard features included 15:1-ratio steering, 7.75 x 14 Rayon Cord tires on red 14-inch Rally-style wheels and a two-speed Super Turbine automatic transmission (or a four-speed manual transmission.) The interior was similar to that of a Special Deluxe model and black, all-vinyl upholstery was the only choice.

1967 SKYLARK GS 400

IN
'67 BUICK
Get in with the In Crowd in a GS-400

The In Crowd knows what's happening, and what's happening is Buick '67. Proof: GS-400, Buick's personal sport car. It has a 400-cu. in., 340-hp V-8, a new brake system with dual master cylinders, energy absorbing steering column, bucket seats, heavy-duty suspension and a list of standard equipment features—including all the new GM safety items—so long it takes a Buick dealer to do it justice. (He'll also tell you how four out of five new-car buyers pay Buick-sized prices to begin with.) The In Crowd's at your Quality Buick dealer's right now. How soon can you join them?

1967 Skylark Gran Sport 400

Are you ready to rock-and-roll?" Buick could have asked its traditionally conservative buyers when the GS 400 hit the ground running in '67. It was a true muscle car capable of going from 0-to-60 mph in 6.9 seconds with an automatic transmission or 6.6 seconds with a four-speed transmission. Its top speed was an eye-opening 122 mph.

The high-performance Skylark took its name from its 400-cid V-8. Three- or four- speed manual or three-speed Super Turbine automatic transmissions were offered. The exterior appearance was strengthened by the use of twin hood scoops, rally stripes and a special grille. The GS name appeared in red letters on the grille and rear deck. F70 x 14 Wide-Oval red or white stripe tires were standard. The GS 400 had no fender skirts. The interior was all-vinyl.

Series Number	Body/Style Number	Body Type & Seating	Factory Price	Shipping Weight	Production Total
SKYLARK GS 400 — SERIES 44600 — V-8					
44600	44607	2d Cpe-6P	$2,956	3,439 lbs.	1,014
44600	44617	2d HT-6P	$3,019	3,500 lbs.	10,659
44600	44667	2d Conv 6P	$3,167	3,505 lbs.	2,140

NOTE 1: 44607 production includes 116 with three-speed manual, 168 with four-speed manual and 730 with THM-400.

NOTE 2: 44617 production includes 373 car with three-speed manual, 2,280 with four-speed manual and 8,006 with THM-400.

NOTE 3: 44667 production includes nine car with three-speed manual, 422 with four-speed manual and 1,628 with THM-400.

ENGINE
BASE V-8: Overhead valves. Cast-iron block and heads. Bore and stroke: 4.04 x 3.90 inches. Displacement: 400 cid. Compression ratio: 10.25:1. Brake hp: 340 at 5000 rpm. Taxable hp: 51.9. Torque: 440 at 300. Hydraulic valve lifters. Five main bearings. Crankcase capacity: 4 qt. (add 1 qt. if new filter installed). Cooling system capacity: 17 qt. (add 1 qt. for heater). Carburetor: Rochester 4MV Quadra-Jet four-barrel. Engine identification code NR.

OPTIONS
L6 air conditioner, heater required ($343.20). P2 carpet savers, all ($6.77). P1 carpet savers and Handi mats ($12.19). U3 electric clock and trunk light ($17.90). 17 heavy-duty cooling package ($42.13). B7 consolette with bucket seats and manual transmission ($36.86). M7 rear window defroster, except convertible ($21.06). 04 door guards ($3.64). G5 economy rear axle ratio (no charge). L1 all tinted glass ($30.54). L2 tinted glass, windshield only ($21.06). 1C driver and passenger headrests with bench seats, all ($41.60). 1D driver and passenger headrest, with bucket seats ($51.93). 18 heater and defroster delete ($71.50 credit). O5 left-hand outside remote-control mirror ($7.10). W5 belt reveal molding ($14.74). Special order paint ($76.25). Two-tone paint, except convertible ($26.33). G1 performance axle with positive-traction differential ($42.13). C1 power disc brakes, not available with wheel covers or chrome wheels ($147.45). R1 power brakes ($100.03). C7 power brakes ($41.60). Q5 4-way tilt-adjustable power seat ($69.51). C6 power steering ($94.79). D1 Sonomatic radio with manual antenna ($64.25). D5 AM/FM radio with manual antenna ($133.76). D6 rear seat speaker, except convertible ($12.84). J1 Custom front and rear seat belts ($6.32). J6 Custom front and rear seat belts, Custom belts and shoulder harness required ($7.90). Vinyl-trimmed Custom notchback ($36.86). J3 front driver and passenger shoulder harness and Custom seat belts ($32.65). J4 front driver and passenger shoulder belt ($23.17). K3 speed alert ($8.43). S7 tilt steering wheel, except with column-shifted three-speed manual transmission ($42.13). U5 tachometer, console required ($47.39). F8 Wide-Oval red line tires on GS 400 (no charge). Custom vinyl top covering with rear quarter belt molding on coupes and sport coupes ($84.26). B3 four-speed manual transmission, not available with console ($184.31). B2 Super Turbine automatic transmission ($236.82). H1 trailer towing package, all without Ride & Handling or Automatic Level Control ($3.69). V1 deluxe wheel covers, on Skylark ($21.06). V3 wire wheel covers ($61.85). V2 chrome-plated wheels ($69.98). U3 Convenience Group, includes electric clock and trunk light ($17.90).

BUICK

1968 SKYLARK GS 350

Like a grassland prairie dog trying hard to outrun a grey-hound, the GS 350 could run a great race , but just didn't have "legs" long enough to win it. Zero-to-60 took 9.5 seconds — about 2 seconds slower than a GS 400.

Trimmed like the Skylark Custom inside, the GS 350 had a more muscular outer appearance. It was coded as a Skylark Custom, although it was more related to the GS 400. Finned simulated air intakes were seen on the front fenders, while a painted lower body accent stripe replaced the bright molding used on Skylark Custom models. The rear suspension was beefed up. Bright wheelhouse moldings were used, but rear fender skirts were not. A GS 350 plaque was found on the center of the deck lid and flashier identification was seen on the grille and rear fenders, with GS monograms appearing in such places — and also on the door panels. Foam-padded all-vinyl bench seats were standard equipment and front bucket seats were optional. A specific grille with a bright crossbar and a textured background was used. An upper level instrument panel ventilation system was a new feature that eliminated the use of front ventipanes. The hood had a scoop at the rear and concealed windshield wipers.

Series Number	Body/Style Number	Body Type & Seating	Factory Price	Shipping Weight	Production Total
GS 350 — SERIES 43400 — V-8					
43400	43437	2d HT-6P	$2,926	3,375 lbs.	8,317

NOTE: lincludes 455 with three-speed manual, 844 with four-speed manual and 7,018 with THM-300.

ENGINE

BASE V-8: Overhead valves. Cast-iron block and heads. Bore and stroke: 3.80 x 3.85 inches. Displacement: 350 cid. Compression ratio: 10.25:1. Brake hp: 280 at 4600 rpm. Taxable hp: 46.20. Torque: 375 at 3200. Hydraulic valve lifters. Five main bearings. Carburetor: Rochester 4MV Quadra-Jet four-barrel. Engine identification code PP.

OPTIONS

16 air conditioner in all models, heater required ($360.20). 17 heavy-duty cooling package ($31.60). X3 non-operating floor console, bucket seats required ($31.60). B7 consolette with bucket seats and manual transmission ($36.86). S6 Cruise Master speed control with V-8 and automatic transmission required ($52.66). Custom trim with notchback bench seat, deluxe armrests, remote door handles and rear courtesy lamps in two-door hardtop ($78.99). Vinyl notchback bench seat in two-door hardtop and convertible ($36.86). Vinyl Strato bucket seats ($68.46). Vinyl Strato bucket seayts ($139.02). M7 rear window defroster ($21.06). C1 disc brakes, power brakes required and not with chrome-plated wheels ($63.19). 04 door guards ($5.27). L1 all tinted glass ($36.86). L2 tinted glass, windshield only ($25.27). 1C driver and passenger headrests with bench seats ($41.60). 1D driver and passenger headrest, with bucket seats ($51.93). O5 left-hand outside remote-control mirror ($9.48). W5 belt reveal molding ($25.27). W5 belt reveal molding ($14.74). Two-tone paint ($31.07). G4 positive-traction differential ($42.13). C7 power brakes ($41.60). Q5 4-way tilt-adjustable power seat ($69.51). C6 power steering ($94.79). R1 power windows ($100.05). D1 Sonomatic radio with manual antenna ($69.51). D5 AM/FM radio with manual antenna ($133.76). D6 rear seat speaker ($16.64). J1 Custom front and rear seat belts iwith bucket seats ($7.90). J3 Custom seat belts front and rear in six-passenger models and two Custom front shoulder belts ($35.81). J3 Custom seat belts front and rear in five-passenger bucket seat models and two Custom front shoulder belts ($34.23). J5 Custom seat belts front and rear in six-passenger models and four Custom front and rear shoulder belts ($62.14). J5 Custom seat belts front and rear in five-passenger bucket seat models and four Custom front and rear shoulder belts ($60.56). K3 speed alert ($8.43). X4 Rallye steering wheel ($45.82). X4 Rallye steering wheel ($31.60). D3 stereo tape player, radio and speaker required ($116.91). U5 tachometer, console required ($47.39). F7 205R-14 radial white sidewall tires ($88.47). Custom vinyl top covering with rear quarter belt molding ($94.79). B9 three-speed manual transmission with floor shift in GS350 without operationg console ($84.26). B3 four-speed manual transmission with floor shift, not available with console ($184.31). B1 Super Turbine automatic transmission ($205.24). V1 deluxe wheel covers ($21.06). V3 wire wheel covers ($80.05). V2 chrome-plated wheels, not available with disc brakes ($90.58). Rallye wheels ($42.66). K4 windshield wipers with depressed park ($18.96). 17 Heavy-duty cooling option ($31.60). U1 Convenience Group, includes dual horns, glove compartment light, ash tray light and trunk light in 43300 ($15.80). U1 Convenience Group, includes dual horns, glove compartment light, ash tray light and trunk light ($11.90). U2 Convenience Group, includes electric clock, glove compartment light, ash tray light and trunk light ($28.75). H4 Rallye Road Control package including 15.0:1 ratio power steering, rear stabilizer bar and Firm Ride front and rear spreings and shocks ($126.38). H6 Rallye Road Control package including rear stabilizer bar and Firm Ride front and rear springs and shocks ($15.80). H1 trailer tow package including special front and rear shocks and special rear springs ($3.69).

1968 GS 400

The '68 GS 400 launched like a jet-propelled swamp boat hightailing it out of the Okeefenokee with a level 7 hurricane on its tail. *Motor Trend* tested a convertible with a bunch of options. Its total weight was 4,300 lbs. At a drag strip it clocked 16.3 seconds at 88 mph. Zero-to-60 performance for the GS 400 hardtop was charted as a snappy 7.5 seconds. *Hot Rod* magazine's Eric Dahlquist did a little bit better with a well-equipped hardtop he wrote about in January 1968. His car had an as-tested price of $4,505 and weighed 3,820 lbs. By using the hood scoop as part of a homemade cold-air package, Dahlquist got the car's quarter-mile performance down to 14.78 seconds and registered a terminal speed of 94 mph.

The GS 400 was another version of the new 112-inch-wheelbase mid-size Buick two-door. It was identified by a GS 400 plaque on each front fender, fake fender vents and functional hood scoops. Folding seatback latches were standard, along with an all-vinyl front bench seat. Front bucket seats were optional. GS 400 styling revisions included an overall swoopier look with an S-shaped body side feature line. The huge air scoop was integrated into the trailing edge of the hood and the chrome finned ornaments decorated the area immediately behind the front wheel openings.

The GS 400 again used the 400-cid V-8 introduced in 1967. There were no changes in the horsepower or torque ratings. Standard equipment included a three-speed manual transmission and a 3.42:1 rear axle.

TOM GLATCH

1968 Gran Sport 400

Series Number	Body/Style Number	Body Type & Seating	Factory Price	Shipping Weight	Production Total
GS 400 — SERIES 44600 — V-8					
44600	44637	2d HT-6P	$3,127	3,514 lbs.	10,743
44600	44667	2d Conv-6P	$3,271	3,547 lbs.	2,454

NOTE 1: 44637 production includes 242 with three-speed manual, 1,632 with four-speed manual and 8,869 with THM-400.

NOTE 2: 44667 production includes 79 with three-speed manual, 351 with four-speed manual and 2,024 with THM-400.

ENGINE

BASE V-8: Overhead valves. Cast-iron block and heads. Bore and stroke: 4.04 x 3.90 inches. Displacement: 400 cid. Compression ratio: 10.25:1. Brake hp: 340 at 5000 rpm. Taxable hp: 52.23. Torque: 440 at 3200. Hydraulic valve lifters. Five main bearings. Carburetor: Rochester 4MV Quadra-Jet four-barrel. Engine identification code PR.

OPTIONS

16 air conditioner in all models, heater required ($360.20). 17 heavy-duty cooling package, without air conditioner ($31.60). X3 non-operating floor console, bucket seats required ($31.60). B4 operating floor console, except GS 400 with Super Turbine automatic transmission, bucket seats required ($57.93). B7 consolette, with bucket seats and manual transmission ($36.86). S6 Cruise Master speed control, automatic transmission required ($52.66). Vinyl notchback bench seat ($36.86). Vinyl Strato bucket seats ($68.46). M7 rear window defroster, except convertible ($21.06). C1 disc brakes, power brakes required; not with chrome-plated wheels ($63.19). 04 door guards ($5.27). L1 all tinted glass ($36.86). L2 tinted glass, windshield only ($25.27). 1C driver and passenger headrests with bench seats ($41.60). 1D driver and passenger headrest, with bucket seats ($51.93). W5 belt reveal molding ($14.74). W8 Rally stripe (no charge). Two-tone paint, not on convertibles ($31.07). G1 performance axle with positive-traction differential ($42.13). G4 positive-traction differential ($42.13). C7 power brakes ($41.60). Q5 4-way tilt-adjustable power seat ($69.51). C6 power steering ($94.79). R1 power windows ($100.05). D1 Sonomatic radio with manual antenna ($69.51). D5 AM/FM radio with manual antenna ($133.76). D6 rear seat speaker ($16.64). J1 Custom front and rear seat belts in all models with bucket seats ($7.90). J3 Custom seat belts front and rear in six-passenger models and two Custom front shoulder belts ($35.81). J3 Custom seat belts front and rear in five-passenger bucket seat models and two Custom front shoulder belts ($34.23). J3 Custom front and rear and third-seat seat belts and two front shoulder belts in three-seat Sportwagon. ($38.97). J5 Custom seat belts front and rear in six-passenger models and four Custom front and rear shoulder belts ($62.14). J5 Custom seat belts front and rear in five-passenger bucket seat models and four Custom front and rear shoulder belts ($60.56). K3 speed alert ($8.43). S7 tilt steering wheel, all except cars with column-shifted three-speed manual transmission ($42.13). X6 Custom steering wheel in 43500-44400 ($10.53). X4 Rallye steering whell in 43435-43500-44000 ($31.60). D3 stereo tape player in 43000-44000, radio and speaker required ($116.91). U5 tachometer, console required ($47.39). F8 F70 x 14 Wide-Oval red line tires (31.60). F8 F70 x 14 Wide-Oval white line tires (31.60). Custom vinyl top covering with rear quarter belt molding ($94.79). B3 four-speed manual transmission in 43437-44600 with floor shift, not available with console ($184.31). B2 Super Turbine automatic transmission ($236.82). V1 deluxe wheel covers, on 44300-44000 ($21.06). V3 wire wheel covers on 43437-44455-44465-44600 ($80.05). V2 chrome-plated wheels; not available with disc brakes ($90.58). Rallye wheels on 43000-44000 ($42.66). 17 Heavy-duty cooling option ($31.60). U3 Convenience group, includes electric clock and trunk light ($18.96). 07 Protection H1 trailer tow package including special front and rear shocks and special rear springs ($3.69).

BUICK

1969 GS 350

JERRY HEASLEY

1969 Gran Sport 350

If you wanted to walk the walk without really taking the ride, the GS 350 was the car for you. "At last a genuine performance machine that doesn't rattle your molars every time you're stopped at a traffic light," said one Buick ad.

The plushest intermediate Buick had better quality vinyl and cloth or all-vinyl interiors, a bright lower body molding and wheelhouse moldings. A chrome sweepspear molding was optional and, at the front, a Buick emblem was centered in the grille. A one-style series for 1969 was the GS 350.

Once again this car combined the Skylark Custom's interior accoutrements with a sporty car's exterior. The front fenders carried neither ventiports or vents this year, but wheelhouse moldings were used. A more prominent hood scoop was hooked to a special air cleaner with twin snorkels. Buick claimed this cold-air-induction system boosted power eight percent and increased torque 6.5 percent. However, the factory output ratings did not change. A GS 350 plaque was used on the center of the deck lid, with monograms on the grille and door panels. All-vinyl, foam padded bbench seats were standard. Front bucket seats were optional. The coupe body used one-piece side glass and an upper-level ventilation system.

Series Number	Body/Style Number	Body Type & Seating	Factory Price	Shipping Weight	Production Total
GS 350 — SERIES 43400 — V-8					
43400	43437	2d HT-6P	$2,980	3,406 lbs.	4,933

NOTE: Includes 233 with three-speed manual, 632 with four-speed manual and 5,440 with THM-350.

ENGINE

BASE V-8: Overhead valves. Cast-iron block and heads. Bore and stroke: 3.80 x 3.85 inches. Displacement: 350 cid. Compression ratio: 10.25:1. Brake hp: 280 at 4600 rpm. Taxable hp: 46.20. Torque: 375 at 3200. Hydraulic valve lifters. Five main bearings. Carburetor: Rochester 4MV Quadra-Jet four-barrel. Engine identification code RP.

OPTIONS

N3 heavy-duty air cleaner ($9.48). 16 air conditioner ($375.99). H3 Automatic Level Control ($78.99). G5 economy rear axle (no charge). G1 performance axle, includes positive-traction differential, automatic transmission required ($42.13). G4 positive-traction rear axle ($42.13). H5 heavy-duty Energizer battery ($7.37). P2 carpet savers ($7.37). P1 Carpet savers and Handy Mats ($14.54). X3 non-operating console ($31.60). B4 full-length console, automatic transmission required ($61.09). B7 consolette, bucket seats and manual transmission with floor shift required ($36.36). 13 heavy-duty cooling with extra-heavy-duty radiator ($21.06). S6 Cruise Master speed control, requires automatic transmissin ($57.93). Q6 custom padded seat cushions, but standard in Skylark Custom and with bucket seats ($15.80). Custom vinyl trim including bucket seats, rear compartment courtesy lights, deluxe armrests and custom compartment shelf with trims 181, 185, 186 and 188 ($149.55). M7 blower type rear window defroster ($22.12). 04 door guards ($5.27). L1 Soft-Ray tinted glass ($38.97). L2 Soft-Ray tinted windshield ($26.33). 27 front headrests ($16.85 and mandatory equipment after January 1, 1969). 05 remote-control left-hand outside rearview mirror ($10.53). W2 Custom belt reveal moldings ($14.74). W4 protective side moldings on Skylarks-Skylark Custom with front fender moldings ($26.33). Two-tone paint ($31.07). C1 power disc brakes ($64.25). C7 power brakes ($41.60). T2 power door locks ($47.39). Q5 4-way tilt seat adjuster ($73.72, but A46 for bucket seats). C6 power steering ($100.05, but not available with Rally Ride Control package). R1 power windows ($105.32). D1 Sonomatic radio with manual antenna ($69.51). D2 Sonomatic radio with power antenna ($100.05). D5 AM/FM radio with electric antenna ($164.30). D7 AM/FM radio with manual antenna ($133.76). D3 stereo tape player, radio and rear speaker required ($116.91). D6 rear speaker ($16.64). J1 Custom front and rear seat belts in six-passenger cars ($10.53). J1 Custom front and rear seat belts in five-passenger cars ($8.74). J3 two Custom front shoulder belts with Custom front and rear seat belts and bucket seats ($11.90). J3 two Custom front shoulder belts in Skylark Custom convertible, Skylark Custom convertible with Custom front and rear seat belts and bench seats ($36.86). J3 two Custom front shoulder belts with Custom front and rear seat belts and bucket seats ($35.07). J5 four Custom front and rear shoulder belts in models with bucket seats and Custom front and rear seat belts ($38.23). J5 four Custom front and rear shoulder belts in models with bench seats and Custom front and rear seat belts ($63.19). 1B Strato Bench seat with right-hand recliner ($31.18). X1 deluxe steering wheel ($15.80). X4 Rallye steering wheel ($15.80). S7 tilt steering, with automatic transmission and non-standard steering wheel ($45.29). K3 speed alert ($11.59). U5 tachometer in, consolette required ($47.39). F1 7.75 x 14 white sidewall tires ($31.60). F2 8.25 x 14 oversize white sidewall tires ($50.56). F3 8.25 x 14 oversize black sidewall tires ($20.01). F3 8.25 x

14 oversize black sidewall tires ($14.74). F7 205R14 radial-ply white sidewall tires ($93.73). E9 Spacesaver spare tire with mini-pump ($15.80). B1 Super Turbine 300 automatic transmission without 350-cid V-8 ($174.24). B1 Super Turbine 300 automatic transmission in with 350-cid V-8. B3 four-speed manual gearbox with floor shift , in cars without full-length console ($184.80). B5 Turbo Hyrda-Matic 350 ($205.92). B9 three-speed manual transmission with floor shift ($84.48). Custom vinyl roof with rear quarter belt molding ($100.05) . V1 de-

luxe wheel covers ($21.06). V3 wire wheel ($80.05). V2 chrome-plated wheels ($94.79, but not available with disc brakes). U3 convenience group including trunk light and map light ($23.17). 17 heavy-duty cooling package including thermostatically controlled fan drive, 55-amp Delcotron and heavy-duty radiator ($33.70, includes fuel return lines with 350-cid V-8, not available with air conditioning). 12 forced upper-level ventilation ($42.13). H4 Rallye Ride control package ($131.65). H1 trailer towing ($3.69).

1969 GS 400

1969 Gran Sport 400

Similar to the GS 350, the most potent Buick had "400" numerals on the hood scoop and rear quarters. A deluxe steering wheel was standard, along with foam padded seats, an ashtray light, a glovebox light and an upper interior light. All-vinyl upholstery was used. A front bench seat was standard. Bucket seats were optional. There was a unique GS 400 grille and a cold-air-induction package. A hot, dealer-installed option was the Stage 1 package, which included a 400-cid/345-hp V-8. Experts said the actual output of this engine was closer to 400 hp.

Stage 1 hardware included a high-lift camshaft, a special modified quadrajet four-barrel carburetor, a large-diameter dual exhaust system with 2 1/4-inch tailpipes and a 3.64:1 Positraction rear axle. Cars so-equipped had "Stage 1" emblems on the front fenders. A three-speed manual transmission with floor-mounted gear selector was standard equipment.

ENGINES

BASE V-8: Overhead valves. Cast-iron block and heads. Bore and stroke: 4.04 x 3.90 inches. Displacement: 400 cid. Compression ratio: 10.25:1. Brake hp: 340 at 5000 rpm. Taxable hp: 52.23. Torque: 440 at 3200. Hydraulic valve lifters. Five main bearings. Carburetor: Rochester 4MV Quadra-Jet four-barrel. Engine identification code RR.

OPTIONAL STAGE 1 V-8: Overhead valves. Cast-iron block and heads. Bore and stroke: 4.04 x 3.90 inches. Displacement: 400 cid. Compression ratio: 10.25:1. Brake hp: 345 at 5800 rpm. Taxable hp: 52.23. Torque: 440 at 3200. Hydraulic valve lifters. Five main bearings. Carburetor: Rochester 4MV Quadra-Jet four-barrel. Engine identification code RR.

OPTIONS

N3 heavy-duty air cleaner ($9.48). 16 air conditioner ($375.99). H3 Automatic Level Control ($78.99). G5 economy rear axle (no charge). G1 performance axle, includes positive-traction differential, automatic transmission required ($42.13). G4 positive-traction rear axle ($42.13). P2 carpet savers ($7.37). P1 Carpet savers and Handy Mats ($14.54). X3 non-operating console, bucket seats required ($31.60). B4 full-length console, bucket seats and automatic transmission required ($61.09). B7 consolette, bucket seats and manual transmission with floor shift required ($36.36). 13 heavy-duty cooling with extra-heavy-duty radiator ($21.06). S6 Cruise Master speed control, requires automatic transmissin ($57.93). Custom vinyl trim in with notchback seats ($36.86). Custom vinyl trim in with Strato bucket seats ($78.99). M7 blower type rear window defroster, except convertible ($22.12). 04 door guards on all two-doors ($5.27). L1 Soft-Ray tinted glass ($38.97). L2 Soft-Ray tinted windshield ($26.33). 27 front headrests $16.85 and mandatory equipment after January 1, 1969). 05 remote-control left-hand outside rearview mirror ($10.53). W2 Custom belt reveal moldings ($14.74). W4 protective side moldings on Skylark-Skylark Custom with front fender moldings ($26.33). Two-tone paint , except convertible, includes rear quarter belt molding ($31.07). Special order paint ($76.25). C1 power disc brakes ($64.25). C7 power brakes ($41.60). T2 power door locks, two-door models ($47.39). Q5 4-way tilt seat adjuster, ($73.72, but A46 for bucket seats). C6 power steering ($100.05, but not available with Rally Ride Control package). R1 power windows ($105.32). D1 Sonomatic radio with manual antenna ($69.51). D2 Sonomatic radio with power antenna, except convertible ($100.05). D5 AM/FM radio with electric antenna, except convertible ($164.30). D7 AM/FM radio

Series Number	Body/Style Number	Body Type & Seating	Factory Price	Shipping Weight	Production Total
GS 400 — SERIES 44600 — V-8					
44600	44637	2d HT-6P	3,181	3,549 lbs.	6,346
44600	44667	2d Conv 6P	3,325	3,594 lbs.	1,564

NOTE 1: 44637 production includes 117 with three-speed manual, 785 with four-speed manual and 5,444 with THM-400.

NOTE 2: 44667 production includes 48 with three-speed manual, 213 with four-speed manual and 1,303 with THM-400.

Series Number	Body/Style Number	Body Type & Seating	Factory Price	Shipping Weight	Production Total
GS 400 (Stage 1) — SERIES 44600 — V-8					
44600	44637	2d HT-6P	$3,380	3,549 lbs.	1,256
44600	44667	2d Conv 6P	$3,524	3,594 lbs.	212

NOTE 3: 44637 production includes nine with three-speed manual, 415 with four-speed manual and 832 with THM-400.

NOTE 4: 44667 production includes four with three-speed manual, 77 with four-speed manual and 131 with THM-400.

with manual antenna ($133.76). D3 stereo tape player, radio and rear speaker required ($116.91). D6 rear speaker ($16.64). J1 Custom front and rear seat belts in six-passenger cars without bucket seats ($10.53). J1 Custom front and rear seat belts in five-passenger cars with bucket seats ($8.74). J3 two Custom front shoulder belts in sport coupe with Custom front and rear seat belts and bucket seats ($11.90). J3 two Custom front shoulder belts in convertible with Custom front and rear seat belts and bench seats ($36.86). J3 two Custom front shoulder belts in convertible with Custom front and rear seat belts and bucket seats ($35.07). J5 four Custom front and rear shoulder belts with bench seats, except convertible ($40.02). J5 four Custom front and rear shoulder belts in Sport Coupe models with bucket seats and Custom front and rear seat belts ($38.23). J5 four Custom front and rear shoulder belts in convertible with bench seats and Custom front and rear seat belts ($61.40). 1B Strato Bench seat with right-hand recliner in ($31.18). S7 tilt steering, in all "Specials" with automatic transmission and non-standard steering wheel ($45.29). K3 speed alert ($11.59). U5 tachometer, consolette required ($47.39). F2 8.25 x 14 oversize white sidewall tires ($18.96). F3 8.25 x 14 oversize black sidewall tires (no charge). F7 205R14 radial-ply white sidewall tires ($56.87). F8 F70-14 Wide-Oval red line tires ($31.60). F9 F70-14 Wide-Oval white line tires ($31.60). E9 Spacesaver spare tire with mini-pump ($15.80). B3 four-speed manual gearbox with floor shift, without full-length console ($184.80). W4 protective side moldings with front fender moldings ($33.68). Custom vinyl roof with rear quarter belt molding on sport coupe ($100.05). V3 wire wheel covers ($80.05). V2 chrome-plated wheels ($94.79, but not available with disc brakes). U3 convenience group including trunk light and map light ($23.17). 17 heavy-duty cooling package including thermostatically-controlled fan drive, 55-amp Delcotron and heavy-duty radiator ($33.70). 12 forced upper-level ventilation ($42.13). H4 Rallye Ride control package ($131.65). H6 Rallye Ride control package ($15.80). A1 Stage 1 option includes 400-cid V-8, specific ornamentation, positive-traction performance axle, heavy-duty cooling and low-restriction dual exhaust system ($199.05).

1970 GS

Driving a stock 1970 GS was like life in the fast-looking lane — you definitely had a go-fast image, but you avoided the Stoplight Gran Prix at all costs. Nevertheless, it was a nice car to own if you wanted good everyday performance and out-of-this-world looks.

A one-model series constituted Buick's "cosmetic" muscle car for 1970. The GS was a more mild-mannered intermediate than the GS 455 or GSX, though it came with all of the trimmings of a rip-roaring charger. A textured black grille was used and there was a functional hood scoops on the panel above. GS signatures appeared on the left-hand grille, front fenders and deck. All-vinyl bench seats in Sandalwood, Blue or Black were standard. An all-vinyl notchback seat was optional, as were individual front bucket seats.

Standard equipment approximated that found on the Skylark Custom and, but also included some true performance-car features like a dual exhaust system, heavy-duty shock absorbers and springs and a semi-enclosed cooling system. A column-mounted gear shifter was standard. This car came standard with a 350-cid V-8, though it was not called a GS 350 in the sales catalog.

Series Number	Body/Style Number	Body Type & Seating	Factory Price	Shipping Weight	Production Total
GS — SERIES 43400 — V-8					
43400	43437	2d HT-6P	$3,098	3,434 lbs.	9,948

NOTE: Includes 224 with three-speed manual, 884 with four-speed manual and 8,840 with THM-350.

ENGINE
BASE V-8: Overhead valves. Cast-iron block and heads. Bore and stroke: 3.80 x 3.85 inches. Displacement: 350 cid. Compression ratio: 10.25:1. Brake hp: 315 at 4800 rpm. Taxable hp: 46.20. Torque: 410 at 3200. Hydraulic valve lifters. Five main bearings. Carburetor: Rochester 4MV Quadra-Jet four-barrel. Engine identification code SP.

OPTIONS
N3 heavy-duty air cleaner ($9.48). 16 air conditioner ($375.99). G5 economy axle (no charge). G8 non-positive-traction performance axle, for trailer towing (no charge). G1 performance axle with positive-traction differential for cars without A1 ($42.13 and automatic transmission required). G4 positive-traction differential, except with A1 ($42.13). H5 heavy-duty Energizer battery ($7.37). P2 carpet savers ($7.37). P1 carpet savers and handi mats ($14.54). B8 front seat floor console without shifter, bucket seats required ($31.60). B4 full-length console, bucket seats and automatic transmission required ($61.09). B7 consolette, bucket seats and floor-shifted manual transmission required ($36.86). 17 heavy-duty cooling, including fan drive Thermo control, fuel return lines on 350-cid V-8, 55-amp Delcotron and extra-heavy-duty radiator, except with air conditioning ($43.18, but not available with A1). 17 heavy-duty cooling with extra-heavy-duty radiator only, air conditioning required ($21.06, but not available with A1). S6 Cruisemaster speed control, V-8 and automatic transmission required ($57.93). M7 rear window defroster ($26.33). 04 door guards on two-door models ($5.27). U6 electric clock ($16.85). E5 evaporative emission system ($36.86). M8 engine block heater, V-8 models ($5.27). L1 Soft-Ray tinted glass ($38.97). L2 Soft-Ray tinted windshield ($26.33). N2 four-note horn ($15.79). U9 full-gauge instrumentation and Rallye clock in GS, GS 455 ($51.60). U5 full-gauge instrumentation and tachometer ($36.86). 05 remote-control mirror ($10.53). Two-tone paint on Sportwagons ($21.38). Two-tone paint ($31.07). Special order paint ($76.25). C1 power disc brakes ($64.25). C7 power brakes ($41.60). T2 power door locks, two-door models ($47.39). Q5 4-Way tilt adjuster, with A46 for bucket seats ($73.72). C6 power steering, automatic transmission required ($105.32). R1 power windows ($105.32). W2 Custom peak molding package ($31.60). D1 Sonomatic radiuo ($69.51). D5 AM/FM radio $133.75. D0 stereo tape player, requires radio and rear speaker, not available with B7 ($116.91). D6 rear speaker ($16.64). J3 two Custom front shoulder belts with six Custom seat belts in Skylark group with bench seat ($13.67). J3 two front shoulder belts with five Custom seat belts, with bucket seats ($11.97). J5 four Custom front and rear shoulder belts with six Custom front and rear seat belts ($40.23). J5 two Custom front shoulder belts with five Custom seat belts, with bucket seats ($38.43). K3 speed alert and trip odometer ($11.70). X2 Rallye steering wheel ($46.09). X3 rim-blow steering wheel ($31.75). S7 tilt steering wheel with automatic transmission and optional steering wheel required ($45.00). F1 G78-14 white sidewall tires ($30.63). F2 H78-14 oversize white sidewall tires ($48.45). F8 G70-14 Wide-Oval red line tires ($62.14). F9 G70-14 Wide-Oval white billboard lettered tires ($62.14). E9 Spacesaver spare tire ($15.80). 12 trailer hitch ($23.17). 13 trailer wiring harness and flasher ($14.74). Turbo Hyrda-Matic 350 transmission ($195.36-205.92). B9 three-speed manual floor shift in GS without B4 ($84.48). B3 four-speed manual floor shift, without B4 ($184.80). Custom vinyl trim ($149.55). Custom vinyl roof ($102.16). 12 forced Comfort-Flo ventilation system ($42.13-57.93). V1 deluxe wheel covers ($21.06). V2 wire wheel covers ($80.05). V2 chrome-plated wheels ($94.79). V7 Super sport wheels ($68.46). H6 Rallye Ride Control package ($15.80, but not available with H1 or H3). A1 Stage 1 option including high-performance 345-hp V-8, specific ornamentation, positive-traction performance axle, heavy-duty radiator and low-restriction dual exhausts ($199.05). H1 trailer towing package ($3.69, but not available with H2 or H3).

1970 GS 455

BUICK

JERRY HEASLEY

1970 Gran Sport Stage 1 455

The GS 455 was a truly muscular Buick with a new big-block V-8 and Hurst-shifted performance transmissions. It could do 0-to-60 mph in 6.5 seconds and had a 129.5-mph top speed. Functional hood scoops dumped cold air into the big V-8's intake. Chrome red-filled lower body and wheelhouse moldings were used with five-spoke, 14 x 6-inch chrome wheels standard. Finned aluminum brake drums with cast-iron liners were used in the front. A GS 455 emblem appeared on the left-hand side of the blacked-out grille, with others showing up on the front fenders and the door trim panels. A GS monogram appeared on the rear deck lid.

Stage I equipment for the GS 455 included of a high-lift camshaft, 10.5:1 compression ratio pistons, a special four-barrel carburetor and a low-restriction dual exhaust system. Stage II equipment for the GS 455 consisted of a hotter cam, 12.0:1 compression ratio forged pistons, an Edelbrock B4B manifold, a Holley carburetor, Mickey Thompson headers and 4.78 differential gears. The Stage II features were only available as a dealer-installed kit.

Series Number	Body/Style Number	Body Type & Seating	Factory Price	Shipping Weight	Production Total
GS 455 — SERIES 44600 — V-8					
44600	44637	2d HT-6P	$3,283	3,562 lbs.	8,732
44600	44667	2d Conv-6P	$3469	3,619 lbs.	1,416

NOTE 1: 44637 production includes 66 with three-speed manual, 510 with four-speed manual and 5,013 with THM-400.

NOTE 2: 44667 production includes 18 with three-speed manual, 67 with four-speed manual and 164 with THM-400.

Series Number	Body/Style Number	Body Type & Seating	Factory Price	Shipping Weight	Production Total
GS 455 STAGE I — SERIES 44600 — V-8					
44600	44637	2d HT-6P	$3,283	3,562 lbs.	8,732
44600	44667	2d Conv-6P	$3,469	3,619 lbs.	1,416

NOTE 3: 44637 production includes 16 with three-speed manual, 664 with four-speed manual and 1,785 with THM-400.

NOTE 4: 44667 production includes one with three-speed manual, 67 with four-speed manual and 164 with THM-400.

ENGINES

GS 455 BASE V-8: Overhead valves. Cast-iron block and heads. Bore and stroke: 4.31 x 3.90 inches. Displacement: 455 cid. Compression ratio: 10.00:1. Brake hp: 350 at 4600 rpm. Taxable hp: 52.20. Torque: 510 at 2800. Hydraulic valve lifters. Five main bearings. Carburetor: Rochester 4MV Quadra-Jet four-barrel. Engine identification code SR.

GS 455 OPTIONAL STAGE 1 V-8: Overhead valves. Cast-iron block and heads. Bore and stroke: 4.31 x 3.90 inches. Displacement: 455 cid. Compression ratio: 10.00:1. Brake hp: 360 at 4600 rpm. Taxable hp: 59.50. Torque: 510 at 2800. Hydraulic valve lifters. Five main bearings. Carburetor: Rochester 4MV Quadra-Jet four-barrel. Engine identification code SS.

OPTIONS

N3 heavy-duty air cleaner ($9.48). 16 air conditioner ($375.99). G1 performance axle with positive-traction differential all Skylarks without A1 ($42.13 and automatic transmission required). G4 positive-traction differential, except with A1 ($42.13). H5 heavy-duty Energizer battery ($7.37). P2 carpet savers ($7.37). P1 carpet savers and handi mats ($14.54). B8 front seat floor console without shifter, bucket seats required ($31.60). B4 full-length console, bucket seats and automatic transmission required ($61.09). B7 consolette, bucket seats and floor-shifted manual transmission required ($36.86). 17 heavy-duty cooling, including fan drive Thermo control, 55-amp. Delcotron and extra-heavy-duty radiator, except with air conditioning ($43.18, but not available with A1). 17 heavy-duty cooling with extra-heavy-duty radiator only, air conditioning required ($21.06, but not available with A1). S6 Cruisemaster speed control, V-8 and automatic transmission required ($57.93). M7 rear window defroster ($26.33). 04 door guards on two-door models ($5.27). U6 electric clock ($16.85). E5 evaporative emission system ($36.86). M8 engine block heater, V-8 models ($5.27). L1 Soft-Ray tinted glass ($38.97). L2 Soft-Ray tinted windshield ($26.33). N2 four-note horn ($15.79). U9 full-gauge instrumentation and Rallye clock ($51.60). U5 full-gauge instrumentation and tachometer ($36.86). 05 remote-control mirror ($10.53). Two-tone paint, except convertible, includes rear quarter belt moldings ($31.07). Special order paint ($76.25). C1 power disc brakes ($64.25). C7 power brakes ($41.60). T2 power door locks, two-door models ($47.39). Q5 4-Way tilt adjuster, with A46 for bucket seats ($73.72). C6 power steering, automatic transmission required ($105.32). R1 power windows ($105.32). W2 Custom upper peak molding package ($14.74). W6 Custom window frame molding package including Custom scalp moldings, roof drip moldings ($40, but not available with vinyl roof). D1 Sonomatic radiuo ($69.51). D5 AM/FM radio $133.75. D0 stereo tape player, requires radio and rear speaker, not available with B7 ($116.91). D6 rear speaker ($16.64). J3 two

Custom front shoulder belts in hardtop with six Custom seat belts and bench seat ($36.74). J3 two Custom front shoulder belts in hardtop with six Custom seat belts with bucket seats ($11.88). J3 two Custom front shoulder belts with six Custom seat belts in convertible with bucket seats ($35.05). J3 two Custom front shoulder belts with five Custom seat belts in two-door hardtop coupe with bucket seats ($11.97). J3 two Custom front shoulder belts with five Custom seat belts in convertible with bucket seats ($35.23). K3 speed alert and trip odometer ($11.70). X2 Rallye steering wheel ($46.09). X3 rim-blow steering wheel ($31.75). S7 tilt steering wheel in Skylarks with automatic transmission and optional steering wheel required ($45.00). F8 G70-14 Wide-Oval red line tires ($62.14). F9 G70-14 Wide-Oval white billboard lettered tires ($62.14). E9 Spacesaver spare tire ($15.80). 12 trailer hitch ($23.17). 13 trailer wiring harness and flasher ($14.74). Turbo Hydra-Matic 400 transmission ($227.04). B3 four-speed manual floor shift in ($184.80). Custom vinyl trim package ($78.99). Custom vinyl roof ($102.16). 12 forced Comfort-Flo ventilation system ($42.13-$57.93). V1 deluxe wheel covers ($21.06). V2 wire wheel covers ($80.05). V2

chrome-plated wheels ($94.79). V7 Super sport wheels ($68.46). H6 Rallye Ride Control package, including rear stabilizer bar, specific heavy-duty wheels, front and rear Firm Ride tuned shock absorbers, a rear lower control arm assembly, and on the LeSabre Custom 455 only Firm Ride rear springs ($15.80, but not available with H1 or H3). H2 Ride & Handling option ($5.27). A1 Stage 1 option including high-performance 455-cid/360-hp V-8, specific ornamentation, positive-traction performance axle, heavy-duty radiator and low-restriction dual exhausts ($199.05).

1970 1/2 OPTION CHANGES AND ADDITIONS: B4 full-length console in two-door hardtop, automatic transmission required ($24.23). C5 fast-variable-ratio power steering for two-door hardtop ($121.12). F4 G60-15 billboard Wide-Oval tires ($162.19). F7 G60-15 billboard Wide-Oval tires with chrome-plated wheels ($230.65). B2 Turbo Hyrda-Matic 400 transmission for two-door hardtop ($42.24). A1 Stage 1 option, includes 455-cid/360-hp high-performance V-8 with four-barrel carburetor for two-door hardtop ($113.75). U3 convenience group including mirror map light and trunk light for two-door hardtop ($6.32).

1970 GSX

Motor Trend said, "Buick's Stage 1 was interesting in '69; now, with the 455 mill, it's an engineering tour de force."

At midyear, Buick introduced its ultra-high-performance GSX package as a $1,196 option for the GS 455 two-door hardtop. Coded as the A9 GSX option, it included a hood-mounted tachometer with available lighting control, special Rallye steering wheel, Rallye instrumentation, a GSX-specific molded plastic front spoiler (look for holes drilled in frame for mounting front spoiler), a rear spoiler with integral baffle and torsion bar support, twin outside rearview Sport-type mirrors, a four-speed manual transmission with Hurst gear shifter, a 3.42:1 ratio rear axle with positive-traction differential, power ront disc brakes, and other muscular stuff.

It came standard with the 455-cid 350-hp V-8 and the Stage I engine was a factory option. The GSX came only in Apollo White or Saturn Yellow with Code 188 black interior trim.

Series Number	Body/Style Number	Body Type & Seating	Factory Price	Shipping Weight	Production Total
GSX — SERIES 44600 — V-8					
44600	44637	2d HT-6P	$4,479	N/A	278
NOTE 1: Includes 81 with four-speed manual and 197 with THM-400.					
GSX STAGE 1 — SERIES 44600 — V-8					
44600	44637	2d HT-6P	$4,479	N/A	400
NOTE 2: Includes 118 with four-speed manual and 282 with THM-400.					
NOTE 3: 187 GSXs were Apollo White and 491 were Saturn Yellow.					

ENGINES

BASE V-8: Overhead valves. Cast-iron block and heads. Bore and stroke: 4.31 x 3.90 inches. Displacement: 455 cid. Compression ratio: 10.00:1. Brake hp: 350 at 4600 rpm. Taxable hp: 52.20. Torque: 510 at 2800. Hydraulic valve lifters. Five main bearings. Carburetor: Rochester 4MV Quadra-Jet four-barrel. Engine identification code SR.

OPTIONAL STAGE 1 V-8: Overhead valves. Cast-iron block and heads. Bore and stroke: 4.31 x 3.90 inches. Displacement: 455 cid. Compression ratio: 10.00:1. Brake hp: 360 at 4600 rpm. Taxable hp: 59.50. Torque: 510 at 2800. Hydraulic valve lifters. Five main bearings. Carburetor: Rochester 4MV Quadra-Jet four-barrel. Engine identification code SS.

OPTIONS

N3 heavy-duty air cleaner ($9.48). 16 air conditioner ($375.99). G1 performance axle with positive-traction differential all Skylarks without A1 ($42.13 and automatic transmission required). G4 positive-traction differential, except with A1 ($42.13). H5 heavy-duty Energizer battery ($7.37). P2 carpet

savers ($7.37). P1 carpet savers and handi mats ($14.54). B8 front seat floor console without shifter, bucket seats required ($31.60). B4 full-length console, bucket seats and automatic transmission required ($61.09). B7 consolette, bucket seats and floor-shifted manual transmission required ($36.86). 17 heavy-duty cooling ($43.18, but not available with A1). 17 heavy-duty cooling with extra-heavy-duty radiator only, air conditioning required ($21.06, but not available with A1). S6 Cruisemaster speed control, V-8 and automatic transmission required ($57.93). M7 rear window defroster ($26.33). 04 door guards on two-door models ($5.27). U6 electric clock ($16.85). E5 evaporative emission system ($36.86). M8 engine block heater, V-8 models ($5.27). L1 Soft-Ray tinted glass ($38.97). L2 Soft-Ray tinted windshield ($26.33). N2 four-note horn ($15.79). U9 full-gauge instrumentation and Rallye clock ($51.60). U5 full-gauge instrumentation and tachometer ($36.86). 05 remote-control mirror ($10.53). Two-tone paint, except convertible, includes rear quarter belt moldings ($31.07). Special order paint ($76.25). C1 power disc brakes ($64.25). C7 power brakes ($41.60). T2 power door locks, two-door models ($47.39). Q5 4-Way tilt adjuster, with A46 for bucket seats ($73.72). C6 power steering, automatic transmission required ($105.32). R1 power windows ($105.32). W2 Custom upper peak molding package ($14.74). W6 Custom window frame molding package ($40, but not available with vinyl roof). D1 Sonomatic radiuo ($69.51). D5 AM/FM radio $133.75. D0 stereo tape player, requires radio and rear speaker, not available with B7 ($116.91). D6 rear speaker ($16.64). J3 two Custom front shoulder belts in hardtop with six Custom seat belts and bench seat ($36.74). J3 two Custom front shoulder belts in hardtop with six Custom seat belts with bucket seats ($11.88). J3 two Custom front shoulder belts with six Custom seat belts in convertible with bucket seats ($35.05). J3 two Custom front shoulder belts with five Custom seat belts in two-door hardtop coupe with bucket seats ($11.97). J3 two Custom front shoulder belts with five Custom seat belts in convertible with bucket seats ($35.23). K3 speed alert and trip odometer ($11.70). X2 Rallye steering wheel ($46.09). X3 rim-blow steering wheel ($31.75). S7 tilt steering wheel in Skylarks with automatic transmission and optional steering wheel required ($45.00). F8 G70-14 Wide-Oval red line tires ($62.14). F9 G70-14 Wide-Oval white billboard lettered tires ($62.14). E9 Spacesaver spare tire ($15.80). 12 trailer hitch ($23.17). 13 trailer wiring harness and flasher ($14.74). Turbo Hyrda-Matic 400 transmission ($227.04). B3 four-speed manual floor shift in ($184.80). Custom vinyl trim package ($78.99). Custom vinyl roof ($102.16). 12 forced Comfort-Flo ventilation system ($42.13-$57.93). V1 deluxe wheel covers ($21.06). V2 wire wheel covers ($80.05). V2 chrome-plated wheels ($94.79). V7 Super sport wheels ($68.46). H6 Rallye Ride Control package ($15.80, but not available with H1 or H3). H2 Ride & Handling option, including specific heavy-duty wheels, heavy-duty front and rear springs, heavy-duty front and rear shock absorbersand a heavy-duty front stabilizer shaft ($5.27). A1 Stage 1 option including high-performance 455-cid/360-hp V-8, specific ornamentation, positive-traction performance axle, heavy-duty radiator and low-restriction dual exhausts ($199.05). H1 trailer towing package ($3.69, but not available with H2 or H3). B4 full-length console in two-door hard-top, automatic transmission required ($24.23). C5 fast-variable-ratio power

1970 Skylark GSX

steering for two-door hardtop ($121.12). F4 G60-15 billboard Wide-Oval tires ($162.19). F7 G60-15 billboard Wide-Oval tires with chrome-plated wheels ($230.65). B2 Turbo Hydra-Matic 400 transmission for two-door hardtop ($42.24). A1 Stage 1 option, includes 455-cid/360-hp high-performance V-8 with four-barrel carburetor for two-door hardtop ($113.75). U3 convenience group for two-door hardtop ($6.32)

1971 GRAN SPORT

The 1971 GS was bread-and-butter muscle car that still offered some degree of poly-unsaturated performance for the highways and byways, if not for the drag strip.

The basic styling of mid-size Buicks used in 1970 was continued for another year. A number of basic safety and convenience features were found on almost all General Motors cars. The GS (Gran Sport) series featured a muscular mid-sized two-door hardtop and a similarlt-equipped convertible. Standard features included Comfort-Flo ventilation, door-operated interior lights, a smoking set, front and rear ashtrays, front and rear armrests, carpeting, dual exhausts, functional air scoops, heavy-duty springs, heavy-duty shock absorbers, a heavy-duty stabilizer bar, a 6,000-mile front lubricated suspension, a 350-cid V-8 with a four-barrel carburetor, a full-flow oil filter, a semi-closed cooling system, a Delcotron alternator, 14-inch wheels, composite finned cast-iron brake drums and G78 x 14 bias-belted black sidewall tires.

Series Number	Body/Style Number	Body Type & Seating	Factory Price	Shipping Weight	Production Total
GS — SERIES 43400 — V-8					
43400	43437	2d HT-5P	$3,285	3,461 lbs.	5,986
43400	43467	2d Conv-5P	$3,476	3,497 lbs.	656

NOTE 1: 43437 includes 25 with three-speed manual, 358 with four-speed manual and 5,603 with THM-350.

NOTE 2: 43467 includes six with three-speed manual, 51 with four-speed manual and 599 with THM-350.

ENGINE

BASE V-8: Overhead valves. Cast-iron block and heads. Bore and stroke: 3.80 x 3.85 inches. Displacement: 350 cid. Compression ratio: 8.50:1. Brake hp: 260 at 4600 rpm. Torque: 360 at 3200. Hydraulic valve lifters. Five main bearings. Carburetor: Rochester 4MV four-barrel. Codes: TD (TH-350) or TB (Three-speed manual or TH-350).

OPTIONS

N3 heavy-duty air cleaner ($9.48). 16 air conditioner ($407.59). G1 performance axle with positive-traction differential with A9 included ($44.23). G4 positive-traction differential, with standard axle ratio ($44.23, but not with A1). H5 heavy-duty Energizer battery ($15.80, but included with A1 or A9). J1 six-seat Custom front and rear seat and shoulder belts in convertibles ($14.74). J3 two Custom front shoulder belts with six Custom seat belts in coupe without bucket seats ($17.90). J3 two Custom front shoulder belts with six Custom seat belts in convertible without bucket seats ($41.07). J3 two Custom front shoulder belts with five Custom seat belts with bucket seats ($13.69). J5 four Custom front and rear shoulder belts with six Custom front and rear seat belts with bench seats ($44.23). J5 four Custom front and rear shoulder belts with six Custom front and rear seat belts in convertible with bench seats ($67.40). J5 four Custom front and rear shoulder belts with five Custom front and rear seat belts in convertible with bucket seats ($40.02). J5 two Custom front shoulder belts with five Custom front and rear seat belts in coupes with bucket seats ($67.36). P2 carpet savers ($8.43). P1 carpet savers and handi mats ($15.80). U6 electric clock ($18.96). B4 full-length console in sport coupe with automatic transmission required ($61.09). B8 short non-shifter console in sport coupes with bucket seats ($36.86). B7 consolette with manual floor shift in Sport Coupes with bucket seats ($36.86). 17 heavy-duty cooling ($43.18, but not available with air conditioning). S6 Cruisemaster speed control, automatic transmission required ($63.19). M7 rear window defroster ($31.60). B2 dual exhausts, A7 required ($30.54). E6 through-the-bumper exhaust extensions on ($26.33). L1 Soft-Ray tinted glass ($43.18). L2 Soft-Ray tinted windshield ($30.54). N5 front and rear bumper guards ($31.60). 04 door guards ($6.32). U7 gauges and tachometer, Skylark GS group ($63.19). U9 gauges and Rally clock ($50.56). 05 remote-control outside rearview mirror ($12.64). 06 Sport-style remote-control outside rearview mirror ($10.53). W2 rear deck lid and quarter panel extewnsion moldings on GS convertible ($16.85). W2 body side upper peak, rear deck lid and rear quarter panel extension moldings ($31.60). W4 body side and front fender protective moldings and lower rear quarter panel extension moldings ($24.23). Two-tone paint, except convertible ($36.86). Special order paint ($115.78). T2 power door locks ($47.39). Q5 4-Way tilt adjuster ($78.99). C6 power steering in ($115.85). R1 power windows ($115.85). 13 heavy-duty radiator, not with A1, air conditioning required ($21.06). D1 Sonomatic radio ($74.78). D5 Sonomatic AM/FM radio

BUICK

JERRY HEASLEY

1971 Buick Gran Sport

($139.02). D6 rear speaker ($18.96). D0 stereo tape player, requires radio and rear speaker ($116.91). Notchback front seats in convertible ($36.86). K3 speed alert and trip odometer ($11.59). X1 deluxe steering wheel ($15.80). X2 Rallye steering wheel ($46.34). X3 rim-blow steering wheel ($36.86). S7 tilt steering wheel, not available with standard transmission or steering wheel ($45.29). H6 Firm Ride & Handling package heavy-duty springs and wheels on cars without H1 or H2 ($15.79, but included in A9). F1 G78-14 white side-wall tires ($32.65). F2 H78-14 oversize white sidewall tires ($50.56). F4 G60-15 super-wide white-letter tires ($162.19). F7 G60-15 super-wide white-letter tires with chrome-plated wheels ($230.65). F8 G70-14 Wide-Oval red-letter tires ($62.14). F9 G70-14 Wide-Oval white-letter tires ($62.14). 12 trailer hitch ($23.17). 13 trailer wiring harness and flasher ($14.74). B2 Turbo Hydra-Matic

400 automatic transmission with A1 or A2 ($242.88). B5 Turbo Hydra-Matic 350 automatic transmission ($221.76). B3 four-speed manual transmission with floor shift in GS ($195.36). Front bucket seat package ($230.65). 12 Comfort-Flo forced ventilation system ($42.13). Sport coupe vinyl roof with Custom rear quarter belt finish molding ($102.16). V1 deluxe wheel covers on cars without super-wide or Wide-Oval tires ($26.33). V3 wire wheel covers on on cars without super-wide or Wide-Oval tires ($84.66). V2 chorome-plated wheels on cars without super-wide or Wide-Oval tires ($94.79). V7 Super Sport wheels on cars without super-wide or Wide-Oval tires ($68.46). A1 Stage 1 high-performance engine kit with 455-cid modified V-8 with four-barrel carburetor ($325.44 over cost of optional regular-compression 455-cid V-8). H1 trailer towing package ($15.80).

1971 GS 455 STAGE 1

Put a GS 455 Stage 1 Buick in your college fund today — especialy the rare ragtop. muscle car expert Scott Lewis once said, "The Stage 1 had the highest torque rating of any engine GM put in a car during the muscle car era."

The $164 Code A9 option package for Gran Sport models included all GS features plus a specific heavy-duty battery, a specific heavy-duty cooling system and a 455-cid V-8 with a four-barrel carburetor. Cars so-equipped wore a "455" call-out under the GS letters on the front fenders.

The $325 Code A1 Stage 1 option with a modified version of the 455-cid V-8 was an additional package that could be added to GS models that already had the lower-priced 455-cid V-8 GS 455 option added. Cars with this engine option had

a "Stage 1" call-out in place of the "455" call-out below the "GS" lettering on each front fender.

Series Number	Body/Style Number	Body Type & Seating	Factory Price	Shipping Weight	Production Total
GS 455 — SERIES 43400 — V-8					
43400	43437	2d HT-5P	$3,449	—	1,481
43400	43467	2d Conv-5P	$3,639	—	165

NOTE 1: 43437 includes 103 with four-speed manual and 1,378 with THM-400.

NOTE 2: 43467 includes 18 with four-speed manual and 147 with THM-400.

Series Number	Body/Style Number	Body Type & Seating	Factory Price	Shipping Weight	Production Total
GS 455 Stage 1 — Series 43400 — V-8					
43400	43437	2d HT-5P	$3,774	—	801
43400	43467	2d Conv-5P	$3,964	—	81

NOTE 3: 43437 includes 114 with four-speed manual and 687 with THM-400.

NOTE 4: 43467 includes nine with four-speed manual and 72 with THM-400.

ENGINES

BASE V-8: Overhead valves. Cast-iron block and heads. Bore and stroke: 4.31 x 3.90 inches. Displacement: 455 cid. Compression ratio: 8.50:1. Brake hp: 315 at 4400 rpm. Taxable hp: 59.50. Torque: 450 at 2800. Hydraulic valve lifters. Five main bearings. Carburetor: Rochester 4MV four-barrel. Engine identification code: TR.

OPTIONAL V-8: Overhead valves. Cast-iron block and heads. Bore and stroke: 4.31 x 3.90 inches. Displacement: 455 cid. Compression ratio: 10.00:1. Brake hp: 345 at 5000 rpm. Taxable hp: 59.50. Torque: 460 at 3000. Hydraulic valve

lifters. Five main bearings. Carburetor: Rochester 4MV four-barrel. Engine identification code: TS.

OPTIONS

N3 heavy-duty air cleaner, all ($9.48). 16 air conditioner, V-8 required ($407.59). J1 six-seat Custom front and rear seat and shoulder belts in convertibles ($14.74). J3 two Custom front shoulder belts with six Custom seat belts in coupes without bucket seats ($17.90). J3 two Custom front shoulder belts with six Custom seat belts in convertible without bucket

1971 Gran Sport Stage 1 455

seats ($41.07). J3 two Custom front shoulder belts with five Custom seat belts with bucket seats ($13.69). J5 four Custom front and rear shoulder belts with six Custom front and rear seat belts in sport coupe with bench seats ($44.23). J5 four Custom front and rear shoulder belts with six Custom front and rear seat belts in convertible with bench seats ($67.40). J5 four Custom front and rear shoulder belts with five Custom front and rear seat belts in convertible with bucket seats ($40.02). J5 two Custom front shoulder belts with five Custom front and rear seat belts in Sport Coupe with bucket seats ($67.36). P2 carpet savers ($8.43). P1 carpet savers and handi mats ($15.80). U6 electric clock ($18.96). B4 full-length console with automatic transmission required ($61.09). B8 short non-shifter console in sport coupe with bucket seats ($36.86). B7 consolette with manual floor shift in sport coupes with bucket seats ($36.86). 17 heavy-duty cooling ($43.18, but not available with air conditioning). S6 Cruisemaster speed control, automatic transmission required ($63.19). M7 rear window defroster ($31.60). E6 through-the-bumper exhaust extensions ($26.33). L1 Soft-Ray tinted glass ($43.18). L2 Soft-Ray tinted windshield ($30.54). N5 front and rear bumper guards ($31.60). 04 door guards ($6.32). U7 gauges and tachometer ($63.19). U9 gauges and Rally clock ($50.56). 06 Sport-style remote-control outside rearview mirror ($10.53). W2 rear deck lid and quarter panel extension moldings on convertible ($16.85). W2 body side upper peak, rear deck lid and rear quarter panel extension moldings ($31.60). Two-tone paint, except convertible , includes rear quarter belt moldings ($36.86). Special order paint ($115.78). C1 power disc brakes ($69.51). C7 power brakes ($47.39). T2 power door locks ($47.39). T3 power door locks and seat locks ($70.56). Q5 4-Way tilt adjuster ($78.99). C6 power steering in ($115.85). R1 power windows ($115.85). 13 heavy-

duty radiator, not with A1, air conditioning required ($21.06). D1 Sonomatic radio ($74.78). D5 Sonomatic AM/FM radio $139.02). D6 rear speaker ($18.96). D0 stereo tape player, requires radio and rear speaker ($116.91). Notchback front seats in convertible ($36.86). Front bucket seats in sport coupe ($81.10). K3 speed alert and trip odometer ($11.59). X1 deluxe steering wheel ($15.80). X2 Rallye steering wheel ($46.34). X2 Rallye steering wheel ($31.60). X3 rim-blow steering wheel ($36.86). S7 tilt steering wheel, not available with standard transmission or steering wheel ($45.29). F1 G78-14 white sidewall tires ($32.65). F2 H78-14 oversize white sidewall tires ($50.56). F4 G60-15 super-wide white-letter tires ($162.19). F7 G60-15 super-wide white-letter tires with chrome-plated wheels ($230.65). F8 G70-14 Wide-Oval red-letter tires ($62.14). F9 G70-14 Wide-Oval white-letter tires ($62.14). 12 trailer hitch ($23.17). 13 trailer wiring harness and flasher ($14.74). B2 Turbo Hydra-Matic 400 automatic transmission with A1 or A2 ($242.88). B3 four-speed manual transmission with floor shift $195.36). Front notchback seat package ($230.65). Front bucket seat package in Skylark Custom two-door hardtop with trim numbers 165, 166, 168 ($230.65). 12 Comfort-Flo forced ventilation system ($42.13). Vinyl roof with Custom rear quarter belt finish molding for sport coupe ($102.16). V1 deluxe wheel covers on cars without super-wide or Wide-Oval tires ($26.33). V3 wire wheel covers on on cars without super-wide or Wide-Oval tires ($84.66). V2 chorome-plated wheels on cars without super-wide or Wide-Oval tires ($94.79). V7 Super Sport wheels on cars without super-wide or Wide-Oval tires ($68.46). A9 high-performance engine option package ($164.30). A1 Stage 1 high-performance engine kit ($325.44 over cost of optional regular-compression 455-cid V-8). H1 trailer towing package ($15.80).

1971 GSX

While nowhere near as muscular as '70 editions, '71 and Skylarks with the GSX package and the Stage 1 engine option are still tremendous performance cars and, since they were rare when new, they are extremely hard to find today. The GSX Registry at www.buickgsx.net says "It is very difficult to identify these cars without paperwork." If you want a rare muscle car that hasn't been slandered in the press, this is the one for you; few people know enough about them to tell the full story.

This year the GSX package was available on the GS sport coupe with any GS engine, including the 350-cid/260-hp V-8, the 455-cid/315-hp V-8 or the 455-cid/345-hp Stage 1 V-8.

The package, which was featured and pictured in the 1971 sales catalog, included body side stripes, hood paint, GSX emblems, painted headlight bezels, black-stripe rocker panel moldings and a color-coordinated rear deck lid spoiler.

GSX buyers could pick simply order the GSX Ornamentation Group and get everything. They could also order various components separately. A hood-mounted tachometer, which was part of the 1970 GSX package, was now a separate option for any GSX. The seats were again trimmed in black vinyl, but had a slightly different grain and pattern. The 1971 GSX also had a different type of steering wheel. The sales catalog indicated that

BUICK

JERRY HEASLEY

1971 GSX

the package could be added to any GS, but historical sources suggest that all 124 installations were made on sport coupes.

Series Number	Body/Style Number	Body Type & Seating	Factory Price	Shipping Weight	Production Total
GSX — SERIES 43400 — V-8					
43400	43437	2d HT-5P	—	—	124

ENGINES

BASE V-8: Overhead valves. Cast-iron block and heads. Bore and stroke: 3.80 x 3.85 inches. Displacement: 350 cid. Compression ratio: 8.50:1. Brake hp: 260 at 4600 rpm. Torque: 360 at 3200. Hydraulic valve lifters. Five main bearings. Carburetor: Rochester 4MV four-barrel. Codes: TD (TH-350) or TB (Three-speed manual or TH-350).

OPTIONAL V-8: Overhead valves. Cast-iron block and heads. Bore and stroke: 4.31 x 3.90 inches. Displacement: 455 cid. Compression ratio: 8.50:1. Brake hp: 315 at 4400 rpm. Taxable hp: 59.50. Torque: 450 at 2800. Hydraulic valve lifters. Five main bearings. Carburetor: Rochester 4MV four-barrel. Engine identification code: TR.

OPTIONAL STAGE 1 V-8: Overhead valves. Cast-iron block and heads. Bore and stroke: 4.31 x 3.90 inches. Displacement: 455 cid. Compression ratio: 10.00:1. Brake hp: 370 at 4600 rpm. Taxable hp: 59.50. Torque: 510 at 2800. Hydraulic valve lifters. Five main bearings. Carburetor: Rochester 4MV four-barrel. Engine identification code: TS.

OPTIONS

N3 heavy-duty air cleaner ($9.48). 16 air conditioner ($407.59). G1 performance axle with positive-traction differential with A9 included ($44.23). G4 positive-traction differential, with standard axle ratio ($44.23, but not with A1). H5 heavy-duty Energizer battery ($15.80, but included with A1 or A9). P2 carpet savers ($8.43). P1 carpet savers and handi mats ($15.80). U6 electric clock ($18.96). B4 full-length console in sport coupe with automatic transmission required ($61.09). B8 short non-shifter console in sport coupes with bucket seats ($36.86). B7 consolette with manual floor shift in sport coupes with bucket seats ($36.86). 17 heavy-duty cooling ($43.18, but not available with air conditioning). S6 Cruisemaster speed control, automatic transmission required ($63.19). M7 rear window defroster ($31.60). B2 dual exhausts, A7

required ($30.54). E6 through-the-bumper exhaust extensions on ($26.33). L1 Soft-Ray tinted glass ($43.18). L2 Soft-Ray tinted windshield ($30.54). N5 front and rear bumper guards ($31.60). 04 door guards ($6.32). U7 gauges and tachometer, Skylark GS group ($63.19). U9 gauges and Rally clock ($50.56). 05 remote-control outside rearview mirror ($12.64). 06 Sport-style remote-control outside rearview mirror ($10.53). W2 rear deck lid and quarter panel extension moldings on GS convertible ($16.85). W2 body side upper peak, rear deck lid and rear quarter panel extension moldings ($31.60). W4 body side and front fender protective moldings and lower rear quarter panel extension moldings ($24.23). Two-tone paint, except convertible ($36.86). Special order paint ($115.78). T2 power door locks ($47.39). Q5 4-Way tilt adjuster ($78.99). C6 power steering in ($115.85). R1 power windows ($115.85). 13 heavy-duty radiator, not with A1, air conditioning required ($21.06). D1 Sonomatic radio ($74.78). D5 Sonomatic AM/FM radio ($139.02). D6 rear speaker ($18.96). D0 stereo tape player, requires radio and rear speaker ($116.91). Notchback front seats in convertible ($36.86). K3 speed alert and trip odometer ($11.59). X1 deluxe steering wheel ($15.80). X2 Rallye steering wheel ($46.34). X3 rim-blow steering wheel ($36.86). S7 tilt steering wheel, not available with standard transmission or steering wheel ($45.29). H6 Firm Ride & Handling package heavy-duty springs and wheels on cars without H1 or H2 ($15.79, but included in A9). F1 G78-14 white sidewall tires ($32.65). F2 H78-14 oversize white sidewall tires ($50.56). F4 G60-15 super-wide white-letter tires ($162.19). F7 G60-15 super-wide white-letter tires with chrome-plated wheels ($230.65). F8 G70-14 Wide-Oval red-letter tires ($62.14). F9 G70-14 Wide-Oval white-letter tires ($62.14). 12 trailer hitch ($23.17). 13 trailer wiring harness and flasher ($14.74). B2 Turbo Hydra-Matic 400 automatic transmission with A1 or A2 ($242.88). B5 Turbo Hydra-Matic 350 automatic transmission ($221.76). B3 four-speed manual transmission with floor shift in GS ($195.36). Front bucket seat package ($230.65). 12 Comfort-Flo forced ventilation system ($42.13). Sport coupe vinyl roof with Custom rear quarter belt finish molding ($102.16). V1 deluxe wheel covers on cars without super-wide or Wide-Oval tires ($26.33). V3 wire wheel covers on on cars without super-wide or Wide-Oval tires ($84.66). V2 chrome-plated wheels ($94.79). V7 Super Sport wheels ($68.46). A1 Stage 1 high-performance engine kit with 455-cid modified V-8 with four-barrel carburetor ($325.44 over cost of optional regular-compression 455-cid V-8). H1 trailer towing package ($15.80).

1972 GS

The '72 Buick GS still had killer "hot car" looks and, with a little tinkering, it can be turned into a reasonable performer, as long as you're not looking to light up the "Christmas tree" at your local quarter-mile. On the other hand, if you prefer going that route, there is the GS 455 to consider. In *CARS Magazine*, Martyn L. Schorr wrote, "The engine in the 350

Gran Sport is a mild 350-cubic-inch four-barrel affair with 8.5:1 compression and a Rochester Quadrajet carburetor. It's a nice all-around street package."

A mild facelift was done on the 1972 Skylark. The front bumper was redesigned and bumper guards were now standard. At the rear, black vinyl surrounds were added to the

JERRY HEASLEY

1972 Gran Sport

tail light and bumper assembly. Standard features included front ashtray, a heater and defroster, a side-terminal Energizer battery, a padded instrument panel and all mandated federal safety features. The Skylark-based GS featured dual exhausts, functional dual hood scoops, a heavy-duty battery, heavy-duty springs, heavy-duty shock absorbers, a stabilizer bar and a muscular look. Appearance enhancements included wide bright rocker moldings, wheelhouse moldings and GS monograms on each front fenders and the rear deck. Black vinyl bench seats were standard.

Series Number	Body/Style Number	Body Type & Seating	Factory Price	Shipping Weight	Production Total
GS SERIES 4G — V-8					
4G	4G37	2d HT-6P	$3,225	3,471 lbs.	5,895
4G	4G67	2d Conv 6P	$3,406	3,525 lbs.	645

NOTE 1: 4G37 included 16 with three-speed manual, 353 with four-speed manual and 5,526 with TH-350.

NOTE 2: 4G67 included five with three-speed manual, 39 with four-speed manual and 601 with TH-350.

ENGINE

GS BASE V-8: Overhead valves. Cast-iron block and heads. Bore and stroke: 3.80 x 3.85 inches. Displacement: 350 cid. Compression ratio: 8.50:1. Net brake hp: 195 at 4000 rpm. Taxable hp: 46.20. Net torque: 290 at 2800. Hydraulic valve lifters. Five main bearings. Carburetor: Rochester 4MV four-barrel. Engine identification code WB.

GS ALTERNATE BASE V-8: Overhead valves. Cast-iron block and heads. Bore and stroke: 3.80 x 3.85 inches. Displacement: 350 cid. Compression ratio: 8.50:1. Net brake hp: 190 at 4000 rpm. Taxable hp: 46.20. Net torque: 285 at 2800. Hydraulic valve lifters. Five main bearings. Carburetor: Rochester 4MV four-barrel. Engine identification code: Probably WB (but we won't swear by it. This was a special low-emissions engine for Califonia market cars only.)

OPTIONS

AM radio. AM/FM radio. AM/FM radio with stereo and tape player ($363). Center console (bucket seats required). Climate Control. Power windows. Electric trunk release. Child safety seat. Remote-control outside rearview mirror. Custom seat and shoulder belts. Custom vinyl top with halo molding for sport coupe. Full vinyl top. Soft-ray tinted glass. Rear window defroster. Mirror map light. Electric clock. Tilt steering wheel. Speed alert. Five-spoke chrome sport wheels. Trailer towing package. Automatic Level Control.

(NOTE: Complete 1972 option information not available at publication; complete list was similar to 1971 in content and prices.)

1972 GS 455

Motor Trend described the 1972 Buick GS 455 Stage 1 as "a well-kept secret, but easily one of the best performing cars of 1972."

When a GS two-door hardtop or convertible had a 455-cid V-8 installed, suitable emblems were added. This car used a version of the bigger Buick engine with the same compression ratio and carburetor as the 350 model, but with 105 extra cubic inches, it generated a whole lot more torque. It also included dual exhausts, functional fresh air hood vents, a heavy-duty battery, heavy-duty springs, heavy-duty shock absorbers and a rear stabilizer bar.

The $325.44 Stage 1 package included a hotter engine with a special hydraulic-lifter cam, special valve springs, direct Ram-Air induction and other go-fast stuff.

When tested by *Motor Trend* in February 1972, a stock 1972 GS 455 Stage 1 turned a best quarter-mile of 14.908 seconds at 93.26 mph. In June 1972, *Hot Rod* magazine ran a chart comparing the performance of the '70 GS 455 Stage 1 with that of a '72 model. The '72 did 0-to-60 mph in 5.8 seconds and covered the quarter-mile in 14.10 seconds at 97 mph. Both cars had a three-speed THM-400 transmission and the '72 had a 4.30:1 rear axle. (See 1970 section also). *Motor Trend* summarized, "Buick has one of the best — if not the best — performance packages now obtainable from Detroit. Though the price is more than a Chevelle buyer is used to, in this case the customer gets what he paid for." *Motor Trend* also pointed out, "No argument about it: Buick didn't start the performance-car movement. But they seem to be the only auto

BUICK

JERRY HEASLEY

1972 Gran Sport 455 Stage 1

maker able to hang onto performance and deliver clean air at the same time. In *Hot Rod*, A.B. Shuman wrote, "The amazing thing, considering all that's happened just in the area of emissions controls, is that a car that runs like the GS Stage 1 could still exist." *CARS Magazine* selected the Skylark Gran Sport 455 as its "Top Performance Car of the Year" in 1972.

Series Number	Body/Style Number	Body Type & Seating	Factory Price	Shipping Weight	Production Total
GS 455 — SERIES 4G — V-8					
4G	37	2d HT-6P	$3,400	3,580 lbs.	1,099
4G	67	2d Conv 6P	$3,581	3,634 lbs.	126

NOTE 1: 4G37 included 84 with four-speed manual and 1,015 with TH-400.

NOTE 2: 4G67 included 12 with four-speed manual and 114 with TH-400.

GS 455 STAGE 1 — SERIES 4G — V-8					
4G	37	2d HT-6P	$3,550	3,580 lbs.	728
4G	67	2d Conv 6P	$3,731	3,634 lbs.	81

NOTE 3: 4G37 included 101 with four-speed manual and 627 with TH-400.

NOTE 4: 4G67 included 15 with four-speed manual and 66 with TH-400.

1972 GSX

If the GS 455 was "Top Performance Car of the Year" and the GS 455 Stage 1 was even hotter, then the ultimate prize for the Buick muscle car collector is the rare '72 GSX 455 Stage 1. No one even knows how many were built.

The GSX version of the Skylark GS hardtop was still available in 1972. Buick built 44 of these cars. The GSX was available with all three GS engines. The 350-cid version could have been ordered with three- or four-speed manual gear boxes or the Turbo Hydra-Matic 350 transmission. The 455-cid four-barrel version could have been ordered with three- or four-speed manual gear boxes or the Turbo Hyrda-Matic 400 transmission. The 455-cid Stage 1 version also could have been ordered with four-speed manual gear boxes or the Turbo Hyrda-Matic 400 transmission.

No breakouts are available indicating how many of these cars were built with each drive train combination and it is

ENGINES

BASE V-8: Overhead valves. Cast-iron block and heads. Bore and stroke: 4.31 x 3.90 inches. Displacement: 455 cid. Compression ratio: 8.50:1. Net brake hp: 225 at 4000 rpm. Taxable hp: 59.50. Net torque: 360 at 2600. Hydraulic valve lifters. Five main bearings. Carburetor: Rochester 4MV four-barrel. Engine identification code WF.

OPTIONAL STAGE 1 V-8: Overhead valves. Cast-iron block and heads. Bore and stroke: 4.31 x 3.90 inches. Displacement: 455 cid. Compression ratio: 8.50:1. Net brake hp: 270 at 4400 rpm. Taxable hp: 59.50. Net torque: 390 at 3000. Hydraulic valve lifters. Five main bearings. Carburetor: Rochester 4MV four-barrel. Engine identification code WS.

OPTIONS

AM radio. AM/FM radio. AM/FM radio with stereo and tape player ($363). Center console (bucket seats required). Climate Control. Power windows. Electric trunk release. Child safety seat. Remote-control outside rear¬view mirror. Custom seat and shoulder belts. Custom vinyl top with halo molding for Sport Coupe. Full vinyl top. Soft-ray tinted glass. Rear window defroster. Mirror map light. Electric clock. Tilt steering wheel. Speed alert. Five-spoke chrome sport wheels. Trailer towing package. Automatic Level Control.

(NOTE: Complete 1972 option information not available at publication; complete list was similar to 1971 in content and prices.)

unknown if examples of all combinations were actually manufactured.

ENGINE

OPTIONAL STAGE 1 V-8: Overhead valves. Cast-iron block and heads. Bore and stroke: 4.31 x 3.90 inches. Displacement: 455 cid. Compression ratio: 8.50:1. Net brake hp: 270 at 4400 rpm. Taxable hp: 59.50. Net torque: 390 at 3000. Hydraulic valve lifters. Five main bearings. Carburetor: Rochester 4MV four-barrel. Engine identification code WS.

OPTIONS

AM radio. AM/FM radio. AM/FM radio with stereo and tape player ($363). Center console (bucket seats required). Climate Control. Power windows. Electric trunk release. Child safety seat. Remote-control outside rearview mirror. Custom seat and shoulder belts. Custom vinyl top with halo molding for sport coupe. Full vinyl top. Soft-ray tinted glass. Rear window defroster. Mirror map light. Electric clock. Tilt steering wheel. Speed alert. Five-spoke chrome sport wheels. Trailer towing package. Automatic Level Control.

(NOTE: Complete 1972 option information not available at publication; complete list was similar to 1971 in content and prices.)

CHEVROLET MUSCLE 1961-1972

While young people scoured used car markets for sharp 1955-1957 models in power-pack form, Chevrolet, responding to criticism of past performance merchandising, toned down the styling of its '60s models. The Chevrolet product line continued to proliferate, with the addition of the traditionally engineered, compact Chevy II in model year 1962. Then came the popular Chevelle, two years later.

1965 would be known as the year of records for the Chevrolet Motor Division. Large Chevrolets were restyled with pleasing, flowing lines. The 1965 Corvette received a four-wheel disc brake system and a robust 396-cid V-8 became Chevy's latest stormer. It replaced the big Chevy's top-option "409," an engine that had become a legend from 1961 to early 1963.

The Camaro, Chevy's belated answer to the enormously successful Ford Mustang, was introduced in model year 1967. First-generation Camaros (1967-1969) are popular among collectors today. Particularly desirable are the Z28 or SS performance packages and all convertible models.

The Corvette started out as Chevrolet's feeble attempt to launch a six-cylinder model that would appeal to true sports-car buffs. The introduction of a V-8 in 1955 took the car on a different tangent. By the time an optional fuel-injected V-8 arrived in 1957, the Corvette was on its way to becoming a true high-performance machine.

The clean, classic styling of 1956 and 1957 was jazzed-up in 1958. Although the basic design was attractive, the chrome-laden 1958 is generally considered the gaudiest Corvette. But, apparently, that's what the public wanted and sales climbed significantly over the previous year's model.

The 327 "Sebring" package of '62 was the first move towards giving the "Vette" some real muscle. Two years later, in a major restyling, the 1963s were an immediate hit. Demand was so great many customers had to wait two months or more to take delivery of their new Sting Ray coupe or ragtop. By now, Corvette's reputation as a powerful sports car was firmly established on the track and street. The arrival of a big-block 396-cid V-8 two years later took Corvette performance to a new level. New aerodynamic styling was introduced in 1968 and remained through the end of the muscle-car era in 1972. Some of most powerful Corvettes ever built arrived in the early '70s and few were produced. After that, Corvettes became significantly tamer. Still, when you mention performance, the American performance car that comes first to most peoples' minds is the Corvette.

(EDITOR'S NOTE: Because of the way that factory options were listed in our sources, it is not always clear if certain options were avaiable only on specific models. Where tire and engine options are listed, the prices given are the amounts added when upgrades were made to the standard tire equipment.)

PHIL KUNZ

CHEVROLET

1961 IMPALA SS 409

JERRY HEASLEY

1961 Impala SS 409

The 1961 Impala SS hardtop with the 409 cid/360 hp V-8 was reported capable of 0-to-60-mph times of 7.8 seconds and 15.8-second quarter-mile runs. Don Nicholson was Top Stock Eliminator at the 1961 National Hot Rod Association Winter Nationals in a 409/409 Super Stock Chevy.

Impalas were easily identified by their triple tail light treatment. They also had crossed racing flags insignia at the center of the rear deck and at the rear fenders with model identification script in the latter location as well. Deluxe wheel discs and wide side moldings, with contrasting insert panels, were other visual distinctions of the top Chevrolet line. Standard equipment lists began with Bel Air features and added parking brake glovebox and back-up lights, anodized aluminum trim, an electric clock and 8.00 x 14 tires on convertibles. All 1961 Chevrolet V-8s had oil filters and oil bath-type air cleaners.

The first Super Sport package was a dealer installed kit available on any Impala model, but most often installed on the two-door styles listed below. It consisted of SS emblems on rear fenders and deck lid, an instrument panel pad, special wheel covers with spinners, power brakes and steering, heavy-duty springs and shocks, sintered metallic brake linings, 7000 rpm tachometer and 8.00 x 14 narrow band white sidewall tires, a dashboard grab bar and a chrome shift housing for the floor-shifted four-speed gear box. The price for the SS equipment

package was in the $54 range. The 409-cid "big-block" V-8 was an extra that turned the '61 SS into a real muscle car.

Series Number	Body/Style Number	Body Type & Seating	Factory Price	Shipping Weight	Production Total
IMPALA SS 409 — SERIES 1800 — V-8					
18	11	2d Sed-6P	$2,771	3,440 lbs.	Note
18	37	2d HT-5P	$2,832	3,480 lbs.	Note
18	67	2d Conv-5P	$3,082	3,600 lbs.	Note

NOTE: 142 Impala SS package were installed. It was possible to get the SS package with other body styles, but it is believed that most were two-door models.

ENGINE

BASE V-8: Overhead valve. Cast-iron block and head. Bore and stroke: 4.312 x 3.50 in. Displacement: 409 cid. Compression ratio: 11.25:1. Brake hp: 360 at 5800 rpm. Taxable hp: 59.50. Torque: 409 at 3600. Five main bearings. Solid valve liftersDual exhaust. Carburetor: Carter AFB four-barrel. Sales code: RPO 580. Engine code: Q and QA.

OPTIONS

Oil bath air cleaner ($5). Deluxe air conditioner, includes heater ($457). Cool pack air conditioner ($317). Positraction rear axle ($43). Heavy-duty battery ($8). Crankcase ventilation system, required on California cars ($5). Temperature controlled radiator fan ($16). Optional generator ($8-$97). Tinted glass, all windows ($38), windshield only ($22). Shaded rear windows on two-door sport coupe ($14). Deluxe heater ($74). Recirculating heater ($47). Padded instrument panel ($18). Two-tone paint ($16). Power brakes ($43). Six-Way power seat ($97), Four-Way power seat ($65). Power steering ($75). Power windows ($102). Heavy-duty radiator ($11). Manual radio ($54). Push-button radio ($62). Heavy-duty rear coil springs ($3). Deluxe steering wheel ($4). Overdrive transmission ($108). Turbo-glide transmission ($210). Four-speed, close-ratio manual transmission ($188). Wheel covers ($15). Windshield washers ($11). Two-speed electric windshield wipers and washers ($16).

1962 BEL AIR 409 (Z11)

JERRY HEASLEY

1962 Bel Air 409

"She's so fine my 409!" Remember the song? "Gonna save my pennies and save my dimes. Gonna buy me a 409, 409, 409." What yearning that Beach Boys pop hit lit in teenagers of the early 1960s. Save your pennies and save your dimes and buy yourself a 409, could it be true? Not really, but put in enough hours in the grocery store or as a pump jockey at the local Esso station, mow a few lawns on the side, get a little help from Dad on the down payment and maybe, just maybe you could buy one. That is, if your dealer would sell a kid a 409. Most local dealers refused, they didn't want a kid getting killed in a car they had sold.

A 409 was killer fast! The 409 engine could be ordered in about anything Chevrolet built, even station wagons, but the heart-stopping combination was a 409 in a "bubble top" Bel Air two-door hardtop. This body style got its nickname from the vast sweeps of front and rear window glass and was a better pick than the imitation convertible Impala hardtop due to its lighter weight. Fit the 409 with a close-ratio four-speed manual transmission, and in the Stoplight Gran Prix nobody else would even come close (unless you missed a shift or your contender had slipped a Chrysler Hemi into that chopped Ford coupe). Take that 409 to the Saturday night drags and you'd get your car's value, that and a documented race with some pretty impressive times — like 115 mph at the end of a stand-

ing-start quarter-mile. A 409 would go! Its power rating? How about 409 hp for the dual four-barrel carburetor version.

Series Number	Body/Style Number	Body Type & Seating	Factory Price	Shipping Weight	Production Total
BEL AIR + Z11 (409 HP) — SERIES 1600 — V-8					
16	11	2dr Sed-5P	$3,047	3,565 lbs.	19,900
16	47	2dr HT-5P	$3,152	3,600 lbs.	5,950

NOTE 1: Prices include 409-hp engine.

NOTE 2: Production is for all Bel Air V-8s of these styles, not just 409s.

ENGINE

OPTIONAL V-8: Overhead valve. Cast-iron block and head. Bore and stroke: 4.312 x 3.50 in. Displacement: 409 cid. Compression ratio: 11.00:1. Brake hp: 409 at 6000 rpm. Taxable hp: 59.50. Torque: 420 at 4000. Five main bearings. Solid valve lifters. Dual exhaust. Carburetors: Dual Carter AFB four-barrel.; (front) 3361-S; (rear) 3362-S. Sales code: RPO 587. Engine code: QB.

OPTIONS

Deluxe air conditioning with automatic transmission, includes heater ($364). Cool Pack air conditioner ($317). Group A body equipment including outside rearview mirror, rear bumper guards, grille guard and inside non-glare mirror ($34). Heavy-duty metallic-faced brakes ($38). Tinted glass, all windows ($38). Tinted glass, windshield only ($22). Shaded sport coupe backlight ($14). Padded dash ($16). Two-tone paint ($16). Power brakes ($43). Six-Way power seat ($97). Power steering ($75). Power windows ($102). Manual radio ($48). Push-button radio ($57). Heavy-duty front and rear shock absorbers ($1). Heavy-duty front coil springs ($1). Heavy-duty rear coil springs ($3). Tachometer for V-8s ($49). Wheel discs ($18). Electric two-speed wipers with washers ($17). Various whitewall and oversize tire options ($31-$36). Positive crankcase ventilation system ($5). Heavy-duty battery ($8). Oil bath air cleaner ($5).

CHEVROLET

1962 CORVETTE "SEBRING"

JERRY HEASLEY

1962 Corvette Sebring 327

A 1962 Corvette with a 327-cid/360-hp fuel-injected V-8 and the 3.70:1 rear axle could go from 0-to-30 mph in 2.5 seconds, from 0-to-60 mph in 5.9 seconds and from 0-to-100 mph in 13.5 seconds. It did the quarter-mile in 14.5 seconds at 104 mph and had an estimated maximum speed of 150 mph. With a 3,080-lb. curb weight, the fuel-injected '62 Vette carried just 8.6 pounds-per-horsepower (the lowest ratio ever up to that point). Until the arrival of the Ford-powered Cobra in late 1962, Corvettes dominated B-production racing in Sports Car Club of America (SCCA) events. This period, in fact, has been called the first "Golden Age" of Corvette racing. The high-performance image didn't hurt in the showroom. An all-time high of 14,531 Corvettes were manufactured in 1962. However, few had the ready-to-race Sebring package with all the competition-oriented options.

The most noticeable changes for 1962 Corvettes were the removal of the side cove chrome trim, a blacked-out grille and ribbed chrome rocker panel molding. For the first time since 1955, Corvettes were offered in solid colors only. This was the last straight-axle Corvette and the first to offer a 327-cid small-block V-8.

There were three versions of the engine and the hottest was part of a package nicknamed after the sports car races at Sebring, Florida. In this format, Vette enthusiasts got a fuel-injected engine. Some say that the high-performance equipment offered for Corvettes of this era was related to the AMA racing ban of 1957 and its effect on Zora Arkus-Duntov. As the story goes, with competition restrictions, the "father" of the Corvette could no longer continue racing with factory support. Therefore, he began to slip some serious racing equip-

ment onto the options list. The story seems plausible when you look at the options list. You could not get power steering, power brakes or air conditioning. However, you could add hot "Duntov" camshafts, thermo-activated cooling fans and aluminum-cased transmissions.

Other competition-oriented Corvette "Sebring" extras included 15 x 5.5-inch wheels (no charge), a direct-flow exhaust system (no charge), a 24-gallon fuel tank ($118.40), a four-speed manual gearbox ($188.30), a positraction rear axle ($43.05), sintered-metallic brake linings ($37.70) and heavy-duty suspension ($333.60). The 327-cid/360-hp Rochester fuel-injection engine was $484.20 by itself.

Series Number	Body/Style Number	Body Type & Seating	Factory Price	Shipping Weight	Production Total
CORVETTE 327 "SEBRING" — SERIES 0800 — V-8					
08	67	2d Conv-5P	$4,038	2,925 lbs.	14,531**

NOTE: Prices include 360-hp engine.
** Production is for all Corvettes.

ENGINE

OPTIONAL "SEBRING" V-8: Overhead valve. Cast-iron block. Bore and stroke: 4.00 x 3.25 inches. Displacement: 327 cid. Compression ratio: 11.25:1. Brake hp: 360 at 6000 rpm. Taxable hp: 51.20. Torque: 352 at 4000 rpm. Five main bearings. Hydraulic valve lifters. Induction: Rochester fuel injection 7017360. Engine code: RF.

OPTIONS

102 Signal-seeking AM radio ($137.75). 276 Five 15 x 5.5-inch wheels (No charge). 313 Powerglide automatic transmission ($199.10). 419 Auxiliary hardtop ($236.75). 426 Electric power windows ($59.20). 441 Direct-Flow exhaust system (no charge). 473 Power-operated folding top mechanism ($161.40). 675 Positraction axle with optional ratio ($43.05). 685 Four-speed manual transmission ($188.30). 686 Metallic brakes ($37.70). 687 Heavy-duty brakes and suspension ($333.60). 1832 Five 6.70 x 15 white sidewall tires ($31.55). 1833 Five 6.70 x 15 nylon tires ($15.75).

1962 IMPALA SS 409

JERRY HEASLEY

1962 Impala SS 409

Chevrolet's top models were in the Impala line. And the SS 409 was also one of the quickest Chevys around — the 1962 Impala SS two-door hardtop with the 409-cid/40-hp engine was reported to do the quarter-mile in 14.9 seconds.

The Option Code 240 Super Sport package added or substituted the following items on regular Impala equipment: Swirl-pattern bodyside moldings, "SS" rear fender emblems, "SS" deck lip badge, specific Super Sport full wheel discs with simulated knock-off spinners, locking center console and passenger assist bar. Super Sport equipment was available on the Impala sport coupe and convertible at $53.80 extra, plus $102.25 for bucket seats. The Turbo-Fire 409-cid/380-hp V-8 with four-barrel carburetor, dual exhaust, high-lift camshaft and solid valve lifters was actually a $428 option package.

ENGINES

OPTIONAL V-8: Overhead valve. Cast-iron block and head. Bore and stroke: 4.312 x 3.50 in. Displacement: 409 cid. Compression ratio: 11.00:1. Brake hp: 380 at 5800 rpm. Taxable hp: 59.50. Torque: 420 at 3200. Five main bearings. Solid valve lifters. Dual exhaust. Carburetor: Carter AFB 3345-SA four-barrel. Sales code: RPO 580. Engine code: QA.

OPTIONAL V-8: Overhead valve. Cast-iron block and head. Bore and stroke: 4.312 x 3.50 in. Displacement: 409 cid. Compression ratio: 11.00:1. Brake hp: 409 at 6000 rpm. Taxable hp: 59.50. Torque: 420 at 4000. Five main bearings. Solid valve lifters. Dual exhaust. Carburetors: Dual Carter AFB four-barrel.; (front) 3361-S; (rear) 3362-S. Sales code: RPO 587. Engine code: QB.

OPTIONS

Deluxe air conditioning with automatic transmission, includes heater ($364). Cool Pack air conditioner ($317). Group A body equipment including outside rearview mirror, rear bumper guards, grille guard and inside non-glare mirror ($34). Heavy-duty metallic-faced brakes ($38). Impala Comfort and Convenience group ($30). Tinted glass, all windows ($38). Tinted glass, windshield only ($22). Shaded sport coupe backlight ($14). Padded dash ($16). Two-tone paint ($16). Power brakes ($43). Six-Way power seat ($97). Power steering ($75). Power windows ($102). Manual radio ($48). Push-button radio ($57). Impala sport coupe and convertible bucket seats ($102). Heavy-duty front and rear shock absorbers ($1). Heavy-duty front coil springs ($1). Heavy-duty rear coil springs ($3). Tachometer for V-8s ($49). Wheel discs ($18). Electric two-speed wipers with washers ($17). Various whitewall and oversize tire options ($31-$36). Positive crankcase ventilation system ($5). Heavy-duty battery ($8). Oil bath air cleaner ($5).

Series Number	Body/Style Number	Body Type & Seating	Factory Price	Shipping Weight	Production Total
IMPALA SS + 409 (380 HP) — SERIES 1800 — V-8					
18	47	2dr HT-5P	$3,204	3,610 lbs.	Note 3
18	67	2dr Conv-5P	$3,454	3,720 lbs.	Note 3

NOTE 1: Prices include 380-hp engine.

Series Number	Body/Style Number	Body Type & Seating	Factory Price	Shipping Weight	Production Total
IMPALA SS + 409 (409 HP) — SERIES 1800 — V-8					
18	47	2dr HT-5P	$3,260	3,610 lbs.	Note 3
18	67	2dr Conv-5P	$3,510	3,720 lbs.	Note 3

NOTE 2: Prices include 409-hp engine.

NOTE 3: Chevy built 78,455 Impala SS hardtops and 20,856 Impala SS convertibles; no engine breakouts are available.

CHEVROLET

1963 CORVETTE Z06

TOM GLATCH

1963 Corvette Z06

The Corvette received major restyling in 1963, including a divided rear window for a new "split-window" fastback coupe. The Z06 Special Performance Package was created to market a tready-to-race version of the Corvette to the public. The option package included dual-circuit power brakes with larger-than-stock sintered metallic linings and vented backing plates, finned oversize brake drums with cooling fans in the drums, forward-acting brake system self adjusters, heavy-duty nine-leaf tranverse rear springs, heavy-duty front springs and specially-calibrated shocks . An oversize 36-gallon racing fuel tank was mandatory early in the year. Aluminum knock-off wheels were initially required as part of the package, but were dropped from the list in January 1963. Mandatory extra-cost options included the L84 V-8, a four-speed manual gearbox and a posi-traction rear end. The Z06 option was only available on the split-window sport coupe. Coupes with the option cannot be distinguished by appearance only.

An L84-powered Corvette could go from 0-to-60 mph in 5.9 seconds and from 0-to-100 mph in 16.5 seconds. The optional knock-off wheels were found to leak due to porosity of the aluminum and poor sealing at the rims. No more than a dozen cars actually got them. Futhermore, only one Corvette has been documented original with original knock-offs. About half of the Z06s built in 1963 are believed to survive. They bring six-figure prices at sales like the RM Classic Auction and Barrett-Jackson.

Series Number	Body/Style Number	Body Type & Seating	Factory Price	Shipping Weight	Production Total
CORVETTE STING RAY — SERIES 0800 — V-8					
0800	37	2dr HT-2P	$6,732	3,300 lbs.	199

ENGINE

OPTIONAL ENGINE: Overhead valve. Cast-iron block. Bore and stroke: 4.00 x 3.25 inches. Displacement: 327 cid. Compression ratio: 11.25:1. Brake hp: 360 at 6000 rpm. Taxable hp: 51.20. Torque: 352 at 4000 rpm. Five main bearings. Hydraulic valve lifters. Induction: Rochester fuel injection 7017360. Sales code: L84. Engine code: RF.

OPTIONS

RPO 898 Genuine leather seat trim ($80); RPO 941 Sebring Silver exterior paint ($80.70). RPO A01 Soft-Ray tinted glass, all windows ($16.15). RPO A02 Soft-Ray tinted glass, windshield ($10). RPO 431 Electric power windows ($59.20). RPO C07 Auxiliary hardtop for convertible ($236.75). RPO C48 Heater and defroster deletion ($100 credit). RPO C60 Air conditioning ($421.80). RPO G81 Positraction rear axle, all ratios ($43.05) RPO G91 Special 3.08:1 "highway" ratio rear axle ($2.20). RPO J50 Power brakes ($43.05). RPO J65 Sintered metallic brakes ($37.70). RPO L84 327-cid 370-hp fuel-injected V-8 ($430.40). RPO M20 Four-speed manual transmission ($188.30). RPO N03 36-gallon fuel tank for "split-window" coupe only ($202.30) RPO N11 Off-road exhaust system ($37.70). RPO N34 Woodgrained plastic steering wheel ($16.15). RPO N40 Power steering ($75.35). RPO P48 Special cast-aluminum knock-off wheels ($322.80). RPO P91 Nylon tires, 6.70 x 15 black sidewall ($15.70) RPO P92 Rayon tires, 6.70 x 15, white sidewall ($31.55). RPO T86 Back-up lamps ($10.80). RPO U65 Signal-seeking AM radio ($137.75). RPO U69 AM-FM radio ($174.35). RPO Z06 Special performance equipment for "split-window" coupe ($1,818.45).

1963 IMPALA SS 409

PHIL KUNZ

1963 Impala SS 409

You could get an Impala SS with a six-cylinder engine or a small V-8, but such a car wouldn't fit the "muscle" theme of this book, so we are focusing on the legendary 409 models. There was a new 340-hp version of the big-block V-8 that used a 10.0:1 compression ratio and a mild hydraulic cam, but the muscle car mills were the 400- and 425-hp versions listed below.

This was a peak year for factory drag racing options, such as improved-for-'63 lightweight Z11 drag package (RPO Z11). This was available for the Model 1847 Impala sport coupe. The $1,245 option now had an aluminum front bumper and stripped interior, in addition to the aluminum front fenders, inner fenders and hood. A new 427-cid/430-hp version of the Chevy big-block used a .100 stroke increase to achieve the extra 18 cubic inches of displacement. It had a bore and stroke of 4.312 x 3.65 inches. This engine also included a new dual four-barrel intake manifold that isolated the intake runners from the engine valves, which were covered by a separate valve cover. The GM decision to adhere strictly to the Auto Manufacturers Association's anti-racing ban put a tragic end to these great engines, but not before the cat was, at least briefly, out of the bag.

ENGINES

OPTIONAL V-8: Overhead valve. Cast-iron block and head. Bore and stroke: 4.312 x 3.50 in. Displacement: 409 cid. Compression ratio: 10.00:1. Brake hp: 340 at 5800 rpm. Taxable hp: 59.50. Torque: 420 at 3200. Five main bearings. Solid valve lifters. Dual exhaust. Carburetor: Carter AFB 3345-SA four-barrel.

OPTIONAL V-8: Overhead valve. Cast-iron block and head. Bore and stroke: 4.312 x 3.50 in. Displacement: 409 cid. Compression ratio: 11.00:1. Brake hp: 400 at 5800 rpm. Taxable hp: 59.50. Torque: 425 at 3600. Five main bearings. Solid valve lifters. Dual exhaust. Carburetor: Carter 3820580 four-barrel. Sales code: RPO L31. Engine code: QA.

OPTIONAL V-8: Overhead valve. Cast-iron block and head. Bore and stroke: 4.312 x 3.50 in. Displacement: 409 cid. Compression ratio: 11.00:1. Brake hp: 425 at 6000 rpm. Taxable hp: 59.50. Torque: 425 at 4200. Five main bearings. Solid valve lifters. Dual exhaust. Carburetors: Dual Carter AFB four-barrel; (front) 3815403; (rear) 3815404. Sales code: RPO L80. Engine code: QB.

OPTIONAL V-8 (Z11): Overhead valve. Cast-iron block and head. Bore and stroke: 4.312 x 3.650 in. Displacement: 427 cid. Compression ratio: 12.50-13.50:1. Brake hp: 420 at 3200. Taxable hp: 57.80. Five main bearings. Solid valve lifters. Dual exhaust. Carburetors: Dual Carter AFB four-barrel. Sales code: RPO Z11. Engine code: QM.

(NOTE: The Z11 package introduced August 1, 1962 included aluminum sheet metal and other special equipment. Only 59 cars with this option were made for drag racing only.)

OPTIONS

Deluxe air conditioning, including heater ($364). Cool Pack air conditioning ($317). Driver seat belt ($10). Pair of front seat belts ($19). Heavy-duty brakes with metallic facings ($38). Comfort and Convenience Group ($31). Tinted glass, all windows ($38), windshield only ($22). Grille guard ($19). Passenger car rear bumper guard ($10). Padded dash ($18). Two-tone paint ($16). Power brakes ($43). Six-Way power seat ($97). Power steering/Power windows ($102). Manual radio ($48). Push-button radio ($57). Push-button radio with antenna and rear speaker ($70). Vinyl roof for sport coupe ($75). Deluxe steering wheel ($4). Super Sport equipment package ($161). Tachometer with V-8s ($48). Wheel discs ($18). Wire wheel discs ($25). Two-speed electric washers and wipers ($17). Turbo-Fire 409-cid/400-hp V-8 with four-barrel carburetor, dual exhaust, high-lift camshaft and solid valve lifters ($428). Turbo-Fire 409-cid/425-hp V-8 with dual four-barrel carburetors, dual exhaust, high-lift camshaft and solid valve lifters ($484). Four-speed transmission ($237). Positraction rear axle ($43). Delcotron 42-amp generator, standard with air conditioning, optional on others at ($11). Heavy-duty radiator ($11). Heavy-duty battery ($8). Delcotron 52-amp generator ($32). Delcotron 62-amp generator ($65-$75).

Series Number	Body/Style Number	Body Type & Seating	Factory Price	Shipping Weight	Production Total
IMPALA SS + 409 (340 HP) — SERIES 1800 — V-8					
18	47	2dr HT-5P	$3,016	3,610 lbs.	Note 1
18	67	2dr Conv-5P	$3,266	3,720 lbs.	Note 1
NOTE 1: Prices include 340-hp engine.					
IMPALA SS + 409 (400 HP) — SERIES 1800 — V-8					
18	47	2dr HT-5P	$3,095	3,610 lbs.	Note 2
18	67	2dr Conv-5P	$3,345	3,720 lbs.	Note 2
NOTE 2: Prices include 400-hp engine.					
IMPALA SS + 409 (425 HP) — SERIES 1800 — V-8					
18	47	2dr HT-5P	$3,151	3,610 lbs.	Note 3
18	67	2dr Conv-5P	$3,391	3,720 lbs.	Note 3

NOTE 3: Prices include 425-hp engine.

NOTE 4: Chevy built 122,644 V-8 powered Impala SS hardtops and 26,860 V-8 powered Impala SS convertibles.

NOTE 5: There is no record of how many Impala SS models had the 409 V-8.

NOTE 6: 16,920 of the 409-cid V-8s were installed in all types of full-size Chevrolets.

CHEVROLET

1964 CORVETTE L84

JERRY HEASLEY

1964 Corvette L84

The Corvette's styling was cleaned up a bit for 1964. The previous year's distinctive rear window divider was replaced by a solid piece of glass. The fake hood vents were eliminated and the roof vents were restyled. A three-speed fan was available in the coupe to aid in ventilation. If you wanted muscle under the hood the fuel-injected L84 was still the hot way to go. It was now rated for 375 hp.

Most 1964 Corvettes (85.7 percent) were equipped with a four-speed manual transmission. An L84-powered 1964 Corvette could go from 0-to-60 mph in 6.3 seconds and from 0-to-100 mph in 14.7 seconds. It had a top speed of 138 mph.

Series Number	Body/Style Number	Body Type & Seating	Factory Price	Shipping Weight	Production Total
CORVETTE STING RAY — SERIES 0800 — V-8					
0800	37	2dr HT-5P	$4,252	2,945 lbs.	8,304
0800	67	2d Conv-2P	$4,037	2,960 lbs.	13,925

NOTE 1: Production totals are for all engines
NOTE 2: 1,325 of the 1964 Corvettes had the L84 V-8

ENGINE

OPTIONAL V-8: Overhead valve. Cast-iron block. Displacement: 327 cid. Bore and stroke: 4.00 x 3.25 inches. Compression ratio: 11.00:1. Brake hp: 375 at 6200 rpm. Torque: 350 lbs.-ft. at 4400 rpm. Five main bearings. Mechanical valve lifters. High-lift camshaft. Induction: Ram-Jet fuel injection. RPO Code: L84.

OPTIONS

RPO 898 Genuine leather seat trim ($80.70); RPO A01 Soft-Ray tinted glass, all windows ($16.15). RPO A02 Soft-Ray tinted glass, windshield ($10). RPO 431 Electric power windows ($59.20). RPO C07 Auxiliary hardtop for convertible ($236.75). RPO C48 Heater and defroster deletion ($100 credit). RPO C60 Air conditioning ($421.80). RPO F40 Special front and rear suspension ($37.70). RPO G81 Positraction rear axle, all ratios ($43.05) RPO G91 Special 3.08:1 "highway" ratio rear axle ($2.20). RPO J50 Power brakes ($43.05). RPO J56 Sintered metallic brakes ($37.70). RPO K66 Transistor ignition system ($65.35). RPO L84 327-cid/375-hp fuel-injected V-8 ($538.40). RPO M20 Four-speed manual transmission ($188.30). RPO M35 Powerglide automatic transmission ($199.10) RPO N03 36-gallon fuel tank for "split-window" coupe only ($202.30) RPO N11 Off-road exhaust system ($37.70). RPO N40 Power steering ($75.35). RPO P48 Special cast-aluminum knock-off wheels ($322.80). RPO P91 Nylon tires, 6.70 x 15 black sidewall ($15.70) RPO P92 Rayon tires, 6.70 x 15, white sidewall ($31.85). RPO T86 Back-up lamps ($10.80). RPO U69 AM-FM radio ($174.35).

1964 IMPALA SS 409

Ban or no ban, the Impala SS 409 hardtop ($2,947) or convertible ($3,196) was still a big, fast car. The hardtop tested out at 7.5 seconds for 0-to-60 mph and 15.3 seconds in the quarter-mile. In 1963, a total of 16,920 big Chevrolets left the factory with 409s under their hoods, but in 1964 orders for these engines dropped and only 8,684 were installed. That makes the 1964 Impala SS 409 much harder to find than a 1963 edition.

Chevrolet's plushest and most sporting model was available only in two-door styles. Exterior distinction came from

the use of a wider upper body molding, filled with a swirl-pattern silver anodized insert. Impala lettering and the SS badge appeared on the rear fenders, with another badge appearing on the deck lid. The rear cove outline moldings were filled with silver anodized inserts. Full wheel covers of specific Super Sport design were used.

For 1964, due to the performance ban that GM brass put into effect the previous year, Chevrolet engine choices stayed about the same as in late 1963. The Turbo-Fire 409 V-8 was again available in three versions. The first had a single four-barrel carburetor and 10.0:1 compression. The second version, costing $428 extra, came with a single four-barrel carburetor, dual exhausts, a high-lift camshaft, solid valve lifters and an 11.0:1 compression ratio. The third 409 was a 425-hp version costing $484 extra. It had dual four-barrel carburetors, dual exhausts, a high-lift camshaft, solid valve lifters and an 11.0:1 compression ratio. In both years, most 409-powered Chevys were Impala Super Sports.

Series Number	Body/Style Number	Body Type & Seating	Factory Price	Shipping Weight	Production Total
IMPALA SS + 409 (340 HP) — SERIES 1800 — V-8					
18	47	2dr HT-5P	$3,296	3,450 lbs.	Note 1
18	67	2dr Conv-5P	$3,545	3,560 lbs.	Note 1
NOTE 1: Prices include 340-hp engine.					
IMPALA SS + 409 (400 HP) — SERIES 1800 — V-8					
18	47	2dr HT-5P	$3,375	3,450 lbs.	Note 1
18	67	2dr Conv-5P	$3,624	3,560 lbs.	Note 1
NOTE 2: Prices include 400-hp engine.					
IMPALA SS + 409 (425 HP) — SERIES 1800 — V-8					
18	47	2dr HT-5P	$3,421	3,450 lbs.	Note 1
18	67	2dr Conv-5P	$3,680	3,560 lbs.	Note 1

NOTE 1: Prices include 425-hp engine.

NOTE 2: Chevy built 154,215 V-8-powered Impala SS hardtops and 27,755 V-8-powered Impala SS convertibles.

NOTE 3: There is no record of how many Impala SS models had the 409 V-8.

NOTE 4: 8,684 of the 409-cid V-8s were installed in all types of full-size Chevrolets.

ENGINES

OPTIONAL V-8: Overhead valve. Cast-iron block and head. Bore and stroke: 4.312 x 3.50 in. Displacement: 409 cid. Compression ratio: 10.00:1. Brake hp: 340 at 5800 rpm. Taxable hp: 59.50. Torque: 420 at 3200. Five main bearings. Solid valve lifters. Dual exhaust. Carburetor: Carter AFB 3345-SA four-barrel.

OPTIONAL V-8: Overhead valve. Cast-iron block and head. Bore and stroke: 4.312 x 3.50 in. Displacement: 409 cid. Compression ratio: 11.00:1. Brake hp: 400 at 5800 rpm. Taxable hp: 59.50. Torque: 425 at 3600. Five main bearings. Solid valve lifters. Dual exhaust. Carburetor: Carter 3820580 four-barrel. Sales code: RPO L31. Engine code: QA.

OPTIONAL V-8: Overhead valve. Cast-iron block and head. Bore and stroke: 4.312 x 3.50 in. Displacement: 409 cid. Compression ratio: 11.00:1. Brake hp: 425 at 6000 rpm. Taxable hp: 59.50. Torque: 425 at 4200. Five main bearings. Solid valve lifters. Dual exhaust. Carburetors: Dual Carter AFB four-barrel.; (front) 3815403; (rear) 3815404. Sales code: RPO L80. Engine code: QB.

OPTIONS

Deluxe air conditioning, including heater ($364). Cool Pack air conditioning ($317). Driver's seat belt ($10). Pair of front seat belts ($19). Heavy-duty brakes with metallic facings ($36). Comfort and Convenience group ($31). Tinted glass, all windows ($36), windshield only ($22). Grille guard ($19). Passenger car rear bumper guard ($10). Padded dash ($18). Two-tone paint ($16). Power brakes ($43). Six-Way power seat ($97). Power steering ($75). Power windows ($102). Manual radio ($46). Push-button radio ($57). Push-button radio with antenna and rear speaker ($70). Vinyl roof for sport coupe ($75). Deluxe steering wheel ($4). Tachometer with V-8s ($48). Wheel discs ($18). Wire wheel discs ($25). Two-speed electric washers and wipers ($17). Tilt steering. Turbo-Fire 409-cid/400-hp V-8 ($349). Turbo-Fire 409-cid/400-hp V-8 with four-barrel carburetor, dual exhaust, high-lift camshaft and solid valve lifters ($428). Turbo-Fire 409-cid/425-hp V-8 with dual four-barrel carburetors, dual exhaust, high-lift camshaft and solid valve lifters ($484). Four-speed transmission with 340-/400-/425-horsepower V-8s ($237). Positraction rear axle ($43). Delcotron 42-amp generator standard with air conditioning ($11). Heavy-duty radiator ($11). Heavy-duty battery, standard with 340 horsepower V-8, optional on others at ($3). Delcotron 52-amp generator ($32). Delcotron 62-amp generator ($65-$75).

1964 MALIBU SS 327

JERRY HEASLEY

1964 Malibu SS 327

Anticipating a general improvement in the market for cars priced and sized below regular models, Chevrolet introduced its all-new Chevelle, a car that fit between the compact Chevy II and full-size models. Assembly was quartered at plants in Baltimore and Kansas City and a brand new factory in Fre-

mont, California. The car was styled with square-looking lines in the Chevy II model, but curved side window glass and an emphasis on width provided a distinctive look. A Super Sport series offered a sport coupe and convertible. These cars had no lower belt trim. Instead, there was a molding running along

CHEVROLET

the full-length of the upper body ridge and continuing along the rear fender edge, plus SS rear fender and rear panel badges and specifically styled wheel covers.

Bucket front seats were popular features in the Chevelle Malibu Super Sport. You could get Super Sport models with a six or a 283-cid V-8, but the hot version was the 327-cid/300-hp edition with a dual exhaust system. The car was Chevrolet Motor Division's original answer to the Pontiac GTO and Oldsmobile 4-4-2.

The 300-hp Chevelle SS could do 0-to-60 mph in 6.3 seconds and the quarter-mile in 12.2 seconds at 103 mph.

Series Number	Body/Style Number	Body Type & Seating	Factory Price	Shipping Weight	Production Total
CHEVELLE MALIBU SUPER SPORT 327- SERIES 58 — V-8					
58	37	2d HT-5P	$2,784	2,975 lbs.	57,445
58	67	2d Conv-5P	$3,283	3,120 lbs.	9,640

NOTE 1: Prices include 327 V-8.
NOTE 2: Production total is for cars with all V-8 engines.
NOTE 3: There is no record of how many Malibu SS models had the 327 V-8.

ENGINE

OPTIONAL V-8: Overhead valve. Cast-iron block and head. Bore and stroke: 4.00 x 3.25 in. Displacement: 327 cid. Compression ratio: 10.50:1. Brake hp: 300 at 5000 rpm. Taxable hp: 51.20. Torque: 360 at 3200. Five main bearings. Hydraulic valve lifters. Dual exhaust. Carburetor: Carter 3826004 four-barrel. Engine code: JR or SS.

OPTIONS

Air conditioning ($317). Rear armrests ($10). Pair of front seat belts ($19). Heavy-duty brakes ($38). Comfort and Conve¬nience Group($39). Tinted glass, all windows ($27), windshield only ($13). Grille guard ($15). Rear bumper guard ($10). Padded dash ($16 Two-tone paint, except con¬vertible ($11). Power brakes ($3). Power steering ($75). Power convertible top ($54). Push-button radio with antenna and rear speaker ($70). Manual radio and antenna ($48). Push-button radio and antenna ($57). Full wheel covers ($13). Wire design wheel covers ($13). Various whitewall and oversize tire options ($9-$42). Posi¬traction rear axle ($38). Heavy-duty clutch ($5). Delcotron 42-amp generator ($11). Heavy-duty radiator ($3). Powerglide transmission ($167). The 327 cid/300 hp V-8 with four-barrel carburetor and 10.5:1 compression was a $138 option.

1965 CHEVELLE SS 396

JERRY HEASLEY

1965 Chevelle SS 396

Chevy out-GTO-ed the GTO with the Z16. It was an over-built car. Zero-to-60 mph took just 6.3 seconds. The quarter-mile could be gobbled up in 12.2 seconds at 103 mph.

Regular production option (RPO) Z16 was the 1965 mid-year SS 396 package, which was installed only on a small number of two-door hardtops (sport coupes). It included a heavy-duty convertible frame structure with two added body mounts, 396-cid/375-hp V-8 with a dual exhaust system with special manifolds, chrome engine compartment accents, a four-speed manual transmission, special shock absorbers, a special reinforced suspension, 11-inch-diameter "big car" drum brakes, stiffer-than-stock springs, a 160-mph speedom-

eter and an AM/FM stereo multiplex radio. Specific exterior trim included Malibu SS emblems mounted on front fenders, a special rear cove panel with an SS emblem and ribbed black molding and "396 Turbo-Jet" front fender emblems. An SS 396 emblem was also mounted in the dash. Fifteen-inch-diameter simulated mag style wheel covers were included.

Model Number	Body/Style Number	Body Type & Seating	Factory Price	Shipping Weight	Production Total
CHEVELLE SS 396 — SERIES 3800 — V-8					
138	37	2d HT-5P	$4,091	3,215 lbs.	201

ENGINE

OPTIONAL V-8: Overhead valve. Cast-iron block and head. Bore and stroke: 4.09 x 3.76 in. Displacement: 396 cid. Compression ratio: 11.0:1. Brake hp:

375 at 5600 rpm. Taxable hp: 53.60. Torque: 415 at 3600. Five main bearings. Solid valve lifters. Carburetor: Holley 3893229 four-barrel. Sales code: L37. Engine code: IX.

OPTIONS

Power brakes ($43). Power steering ($86). Four season air conditioning ($364). Rear antenna (no charge). Front bumper guards ($10), rear bumper guards ($10). Rear windshield defroster ($22). Tinted glass on all windows ($31), windshield only ($20). Heater and defroster deletion ($72 credit, not available with air). Tri-volume horn ($14). Instrument panel safety pad ($18). Two-tone paint ($16). Power top on convertible ($54). Power windows ($102). Manual radio ($50). Push-button radio ($58). Push-button radio with rear seat speaker, not available on convertibles ($72). AM/FM radio ($137). Black vinyl roof cover on sport coupes ($75). Deluxe seat belts with retractors ($8). Sport-styled steering wheel ($32). Comfort-lift steering wheel with four-speed or Powerglide ($43). Tachometer on V-8s ($48). Positive traction rear axle ($38). Heavy-duty clutch, on six-cylinder only ($5). Available rear axle gear ratios: 3.08:1, 3.31:1, 4.70:1, 2.73:1. RPO Z16 package ($1,501)

1965 CORVETTE STING RAY 396

PHIL KUNZ

1965 Corvette Sting Ray 396

Three functional, vertical front, slanting louvers on the sides of the front fenders; a blacked-out, horizontal-bars grille and different rocker panel moldings were the main styling changes for 1965 Corvettes. A new hood without indentations was standard, but Corvettes with a newly optional 396-cid "big-block" V-8 used a special hood with a funnel-shaped "power blister" air scoop. Inside the car the instruments were changed to a flat-dial, straight-needle design with an aircraft-type influence. The seats had improved support and one-piece molded inside door panels were introduced.

Standard equipment included: tachometer, safety belts, heater and defroster, windshield washer, outside rear view mirror, dual exhaust, electric clock, carpeting, manually operated top (convertible) and sun visors. A four-wheel disc-brake system was standard, although drum brakes could be substituted for a $64.50 credit. Fuel injection was phased out at the end of the 1965 model year. New options included a nasty-looking side exhaust system and telescoping steering wheel.

An L78-powered 1965 Corvette could go from 0-to-60 mph in 5.7 seconds, and from 0-to-100 mph in 13.4 seconds.

ENGINE

1965 1/2 OPTIONAL V-8: Overhead valve. Cast-iron block. Displacement: 396 cid. Bore and stroke: 4.094 x 3.76 inches. Compression ratio: 11.00:1. Brake hp: 425 at 6400 rpm. Torque: 415 lbs.-ft. at 4000 rpm. Five main bearings. Mechanical valve lifters. High-lift camshaft. Carburetor: Holley four-barrel. RPO code L78.

OPTIONS

RPO 898 Genuine leather seat trim ($80.70); RPO A01 Soft-Ray tinted glass, all windows ($16.15). RPO A02 Soft-Ray tinted glass, windshield ($10.80). RPO 431 Electric power windows ($59.20). RPO C07 Auxiliary hardtop for convertible ($236.75). RPO C48 Heater and defroster deletion ($100 credit). RPO C60 Air conditioning ($421.80). RPO F40 Special front and rear suspension ($37.70). RPO G81 Positraction rear axle, all ratios ($43.05) RPO G91 Special 3.08:1 "highway" ratio rear axle ($2.20). RPO J50 Power brakes ($43.05). RPO J61 Drum brake substitution ($64.50 credit). RPO K66 Transistor ignition system ($75.35). RPO L78 396-cid/425-hp V-8 ($292.70). RPO M20 Four-speed manual transmission ($188.30). RPO M22 Close-ratio four-speed manual transmission ($236.95). RPO M35 Powerglide automatic transmission ($199.10) RPO N03 36-gallon fuel tank for "split-window" coupe only ($202.30) RPO N11 Off-road exhaust system ($37.70). RPO N14 Side-mount exhaust system ($134.50). N32 Teakwood steering wheel ($48.45). N36 Telescopic steering wheel ($43.05). RPO N40 Power steering ($96.85). RPO P48 Special cast-aluminum knock-off wheels ($322.80). RPO P92 7.75 x 15 white sidewall tires ($31.85). RPO T01 7.75 x 15 gold sidewall tires ($50.05). RPO U69 AM-FM radio ($203.40). RPO Z01 Back-up lamps and inside day/night mirror ($16.15).

Model Number	Body/Style Number	Body Type & Seating	Factory Price	Shipping Weight	Production Total
CORVETTE STING RAY — SERIES 9400 — V-8					
194	37	2d HT-6P	$4,233	2,980 lbs.	8,186
194	67	2d Conv-6P	$4,022	2,985 lbs.	15,376

CHEVROLET

1965 IMPALA SS 409

PHIL KUNZ

1965 Impala SS 409

This year was the end of an era. The great W-block introduced in 1958 as a 348-cid mill, and later the 409 of 1961, was phased out, and the Mark IV production version of the 1963 Mark II NASCAR engine in its 396-cid version superseded the 409.

The Impala SS featured bright wheelhouse moldings (without bright lower body moldings), Super Sport front fender script, a black-filled rear cove band with an Impala SS badge at the right-hand side and a similar badge on the left-hand side of the radiator grille. Specific Super Sport full wheel covers were used. The SS interior featured full carpeting, all-vinyl trim with front bucket seats, bright front seatback outline moldings, combination vinyl-and-carpet door trim (with bright accents), foam seat cushions, courtesy lights, SS identification on the door panels, a center console with a built-in Rally-type clock and a vacuum gauge.

Model Number	Body/Style Number	Body Type & Seating	Factory Price	Shipping Weight	Production Total
IMPALA SS 409 — SERIES 6600 — V-8					
166	37	2d HT-6P	$3,189	3,570 lbs.	212,027
166	67	2d Conv-6P	$3,454	3,645 lbs.	27,443

NOTE 1: Prices are for 409-cid/340-hp cars. Add $79 for 400 hp.
NOTE 2: Price of 409-cid/425-hp option not available.
NOTE 3: Production totals are for all V-8-powered Impala SS models.
NOTE 4: Chevrolet installed 2,828 of the 409-cid V-8s in model year 1965. Most or all were put in Super Sports.

ENGINES

OPTIONAL V-8: Overhead valve. Cast-iron block and head. Bore and stroke: 4.312 x 3.50 in. Displacement: 409 cid. Compression ratio: 10.00:1. Brake hp: 340 at 5000 rpm. Taxable hp: 59.50. Torque: 420 at 3200. Five main bearings. Hydraulic valve lifters. Dual exhaust. Carburetor: Rochester 7025123 four-barrel. Sales code: RPO L33. Engine code: JB, JC, JE or JF.

OPTIONAL V-8: Overhead valve. Cast-iron block and head. Bore and stroke: 4.312 x 3.50 in. Displacement: 409 cid. Compression ratio: 11.00:1. Brake hp: 400 at 5800 rpm. Taxable hp: 59.50. Torque: 425 at 3600. Five main bearings. Solid valve lifters. Dual exhaust. Carburetor: Carter 3855581 four-barrel. Sales code: RPO L31. Engine code: JA or JD.

(NOTE: The 425-hp engine was a racing-only option.)

OPTIONS

Power brakes ($43). Power steering ($96). Deluxe front seat belts with retractors ($8). Rear window defroster ($22). Tinted glass on all windows ($38), windshield only ($22). Rear bumper guards ($10). Front bumper guards ($16). Heater/defroster delete ($72 credit). Tri-volume horn ($14). Padded instrument panel ($18.30). Power windows ($102.25). Manual radio ($50). Push-button radio ($59). AM/FM push-button radio ($137). AM/FM radio with stereo ($244). Rear seat speaker ($13). Vinyl roof cover on sport coupe ($75). Sport-styled steering wheel ($32). Comfort-lift steering wheel ($43). Wire wheel design wheel covers ($57). Electric two-speed windshield wipers with washer ($17). Three-speed manual transmission was standard in all models. Overdrive transmission ($107.60). Four-speed manual floor shift transmission ($236.75). V-8 409-cid/340-hp L33 engine ($242.10). V-8 409-cid/400-hp L31 engine ($320.65). V-8 409-cid/425-hp L31-L80. Positive traction rear axle ($43). Heavy-duty air cleaner ($5.40). Heavy-duty clutch ($11). Available rear axle gear ratios: 3.35:1, 3.55:1.

1965 NOVA SS 327

Chevy ll's for 1965 were mildly restyled with a new grille, new rear cove treatment and revised bright trim. In addition to or replacing Nova equipment, Nova SS models also had color-accented body side and rear quarter moldings, front and

rear wheel opening moldings, belt moldings, Nova SS rear fender nameplates and SS emblems, a "Nova SS" deck lid nameplate and emblem, a rear cove outline molding, a silver-painted rear cove area, special Super Sport wheel covers with

14-inch wheels and tires, luxurious all-vinyl seat trim, a all-vinyl headliner, front bucket seats, a floor-mounted shift and special trim plate (with optional four-speed and Powerglide transmissions), an oil pressure gauge, a temperature gauge and an ammeter (in place of warning lights), bright front seat outer end panels, SS glove compartment door nameplates and an electric clock.

This year, the 327-cid V-87 was a factory option. It was offered in 250-hp form, as well as the more muscular 300-hp version. The L30 combo in the Nova was good for 0-to-60 mph in 8.6 seconds and a 16.4-second quarter-mile at 85.87 mph.

Series Number	Body/Style Number	Body Type & Seating	Factory Price	Shipping Weight	Production Total
NOVA SS 327 (250 HP) — SERIES 04 — V-8					
17	37	2dr HT-5P	$2,582	2,885 lbs.	Note 1
NOVA SS 327 (250 HP) — SERIES 04 — V-8					
17	37	2dr HT-5P	$2,625	2,885 lbs.	Note 1

NOTE 1: Production total is for all V-8 powered Nova SS models was 4,801.
NOTE 2: Price estimates include cost of 327 V-8 but no other options.

ENGINES

OPTIONAL V-8: Overhead valve. Cast-iron block and head. Bore and stroke: 4.00 x 3.25 in. Displacement: 327 cid. Compression ratio: 10.50:1. Brake hp: 250 at 4400 rpm. Taxable hp: 51.20. Torque: 350 at 2800. Five main bearings. Hydraulic valve lifters. Carburetor: Rochester 7024225four-barrel. Engine code: ZA, ZE, ZK or ZM.

OPTIONAL V-8: Overhead valve. Cast-iron block and head. Bore and stroke: 4.00 x 3.25 in. Displacement: 327 cid. Compression ratio: 10.50:1. Brake hp: 300 at 5000 rpm. Taxable hp: 51.20. Torque: 360 at 3200. Five main bearings. Hydraulic valve lifters. Dual exhaust. Carburetor: Carter 3851761 four-barrel. Engine code: ZB, ZF, ZL or ZN.

OPTIONS

Power brakes ($43). Power steering ($86). Air conditioning ($317). Rear antenna (no charge). Front Custom Deluxe retractable seat belts ($8). Tinted glass on all windows ($27), on windshield only ($13). Grille guard ($15). Rear bumper guard ($10). Tri-Volume horn, not available with A/C ($14). Padded instrument panel ($16). Two-tone paint ($11). Push-button radio with front speaker ($59). Manual radio ($50). Push-button radio with front and rear speakers ($72). Push-button AM/FM radio ($137). Tachometer ($48). Super Sport wire wheel covers ($57). Three-speed manual transmission was standard. Automatic transmission ($178). Four-speed manual floor shift transmission on V-8 only ($188). V-8 327-cid/250-hp L30 engine ($95). V-8 327-cid/300-hp L74 engine ($138). Positive traction rear axle ($38). Heavy-duty clutch, not available on V-8 with A/C ($5). Available rear axle gear ratios: 3.08:1, 3.55:1, 3.36:1, 3.07:1.

1966 CHEVELLE SS 396

JERRY HEASLEY

1966 Chevelle SS 396

This apple-pie-in-your-face mid-sized Chevy could burn rubber faster than you burn your latest apple pie. Car and Driver said the SS 396 "was a ball to drive." Even the mid-range L34 version was good for 7.9-second 0-to-60 runs and a 14.66-second quarter-mile at 99.88 mph

A new body graced 1966 Chevelles. It had forward-thrusting front fenders, new body contour lines, a wider-appearing anodized aluminum grille and a new rear cove treatment. The new body was more curvaceous and had a slight "Coke-bottle" shape with the rear fenders bulging upwards. The dual round headlights were moved closer together, like they had been in 1964. The grille had nine vertical members behind four full-width horizontal moldings. The rear of the sport coupe had a unique "flying buttress" treatment with the backlight hooded by the sail panels.

The Chevelle performance package was no longer the Malibu SS, but simply the Chevelle SS 396. It featured twin simulated air intakes on its hood, a blacked-out grille, wheelhouse moldings, ribbed and color-accented body sill moldings, ribbed and color-accented lower rear fender moldings, an SS 396 grille emblem, an SS 396 rear cove emblem and Super Sport script on the rear fenders. Specific mag-style wheel covers were included, as were five nylon red stripe tires (although white sidewall tires were a no-cost option).

Chevelle SS 396 buyers also got a standard Turbo-Jet big-block V-8, a special suspension, a fully synchronized three-speed manual transmission and a floor-mounted gear shifter.

CHEVROLET

Model Number	Body/Style Number	Body Type & Seating	Factory Price	Shipping Weight	Production Total
CHEVELLE SS-396 — SERIES 3800 — V-8					
38	17	2d HT-6P	$2,776	3,375 lbs.	66,843
38	67	2d Conv-6P	$2,984	3,470 lbs.	5,429

ENGINES

BASE V-8: Overhead valve. Cast-iron block and head. Bore and stroke: 4.09 x 3.76 in. Displacement: 396 cid. Compression ratio: 10.25:1. Brake hp: 325 at 4800 rpm. Taxable hp: 53.60. Torque: 410 at 3200. Five main bearings. Hydraulic valve lifters. Carburetor: Holley 3874898 or Rochester 7026201 four-barrel. Sales code: L35. Engine code: (Chevelle) ED, EH, EK and EM; (Chevrolet) IA, IB, IG, IV, IC and IN.

OPTIONAL V-8: Overhead valve. Cast-iron block and head. Bore and stroke: 4.09 x 3.76 in. Displacement: 396 cid. Compression ratio: 10.25:1. Brake hp: 360 at 5200 rpm. Taxable hp: 53.60. Torque: 420 at 3600. Five main bearings. Hydraulic valve lifters. Carburetor: Holley 3886087 or Rochester 7026201 four-barrel. Sales code: L34. Engine code: EF, EJ, EL and EN.

OPTIONAL V-8: Overhead valve. Cast-iron block and head. Bore and stroke: 4.09 x 3.76 in. Displacement: 396 cid. Compression ratio: 11.0:1. Brake hp: 375 at 5600 rpm. Taxable hp: 53.60. Torque: 415 at 3600. Five main bearings. Hydraulic valve lifters. Carburetor: Holley 3893229 four-barrel. Sales code: L78. Engine code: EG.

(NOTE: The L78 V-8 option was released at midyear.)

OPTIONS

RPO L35 325-hp V-8 ($182.95). RPO L34 360-hp V-8 in SS 396 ($105.35). RPO L78 375-hp V-8 in SS 396($236). RPO N10 dual exhaust ($21.10). RPO M13 heavy-duty three-speed manual transmission in SS 396 (no charge). RPO M35 Powerglide transmission in SS 396 ($115.90). RPO M20 wide-ratio four-speed manual transmission in SS 396 ($105.35). RPO M21 close-ratio four-speed manual transmission ($105.35). RPO G80 Positraction rear axle ($36.90). RPO J65 sintered metallic brake linings ($36.90). RPO G66 Superlift rear air shocks ($36.90). RPO F40 special suspension ($4.75). RPO J50 power brakes ($42.15). RPO N40 power steering ($84.30). RPO A31 power windows ($100.10). RPO K30 Cruise-Master speed control ($76.40). RPO CO8 vinyl roof ($73.75). RPO A51 power front seats ($69.55). RPO A51 Astro bucket front seats ($110.60). RPO C60 Four-Season air conditioning ($356). RPO Z19 Comfort & Convenience group ($21.10). RPO AO1 tinted glass in all windows ($30.55). RPO AO2 tinted windshield ($19.50). RPO V31 front bumper guards ($9.70). RPO V32 rear bumper guards ($9.70). RPO U14 special instrumentation including ammeter, oil pressure gauge, engine coolant temperature gauge and tachometer ($79). RPO N33 Comfortilt steering wheel ($42.15). RPO D55 center console ($47.40). RPO U16 tachometer ($47.40). RPO V74 hazard warning lights ($21.10). RPO U63 AM push-button radio ($57.40). RPO U69 AM/FM push-button radio ($133.80). RPO U80 rear seat speaker ($13.20).

1966 CORVETTE STING RAY 427

1966 Corvette Sting Ray 427

In 1966, you could get your Corvette with a big old 427 crammed under the hood. The new 'Vette big block came in 390- (L30) and 425-hp (L72) versions, and both of them could make for a pretty hairy ride. With a weight-to-power ratio of 8.5:1, the L72 'Vette was good for 0-to-60 mph in 5.7 seconds and a 14-second quarter-mile at 102 mph.

A plated, cast-metal grille with an "egg crate" insert; ribbed rocker panel moldings; chrome-plated exhaust bezels; spoke-style wheel covers; a vinyl covered headliner and the elimination of roof vents helped set the 1966 Corvette apart from the previous year's model. The front fender sides again had thee slanting vertical air louvers. Inside, the seats had an extra amount of pleats.

Corvettes equipped with the new 427-cid V-8 came with a power-bulge hood.

Model Number	Body/Style Number	Body Type & Seating	Factory Price	Shipping Weight	Production Total
CORVETTE — SERIES 9400 — V-8					
94	37	2d HT-6P	$4,295	2,985 lbs.	9,958
94	67	2d Conv-6P	$4,084	3,000 lbs.	17,762

NOTE: The production totals above are for all 1966 Corvettes.

ENGINES

OPTIONAL V-8: Overhead valve. Cast-iron block. Displacement: 427 cid. Bore and stroke: 4.251 x 3.76 inches. Compression ratio: 10:25:1. Brake hp: 390 at 5200 rpm. Taxable hp: 57.80. Torque: 460 at 3600 rpm. Five main bearings. Hydraulic valve lifters. High-performance camshaft. Carburetor: Holley 3882835 four-barrel. Sales code: L30. Engine code: IL, IM, IQ or IR.

OPTIONAL V-8: Overhead valve. Cast-iron block. Displacement: 427 cid. Bore and stroke: 4.251 x 3.76 inches. Compression ratio: 11.00:1. Brake hp: 425 at 5600 rpm. Taxable hp: 57.80. Torque: 460 at 4000 rpm. Five main bearings. Mechanical valve lifters. Special-performance camshaft. Carburetor: Holley 3886101 four-barrel. Sales code: L72. Engine code: IK or IP.

OPTIONS

RPO 898 Genuine leather seat trim ($79); RPO A01 Soft-Ray tinted glass, all windows ($15.80). RPO A02 Soft-Ray tinted glass, windshield ($10.55). RPO 431 Electric power windows ($59.20). RPO A82 Headrests ($42.15). RPO A85 Shoulder harness ($26.35). RPO C07 Auxiliary hardtop for convertible ($231.75). RPO C48 Heater and defroster deletion ($97.85 credit). RPO C60 Air conditioning ($412.90). RPO F41 Special front and rear suspension ($36.90). RPO G81 Positraction rear axle, all ratios ($42.15) RPO J50 Power brakes ($43.05). RPO J56 Special heavy-duty brakes ($342.30). RPO K66 Transistor ignition system ($73.75). RPO L36 427-cid 390-hp V-8 ($181.20). RPO L72 427-cid 427-hp V-8 ($312.85). RPO M20 Four-speed manual transmission ($184.30). RPO M21 Four-speed close-ratio manual transmission ($184.30). RPO M22 Heavy-duty close-ratio four-speed manual transmission ($237.00). RPO M35 Powerglide automatic transmission ($194.85) RPO N03 36-gallon fuel tank for ($198.05) RPO N11 Off-road exhaust system ($36.90). RPO N14 Side-mount exhaust system ($131.65). N32 Teakwood steering wheel ($48.45). N36 Telescopic steering wheel ($42.15). RPO N40 Power steering ($94.80). RPO P48 Special cast-aluminum knock-off wheels ($326.00). RPO P92 7.75 x 15, white sidewall tires ($31.30). RPO T01 7.75 x 15 gold sidewall tires ($46.55). RPO U69 AM-FM radio ($199.10). RPO V74 Traffic hazard lamp switch ($11.60).

1966 IMPALA SS 396/SS 427

1966 Impala SS

Any 1966 car buyer with muscle-car tendencies needed a V-8 and Chevrolet's hotter offerings started with a 327-cid 275-hp engine. That was mild compared to the Turbo-Fire 396 option. However, real muscle-car fanatics were sure not to settle for anything less than 427 cubic inches.

The new 427-cid V-8 grew out of the Chevrolet racing cars that Bill Thomas had whipped up for NASCAR competition. Big Chevrolets had not been competitive in circle-track racing since 1963, so Thomas took a 396 to his home garage, reworked it to 427 cid, got NASCAR to accept it and talked to the factory about his project. By November 1965, *Car Life* magazine reported that Chevy had enlarged the production 396 to 427. Chevrolet decided to offer the so-called "Rat" motor in showroom cars in two editions.

The RPO L36 version had a 10.25:1 compression ratio and generated 390 hp at 5200 rpm and 460 ft. lbs. of torque at 3600 rpm. With its higher 11.0:1 compression ratio and solid valve lifters, the RPO L72 "special purpose" version of the 427 was

rated for 425 hp at 5600 rpm and 480 lbs.-ft. of torque at 4000 rpm. Fitted with a 390-hp 427, a big '66 Chevy carried about 10.8 lbs. per horsepower and could do 0-to-60 mph in 7.9 seconds or so. The quarter-mile took about 15.5 seconds. According to Robert C. Ackerson's research for his book *Chevrolet High-Performance,* both versions of the 427 were relatively scarce in 1966. A total of 3,287 full-size Chevys carried the L36 and only 1,856 had the L72 installed. Ironically, the rarest Impala SS was the six-cylinder convertible, of which only 46 were built.

Chevrolet was in the second season of a totally new body change, so a mild facelift sufficed for 1966.

Model Number	Body/Style Number	Body Type & Seating	Factory Price	Shipping Weight	Production Total
IMPALA SUPER SPORT — SERIES 6800 — V-8					
68	37	2d HT-6P	3,003	3,615 lbs.	64,058
68	67	2d Conv-6P	3,254	3,650 lbs.	9,498

NOTE 1: The production total above is for all V-8 powered Impala SS models.
NOTE 2: Only 5.143 full-sized Chevrolets had a 427-cid V-8, but not all of them were Impala SS models.

CHEVROLET

ENGINES

OPTIONAL V-8: Overhead valve. Cast-iron block and head. Bore and stroke: 4.09 x 3.76 in. Displacement: 396 cid. Compression ratio: 10.25:1. Brake hp: 325 at 4800 rpm. Taxable hp: 53.60. Torque: 410 at 3200. Five main bearings. Carburetor: Holley 3874898 or Rochester 7026201 four-barrel. Sales code: L35. Engine code: (Chevelle) ED, EH, EK and EM; (Chevrolet) IA, IB, IG, IV, IC and IN.

OPTIONAL V-8: Overhead valve. Cast-iron block and head. Bore and stroke: 4.25 x 3.76 in. Displacement: 427 cid. Compression ratio: 11.0:1. Brake hp: 390 at 5200 rpm. Taxable hp: 57.80. Torque: 460 at 3600. Five main bearings. Dual exhaust. Carburetor: Rochester 7025123 four-barrel. Engine code: IH, IJ and II.

OPTIONAL V-8: Overhead valve. Cast-iron block and head. Bore and stroke: 4.25 x 3.76 in. Displacement: 427 cid. Compression ratio: 10.25:1. Brake hp: 425 at 5600 rpm. Taxable hp: 57.80. Torque: 460 at 4000. Five main bearings. Solid valve lifters. Dual exhaust. Carburetor: Holley 3885067 four-barrel. Engine code: ID and IO.

OPTIONS

Power brakes ($42). Power steering ($95). Four-Season comfort air conditioning. Power rear antenna ($26). Rear window defroster. Emergency road kit. Tinted Soft-Ray glass on all windows ($37), windshield only ($21). Front bumper guards ($16), rear bumper guards ($16). Strato-ease front seat

headrests ($53). Deletion heater and defroster ($71 credit). Tri-volume horn ($14). Special instrumentation ($79). Spare wheel lock. AM/FM push-button radio with front antenna ($134). AM/FM push-button radio with front antenna and rear speaker ($147). AM/FM push-button stereo radio with front antenna ($239). AM push-button radio with front antenna ($57). AM push-button radio with front antenna and rear speaker ($71). Vinyl roof cover in black or beige ($79). Front and rear Custom Deluxe color matched seat belts with front retractors. Four-Way power driver's seat ($70). Comfort-Tilt steering wheel ($42). Sport-styled steering wheel ($32). Tilt-telescopic steering wheel. Tachometer. Traffic hazard warning system. Set of five 14-inch wheels with 6JK rims ($21). Mag style wheel covers ($53). Simulated wire wheel covers ($56). Power windows ($100). A heavy-duty three-speed transmission with floor shift was optional (required) with 396-cid and 427-cid V-8s ($79). A four-speed manual transmission was optional for V-8 engines ($184). Close ratio version (2.20:1 low) was available for 396-427 V-8s. Powerglide two-speed automatic transmission was available with column shift (floor lever on bucket-seat equipped Series 163, 166, 167 cars) for 325-hp/396 V-8s ($195). Turbo Hydra-Matic was optional on 396 V-8 and 427-cid/390-hp V-8 ($226). Optional engines included: 396-cid/325-hp Turbo-Jet V-8 (RPO L35) ($158). 427-cid/390-hp Turbo-Jet V-8 (RPO L36) ($316). 427-cid/425-hp Turbo-Jet V-8 (RPO L72).

1966 NOVA SS 327

JERRY HEASLEY

1966 Nova SS 327

Only 200 Nova SS sport coupes with the RPO L79 V-8 were built. Those cars could do 0-to-60 mph in 7.2 seconds and cover the quarter-mile in 15.1 seconds at 93 mph.

The sporty Nova SS was identified on the exterior by color-accented wide body sill moldings, front and rear wheel opening moldings with extensions on both lower fenders, door and rear quarter upper bodyside moldings, an SS grille emblem, a Nova SS rear fender script, a full-width ribbed rear deck panel with Chevy II nameplate and SS badge and special 14-inch Super Sport wheel covers. Interiors included all-vinyl front bucket seats (console with four-speed or automatic) and most features found on Nova models. An SS emblem was found on the glovebox door. The 327-cid V-8 was again optional.

Model Number	Body/Style Number	Body Type & Seating	Factory Price	Shipping Weight	Production Total
NOVA SS 327 (275 HP) — SERIES 17 — V-8					
17	37	2d HT-6P	$2,628	2,920 lbs.	Note 1
NOVA SS 327 (350 HP) — SERIES 17 — V-8					
17	37	2d HT-6P	$2,671	2,920 lbs.	Note 1

NOTE 1: Production total for all V-8 powered Nova SS models was 16,311.
NOTE 2: Price incudes cost of the base 327-cid V-8, but no other options.

ENGINES

OPTIONAL V-8: Overhead valve. Cast-iron block and head. Bore and stroke: 4.00 x 3.25 in. Displacement: 327 cid. Compression ratio: 10.25:1. Brake hp: 275 at 4800 rpm. Taxable hp: 51.20. Torque: 355 at 3200. Five main bearings. Hydraulic valve lifters. Carburetor: Holley 3876747 or Carter 3876749 four-barrel. Sales code: L30. Engine code: ZA, ZE, ZB, ZC, ZK, ZM, ZD and ZF.

OPTIONAL V-8: Overhead valve. Cast-iron block and head. Bore and stroke: 4.00 x 3.25 in. Displacement: 327 cid. Compression ratio: 11.00:1. Brake hp: 350 at 6000 rpm. Five main bearings. Hydraulic valve lifters. Dual exhaust. Carburetor: Holley 3877413 four-barrel. Sales code: L79. Engine code: ZI, ZG, ZJ and ZH.

OPTIONS

Power brakes ($42). Power steering ($84). All-Weather air conditioning ($310). Cen¬ter console for strato-bucket seats. Rear window defroster. Tinted Soft-Ray glass on all windows ($31), on windshield only ($21). Front bumper guards ($10), rear bumper guards ($10). Strato-Rest headrest ($53). Tri-volume horn. AM push-button radio ($57). AM push-button radio with rear seat speaker ($71). Vinyl roof cover ($74). Custom Deluxe color matched seat belts ($8). Sport-styled steering wheel ($32). Power-operated convertible top. Wheel covers ($21). Mag-styled wheel covers ($74). Simulated wire wheel covers ($73). A three-speed manual transmission was standard in all models. A four-speed manual transmission was optional for cars equipped with V-8s ($184). Powerglide two-speed automatic transmission was optional for all engines ($164-$174). 327-cid/275-hp V-8 RPO L30 ($93). 327-cid/350-hp V-8 RPO L79 (only 200 built).

1967 CAMARO SS 350/SS 396

JERRY HEASLEY

1967 Camaro SS

While inspired by the "pony car" segment that the Mustang had carved out of the marketplace, the first Camaro was really promoted as more of a "Junior Corvette" that gave the family man with a hunkering for a real sports car the opportunity to buy one with four seats. Chevrolet described the Camaro as a "road machine" and promised buyers "wide stance stability and big-car power." It rode a 108-inch wheelbase and measured 185 inches stem-to-stern.

A factory Rally Sport option package could be added to any Camaro with any engine. "From hideaway headlights to unique tail lights this Camaro says swinger from all angles," boasted the 1967 Camaro sales catalog in the section devoted to the Rally Sport model-option.

Car and Driver tested an SS 350 at 0-to-60 mph in 7.8 seconds and the quarter-mile in 16.1 seconds at 86.5 mph. *Motor Trend* needed 8 seconds to get to 60 mph, but did the quarter in 15.4 at 90 mph. *Motor Trend* tested an L35 SS 396 Camaro with four-speed gearbox at 6 seconds for 0-to-60 mph and a 14.5-second quarter-mile at 95 mph. *Car Life* (May 1967) drove a similar car with Powerglide and registered a 6.8-second 0-to-60 time and 15.1-second quarter-mile at 91.8 mph. Unofficially, since a total of 34,411 Super Sports were built and 29,270 were SS 350 models, that leaves 5,141 that were built as SS 396s.

Model Number	Body/Style Number	Body Type & Seating	Factory Price	Shipping Weight	Production Total
CAMARO SS — SERIES 24 + Z27 —					
(RPO L48 "TURBO-FIRE 350" V-8/THREE-SPEED MANUAL TRANSMISSION)					
24	37	2d HT	$2,783	—	Notes 1/2
24	67	2d Conv	$3,019	—	Notes 1/2
CAMARO SS — SERIES 24 + Z27 —					
(RPO L35 "TURBO-JET 396" V-8/ THREE-SPEED MANUAL TRANSMISSION)					
24	37	2d HT	$2,835	—	Notes 1/2
24	67	2d Conv	$3,072	—	Notes 1/2
CAMARO SS — SERIES 24 + Z27 —					
(RPO L78 "TURBO-JET 396" V-8/ THREE-SPEED MANUAL TRANSMISSION)					
24	37	2d HT	$3,072	—	Notes 1/2
24	67	2d Conv	$3,309	—	Notes 1/2

NOTE 1: Combined model-year production of all 1967 Camaros was 220,906.

NOTE 2: Combined production of all 1967 Camaros included 34,411 total SS models (sport coupes and convertibles combined).

ENGINES

DELETE OPTION V-8: 90-degree, overhead valve. Cast-iron block and head. Bore & stroke: 4.00 x 3.25 in. Displacement: 327 cid. Compression ratio: 10.0:1. Brake hp: 275 at 4800 rpm. Torque: 355 lbs.-ft. at 3200 rpm. Five main bearings. Hydraulic valve lifters. Rochester four-barrel carburetor. RPO code: L30.

CAMARO SS 350 BASE V-8: 90-degree, overhead valve. Cast-iron block and head. Bore & stroke: 4.00 x 3.48 in. Displacement: 350 cid (5.7 liters). Compression ratio: 10.25:1. Brake hp: 295 at 4800 rpm. Torque: 380 lbs.-ft. at 3200 rpm. Five main bearings. Hydraulic valve lifters. Rochester four-barrel carburetor. Standard in Camaro SS; not available in other models. RPO code: L48.

CHEVROLET

CAMARO SS 396 BASE V-8: 90-degree, overhead valve. Cast-iron block and head. Bore & stroke: 4.09 x 3.76 in. Displacement: 396 cid. Compression ratio: 10.25:1. Brake hp: 325 at 4800 rpm. Torque: 410 lbs.-ft. at 3200 rpm. Five main bearings. Hydraulic valve lifters. Rochester four-barrel carburetor. Optional in Camaro SS; not available in other models. RPO code: L35.

CAMARO SS 396 BASE V-8: 90-degree, overhead valve. Cast-iron block and head. Bore & stroke: 4.09 x 3.76 in. Displacement: 396 cid. Compression ratio: 11.0:1. Brake hp: 375 at 5600 rpm. Torque: 415 lbs.-ft. at 3600 rpm. Five main bearings. Hydraulic valve lifters. Rochester four-barrel carburetor. Optional in Camaro SS; not available in other models. RPO code: L78.

OPTIONS

AL4 Strato-Back front bench seat ($26.35). AS1 front shoulder belts ($23.20). AS2 Strato-Ease headrests ($52.70). A01 Soft-Ray all tinted glass ($30.55). A02 Soft-Ray tinted windshield only ($21.10). A31 power windows ($100.10). A39 custom deluxe front and rear belts ($6.35). A67 rear folding seat ($31.60). A85 custom deluxe front shoulder belts ($26.35). B37 color-keyed floor mats ($10.55). B93 door edge guards ($3.20). C06 power convertible top ($52.70). C08 vinyl roof cover ($73.75). C48 heater and defroster deletion ($31.65 credit). C50 rear window defroster with sport coupe ($21.10). C50 rear window defroster with convertible ($31.60). C60 air conditioning ($356). D33 left-hand remote-controlled outside rearview mirror ($9.50). D55 center front seat console ($47.40). D91 Front end "bumblebee" stripe ($14.75). F41 heavy-duty Sport suspension ($10.55). G80 positraction rear axle ($42.15). Optional axle ratios 3.31:1, 3.55:1, 2.73:1, 3.07:1 and 7.73:1 ($2.15 each). J50 power brakes ($42.15). J52 front disc brakes ($79). J56 heavy-duty front disc brakes ($105.35) J65 special metallic brake facings ($36.90). K02 tem- perature-controlled de-clutching fan ($15.80). K19 Air Injector Reactor for California car ($44.75). K24 closed positive crankcase ventilation system ($5.25). K30 speed and cruise control ($50.05). K76 61-amp Delcotron alternator ($21.10). K79 42-amp Delcotron alternator ($10.55). L35 396-cid/325-hp V-8 in Camaro SS only ($263.30). L48 350-cid/295-hp V-8 ($210.65). L78 396-cid/375-hp V-8 ($500.30). M11 floor-mounted gearshift lever ($10.55). M13 special three-speed manual transmission ($79). M20 wide-ratio four-speed manual transmission ($184.35). M21 close-ratio four-speed manual transmission ($184.35). M35 Powerglide automatic transmission with small-block V-8s ($194.35). M40 Turbo Hydra-Matic transmission ($226.45). N10 dual exhaust system ($22.10). N30 deluxe steering wheel ($7.40). N33 Comfortilt steering wheel ($42.15). N34 walnut grained steering wheel ($31.60). N40 power steering ($84.30). N44 "Quick-Response" variable-ratio steering ($15.80). N61 dual exhaust system ($21.10). N96 mag-style wheel covers ($73.75). PQ2 7.35 x 14 nylon white sidewall tires ($52.00). PW6 D70-14 red stripe tires ($62.50). P01 bright metal wheel covers ($21.10). P12 five 14 x 6 in. wheels ($5.30). P58 7.35 x 14-inch white sidewall tires ($31.35). T60 heavy-duty battery ($7.40). U03 tri-volume horn ($13.70). U15 speed warning indicator ($10.55). U17 special instrumentation ($79.00). U25 luggage compartment light ($2.65). U26 underhood light ($2.65). U27 glove compartment light ($2.65). U28 ashtray light ($2.65). U29 courtesy lights ($4.25). U35 electric clock ($15.80). U57 stereo tape player ($128.50). U63 AM radio ($57.40). U69 AM/FM radio ($133.80). U73 manual rear-mounted radio antenna ($9.50). U80 rear seat speaker ($13.90). V01 heavy-duty radiator ($10.55). V31 front bumper guard ($12.65). V32 rear bumper guard ($9.50). Z21 style trim ($40.05). Z22 Rally Sport package ($105.35). Z23 special interior group ($10.55). Z28 Special Performance package ($358.10).

1967 CAMARO Z/28

JERRY HEASLEY

1967 Camaro Z/28

The Z/28 package first appeared in December 1966. During the second half of 1967 a limited number of Camaros were built with the new option, which was available for Camaro sport coupes only. It was most sought after by enthusiasts with a serious interest in racing.

The May 1967 edition of *Motor Trend* road tested a Camaro Z/28 coupe with the 302-cid/290-hp V-8 and four-speed manual transmission. It did 0-to-60 mph in 7.0 seconds and the quarter-mile in 14.8 seconds at 96 mph. The magazine noted that this engine was "rumored to bring more than 400 true hp to the starting line." It also pointed out that the Z/28 ran a slower 0-to-60 mph time than an SS 396 Camaro, but a faster quarter-mile.

All Z/28s included a high-performance 302-cid small-block V-8 engine, a 2 1/4-inch diameter dual exhaust system, dual deep-tone mufflers, a heavy-duty suspension, special front coil springs, special multi-leaf rear springs, heavy-duty front and rear shock absorbers, 21.4:1 quick-ratio steering, 15 x 6-in. wheel rims, E70 x 15 special red stripe nylon cord high-performance tires, a 3.73:1 rear axle ratio, paint stripes on the hood, paint stripes on the rear deck lid and Z/28 fender emblems.

Model Number	Body/Style Number	Body Type & Seating	Factory Price	Shipping Weight	Production Total
CAMARO Z/281 — SERIES 24 + Z/28 —					
(V-8 WITH 4-SPEED MANUAL TRANSMISSION AND POWER BRAKES)					
24	37	2d HT	$3,273	3,520 lbs.	602

NOTE 1: Combined model-year production of all 1967 Camaros was 220,906.

NOTE 2: Combined production of all 1967 Camaros included 602 Z/28s.

ENGINE

Z/28 BASE V-8: 90-degree, overhead valve. Cast-iron block. Cast-iron head. Bore & stroke: 4.002 x 3.005 in. Displacement: 302 cid (5.0 liters). Compression ratio: 11.0:1. Brake hp: 290 at 5800 rpm. Torque: 290 lbs.-ft. at 4200 rpm. Five four-bolt main bearings with nodular iron main caps. Solid valve lifters. Holley no. 3923289 (R4055A) four-barrel carburetor. Four-bolt main bearings. Special solid lifter camshaft. Dual exhaust system (2 1/4-in. diameter) with dual deep-tone mufflers.

OPTIONS

AL4 Strato-Back front bench seat ($26.35). AS1 front shoulder belts ($23.20). AS2 Strato-Ease headrests ($52.70). A01 Soft-Ray all tinted glass ($30.55). A02 Soft-Ray tinted windshield only ($21.10). A31 power windows ($100.10). A39 custom deluxe front and rear belts ($6.35). A67 rear folding seat ($31.60). A85 custom deluxe front shoulder belts ($26.35). B37 color-keyed floor mats ($10.55). B93 door edge guards ($3.20). C06 power convertible top ($52.70). C08 vinyl roof cover ($73.75). C48 heater and defroster deletion ($31.65 credit). C50 rear window defroster with Sport Coupe ($21.10). C50 rear window defroster with convertible ($31.60). C60 air conditioning ($356). D33 left-hand remote-controlled outside rearview mirror ($9.50). D55 center front seat console ($47.40). D91 Front end "bumblebee" stripe ($14.75). F41 heavy-duty Sport suspension ($10.55). G80 positraction rear axle ($42.15). Optional axle ratios 3.31:1, 3.55:1, 2.73:1, 3.07:1 and 7.73:1 ($2.15 each). J50 power brakes ($42.15). J52 front disc brakes ($79). J56 heavy-duty front disc brakes ($105.35). J65 special metallic brake facings ($36.90). K02 temperature-controlled de-clutching fan ($15.80). K19 Air Injector Reactor for California car ($44.75). K24 closed positive crankcase ventilation system ($5.25). K30 speed and cruise control ($50.05). K76 61-amp Delcotron alternator ($21.10). K79 42-amp Delcotron alternator ($10.55). L22 250-cid inline six-cylinder engine ($26.35). L30 327-cid/275-hp V-8 ($92.70). L35 396-cid/325-hp V-8 in Camaro SS only ($263.30). L48 350-cid/295-hp V-8 ($210.65). L78 396-cid/375-hp V-8 ($500.30). M11 floor-mounted gearshift lever ($10.55). M13 special three-speed manual transmission ($79). M20 wide-ratio four-speed manual transmission ($184.35). M21 close-ratio four-speed manual transmission ($184.35). M35 Powerglide automatic transmission with six-cylinder engines ($184.35). M35 Powerglide automatic transmission with small-block V-8s ($194.35). M40 Turbo Hydra-Matic transmission ($226.45). N10 dual exhaust system ($22.10). N30 deluxe steering wheel ($7.40). N33 Comfortilt steering wheel ($42.15). N34 walnut grained steering wheel ($31.60). N40 power steering ($84.30). N44 "Quick-Response" variable-ratio steering ($15.80). N61 dual exhaust system ($21.10). N96 mag-style wheel covers ($73.75). PQ2 7.35 x 14 nylon white sidewall tires ($52.00). PW6 D70-14 red stripe tires ($62.50). P01 bright metal wheel covers ($21.10). P12 five 14 x 6 in. wheels ($5.30). P58 7.35 x 14 in. white sidewall tires ($31.35). T60 heavy-duty battery ($7.40). U03 tri-volume horn ($13.70). U15 speed warning indicator ($10.55). U17 special instrumentation ($79.00). U25 luggage compartment light ($2.65). U26 underhood light ($2.65). U27 glove compartment light ($2.65). U28 ashtray light ($2.65). U29 courtesy lights ($4.25). U35 electric clock ($15.80). U57 stereo tape player ($128.50). U63 AM radio ($57.40). U69 AM/FM radio ($133.80). U73 manual rear-mounted radio antenna ($9.50). U80 rear seat speaker ($13.90). V01 heavy-duty radiator ($10.55). V31 front bumper guard ($12.65). V32 rear bumper guard ($9.50). Z21 style trim ($40.05). Z22 Rally Sport package ($105.35). Z23 special interior group ($10.55). Z28 Special Performance package ($358.10). Z28 Special Performance package ($779.40). Z28 Special Performance package ($858.40). Z87 custom interior ($94.80).

1967 CAMARO 427

1967 Dana Camaro

JERRY HEASLEY

Camaros fitted with big-block 427-cid Chevrolet V-8s were evaluated by Chevrolet's engineering department in early 1967, just a few months after the new model first hit the showrooms. At about that time, one of these creations was demonstrated to the press by Chevrolet technical projects manager Walter R. Mackenzie. As you might guess, the experimental 427-powered Camaro topped the performance of even the hottest of the production versions of the car.

These cars were constructed as "semi-factory-built" racing cars by a small number of high-volume Chevrolet dealerships that had close links to drag racing and Chevrolet Motor Division's Product Promotion Network. The managers and salesmen at such dealerships became key players in the development, sales and promotion of the 427 Camaros. The specialized Chevrolet dealers involved in such programs included Don Yenko Chevrolet in Canonsburg, Pennsylvania, Baldwin Motion Chevrolet of Baldwin, Long Island, New York, Dana Chevrolet in South Gate, California, Nickey Chevrolet in Chicago, Illinois, and the Fred Gibb Agency of La Harpe, Illinois. Don Yenko, Dana Chevrolet and Nicky Chevrolet all started selling Camaros fitted with L72 Corvette engines (the 427-cid/425-hp V-8) in 1967.

Dana's basic version listed for $3,995. In addition to the big motor, the package included a Muncie four-speed manual gearbox, a 3.55:1 Positraction axle, 14 x 6-inch wheels with D70-14 Firestone wide-oval nylon red line tires, metallic brake linings, headers and dual exhausts, heavy-duty clutch and pressure plate, a fat front stabilizer bar, heavy-duty shocks and a 17-quart radiator. *Motor Trend* tested a Dana 427 Camaro with a 3.73:1 axle and 9.00/9.50 x 14 tires. It did the quarter-mile in 12.75 seconds at over 110 mph.

Model Number	Body/Style Number	Body Type & Seating	Factory Price	Shipping Weight	Production Total
CAMARO 427 — SERIES 24 (MODIFIED) — V-8					
24	37	2d HT	$3,995*	3,701 lbs.	N/A

NOTE: Price of Dana Chevrolet's "basic" 427 conversion.

ENGINE

OPTIONAL DEALER-INSTALLED ENGINE: Overhead valve. Cast-iron block. Displacement: 427 cid. Bore and stroke: 4.251 x 3.76 inches. Compression ratio: 11.0:1. Brake hp: 425 at 5600 rpm. Taxable hp: 57.80. Torque: 460 at 3800 rpm. Five main bearings. Mechanical valve lifters. Special-performance camshaft. Carburetor: Four-barrel. Sales code: L72. Engine code: Various.

OPTIONS

The 427 Camaros were essentially built to order. The specialized dealers utilized a combination of actory options as well as some non-factory options.

1967 CHEVELLE SS 396

1967 Chevelle SS 396

Chevelle sales set a record in 1967 and it's clear that the SS 396 was the muscular motivator of increased showroom activity. The 1967 SS 396 sport coupe with 375 hp did 0-to-60 mph in 6.5 seconds and did the quarter-mile in 14.9 seconds. *Car and Driver* said that the SS 396, "scored very high with us because of its intrinsic balance. It handled nicely and was therefore a ball to drive."

The Chevelle SS 396 had a youthful flair and a 396-cid/325-hp "big-block" V-8 engine.

A 350-hp version of the 396-cid V-8 was a regular production option. The 375-hp version of the 396-cid V-8 was not listed on Chevrolet Motor Division's internal specification sheets, but it was possible to purchase the necessary components from a Chevrolet dealer to convert the 350-hp V-8 to a

375-hp job. The cost of this conversion was $475.80. A "dual-purpose" Turbo Hydra-Matic 350 transmission was a newly available extra for the SS 396 only. This option allowed shifting gears with an automatic transmission, as well as "shiftless" operation in the "D" range.

Model Number	Body/Style Number	Body Type & Seating	Factory Price	Shipping Weight	Production Total
CHEVELLE SS-396 — SERIES 3800 — V-8					
38	17	2d HT-6P	$2,590	3,115 lbs.	64,532
38	67	2d Conv-6P	$2,796	3,210 lbs.	7,995

ENGINES

BASE V-8: Overhead-valve. Cast-iron block and head. Bore and stroke: 4.09 x 3.76 in. Displacement: 396 cid. Compression ratio: 10.25:1. Brake hp: 325 at 4800 rpm. Taxable hp: 53.60. Torque: 410 lbs.-ft. at 3200. Five main bearings. Hydraulic valve lifters. Carburetor: Rochester 7027201 four-barrel. Sales code: L35.

OPTIONAL V-8: Overhead-valve. Cast-iron block and head. Bore and stroke: 4.09 x 3.76 in. Displacement: 396 cid. Compression ratio: 10.25:1. Brake hp: 350 at 5200 rpm. Taxable hp: 53.60. Torque: 415 lbs.-ft. at 3400. Five main bearings. Hydraulic valve lifters. Carburetor: Four-barrel. Sales code: L34.

OPTIONAL V-8: Overhead-valve. Cast-iron block and head. Bore and stroke: 4.09 x 3.76 in. Displacement: 396 cid. Compression ratio: 11.00:1. Brake hp: 375 at 5600 rpm. Taxable hp: 53.60. Torque: 415 lbs.-ft. at 3600. Five main bearings. Solid valve lifters. Carburetor: Four-barrel.

(NOTE: This engine was not listed in 1967 Chevelle sales literature, but did have a limited installation rate.)

OPTIONS

Four-Season air conditioning, including 61-amp Delcotron, heavy-duty radiator and temperature-controlled fan and requiring larger tires with some Chevelles ($356). Station wagon rear window air deflector ($19). Air Injection Reactor, requiring closed ventilation system ($44.75). Rear antenna, except station with AM/FM radio ($9.50). Positraction rear axle ($42.15). Special economy or high-performance rear axle ($2.15). Heavy-duty battery ($7.40). Center rear seat belts for cars with standard belts ($6.35). Front and rear Custom Deluxe seat belts ($6.35). Center rear Custom Deluxe seat belts for cars with Custom Deluxe seat belts or Custom Appearance group ($7.90). Standard type shoulder belts, in cars with standard seat belts ($23.20). Custom Deluxe shoulder belts, for cars with Custom Deluxe seat belts or Custom Appearance package ($26.35). Front disc brakes, not available with metallic brakes ($79). Sintered metallic brake linings ($36.90). Front bumper guards ($12.65). Rear bumper guards ($12.65). Rear windshield defroster in sport coupe ($21.10). Door edge guards, two-door models ($3.20). 396-cid/350-hp V-8 engine, SS 396 only ($105.35). Temperature-controlled fan, V-8s, standard with air conditioning ($15.80). 42-amp Delcotron generator, not available with air conditioning ($15.80). 61-amp Delcotron generator, standard with air conditioning ($21.10). All windows tinted ($30.55). Tinted windshield only ($21.10). Driver and passenger Strato-Ease headrests, with front bucket seats ($52.70). Driver and passenger Strato-Ease headrests, with standard front bench seat ($42.15). Heater and defroster deletion ($70.70 credit). Tri-volume horn ($13.70). Special instrumentation with ammeter, temperature gauge, oil pressure gauge and tachometer ($79). Ash tray light ($1.60). Courtesy light, all except convertibles ($4.25). Luggage light ($2.65). Underhood light ($2.65). Twin front and rear floor mats ($10.55). Left-hand outside remote-control mirror ($9.50). Two-tone paint ($15.80). Power brakes ($42.15). Four-way power front seat, except with floor-mounted transmission ($69.55). Power steering ($84.30). Power convertible top in white, black or blue ($52.70) Power windows ($100.10). Heavy-duty radiator, except with air conditioning ($10.55). AM/FM push-button radio with front antenna ($133.80). Push-button radio with front antenna ($57.40). AM/FM push-button radio with front antenna ($70.60). AM/FM push-button radio with front antenna and rear speaker ($147). Rear seat speaker ($13.20) Vinyl roof cover, for sport coupe ($73.75). Strato bucket seats in sport coupe and convertible ($110.60). Superlift rear shock absorbers ($36.90). Speed and cruise control, V-8s with automatic transmissions ($50.05). Speed warning indicator ($10.55). Comfortilt steering wheel, requires four-speed manual or automatic transmissions ($42.15). Sport styled steering wheel ($31.60). Stereo tape system with four speakers, not available with rear speaker systems ($128.50). Special front and rear suspension ($4.75). Tachometer, for V-8s, standard with special instrumentation group ($47.40). F70 x 14 four-ply rated white stripe tires in place of red stripe (no cost). Close-ratio four-speed manual transmission ($105.35). Wide-ratio four-speed manual transmission ($105.35). Turbo Hydra-Matic transmission ($147.45). Special floor-mounted three-speed manual transmission for SS 396 (standard). Powerglide automatic transmission for SS 396 ($115.90). Positive crankcase ventilation, standard with 325- and 350-hp engines; on other engines ($5.25). Wheel covers with non-disc brakes ($21.10). Mag-styled wheel covers with non-disc brakes ($73.75). Simulated wire wheel covers with non-disc brakes ($73.75). Appearance group ($45.40). Auxiliary lighting group ($6.90); for sport coupe includes items 1, 2, 3 and 4 ($11.15). Operating convenience group ($30.60).

Some consider the 1967 the best looking of the early Sting Rays. Its styling, although basically the same as in 1966, was a bit cleaner. The same eggcrate-style grille with Argent Silver finish was carried over. Big-block cars had a large front-opening air scoop over the center bulge. The crossed flags badge on the nose of the 1967 Corvette had a widened "V" at its top. On the sides of the front fenders were five vertical and functional louvers that slanted towards the front of the car.

At the rear there were now dual round tail lights on each side (instead of a tail light and optional back-up light). The twin back-up lights were now mounted in the center of the rear panel. Optional finned aluminum wheels were changed in design and had a one-year-only, non-knock-off center.

A 427-cid/435-hp 1967 Corvette convertible carried on 7.7 lbs. per horsepower. It could hit 60 mph in 5.5 seconds and do the quarter-mile in 13.8 seconds. Extremely rare (only 20 were built) — and off in a class by itself — was the aluminum-head

1967 CORVETTE 427

L88. This powerhouse was officially rated at only 430 hp, but really developed nearly 600 hp!

Model Number	Body/Style Number	Body Type & Seating	Factory Price	Shipping Weight	Production Total
CORVETTE — SERIES 9400 — V-8					
94	37	2d HT-6P	$4,553	3,000 lbs.	8,504
94	67	2d Conv-6P	$4,341	3,020 lbs.	14,436

NOTE 1: The prices above include the cost of the L36 V-8 but no other extras.

NOTE 2: The production totals above are for all 1967 Corvettes.

NOTE 3: Engine breakouts included: (L36) 3,832 built, (L68) 2,101 built, (L71) 3,754 built, (L82) 20 built, (L71/L89) 16 built, (L88) 20 built.

ENGINES

OPTIONAL V-8: Overhead valve. Cast-iron block. Displacement: 427 cid. Bore and stroke: 4.251 x 3.76 inches. Compression ratio: 10:25:1. Brake hp: 390 at 5400 rpm. Taxable hp: 57.80. Torque: 460 at 3600 rpm. Five main bearings. Hydraulic valve lifters. High-performance camshaft. Carburetor: Holley four-barrel. Sales code: L36. Engine code: IL, IM, IQ and IR.

OPTIONAL V-8: Overhead valve. Cast-iron block. Displacement: 427 cid. Bore and stroke: 4.251 x 3.76 inches. Compression ratio: 10.25:1. Brake hp: 400 at

CHEVROLET

PHIL KUNZ

1967 Corvette 427

5400 rpm. Taxable hp: 57.80. Torque: 460 at 3600 rpm. Five main bearings. Hydraulic valve lifters. Special-performance camshaft. Carburetor: Three Holley two-barrel. Sales code: L68. Engine code: JC, JF, JD and JG.

OPTIONAL V-8: Overhead valve. Cast-iron block. Displacement: 427 cid. Bore and stroke: 4.251 x 3.76 inches. Compression ratio: 11.0:1. Brake hp: 430 at 5600 rpm. Taxable hp: 57.80. Torque: 460 at 3800 rpm. Five main bearings. Mechanical valve lifters. Special-performance camshaft. Carburetor: Four-barrel. Sales code: L82. Engine code: IT.

OPTIONAL V-8: Overhead valve. Cast-iron block. Displacement: 427 cid. Bore and stroke: 4.251 x 3.76 inches. Compression ratio: 11.0:1. Brake hp: 435 at 5800 rpm. Taxable hp: 57.80. Torque: 460 at 4000 rpm. Five main bearings. Mechanical valve lifters. Special-performance camshaft. Carburetor: Three Holley two-barrels. Sales code: L71. Engine code: JE, IU, JH and JA.

OPTIONAL V-8: Overhead valve. Cast-iron block. Displacement: 427 cid. Bore and stroke: 4.251 x 3.76 inches. Compression ratio: 11.0:1. Brake hp: 435 at 5800 rpm. Taxable hp: 57.80. Torque: 460 at 4000 rpm. Five main bearings. Mechanical valve lifters. Aluminum cylinder heads. Extra-large exhaust valves. Special-performance camshaft. Carburetor: Three Holley two-barrels. Sales code: L71/L89. Engine code: IU. (NOTE: Only 16 of the L71 Corvettes had the optional aluminum cylinder heads installed in 1967.)

OPTIONAL V-8 (MIDYEAR): Overhead valve. Displacement: 427 cid. Bore and stroke: 4.251 x 3.76 inches. Compression ratio: 12.50:1. Brake hp: 560 at 6400 rpm. Taxable hp: 57.80. Five main bearings. Mechanical valve lifters. Special-ultra-high-performance camshaft with .5365-in. intakes. Carburetor:

Single Holley 850CFM four-barrel. Sales code: L88. (NOTE: Only 20 Corvettes with this engine were built in 1967.)

OPTIONS

RPO 898 Genuine leather seat trim ($79); RPO A01 Soft-Ray tinted glass, all windows ($15.80). RPO A02 Soft-Ray tinted glass, windshield ($10.55). RPO A31 Electric power windows ($57.95). RPO A82 Headrests ($42.15). RPO A85 Shoulder harness for coupe only ($26.35). RPO C07 Auxiliary hardtop for convertible ($231.75). RPO C48 Heater and defroster deletion ($97.85 credit). RPO C60 Air conditioning ($412.90). RPO F41 Special front and rear suspension ($36.90). RPO J50 Power brakes ($42.15). RPO J56 Special heavy-duty brakes ($342.30). RPO K66 Transistor ignition system ($73.75). RPO L36 427-cid/390-hp V-8 ($200.15). RPO L68 427-cid/400-hp V-8 ($305.50). L71 427-cid/435-hp ($437.10). RPO L79 327-cid/350-hp V-8 ($105.35). RPO L88 427-cid/430-hp V-8 (actual hp estimated at 560) ($947.90). L89 Aluminum cylinder heads for RPO L71 V-8 ($368.65). RPO M20 Four-speed manual transmission ($184.30). RPO M21 Four-speed close-ratio manual transmission ($184.30). RPO M22 Heavy-duty close-ratio four-speed manual transmission ($237.00). RPO M35 Powerglide automatic transmission ($194.85) RPO N03 36-gallon fuel tank for ($198.05). RPO N11 Off-road exhaust system ($36.90). RPO N14 Side Mount exhaust system ($131.65). N36 Telescopic steering wheel ($42.15). RPO N40 Power steering ($94.80). RPO P48 Special cast-aluminum knock-off wheels ($263.30). RPO P92 7.75 x 15, white sidewall tires ($31.35). RPO QB1 7.75 x 15 red-line tires ($46.65). U15 Speed-warning indicator ($10.55). RPO U69 AM/FM radio ($199.10).

1967 IMPALA SS 396/SS 427

The '67 Impala SS 396 was not just a go-to-work car with a hood scoop. It offered gunboat lovers a "no-excuses-sir" big-car alternative to mid-size muscle. The Impala SS 396 could move from 0-to-60 mph in about 8.5 seconds and did the quarter-mile in around 16.3 seconds. The Impala SS 427 was strictly intended to be an "image" car, though one of larger proportions.

While the 427-cid engine was made available in other Chevrolets, only the SS 427 came with a full assortment of

muscle-car goodies. The '67 version was road tested at 8.4 seconds for 0-to-60 mph and 15.8 seconds for the quarter-mile. That's just slightly slower than a 1970 SS 396 Chevelle with 350 hp, which isn't bad at all for a full-sized Chevy.

Exterior items giving the Impala its status included roof drip cap and reveal moldings on hardtops, deck lid center panel accents in silver and black-accented tail light surrounds. Full wheel covers were included. The following features were added to (or replaced) the equipment found on lower-priced lines:

Everything new that could happen... *happened!*

in styling... in safety... and in all these things for your pure personal pleasure

You're protected by all kinds of new safety features; your ride's smoother and your steering's easier; your music's in true stereo on tape or radio you can add; you've never looked better, going the Chevrolet Way.

'67 CHEVROLET

1967 Impala SS

a brushed metal bright-outlined lower instrument panel facing, electric clock, fingertip door releases, foam-cushioned rear seat, bright seat end panels, bright garnish moldings on sport coupes, bright foot pedal trim outlines (with power brakes), roof side rail lights, courtesy instrument panel (on sport coupe and convertible) and a power-operated convertible top.

The sporty Impala SS once again featured an all-vinyl interior, Strato bucket front seats and a center console housing the shift lever.

Series Number	Body/Style Number	Body Type & Seating	Factory Price	Shipping Weight	Production Total
IMPALA SS 396/SS 427 — SERIES 6800 — V-8					
68	37	2d HT-6P	$3,003	3,615 lbs.	64,058
68	67	2d Conv-6P	$3,254	3,650 lbs.	9,498

NOTE 1: Production totals are for all Impala SS V-8 models.
NOTE 2: Only 2,124 of the Impala SS models built had the 427-cid V-8.

ENGINES

OPTIONAL V-8: Overhead valve. Cast-iron block and head. Bore and stroke: 4.09 x 3.76 in. Displacement: 396 cid. Compression ratio: 10.25:1. Brake hp: 325 at 4800 rpm. Taxable hp: 53.60. Torque: 410 at 3200. Five main bearings. Hydraulic valve lifters. Carburetor: Rochester 7027201 four-barrel. Sales code: L35. Engine code: IA, IB, IG, IV, IC and IN.

OPTIONAL V-8: Overhead valve. Cast-iron block and head. Bore and stroke: 4.25 x 3.76 in. Displacement: 427 cid. Compression ratio: 11.0:1. Brake hp: 385 at 5200 rpm. Taxable hp: 57.80. Torque: 460 at 3400. Five main bearings. Hydraulic valve lifters. Dual exhaust. Carburetor: Four-barrel. Sales code: L36. Engine code: IE, IH, IJ, IS, II, IX, IF and IO.

OPTIONAL V-8: Overhead valve. Cast-iron block and head. Bore and stroke:

4.25 x 3.76 in. Displacement: 427 cid. Compression ratio: 10.25:1. Brake hp: 425 at 5600 rpm. Taxable hp: 57.80. Torque: 460 at 4000. Five main bearings. Solid valve lifters. Dual exhaust. Carburetor: Holley 3885067 four-barrel. Sales code L72. Engine code: ID and IK.

OPTIONS

Power brakes ($42). Power steering ($95). Four Season air conditioning ($356). Comfort-On air conditioning ($435). Rear window air deflector on wagons ($19). Rear manual antenna, not available with AM/FM radio ($9.50). Custom Deluxe front and rear seat belts ($6). Front shoulder belts ($23). Rear window defroster ($21). Tinted glass on all windows ($37), windshield only ($21). Door edge guards on two-doors ($3). Rear bumper guards ($16). Front bumper guards ($16). Head rest with Strato-Back or bucket seats ($53). Head rests with standard bench front seats ($42). Heater and defroster deletion ($71 credit). Tri-Volume horn ($14). Special instrumentation, V-8 only ($79). Automatic superlift level control. Color-keyed floor mats ($11). Left-hand outside remote control mirror ($10). Two-tone paint ($16). Rear power antenna ($28). Four-Way power seat with bucket seats ($70). Power windows ($100). Push-button radio with front antenna ($57). Push-button AM/FM radio with front antenna ($134). Push-button AM/FM radio with front antenna and rear speaker ($147). AM/FM stereo radio with front antenna ($239). Rear seat speaker ($13). Vinyl roof cover on Black or Beige sport coupes ($79). Strato-back vinyl seat (no charge). Strato-back seats including console floor-mounted shift ($158). Rear fender skirts ($26). Speed and cruise control ($50). Speed warning indicator ($11). Comfort-lift steering wheel with Powerglide Hydra-Matic or four-speed manual transmission required ($42). Sport-styled steering wheel ($32). Stereo tape system with four speakers ($129). Mag-style wheel covers ($53). Simulated wire wheel covers ($56). A three-speed manual transmission with floor shift was optional for 396-cid/427-cid V-8s (RPO M13). A four-speed manual transmission with floor shift coded RPO M20 was optional for all V-8 engines ($184). Powerglide two-speed automatic transmission was optional for SS 396 ($195). Turbo Hydra-Matic three-speed automatic transmissions ($226). Optional engines included: RPO L35: 396-cid/325-hp V-8 ($158); RPO L36: 427-cid/385-hp V-8 (included with SS-427 package for $316 total). Positraction rear axle.

1967 NOVA SS 327

PHIL KUNZ

1967 Nova SS 327

Revised for 1967, the taut, small Nova continued to make an excellent high-performance car when equipped with the SS model-option. The 1967 Nova Super Sport had these additional exterior distinctions: a special black-accented grille with a Nova SS emblem low on the driver's side, lower body moldings (above black-painted sill area), body side accent stripes, front and rear bright wheelhouse moldings (with extensions along lower fender edges), specific Super Sport full wheel covers, Super Sport rear fender scripts and a full-width color-accented deck lid trim panel with center emblem and Nova SS signature. The SS interiors were all-vinyl,-trimmed with front Strato bucket seats and bright seat end panels standard. A floor shift trim plate was included on cars with a four-speed manual or automatic transmission. A three-spoke steering wheel was used.

The RPO L30 327-cid V-8 was a separate option. Officially, the RPO L79 327 was not a factory option, although it has been found that a few such cars were actually built by Chevrolet.

Series Number	Body/Style Number	Body Type & Seating	Factory Price	Shipping Weight	Production Total
NOVA SS — SERIES 1700 — V-8					
17	1173	72-dr HT Cpe-5P	$2,592	2,820 lbs.	8,214

NOTE 1: The factory price above does not include the 327-cid V-8.; 327 prices are listed under options.
NOTE 2: The production total above is for all V-8 powered Nova SS models.

ENGINES

OPTIONAL V-8: Overhead valve. Cast-iron block and head. Bore and stroke: 4.00 x 3.25 in. Displacement: 327 cid. Compression ratio: 10.25:1. Brake hp: 275 at 4800 rpm. Taxable hp: 51.20. Torque: 355 at 3200. Five main bearings. Hydraulic valve lifters. Carburetor: Four-barrel. Sales code: L30. Engine code: ZA, ZB, ZD, ZE, ZK and ZM.

OPTIONAL V-8: Overhead valve. Cast-iron block and head. Bore and stroke: 4.00 x 3.25 in. Displacement: 327 cid. Compression ratio: 11.00:1. Brake hp: 350 at 6000 rpm. Taxable hp: 51.20. Torque: 360 at 3200. Five main bearings. Hydraulic valve lifters. Dual exhaust. Carburetor: Holley 3877413 four-barrel. Sales code: L79. Engine code: ZI, ZG and ZJ. (Available as a limited-production or Special Production Option (SPO) only.)

OPTIONS

Power brakes ($42). Power steering ($84). All-Weather air conditioning ($311). Rear antenna ($10). Custom Deluxe front and rear seat belts ($6). Driver and passenger front shoulder belts, standard type ($23), Custom Deluxe type ($26). Front bumper guards ($10). Rear bumper guards ($10). Electric clock ($16). Rear window defroster in sport coupe ($21). Door edge guards, two- doors ($3). Tinted glass, all windows ($31), windshield only ($21). Driver and passenger Strato-Ease headrests ($53). Heater and defroster deletion ($70 credit). Tri-Volume horn ($14). Front and rear color-keyed floor mats ($11). Left-hand outside remote control mirror ($10). Two-tone paint ($16). Push-button radio with front antenna and rear speaker ($71). Push-button radio with front antenna ($57). Rear speaker ($13). Speed warning indicator ($10). Sport-styled steering wheel ($32). Mag styled wheel covers ($74). Simulated wire wheel covers ($74). A three-speed manual transmission, with column shift, was standard. A four-speed manual transmission was available with optional V-8s ($184). Powerglide two-speed automatic transmission was available with all engines ($174 with V-8). RPO L30: 327-cid/275-hp V-8 ($93). Posi-Traction rear axle ($42).

1968 CAMARO SS 396

Chevrolet boasted that the 1968 Camaro SS (Super Sport) was dedicated to the "fun crowd." The sales catalog said it was "a husky performer and looks it." Big engines, a beefed-up suspension and special equipment features made this model-option stand out.

The SS 396 package included unique hood with twin banks of four square simulated air intakes, a big SS emblem for the center of the grille, special hood insulation, special chassis components, a 396-cid V-8 engine, a color-keyed bumblebee type front accent band (black with light colors and white with darker colors), SS identification below the Camaro front fender script and SS identification on the round fuel filler cap at the center of the rear body panel. A dual exhaust system was included at no additional cost. A 375-hp SS 396 with cold-air induction did 0-to-60 mph in 6.8 seconds and the quarter-mile in 14.77 seconds at 98.72 mph. Its top speed was 126 mph.

JERRY HEASLEY

1968 Camaro SS 396

Model Number	Body/Style Number	Body Type & Seating	Factory Price	Shipping Weight	Production Total
CAMARO SS — SERIES 24 + Z27 —					
(RPO L35 "TURBO-JET 396" V-8/THREE-SPEED MANUAL TRANSMISSION)					
24	37	2d HT	$2,933	2,955 lbs.	Note 1
24	67	2d Conv	$3,171	3,245 lbs.	Note 1
CAMARO SS — SERIES 24 + Z27 —					
(RPO L34 "TURBO-JET 396" V-8/THREE-SPEED MANUAL TRANSMISSION)					
24	37	2d HT	$3,039	2,955 lbs.	Note 2
24	67	2d Conv	$3,277	3,245 lbs.	Note 2
CAMARO SS — SERIES 24 + Z27 —					
(RPO L78 "TURBO-JET 396" V-8/THREE-SPEED MANUAL TRANSMISSION)					
24	37	2d HT	$3,170	2,955 lbs.	4,250
24	67	2d Conv	$3,408	3,245 lbs.	329
CAMARO SS — SERIES 24 + Z27 —					
(RPO L78/L89 "TURBO-JET 396" V-8/THREE-SPEED MANUAL TRANSMISSION)					
24	37	2d HT	$3,539	2,955 lbs.	252
24	67	2d Conv	$3,777	3,245 lbs.	20

NOTE 1: 10,773 L35 cars built and 2,579 L34 cars built (sport coupes and convertibles combined).

ENGINES

OPTIONAL V-8: 90-degree, overhead valve. Cast-iron block and head. Bore & stroke: 4.09 x 3.76 in. Displacement: 396 cid. Compression ratio: 10.25:1. Brake hp: 325 at 4800 rpm. Torque: 410 at 3200 rpm. Five main bearings. Hydraulic valve lifters. Rochester four-barrel carburetor. Optional in Camaro SS; not available in other models. RPO code L35.

OPTIONAL V-8: 90-degree, overhead valve. Cast-iron block and head. Bore & stroke: 4.09 x 3.76 in. Displacement: 396 cid. Compression ratio: 10.25:1. Brake hp: 350 at 5200 rpm. Rochester four-barrel carburetor. Optional in Camaro SS; not available in other models. RPO code L34.

OPTIONAL V-8: 90-degree, overhead valve V-8. Cast-iron block and head. Bore & stroke: 4.09 x 3.76 in. Displacement: 396 cid. Compression ratio: 11.0:1. Brake hp: 375 at 5600 rpm. Rochester four-barrel carburetor. Optional in Camaro SS; not available in other models. RPO code L78.

OPTIONAL V-8: 90-degree, overhead valve. Cast-iron block. Aluminum head with large valves. Bore & stroke: 4.09 x 3.76 in. Displacement: 396 cid. Compression ratio: 11.0:1. Brake hp: 375 at 5600 rpm. Rochester four-barrel carburetor.

OPTIONS

C60 air conditioning ($360.20). D33 left-hand remote-controlled outside rearview mirror ($9.50). D55 center front seat console ($50.60). D80 rear deck lid spoiler ($32.65). D90 Sport striping ($25.30). D91 Front end "bumblebee" stripe ($14.75. D96 accent striping ($13.70). F41 heavy-duty Sport suspension ($10.55). G31 special heavy-duty rear springs ($20.05). G80 positraction rear axle ($42.15). Optional axle ratios ($2.15). J50 power brakes ($42.15). J52 front disc brakes ($100.10). KD5 positive crankcase ventilation ($6.35). K02 temperature-controlled de-clutching fan ($15.80). K30 speed and cruise control ($52.70). K76 61-amp Delcotron alternator ($26.35). K79 42-amp Delcotron alternator ($10.55). L34 396-cid/350-hp in Camaro SS only ($368.65). L35 396-cid/325-hp V-8 in Camaro SS only ($263.30). L78 396-cid/375-hp V-8 ($500.30). L78/L89 396-cid/375-hp V-8 with aluminum cylinder heads in Camaro SS only ($868.95). MB1 Torque drive transmission ($68.65). M11 floor-mounted gearshift lever ($10.55). M13 special three-speed manual transmission ($79). M20 wide-ratio four-speed manual transmission ($184.35). M21 close-ratio four-speed manual transmission ($184.35). M22 close-ratio heavy-duty four-speed manual transmission ($310.70). M40 Turbo Hydra-Matic transmission ($237.00). NF2 Deep-Tone dual exhaust system ($27.40). N10 dual exhaust system ($27.40). N33 Comfortilt steering wheel ($42.15). N34 walnut grained steering wheel ($31.60). N40 power steering ($84.30). N44 "Quick-Response" variable-ratio steering ($15.80). N65 Spacesaver spare tire ($19.35). N95 simulated wire wheel covers ($73.75). N96 mag-style wheel covers ($73.75). PA2 mag-spoke wheel covers ($73.75). PW7 F70-14 white sidewall tires ($64.75). PW8 F70-14 red stripe tires ($64.75). PY4 F70-14 fiberglass-belted tires ($26.55). PY5 fiberglass-belted red stripe tires ($26.55). P01 bright metal wheel covers ($21.10). P58 7.35 x 14 white sidewall tires ($31.35). T60 heavy-duty battery ($7.40). U03 tri-volume horn ($13.70). U15 speed warning indicator ($10.55). U17 special instrumentation ($94.80). U46 light monitoring system ($26.35). U57 stereo tape player ($133.80). U63 AM radio ($61.10). U69 AM/FM radio ($133.80). U73 manual rear-mounted radio antenna ($9.50). U79 push-button AM/FM stereo radio ($239.15). U80 rear seat speaker ($13.20). V01 heavy-duty radiator ($13.70). V31 front bumper guard ($12.65). V32 rear bumper guard ($12.65). ZJ7 Rally wheels ($31.60). ZJ9 auxiliary lighting in sport coupe without custom interior option ($13.70). ZJ9 auxiliary lighting in sport coupe with custom interior option ($11.10). ZJ9 auxiliary lighting in convertible without custom interior option ($9.50). ZJ9 auxiliary lighting in convertible with custom interior option ($6.85). Z21 style trim ($47.40). Z22 Rally Sport package ($105.35). Z23 special interior group ($17.95). Z27 Camaro SS package ($210.65-$868.95). Z28 Special Performance package ($400.25-$858.40). Z87 custom interior ($110.60).

CHEVROLET

1968 CAMARO Z/28

JERRY HEASLEY

1968 Camaro Z/28

In 1968, the popularity of the Camaro Z/28 Special Performance package started to climb based on the car's first-year racing reputation. During the later part of the 1967 model year, only 602 Z/28s had been released and Chevrolet wasn't sure if it wanted to market the option strictly for racing or to the public. Output climbed to 7,199 cars in 1968, making it clear that a decision had been made.

The Z/28 package was available for Camaro sport coupes only. It came in four different variations. All Z/28s included a high-performance 302-cid small-block V-8 engine, a dual exhaust system, special front and rear suspensions, a heavy-duty radiator, a temperature-controlled de-clutching radiator fan, quick-ratio steering, 15 x 6-inch wheel rims, E70 x 15 special red stripe nylon tires, a 3.73:1 rear axle ratio, paint stripes on the hood and paint stripes on the rear deck lid.

The 1968 Z/28 was road tested by several major magazines with varying results. *Road & Track* (June 1968) recorded a 14.90-second quarter-mile at 100 mph. *Car Life* (July 1968) recorded a 14.85-second quarter-mile at 101.40 mph. *Car and Driver* (June 1968) recorded a 13.77-second quarter-mile at 107.39 mph.

Model Number	Body/Style Number	Body Type & Seating	Factory Price	Shipping Weight	Production Total
CAMARO Z/281 — SERIES 24 + Z/28 —					
(V-8 WITH 4-SPEED MANUAL TRANSMISSION AND POWER BRAKES)					
24	37	2d HT	$3,297	—	Note 1
CAMARO Z/282 — SERIES 24 + Z/28 -					
(V-8 WITH 4-SPEED MANUAL TRANSMISSION AND POWER BRAKES)					
24	37	2d HT	$3,376	—	Note 1
CAMARO Z/283 — SERIES 24 + Z/28 —					
(V-8 WITH 4-SPEED MANUAL TRANSMISSION AND POWER BRAKES)					
24	37	2d HT	$3,755	—	Note 1
CAMARO Z/283 — SERIES 24 + Z/28 —					
(V-8 WITH 4-SPEED MANUAL TRANSMISSION AND POWER BRAKES)					
24	37	2d HT	$3,834	—	Note 1

NOTE 1: In the 1968 model year a total of 7,199 Camaro Z/28s were built.

ENGINE

OPTIONAL V-8: 90-degree, overhead valve V-8. Cast-iron block. Cast-iron head. Bore & stroke: 4.002 x 3.005 in. Displacement: 302 cid (5.0 liters). Compression ratio: 11.0:1. Brake hp: 290 at 5800 rpm. Torque: 290 lbs.-ft. at 4200 rpm. Five four-bolt main bearings with nodular iron main caps. Solid valve lifters. Induction system: 800-cfm Holley no. 3923289 (R4055A) four-barrel carburetor. Dual exhaust system (2 1/4-inch diameter) with dual deep-tone mufflers

OPTIONS

AK1 custom deluxe seat and shoulder belts ($11.10). AL4 Strato-Back front bench seat ($32.65). AS1 front shoulder belts ($23.20). AS2 Strato-Ease headrests ($52.70). AS4 custom deluxe rear shoulder belts ($26.35). AS5 standard rear shoulder belts ($23.20). A01 Soft-Ray all tinted glass ($30.55). A02 Soft-Ray tinted windshield only ($21.10). A31 power windows ($100.10). A39 custom deluxe front and rear belts ($7.90). A67 rear folding seat ($42.15). A85 custom deluxe front shoulder belts ($26.35). B37 color-keyed floor mats ($10.55). B93 door edge guards ($4.25). C08 vinyl roof cover ($73.75). C50 rear window defroster with sport coupe ($21.10). C60 air conditioning ($360.20). D33 left-hand remote-controlled outside rearview mirror ($9.50). D55 center front seat console ($50.60). D80 rear deck lid spoiler ($32.65). D90 Sport striping ($25.30). D96 accent striping ($13.70). F41 heavy-duty Sport suspension ($10.55). G31 special heavy-duty rear springs ($20.05). G80 Positraction rear axle ($42.15). Optional axle ratios ($2.15). J50 power brakes ($42.15). J52 front disc brakes ($100.10). KD5 positive crankcase ventilation ($6.35). K02 temperature-controlled de-clutching fan ($15.80). K30 speed and cruise control ($52.70). K76 61-amp Delcotron alternator ($26.35). K79 42-amp Delcotron alternator ($10.55). MB1 Torque drive transmission ($68.65). M11 floor-mounted gearshift lever ($10.55). M22 close-ratio heavy-duty four-speed manual transmission (mandatory $310.70 option). N33 Comfortilt steering wheel ($42.15). N34 walnut grained steering wheel ($31.60). N40 power steering ($84.30). N44 "Quick-Response" variable-ratio steering ($15.80). N65 Spacesaver spare tire ($19.35). N95 simulated wire wheel covers ($73.75). N96 mag-style wheel covers ($73.75). PA2 mag-spoke wheel covers ($73.75). PW7 F70-14 white sidewall tires ($64.75). PW8 F70-14 red stripe tires ($64.75). PY4 F70-14 fiberglass-belted tires ($26.55). PY5 fiberglass-belted red stripe tires ($26.55). P01 bright metal wheel covers ($21.10). P58 7.35 x 14 white sidewall tires ($31.35). T60 heavy-duty battery ($7.40). U03 tri-volume horn ($13.70). U15 speed warning indicator ($10.55). U17 special instrumentation ($94.80). U46 light monitoring system ($26.35). U57 stereo tape player ($133.80). U63 AM radio ($61.10). U69 AM/FM radio ($133.80). U73 manual rear-mounted radio antenna ($9.50). U79 push-button AM/FM stereo radio ($239.15). U80 rear seat speaker ($13.20). V01 heavy-duty radiator ($13.70). V31 front bumper guard ($12.65). V32 rear bumper guard ($12.65). ZJ7 Rally wheels ($31.60). ZJ9 auxiliary lighting in sport coupe without custom interior option ($13.70). ZJ9 auxiliary lighting in sport coupe with custom interior option ($11.10). ZJ9 auxiliary lighting in convertible without custom interior option ($9.50). ZJ9 auxiliary lighting in convertible with custom interior option ($6.85). Z21 style trim ($47.40). Z22 Rally Sport package ($105.35). Z23 special interior group ($17.95). Z28 Special Performance package ($400.25-$858.40). Z87 custom interior ($110.60).

1968 YENKO SYC CAMARO

JERRY HEASLEY

1968 Yenko SYC Camaro

Ten pounds stuffed into a 5-pound sack. That describes the Yenko SYC, a Camaro stuffed with 427 massive cubes of big-block V-8 power. Don Yenko, of Canonsburg, Pennsylvania, operated Yenko Sportscars. He was one of the first Chevy dealers to turn Camaros into hot rods. Yenko had previously turned out race-modified Corvettes and Corvairs. After the Camaro was introduced, he dreamed up the "Super Yenko Camaro."

The Yenko SYC was essentially a new Camaro V-8 that had the factory small-block replaced with an L72 Corvette engine. This 427 dropped right in the Camaro chassis, then Yenko's racing team mechanics added some heavy-duty bits and did some performance tuning. Yenko Sportscars offered 427-powered Camaros with two horsepower ratings, 435 or 450. Most cars also received a Yenko data plate, special Yenko badges, 427 emblems and a clone of the "Yenko Stinger" Corvette hood. The basic '67 Yenko Camaro sold for about $3,800. The exact number made that year is unknown. For years, it was thought that 54 cars were made the first year, but some experts feel the total may have been closer to 100.

Don Yenko helped to establish a distributorship called Span, Inc., based in Chicago, that marketed the muscular Camaros nationally. It is likely that many of the cars were actually modified in Chicago. When they were shipped to Canonsburg, Yenko added decals, badges and other special features. For 1968, Yenko started with cars that had the L78 version of the 396, which had become the top factory option. These units already had heavy-duty parts and Yenko merely dropped the L72 V-8 onto the stock motor mounts.

These "Keystone State Killers" were regarded as the ultimate muscle cars. A genuine Yenko SYC Camaro can get down a drag strip in the low 12-second range. One run of 11.94 seconds @ 115 mph has been documented. These cars could go from a standing start to 60 mph in 3.8 seconds.

Model Number	Body/Style Number	Body Type & Seating	Factory Price	Shipping Weight	Production Total
YENKO SYC CAMARO 427 — SERIES 2400 — V-8					
24	37	2d HT	$3,800	3,500 lbs.	68-100

NOTE 1: All statistics are estimates.

ENGINES

BASE SYC V-8: 90-degree, overhead valve. Cast-iron block and head. Bore & stroke: 4.251 x 3.76 in. Displacement: 427 cid. Compression ratio: 11.00:1. Brake hp: 400 at 5400 rpm. Torque: 460 lbs.-ft. at 3600 rpm. Five main bearings. Solid valve lifters. Induction system: Rochester four-barrel carburetor.

OPTIONAL SYC V-8: 90-degree, overhead valve V-8. Cast-iron block and head. Bore & stroke: 4.251 x 3.76 in. Displacement: 427 cid. Compression ratio: 11.25:1. Brake hp: 435 at 5800 rpm. Torque: 460 lbs.-ft. at 4000 rpm. Five main bearings. Solid valve lifters. Induction system: Rochester four-barrel carburetor.

OPTIONS

F41 heavy-duty Sport suspension ($10.55). G31 special heavy-duty rear springs ($20.05). G80 positraction rear axle ($42.15). Optional axle ratios ($2.15). J50 power brakes ($42.15). J52 front disc brakes ($100.10). KD5 positive crankcase ventilation ($6.35). K02 temperature-controlled de-clutching fan ($15.80). K76 61-amp Delcotron alternator ($26.35). K79 42-amp Delcotron alternator ($10.55). M21 close-ratio four-speed manual transmission ($184.35). M22 close-ratio heavy-duty four-speed manual transmission ($310.70). M40 Turbo Hydra-Matic transmission ($237.00). N44 "Quick-Response" variable-ratio steering ($15.80). N65 Spacesaver spare tire ($19.35). T60 heavy-duty battery ($7.40). U17 special instrumentation ($94.80). V01 heavy-duty radiator ($13.70). (Note: various other factory and aftermarket options selected by buyer.)

CHEVROLET

1968 CORVETTE 427

JERRY HEASLEY

1968 Corvette 427

The Corvette's first major restyling since 1963 occurred in this year. Chevrolet's big-block, 4.251 x 3.76-inch bore and stroke, 427-cid V-8 was available in the Corvette in four different muscular versions. The least powerful was RPO L36. The second-most powerful 427 was the L68 version. Next came RPO L71, which was a step up the performance ladder with its special-performance, solid-lifter camshaft, three Holley two-barrels and an 11.0:1 compression ratio. The ultimate option was the super-powerful RPO L88 aluminum-head V-8, a $947 option intended primarily for racing. The L88 had mechanical valve lifters, a special ultra-high-performance camshaft with .5365-inch intake and a single Holley 850CFM four-barrel.

Car and Driver tested an L68 Corvette with a four-speed manual gearbox and 3.70:1 rear axle, in its May 1968 issue. It did the standing-start quarter-mile in 14.1 seconds at 102 mph. Its top speed was estimated to be 119 mph. An L71 with a four-speed manual transmission and 3.55:1 rear axle was tested by *Car Life* in June 1968. It did the quarter-mile in 13.41 seconds at 109.5 mph. Its top speed was 142 mph. The L88 with a 3.36:1 rear axle did the quarter-mile in 13.56 seconds at 111.10 mph.

Model Number	Body/Style Number	Body Type & Seating	Factory Price	Shipping Weight	Production Total
CORVETTE 427 — SERIES 9400 — V-8					
94	37	2-dr HT-2P	$4,863	3,055 lbs.	9,936
94	67	2-dr Conv-2P	$4,547	3,070 lbs.	18,630

NOTE 1: The production totals above are for all 1968 Corvettes.
NOTE 2: The prices above include the cost of the L36 V-8 but no other extras.
NOTE 3: Engine breakouts included: (L36) 7,717 built, (L68) 1,932 built (L71) 2,898 built, (L71/L89) 624 built, (L88) 80 built.

ENGINES

OPTIONAL V-8: Overhead valve. Cast-iron block. Bore and stroke: 4.251 x 3.76 inches. Displacement: 427 cid. Compression ratio: 10:25:1. Brake hp: 390 at 5400 rpm. Taxable hp: 57.80. Torque: 460 at 3600 rpm. Five main bearings. Hydraulic valve lifters. High-performance camshaft. Carburetor: Holley four-barrel. Sales code: L36. Engine code: IL or IQ.

OPTIONAL V-8: Overhead valve. Cast-iron block. Bore and stroke: 4.251 x 3.76 inches. Displacement: 427 cid. Compression ratio: 10.25:1. Brake hp: 400 at 5400 rpm. Taxable hp: 57.80. Torque: 460 at 3600 rpm. Five main bearings. Hydraulic valve lifters. Special-performance camshaft. Carburetor: Three Holley two-barrel. Sales code: L68. Engine code: IM or IO.

OPTIONAL V-8: Overhead valve. Cast-iron block. Bore and stroke: 4.251 x 3.76 inches. Displacement: 427 cid. Compression ratio: 11.0:1. Brake hp: 435 at 5800 rpm. Taxable hp: 57.80. Torque: 460 at 4000 rpm. Five main bearings. Mechanical valve lifters. Special-performance camshaft. Carburetor: Three Holley two-barrels. Sales code: L71. Engine code IR.

OPTIONAL V-8: Overhead valve. Cast-iron block. Bore and stroke: 4.251 x 3.76 inches. Displacement: 427 cid. Compression ratio: 11.0:1. Brake hp: 435 at 5800 rpm. Taxable hp: 57.80. Torque: 460 at 4000 rpm. Five main bearings. Mechanical valve lifters. Aluminum cylinder heads. Extra-large exhaust valves. Special-performance camshaft. Carburetor: Three Holley two-barrels. Sales code: L71/L89. Engine code IU.

OPTIONAL V-8: Overhead valve. Bore and stroke: 4.251 x 3.76 inches. Displacement: 427 cid. Compression ratio: 12.50:1. Brake hp: (Advertised) 430 hp; (Actual) 560 at 6400 rpm. Taxable hp: 57.80. Five main bearings. Mechanical valve lifters. Special-ultra-high-performance camshaft with .5365-in. intakes. Carburetor: Single Holley 850CFM four-barrel. Sales code: L88. Engine code: IT.

OPTIONS

RPO 898 Genuine leather seat trim ($79). RPO A01 Soft-Ray tinted glass, all windows ($15.80). RPO A31 Electric power windows ($57.95). RPO A82 Restraints ($42.15). RPO A85 Custom shoulder belts ($26.35). RPO C07 Auxiliary hardtop for convertible ($231.75). RPO C08 Vinyl cover for auxiliary hardtop ($52.70). RPO C50 Rear window defroster ($31.60). RPO C60 Air conditioning ($412.90). RPO F41 Special front and rear suspension ($36.90). G81 Positraction rear axle, all ratios ($46.35). RPO J50 Power brakes ($42.15). RPO J56 Special heavy-duty brakes ($384.45). RPO K66 Transistor ignition system ($73.75). RPO L36 427-cid/390-hp V-8 ($200.15). RPO L68 427-cid/400-hp V-8 ($305.50). L71 427-cid/435-hp ($437.10). L71/ L89 427-cid/435-hp V-8 with aluminum cylinder heads ($947.90). RPO L88 427-cid/560-hp V-8 ($805.75). RPO M20 Four-speed manual transmission ($184.30). RPO M21 Four-speed close-ratio manual transmission ($184.30). RPO M22 Heavy-duty close-ratio four-speed manual transmission ($263.30). RPO M35 Turbo Hydra-Matic automatic transmission ($226.45) RPO N11 Off-road exhaust system ($36.90). N36 Telescopic steering wheel ($42.15). RPO N40 Power steering ($94.80). RPO P01 Bright metal wheel cover ($57.95). RPO PT6 Red stripe nylon tires F70 x 15 ($31.30). RPO PT7 F70 x 15, White stripe tires ($31.35). RPO UA6 Alarm system ($26.35). RPO U15 Speed-warning indicator ($10.55). RPO U69 AM-FM radio ($172.75). RPO U79 Stereo radio ($278.10). Available rear axle gear ratios: 2.73:1, 3.08:1, 3.36:1, 3.55:1, 4.11:1.

1968 CHEVELLE SS 396

CHEVROLET

JERRY HEASLEY

1968 Chevelle SS 396

The "flying buttress" roofline of the Chevelle sport coupe was replaced by a more fastback style and the rear windows had a "veed" appearance (also used on pillared coupes). The round-lens headlights were placed in square, hooded chrome housing that edged up into the hood line. The Chevelle muscle car again wore an exclusive hood with twin power domes. This year the ornamentation was a smaller section of grille work at the rear of each dome.

The heart of the car was the base engine, a 396-cid "big-block" V-8 with 325 hp. Two more-powerful versions of this motor were optional. The 325- and 350-hp versions of the 396-cid V-8 were available with a special three-speed Synchromesh transmission as standard equipment. A four-speed manual gearbox and Powerglide or Turbo Hydra-Matic automatic transmissions were optional. The 375-hp versions, which had to be special ordered, were installed in no more than 2,000 cars. There was a two- to three-month waiting period to get one. A power convertible top was optional.

Series Number	Body/Style Number	Body Type & Seating	Factory Price	Shipping Weight	Production Total
CHEVELLE SS 396 — SERIES 3800 — V-8					
38	37	2d Spt Cpe-6P	$2,899	3,475 lbs.	55,309
38	67	2d Conv-6P	$3,102	3,551 lbs.	2,286

ENGINES

BASE V-8: Overhead-valve. Cast-iron block and head. Bore and stroke: 4.09 x 3.76 in. Displacement: 396 cid. Compression ratio: 10.25:1. Brake hp: 325 at 4800 rpm. Torque: 410 lbs.-ft. at 3200. Five main bearings. Hydraulic valve lifters. Carburetor: Rochester 7028211 four-barrel. Sales code: L35.

OPTIONAL V-8: Overhead-valve. Cast-iron block and head. Bore and stroke: 4.09 x 3.76 in. Displacement: 396 cid. Compression ratio: 10.25:1. Brake hp: 350 at 5200 rpm. Torque: 415 lbs.-ft. at 3400. Five main bearings. Hydraulic valve lifters. Carburetor: Four-barrel. Sales code: L34.

OPTIONAL V-8: Overhead-valve. Cast-iron block and head. Bore and stroke: 4.09 x 3.76 in. Displacement: 396 cid. Compression ratio: 11.00:1. Brake hp: 375 at 5600 rpm. Torque: 415 lbs.-ft. at 3600. Five main bearings. Solid valve lifters. Carburetor: Four-barrel. Sales code L78.

OPTIONAL V-8: Overhead-valve. Cast-iron block and head. Bore and stroke: 4.09 x 3.76 in. Displacement: 396 cid. Compression ratio: 11.00:1. Brake hp: 375 at 5600 rpm. Torque: 415 lbs.-ft. at 3600. Five main bearings. Solid valve lifters. Carburetor: Four-barrel. Sales code L89.

OPTIONS

C60 Four-Season air conditioning, including 61-amp Delcotron, heavy-duty radiator and temperature-controlled fan ($360.20). G80 Positraction rear axle ($42.15). AXL1 Special economy or high-performance rear axle ($2.15). T60 heavy-duty battery ($7.40). A51 Standard-type front shoulder belts, in cars with standard seat belts ($23.20). AS1/S5 Standard-type rear shoulder belts, in cars with standard seat belts ($46.40). A39 Custom Deluxe front and rear seat belts, for cars with bucket seats ($7.90). A39 Custom Deluxe front and rear seat belts, for cars with bench front seats ($9.50). A85 Custom Deluxe front shoulder belts, requires Custom Deluxe seat belts ($26.35). A85/S4 Custom Deluxe front and rear shoulder belts, requires Custom Deluxe seat belts ($52.70). V31 Front bumper guards ($15.80). V32 Rear bumper guards ($15.80). D55 Console, including electric clock, requires bucket seats ($50.60). C50 Rear windshield defroster, all except convertibles and wagons ($21.10). B93 Door edge guards, two-door models ($4.25). L34 396-cid/350-hp V-8 engine, SS 396 only ($105.35). L78 396-cid/375-hp V-8 SS 396 only ($237). K02 Temperature-controlled fan, standard witrh air conditioning ($15.80). K79 42-amp Delcotron generator, not available with air conditioning or with C60 ($10.55). K76 61-amp Delcotron generator, with air conditioning ($5.30); without air conditioning ($26.35). A01 All windows tinted ($34.80). A02 Tinted windshield only ($23.20). A81 Driver and passenger headrests, with front Strato bucket seats ($52.70). A82 Driver and passenger headrests, with standard front bench seat ($42.15). U03 Tri-volume horn ($13.70). Special instrumentation with ammeter, temperature gauge, oil pressure gauge and tachometer ($94.80). U46 light monitoring system ($26.35). ZJ19 auxiliary lighting groups with A) ash tray, B) courtesy, C) glove box, D) luggage and E) underhood lights; in convertibles includes A, D and E ($6.85); in SS 396 sport coupe includes A and B ($11.10). B37 Twin front and rear floor mats ($10.55). D33 Left-hand outside remote-control mirror ($9.50). J50 Power drum brakes ($42.15). J50 Power disc front brakes ($100.10). N40 Power steering ($94.80). C06 Power convertible top in White, Black or Blue ($52.70). A31 Power windows ($100.10). V01 Heavy-duty radiator, except with air conditioning ($10.55). U63 AM push-button radio with front antenna ($61.10). U69 AM/FM radio with front antenna ($133.80). U69/79 AM/FM radio with front antenna and stereo ($239.15). U57 Stereo tape system with four speakers ($133.80). U80 Rear seat speaker, not available with U79 ($13.20) U73 rear antenna, all except AM/FM ($9.50). CO81/82 Vinyl roof cover, for Sport Coupes ($84.30). A51 Strato bucket seats ($110.60). G66 Superlift rear shock absorbers ($42.15). K30 Speed and cruise control, with automatic transmission ($52.70). U15 Speed warning indicator ($10.55). N33 Comfortilt steering wheel, requires floor shifter or automatic transmissions ($42.15). N34 Sport styled steering wheel ($31.60). D96 accent striping ($29.50). F40 Special front and rear suspension ($4.75). M22 Close-ratio four-speed manual transmission for SS 396/375 hp ($237). M21 Close-ratio four-speed manual transmission for other SS 396s ($184.35). M20 Wide-ratio four-speed manual transmission for all ($184.35). M40 Turbo Hydra-Matic transmission for SS 396 with 350-hp or 325-hp V-8 only ($237). M13 Special

CHEVROLET

floor-mounted three-speed manual transmission for all except SS 396 ($79 and standard on SS 396). M10 Overdrive transmission with 140-, 155-, 200- or 250-hp engines ($115.90). KD5 Heavy-duty closed engine positive crankcase ventilation system ($6.35). P01 Four bright metal wheel covers ($21.10). N96 Mag-styled wheel covers with non disc brakes ($73.75). N95 simulated wire wheel covers with non-disc brakes ($73.75). PA2 Mag spoke wheel covers ($73.75). ZJ7 Rallye wheels, including special wheels, hubcaps and trim rings ($31.60). P1 Appearance group ($46.40). P4 Operating convenience group ($46.40). P4 Operating convenience group for SS 396 with U14 special instrumentation ($30.60). P4 Operating convenience group ($9.50).

1968 CHEVY II 427

JERRY HEASLEY

1968 Chevy II 427

Despite adapting a Chevelle-like image, the all-new '68 Chevy II was actually more of a five-passenger version of the Camaro. Both of these Chevys shared the same basic platform floor, forward subframe and front suspension. Also common was the use of a rear suspension with staggered shock absorbers. The relationship between the Chevy II and the Camaro meant that all engines that fit in Chevy's "pony car" could also be stuffed into a Chevy II.

It didn't take too long before well-known drag racers like Dickie Harrell and high-performance factory dealers (like Don Yenko Chevrolet of Cannonsburg, Pennsylvania and Nickey Chevrolet of Chicago, Illinois realized that the Chevy II's Camaro-type engine bay could also accommodate a 427-cid Chevrolet big-block V-8. A small number of such cars were constructed, mainly with drag racing in mind. Since 427-powered Novas were not a factory-issued item, it's hard to pin down specifics on them. When installed in Camaros, the 427 was made available in 410- and 450-hp versions and it's likely the output was roughly the same in the Chevy II. A 427-powered Camaro sold for just under $4,000 in 1968, so logic suggests that a 427-powered Chevy II would have cost a bit less than that.

The performance of the 427 Chevy II was probably in the same general bracket as that of a 427 Camaro, which was around 13 seconds for the quarter-mile at a bit over 100 mph.

Series Number	Body/Style Number	Body Type & Seating	Factory Price	Shipping Weight	Production Total
CHEVY II 427 — SERIES 1300 — V-8					
427 V-8 (410 HP)					
13	27	2d Cpe-6P	$3,999	3,200 lbs.	Note 2

NOTE 1: Price/weight are estimates.

NOTE 2: Not officially documented. It is believed that only 15 to 25 such cars were built.

ENGINES

OPTIONAL V-8 (DEALER-INSTALLED): Overhead valve. Cast-iron block and head. Bore and stroke: 4.25 x 3.76 in. Displacement: 427 cid. Compression ratio: 10.25:1. Estimated brake hp: 410. Five main bearings. Hydraulic valve lifters. Dual exhaust. Carburetor: Holley 3885067 four-barrel. Sales code: L72. Engine code: Various.

CHEVY II OPTIONAL V-8 (DEALER-INSTALLED): Overhead valve. Cast-iron block and head. Bore and stroke: 4.25 x 3.76 in. Displacement: 427 cid. Compression ratio: 11.00:1. Estimated brake hp: 450. Five main bearings. Hydraulic valve lifters. Dual exhaust. Carburetor: Holley 800-cfm four-barrel. Sales code: Special COPO only version. Engine code: Various.

OPTIONS

Rear positraction axle ($42.15). Console with floor-mounted shift. bucket seats required ($50.60). Heavy-duty clutch ($5.30). Left-hand outside remote-control mirror ($9.50). Power brakes, with drum-type brakes ($42.15). Power brakes, with disc-type brakes ($100.10). Power steering ($84.30). Sport-styled steering wheel ($31.60). Four-speed wide-ratio transmission ($184.35). Four-speed close-ratio transmission ($79.00). Mag-style wheel covers ($73.75). Mag spoke wheel covers ($31.60). Custom Exterior group ($68.50). Exterior Decor package ($31.60). Special Interior group ($15.60).

1968 IMPALA SS 427

CHEVROLET

1968 Impala SS 427

Chevrolets grew longer in 1968, with the addition of some bumper, grille, hood and fender modifications. The change that stood out the most was in the tail light design, which now featured recessed lenses housed in rear bumper apertures. The hood was restyled to cover recessed windshield wipers. The front end featured a "floating" type bumper design, in which a grille with slightly finer gridwork showed through below the bumper bar. The headlights were now mounted in rectangular bezels.

Unfortunately, the 1968 Impala SS 427 proved ineffective in boosting big-car sales to enthusiasts. Experts say the 1968s are the more desirable to collectors, but they also represent the easiest SS 427 model to fake. This is because they were not coded as an individual series model.

The RPO Z03 Impala Super Sport option included a special all-vinyl interior, Strato-Bucket seats, a center console, SS wheel covers and a console-mounted shifter with automatic or four-speed manual transmissions.

Series Number	Body/Style Number	Body Type & Seating	Factory Price	Shipping Weight	Production Total
IMPALA SS 427 — SERIES 6400 — V-8					
64	87	2d Spt Cpe-6P	$3,331	3,630 lbs.	14,881
64	47	2d Cus Cpe-6P	$3,384	3,645 lbs.	17,058
64	67	2d Conv-6P	$3,560	3,680 lbs.	4,493

NOTE 1: Prices shown above include additional cost of SS 427 option.

NOTE 2: Weights are for base Impala SS models with 307-cid V-8s.

NOTE 3: Production totals are for all Impala SS regardless of engine.

NOTE 4: Only 1,778 cars combined carried the SS 427 option.

ENGINES

BASE V-8: Overhead valve. Cast-iron block and head. Bore and stroke: 4.25 x 3.76 in. Displacement: 427 cid. Compression ratio: 11.0:1. Brake hp: 385 at 5200 rpm. Torque: 460 at 3400. Five main bearings. Hydraulic valve lifters. Dual exhaust. Carburetor: Four-barrel. Sales code: L36. Engine code: IB, IE, IH, IJ, IS and IC.

IMPALA SS 427 OPTIONAL V-8: Overhead valve. Cast-iron block and head. Bore and stroke: 4.25 x 3.76 in. Displacement: 427 cid. Compression ratio: 10.25:1. Brake hp: 425 at 5600 rpm. Torque: 460 at 4000. Five main bearings. Solid valve lifters. Dual exhaust. Carburetor: Holley 3885067 four-barrel. Sales code L72. Engine code: ID.

OPTIONS

Four Season air conditioning, except with 425-hp V-8 ($368.65). Comfort-On automatic temperature control air conditioning, except with 425-hp V-8 ($447.65). Positraction rear axle ($42.15). Electric clock ($15.80). Heavy-duty clutch ($10.55). Rear window defroster ($21.10). Turbo-Jet 427-cid/385-hp V-8, included with SS-427 option ($263.30). Turbo-Jet 427-cid/425-hp V-8 ($447.65). Tinted glass, windshield ($25.30), all windows ($39.50). Headrests with Strato bucket seats ($52.70), with bench seats ($42.15). Special instrumentation including ammeter, oil pressure, tempera¬ture gauges and tachometer and including clock ($94 80). Remote control left and outside rearview mirror ($9.50). Power rear antenna ($28.45). Power drum brakes ($42.15). Power disc brakes, includes 15-inch hubcaps, wheels and tires ($121.15). Power door lock system, two-door ($44.80. Six-Way power seat, except with bucket seats or four-speed manual transmission ($94.60). Four-Way power left-hand bucket seat ($69.55). Power steering ($94.60). Power windows ($100.10). Heavy-duty radiator ($13.70). Push-button AM radio with antenna ($61.10). Push-button AM/FM radio with front antenna ($133.80). AM/FM radio and stereo ($239.15). Rear manual antenna ($9 50). Rear speaker ($13.20). Stereotape system with four speakers ($133.80). White or Black vinyl roof for Sport Coupe ($89.55). Cloth Strato-Back seats ($105.35). Strato-Back seats, bucket style ($158). Superlift shock absorbers, standard type ($42.15), automatic level control type ($89.55). Cruise Master speed control ($92.70). Rear fender skirts, except with disc brakes ($26.35). Speed warning indicator ($10.55). Deluxe steering wheel ($4.25). Comfort-Tilt steering wheel ($42.15). Sport steering wheel ($31.60). Front and rear special purpose suspension ($21.10). Close-Range four-speed manual transmission ($184.35). Heavy-duty close-range four-speed manual transmission ($310.70). Wide-Range four-speed manual transmission ($184.35). Turbo Hydra-Matic transmission ($226.45-$237). Mag-style 14-inch wheel covers $52.70). Simulated wire type wheel covers ($55.85). Mag spoke 14-inch wheel covers ($52.70). Rallye wheels, on SS-427 without disc brakes, ($21.10), others ($31.60), with discs ($10.55). Appearance Guard group ($26.35-$49.55). Auxiliary Lighting group ($2.65-$39). Convenience Operating Group ($9.50-$46.40). Decor group ($21.10-$72.60). RPO Z03 Impala Super Sport Option, includes special all-vinyl interior, Strato-Bucket seats, center console, SS wheel covers and console shift with automatic or four-speed manual transmissions, on Impala Custom coupe, sport coupe or convertible ($179.05). RPO Z24 Impala SS-427 Option, includes all the above plus special hood, red stripe tires, ornamentation, special suspension features and 15-inch wheels, with RPO L36 Turbo-Jet 385-hp V-8 ($358.10), with RPO L72 Turbo-Jet 425-hp V-8 ($542.45).

CHEVROLET

1968 NOVA SS 396

PHIL KUNZ

1968 Nova SS 396

Chevrolet's senior compact underwent a basic styling change for the 1968 model year. The new body was longer and wider and featured a Chevelle-inspired semi-fastback roofline with wide, flaring sail panels. However, the 1968 model can be identified by the positioning of the model name at the center of the upper grille surround. Other features included single headlights set into square bezels, a full-width multiple bar grille and a more Chevelle-like rear end look.

The Nova SS Option included the 350-cid/295-hp Turbo-Fire V-8, a special steering wheel, hood ornaments, a black-accented grille, a black-accented rear deck plate, hood insulation, an SS nameplate, SS deck emblems, an SS grille and red stripe tires on 6-inch rims.

The image of the Nova SS began to change by the time the sales year was half over. The Nova's new stub frame was borrowed from the Camaro parts bin and, by January 1968, Nova buyers were being offered some new "big-block" engine options that fit comfortably in the new power plant cradle. The 396-cid V-8 was offered for serious muscle-car lovers, but was not advertised by Chevrolet. It provided 6-second 0-to-60-mph performance and was good for 14-second quarter-mile runs. The Nova's standard transmission was a column-mounted three-speed. Options included a three-speed with floor shifter, a four-speed stick (commonly ordered by muscle car fans) and Powerglide automatic. The "Gen II" Chevy II/Nova is becoming one of the hottest collectible Chevrolets in today's youth-oriented enthusiast marketplace.

Series Number	Body/Style Number	Body Type & Seating	Factory Price	Shipping Weight	Production Total
NOVA SS 396 — SERIES 1300 — V-8					
TURBO-JET 396 V-8 (350 HP)					
13	27	2d Cpe-6P	$2,970	3,107 lbs.	234
TURBO-JET 396 V-8 (375 HP)					
13	27	2d Cpe-6P	$3,101	3,107 lbs.	667

NOTE 1: Prices shown include cost of 396-cid engine, but no other options.

NOTE 2: Weight shown is for base Nova SS V-8.

NOTE 3: Total production of 1968 Nova SS coupes was 4,670.

ENGINES

OPTIONAL V-8: Overhead valve. Cast-iron block and head. Bore and stroke: 4.09 x 3.76 in. Displacement: 396 cid. Compression ratio: 10.25:1. Brake hp: 350 at 5200 rpm. Taxable hp: 53.60. Torque: 415 at 3400. Five main bearings. Hydraulic valve lifters. Carburetor: Four-barrel. Sales code: L34. Engine code: MX.

OPTIONAL V-8: Overhead valve. Cast-iron block and head. Bore and stroke: 4.09 x 3.76 in. Displacement: 396 cid. Compression ratio: 11.00:1. Brake hp: 375 at 5600 rpm. Taxable hp: 53.60. Torque: 415 at 3600. Five main bearings. Solid valve lifters. Carburetor: Four-barrel. Engine code: MQ or MR.

OPTIONS

All-Season air conditioning ($347.60). Rear posi-traction axle ($42.15). Console with floor-mounted shift. bucket seats required ($50.60). Electric clock ($15.80). Heavy-duty clutch ($5.30). 350-hp L34 dual-exhaust V-8 ($368.65). 375-hp L78 dual-exhaust V-8 ($500.30). Tinted glass, all windows ($30.55), windshield only ($21.10). Special instrumentation, with console ($94.80). Left-hand outside remote-control mirror ($9.50). Power brakes, with drum-type brakes ($42.15). Power brakes, with disc-type brakes ($100.10). Power steering ($84.30). Vinyl roof cover in white or black ($73.75). Sport-styled steering wheel ($31.60). Stereo tape system ($133.80). Automatic transmission ($174.25). Four-speed wide-ratio transmission ($184.35). Four-speed close-ratio transmission ($79.00). Simulated wire wheel covers ($73.75). Mag-style wheel covers ($73.75). Mag spoke wheel covers ($31.60). Custom Exterior group ($68.50). Exterior Decor package ($31.60). Special Interior group ($15.60).

1969 CHEVELE SS 396

CHEVROLET

JERRY HEASLEY

1969 Chevelle SS 396

The 1969 Chevelle was a gorgeous update of the 1968 design. The SS 396 was no longer a separate series, but became the Z25 option, which could be ordered for the Chevelle 300 Deluxe coupe, the Chevelle 300 Deluxe sport coupe, the Malibu sport coupe and the Malibu convertible.

The Chevelle SS 396 with the 325-hp V-8 and automatic transmission that *Car and Driver* comparison road tested in January 1969 did 0-to-60 mph in 5.8 seconds and covered the quarter-mile in 14.41 seconds at 97.35 mph. You could order the SS 396 option for the Chevelle 300 Deluxe two-door coupe over the counter for $3,409 or more than $300 less than a Dodge Super Bee.

Series Number	Body/Style Number	Body Type & Seating	Factory Price	Shipping Weight	Production Total
CHEVELLE 300 DELUXE + RPO Z25 (SS 396) — SERIES 3400 — V-8					
34	37	2d HT-6P	$2,959	—	Note 3
34	11	2d Cpe-6P	$2,896	—	Note 3
CHEVELLE MALIBU + RPO Z25 (SS 396) — SERIES 3600 — V-8					
36	37	2d HT-6P	$3,038	—	Note 3
36	67	2d Conv-6P	$3,237	—	Note 3

NOTE 1: Prices include RPO Z25 package. With L35 version of 396-cid V-8.
NOTE 2: See options section for prices of other 396-cid V-8s.
NOTE 3: 86,307 Chevelles had the SS 396 option.

ENGINES

OPTIONAL V-8: Overhead-valve. Cast-iron block and head. Bore and stroke: 4.09 x 3.76 in. Displacement: 396 cid (actually 402 cid). Compression ratio: 10.25:1. Brake hp: 325 at 4800 rpm. Taxable hp: 53.60. Torque: 410 at 3200. Five main bearings. Hydraulic valve lifters. Carburetor: Four-barrel. Sales code L35.

OPTIONAL V-8: Overhead-valve. Cast-iron block and head. Bore and stroke: 4.09 x 3.76 in. Displacement: 396 cid (actually 402 cid). Compression ratio: 10.25:1. Brake hp: 350 at 5200 rpm. Taxable hp: 53.60. Torque: 415 at 3400. Five main bearings. Hydraulic valve lifters. Carburetor: Four-barrel. Sales code L34.

OPTIONAL V-8: Overhead-valve. Cast-iron block and head. Bore and stroke: 4.09 x 3.76 in. Displacement: 396 cid (actually 402 cid). Compression ratio: 11.00:1. Brake hp: 375 at 5600 rpm. Taxable hp: 53.60. Torque: 415 at 3600. Five main bearings. Hydraulic valve lifters. Carburetor: Four-barrel. Sales code: L78.

OPTIONAL V-8: Overhead-valve. Cast-iron block. Aluminum head with large valves. Bore and stroke: 4.09 x 3.76 in. Displacement: 396 cid (actually 402 cid). Compression ratio: 11.00:1. Brake hp: 375 at 5600. Taxable hp: 53.60. Torque: 415 at 3600. Five main bearings. Solid valve lifters. Carburetor: Holley four-barrel carburetor on high-rise aluminum intake manifold. Sales code L78/L89.

OPTIONS (PARTIAL LIST)

C60 Four-Season air conditioning, including 61-amp Delcotron alternator, heavy-duty radiator and temperature-controlled fan and requiring larger tires with some Chevelles ($376). ZP5 Appearance group ($50.65). G80 Positraction rear axle ($42.15). ZQ8/9 economy, performance or special rear axle ($2.15). T/60 Heavy-duty battery with 396-cid V-8 ($15.80). AS1 Standard type front shoulder belts, in convertible ($23.20). J50 power drum brakes ($42.15). J50/52 power front disc brakes ($64.25). MA6, Heavy-duty 10-in. dual plate clutch with 350-hp V-8 ($47.40). C50 Rear windshield defroster, for coupe and sport coupe ($22.15). A93 Power door locks for two-door models ($44.80). L34 396-cid/350-hp V-8 engine ($121.15). L78 396-cid/375-hp V-8 ($252.80). L78/L89 396-cid/375-hp V-8 with aluminum heads ($647.75). Solid color Monaco Orange or Daytona Yellow paint ($42.15). Two-tone paint ($23.20). V01 Heavy-duty radiator ($14.75). U63 AM push-button radio with front antenna ($61.10). U69 AM/FM radio with front antenna ($133.80). U69/79 AM/FM radio with front antenna and stereo ($239.15). U73 Rear antenna, all except AM/FM ($9.50). CO8 Vinyl roof cover, for hardtop models ($89.55). Z25 SS 396 option package for Chevelle sport coupe or convertible, includes 396-cid/325-hp V-8, black-accented grille, special hood, special ornamentation, special suspension, sport wheels, wide-oval white lettered tires, power disc brakes and special three-speed manual transmission ($347.60). A51 Strato bucket seats in Malibu sport coupe and convertible ($111.15). K30 Speed and cruise control, V-8s with automatic transmissions ($52.70). U15 Speed warning indicator ($10.55). N30 Deluxe steering wheel in Chevelle 300s ($7.40). N30 Deluxe steering wheel in Chevelle 300 Deluxe ($4.25). N33 Comfortilt steering wheel, requires floor shifter or automatic transmissions ($57.95). U15 speed warning indicator ($11.60). N40 Power steering for SS 396 ($105.35). N33 Comfortilt steering wheel ($45.30). N34 Sport styled steering wheel ($34.80). D96 accent striping ($26.35). M20 wide-ratio four-speed manual transmission ($184.80). M22 Close-ratio four-speed manual transmission ($264). M21 Close-ratio four-speed manual transmission ($184.80). M40 Turbo Hydra-Matic transmission for six-cylinder Chevelles ($190.10). M40 Turbo Hydra-Matic transmission for 375-hp Chevelles ($290.40). M40 Turbo Hydra-Matic transmission for other V-8 Chevelles ($221.80). MC1 Special three-speed manual transmission ($79). Vinyl trim interior for 300 series and Malibu Sport Coupe ($12.65). KD5 Heavy-duty closed engine positive crankcase ventilation system ($6.35). A31 power windows ($100.35). C224 Hide-A-way windshield wipers ($19). P01 Four bright metal wheel covers ($21.10). PA2 Mag spoke wheel covers ($73.75). ZJ7 Rallye wheels, including special wheels, hubcaps and trim rings ($31.60).

CHEVROLET

1969 CAMARO SS 396

PHIL KUNZ

1969 Camaro SS 396

The last of the first-generation Camaros is considered by many enthusiasts to be the best one. The concept behind the new design was to make the Camaro look more "aggressive." The heavily restyled body looked longer and lower. The wheel wells were flattened with sculptured feature lines flowing off them towards the rear of the car and rear-slanting air slots ahead of the rear wheel.

The SS option added a 300-hp Turbo-Fire 350 V-8, a neat-looking hood with exclusive bright-finished simulated intake ports, "hockey-stick" style sport striping, simulated rear fender louvers, power front disc brakes, F70-14 raised white-letter tires and other stuff. Three different "Turbo-Jet 396" (396-cid) V-8s were available as options for the Camaro SS, the RPO L34 version, the RPO L78 version and the RPO L89 version. When these engines were added, the rear panel of the standard Camaro SS was painted black (except on Indy 500 Pace Cars).

In May 1969 *Car Life* magazine road tested a 375-hp SS 396 Camaro with the close-ratio four-speed manual transmission and cold-air-induction hood. The car did the quarter-mile in 14.77 seconds at 98.72 mph. It had a top speed of 126 mph.

Model Number	Body/Style Number	Body Type & Seating	Factory Price	Shipping Weight	Production Total
CAMARO SS — SERIES 24 + Z27 —					
(RPO L34 "TURBO-JET 396" V-8/ THREE-SPEED MANUAL TRANSMISSION)					
24	37	2d HT	$3,207	—	Note 1
24	67	2d Conv	$3,420	—	Note 1
CAMARO SS — SERIES 24 + Z27 —					
(RPO L35 "TURBO-JET 396" V-8/ THREE-SPEED MANUAL TRANSMISSION)					
24	37	2d HT	$3,086	—	Note 1
24	67	2d Conv	$3,299	—	Note 1
CAMARO SS — SERIES 24 + Z27 —					
(RPO L34 "TURBO-JET 396" V-8/ THREE-SPEED MANUAL TRANSMISSION)					
24	37	2d HT	$3,207	—	Note 1
24	67	2d Conv	$3,420	—	Note 1
CAMARO SS — SERIES 24 + Z27 —					
(RPO L89 "TURBO-JET 396" V-8/ THREE-SPEED MANUAL TRANSMISSION)					
24	37	2d HT	$3,734	—	Note 1
24	67	2d Conv	$3,947	—	Note 1
CAMARO SS INDY PACE CAR — MODEL 12467 + Z11 (396-CID V-8)					
24	67	2d Conv	$3,405	—	Note 2
CAMARO SS INDY PACE CAR — MODEL 12437 + Z10 — (350-CID V-8)					
24	37	2d HT	$3,192	—	Note 3

NOTE 1: 2,018 Camaro SS cars were equipped with the L34 engine; 6,752 cars factory equipped with the L35 engine; 4,889 equipped with the L78 engine; 311 equipped with the L78 engine plus L89 aluminum cylinder.

NOTE 2: 3,675 Indy Pace Car convertibles were built (all engines included).

NOTE 3: 200-300 Indy Pace Car coupes were built (all engines included).

ENGINES

OPTIONAL V-8: Overhead valve. Cast-iron block and head. Bore and stroke: 4.09 x 3.76 in. Displacement: 396 cid (actually 402 cid). Compression ratio: 10.25:1. Brake hp: 325 at 4800 rpm. Taxable hp: 53.60. Torque: 410 at 3200. Five main bearings. Hydraulic valve lifters. Carburetor: Four-barrel. Sales code: L34. Engine code: JB, JG and JU.

OPTIONAL V-8: Overhead valve. Cast-iron block and head. Bore and stroke: 4.09 x 3.76 in. Displacement: 396 cid (actually 402 cid). Compression ratio: 10.25:1. Brake hp: 350 at 5200 rpm. Taxable hp: 53.60. Torque: 415 at 3400. Five main bearings. Hydraulic valve lifters. Carburetor: Four-barrel. Sales code L35. Engine code: JF, JI and KA.

OPTIONAL V-8: Overhead valve. Cast-iron block and head. Bore and stroke: 4.09 x 3.76 in. Displacement: 396 cid (actually 402 cid). Compression ratio: 11.00:1. Brake hp: 375 at 5600 rpm. Taxable hp: 53.60. Torque: 415 at 3600. Five main bearings. Hydraulic valve lifters. Carburetor: Four-barrel. Sales code: L78. Engine code: JH, KL, JL, KC, JJ, JM and KE.

OPTIONAL V-8: Overhead valve. Cast-iron block. Aluminum head with large valves. Bore and stroke: 4.09 x 3.76 in. Displacement: 396 cid (actually 402 cid). Compression ratio: 11.00:1. Brake hp: 375 at 5600 rpm. Taxable hp: 53.60. Torque: 415 at 3600. Five main bearings. Solid valve lifters. Carburetor: Holley four-barrel carburetor on high-rise aluminum intake manifold. Sales code L78/L89. Engine code: JH, KL, JL, KC, JJ, JM and KE.

OPTIONS (PARTIAL LIST)

C06 power convertible top ($52.70). C60 air conditioning ($376). DX1 front accent striping ($25.30). D33 left-hand remote-controlled outside rearview mirror ($10.55). D34 visor-vanity mirror ($3.20). D55 center front seat console ($53.75). D90 Sport striping ($25.30). D96 fender striping ($15.80). F41 heavy-duty Sport suspension ($10.55). G31 special heavy-duty rear springs ($20.05). G80 Positraction rear axle ($42.15). Optional axle ratios ($2.15). JL8 power four-wheel disc brakes ($500.30). J52 power front disc brakes ($64.25). J50 power brakes ($42.15). KD5 positive crankcase ventilation ($6.35). K02 temperature-controlled de-clutching fan ($15.80). K05 engine block heater ($10.55). K79 42-amp Delcotron alternator ($10.55). K85 63-amp Delcotron alternator ($26.35). L34 396-cid 350-hp in Camaro SS only ($184.35). L35 396-cid/325-hp V-8 in Camaro SS only ($63.20). L78/L89 396-cid/375-hp V-8 with aluminum cylinder heads in Camaro SS only ($710.95). MB1 Torque drive transmission ($68.65). MC1 special three-speed manual transmission ($79). MC11 floor-mounted gear shift lever ($10.55). M20 wide-ratio four-speed manual transmission ($195.40). M21 close-ratio four-speed manual transmission ($195.40). M22 close-ratio heavy-duty four-speed manual transmission ($322.10). M40 Turbo Hydra-Matic transmission ($190.10). NC8 chambered dual exhaust system ($15.80). N10 dual exhaust system ($30.55). N33 Comfortilt steering wheel ($45.30). N34 wood-grained steering wheel ($34.80). N40 power steering ($94.80). N44 "Quick-Response" variable-ratio steering ($15.80). N65 Spacesaver spare tire ($19). N95 simulated wire wheel covers ($73.75). N96 mag-style wheel covers ($73.75). PA2 mag-spoke wheel covers ($73.75). PY4 F0-14 fiberglass-belted white sidewall tires on Camaro SS ($26.25). PY5 fiberglass-belted red stripe tires ($88.60). PY5 fiberglass-belted red stripe tires ($26.25). P01 bright metal wheel covers ($21.10). P06 wheel trim rings ($21.10). T60 heavy-duty battery ($8.45). U16 tachometer ($52.70). U46 light monitoring system ($26.35). U57 stereo tape player ($133.80). U63 AM radio ($61.10). U69 AM/FM radio ($133.80). U73 manual rear-mounted radio antenna ($9.50). U79 push-button AM/FM stereo radio ($239.10). U80 rear seat speaker ($13.20). VE3 special body-color front bumper ($42.15). V01 heavy-duty radiator ($14.75). V31 front bumper guard ($12.65). V32 rear bumper guard ($12.65). ZL2 special cold-air-induction hood for ($79). Z11 special Indy 500 convertible package ($36.90). Z21 style trim ($47.40). Z22 Rally Sport package ($131.65). Z23 special interior group ($17.95). Z27 Camaro Super Sport package ($295.95). Z28 Special Performance package ($458.15). Z87 custom interior ($110.60). Two-tone paint ($31.60).

1969 CAMARO Z/28

JERRY HEASLEY

1969 Camaro Z/28

In 1969, the popularity of the Camaro Z/28 achieved a three-year high with production climbing from 602 in 1967 to 7,199 in 1968 to 20,302 in 1969. To a large degree, the boom in interest was generated by the 1969 Z/28s that Roger Penske's racing team campaigned in the Sports Car Club of America's Trans-Am series. Penzke's dark blue-with-yellow lettering Camaros appeared in Sunoco gasoline advertisements, as well as in promotions for Sears Die-Hard batteries.

The Z/28 package was available for Camaro sport coupes with power brakes and a four-speed manual transmission. A positraction rear axle (as an extra-cost option) was recommended to go with the package. The Z/28 featured a very special 302-cid V-8, a dual exhaust system with deep-tone mufflers, a special front suspension, a special rear suspension, quick-ratio steering, 15 x 7-inch Rally wheel rims, special E70-15 white-letter tires, a 3.73:1 ratio rear axle and special rally stripes on the hood and rear deck lid.

The Z/28 was tested to do 0-to-60 mph in 7.4 seconds and the quarter-mile in 15.12 seconds at 94.8 mph.

Model Number	Body/Style Number	Body Type & Seating	Factory Price	Shipping Weight	Production Total
CAMARO Z/28 — SERIES 24 + Z/28 —					
(V-8 WITH FOUR-SPEED MANUAL TRANSMISSION)					
24	37	2d HT	$3,588	—	20,302

Note: Price reflects computed price with least-expensive mandatory options array early in model year.

CHEVROLET

ENGINES

BASE Z/28 V-8: 90-degree, overhead valve. Cast-iron block. Large-port cylinder head with 2.02-in. intake valves and 1.60-in. exhaust valves. Bore & stroke: 4.002 x 3.005 in. Displacement: 302 cid (5.0 liters). Compression ratio: 11.1:1. Brake hp: 290 at 5800 rpm. Torque: 290 at 4200 rpm. Five four-bolt main bearings with nodular iron main caps. Solid valve lifters. Induction system: Holley no. 4053 four-barrel carburetor. Four-bolt main bearings. Special 30/30 lash solid lifter camshaft. Aluminum high-rise manifold.

OPTIONS

AS1 front shoulder belts ($23.20). AS4 custom deluxe rear shoulder belts ($26.35). AS5 standard rear shoulder belts ($23.20). A01 Soft-Ray tinted glass ($32.65). A31 power windows ($105.35). A39 custom deluxe front and rear belts ($9). A67 rear folding seat ($42.15). A85 custom deluxe front shoulder belts ($26.35). B37 color-keyed floor mats ($11.60). B93 door edge guards ($4.25). CE1 headlight flasher ($15.80). C08 vinyl roof cover ($84.30). C50 rear window defroster ($22.15). C60 air conditioning ($376). DX1 front accent striping ($25.30). D33 left-hand remote-controlled outside rearview mirror ($10.55). D34 visor-vanity mirror ($3.20). D55 center front seat console ($53.75). D90 Sport striping ($25.30). D96 fender striping ($15.80). F41 heavy-duty Sport suspension ($10.55). G31 special heavy-duty rear springs ($20.05). G80 positraction rear axle ($42.15). Optional axle ratios ($2.15). JL8 power four-wheel disc brakes ($500.30). J52 power front disc brakes ($64.25). J50 power brakes ($42.15). KD5 positive crankcase ventilation ($6.35). K02 temperature-controlled de-clutching fan ($15.80). K05 engine block heater ($10.55). M20 wide-ratio four-speed manual transmission ($195.40). M21 close-ratio four-speed manual transmission ($195.40). M22 close-ratio heavy-duty four-speed manual transmission ($322.10). NC8 chambered dual exhaust system ($15.80). N33 Comfortilt steering wheel ($45.30). N34 woodgrained steering wheel ($34.80). N40 power steering ($94.80). N44 "Quick-Response" variable-ratio steering ($15.80). N65 Spacesaver spare tire ($19). N95 simulated wire wheel covers ($73.75). N96 mag-style wheel covers ($73.75). PA2 mag-spoke wheel covers ($73.75). P01 bright metal wheel covers ($21.10). P06 wheel trim rings ($21.10). T60 heavy-duty battery ($8.45). U15 speed warning indicator ($11.60). U17 special instrumentation ($94.80). U35 electric clock ($15.80). U16 tachometer ($52.70). U46 light monitoring system ($26.35). U57 stereo tape player ($133.80). U63 AM radio ($61.10). U69 AM/FM radio ($133.80). U73 manual rear-mounted radio antenna ($9.50). U79 push-button AM/FM stereo radio ($239.10). U80 rear seat speaker ($13.20). VE3 special body-color front bumper ($42.15). V01 heavy-duty radiator ($14.75). V31 front bumper guard ($12.65). V32 rear bumper guard ($12.65). ZJ9 auxiliary lighting in sport coupe without custom interior option ($13.70). ZJ9 auxiliary lighting with custom interior option ($11.10). ZJ9 auxiliary lighting in convertible without custom interior option ($9.50). ZK3 custom deluxe seat and shoulder belts ($12.15). ZL2 special cold-air-induction hood ($79). Z21 style trim ($47.40). Z22 Rally Sport package ($131.65). Z23 special interior group ($17.95). Z/28 Special Performance Package ($458.12 and also priced at $473.95 and $522.40 during 1969). Z87 custom interior ($110.60). Two-tone paint ($31.60).

1969 CAMARO ZL1

JERRY HEASLEY

1969 Camaro ZL1

In 1968, Chevrolet dealer Fred Gibb was well known to drag racing enthusiasts for his energetic support of their sport. Gibb — the owner of the Fred Gibb Agency of La Harpe, Illinois — talked to Vince Piggins about constructing the "ultimate" muscle car. The idea was to use an all-aluminum 427-cid V-8 in the compact Camaro body to create a Super Stock racing car. Piggins, who is now a high-performance legend — was in charge of such projects for Chevrolet Motor Division. National Hot Rod Association (NHRA) rules said that a minimum of 50 cars had to be built to qualify the super-hot ZL1 Camaros for competition. Chevrolet general manager E.M. "Pete" Estes gave Fred Gibbs his word that Chevrolet Motor Division would build the first ZL1s before the end of the year, on the condition that the Illinois dealer would take 50 of the cars at a proposed price of $4,900. Gibbs accepted Estes' offer and General Motors Central Office Production Order system was utilized to order the cars.

The first ZL1s built were a pair of Dusk Blue cars made at the Norwood, Ohio, assembly plant on December 30, 1968. They arrived at the LeHarpe, Illinois, dealership the next day, covered with snow. Unfortunately, the factory invoice price had climbed to $7,269! All 50 cars that were shipped to Gibbs were virtually identical, except for the choice of color and transmission. They had the COPO 9560 option with the aluminum 427 V-8. Nineteen additional cars were also built for other Chevrolet dealers around the country. The equipment on all 69 cars included the Z22 Rally Sport package, J50 power brakes, N40 power steering, a V10 tachometer, racing style outside rearview mirrors, exhaust resonators, a dual exhaust system with tailpipe extensions, a special steering wheel, F70-15 black sidewall tires with raised gold letters, special lug nuts, special wheel center caps, special identification decals on the hood, grille and rear panel, a special instrument cluster and an extra-wide front valance panel.

According to the February 1969 issue of *Super Stock* magazine, the ZL1 Camaro in racing trim could cover the quarter-mile in as little as 10.41 seconds at 128.10 mph. That was with the "stock" Holley 850-cfm carburetor.

Model Number	Body/Style Number	Body Type & Seating	Factory Price	Shipping Weight	Production Total
CAMARO ZL1 — SERIES 2400 — V-8					
24	37	2d HT	$7,269	—	69

ENGINE

OPTIONAL COPO V-8: Overhead valve V-8. Aluminum block and "open-chamber" aluminum heads. Bore and stroke: 4.251 x 3.76 in. Displacement: 427 cid. Compression ratio: 12.5:1. Brake hp: 430 at 5800 rpm. Torque: 460 at 4000 rpm. Five main bearings. Solid valve lifters. Induction system: special 850 cfm Holley four-barrel carburetor on top of a special high-rise aluminum manifold.

OPTIONS

Specific information on optional equipment used on ZL1 Camaros is not available. These were basically purpose-built drag racing cars. Check other 1969 Camaro listings for a list of factory options offered for regular production models.

1969 YENKO SYC CAMARO

1969 Yenko SYC Camaro

JERRY HEASLEY

In the early days of drag racing, enthusiasts modified old cars in their home garages (or even under the old shade tree) and raced them on the weekend. In many cases, the same machine provided daily transportation and weekend sport. After the factory muscle car was invented, interest in drag racing boomed and the sport grew more professional. Those getting into the field turned to specialized car dealers to get the hottest rides.

In 1968, Don Yenko Chevrolet of Canonsburg, Pennsylvania, decided to expand his high-performance car operation (called Yenko Sports Cars) by making SYC (Super Yenko Camaro) models available to enthusiasts through a small number of selected factory dealers nationwide. The plan was to base these cars on 1969 Camaros ordered from Chevrolet via a COPO (Central Office Production Order) arrangement. This type of purchase allowed dealers to order special equipment on a Chevrolet as long as building the car did not upset the normal stream of output at the factory. Yenko's cars were produced under order number 9561 and were fitted with 427-cid/425-hp L72 V-8 engines, M21 or M22 four-speed manual gear boxes (or an M40 Turbo Hydra-Matic), front disc brakes, a special ducted hood, a heavy-duty radiator, a special suspension, a 4.10:1 positraction rear axle and a rear deck lid spoiler.

Originally, Don Yenko had planned to take all of the COPO 9561 cars, but other Chevrolet dealers wanted a piece of the same action and also placed additional orders. As a result, about 100 cars were sold. However, Yenko also ordered a batch of COPOI 9737 Camaros, which had 15-inch wheels, Goodyear Wide Tread GT tires, a 140-mph speedometer and a beefy one-inch front stabilizer bar. Experts estimate that between 199 and 201 cars were built, but some enthusiasts believe that as many as 350 Yenkos were made. There is an old photo of Don Yenko standing in front of a transporter truck and he is holding a handwritten sign that reads "Our 350th Camaro." Hard evidence is lacking though. The total of 350 could be for all cars built since 1967. No one knows for sure. Yenko's SYC Camaros came only in seven exterior body colors: Hugger Orange, LeMans Blue, Fathom Green, Daytona Yellow, Rally Green and Olympic Gold. The cars had a base price of $3,895, including shipping.

On April 19, 1969 a Yenko Camaro with factory-installed headers and racing slicks, driven by Ed Hedrick, did the quarter-mile at a drag strip in York, Pennsylvania, in 11.94 seconds at 114.5 mph.

Model Number	Body/Style Number	Body Type & Seating	Factory Price	Shipping Weight	Production Total
YENKO SYC CAMARO — SERIES 2400 — V-8					
24	37	2d HT	3$,895	—	100-201

CHEVROLET

ENGINE

YENKO SYC CAMARO BASE V-8 (COPO): Overhead valve. Cast-iron block and head. Bore and stroke: 4.25 x 3.76 in. Displacement: 427 cid. Compression ratio: 11.00:1. Brake hp: 425 at 5600 rpm. Taxable hp: 57.80. Torque: 460 at 4000. Five main bearings. Hydraulic valve lifters. Dual exhaust. Carburetor: Holley 800-cfm four-barrel. Sales code: Special COPO only version. Engine code: LD, LS and MD.

OPTIONS

Available options included front and rear bumper guards ($25), front and rear floor mats ($12), an AM-FM push-button radio ($134), heavy-duty Air Lift shocks ($45), traction bars ($50) and chrome exhaust extensions ($38).

1969 CAMARO COPO 427

JERRY HEASLEY

1969 Camaro COPO 427

Chevy designers did a lot of work updating the styling of the '69 Camaro and the result was a car that won instant recognition as a classic among the ranks of enthusiasts. With additional body sculpturing, raised feature lines streaming off the fenders and dummy rear brake cooling louvers just ahead of the rear wheel openings, this was an instant icon of the muscle car era. In '69, the Central Office Production Order (COPO) remained the key to doing an "end run" around GM's anti-performance policies.

The '69s were built as COPO 9561 and 9737 cars. The '69 edition of the big-block 427 Camaro could be ordered with either the M22 four-speed manual gear box or the Turbo Hydra-Matic transmission. In either case, it listed for $4,245. In '69, $4,245 was considered a huge sum of money for any Chevy and the COPO cars were difficult to move. However, people are beginning to research all of the high-performance dealerships more closely.

The performance of COPO Camaros was awesome. The 427-cid/425-hp cars built under COPO 9561 did 0-to-60 in 5.4 seconds and the quarter-mile in 13.5 seconds at 102 mph. The 427-cid/430-hp cars built under COPO 9560 did 0-to-60 in 5.3 seconds and the quarter-mile in 13.16 seconds at 110 mph.

Model Number	Body/Style Number	Body Type & Seating	Factory Price	Shipping Weight	Production Total
CAMARO COPO 427 — SERIES 2400 — V-8					
24	37	2d HT	$4,245	—	—

ENGINE

YENKO SYC BASE V-8 (COPO): Overhead valve. Cast-iron block and head. Bore and stroke: 4.25 x 3.76 in. Displacement: 427 cid. Compression ratio: 11.00:1. Brake hp: 425 at 5600 rpm. Taxable hp: 57.80. Torque: 460 at 4000. Five main bearings. Hydraulic valve lifters. Dual exhaust. Carburetor: Holley 800-cfm four-barrel. Sales code: Special COPO only version. Engine code: LD, LS and MD.

OPTIONS

Specific information on optional equipment used on ZL1 Camaros is not available. These were basically purpose-built drag racing cars. Check other 1969 Camaro listings for a list of factory options offered for regular production models.

1969 CORVETTE 427

PHIL KUNZ

1969 Corvette 427

"With this one beautiful exception, there is no such thing as an American sports car," said *Car Life* magazine about the '69 Corvette. Cars with the 400-hp L68 version of the 427 did 0-to-60 mph in 6.5 seconds. The 430-hp L88 version did the quarter-mile in 14.10 seconds at 106.89 mph. The 435-hp L71 version did the quarter-mile in 13.94 seconds at 105.63 mph and had a 151-mph top speed.

After a year's absence, the Stingray name (now spelled as one word) re-appeared on the front fenders. The back-up lights were integrated into the center tail lights. The ignition was now on the steering column and the door depression button used in 1968 was eliminated. (A key lock was put in its place.) Front and rear disc brakes, headlight washers, center console, wheel trim rings, carpeting and all-vinyl upholstery were standard.

Model Number	Body/Style Number	Body Type & Seating	Factory Price	Shipping Weight	Production Total
CORVETTE STINGRAY 427 —SERIES 9000 — V-8:					
94	37	2d HT-2P	$4,984	3,091 lbs.	22,129
94	67	2d Conv-2P	$4,641	3,096 lbs.	16,633

NOTE 1: The production totals above are for all 1969 Corvettes.
NOTE 2: The prices above include the cost of the L36 V-8 but no other extras.
NOTE 3: Engine breakouts included: (L36) 10,531 built; (L68) 2,072 built; (L71) 2,722 built; (L71/L89) 390 built; (L88) 116 built

ENGINES

OPTIONAL V-8: Overhead valve. Cast-iron block. Bore and stroke: 4.251 x 3.76 inches. Displacement: 427 cid. Compression ratio: 10:25:1. Brake hp: 390 at 5400 rpm. Taxable hp: 57.80. Torque: 460 at 3600 rpm. Five main bearings. Hydraulic valve lifters. High-performance camshaft. Carburetor: Holley four-barrel. Sales code: L36. Engine code: LM, LL, MH or MI.

OPTIONAL V-8: Overhead valve. Cast-iron block. Bore and stroke: 4.251 x 3.76 inches. Displacement: 427 cid. Compression ratio: 10.25:1. Brake hp: 400 at 5400 rpm. Taxable hp: 57.80. Torque: 460 at 3600 rpm. Five main bearings. Hydraulic valve lifters. Special-performance camshaft. Carburetor: Three Holley two-barrel. Sales code: L68. Engine code: LQ, LN, MJ or MK.

OPTIONAL V-8: Overhead valve. Cast-iron block. Bore and stroke: 4.251 x 3.76 inches. Displacement: 427 cid. Compression ratio: 11.0:1. Brake hp: 435 at 5800 rpm. Taxable hp: 57.80. Torque: 460 at 4000 rpm. Five main bearings. Mechanical valve lifters. Special-performance camshaft. Carburetor: Three Holley two-barrels. Sales code: L71. Engine code: LR, LX, LP, LW, LT and LU.

OPTIONAL V-8: Overhead valve. Cast-iron block. Bore and stroke: 4.251 x 3.76 inches. Displacement: 427 cid. Compression ratio: 11.0:1. Brake hp: 435 at 5800 rpm. Taxable hp: 57.80. Torque: 460 at 4000 rpm. Five main bearings. Mechanical valve lifters. Aluminum cylinder heads. Extra-large exhaust valves. Special-performance camshaft. Carburetor: Three Holley two-barrels. Sales code: L71/L89.

OPTIONAL V-8: Overhead valve. Bore and stroke: 4.251 x 3.76 inches. Displacement: 427 cid. Compression ratio: 12.50:1. Brake hp: (advertised) 430 hp; (actual) 560 at 6400 rpm. Taxable hp: 57.80. Five main bearings. Mechanical valve lifters. Special-ultra-high-performance camshaft with .5365-in. intakes. Carburetor: Single Holley 850CFM four-barrel. Sales code: L88. Engine code: ME, MG and MR.

OPTIONS

RPO 898 Genuine leather seat trim ($79); RPO A01 Soft-Ray tinted glass, all windows ($16.90). RPO A31 Electric power windows ($63.20). RPO A85 Custom shoulder belts ($42.15). RPO C07 Auxiliary hardtop for convertible ($252.80). RPO C08 Vinyl cover for auxiliary hardtop ($57.95). RPO C50 Rear window defroster ($32.65). RPO C60 Air conditioning ($428.70). RPO F41 Special front and rear suspension ($36.90). G81 Positraction rear axle, all ratios ($46.35). RPO J50 Power brakes ($42.15). RPO K05 Engine block heater ($10.55). RPO K66 Transistor ignition system ($81.10). RPO L36 427-cid/390-hp V-8 ($221.20). RPO L68 427-cid/400-hp V-8 ($326.55). L71 427-cid/435-hp ($437.10). RPO L88 427-cid/435-hp V-8 ($1032.15). RPO L89 427-cid/435-hp V-8 ($832.05). RPO ZL1 Optional special 427-cid aluminum V-8 ($3,000). RPO M20 Four-speed manual transmission ($184.80). RPO M21 Four-speed close-ratio manual transmission ($184.80). RPO M22 Heavy-duty close-ratio four-speed manual transmission ($290.40). RPO M40 Turbo Hydra-Matic automatic transmission ($221.80) RPO N14 Side mount exhaust system ($147.45). N37 Tilt-Telescopic steering wheel ($84.30). RPO N40 Power steering ($105.35). RPO P02 Wheel covers ($57.95). RPO PT6 Red Stripe nylon tires F70 x 15 ($31.30). RPO PT7 F70 x 15, White Stripe tires ($31.30). TJ2 Front fender louver trim ($21.10). RPO UA6 Alarm system ($26.35). RPO U15 Speed-warning indicator ($11.60). RPO U69 AM-FM radio ($172.45). RPO U79 Stereo radio ($278.10).

CHEVROLET

1969 CORVETTE ZL1

JERRY HEASLEY

1969 Corvette ZL1

Perhaps the wildest, most exotic, highest-performance muscle engine ever offered to the public was the ZL1. It was an all-aluminum, 427-cid, Chevy "Rat" engine. Just 69 engines were installed in '69 Camaros and only two went into '69 Corvettes. That was it!

The use of the ZL1 in Camaros was intended to homologate the engine for National Hot Rod Association competition. A minimum of 50 had to be built for it to be eligible for "stock" class drag racing. But, in the Corvette, the ZL1 wasn't homologated. It was more a case of optioning the ultimate high-performance Chevrolet with the ultimate high-performance big-block. You might say it was a matter of pride. There were 10-12 engineering test Corvette "mules" built with ZL1s. They were used in magazine road tests, engineering and track evaluations and driven by the likes of Zora Arkus-Duntov and GM VIPs. Of course, these ZL1 evaluation vehicles had to be destroyed—eventually. In the process, two 'Vettes went out the door as RPO ZL1s. They included a Canary Yellow car with side pipes and a Can-Am White T-top coupe with black ZLl side stripes. In 1989, the yellow car, also a T-top, was confiscated by the U.S. government. It had been in the possession of a convicted cocaine dealer serving a sentence in an Alabama prison. Earlier, someone had paid $225,000 for the car, which had 55,317 original miles. The government estimated its value at around $500,000 but sold it for the minimum reserve bid of $300,000.

Greg Joseph, a history professor at Long Beach College, in California, researched ZL1 history. This led him to *Hot Rod* magazine (December 1968), with a cover story on Chevy's new all-aluminum 427. The article told of a "painted-block ZL1" engine in a test Corvette driven by the automotive press. A parenthetical statement added: "And all those guys at the '69 Chevy preview thought it was an L88. Forgot your pocket magnets, right, guys?" Chevrolet had painted the ZL1s, possibly to hide them from the press, as had been the case with one of the test cars spotlighted in *Hot Rod*. To the journalists, the ZL1 (a $3,010 assortment of aluminum cylinder block and heads) was a $1,032.15 RPO L88 package.

Model Number	Body/Style Number	Body Type & Seating	Factory Price	Shipping Weight	Production Total
CORVETTE STINGRAY 427 — SERIES 9400 — V-8:					
94	37	2d HT-2P	$7,994	—	2

NOTE 1: 10-12 engineering test mules with ZL1s were also built (and destroyed).
NOTE 2: The prices above include the cost of the ZL1 option but no other extras.

ENGINE

OPTIONAL V-8: Overhead valve. Bore and stroke: 4.251 x 3.76 inches. Displacement: 427 cid. Compression ratio: 12.50:1. Brake hp: (advertised) 430 hp; (actual) 560 at 6400 rpm. Taxable hp: 57.80. Five main bearings. Mechanical valve lifters. Special-ultra-high-performance camshaft with .5365-in. intakes. Carburetor: Single Holley 850CFM four-barrel. Sales code: L88 +ZL1. Engine code: ME, MG and MR.

1969 IMPALA SS 427

1969 Impala SS 427

Full-size Chevrolets were completely redesigned. While wheelbase was unchanged, the cars grew an inch in length. A new, integrated bumper/grille imparted a narrower look, although the width of 80 inches was the same as the previous year. The area around the front and rear wheelhousings was flared out, giving a more highly sculptured appearance.

There was not a Super Sport series and buyers could not order a Super Sport option package without the 427-cid big-block V-8. They had to order the SS 427 option, which included both the big-block V-8 and the typical SS trimmings as a buyer-takes-all package. So, if you wanted to get a full-sized Chevy muscle car, you had to go all the way! The Z24 code was again used to identify the option. The SS 427 package could also be ordered for the Custom coupes, sport coupes and convertible. The package retailed for $422.35. It included power disc brakes, a special three-speed transmission, special ornamentation, chassis and suspension upgrades, 15-inch wheels, red stripe tires and the 427-cid V-8. The '69 SS 427 was the most similar to the SS 396 Chevelle, since it was all-inclusive. If you wanted SS badges, you had to order an SS 427.

The '69 396 Impala was road tested at 8.4 seconds for 0-to-60 mph and 15.8 seconds for the quarter-mile. That's just slightly slower than a 1970 SS 396 with 350 hp, but not bad at all for a full-sized Chevy.

ENGINES

BASE V-8: Overhead valve. Cast-iron block and head. Bore and stroke: 4.25 x 3.76 in. Displacement: 427 cid. Compression ratio: 10.25:1. Brake hp: 390 at 4800 rpm. Taxable hp: 57.80. Torque: 460 lbs.-ft. at 3600. Five main bearings. Hydraulic valve lifters. Sales code: L72. Engine code: LA, LC, LG, LF, LZ, MB, LH, MC and LI.

OPTIONAL COPO V-8: Overhead valve. Cast-iron block and head. Bore and stroke: 4.25 x 3.76 in. Displacement: 427 cid. Compression ratio: 11.00:1. Brake hp: 425 at 5600 rpm. Taxable hp: 57.80. Torque: 460 460 lbs.-ft. at 4000. Five main bearings. Hydraulic valve lifters. Dual exhaust. Carburetor: Holley 800-cfm four-barrel. Sales code: Special COPO only version. Engine code: LD, LS and MD.

OPTIONS

Four-Season air conditioning ($363.40-$384.45). Comfort-On air conditioning ($463.45). Custom Deluxe shoulder belts ($12.15-$16.90). Power drum brakes ($42.15). Power front disc brakes ($64.25). Electric clock ($15.80). Heavy-duty clutch ($47.50-$52.00). Console with courtesy light ($53.75). ElectroClear rear defroster ($32.65). Headlight washer ($15.80). Light monitoring system ($26.35). Two-tone paint ($23.20). AM push-button radio ($61.10). AM/FM push-button radio ($133.60). AM/FM radio and stereo ($239.10). Rear manual antenna ($9.50-$10.55). Vinyl roof ($79.00-$88.55). Six-Way power seat ($100.10). Automatic level control ($89.66). Speed and Cruise Control, V-8 and automatic required ($57.95). Power steering ($89.55-$105.35). Comfort-Tilt steering column ($45.30). Sport-styled steering wheel, except Nova ($34.80). Liquid tire chain ($23.20). Power trunk opener ($14.75). Full wheel covers ($21.10). Mag-spoke wheel covers ($73.75). Simulated wire wheels ($55.85). Special wheel covers ($57.95), on other full-size Chevrolets ($79.00). May 1, 1969, changes: ElectroClear rear defroster ($47.40). RPO L36 427-cid/390-hp Turbo-Jet V-8, in Chevrolet ($237.00). RPO L72 427-cid/425-hp Turbo-Jet V-8, in Chevrolet with SS option ($183.35). Wide-Range four-speed manual transmission ($195.40). Close-ratio four-speed manual transmission ($184.80). Heavy-duty four-speed manual transmission ($313.00). Special three-speed manual transmission standard with SS- 427($68.65). Turbo Hydra-Matic M40 type ($221.80). Floor-mounted shift lever, as optional equipment ($10.55). Positraction axle ($42.15).

Series Number	Body/Style Number	Body Type & Seating	Factory Price	Shipping Weight	Production Total
IMPALA SS 427— SERIES 6400 + Z24 — V-8					
64	37	2d HT-6P	$3,455	3,775 lbs.	Note 1
64	47	2d Fml HT-6P	$3,507	3,800 lbs.	Note 1
64	67	2d Conv-6P	$3,683	3,835 lbs.	Note 1

NOTE 1: The SS 427 package was installed on 2,455 cars of all body style combined.

CHEVROLET

1969 NOVA SS 396

JERRY HEASLEY

1969 Nova SS 396

Following the age-old advice "don't mess with success" Chevrolet left the Nova largely unchanged in 1968. The Chevy II name was dropped from the "senior" compact cars, which were now simply called Novas. Due to this change, a Chevrolet emblem was placed on the center of the upper grille bar to emphasize that this was a real Chevy and not a "Chevy, too."

A vast selection of options, including Super Sport equipment, could be ordered. The base Nova SS (Super Sport) had a 350-cid/ 300-hp V-8. Power disc brakes were now standard content with the Nova Super Sport option package. The Nova SS 396 was an even more potent possibility.

The milder version of this monster motor had hydraulic valve lifters, while the king-of-the-streets L78 edition was the heavy-breathing solid-lifter version. The milder version of the Nova SS 396 coupe ran the quarter-mile in about 14.5 seconds at over 101 mph. With some super tuning, un-corked headers and racing slicks, the Nova SS 396 ran in the mid-to-low 13-second bracket.

Series Number	Body/Style Number	Body Type & Seating	Factory Price	Shipping Weight	Production Total
NOVA SS 396 (350-HP) — SERIES 1400 — V-8					
14	27	2d Cpe-6P	$2,589	N/A	1,947
NOVA SS 396 (375-HP) — SERIES 1400 — V-8					
14	27	2d Cpe-6P	$2,684	N/A	5,262

NOTE 1: Prices above include cost of 396-cid V-8.
NOTE 2: A total of 17,654 Novas (all engines) were equipped with the Super Sport option.

ENGINES

OPTIONAL V-8: Overhead valve. Cast-iron block and head. Bore and stroke: 4.09 x 3.76 in. Displacement: 396 cid (actually 402 cid). Compression ratio: 10.25:1. Brake hp: 350 at 5200 rpm. Taxable hp: 53.60. Torque: 415 at 3400. Five main bearings. Hydraulic valve lifters. Carburetor: Four-barrel. Engine code: JF, JI, JM, JU, KA and KE.

OPTIONAL V-8: Overhead valve. Cast-iron block and head. Bore and stroke: 4.09 x 3.76 in. Displacement: 396 cid (actually 402 cid). Compression ratio: 11.00:1. Brake hp: 375 at 5600 rpm. Taxable hp: 53.60. Torque: 415 at 3600. Five main bearings. Hydraulic valve lifters. Carburetor: Four-barrel. Sales code: L78. Engine code: JH, JL and KC.

OPTIONS

Four-Season air conditioning ($363.40-$384.45). Custom Deluxe shoulder belts ($12.15-$16.90). Power drum brakes ($42.15). Power front disc brakes ($64.25). Electric clock ($15.80). Heavy-duty clutch ($47.50-$52.00). Console with courtesy light ($53.75). ElectroClear rear defroster ($32.65). Power door locks ($44.80. Light monitoring system ($26.35). Two-tone paint ($23.20). AM push-button radio ($61.10). AM/FM push- button radio ($133.60). AM/FM radio and stereo ($239.10). Rear manual antenna ($9.50-$10.55). Vinyl roof ($79.00-$88.55). Six-Way power seat ($100.10). Speed and Cruise Control, V-8 and automatic required ($57.95). Power steering ($89.55-$105.35). Com¬fort-Tilt steering column ($45.30). Liquid tire chain ($23.20). Full wheel covers ($21.10). Mag-spoke wheel covers ($73.75). RPO L34 396-cid/350-hp Turbo-Jet V-8 ($121.15). RPO L78 396-cid/375-hp Turbo-Jet V-8 ($316.00). Wide-Range four-speed manual transmission ($184.80). Close-ratio four-speed manual transmission ($184.80). Heavy-duty four-speed manual trans¬mission ($312.55). Powerglide automatic transmission ($158.40). Special three-speed manual transmission, standard Turbo Hydra-Matic (M40 type) in Nova with 350 hp V-8 ($190.10), with 375 hp V-8 ($290.40). Floor-mounted shift lever, as optional equipment ($10.55). Positraction axle ($42.15). RPO Z26: Nova SS option package, on coupe only, includes simulated air intakes on hood, simulated front fender louvers, black accents, black accent grille and rear panel, SS emblems, Red Stripe F70-14 tires, 14 x 7-inch wheels, special suspension and three-speed gearbox, power disc brakes, bright engine accents, hood insulation, and 350-cid/300-hp V-8 ($280.20).

1969 Yenko SYC Nova

1969 YENKO SYC NOVA

Don Yenko once said in an interview that his 427 Nova was "a beast, almost lethal." That is precisely why the insurance companies stepped in and virtually ended its production. They didn't want to insure it and, after 30 were converted at Yenko's Chevrolet agency, the other seven that had been slated to get 427s remained SS 396 Novas with 4.10:1 Positraction rear ends. SYC Novas supposedly started out as SS 396s, although at least one was a base Nova without SS equipment. The stock L78-optioned 396 engine, less heads, intake, carburetor, water pump and other top end components, was pulled and replaced with a crate-type 427 short-block. That's how easy the swap was, which is why it was so popular in the '60s. Many dealerships did these conversions for customers, but only certain dealers did them when the cars were brand new. Yenko went one step further and gave these cars special names. Every car — whether Camaro, Chevelle or Nova — was an SYC. The initials stood for "Yenko Super Cars."

Zero-to-60 mph times for such cars fell in the under-four-second bracket, according to Don Yenko, and the quarter-mile elapsed times were radical, too

On paper, the SYC 427 Nova, built by Don Yenko Chevrolet in Canonsburg, Pennsylvania, is one of the most outrageous muscle cars to ever hit the highway and be street legal. It was a compact Nova with Chevrolet's monster 427-cid/425-hp V-8 stuffed into it. This RPO L72 solid-lifter big-block engine was made famous in the 1966 Corvette. In 1969, it was offered as a COPO (Central Office Production Order) option in the Chevelle and Camaro.

If a mid-sized Chevy 427 was a terror on the street, then a lighter 427 Camaro would have an even better power-to-weight ratio, second only to the Corvette. That's how things were until the absolutely wicked 427 Nova was produced.

ENGINES

OPTIONAL V-8: Overhead valve. Cast-iron block and head. Bore and stroke: 4.25 x 3.76 in. Displacement: 427 cid. Compression ratio: 11.00:1. Brake hp: 425 at 5600 rpm. Taxable hp: 57.80. Torque: 460 at 4000. Five main bearings. Hydraulic valve lifters. Dual exhaust. Carburetor: Holley 800-cfm four-barrel. Sales code: L72.

OPTIONS

Four-Season air conditioning ($363.40-$384.45). Custom Deluxe shoulder belts ($12.15-$16.90). Power drum brakes ($42.15). Power front disc brakes ($64.25). Electric clock ($15.80). Heavy-duty clutch ($47.50-$52.00). Console with courtesy light ($53.75). ElectroClear rear defroster ($32.65). Power door locks ($44.80). Light monitoring system ($26.35). Two-tone paint ($23.20). AM push-button radio ($61.10). AM/FM push- button radio ($133.60). AM/FM ra-

Series Number	Body/Style Number	Body Type & Seating	Factory Price	Shipping Weight	Production Total
YENKO SYC NOVA 427 — SERIES 1400 — V-8					
14	27	2d HT-6P	NA	N/A	30

dio and stereo ($239.10). Rear manual antenna ($9.50-$10.55). Vinyl roof ($79.00-$88.55). Six-Way power seat ($100.10). Speed and Cruise Control, V-8 and automatic required ($57.95). Power steering ($89.55-$105.35). Com¬fort-Tilt steering column ($45.30). Liquid tire chain ($23.20). Full wheel covers ($21.10). Mag-spoke wheel covers ($73.75). RPO L34 396 cid/350 hp Turbo-Jet V-8 ($121.15). RPO L78 396-cid/375-hp Turbo-Jet V-8 ($316.00). Wide-Range four-speed manual transmission ($184.80). Close-ratio four-speed manual transmission ($184.80). Heavy-duty four-speed manual transmission ($312.55). Powerglide automatic transmission ($158.40). Special three-speed manual transmission, standard Turbo Hydra-Matic (M40 type) in Nova with 350-hp V-8 ($190.10), with 375-hp V-8 ($290.40). Floor-mounted shift lever, as optional equipment ($10.55). Positraction axle ($42.15). RPO Z26: Nova SS option package, on coupe only ($280.20).

1970 CAMARO RS/SS 396

The introduction of an all-new Chevrolet Camaro was pushed back to mid-1970 by a union strike at the General Motors factory in Norwood, Ohio. This delayed production of the all-new 1970 Camaro model until January 5, 1970. As a result, the second-generation F-cars were not introduced to the public until December 26, 1970. However, a gorgeous design inspired by European sports cars gave the new Camaro immediate appeal. The sleek long hood-short deck fastback body was longer, lower and wider than that of the first-generation Camaro.

The Camaro SS or Super Sport was a real muscle car for the streets. The RPO Z27 SS package was a factory option that retailed for $289.65 in 1970. It was available for V-8-powered

Camaros with four-speed or Turbo Hydra-Matic transmission. The SS packaged included the 270-hp Turbo-Fire 350 V-8, a black-finished grille with a bright outline and SS identification, a remote-control left-hand outside sport type rearview mirror, power brakes, special hood insulation, dual exhaust outlets, Hide-A-Way windshield wipers, 14 x 7-inch wheels, F70 x 14 wide-oval white-letter bias-belted tires and special SS ornamentation on fenders, steering wheel and rear deck lid. A 300-hp "396 Turbo-Jet" V-8 was optional for cars with the SS package.

The Camaro SS 396 did 0-to-60 mph in 6.8 seconds and ran the quarter-mile in 14.77 seconds at 98.72 mph. It had a top speed of 126 mph.

CHEVROLET

JERRY HEASLEY

1970 Camaro SS

Model Number	Body/Style Number	Body Type & Seating	Factory Price	Shipping Weight	Production Total
CAMARO SS — SERIES 24 + Z27 — (RPO L48 "TURBO-FIRE 350" V-8/FOUR-SPEED MANUAL TRANSMISSION)					
23	87	2d HT	$3,336	—	Note 1
CAMARO SS — SERIES 24 + Z22 — (RPO L34 "TURBO-JET 396" V-8/FOUR-SPEED MANUAL TRANSMISSION)					
24	87	2d HT	$3,491	—	Note 1
CAMARO SS — SERIES 24 + Z22 — (RPO L78 "TURBO-JET 396" V-8/FOUR-SPEED MANUAL TRANSMISSION)					
24	87	2d HT	$3,724	—	Note 1

NOTE 1: Model year production of 1970 Camaro SS sport coupes was 15,201.

ENGINES

BASE V-8: Overhead valve. Cast-iron block and head. Bore and stroke: 4.13 x 3.76 in. Displacement: 396 cid (actually 402 cid). Compression ratio: 10.25:1. Brake hp: 350 at 5200 rpm. Taxable hp: 54.50. Torque: 415 at 3400. Five main bearings. Hydraulic valve lifters. Carburetor: Four-barrel. Engine code: (CJF, CJI, CTW and CTX.

OPTIONAL V-8: Overhead valve. Cast-iron block and head. Bore and stroke: 4.09 x 3.76 in. Displacement: 396 cid (actually 402 cid). Compression ratio: 11.00:1. Brake hp: 375 at 5600 rpm. Taxable hp: 53.60. Torque: 415 at 3600. Five main bearings. Hydraulic valve lifters. Carburetor: Four-barrel. Sales code: L78. Engine code: CJL, CJH, CTY and CKO.

OPTIONS

AK1 color-keyed seat and shoulder belts ($12.15). AS4 rear shoulder belts ($26.35). A01 Soft-Ray tinted glass ($37.95). B37 color-keyed floor mats ($11.60). B93 door edge guard moldings ($5.30). C08 vinyl roof cover ($89.55). C24 Hide-A-Way windshield wipers ($19). C50 rear window defogger ($26.35). C60 Four-Season air conditioning ($380.25). D34 visor-vanity mirror ($3.20). D35 sport mirrors ($26.35). D55 center console ($59). D80 rear deck lid spoiler ($32.65). F41 sport suspension ($30.55). G80 positraction rear axle ($44.25). J50 power brakes ($47.30). L34 "396 Turbo-Jet" 402-cid/350-hp V-8 ($152.75). L78 "396 Turbo-Jet" 402-cid/375-hp V-8 ($385.50). M20 four-speed wide-ratio manual transmission ($205.95). M35 Powerglide automatic transmission with six-cylinder engine ($174.25). M40 Turbo Hydra-Matic automatic transmission with Z/28 ($290.40). M40 Turbo Hydra-Matic automatic transmission with Camaros SS with optional L34 V-8 ($221.80). NA9 California emission controls ($36.90). N33 Comfortilt steering wheel ($45.30). N40 power steering ($105.35). PY4 F70-14 white sidewall tires ($65.70). PO1 bright metal wheel trim covers ($26.35). P02 custom wheel trim covers ($79). T60 heavy-duty battery ($15.80). U14 special instrumentation ($84.30). U35 electric clock ($15.80). U63 AM radio ($61.10). U69 AM/FM radio ($133.80). U80 rear seat speaker ($14.75). VF3 deluxe front and rear bumpers ($36.90). V01 heavy-duty radiator ($14.75). YD1 trailering axle ratio ($12.65). ZJ7 Rally wheels with trim rings ($42.15). ZJ9 auxiliary lighting without custom interior option ($13.70). ZJ9 auxiliary lighting with custom interior option ($11.10). ZQ9 performance axle ratio ($12.65). Z21 style trim ($52.70). Z22 Rally Sport package ($168.55). Z23 interior accent group ($21.10). Z27 Camaro Super Sport package ($289.65). Z87 custom interior ($115.90).

1970 CAMARO Z/28

CHEVROLET

JERRY HEASLEY

1970 Camaro Z/28

The Camaro Z/28 grew out of Chevrolet's desire to field a car in the popular Sports Car Club of America Trans-Am racing series. SCCA rules put maximum displacement restrictions on the so-called sedan racers. The rules were changed in 1970 and, as a result, the Z/28's high-performance small-block V-8 was increased from 302 cid to 350 cid. However, it was a very special 350-cid engine that was virtually identical to the LT1 Corvette engine. The major difference was that the Camaro had a more restrictive exhaust system that robbed away about 10 hp and gave the engine a 360-hp rating. The combination of the new body with this outstanding motor made the 1970 Z/28 an instant classic.

The RPO Z/28 Special Performance package retailed for $572.95 in 1970. It was available for V-8-powered Camaros with special instrumentation, a four-speed manual or Turbo Hydra-Matic transmission, power brakes and a positraction rear axle. Standard equipment included a heavy-duty radiator, the F41 performance suspension, heavy-duty front and rear springs, 15 x 7-in. wheels, a rear deck lid spoiler and special paint stripes on the hood and rear deck lid.

In May 1970, *Car Life* tested a Z/28 with Turbo Hydra-Matic transmission and a 4.10:1 rear axle. This car 0-to-60 mph in 6.5 seconds. And the quarter-mile in 14.51 seconds At 98.79 mph. Top speed was given as 119 mph. *Car and Driver* tested a similar car the same month and registered a 0-to-60 mph time and a 14.2 second quarter-mile at 100.3 mph.

Model Number	Body/Style Number	Body Type & Seating	Factory Price	Shipping Weight	Production Total
CAMARO Z/28 — SERIES 24 + Z/28 — (V-8 WITH FOUR-SPEED MANUAL TRANSMISSION)					
24	87	2d HT	$3,794	—	Note 1
CAMARO Z/28 — SERIES 24 + Z/28 — (V-8 WITH TURBO HYDRA-MATIC TRANSMISSION)					
24	87	2d HT	$3,878	—	Note 1

NOTE 1: Model year production of 1970 Camaro Z/28 coupes was 8,733.

ENGINE

BASE V-8: 90-degree, overhead valve V-8. Cast-iron block and head. Bore & stroke: 4.00 x 3.48 in. Displacement: 350 cid (5.7 liters). Compression ratio: 11.0:1. Brake hp: 360 at 6000 rpm. Torque: 380 lbs.-ft. at 4000 rpm. Five main bearings. Solid valve lifters. Induction system: Holley four-barrel carburetor. Four-bolt main bearings. Big valve heads. Special cam. Aluminum high-rise manifold. Standard in Camaro Z/28; not available in other Camaros.

OPTIONS

AK1 color-keyed seat and shoulder belts ($12.15). AS4 rear shoulder belts ($26.35). A01 Soft-Ray tinted glass ($37.95). B37 color-keyed floor mats ($11.60). B93 door edge guard moldings ($5.30). C08 vinyl roof cover ($89.55). C24 Hide-A-Way windshield wipers ($19). C50 rear window defogger ($26.35). C60 Four-Season air conditioning ($380.25). D34 visor-vanity mirror ($3.20). D35 sport mirrors ($26.35). D55 center console ($59). D80 rear deck lid spoiler ($32.65). F41 sport suspension ($30.55). G80 Positraction rear axle ($44.25). J50 power brakes ($47.30). M20 four-speed wide-ratio manual transmission ($205.95). M40 Turbo Hydra-Matic automatic transmission ($290.40). NA9 California emission controls ($36.90). N33 Comfortilt steering wheel ($45.30). N40 power steering ($105.35). P02 custom wheel trim covers ($79). T60 heavy-duty battery ($15.80). U14 special instrumentation ($84.30). U35 electric clock ($15.80). U63 AM radio ($61.10). U69 AM/FM radio ($133.80). U80 rear seat speaker ($14.75). VF3 deluxe front and rear bumpers ($36.90). V01 heavy-duty radiator ($14.75). YD1 trailering axle ratio ($12.65). ZJ7 Rally wheels with trim rings ($42.15). ZJ9 auxiliary lighting without custom interior option ($13.70). ZJ9 auxiliary lighting with custom interior option ($11.10). ZQ9 performance axle ratio ($12.65). Z21 style trim ($52.70). Z22 Rally Sport package ($168.55). Z23 interior accent group ($21.10). Z28 Special Performance package ($572.95). Z87 custom interior ($115.90).

CHEVROLET

1970 CHEVELLE SS 396

JERRY HEASLEY

1970 Chevelle SS 396

The more highly sculptured 1970 Chevelle featured a bold-looking frontal treatment with a horizontally split grille opening and dual headlights. The Z25 Super Sport option was available to turn any 1970 Chevelle V-8 sport coupe or convertible into an SS 396. Of these body styles, only the sport coupe was included in the base Series 3400 Chevelle line. The Malibu line included both body styles. After January 1970, the 396-cid V-8 was actually a 402-cid V-8, although the SS 396 name was still used.

The Chevelle SS 396 with the 325-hp V-8 and automatic transmission that *Car and Driver* comparison road tested in January 1969 did 0-to-60 mph in 5.8 seconds and covered the quarter-mile in 14.41 seconds at 97.35 mph. The magazine noted that you could order the SS 396 option for the Chevelle 300 Deluxe two-door coupe over the counter for $3,409 or more than $300 less than a Dodge Super Bee.

Series Number	Body/Style Number	Body Type & Seating	Factory Price	Shipping Weight	Production Total
CHEVELLE 300 DELUXE + RPO Z25 (SS 396) — SERIES 3400 — V-8					
34	37	2d HT-6P	$3,108	—	Note 1
CHEVELLE MALIBU + RPO Z25 (SS 396) — SERIES 3600 — V-8					
36	37	2d HT-6P	$3,255	—	Note 1
36	67	2d Conv-6P	$3,455	—	Note 1

NOTE 1: Prices include RPO Z25 package. With L34 version of 396-cid V-8.
NOTE 2: See options section for prices of other 396-cid V-8s.
NOTE 3: 49,826 Chevelles had the SS 396 option.

ENGINES

BASE V-8: Overhead-valve. Cast-iron block and head. Bore and stroke: 4.13 x 3.76 in. Displacement: 402 cid (396 cid). Compression ratio: 10.25:1. Brake hp: 350 at 5200 rpm. Taxable hp: 54.50. Torque: 415 at 3400. Five main bearings. Hydraulic valve lifters. Carburetor: Four-barrel. Sales code: L34.

OPTIONAL V-8: Overhead-valve. Cast-iron block and head. Bore and stroke: 4.09 x 3.76 in. Displacement: 396 cid (actually 402 cid). Compression ratio: 11.00:1. Brake hp: 375 at 5600 rpm. Taxable hp: 53.60. Torque: 415 at 3600. Five main bearings. Hydraulic valve lifters. Carburetor: Four-barrel. Sales code: L78.

OPTIONAL V-8: Overhead-valve. Cast-iron block. Aluminum head with large valves. Bore and stroke: 4.09 x 3.76 in. Displacement: 396 cid (actually 402 cid). Compression ratio: 11.00:1. Brake hp: 375 at 5600 rpm. Taxable hp: 53.60. Torque: 415 at 3600. Five main bearings. Solid valve lifters. Carburetor: Holley four-barrel. Sales code: L78/L89.

OPTIONS (PARTIAL LIST)

C60 Four-Season air conditioning, including 61-amp Delcotron, heavy-duty radiator and temperature-controlled fan and requiring larger tires with some Chevelles ($376). ZP5 appearance group ($34.85). G80 Positraction rear axle ($42.15). ZQ9 performance rear axle on Malibu with 375-hp V-8 and Positraction ($25.30). T60 J50 power drum brakes ($42.15). JL2 power front disc brakes ($64.25). U35 electric clock, included with special instrumentation ($15.80). D55 console with courtesy light ($53.75). C50 rear windshield defroster ($20.85 in coupe, $29.20 in convertible). AU3 power door locks ($44.80). L48 350-cid/300-hp V-8 engine, all except SS 396 ($68.50). LS3 402-cid/330-hp V-8 engine, all except SS 396 ($162.20). L34 396-cid/350-hp V-8 engine, SS 396 only ($121.15). L78 396-cid/375-hp V-8 SS 396 only ($250.00). L78/L89 396-cid 375-hp V-8 with aluminum heads, for SS 396 only ($647.75). ZL2 cowl-induction hood ($147.45). U14 special instrumentation with ammeter, temperature gauge, oil pressure gauge and tachometer ($94.80). U46 "Vigilite" light monitoring system ($26.35). Two-tone paint ($23.20). V01 heavy-duty radiator ($14.75). U63 AM push-button radio with front antenna ($61.10). U69 AM/FM radio with front antenna ($133.80). U79 AM/FM radio with front antenna and stereo ($239.15). UM1 AM radio with stereo tape deck ($194.85). UM2 AM/FM radio with stereo tape deck ($372.85). U80 rear seat speaker, not available with stereo ($13.20). Vinyl roof ($94.80). U73 rear antenna, all except AM/FM ($9.50). CO8 vinyl roof cover for hardtop models ($89.55). Z25 SS 396 option package for Chevelle/Malibu sport coupe or convertible ($445.55). Z25 SS 396 option package with L78 engine for Chevelle/Malibu sport coupe ($656.20). Z25 SS 396 option package with L78/L89 engine and special three-speed manual transmission ($840.50). Z25 SS 396 option package with L78/L89 and special three-speed manual transmission ($858.65). Electric seat back latch ($23.70). A51 Strato bucket seats in Malibu sport coupe and convertible ($121.15). K30 speed and cruise control, V-8s with automatic transmissions ($57.95). N40 power steering for SS 396 ($105.35). N33 Comfortilt steering wheel ($45.30). Cushioned rim steering wheel ($34.80). N34 Sport styled steering wheel ($34.80). D96 sport striping for SS 396 only, standard with ZL2 ($68.50). F40 special front and rear suspension ($17.25). Power convertible top ($52.70). M20 wide-ratio four-speed manual transmission ($184.80). M21 Close-ratio four-speed manual transmission ($184.80,). M40 Turbo Hydra-Matic transmission for 375-hp Chevelles ($290.40). M40 Turbo Hydra-Matic transmission for other V-8s ($221.80). Vinyl trim interior for Chevelle and Malibu sport coupe ($12.65). A31 power windows ($105.35). PO1 four bright metal wheel covers ($21.10). ZJ7 Rallye wheels, including special wheels, hubcaps and trim rings ($35.85). PY4 five F70-14/B white stripe tires replacing PL4-SS 396 option (no cost).

1970 CHEVELLE SS 454

JERRY HEASLEY

1970 Chevelle SS 454

Some enthusiasts contend that the LS6 was the fastest production car ever built. A test car powered by the LS6 engine moved from 0 to 60 mph in 5.4 seconds and did the standing-start quarter mile in 13.81 seconds at 103.8 mph. Those numbers were racked up with a Turbo Hydra-Matic transmission and a 3.77:1 rear axle. You could also order either 454-cid engine with one of three available four-speed manual transmissions. The LS6 was a super-high-performance 450-hp engine featuring things like four-bolt main bearings, nodular iron bearing caps, heavy-duty connecting rods, big-diameter exhaust valves and a solid-lifter camshaft.

Sometime after the start of the 1970 model year, a new Z15 option was released and allowed Malibu V-8 sport coupe or convertible buyers to turn their car into an SS 454. The SS 454 package included bright engine accents, dual exhausts with bright tips, power front disc brakes, a black-painted grille, wheel opening moldings, a special rear bumper with a resilient black insert, a special domed hood, a special heavy-duty suspension, 14 x 7-inch Sport wheels, F70 x 14 Wide-Oval white lettered tires and a 454-cid Turbo-Jet 360-hp base V-8.

Series Number	Body/Style Number	Body Type & Seating	Factory Price	Shipping Weight	Production Total
CHEVELLE MALIBU SS 454 + RPO Z15 (SS 454) — SERIES 3600 — V-8					
36	37	2d HT-6P	$3,312	—	Note 3
36	67	2d Conv-6P	$3,512	—	Note 3

NOTE 1: Prices include RPO Z15 package.

NOTE 2: See options section for LS6 prices.

NOTE 3: 3,773 Malibus had the SS 354 option.

ENGINES

BASE V-8: Overhead-valve. Cast-iron block and head. Bore and stroke: 4.25 x 4.00 in. Displacement: 454 cid. Compression ratio: 10.25:1. Brake hp: 360 at 4400 rpm. Taxable hp: 57.80. Torque: 500 at 3200. Five main bearings. Hy-draulic valve lifters. Dual exhaust. Carburetor: Four-barrel. Sales code: LS5 (added midyear).

OPTIONAL V-8: Overhead-valve. Cast-iron block. Bore and stroke: 4.251 x 4.00 in. Displacement: 454 cid. Compression ratio: 11:25:1. Brake hp: 450 at 5600 rpm. Taxable hp: 57.80. Torque: 500 at 3600 rpm. Five main bearings. Solid valve lifters. High-performance camshaft. Carburetor: Holley four-barrel. Sales code: LS6 (added midyear).

OPTIONS (PARTIAL LIST)

C60 Four-Season air conditioning, including 61-amp Delcotron, heavy-duty radiator and temperature-controlled fan and requiring larger tires with some Chevelles ($376). ZP5 appearance group ($34.85). G80 Positraction rear axle ($42.15). ZQ9 performance rear axle on Malibu with 375-hp V-8 and Positraction ($25.30). J50 power drum brakes ($42.15). JL2 power front disc brakes ($64.25). U35 Electric clock, included with special instrumentation ($15.80). D55 console with courtesy light ($53.75). C50 rear windshield defroster ($20.85 in coupe, $29.20 in convertible). AU3 power door locks ($44.80). K85 63-amp Delcotron generator, with air conditioning ($5.30); without air conditioning ($26.35). A01 all windows tinted ($36.90). V31/32 front or rear bumper guards ($15.80). B93 door edge guards ($4.25). K05 engine block heater ($10.55). ZL2 cowl-induction hood, requires Super Sport packages ($147.45). U14 special instrumentation with ammeter, temperature gauge, oil pressure gauge and tachometer ($94.80). U46 "Vigilite" light monitoring system ($26.35). Two-tone paint ($23.20). V01 heavy-duty radiator ($14.75). U63 AM push-button radio with front antenna ($61.10). U69 AM/FM radio with front antenna ($133.80). U79 AM/FM radio with front antenna and stereo ($239.15). UM1 AM radio with stereo tape deck ($194.85). UM2 AM/FM radio with stereo tape deck ($372.85). U80 rear seat speaker, not available with stereo ($13.20). Vinyl roof ($94.80). U73 rear antenna, all except AM/FM ($9.50). CO8 vinyl roof cover for hardtop models ($89.55). Electric seat back latch ($23.70). A51 Strato bucket seats in Malibu ($121.15). K30 speed and cruise control, V-8s with automatic transmissions ($57.95). N40 power steering for SS 396 ($105.35). N33 Comfortilt steering wheel ($45.30). Cushioned rim steering wheel ($34.80). N34 Sport styled steering wheel ($34.80). D96 sport striping for SS 396 only, standard with ZL2 ($68.50). F40 Special front and rear suspension ($17.25). Power convertible top ($52.70). Vinyl trim interior for Chevelle and Malibu sport coupe ($12.65). A31 power windows ($105.35). PO1 Four bright metal wheel covers ($21.10). ZJ7 Rallye wheels ($35.85). PY4 five F70-14/B White Stripe tires replacing PL4-SS 454 option (no cost).

1970 CORVETTE 454

CHEVROLET

PHIL KUNZ

1970 Corvette 454

Now in its third year, the "Shark"-bodied Corvette still had plenty of teeth, especially with a big-block V-8 rumbling under the fiberglass hood.

Refinements were made to the basic styling used since 1968. A new ice-cube-tray design grille and matching side fender louvers; rectangular, amber front signal lights; fender flares and square exhaust exits were exterior changes. The bucket seats and safety belt retractor containers were also improved. Standard equipment included: front and rear disc brakes, headlight washers, wheel trim rings, carpeting, center console and all-vinyl upholstery (in either Black, Blue, Green, Saddle or Red).

RPO LS5 was a big-block 454 with an advertised 390 hp and 500 lbs.-ft. of torque at 3400 rpm. It was a step up the muscle car ladder from LT1, which was based on the small-block 350 rated at 370 hp.

ENGINES

OPTIONAL V-8: Overhead valve. Cast-iron block. Displacement: 454 cid. Bore and stroke: 4.251 x 4.00 inches. Compression ratio: 10:25:1. Brake hp: 390 at 4800 rpm. Torque: 500 lbs.-ft. at 3400 rpm. Five main bearings. Hydraulic valve lifters. High-performance camshaft. Rochester 750CFM Quadra-Jet four-barrel. RPO Code LS5.

OPTIONS

Custom interior trim ($158); RPO A31 Electric power windows ($63.20). RPO A85 Custom shoulder belts ($42.15). RPO C07 Auxiliary hardtop for convertible ($273.85). RPO C08 Vinyl cover for auxiliary hardtop ($63.20). RPO C50 Rear window defroster ($36.90). RPO C60 Air conditioning ($447.65). G81 Positraction rear axle, all ratios ($12.65). RPO J50 Power brakes ($47.40). RPO LS5 454-cid/390-hp V-8 ($289.65). RPO M21 Four-speed close-ratio manual transmission (no cost option). RPO M22 Heavy-duty close-ratio four-speed manual transmission ($95.00). RPO M40 Turbo Hydra-Matic automatic transmission (no cost option). N37 Tilt-Telescopic steering wheel ($84.30). RPO N40 Power steering ($105.35). RPO P01 Custom wheel covers ($57.95). RPO PT7 white stripe nylon tires F70 x 15 ($31.30). RPO PU9 F70 x 15 raised-white-letter tires ($33.15). T60 Heavy-duty battery ($15.80). RPO UA6 Alarm system ($31.60). RPO U69 AM-FM radio ($172.75). RPO U79 Stereo radio ($278.10).

Model Number	Body/Style Number	Body Type & Seating	Factory Price	Shipping Weight	Production Total
CORVETTE STINGRAY 454 — SERIES 9000 + LS5 — V-8					
94	37	2d HT-2P	$,482	3,153 lbs.	Note 2
94	67	2d Conv-2P	$5,139	3,167 lbs.	Note 2

NOTE 1: Prices include cost of LS5 engine but no other extras.
NOTE 2: A total of 4,473 cars were equipped with the 454-cid LS5 V-8.
NOTE 3: One car was built with the experimental 454-cid LS7 V-8.

1970 MONTE CARLO SS 454

JERRY HEASLEY

1970 Monte Carlo SS 454

The original Monte Carlo was said to combine action and elegance in a sporty, personal luxury package. Based on the same platform as the re-designed 1969 Pontiac Grand Prix, the Monte Carlo was bigger than the Chevelle and had a price tag in the Impala range. A long hood/short deck image and smart interior and exterior appointments were incorporated. Styling features included large, single headlamps mounted in square-shaped bright housings, a rectangular front opening with a grid-textured grille of thin bright horizontal moldings (with a center badge), and a profile emphasizing the popular 'venturi' shape, enhanced by a crisply sculptured upper feature line.

Although mainly luxurious in overall character, the Monte Carlo turned out to be quite a fine high-performance machine. The potent, SS 454 version was capable of 0-to-60 mph in under 8 seconds. This package was found to be extremely suitable to short-track stock car racing. This was due to a combination of good power-to-weight distribution along with aerodynamic factors. The only available body style was a coupe. Standard equipment included power front disc brakes, an electric clock, assist straps, elm-burl dash panel inlays, G78-15-B bias-belted black sidewall tires and a 350-cid V-8. Although commonly seen on most Monte Carlos, fender skirts were optional.

ENGINES

BASE V-8: Overhead valve. Cast-iron block and head. Bore and stroke: 4.25 x 4.00 in. Displacement: 454 cid. Compression ratio: 8.50:1. Gross Brake hp: 365 at 4800 rpm. Net brake hp: 285 at 4000 rpm. Net torque: 390 at 3200 rpm. Five main bearings. Hydraulic valve lifters. Dual exhaust. Carburetor: Four-barrel.

OPTIONAL V-8: Overhead valve. Cast-iron block and head. Bore and stroke: 4.25 x 4.00 in. Displacement: 454 cid. Compression ratio: 9.00:1. Net brake hp: 325 at 5600 rpm. Taxable hp: 57.80. Net torque. 390 at 3600 rpm. Five main bearings. Hydraulic valve lifters. Dual exhaust. Carburetor: Four-barrel.

OPTIONS

Comfort-On air conditioning ($463.45). Four-Season air conditioning ($363.40-$384.15). Power drum brakes ($41.15-$43.05). Power front disc brakes ($64.25-$65.65). Console ($52.75). Electro-Clear rear defroster ($41.70). Standard rear defroster ($20.85-$29.20). Power door locks ($35.45). Tinted glass ($24.83-$30.00). Headlight delay system ($18.36). Special instrumentation, includes tachometer, ammeter and temperature gauges ($68.50). Vigilante light monitoring system,($26.35). AM push-button radio ($61.10). AM/FM push-button radio ($133.80). AM/FM radio with FM stereo ($239.10). Stereotape, with AM radio ($194.85), with AM/FM radio and FM stereo ($372.85). Black, blue, dark gold, green or white vinyl top ($126.40). Six-Way power front seat ($100.10). Power Strato-Bucket seat ($121.15). Rear fender skirts ($31.60). Power steering ($89.55-$105.35). Comfort-Tilt steering wheel ($46). Wheel covers ($21). Color-keyed wheel covers ($15.80). Special wheel covers ($57.95-$80.70). Six 15 x 7JK wheels ($10.55). Rally-styled wheels ($36). Fingertip windshield wiper control ($19). RPO LS6 454-cid/450-hp Turbo-Jet V-8, in Monte Carlo with SS-454 option package ($263.30). Wide-range type four-speed manual transmission ($184.80). Turbo Hydra-Matic 400 transmission ($221.80). Positraction axle ($42.15). Heavy-duty battery ($15.80). Dual exhaust ($24.17). 63-amp generator without air conditioning ($21.00), with air conditioning ($4). Engine block heater ($10.55). Heavy-duty radiator ($32.00). RPO Z20 Monte Carlo SS Package, includes 454-cid/360-hp V-8, Superlift with Automatic Level Control, dual exhaust, G70-15/B white-letter tires, 15 x 7-inch wheels, 454 emblems on bodysill moldings, and requires Turbo Hydra-Matic ($420.25).

Series Number	Body/Style Number	Body Type & Seating	Factory Price	Shipping Weight	Production Total
MONTE CARLO SS 454 —SERIES 138 + Z20 — V-8					
36	57	2d HT-5P	$3,543	3,460 lbs.	3,823

NOTE: The production total includes 10 cars ordered with the LS-6 454-cid V-8 rated at 450 hp.

1970 Nova SS 396

CHEVROLET

1970 Nova SS 396

Perfect for younger car buffs, high-performance versions of the Nova were real "sleepers" in the Stoplight Grand Prix. The Nova was a small, light basic car which normally appealed to factory workers and school teachers who wanted reliable, economical transportation. But since the car's underpinnings were derived from the Camaro, it was possible to stuff Camaro-type performance under the Nova's hood. Adding a few heavy-duty components and fat tires could turn the tiny "taxi" into a fairly respectable weekend cruiser.

For 1970 updates, the Nova got a new grille insert with squarer openings than the previous year's model. Chevrolet's senior compact continued to use the same platform introduced two years earlier. The "Coke-bottle" body shape had the popular long hood/short rear deck look and a trim overall length. Variable-ratio power steering was a new extra for 1970.

Naturally, muscle car fans did not want the base 307-cid V-8. Most of them preferred moving up to the RPO Z26 Nova Super Sport package. Its basic "SS" ingredients included a 350-cid/300-hp V-8, dual exhausts, power front disc brakes, a simulated air intake on the hood, simulated front fender louvers, and "SS" emblems. A four-speed manual or Turbo Hydra-Matic transmission was mandatory with the Super Sport option. Two optional Turbo-Jet V-8s were available for those who wanted to compete at a drag strip or on the downtown cruising strip. The first big-block package, coded RPO L34, came with the 396-cid (actually 402 cubic inches) 350-hp engine and was priced at $184.35 extra. The second package, coded RPO L78, included the 396-cid/375-hp engine at $316 above the cost of the base 350-cid V-8.

Model Number	Body/Style Number	Body Type & Seating	Factory Price	Shipping Weight	Production Total
NOVA SS 396 — SERIES 1400 — V-8 (L34)					
14 27	2d Cpe-6P	$3,200	N/A	1,947	
NOVA SS 396 — SERIES 1400 — V-8 (L78)					
14 27	2d Cpe-6P	$3,332	N/A	5,262	

NOTE 1: Prices above include SS package, Hydra-Matic and cost of Turbo-Jet V-8.
NOTE2: A total of 19,558 cars got the Nova SS package.
NOTE 3: A total of 7,209 cars had a 396-cid V-8.

ENGINES

OPTIONAL V-8: Overhead valve. Cast-iron block and head. Bore and stroke: 4.13 x 3.76 in. Displacement: 396 cid (actually 402 cid). Compression ratio: 10.25:1. Brake hp: 350 at 5200 rpm. Taxable hp: 54.50. Torque: 415 at 3400. Five main bearings. Hydraulic valve lifters. Four-barrel. Sales code: L34. Engine code: CTW, CTX or CTZ.

OPTIONAL V-8: Overhead valve. Cast-iron block and head. Bore and stroke: 4.09 x 3.76 in. Displacement: 396 cid (actually 402 cid). Compression ratio: 11.00:1. Brake hp: 375 at 5600 rpm. Taxable hp: 53.60. Torque: 415 at 3600. Five main bearings. Hydraulic valve lifters. Carburetor: Four-barrel. Sales code: L78. Engine code: CTY, CKO, CKP, CTY, CKQ, CKT and CKU.

OPTIONS

Four Season air conditioning ($363.40-$384.15). Power drum brakes ($41.15-$43.05). Power front disc brakes ($64.25-$65.65). Console, with bucket seats only ($53.75). Standard rear defroster ($20.85- $29.20). Power door locks ($35.45). Tinted glass ($24.83-$30.00). Headlight delay system ($18.36). Special instrumentation, includes tachometer, ammeter and temperature gauges in Nova V-8 with console ($94.80). AM push-button radio ($61.10). AM/FM push-button radio ($133.80). AM/FM radio with FM stereo ($239.10). Stereotape, with AM radio ($194.85), with AM/FM radio and FM stereo ($372.85). Black, blue, dark gold, green or white vinyl top ($84.30). Six-Way power front seat ($100.10). Power Strato-Bucket seat ($121.15). Power steering ($89.55-$105.35). Comfort-Tilt steering wheel ($46). Wheel covers ($21). Special wheel covers ($57.95-$80.70). Sport-styled wheels ($79). Fingertip windshield wiper control ($19). RPO L34 396-cid/350-hp V-8 ($184.35). RPO L78 396-cid/375-hp V-8 ($316.50). Wide-range type four-speed manual transmission ($184.80). Regular close-ratio four-speed manual transmission ($184.80), Turbo Hydra-Matic transmission ($221.80. Positraction axle ($42.15). Heavy-duty battery ($15.80). Dual exhaust ($24.17). 63-amp generator without air conditioning ($21.00), with air conditioning ($4). Engine block heater ($10.55). Heavy-duty radiator ($15-$32). Custom Exterior Package ($97.95), on sedans ($79.00). Custom Interior package (cost not available).

1971 CAMARO SS 350/400

1971 Camaro SS 350/400

Motor Trend (December 1970) said, "If the pony car concept wanes in the next decade, the latest Camaros will be remembered as the zenith of development of that particular genre." The RS/SS 396 was recommended by *Motor Trend* for "effortless cruising" and proved that Chevy "had it all together" as far as the sports-compact musclecar niche went.

There were few basic changes in the 1971 Camaro, the most obvious being the addition of "high-back" front bucket seats with integral head restraints. Engines were modified to operate on low-lead or lead-free gasoline blends. This meant lower compression ratios and horsepower ratings.

The RPO Z27 Super Sport or SS package was a factory option that cost Chevrolet dealers $248.34 and retailed for $313.90. It was available for V-8-powered Camaros with four-speed or Turbo Hydra-Matic transmission.

The RS package could be added to six-cylinder or V-8 Camaros. It could also be combined with the SS package or the Z/28 Special Performance package by adding $179.05 to the prices shown further below for these model-options. RS emblems were deleted from the package when it was ordered in combination with the Camaro SS package or when the Z/28 Special Performance package was also ordered.

Model Number	Body/Style Number	Body Type & Seating	Factory Price	Shipping Weight	Production Total
CAMARO SS — SERIES 24 + Z27 — (RPO L48 "TURBO-FIRE 350" V-8)					
23	87	2d HT	$3,126	—	Note 1
CAMARO SS — SERIES 24 + Z22 — (RPO LS3 "TURBO-JET 396" V-8)					
24	87	2d HT	$3,222	—	Note 1

NOTE 1: Model year production of 1971 Camaro SS coupes was 18,287.

ENGINES

BASE V-8: 90-degree, overhead valve. Cast-iron block and head. Bore & stroke: 4.00 x 3.48 in. Displacement: 350 cid (5.7 liters). Compression ratio: 8.5:1. Gross hp: 270 at 4800 rpm. Net hp: 210 at 4400 rpm. Net torque: 300 at 2800 rpm. Five main bearings. Hydraulic valve lifters. Induction system: Rochester four-barrel carburetor. Standard in Camaro SS; not available in other models. RPO code L48.

OPTIONAL V-8: 90-degree, overhead valve V-8. Cast-iron block and head. Bore & stroke: 4.13 x 3.76 in. Displacement: 402 cid. Compression ratio: 8.5:1. Gross hp: 300 at 4800 rpm. Net hp: 260 at 4400 rpm. Net torque: 345 at 3200 rpm. Five main bearings. Hydraulic valve lifters. Induction system: Rochester no. 7042118 four-barrel carburetor. Optional in Camaro SS; not available in other models. RPO LS3.

OPTIONS

AK1 color-keyed seat and shoulder belts ($15.30). AN6 adjustable seatback ($19). AS4 rear shoulder belts ($26.35). A01 Soft-Ray tinted glass ($40.05). B37 color-keyed floor mats ($12.65). B93 door edge guard moldings ($6.35). C08 vinyl roof cover ($89.55). C24 Hide-A-Way windshield wipers ($21.10). C50 rear window defogger ($31.60). C60 Four-Season air conditioning ($402.35). D34 visor-vanity mirror ($3.20). D35 sport mirror ($15.80). D55 center console ($59). D80 front and rear spoilers ($79). F41 sport suspension ($30.55). G80 positraction rear axle ($44.25). J50 power brakes ($47.30). LS3 "396 Turbo-Jet V-8 ($99.05). L65 350-cid Turbo-Fire four-barrel V-8 ($26.35). M20 four-speed wide-ratio manual transmission ($205.95). M21 four-speed close-ratio manual transmission ($205.95). M22 heavy-duty four-speed close-ratio manual transmission ($237.60). M40 Turbo Hydra-Matic automatic transmission with Camaros SS with optional LS3 V-8 ($237.60). NK2 custom steering wheel ($15.80). NK4 sport steering wheel ($15.80). N33 Comfortilt steering wheel ($45.30). N40 power steering ($110.60). PL3 E-78-14 white sidewall tires ($26.05). PL4 F70-14 white letter tires ($81.50). PY4 F70-14 white sidewall tires ($68.05). PO1 bright metal wheel trim covers ($26.35). P02 custom wheel trim covers ($84.30). T60 heavy-duty battery ($15.80). U14 special instrumentation ($84.30). U35 electric clock ($16.90). U63 AM radio ($66.40). U69 AM/FM radio ($139.05). U80 rear seat speaker ($15.80). VF3 deluxe front and rear bumpers ($36.90). V01 heavy-duty radiator ($14.75). YD1 trailering axle ratio ($12.65). ZJ7 Rally wheels with trim rings ($45.30). ZJ9 auxiliary lighting without custom interior option ($18.45). ZJ9 auxiliary lighting with custom interior option ($15.80). ZQ9 performance axle ratio ($12.65). Z21 style trim ($57.95). Z22 Rally Sport package ($179.05). Z23 interior accent group ($21.10). Z27 Camaro Super Sport package ($313.90). Z87 custom interior ($115.90).

1971 CAMARO Z/28

CHEVROLET

1971 Camaro Z/28

JERRY HEASLEY

The RPO Z/28 Special Performance package was a factory option that cost Chevrolet dealers $622.41 and retailed for $786.75. It was available for V-8-powered Camaros with a four-speed manual or Turbo Hydra-Matic transmission. The Z/28 came with an exclusive 330-hp Turbo-Fire 350 V-8, bright engine accents, a left-hand remote-controlled sport style outside rearview mirror, special instrumentation, power brakes, a 3.73:1 Positraction rear axle, a heavy-duty radiator, dual exhausts, a black-finished grille, Z/28 emblems on the front fender, rear bumper guards, a sport suspension, heavy-duty springs and front and rear springs, 15 x 7-inch wheels with bright lug nuts, special wheel center caps, wheel trim rings, F60-15/B bias-belted white-letter tires, a rear deck lid spoiler with Z/28 decal and special black or white paint stripes (except with a vinyl top or a black or white painted roof).

The four-speed manual or Turbo Hydra-Matic transmission was required at extra cost. Air conditioning, wheel covers or Rally wheels were not available.

A road test in the August 1972 issue of *Motor Trend* involved a Z/28 with the 350-cid/255-hp V-8, four-speed manual transmission and 3.73:1 rear axle. The car did 0-to-60 mph in 7.7 seconds and the quarter-mile in 15.2 seconds at 86.6 mph.

ENGINE

BASE V-8: Overhead valve V-8. Cast-iron block and head. Bore & stroke: 4.00 x 3.48 in. Displacement: 350 cid (5.7 liters). Compression ratio: 9.0:1. Gross horsepower: 330 at 5600 rpm. Net horsepower: 275 at 5600 rpm. Gross torque: 360 lbs.-ft. at 4000 rpm. Net torque: 300 lbs.-ft. at 4000 rpm. Five main bearings. Hydraulic valve lifters. Induction system: Rochester no. 7042202 four-barrel carburetor. Four-bolt main bearings. Big valve heads. Special cam. Aluminum high-rise manifold. Standard in Camaro Z/28; not available in other Camaros.

OPTIONS

AK1 color-keyed seat and shoulder belts ($15.30). AN6 adjustable seatback ($19). AS4 rear shoulder belts ($26.35). A01 Soft-Ray tinted glass ($40.05). B37 color-keyed floor mats ($12.65). B93 door edge guard moldings ($6.35). C08 vinyl roof cover ($89.55). C24 Hide-A-Way windshield wipers ($21.10). C50 rear window defogger ($31.60). C60 Four-Season air conditioning ($402.35). D34 visor-vanity mirror ($3.20). D35 sport mirror ($15.80). D55 center console ($59). D80 front and rear spoilers ($79). F41 sport suspension ($30.55). G80 positraction rear axle ($44.25). J50 power brakes ($47.30). M20 four-speed wide-ratio manual transmission ($205.95). M21 four-speed close-ratio manual transmission ($205.95). M22 heavy-duty four-speed close-ratio manual transmission ($237.60). M40 Turbo Hydra-Matic automatic transmission with Z/28 ($306.25). NK2 custom steering wheel ($15.80). NK4 sport steering wheel ($15.80). N33 Comfortilt steering wheel ($45.30). N40 power steering ($110.60). PL3 E-78-14 white sidewall tires ($26.05). PL4 F70-14 white letter tires ($81.50). PY4 F70-14 white sidewall tires ($68.05). PO1 bright metal wheel trim covers ($26.35). P02 custom wheel trim covers ($84.30). T60 heavy-duty battery ($15.80). U14 special instrumentation ($84.30). U35 electric clock ($16.90). U63 AM radio ($66.40). U69 AM/FM radio ($139.05). U80 rear seat speaker ($15.80). VF3 deluxe front and rear bumpers ($36.90). V01 heavy-duty radiator ($14.75). YD1 trailering axle ratio ($12.65). ZJ9 auxiliary lighting without custom interior option ($18.45). ZJ9 auxiliary lighting with custom interior option ($15.80). ZQ9 performance axle ratio ($12.65). Z21 style trim ($57.95). Z22 Rally Sport package ($179.05). Z23 interior accent group ($21.10). Z28 Special Performance package ($786.75). Z87 custom interior ($115.90).

Model Number	Body/Style Number	Body Type & Seating	Factory Price	Shipping Weight	Production Total
CAMARO Z/28 — SERIES 24 + Z/28 —					
(V-8 WITH FOUR-SPEED MANUAL TRANSMISSION)					
24	87	2d HT	$3,841	—	Note 1
CAMARO Z/28 — SERIES 24 + Z/28 —					
(V-8 WITH TURBO HYDRA-MATIC TRANSMISSION)					
24	87	2d HT	$3,941	—	Note 1

NOTE 1: Model year production of 1971 Camaro Z/28 coupes was 4,862.

1971 CORVETTE 454

TOM GLATCH

1971 Corvette 454

If you liked the 1970 Corvette, you'd like the 1971 version. They were virtually the same car.

A new resin process (that supposedly improved the body) and a different interior were the major changes. Under the hood, the compression ratios were dropped a bit to enable Corvette engines to run on lower octane fuel.

Standard equipment included: all-vinyl upholstery; dual exhaust; outside rearview mirror; carpeting; center console; wheel trim rings; electric clock; tachometer; heavy-duty battery; front and rear disc brakes with warning light; and tinted glass. Buyers had their choice of 10 exterior colors: Mulsanne Blue, Bridgehampton Blue, Brands Hatch Green, Steel Cities Gray, Ontario Orange, Millie Miglia Red, Nevada Silver, Classic White, Sunflower Yellow and War Bonnet Yellow. All convertibles came with a choice of Black or White soft tops. Interior colors were: Black, Dark Blue, Dark Green, Red and Saddle.

A 1971 Corvette with the LS5 engine could go 0-to-60 mph in 5.7 seconds, 0-to-100 mph in 14.1 seconds and do the standing-start quarter-mile in 14.2 seconds at 100.33 mph. A 1971 Corvette with the LS6 engine and 3.36:1 rear axle was rested by *Car and Driver* magazine in June 1971. It moved from 0-to-60 mph in 5.3 seconds, from 0-to-80 mph in 8.5 seconds and from 0-to-100 mph in 12.7 seconds. The same car did the quarter-mile in 13.8 seconds at 104.65 mph.

Model Number	Body/Style Number	Body Type & Seating	Factory Price	Shipping Weight	Production Total
CORVETTE STINGRAY SERIES — SERIES 9000 — V-8 (LS5)					
94	37	2d HT-2P	$5,831	3,153 lbs.	Note 2
94	67	2d Conv-2P	$5,594	3,167 lbs.	Note 2
CORVETTE STINGRAY SERIES — SERIES 9000 — V-8 (LS6)					
94	37	2d HT-2P	$6,757	3,153 lbs.	Note 3
94	67	2d Conv-2P	$6,520	3,167 lbs.	Note 3

NOTE 1: Prices include the indicated engine.
NOTE 2: 5,097 Corvettes carried the LS5 V-8.
NOTE 3: 188 Corvettes carried the LS6 V-8.

ENGINES

OPTIONAL V-8: Overhead valve. Cast-iron block. Displacement: 454 cid. Bore and stroke: 4.251 x 4.00 inches. Compression ratio: 8.5:1. Brake hp: 365 at 4800 rpm. Torque: 465 at 3200 rpm. Five main bearings. Hydraulic valve lifters. High-performance camshaft. Rochester 750CFM Quadra-Jet four-barrel. RPO code LS5.

OPTIONAL V-8: Overhead valve. Cast-iron block. Displacement: 454 cid. Bore and stroke: 4.251 x 4.00 inches. Compression ratio: 8.5:1. Brake hp: 425 at 5600 rpm. Torque: 475 at 4000 rpm. Five main bearings. Hydraulic valve lifters. High-performance camshaft. Holley 880CFM four-barrel. RPO code LS6.

OPTIONS

Custom interior trim ($158). RPO A31 Electric power windows ($79). RPO A85 Custom shoulder belts ($42). RPO C07 Auxiliary hardtop for convertible ($274). RPO C08 Vinyl cover for auxiliary hardtop ($63). RPO C50 Rear window defroster ($42). RPO C60 Air conditioning ($459). G81 Positraction rear axle, all ratios ($13). RPO J50 Power brakes ($47). RPO LS5 454-cid/365-hp V-8 ($295). RPO LS6 454-cid/425-hp V-8 ($1,221). RPO M21 Four-speed close-ratio manual transmission (no cost option). RPO M22 Heavy-duty close-ratio four-speed manual transmission ($100.00). RPO M40 Turbo Hydra-Matic automatic transmission (no cost option). N37 Tilt-Telescopic steering wheel ($84.30). RPO N40 Power steering ($115.90). RPO P02 Custom wheel covers ($63). RPO PT7 White stripe nylon tires F70 x 15 ($28). RPO PU9 F70 x 15 raised-white-letter tires ($42). T60 Heavy-duty battery ($15.80). RPO U69 AM-FM radio ($178). RPO U79 Stereo radio ($283).

CHEVROLET

1971 CHEVELLE SS "400/454"

JERRY HEASLEY

1971 Chevelle SS

These cars were a smogged version of the SS 396 without its stripes. Though often overlooked, these cars are getting a second look today. A couple of visits to eBay can help you turn one of these into a racer to reckon with. On the other hand, if you find one with a 454 already in it, you'll save a bunch in Paypal fees.

The '71 Super Sport package came in lower-priced Chevelle SS version. A glance at the engine call-outs under the SS logos on the grille, fenders and bumper told you which you were looking at. The base engine in the SS was only a 245-hp version of the 350-cid small-block V-8. A 270-hp "Corvette" version of the 350 was optional. You could also get a 400-cid/300-hp Turbo-Jet big-block V-8 (which was was the 402-cid version of the old Turbo-Jet 396. The SS package had a dealer cost of $282.44 and a retail price of $357.05.

The complete contents of the SS equipment package included power front disc rear drum brakes, a black-finished grille, a special domed hood with locking pins, Sport suspension, 15 x 7-inch wheels and other goodies.

Series Number	Body/Style Number	Body Type & Seating	Factory Price	Shipping Weight	Production Total
CHEVELLE SS "400" — SERIES 3600 + YF3 + LS3 — V-8					
36	37	2d HT-5P	3,337	3,460 lbs.	—
CHEVELLE SS "454" — SERIES 3600 + YF3 + LS5 — V-8					
36	37	2d HT-5P	3,616	3,460 lbs.	—
CHEVELLE SS "454" — SERIES 3600 + YF3 + LS5 — V-8					
36	37	2d HT-5P	3,627	3,460 lbs.	—

NOTE 1: Chevrolet built an estimated 80,000 cars with the SS package.

NOTE 2: A total of 19,292 Chevelle SS models were equipped with 454-cid V-8s.

ENGINE

OPTIONAL V-8: Overhead-valve. Cast-iron block and head. Bore and stroke: 4.13 x 3.76 in. Displacement: 402 cid (400 cid). Compression ratio: 8.50:1. Gross brake hp: 300 at 4800 rpm. Net brake hp: 260 at 4400 rpm. Taxable hp: 54.50.

Gross torque: 400 at 3200. Net torque: 345 at 3200 rpm. Five main bearings. Hydraulic valve lifters. Carburetor: Four-barrel. Sales code LS3.

OPTIONS

C60 Four-Season air conditioning, including 61-amp Delcotron generator, heavy-duty radiator and temperature-controlled fan and requiring larger tires with some Chevelles ($407.60). G80 Positraction rear axle (Chevelles $46.35). YD1 trailering axle ratio ($12.65). T60 heavy-duty 80-amp battery ($15.60). AK1 Custom Deluxe front shoulder belts for bench seat cars ($16.90). AK1 Custom Deluxe front shoulder belts for coupe with bucket seats ($15.30). AS4 Custom Deluxe rear shoulder belts ($26.35). U35 Electric clock, included with special instrumentation ($16.90). D55 Console with courtesy light, not available with standard three-speed manual transmission ($59). C50 Rear windshield defroster ($31.60). AU3 power door locks ($44.80). LS3 402-cid/300-hp V-8 engine with E78 x 14 tires or Super Sport package ($172.75). K85 63-amp Delcotron generator, with air conditioning ($5.30); without air conditioning ($26.35). A01 All windows tinted ($43.20). V30 front and rear bumper guards ($31.60). B93 door edge guards ($6.35). U14 Special instrumentation with ammeter, temperature gauge, oil pressure gauge and tachometer ($94.80). ZJ9 auxiliary lighting groups ($21.10). B37 twin front and rear floor mats ($12.65). B37 color-keyed front and rear floor mats ($12.65). D33 left-hand outside remote-control mirror ($12.65). D34 visor vanity mirror ($3.20). B90 window moldings ($26.35). Two-tone paint with bright metal outline moldings ($31.60). J50 power drum brakes ($47.40). JL2 power disc brakes ($69.55). AU3 power door locks system ($46.35). N40 power steering ($115.90). V01 heavy-duty radiator with V-8 engine ($21.10). U63 AM push-button radio with front antenna ($66.40). U69 AM/FM radio with front antenna ($139.05). U79 AM/FM radio with front antenna and stereo ($239.10). UM1 AM radio with stereo tape deck ($200.15). UM2 AM/FM radio with setero tape deck ($372.85). U80 rear seat speaker, not available with stereo ($15.80). Vinyl roof ($94.80). K30 cruise control, requires power brakes and Turbo Hydra-Matic transmission ($63.20). N33 Comfortilt steering, requires automatic transmission ($45.35). NK2 Custom black four-spoke steering wheel, not available with N33 ($15.80). NK4 black four-spoke Sport steering wheel ($15.80). F40 heavy-duty front and rear suspension with special springs and matching shocks ($17.95). F41 Sport suspension with special front and rear stabilizers, matching rear shocks and rear axle control arms,($30.35). M40 Turbo Hydra-Matic transmission ($237.60). M20 wide-range four-speed manual transmission ($195.40). MC1 floor-mounted three-speed manual transmission ($132). Trim interior with vinyl bench seats ($19). P01 bright metal wheel covers ($26.35). ZP5 Appearance Guard group ($53.80). ZQ2 Operating Convenience group ($44.25), on sport coupe without special instrumentation includes A, B, D ($61.15). Z15 SS equipment package ($357.05). LS5 454-cid/365-hp V-8 engine in Chevelle or Malibu with Super Sport equipment, heavy-duty battery and Sport suspension

($279.10). LS6 454-cid/425-hp V-8 engine in Chevelle or Malibu with Super Sport equipment, heavy-duty battery and Sport suspension ($290.40).

1971 "HEAVY CHEVY" 400

1971 Heavy Chevy

In 1971, Chevy came out with a totally new stripped-down muscle car called the "Heavy Chevy." It came as a sports coupe only and was promoted as a car that could save enthusiasts from the high insurance rates being charged to Chevelle Super Sport owners.

The RPO YF3 Heavy Chevy option-created-model was a version of the $2,980 Malibu V-8 two-door hardtop. The package added side striping, a blacked-out grille, base Rally wheels and appropriate front fender decals that read "Heavy Chevy." An air induction hood — complete with hood pins — was an option.

How "heavy" your Heavy Chevy got was up to you. Under the hood, options started with the standard 307-cid/200-hp small-block V-8 engine. You could check other boxes for the RPO L65 power plant, which was a 350-cid V-8 with a two-barrel carburetor and 245 hp. If you needed more than that, you could opt for a 270-hp four-barrel RPO L48 version of the 350-cid engine or go all the way up to the 300-hp/400-cid (actually 402) big-block.

The Heavy Chevy coupe was available with the 300-hp V-8 was tested. A typical 0-to-60-mph time with Turbo Hydra-Matic transmission was 10.5 seconds. The quarter-mile took 16.9 seconds at 812 mph.

Series Number	Body/Style Number	Body Type & Seating	Factory Price	Shipping Weight	Production Total
MALIBU "HEAVY CHEVY" 400 — SERIES 3600 + YF3 + LS3 — V-8					
36	37	2d HT-5P	$3,295	3,460 lbs.	6,727

ENGINE

Overhead-valve. Cast-iron block and head. Bore and stroke: 4.13 x 3.76 in. Displacement: 402 cid (400 cid). Compression ratio: 8.50:1. Net brake hp: 260 at 4400 rpm. Taxable hp: 54.50. Net torque. lbs.-ft. 345 at 3200 rpm. Five main bearings. Hydraulic valve lifters. Carburetor: Four-barrel. Sales code LS3. Promoted as SS 396.

OPTIONS

C60 Four-Season air conditioning, including 61-amp Delcotron generator, heavy-duty radiator and temperature-controlled fan and requiring larger tires with some Chevelles ($407.60). G80 Positraction rear axle ($46.35). YD1 traile-ring axle ratio ($12.65). ZQ9 performance rear axle on Malibu with standard V-8 and Positraction ($12.65). T60 heavy-duty 80-amp battery ($15.60). AK1 Custom Deluxe front shoulder belts for bench seat cars ($16.90). AK1 Custom Deluxe front shoulder belts for coupe with bucket seats ($15.30). A85 Custom Deluxe front shoulder belts with bench seats ($26.35). AS4 Custom Deluxe rear shoulder belts, requires Custom deluxe seat belts ($26.35). U35 Electric clock, included with special instrumentation ($16.90). D55 Console with courtesy light, not available with standard three-speed manual transmission ($59). C50 Rear windshield defroster ($31.60). AU3 power door locks ($44.80). LS3 402-cid/300-hp V-8 engine with E78 x 14 tires ($172.75). K85 63-amp Delcotron generator with air conditioning ($5.30); without air conditioning ($26.35). A01 All windows tinted ($43.20). V30 front and rear bumper guards ($31.60). B93 door edge guards ($6.35). U14 Special instrumentation with ammeter, temperature gauge, oil pressure gauge and tachometer ($94.80). ZJ9 auxiliary lighting groups ($15.80). B37 twin front and rear floor mats ($12.65). B37 color-keyed front and rear floor mats ($12.65). D33 left-hand outside remote-control mirror ($12.65). D34 visor vanity mirror ($3.20). Two-tone paint with bright metal outline moldings ($31.60). J50 power drum brakes ($47.40). JL2 power disc brakes ($69.55). AU3 power door locks system ($46.35). N40 power steering ($115.90). V01 heavy-duty radiator with V-8 ($21.10). U63 AM push-button radio with front antenna ($66.40). U69 AM/FM radio with front antenna ($139.05). U79 AM/FM radio with front antenna and stereo ($239.10). UM1 AM radio with stereo tape deck ($200.15). UM2 AM/FM radio with setero tape deck ($372.85). U80 rear seat speaker, not available with stereo ($15.80). Vinyl roof ($94.80). K30 cruise control, requires power brakes and Turbo Hydra-Matic transmission ($63.20). N33 Comfortilt steering, requires automatic transmission ($45.35). NK2 Custom black four-spoke steering wheel, not available with N33 ($15.80). NK4 black four-spoke Sport steering wheel ($15.80). D88 Malibu sport striping package ($79 or standard with ZL2 option). F40 heavy-duty front and rear suspension with special springs and matching shocks ($17.95). F41 Sport suspension ($30.35). M40 Turbo Hydra-Matic transmission ($237.60). M20 wide-range four-speed manual transmission ($195.40). MC1 floor-mounted three-speed manual transmission with 300-hp V-8 ($132). Trim interior with vinyl bench seats ($19). A51 Strato-bucket vinyl seats ($136.95). P01 bright metal wheel covers ($26.35). P02 custom wheel covers, not available with SS equipment or special performance package ($84.30). ZP5 Appearance Guard group ($53.80). ZQ2 Operating Convenience group ($44.25), on sport coupe without special instrumentation includes A, B, D ($61.15). PX5 five F78-14/B black sidewall tires replacing five E78-14/B black sidewall tires on Malibu with 300-hp engine, includes 14 x 6-inch wheels ($23.20). PX6 five F78-14/B white stripe tires replacing five E78-14/B black sidewall tires on Malibu with 300-hp engine, includes 14 x 6-inch wheels ($53.35). Midyear Addition: VF3 Heavy Chevy package ($142.20).

CHEVROLET

1971 MALIBU SS 454

"There's still an SS 454," Chevy advised. "Any car that was named the best of its kind in *Car and Driver's* reader's choice (the 1970 Chevelle SS 454) is sure to stay around." If the muscle car era was singing its swan song, the SS 454 at least let it go out carrying a tune.

Chevelle models received changes to the front end in 1971. A new twin-level grille was divided by a bright horizontal bar. The front parking lights were moved from the bumper into the fender tips.

Although the muscle car era was in decline, there were still some hot options left. The early '70s was the era of low-cost muscle cars and "lick-'em-stick-'em" muscle cars that had the decals, but not the big-cube engines, of the recent past. Chevrolet set things up so buyers could order all of the Super Sport goodies on any Malibu sport coupe or convertible as long as it had at least a 350-cid V-8. The 400-cid V-8 was optional and the 454-cid V-8 was an exclusive option. The RPO Z15 SS package sold for $357. It included: power brakes with disc brakes up front, a black-accented grille, a special suspension, a special domed hood with functional hood lock pins, SS identification for the hood, rear deck and fenders and other stuff.

This year Chevrolet listed the net horsepower rating and gross horsepower rating for both engines. The LS5 version produced 285 net hp and 365 gross hp. The LS6 version generated 325 nhp and 425 ghp. Both came with a choice of a four-speed manual transmission or a three-speed Turbo Hydra-Matic transmission.

Series Number	Body/Style Number	Body Type & Seating	Factory Price	Shipping Weight	Production Total
MALIBU SS 454 — SERIES 3600 + Z15 + LS 5 — V-8					
36	37	2d HT-5P	$3,617	3,442 lbs.	—
36	67	2d Conv-5P	$3,897	3,767 lbs.	—
MALIBU SS 454 — SERIES 3600 + Z15 + LS 5 — V-8					
36	37	2d HT-5P	$3,628	3,442 lbs.	—
36	67	2d Conv-5P	$3,908	3,767 lbs.	—

NOTE 1: Chevrolet built an estimated 80,000 cars with the SS package.
NOTE 2: A total of 19,292 Chevelle SS models were equipped with 454-cid V-8s.

ENGINES

OPTIONAL V-8: Overhead-valve. Cast-iron block and head. Bore and stroke: 4.25 x 4.00 in. Displacement: 454 cid. Compression ratio: 8.50:1. Net brake hp: 285 at 4000 rpm. Taxable hp: 57.80. Net torque. 390 lbs.-ft. at 3200 rpm. Five main bearings. Hydraulic valve lifters. Dual exhaust. Carburetor: Four-barrel. Sales code LS5.

OPTIONAL V-8: Overhead-valve. Cast-iron block and head. Bore and stroke: 4.25 x 4.00 in. Displacement: 454 cid. Compression ratio: 9.00:1. Net brake hp: 325 at 5600 rpm. Taxable hp: 57.80. Net torque. 390 lbs.-ft. at 3600 rpm. Five main bearings. Hydraulic valve lifters. Dual exhaust. Carburetor: Four-barrel. Sales code LS6.

OPTIONS

C60 Four-Season air conditioning ($407.60). G80 Positraction rear axle (Chevelles $46.35). YD1 trailering axle ratio ($12.65). T60 heavy-duty 80-amp battery ($15.60). AK1 Custom Deluxe front shoulder belts for bench seat cars ($16.90). AK1 Custom Deluxe front shoulder belts for coupe with bucket seats ($15.30). AS4 Custom Deluxe rear shoulder belts ($26.35). U35 Electric clock, included with special instrumentation ($16.90). D55 Console with courtesy light, not available with standard three-speed manual transmission ($59). C50 Rear windshield defroster ($31.60). AU3 power door locks ($44.80). LS3 402-cid 300-hp V-8 engine with E78 x 14 tires or Super Sport package ($172.75). K85 63-amp Delcotron generator, with air conditioning ($5.30); without air conditioning ($26.35). A01 All windows tinted ($43.20). V30 front and rear bumper guards ($31.60). B93 door edge guards ($6.35). U14 Special instrumentation with ammeter, temperature gauge, oil pressure gauge and tachometer ($94.80). ZJ9 auxiliary lighting groups ($21.10). B37 twin front and rear floor mats ($12.65). B37 color-keyed front and rear floor mats ($12.65). D33 left-hand outside remote-control mirror ($12.65). D34 visor vanity mirror ($3.20). B90 window moldings ($26.35). Two-tone paint with bright metal outline moldings ($31.60). J50 power drum brakes ($47.40). JL2 power disc brakes ($69.55). AU3 power door locks system ($46.35). N40 power steering ($115.90). V01 heavy-duty radiator with V-8 engine ($21.10). U63 AM push-button radio with front antenna ($66.40). U69 AM/FM radio with front antenna ($139.05). U79 AM/FM radio with front antenna and stereo ($239.10). UM1 AM radio with stereo tape deck ($200.15). UM2 AM/FM radio with setero tape deck ($372.85). U80 rear seat speaker, not available with stereo ($15.80). Vinyl roof (Chevelle $94.80). K30 cruise control, requires power brakes and Turbo Hydra-Matic transmission ($63.20). N33 Comfortilt steering, requires automatic transmission ($45.35). NK2 Custom black four-spoke steering wheel, not available with N33 ($15.80). NK4 black four-spoke Sport steering wheel ($15.80). F40 heavy-duty front and rear suspension with special springs and matching shocks ($17.95). F41 Sport suspension with special front and rear stabilizers, matching rear shocks and rear axle control arms,($30.35). M40 Turbo Hydra-Matic transmission ($237.60). M20 wide-range four-speed manual transmission ($195.40). MC1 floor-mounted three-speed manual transmission ($132). Trim interior with vinyl bench seats ($19). P01 bright metal wheel covers ($26.35). ZP5 Appearance Guard group ($53.80). ZQ2 Operating Convenience group on sport coupe with special instrumentation includes B, D ($44.25), on sport coupe without special instrumentation includes A, B, D ($61.15). Z15 SS equipment package for sport soupe with optional V-8 ($357.05). LS5 454-cid/365-hp V-8 engine in Chevelle or Malibu with Super Sport equipment, heavy-duty battery and Sport suspension ($279.10). LS6 454-cid/365-hp V-8 engine in Chevelle or Malibu with Super Sport equipment, heavy-duty battery and Sport suspension ($290.40).

1971 MONTE CARLO SS 454

The muscle car era was winding to its untimely end, but it wasn't for lack of enthusiasts willing to buy such cars. Nor was it the doing of Detroit's "Big Three." New government rules about pollution and safety were forcing the issue, while insurance companies were using drastic rate hikes to make muscle cars prohibitively expensive to operate. The government requirements for product certification also absorbed money and time, making it harder and expensive to do annual product revisions. A touch of greater distinction was added to the Monte Carlo Super Sport option, which now featured a blackout-style rear beauty panel and "SS 454" identification on the lower front fenders. There was also an "SS" badge on the rear beauty panel.

The best news was that muscle car lovers could now order two versions of the 454-cid V-8 in the Monte Carlo and both provided more horsepower than the base 350.. Monte Carlo SS 454s came standard with a three-speed Turbo Hydra-Matic automatic transmission. The only transmission option was a fully synchronized four-speed manual transmission with a floor-mounted gear shifter, and this option was a special-order item only. The SS 454 package included all of the same goodies it featured in 1970, such as heavy-duty front and rear springs, heavy-duty shocks with automatic level control and heavy front and rear stabilizer bars.

Of course, with the government and the insurance industry breathing down its neck, Chevrolet didn't promote the Monte Carlo SS very heavily and production for the model year dropped nearly 50 percent. It was the last year for the Monte Carlo SS 454. Only 1,919 of these cars were built.

Series Number	Body/Style Number	Body Type & Seating	Factory Price	Shipping Weight	Production Total
MONTE CARLO SS 454 — SERIES 3800 — V-8					
38	57	2d HT-5P	$3,901	3,488 lbs.	1,919

NOTE 1: An unspecified, but extremely limited number of cars were ordered with the LS6 454-cid V-8.

ENGINES

BASE V-8: Overhead valve. Cast-iron block and head. Bore and stroke: 4.25 x 4.00 in. Displacement: 454 cid. Compression ratio: 8.50:1. Gross Brake hp: 365 at 4800 rpm. Net brake hp: 285 at 4000 rpm. Taxable hp: 57.80. Net torque: 390 at 3200 rpm. Five main bearings. Dual exhaust. Carburetor: Four-barrel. Engine code: CPA, CPG, CPP, CPR and CPD.

OPTIONAL V-8: Overhead valve. Cast-iron block and head. Bore and stroke: 4.25 x 4.00 in. Displacement: 454 cid. Compression ratio: 9.00:1. Net brake hp: 325 at 5600 rpm. Taxable hp: 57.80. Net torque: 390 at 3600 rpm. Five main bearings. Dual exhaust. Carburetor: Four-barrel. Engine code: CPP, CPR and CPZ.

OPTIONS

Air conditioning ($408). Vinyl top ($126). AM/FM stereo ($239). Power windows ($127). Monte Carlo SS 454 package ($485). Wide-ratio four-speed manual transmission with floor shift.

1972 "HEAVY CHEVY" 400 (402)

This car was Chevy's last-ditch effort to keep the muscle car flame burning, but not too many folks drove their Heavy Chevy to the levy and the package died off after just 18 months. A few of the cars carried enough performance options to put them in the muscle car category and there's no doubt that they are rare.

The RPO YF3 Heavy Chevy option-created-model was again a "muscle-car-image" version of the Malibu V-8 two-door hardtop. It added special side striping (in a choice of black or white colors), a black-accented radiator grille, Heavy Chevy decals, a special domed hood with hood locking pins, 4 x 6-inch Rally-type wheels with bright lug nuts and special Rally wheel center caps. The package had a wholesale price of $107.64 and a retail price of $138. With that kind or mark-up, it's no wonder that dealers didn't push them out the door.

You could order a Heavy Chevy with engine options up to the "400." The 400-cid V-8 was available in only one version with a 240-hp rating.

Series Number	Body/Style Number	Body Type & Seating	Factory Price	Shipping Weight	Production Total
MALIBU "HEAVY CHEVY" 400 —SERIES D + YF3 + LS3 — V-8					
D	37	2d HT-5P	$3,232	3,460 lbs.	9,508

ENGINE

OPTIONAL V-8: Overhead valve. Cast-iron block and head. Bore and stroke: 4.13 x 3.76 in. Displacement: 402 cid (400 cid). Compression ratio: 8.50:1. Net brake hp: 240 at 4400 rpm. Taxable hp: 54.50. Net torque. 345 at 3200 rpm. Five main bearings. Hydraulic valve lifters. Carburetor: CLA, CLB, CTA, CTB, CLS, CTJ and CTH. VIN code: U.

OPTIONS

C60 Four-Season air conditioning, including 61-amp Delcotron generator, heavy-duty radiator and temperature-controlled fan and requiring larger tires with some Chevelles ($397.60). G80 Positraction rear axle ($45). ZQ9 performance rear axle on Malibu with standard V-8 and Positraction ($12). YD1 trailering axle ratio with 350-cid V-8s or 402-cid V-8, required heavy-duty suspension and positraction ($12). Y60 heavy-duty 80-amp battery ($15). AK1 Custom Deluxe color-keyed seat belts ($16). AK1 Custom Deluxe color-keyed seat belts with bucket seats and two front shoulder belts ($14.50). V30 front and rear bumper guards ($31). U35 Electric clock, included with special instrumentation ($16). D55 Console with floor-mounted shift, rear seat courtesy light and luggage compartment light, bucket seats and optional transmission required ($57). C50 rear windshield defroster ($31). AU3 power door locks ($44.80). LS3 402-cid V-8 engine in Malibu with E78 x 14 tires ($168). K85 63-amp Delcotron generator, with air conditioning ($5); without air conditioning ($26). A01 all windows tinted ($42). ZL2/YF8 cowl-induction hood, includes white or black striping ($154). U14 special instrumentation package ($82). ZJ9 auxiliary lighting group ($21). B37 twin front and rear floor mats ($12). D33 Left-hand outside remote-control mirror ($12). D34 visor vanity mirror ($3). Two-tone paint with bright metal outline moldings ($31). J50 power drum brakes ($46). JL2 power disc brakes ($68). AU3 power door locks system ($45). N40 power steering ($113). V01 heavy-duty radiator with six-cylinder engine ($14). V01 heavy-duty radiator with V-8 engine ($21). U63 AM push-button radio with front antenna ($65). U69 AM/FM radio with front antenna ($135). U79 AM/FM radio with front antenna and stereo ($233). UM1 AM radio with stereo tape deck ($195). UM2 AM/FM radio with setero tape deck ($363). U80 rear seat speaker ($15). Vinyl roof ($92). K30 cruise control, requires power brakes and Turbo Hydra-Matic transmission ($62). N33 Comfortilt steering, requires automatic transmission ($44). NK2 Custom black four-spoke steering wheel, not available with N33 ($15). NK4 black four-spoke sport steering wheel ($15). D88 Malibu sport striping package ($77). F40 special front and rear suspension ($17). F41 Sport suspension for Chevelle/Malibu with 240-hp V-8 ($30). M40 Turbo Hydra-Matic transmission ($231). M20 wide-range four-speed manual transmission ($190). M22 special close-ratio four-speed manual transmission ($231). MC1 floor-mounted three-speed manual transmission for Chevelles with 240-hp V-8 ($128). A51 vinyl bench seat for Chevelles ($18). A51 Strato-bucket cloth or vinyl ($133). F01 bright metal wheel covers ($26). F02 Custom wheel covers, not available with special performance package ($82). ZJ7 Rallye wheels, including special wheels, hubcaps and trim rings ($44). ZP5 Appearance Guard group ($52). ZQ2 Operating Convenience group ($43), on sport coupe without special instrumentation includes A, B, D ($59). VF3 Heavy Chevy package for Chevelle V-8 coupes, includes black-accented grille, special side striping, "Heavy Chevy" hood decal, "Heavy Chevy" front fender decal, "Heavy Chevy" rear deck lid decal, special domed hood with locking pins and 14 x 6-in. Rallye-type wheels with bright lug nuts and center caps ($142.20). ZL2/YF8 Cowl-induction hood package ($154). PK2 G78-14 white sidewall tires. PL3 E78-14 white stripe tires. PM6 G78-14 white stripe tires. PM7 F60-15 white-letter tires. PU8 G78-15 white stripe tires. PX6 F78-14 white sidewall tires.

CHEVROLET

1972 CAMARO RS/SS 396

JERRY HEASLEY

1972 Camaro SS

This was the last year for the SS package and the last year for the big-block. Chevy was backing out of the muscle car niche and the '72 SS 396 was another step in that direction. Oh how things had changed in a few short years — and not for the best.

The 1972 Camaro was promoted as "the closest thing to a Vette yet." It was almost identical in general appearance to the 1971 model, but had a slightly coarser grille mesh and high-back bucket seats. The RPO Z27 Super Sport or SS package was a factory option that cost Chevrolet dealers $237.90 and retailed for $306.35. It was available for V-8-powered Camaros with four-speed or Turbo Hydra-Matic transmission.

The SS option added the 200-hp Turbo-Fire 350 V-8. A 240-hp "396 Turbo-Jet" (actually 402-cid) V-8 was optional for cars with the SS package. Like the smaller 350, the optional "396" V-8 came with chrome dress-up parts, heavy-duty engine mounts and a heavy-duty starter. On Camaro SS 396 models the rear body panel was finished in black and the buyer got a heavy-duty Sport suspension with front and rear stabilizer bars and special shock absorbers. The 240-hp engine was not available for cars being registered in California.

The RPO Z22 Rally Sport package was a factory option that cost Chevrolet dealers $92.04 and retailed for $118. The Rally Sport option added a special black-finished grille with Argent Silver accents, a special rubber-tipped vertical grille center bar, a smaller grille grid pattern (identical to the 1971 Rally Sport grille), and other exterior goodies.

Model Number	Body/Style Number	Body Type & Seating	Factory Price	Shipping Weight	Production Total
CAMARO SS 396 — SERIES 24 — V-8					
24	87	2d HT	$3,222	—	970

ENGINE

OPTIONAL V-8: 90-degree, overhead valve. Cast-iron block and head. Bore & stroke: 4.13 x 3.76 in. Displacement: 402 cid . Compression ratio: 8.5:1. Brakehp: 240 at 4400 rpm. Torque: 345 at 3200 rpm. Five main bearings. Hydraulic valve lifters. Induction system: Rochester no. 7042118 four-barrel carburetor. Optional in Camaro SS; not available in other models. Sales code: LS3. VIN Code: U.

OPTIONS

AK1 color-keyed seat and shoulder belts ($14.50). AN6 adjustable seatback ($18). A01 Soft-Ray tinted glass ($39). 37 color-keyed floor mats ($12). B84 body side moldings ($33). B93 door edge guard moldings ($6). C08 vinyl roof cover ($87). C24 Hide-A-Way windshield wipers ($21). C50 rear window defogger ($31). C60 Four-Season air conditioning ($397). D34 visor-vanity mirror ($3). D35 sport mirror ($15). D55 center console ($57). D80 front and rear spoilers ($77). F41 sport suspension ($30). G80 positraction rear axle ($45). J50 power brakes ($46). LS3 402-cid "396 Turbo-Jet 240-hp V-8 ($96). M20 four-speed wide-ratio manual transmission ($200). M21 four-speed close-ratio manual transmission ($200). M40 Turbo Hydra-Matic automatic transmission with Camaros SS with optional LS3 V-8 ($231). NK4 sport steering wheel ($15). N33 Comfortilt steering wheel ($44). N40 power steering ($130). PL3 E-78-14 white sidewall tires ($28). PL4 F70-14 white letter tires ($82.85). PY4 F70-14 white sidewall tires ($69.85). PO1 bright metal wheel trim covers ($26). P02 custom wheel trim covers ($82). U35 electric clock ($16). U63 AM radio ($65). U69 AM/FM radio ($135). U80 rear seat speaker ($15). VF3 deluxe front and rear bumpers ($36). V01 heavy-duty radiator ($14). YD1 trailering axle ratio ($12). YF5 California emissions test ($15). ZJ7 Rally wheels with trim rings ($44). ZJ9 auxiliary lighting ($17.50). ZJ9 auxiliary lighting with Z54 Quiet Sound group or Type LT ($15). Z21 style trim ($56). Z22 Rally Sport package ($118). Z27 Camaro Super Sport package ($306.35).

1972 CAMARO Z28

CHEVROLET

DAN LYONS

1972 Camaro Z28

The RPO Z/28 Special Performance package was a factory option that cost Chevrolet dealers $597.48 and retailed for $769.15. It was available for V-8-powered Camaros in two versions.

The Z28/YF8 version included black striping and the Z28/ZR8 version included white striping. In addition, the Z28 came with an exclusive 255-hp Turbo-Fire 350 V-8, finned aluminum rocker covers, bright engine accents, dual sport style outside rearview mirrors (left-hand remote-control), special instrumentation, power brakes, a 3.73:1 positraction rear axle, dual exhausts, a black-finished grille, Z28 emblems, rear bumper guards, a sport suspension with heavy-duty springs and front and rear stabilizer bars, heavy-duty engine mounts, a heavy-duty starter, a heavy-duty radiator, 15 x 7-in. wheels with bright lug nuts, special wheel center caps, wheel trim rings, F60-15/B bias-belted white-letter tires, Z28 decals and special paint stripes on the hood and rear deck lid.

A four-speed manual or Turbo Hydra-Matic transmission was required at extra cost and air conditioning, wheel covers or Rally wheels were not available. It was possible to order a Z28 in 1972 and delete the hood and deck lid stripes.

A road test in the August 1972 issue of *Motor Trend* involved a Z/28 with the 350-cid/255-hp V-8, four-speed manual transmission and 3.73:1 rear axle. The car did 0-to-60 mph in 7.7 seconds and the quarter-mile in 15.2 seconds at 86.6 mph.

ENGINE

ENGINE: 90-degree, overhead valve. Cast-iron block and head. Bore & stroke: 4.00 x 3.48 in. Displacement: 350 cid (5.7 liters). Compression ratio: 9.0:1. Brake hp: 255 at 5600 rpm. Torque: 280 at 4000 rpm. Five main bearings. Hydraulic valve lifters. Induction system: Rochester no. 7042202 four-barrel carburetor. Standard in Camaro Z/28; not available in other Camaros. VIN Code: L.

Model Number	Body/Style Number	Body Type & Seating	Factory Price	Shipping Weight	Production Total
CAMARO Z/28 — SERIES 24 + Z/28 —					
(V-8 WITH FOUR-SPEED MANUAL TRANSMISSION)					
24	87	2d HT	$3,789	—	Note 1
CAMARO Z/28 — SERIES 24 + Z/28 —					
(V-8 WITH TURBO HYDRA-MATIC TRANSMISSION)					
24	87	2d HT	$3,886	—	Note 1

NOTE 1: Model year production of 1972 Camaro Z/28 coupes was 2,575.

OPTIONS

AK1 color-keyed seat and shoulder belts ($14.50). AN6 adjustable seatback ($18). A01 Soft-Ray tinted glass ($39). 37 color-keyed floor mats ($12). B84 body side moldings ($33). B93 door edge guard moldings ($6). C08 vinyl roof cover ($87). C24 Hide-A-Way windshield wipers ($21). C50 rear window defogger ($31). C60 Four-Season air conditioning ($397). D34 visor-vanity mirror ($3). D35 sport mirror ($15). D55 center console ($57). D80 front and rear spoilers ($77). F41 sport suspension ($30). G80 positraction rear axle ($45). J50 power brakes ($46). LS3 402-cid "396 Turbo-Jet 240-hp V-8 ($96). L65 350-cid 165-hp four-barrel V-8 ($26). M20 four-speed wide-ratio manual transmission ($200). M21 four-speed close-ratio manual transmission ($200). M22 heavy-duty four-speed close-ratio manual transmission. M35 Powerglide automatic transmission with six-cylinder engine ($174). M35 Powerglide automatic transmission with V-8 engine ($185). M40 Turbo Hydra-Matic automatic transmission with Z/28 ($297). M40 Turbo Hydra-Matic automatic transmission with Camaros SS with optional LS3 V-8 ($231). M40 Turbo Hydra-Matic automatic transmission with other Camaros ($210). NK4 sport steering wheel ($15). N33 Comfortilt steering wheel ($44). N40 power steering ($130). PL3 E-78-14 white sidewall tires ($28). PL4 F70-14 white letter tires ($82.85). PY4 F70-14 white sidewall tires ($69.85). PO1 bright metal wheel trim covers ($26). P02 custom wheel trim covers ($82). U35 electric clock ($16). U63 AM radio ($65). U69 AM/FM radio ($135). U80 rear seat speaker ($15). VF3 deluxe front and rear bumpers ($36). V01 heavy-duty radiator ($14). YD1 trailering axle ratio ($12). YF5 California emissions test ($15). ZJ7 Rally wheels with trim rings ($44). ZJ9 auxiliary lighting ($17.50). ZJ9 auxiliary lighting with Z54 Quiet Sound group or Type LT ($15). Z21 style trim ($56). Z22 Rally Sport package ($118). Z27 Camaro Super Sport package ($306.35). Z/28 special performance package ($769.15). Z87 custom interior ($113).

CHRYSLER

CHRYSLER MUSCLE 1960-65

The year 1955 also brought the introduction of the mighty Chrysler 300 Letter Car, which was immediately embraced by enthusiastic buyers. The Chrysler 300 earned championship titles in both NASCAR Grand National and AAA stock car racing.

In 1956, the second Chrysler Letter Car, dubbed the 300B, was offered in two horsepower ratings. This helped it bring more fame to the company through repeated achievements on the nation's stock car racing tracks. The 300B broke the world's passenger car speed record in competition at Daytona Beach, Fla., with an average of nearly 140 mph.

By 1957, a new direction in styling was unleashed by Exner and his talented staff. This new "Forward Look," with its graceful tailfins, took numerous styling awards. The major chassis development, which was to remain a Chrysler forte into the 1980s (on some models), was a torsion bar front suspension. *Motor Trend* magazine awarded the 1957 Chrysler its highest honor — the "Car of the Year" title. Its superb handling qualities and engineering characteristics were the main reasons for the award.

Model year 1958 brought a minor face lifting. The first-generation hemispherical (Hemi) engine was also in its last year. An electronic fuel injection system, designed by Bendix, was briefly made available as an option on the latest 300D Letter Car. In 1959, Chrysler 300 styling was modestly changed, but a brand-new "Golden Lion" V-8 arrived. It was larger in displacement than its predecessor and used a wedge-shaped combustion chamber design.

A new era for Chrysler began in 1960, as a switch to building unitized bodies was made. These "Uni-Body" cars were styled with the customary tailfins, although they were more rakish in overall design. A major engineering feat was the introduction of ram-induction manifolding.

The 1961 models were again slightly facelifted. The major degree of change was reflected in frontal appearance and at the rear, with alterations to the headlights and taillamps. By 1962, tailfins were no longer the order of the day. A new mid-priced 300 series was offered, but the true high-performance Letter Car 300 series continued.

Styling in 1963 was totally revamped. A clean, slab-sided look evolved. To the dismay of management, sales dropped and Chrysler remained America's 11th-largest automaker. A five-year or 50,000-mile warranty on all drivetrain components became a marketing tool to boost confidence and spur extra sales. A slight styling revision was seen for 1964 and sales climbed over 30 percent. Unfortunately, the company remained at the number 11 slot.

Freshly styled 1965 models helped set a blistering, all-time sales record. National economic gains, combined with the extended warranty program, established an excellent business climate and generated a 65 percent sales gain. But, thereafter, styling stayed basically unchanged until the 1969 model year. And why not, since Chrysler had continued to break records, reaching more and more buyers every season. For the 1966 to 1968 period, the company placed ninth or 10th in sales each year.

1960 CHRYSLER 300F

1960 Chrysler 300F

The sixth edition of the letter series 300 continued its tradition as a high-performance vehicle. Besides the all-new styling and unibody construction, big improvements in engineering were evident with the unveiling of a Ram-Tuned induction manifold option. Chrysler's dropping the Hemi in 1959 hurt the 300's high-performance image. Even though the first "Golden Lion" wedge-head V-8 was shown to be equally as potent (92 mph in the quarter-mile), the loss of the Hemi created a vacuum. In 1960, the vacuum was filled by providing the 300F with a ram-inducted 413-cid V-8. Ram-tuning had long been a means of raising torque and horsepower for drag racing. Chrysler engineers adapted this idea with cross-over ram induction manifolds, which placed one bank of cylinder's carburetor on the far side of the opposing bank of cylinder's carburetor. No longer were the carburetors placed inline, between the cylinder heads, as on previous dual-carbureted 300s.

Two horsepower versions were available in 1960 and a few cars (seven to 10, including at least one convertible) were built with the French Pont-A-Mousson four-speed gearbox. Engine hardware common to both ram-tuned engines included a hot cam, heavy-duty valve springs, a low-back-pressure exhaust system, a dual-point distributor, a low-restriction air cleaner, special spark plugs and the dual-quad carbs. The carbs were mounted on a wild-looking cross-ram manifold that put one air cleaner on each side of the engine. The stacks were 30 inches long and had to be crisscrossed to fit under the hood. At low speeds, the "long" rams worked great, but they hurt performance above 4,000 rpm. To solve the problem, engineers

removed a section of the inner walls of the manifolds to create the optional 400-hp engine. On the outside, these "short" rams looked the same, but they were effectively 15 inches long.

All New Yorker standard features were included on the 300F, plus power swivel seats. White sidewall nylon tires were also standard.

Model Number	Body/Style Number	Body Type & Seating	Factory Price	Shipping Weight	Production Total
300F — SERIES PC3-300 — V-8					
PC3-300	842	2d HT-5P	$5,411	4,270 lbs.	964
PC3-300	845	2dr Conv-5P	$5,841	4,310 lbs.	248

ENGINES

BASE "LONG RAM" V-8: Overhead valve. Cast-iron block. Bore and stroke: 4.18 x 3.75 inches. Displacement: 413 cid. Compression ratio: 10.10:1. Brake hp: 375 at 5000 rpm. Taxable hp: 55.90. Torque: 495 at 2800 rpm. Five main bearings. Hydraulic valve lifters. Dual exhaust. Carburetor: "Long" Ram Induction intake manifold with two Carter AFB-2903-S four-barrel carburetors. Engine code: P-41.

OPTIONAL "SHORT RAM" V-8: Overhead valve. Cast-iron block. Bore and stroke: 4.18 x 3.75 inches. Displacement: 413 cid. Compression ratio: 10.10:1. Brake hp: 400 at 5200 rpm. Taxable hp: 55.90. Torque: 465 at 3600 rpm. Five main bearings. Solid valve lifters. Dual exhaust. Carburetor: "Short" Ram Induction intake manifold with two Carter AFB-2903-S four-barrel carburetors. Engine code: P-41. (NOTE: Limited production V-8. The external legnth of the "long" and "short" rams was the same, but the interior length varied.)

OPTIONS

Power seat ($102). Air conditioning ($510). Heater ($102). Golden tone radio ($100). Golden tone with touch tuner ($124). Rear seat speaker ($17). Power antenna ($26). Auto-Pilot ($486). Automatic beam changer ($44). Rear window defogger ($21). Sure Grip differential ($52). Solex glass ($43). Two-tone paint ($20). Vacuum door locks ($37).

1961 CHRYSLER 300G

CHRYSLER

CLIFF GROMER

1961 Chrysler 300G

Car Life called the Chrysler 300G "the best road car on the market." Chrysler called it "the brand-new 1961 version of Chrysler's championship breed of rare motorcars. The 300G could do 0-to-60 mph in 8.4 seconds, and 0-to-100 mph in 21.2 seconds. The quarter mile took 16.2 seconds at 87.4 mph. Top speed of the 300G was reported by *Car Life* to be 131 mph. At Daytona, a 300G running with the optional 2.93:1 axle ratio won the NASCAR Flying Mile Championship with a two-way average of 143.0 mph. A 300G also won the NASCAR Standing Mile Championship with a speed of 90.7 mph.

The 300G was still considered a part of the high-performance market by those who appreciated brute horsepower in a luxury automobile. It was a limited-edition automobile, precision built for the connoisseur of careful craftsmanship and superb engineering.

Its styling mirrored the minor styling changes found in the other 1961 Chryslers. The car's appearance was altered by the use of an inverted grille shape and the relocation of the tail lights from the fins to above the rear bumper.

The 300G continued to use Chrysler's 413-cid wedge V-8 with 375 hp at 5000 rpm and 495 lbs.-ft. of torque at 2800 rpm. This engine had 30-inch ram-induction tubes that increased torque up to 10 percent in the mid-engine range. Dual Carter four-barrel carbs were carried over. As with the 300F, Chrysler offered a 400-hp option for the 300G. This V-8 had solid lifters, "short" induction tubes, slightly larger carburetors and a longer-duration (284- to 268-degree) cam. The short rams reduced maximum torque to 465 lbs.-ft. at 3600 rpm. The 300G's standard axle ratio was 3.23:1. This change gave

the G a slight top speed advantage over the F. The standard transmission for the 300G was a heavy-duty TorqueFlite with increased oil pressure and stronger internal components. With ratios of 2.45, 1.45 and 1.00:1 plus a maximum stall ratio of 2.2:1, this push-button-controlled transmission gave outstanding performance. Replacing the four-speed Pont-a-Mousson manual transmission as an alternative to TorqueFlite was a heavy-duty three-speed Chrysler-built gearbox. A manual transmission 300G had almost identical acceleration times as the TorqueFlite version.

Model Number	Body/Style Number	Body Type & Seating	Factory Price	Shipping Weight	Production Total
300G — SERIES RC4P — V-8					
RC4-P	842	2d HT-5P	$5,411	4,260 lbs.	1,280
RC4-P	845	2d Conv-5P	$5,841	4,315 lbs.	337

ENGINES

BASE "LONG RAM" V-8: Overhead valve. Cast-iron block. Bore and stroke: 4.18 x 3.75 inches. Displacement: 413 cid. Compression ratio: 10.10:1. Brake hp: 375 at 5000 rpm. Taxable hp: 55.90. Torque: 495 at 2800 rpm. Five main bearings. Hydraulic valve lifters. Dual exhaust. Carburetors: Two Carter Type AFB Model 2903S four-barrel. Engine code: R-41.

OPTIONAL "SHORT RAM" V-8: Overhead valve. Cast-iron block. Bore and stroke: 4.18 x 3.75 inches. Displacement: 413 cid. Compression ratio: 10.10:1. Brake hp: 400 at 5000 rpm. Taxable hp: 55.90. Torque: 465 at 3600 rpm. Five main bearings. Solid valve lifters. Dual exhaust. Carburetors: Two Carter Type AFB Model 2903S four-barrel. Engine code: R-41.

OPTIONS

Power seat ($102). Swivel seat ($87). Heater ($102). Air conditioner, all except station wagons ($510). Air conditioner, in station wagons ($714). Golden Tone radio ($100). Golden Touch Tuner radio ($124). Power antenna ($26). Rear window defogger ($21). Sure Grip differential ($52). Left-hand outside remote mirror ($18). Tinted glass ($43). Closed crankcase vent system ($5).

1962 CHRYSLER 300H

CHRYSLER

PHIL KUNZ

1962 Chrysler 300H

The Chrysler Letter Car was a legend in its own time, but after eight years, its time was beginning to run out. For 1962, Highland Park (Chrysler headquarters) decided to cash in on the 300's high-performance reputation by offering a series of non-letter Sport 300s. These cars used a milder 383-cid two-barrel V-8 as standard equipment and shared their 122-inch wheelbase with Chrysler's low-priced Newport line.

The real Letter Car was still offered. The true high-performance 300 used the same series designation as the Sport Series 300, but serial number identification was different. However, it was now based on the same, smaller platform to hold down production costs. This 300H came in the traditional two-door hardtop and convertible models. The shorter wheelbase actually shaved about 300 lbs. off its curb weight and therefore increased the horsepower-per-pound factor. At the same time, the standard 413-cid V-8 was boosted to 380 hp, five more than the 1961 300G offered.

The lighter weight and higher horsepower resulted in an excellent performing car. With just 10.6 lbs. to move with each unit of power, the H had the best power-to-weight ratio seen in any Letter Car. It did 0-to-60 mph in the same 7.7 seconds as the Hemi-motivated 1957 300C. And it covered the quarter-mile in 16 seconds. This tied the Ram-tuned 1960 Chrysler 300F for elapsed time.

A very interesting item was mentioned in *Motor Trend's* "Spotlight on Detroit" column in the magazine's June 1962 issue. It read, "You can now order 426 cubic inches on any

Chrysler 300 or 300H. Factory 413-cid blocks bored .060 are available on special order ... This top engine is rated 421 hp at 5400 rpm. Chrysler Division isn't going in for any dragging like Dodge and Plymouth, but they will supply the hot stuff if you want it." The 426-cid V-8 came in 373-, 385-, 413- and 421-hp versions with the top options featuring dual four-barrel carburetors. The 426 engine carried the code S-42.

Standard equipment for the 300H didn't cut any corners, either. It included an interior with four bucket seats done in tan leather. Other colors of leather were available on special order. Two big four-barrel carburetors sat atop the base engine, continuing a long-standing Letter Car feature. And a 405-hp Ram-tuned engine was an exclusive-to-the-300H option. Another big difference between the 300H and earlier Letter Cars was its lack of tailfins. The combination of decreased size, less distinction and corporate changes in thinking teamed up to make the Chrysler 300H a rare car.

Model Number	Body/Style Number	Body Type & Seating	Factory Price	Shipping Weight	Production Total
300H — SERIES SC2-M — V-8					
SC2-M	842	2d HT-5P	$5,090	4,050 lbs.	435
SC2-M	845	2d Conv-5P	$5,461	4,105 lbs.	123

ENGINES

BASE V-8: Overhead valve. Cast-iron block. Bore and stroke: 4.18 x 3.75 inches. Displacement: 413 cid. Compression ratio: 10.10:1. Brake hp: 380 at 5200 rpm. Taxable hp: 55.90. Torque: 450 at 3600 rpm. Five main bearings. Solid valve lifters. Dual exhaust. Carburetor: Two Carter carburetors, (front) AFB Model 3258-S four-barrel; (rear) AFB Model 3259-S four-barrel. Engine code: S-41.

CHRYSLER

OPTIONAL V-8 (SHORT RAM): Overhead valve. Cast-iron block. Bore and stroke: 4.18 x 3.75 inches. Displacement: 413 cid. Compression ratio: 10.10:1. Brake hp: 405. Taxable hp: 55.90. Five main bearings. Solid valve lifters. Dual exhaust. Carburetors: Two Carter Type AFB Model 2903S four-barrel. Engine code: R-41.

OPTIONS

Power brakes ($48). Power steering ($108). Air conditioning ($510). Dual Deluxe air conditioning ($714). Power radio antenna ($26). Auto-Pilot ($86).

Rear window defogger ($21). Vacuum door locks ($56). Custom Conditionaire heater ($102). Left outside remote con¬trol mirror ($18). Power door locks ($56). Front power seat ($102). Rear shelf radio speaker ($17). Golden Tone radio ($93). Golden Touch Tone radio ($129). Tinted windshield ($29). Tinted glass, all windows ($43). Shaded backlight ($74). Leather front bucket seats ($201). Variable speed windshield wipers ($6). Undercoating ($18). V-8 413-cid/405-hp ram-induction engine. Positive traction rear axle ($52). Available rear axle gear ratios: 2.93:1; 3.23:1.

1963 CHRYSLER 300J

1963 Chrysler 300J

All Chrysler 300 Letter Cars deserve recognition as "beautiful brutes," but the 300J has the added distinction of also being a rare, beautiful brute when new. Only 400 were produced, so a sighting nowadays is worth celebrating.

Like the original C300 and 300B models, the 300J was available only as a two-door hardtop. The 300J was available in five colors: Formal Black, Alabaster, Madison Gray, Oyster White and Claret. Adding a touch of class were the two pin stripes (in a contrasting color) that ran the length of the body and 300J medallions situated on the C-pillar and the rear deck. The interior featured the controversial square steering wheel that many drivers found uncomfortable, but the outstanding design of the front bucket seats (finished in claret red leather), plus vinyl door panel trimming, color-coordinated claret carpeting and a center console with a built-in tachometer served as at least partial redemptions for this lapse of judgment by Chrysler. A feature unique to Chryslers that was found on the 300J were windshield wiper blades fitted with airfoils to press the blade against the windshield at high speeds.

Only one engine was offered for the 300J — Chrysler's 413-cid wedge-head V-8. This engine, with mechanical lifters and a compression ratio of 10.0:1, had ratings of 390 hp at 4800 rpm and 485 lbs.-ft. of torque at 3600 rpm. Dual four-barrel AFB 3505S carburetors were used on a special cross-ram intake manifold.

Performance of the 300J paralleled or exceeded that of many smaller and lighter vehicles. *Motor Trend*, April 1963, reported a 0-to-60-mph time of 8.0 seconds and a quarter-mile time and speed of 15.8 seconds at 89 mph in a Torqueflite-equipped 300J running with a 3.23:1 axle ratio. The true forte of the 300J was its top speed, which was in excess of 142 mph. Some sources indicate that the 426-cid V-8 (see 1962) was offered for 1963 Chryslers with 373-, 415- and 425-hp ratings. The 426 engine code was T-42.

The 300J was a thoroughbred American grand touring car that maintained a tradition of excellence, which today gives it a status unique among performance automobiles. What a pity there aren't enough to go around!

Model Number	Body/Style Number	Body Type & Seating	Factory Price	Shipping Weight	Production Total
300J — SERIES TC2-M — V-8					
TC2-M	842	2dr HT-6P	$5,260	4,000 lbs.	400

ENGINE

BASE V-8: Overhead valve. Cast-iron block. Bore and stroke: 4.18 x 3.75 inches. Displacement: 413 cid. Compression ratio: 9.60:1. Brake hp: 390 at 4800 rpm. Taxable hp: 56.20. Torque: 485 at 3600 rpm. Five main bearings. Solid valve lifters. Dual exhaust. Carburetor: Two Carter Type AFB four-barrel Model 3505-S. Engine code: T-41.

OPTIONS

Air conditioning with heater ($150). Power antenna, except station wag¬ons ($26). Auto-Pilot ($86). Front console in 300 ($165). Rear window defogger ($21). Custom Conditionaire heater ($102). Left outside remote control mirror ($18). Left or right power bucket seat ($93). Power door locks in four-door ($56). Power front bench seat ($102). Power windows ($108). Golden Tone radio ($93). Golden Touch Tune radio ($13). Rear speaker, except convertible ($17). Pair of front seat belts ($24). Tinted windshield ($29). All tinted glass ($43). Leather trim in 300 hardtop and convertible ($93). Undercoating ($18). V-8 413-cid/360-hp twin four-barrel carb engine ($162). V-8 413-cid/365-hp twin four-barrel carb engine. V-8 426-cid/373-hp twin four-barrel carb engine. V-8 426-cid/415-hp short ram engine. V-8 426-cid/425-hp short ram engine. Positive traction rear axle ($52).

1964 CHRYSLER 300K

BOB SCHWARTZ

1964 Chrysler 300K

The convertible returned to the Chrysler 300 Letter Car series lineup after a one-year hiatus. Styling paralleled the regular 300 series, although interiors were more luxuriously detailed. A between-the-seat console was standard and leather trim was optional. A Ram-Tuned induction manifold setup was available as an option. The 1964 Chrysler 300-K was the most popular Chrysler Letter Car — at least with new-car buyers. While it can be argued that the later Letter Cars lacked the performance that the earlier models abounded in, they were still among the fastest-accelerating cars of their era. Hoever, the competition was getting hotter and would soon pull ahead.

The 300K's standard engine was the 413-cid V-8 with a 360-hp rating, but for $375 you could order the 390-hp/413-cid power plant that featured twin Carter AFB four-barrel carbs on a short-ram intake manifold. This was the last year for the optional availability of the Ram-tuned induction V-8. For transmissions, a TorqueFlite automatic was standard and a new four-speed manual gearbox was optional.

The 1964 Chrysler got only mild styling changes, but the Chrysler 300-K did get some much-needed attention. A convertible returned along with lower prices. The 300K's attractively styled interior also featured bucket-type seats and a console. Leather trim was now optional at just $93 extra. When the counting of 300-K's was done at the end of the 1964 model year, a grand total of 3,647 units had been. That topped the 1957 Chrysler 300-C's record of 2,402.

Model Number	Body/Style Number	Body Type & Seating	Factory Price	Shipping Weight	Production Total
300K — SERIES VC2-M — V-8					
VC2-M	300842	2d HT-4P	$4,056	3,965 lbs.	3,022
VC2-M	300845	2d Conv-4P	$4,522	3,990 lbs.	625

ENGINES

BASE V-8: Overhead valve. Cast-iron block. Bore and stroke: 4.18 x 3.75 inches. Displacement: 413 cid. Compression ratio: 10.10:1. Brake hp: 360 at 4800 rpm. Taxable hp: 56.20. Torque: 470 at 3200 rpm. Five main bearings. Hydraulic valve lifters. Dual exhaust. Carburetor: Carter AFB-3614-S four-barrel. Engine code: V-41.

OPTIONAL V-8: Overhead valve. Cast-iron block. Bore and stroke: 4.18 x 3.75 inches. Displacement: 413 cid. Compression ratio: 9.60:1. Brake hp: 390 at 4800 rpm. Taxable hp: 56.20. Torque: 485 at 3600 rpm. Five main bearings. Solid valve lifters. Dual exhaust. Carburetor: Two Carter Type AFB four-barrel Model 3505-SA. Engine code: V-41.

OPTIONS

Power windows ($108). Heater and defroster all models ($102). Air conditioning ($510). Deluxe dual air conditioning, all except convertibles ($714). Golden Tone radio ($93). AM/FM radio ($157). Golden Touch Tuner radio ($129). Center Console in all 300 models ($129). Leather trim in 300K ($94). Leather trim ($72). Seat belts ($7). Heavy-duty springs, shocks, sway bar and brakes ($36). Adjustable steering wheel ($47). Undercoating ($18). Tinted glass, all windows ($43). Close-ratio four-speed manual floor shift was optional ($227). V-8 413-cid/360-hp four-barrel carb engine ($43). V-8 413-cid/390-hp dual four-barrel Ram-Tuned induction engine ($375). Positive traction rear axle ($52). Available rear axle gear ratios: 3.23:1; 3.91:1; 2.76:1.

CHRYSLER

1965 CHRYSLER 300L

1965 Chrysler 300L

The last of the legendary Chrysler 300 "Letter Cars" was the 1965 300L. It closed 10 years of milestone Mopar performance history. Some automotive historians and enthusiasts feel that the 1955 Chrysler C-300 was the first real "muscle car." If so, the last Letter Car has to be considered a significant automobile for serious collectors.

As the last edition of Chrysler's "beautiful brute," the 300L was perhaps a bit tamed by old age. Nevertheless, the 300 Letter Car series did end with a car that was a capable performer. The Chrysler 300L, with its standard 413-cid/390-hp engine, could hurl its 4,660 lbs. from 0-to-60 mph in 8.8 seconds and could scat down the quarter-mile in 17.3 seconds. That was slower than a 396-cid/325-hp Chevrolet Caprice, but faster than a 390-cid/300-hp T-Bird.

In the process, it coddled its passengers in beautiful vinyl front bucket seats and a notchback rear seat. The elegant dashboard used on all 1965 Chryslers was strewn prettily across the 300L's interior and was complemented by a commanding center console between the bucket seats. Aside from its massive, high-output power plant, the 300 L's only major distinction was a lighted medallion at the center of its silver crossbar grille. At night, the medallion glowed softly when the headlights were switched on. It also managed to attract a good number of buyers, with 2,405 driving away in a 300L hardtop and an additional 440 taking off in a rare 300L convertible. Even with such modest production totals, the Chrysler 300L models were the second-best selling Letter Cars in history.

Alas, this achievement went largely unnoticed and plans for the 1966 Chrysler 300M were cancelled. A great Chrysler

tradition had come to an end with the 300L. This was the last year for the Letter Series high-performance specialty car. It closely resembled the standard 300. The letter "L" in the center of the grille cross-bar lit-up when the lights were turned on. The 300L used high-performance tires and suspension. Coupled with a high-output 413-cid single-carb engine, this set it apart from the regular 300. Styling touches used to distinguish the Chrysler 300L were a painted insert in the upper body molding and a damascened insert between the rear taillamps. There were also special interior appointments and appropriate Letter Series medallions.

Model Number	Body/Style Number	Body Type & Seating	Factory Price	Shipping Weight	Production Total
300L — SERIES AC2-P — V-8					
AC2-P	C42	2d HT-5P	$4,090	4,225 lbs.	2,405
AC2-P	C45	2d Conv-5P	$4,545	4,155 lbs.	440

ENGINE

BASE V-8: Overhead valve. Cast-iron block. Bore and stroke: 4.18 x 3.75 inches. Displacement: 413 cid. Compression ratio: 10.10:1. Brake hp: 360 at 4800 rpm. Taxable hp: 56.20. Torque: 470 at 3200 rpm. Five main bearings. Hydraulic valve lifters. Dual exhaust. Carburetor: Carter AFB-3860-S four-barrel. Engine code: A-413.

OPTIONS

Power windows. Power seat. Reclining bucket seats. Power door locks. Heater and defroster. Air conditioner (dual air conditioning on all except convertible). Golden Tone radio. AM/FM radio. Golden Touch tuner. Rear seat speaker. Console. Seat belts. Heavy-duty springs, shocks, sway bar and brakes. Adjustable steering wheel. Undercoating. Tinted glass. Day/Night rearview mirror. Remote control mirror. Column-shift automatic transmission was standard. Four-speed manual floor shift transmission optional Positive traction rear axle was optional in all models at extra cost.

DODGE MUSCLE 1962-72

You could trace the start of the high-performance Dodge back to 1953, when the "Red Ram" Hemi V-8 arrived in some series. In 1954, a Dodge V-8 set 196 speed records at the Bonneville Salt Flats. By the early '60s the muscle car era was starting to unfold and Dodge Division's racing image was evident at dragstrips across the United States. A few years later, the 426 Wedge made drag racing history in the hands of race teams like the Ramchargers and drivers like "Dandy" Dick Landy. From 1962 through 1964, Dodge's big performance V-8s ranged from 265 to 425 hp.

A 273-cid "small-block" V-8 was also developed in the early '60s for the compact Dodge Dart. This was quickly bored to 318 and 340 cid with the latter engine producing upwards of 290 hp when equipped with a "Six-Pack" of three two-barrel carbs. Speed legend Andy Granatelli employed the small Mopar V-8 as the basis of his fuel-injected Indy car engines in the late '60s.

Dodge re-introduced the Hemi V-8 in 1964, but this version was strictly for racing. It had a short tenure in NASCAR racing, but started tearing up America's drag strips and it remains a formidable force in quarter-mile competition today.

The year 1965 brought a long list of muscle car options including the 426 "Street Hemi," floor shifts, bucket seats and consoles. The '66 Dodge Charger was a fastback show car brought to life. It was based on the new Coronet and both models combined high-performance and luxury. Advertised as Dodge's "Rebellion," the sales trend registered a gain, with

Dodge capturing a 6.6-percent market share. The face-lifted 1967 Charger/Coronet received a new R/T option package for the performance crowd.

Moderate styling changes were seen on the smallest and largest 1968 Dodges, while Coronet/Chargers adopted a slim, rounded, "Coke-bottle" theme. No longer slope-backed, the Charger had conventional hardtop styling on a Coronet body tipped by a unique wind-splitting nose. It came V-8-powered only, up to the hefty Hemi Charger. The popular 1968 lineup gave Dodge its fifth sales record in six years. Hailed as a year of "Dodge Fever," 1969 was the second best 12 months in Dodge history.

As the 1970s dawned, Dodge continued to emphasize sportiness and performance, but the market began to change rapidly with governmental regulation and oil embargoes. The sporty, all-new Challenger, introduced in 1970 as a companion to Plymouth's Barracuda, was too late to find large success in the waning days of the muscle car era. It survived only through 1974, although the name was reintroduced later for a Japanese model imported by Dodge.

Restyled for 1971, the mid-range was split between the Charger two-door sport models and other Coronets. There was more buyer interest in the Dart line, which in response expanded to include additional luxury sedans and sporty, performance coupes with names such as Demon and Swinger. After 1972, Dodge — like other automakers — was forced to join the trend towards smaller, less-powerful cars.

JERRY HEASLEY

DODGE

DODGE

1962 POLARA 500 "413"

JERRY HEASLEY

1962 Polara

Polara 500 was the top trim level Dodge for 1962. It shared body and chassis components with the Dart series and included all the features of the Dart 440 plus bucket seats, carpeting, a dual exhaust system, a base 361-cid V-8 engine, a padded instrument panel, a deluxe steering wheel, full wheel covers, an outside rearview mirror on the left-hand driver's door and the Polara name, in script. Special exterior trim, in contrasting colors, was also a part of the Polara 500 package. When fitted with performance versions of the 413-cid big-block V-8, the Polara 500 two-door hardtop and convertible became somewhat of an early muscle car.

While the Ram-tuned engines of 1961 were extremely powerful, with their huge intake manifolds, they were a mechanic's nightmare. Chrysler Corp. solved this problem with the midyear introduction of the famous Ram-Charger 413 engine, which utilized ram passages only 15 inches long. As the name implied, this engine represented the maximum performance state of tune for the 413-cid V-8. The intake and exhaust ports were 25 percent larger than in 1961 and there were dozens of other performance features, such as mechanical valve lifters and a cast-aluminum ram-induction manifold. Dodges proved themselves to be the car to beat on the dragstrip in 1962.

Model Number	Body/Style Number	Body Type & Seating	Factory Price	Shipping Weight	Production Total
POLARA 500 — SERIES SD2P —V-8					
SD2P	542	2d HT-6P	$3,019	3,315 lbs.	6,973
SD2P	545	2d Conv-6P	$3,263	3,430 lbs.	2,077

NOTE 1: Production totals above are for all Polara V-8s, not just 413s.

ENGINES

OPTIONAL V-8: Overhead valve. Cast-iron block. Bore and stroke: 4.19 x 3.75 inches. Displacement: 413 cid. Compression ratio: 11.00:1. Brake hp: 365 at 4600 rpm. Taxable hp: 55.90. Torque: 460 at 2800 rpm. Five main bearings. Hydraulic valve lifters. Carburetor: Carter AFB 3251-S four-barrel. Engine code: S-41.

OPTIONAL V-8: Overhead valve. Cast-iron block. Bore and stroke: 4.19 x 3.75 inches. Displacement: 413 cid. Compression ratio: 11.00:1. Brake hp: 385 at 5200 rpm. Taxable hp: 55.90. Torque: 455 at 3600 rpm. Five main bearings. Hydraulic valve lifters. Carburetor: Two Carter AFB four-barrels: (front) 2970-S; (rear) 2971-S. Engine code: S-41.

OPTIONAL V-8: Overhead valve. Cast-iron block. Bore and stroke: 4.19 x 3.75 inches. Displacement: 413 cid. Compression ratio: 11.00:1. Brake hp: 410 at 5200 rpm. Taxable hp: 55.90. Torque: 460 at 4400 rpm. Five main bearings.

Solid valve lifters. Carburetor: Two Carter AFB 2903-S four-barrels. Engine code: S-41.

OPTIONAL V-8: Overhead valve. Cast-iron block. Bore and stroke: 4.19 x 3.75 inches. Displacement: 413 cid. Compression ratio: 13.50:1. Brake hp: 420 at 5400 rpm. Five main bearings. Solid valve lifters. Carburetor: Two Carter AFB 3084-S four-barrels. Engine code: S-41. (Midyear option.)

OPTIONS

Electric clock ($16). Music Master radio ($58). TorqueFlite automatic transmission on six-cylinders ($192); on V-8s ($211). Power steering ($77). Power brakes ($43). Power seats ($96). Power windows ($102). Air Temp air conditioning ($445). Windshield washer ($12). 413-cid Ramcharger V-8 engine ($400). Four-speed manual transmission ($146). White sidewall tires ($33-$48).

1963 POLARA 500

DODGE

DOUG MITCHEL

1963 Polara 500 (with optional 426)

With its 119-inch wheelbase and 3,985-lb. curb weight, it is a bit hard to think of the 1963 Dodge Polara 500 convertible as a muscle car, until you see the results that Jim Wright recorded when he test drove such a car for *Motor Trend* magazine. His ragtop was equipped with the 383-cid/330-hp V-8 and managed to get from 0-to-60 mph in a mere 7.7 seconds. The quarter-mile took 15.8 seconds, by which time the big, open-top Dodge was moving at 92 mph. A lighter Sport Coupe would have done even better.

"Barring the all-out drag-strip engines, there aren't many that can stay with the 330-hp "383" in acceleration," said Wright. He noted that the Polara 500's times through various speeds and the quarter-mile were "very impressive," especially considering that it used a 3.23.0:1 rear axle.

The Polara 500 was a special high-performance sport model that included all the features of the Polara, plus bucket seats, rear foam seat cushions, a padded instrument panel, a deluxe steering wheel, special wheel covers and a new 383-cid/265-hp V-8. Polara 500 models also included special exterior trim on the rear quarter panels behind the rear wheelwell. With its 4.25 x 3.38-inch bore and stroke the base 383 was considered a Chrysler big-block engine and it was one of the best for all-around driving. It used 10.0:1 aluminum pistons and the 330-hp version had a Carter four-barrel carburetor that let the

engine breathe deeply and rev to a 5,500-rpm redline above its 4,600-rpm horsepower peak. The torque output was a strong 425 lbs-ft. at 2,800 rpm. It was available attached to a Borg-Warner T-10 four-speed with a 2.20.0:1 low gear, which didn't hurt its drag-strip performance one bit.

Model Number	Body/Style Number	Body Type & Seating	Factory Price	Shipping Weight	Production Total
POLARA 500 — SERIES TD2P — V-8					
TD2P	642	2d HT-6P	$2,965	3,426 lbs.	5,629
TD2P	645	2d Conv-6P	$3,196	3,546 lbs.	1,634

NOTE 1: Production totals above are for all Polara V-8s.

ENGINES

BASE V-8: Overhead valve. Cast-iron block. Bore and stroke: 4.25 x 3.38 inches. Displacement: 383 cid. Compression ratio: 10.0:1. Brake hp: 305 at 4600 rpm. Taxable hp: 57.80. Torque: 410 at 2400 rpm. Five main bearings. Hydraulic valve lifters. Carburetor: Carter BBD-3476-S two-barrel. Engine code: V-38.

OPTIONAL V-8: Overhead valve. Cast-iron block. Displacement: 383 cid. Bore and stroke: 4.25 x 3.38 inches. Compression ratio: 10.0:1. Brake hp: 330 at 4600 rpm. Taxable hp: 57.80. Torque: 425 at 2800 rpm. Five main bearings. Hydraulic valve lifters. Carburetor: Carter BBD-3684-S four-barrel. Engine code: V-38.

OPTIONS

Electric clock ($16). Music Master radio ($58). TorqueFlite automatic transmission ($211). Power steering ($77). Power brakes ($43). Power seats ($96). Power windows ($102). Air Temp air conditioning ($45). Windshield washer ($12). 426-cid Ramcharger V-8 engine ($445). Four-speed manual transmission ($146). White sidewall tires ($33-$48). Sure-Grip differential. Sun tachometer. Seat belts.

DODGE

1963-64 DODGE "MAX WEDGE" RAMCHARGER

PHIL KUNZ

1963 Dodge Ramcharger

Dodge built high-performance hemi-head V-8s from 1953 to 1958. By the last year, up to 320 hp was available in the Super D-500 version. There had been an even more brutal 340-hp D-501 option in mid-1957, before automakers were forced to apply brakes to the horsepower race. Also interesting was the 330-hp V-8 with electrionic fuel injection offered for a short time in early 1958. Cars ordered with this option were recalled and retro-fitted with "only" two four-barrel carbs. A new, cheaper-to-build "wedge" V-8 arrived in 1959. It became well known in its early 383-, and 413- configurations. In the early '60s, it was available with wild-looking cross-ram intake manifolds in a 375-hp package.

The 413 was the first Mopar engine to have an impact on drag racing. Chrysler's own factory literature said that it was designed for use in "acceleration trials." The "Max Wedge" 413 was released in 1962. It had big intake and exhaust ports, stainless steel head gaskets, big valves, a hot cam, dual valve springs, solid valve lifters and cast nodular rocker arms. A special aluminum ram-induction intake manifold with no heat crossover passage carried twin Carter AFB four-barrel carburetors. The engine was offered with two different compression ratios — 11.0:1 or 13.5:1 — and TRW built two types of special pistons for it. Other content included forged rods that were factory magnafluxed, free-flowing exhaust headers and a number of features usually associated with racing engines.

This potent big block could be hooked to a three-speed gearbox with a floor shifter or a beefy version of Chrysler's TorqueFlight automatic transmission. The 413 soon made

drag racing history in cars such as Dandy Dick Landy's SS/S class Dodge. By the way, Dodge called it the "Ram-Charger 413" while Plymouth dubbed what was essentially the same engine its "Super Stock 413." Also making its first appearance in 1962 was the 426-cid Wedge-head V-8. That year, you could not order this engine in a Dodge (or Plymouth), it came only in big Chryslers.

Motor Trend's "Spotlight on Detroit" column (June 1962) said, "You can now order 426 cubic inches on any Chrysler 300 or 300-H. Factory 413-cubic-inch blocks bored .060 are available on special order, with component combinations including forged pistons of 12-to-1 compression, 292-degree-duration cam with solid lifters, big exhaust valves, streamlined exhaust headers, and the original dual-four-barrel ram manifolds with passages shortened to "tune" above 4000 rpm. This top engine is rated 421 hp at 5400 rpm.

For 1964, Dodges were totally restyled once again. Many Dodge enthusiasts consider the 1964 models to be one of the most attractive ever built. Smooth styling was the keynote and every line seemed to flow into the next line. The grille was the epitome of simplicity. It began as small chrome moldings around the outboard headlights, narrowed slightly at the inboard headlights and featured a vertical bar theme. The Dodge name, in block letters, was spaced equally across the front of the hood. From the windshield back, the 1964 Dodges shared bodies with the previous models, except at the "C" pillar of two-door hardtops, which was wider at the top than at the bottom. The basic 1963 body shell, combined with the new front end, produced an attractive car, indeed.

Model Number	Body/Style Number	Body Type & Seating	Factory Price	Shipping Weight	Production Total
1963 DODGE 330 — SERIES VD2L — V-8					
VD2L	642	2d Sed-6P	$2,372	3,270 lbs.	10,350

NOTE 1: It is believed that most cars built for drag racing were based Dodge's cheapest and lightest V-8 model, the Dodge 330 two-door sedan.

NOTE 2: Prices are for the base V-8 model without drag racing options and special equipmernt, which could add considerably to price.

NOTE 3: Production is given for the base V-8 model. The number of drag racing cars built is unknown.

NOTE 4: During model-year 1963 Chrysler built only 2,130 426-cid V-8s for all cars in all divisions.

Model Number	Body/Style Number	Body Type & Seating	Factory Price	Shipping Weight	Production Total
1964 DODGE 330 SERIES — VD2L — V-8					
VD2L	611	2d Sed-6P	$2,372	3,270 lbs.	9697

NOTE 1: It is believed that most cars built for drag racing were based Dodge's cheapest and lightest V-8 model, the Dodge 330 two-door sedan.

NOTE 2: Prices are for the base V-8 model without drag racing options and special equipmernt, which could add considerably to price.

NOTE 3: Production is given for the base V-8 model. The number of drag racing cars built is unknown.

NOTE 4: During model-year 1964 Chrysler built only 6,359 426-cid V-8s of all types for all cars in all its divisions. Of these, 6,088 were 426-cid Wedge V-8s.

ENGINES

OPTIONAL V-8: Overhead valve. Cast-iron block. Displacement: 426 cid. Bore and stroke: 4.25 x 3.75 inches. Compression ratio: 10.30:1. Brake hp: 365 at 4800 rpm. Taxable hp: 57.80. Torque: 475 at 3200 rpm. Five main bearings. Hydraulic valve lifters. Carburetor: Carter AFB 3859-S four-barrel. Engine code: V-42.

OPTIONAL WEDGE V-8: Overhead valve. Cast-iron block. Displacement: 426 cid. Bore and stroke: 4.25 x 3.75 inches. Compression ratio: 11.00:1. Brake hp: 415 at 5600 rpm. Taxable hp: 57.80. Torque: 470 at 4400 rpm. Five main bearings. Solid valve lifters. Carburetor: Two Carter AFB four-barrel. Engine code: 426VMP.

OPTIONAL V-8: Overhead valve. Cast-iron block. Displacement: 426 cid. Bore and stroke: 4.25 x 3.75 inches. Compression ratio: 13.50:1. Brake hp: 425 at 5600 rpm. Taxable hp: 57.80. Torque: 480 at 4400 rpm. Five main bearings. Solid valve lifters. Carburetor: Two Carter AFB 3084-S four-barrel. Engine code: 426VMPHC.

OPTIONS

TorqueFlite automatic transmission ($211). Power steering ($77). Power brakes ($43). 426-cid Ramcharger V-8 engine ($445). Four-speed manual transmission ($146). Sure-Grip differential. Sun tachometer. Seat belts.

1965 CORONET 426 WEDGE

PHIL KUNZ

1965 Coronet

The Coronet name, last used by Dodge in 1959, was revived for the intermediate-size Dodge models for 1965. While larger than Ford's Fairlane and Chevrolet's Chevelle, it was nevertheless smaller than full-size Polara models. It was built on a 117-inch wheelbase platform, 2 inches shorter than the 1964 Polara/440/330 models. Styling was simple. The grille and rear end treatments were quite flat. There was a slab-sided look with only a belt-level feature line. Vertical bars patterned the grille and the taillights were also vertically positioned.

The Coronet 500 was the top trim level of the Coronet series and included a padded instrument panel, a center console, bucket seats, full wheel covers, a V-8 engine, a a single horizontal chrome strip at the beltline and the Coronet 500 name, in script, at the rear of the wheel well on the front fenders.

The 1965 Coronet was tapped to carry the Dodge emblem in the high-performance market and big engines went into Coronet 330s and Cornet 440s, as well as the 500. However, it was the Coronet 500 that had the full muscle car image with

DODGE

a standard V-8, bucket seats and a center console. Initially, the 426 Wedge was the hottest engine option. For street driving, Dodge offered the single four-barrel version. The dual four-barrel counterpart was for the racers. The Coronet's limited-production-options sheet included the Ramcharger drag package, but with steel fenders and hood due to new National Hot Rod Association S/S class ruleswhich madated heavier racing weights At the NHRA Nats, Bob Harrop's '65 Coronet took the checkered flag.

Model Number	Body/Style Number	Body Type & Seating	Factory Price	Shipping Weight	Production Total
CORONET — SERIES AW2P — V-8					
AW2L	W21	2d Sed-6P	$2,627	3,145 lbs.	16
CORONET DELUXE — SERIES AW2P — V-8					
AW2L	W11	2d Sed-6P	$2,666	3,160 lbs.	175
CORONET 440 — SERIES AW2P — V-8					
AW2H	W33	2d HT-6P	$2,809	3,255 lbs.	585
AW2H	W35	2d Conv-6P	$3,196	3,340 lbs.	31
CORONET 500 — SERIES AW2P — V-8					
AW2P	W42	2d HT-6P	$3,024	3,255 lbs.	1,169
AW2P	W45	2d Conv-6P	$3,196	3,340 lbs.	124

NOTE 1: Prices are for the base V-8 model with the 426 Wedge V-8 added and no other options.

NOTE 2: Production is given for Coronets with the 426-cid four-barrel SW (Wedge) V-8

NOTE 3: Of the 426 Wedge cars listed above, the four-speed manual transmission was used in 11 Coronet two-door sedans, 131 Coronet Deluxe two-door sedans, 403 Coronet 440 two-door hardtops, 21 Coronet 440 convertibles, 729 Coronet 500 two-door hardtops and 77 Coronet 500 convertibles.

NOTE 4: Total production of Cornets with the 426 SW (Wedge) V-8 was 2,100 cars.

ENGINES

OPTIONAL V-8: Overhead valve. Cast-iron block. Displacement: 426 cid. Bore and stroke: 4.25 x 3.75 inches. Compression ratio: 10.10:1. Brake hp: 365 at 4800 rpm. Taxable hp: 57.80. Torque: 470 at 3200 rpm. Five main bearings. Hydraulic valve lifters. Carburetor: Carter AFB 3959-S four-barrel. Engine code: A-426.

OPTIONAL "WEDGE" V-8: Overhead valve. Cast-iron block. Displacement: 426 cid. Bore and stroke: 4.25 x 3.75 inches. Compression ratio: 13.50:1. Brake hp: 425 at 5600 rpm. Taxable hp: 57.80. Torque: 480 at 4400 rpm. Five main bearings. Solid valve lifters. Carburetor: Two Carter AFB 3084-S four-barrel. Engine code: AH-426

OPTIONS

Music Master AM radio ($45). Astrophonic AM radio ($69). AM/FM radio ($103). Rear speaker with reverberation ($28-$41 depending on model). Air conditioning ($282-$315). Auto Pilot ($66). Power steering ($67-$74). Power brakes ($33). Electric clock ($12). Rear window defogger ($16). Sure-Grip differential ($39). Power door locks ($43). Tinted glass ($31). Two-tone paint ($13). Power bench seats ($74). Tachometer ($39). TorqueFlite automatic transmission ($165-$181). Four-speed manual transmission ($146-$180). 365-hp V-8 engine ($344). 425-hp V-8 engine ($444).

1965 CORONET 500 426 HEMICHARGER

Early in model year 1965 a factory-installed Race Hemi was not on the Coronet options list. However, if you were willing to pay the roughly $1,800 price tag and sign away rights to a new-car warranty, you could get one. The hot engine was also available for "off-road" (racing) purposes.

The 426-cid "Hemicharger"-powered Dodges continued to dominate the action on the dragstrips across the country. A few Hemis were produced for street use and were sold "as is," meaning Chrysler Corp. was not responsible for their use and all warranty provisions, normally associated with a new car, did not apply to the Hemi Dodges.

The two Race Hemis were rated at 415 and 425 hp. A total of 360 of these engines went into 1965 Dodges, making any '65 Dodge with a one of these motors a collector gem, not to mention a very fast machine.

Model Number	Body/Style Number	Body Type & Seating	Factory Price	Shipping Weight	Production Total
CORONET — SERIES AW2P — V-8					
AW2L	W21	2d Sed-6P	$4,083	3,145 lbs.	Note 3
CORONET DELUXE — SERIES AW2P — V-8					
AW2L	W11	2d Sed-6P	$4,122	3,160 lbs.	Note 3
CORONET 440 — SERIES AW2P — V-8					
AW2H	W33	2d HT-6P	$4,265	3,255 lbs.	Note 3
AW2H	W35	2d Conv-6P	$4,480	3,340 lbs.	Note 3
CORONET 500 — SERIES AW2P — V-8					
AW2P	W42	2d HT-6P	$4,437	3,255 lbs.	Note 3
AW2P	W45	2d Conv-6P	$4,652	3,340 lbs.	Note 3

NOTE 1: Prices are for the base V-8 model with the 426 Hemi V-8 added and no other options.

NOTE 2: Production totals above are for all Coronets with all V-8 engines (sixes not included).

NOTE 3: 101 Coronet S/S models with the 426-cid Hemi were shipped.

NOTE 4: During model-year 1965 Chrysler built only 6,929 426-cid V-8s of all types for all cars in all its divisions. Of these, 360 were Race Hemis.

ENGINES

OPTIONAL V-8: Overhead valve. Cast-iron block. Displacement: 426 cid. Bore and stroke: 4.25 x 3.75 inches. Compression ratio: 11.00:1. Brake hp: 415 at 5600 rpm. Taxable hp: 57.80. Torque: 470 at 4400 rpm. Five main bearings. Solid valve lifters. Carburetor: Two Carter AFB 3859-S four-barrel. Engine code: AH-426.

OPTIONAL V-8: Overhead valve with hemispherical segment combustion chambers. Cast-iron block. Displacement: 426 cid. Bore and stroke: 4.25 x 3.75 inches. Compression ratio: 12.0:1. Brake hp: 425 at 5600 rpm. Taxable hp: 57.80. Torque: 480 at 4600 rpm. Five main bearings. Solid valve lifters. Carburetor: Two Carter AFB 3084-S four-barrel. Engine code: AH-426HC.

OPTIONS

Power steering ($67-$74). Power brakes ($33). Sure-Grip differential ($39). Power door locks ($43). Tinted glass ($31). Two-tone paint ($13). Tachometer ($39). TorqueFlite automatic transmission ($165-$181). Four-speed manual transmission ($146-$180). Hemi V-8 engine ($1,800 approximately).

1966 CHARGER 383/HEMI

JERRY HEASLEY

1966 Hemi Charger

The Charger was Dodge's answer to the fastback trend. It was dramatically different than all competitors when it arrived. It was big and wide, which gave it a distinctive "flat" look to distinguish it from other muscle cars. It combined MoPar's bright, clean interior styling with some of the company's best engine options to create a package that had no peers. Dodge called the 1966 Charger a "Sports Sedan," even though it was really a sport coupe. This was an attempt to widen its sales appeal beyond the youth market and to stress its cargo-carrying abilities.

The Charger used Coronet chassis and running gear, but the body was completely different. With a full-size 117-inch wheelbase and 203.6 inches of overall length, the Charger was certainly roomy. And its 75.3-inch width didn't hurt either. With seating for only four on its front and rear bucket seats, the Charger was not really sedan-like in the passenger-carrying category, either. Its real appeal was its sporty flavor. Nevertheless, young-at-heart American dads canny enough to convince their better half that the Charger was really a "kind of station wagon" were likely to go for the base 318-cid/230-hp V-8 or the one-step-up 361-cid/265-hp option. Once you got to the big-block 383 you were talking "muscle car."

Most magazines tested the 383 Charger. *Motor Trend* reported an 8.9-second 0-to-60 time and 16.3 seconds for the quarter-mile at 85 mph.

Though the car itself was large, lush and heavy, the availability of the optional 426-cid Hemi V-8 engine made the Charger a genuine contender for the hottest niche in the muscle car market. The 425-hp big-block V-8 featured a pair of four-barrel carburetors, extra-wide dual exhausts and all sorts of heavy-duty performance hardware. The huffing-and-puffing Hemi could shave two seconds or more off the acceleration times of the 383-powered Charger. NASCAR drivers thought the fastback roof would enhance the Charger's aerodynamics in Grand National stock car racing. However, they actually tended to lift at the rear, a problem that the race car builders solved by adding a small rear deck lid spoiler. After that, the Chargers won 18 races.

Model Number	Body/Style Number	Body Type & Seating	Factory Price	Shipping Weight	Production Total
CHARGER (383) — SERIES BX2P — V-8					
BX2P	29	2d HT-4P	$4,054	3,504 lbs.	12,328

NOTE 1: Price above is for the Charger with the 383-cid/325-hp V-8.

NOTE 2: Production total above is for cars with the 383-cid/325-hp V-8.

Model Number	Body/Style Number	Body Type & Seating	Factory Price	Shipping Weight	Production Total
CHARGER (HEMI) — SERIES BX2P — V-8					
BX2P	29	2d HT-4P	$3,603	3,504 lbs.	468

NOTE 1: Price above is for the Charger with the 426-cid/425-hp Hemi V-8. The engine listed for $907.60.

NOTE 2: A four-speed manual transmission ($184.20) was mandatory. This meant that $1,091.80 was the minimum added cost of a Hemi..

NOTE 3: Production total above is for all Chargers with the Hemi. Of these, 218 had TorqueFlite automatic transmission.

ENGINES

OPTIONAL V-8: Overhead valve. Cast-iron block. Displacement: 383 cid. Bore and stroke: 4.25 x 3.38 inches. Compression ratio: 10.0:1. Brake hp: 325 at 4800 rpm. Taxable hp: 57.80. Torque: 425 at 2800 rpm. Five main bearings. Hydraulic valve lifters. Carburetor: Carter BBD-3855-S four-barrel. Engine code: B-383. VIN code: G.

OPTIONAL V-8: Overhead valve with hemispherical segment combustion chambers. Cast-iron block. Displacement: 426 cid. Bore and stroke: 4.25 x 3.75 inches. Compression ratio: 10.25:1. Brake hp: 425 at 5000 rpm. Taxable hp: 57.80. Torque: 490 at 4000 rpm. Five main bearings. Hydraulic valve lifters. Carburetor: Two Carter AFB 3084-S four-barrel. Engine code: B-426. VIN code: H.

OPTIONAL V-8: Overhead valve with hemispherical segment combustion chambers. Cast-iron block. Displacement: 426 cid. Bore and stroke: 4.25 x 3.75 inches. Compression ratio: 10.25:1. Compression ratio: 12.0:1. Brake hp: 425 at 5600 rpm. Taxable hp: 57.80. Torque: 480 at 4600 rpm. Five main bearings. Solid valve lifters. Carburetor: Two Carter AFB 3084-S four-barrel. Engine code: B-426. VIN code: K.

OPTIONS

426 Hemi V-8. Music Master AM radio ($45). Astrophonic AM radio ($69). AM/FM radio ($103). Rear speaker with reverberation ($28-$41 depending on model). Air conditioning ($282-$315). Auto Pilot ($66). Power steering ($67-$74). Power brakes ($33). Electric clock ($12). Rear window defogger ($16). Sure-Grip differential ($39). Power door locks ($43). Tinted glass ($31). Two-tone paint ($13). Power bench seats ($74). Tachometer ($39). TorqueFlite automatic transmission ($165-$181). Four-speed manual transmission ($146-$180).

DODGE

1966 HEMI CORONET

JERRY HEASLEY

1966 Hemi Coronet

When it was introduced in 1965, the mid-sized Coronet immediately became the centerpiece of Dodge's muscle car fleet. An ad that ran that year asked "Why not drop a Hemi in the new Coronet 500?" The '65 Coronets had come only with the 12.5:1 compression ratio Race Hemi. That engine created more of a drag racing machine than a street-prowling muscle car. This was corrected by making the 426-cid/425-hp dual-quad Street Hemi available in 1966. Displacement-wise and power-wise, it matched the race version, but the big differences were a hydraulic lifter cam and a 10.5:1 compression ratio.

The Hemi was the most powerful production car engine ever built until just recently, but it was still well suited to street use. You really had to open the hood to see if there was a Hemi lurking underneath. Hemi Coronets could hit 60 mph in 6.1 seconds and do the quarter-mile in 14.5. Only 340 Coronet 500 hardtops (204 of them four-speeds) got the Hemi, along with just 21 convertibles (12 with four-speeds). Another 379 of the other Coronets also had this engine added to them.

The Coronet was one of those automobiles capable of "wearing many hats." In its six-cylinder, four-door format it made a great grocery getter or salesman's "company car." When you reduced the number of doors by two and increased the number of cylinders by a like amount (packing them in a V-block format along the way) you got the makings of a muscle car. Then, by installing the ultimate V-8 and slapping "Hemi" badges on the sides, you wound up with a King Kong Coronet that could pound pavement with the best of them. This smooth-lined rendition of the classic big-engine-stuffed-in-small-body "factory hot rod" was a royal pain in the butt for GM and FoMoCo fans.

Model Number	Body/Style Number	Body Type & Seating	Factory Price	Shipping Weight	Production Total
CORONET — SERIES BW2P — V-8					
BW2E	WE21	2d Sed-6P	$3,266	3,215 lbs.	34*
CORONET DELUXE — SERIES BW2P — V-8					
BW2L	WL211	2d Sed-6P	$3,305	3,220 lbs.	49*
CORONET 440 — SERIES BW2P — V-8					
BW2H	WH23	2d HT-6P	$3,459	3,240 lbs.	288*
BW2H	WH27	2d Conv-6P	$3,674	3,345 lbs.	6*
CORONET 500 — SERIES BW2P — V-8					
BW2P	WP23	2d HT-6P	$3,613	3,315 lbs.	340*
BW2P	WP27	2d Conv-6P	$3,829	3,390 lbs.	21*

*Production totals are for Coronets with the 426 Hemi.

NOTE 1: Prices are for the base V-8 model with the 426 Hemi added and no other options. The engine listed for $907.60.

NOTE 2: A four-speed manual transmission ($184.20) was mandatory. This meant that $1,091.80 was the minimum added cost of a Hemi.

NOTE 3: Of the 426 Hemi cars listed above the four-speed manual transmission was used in 11 Coronet two-door sedans, 31 Coronet Deluxe two-door sedans, 160 Coronet 440 two-door hardtops, three Coronet 440 convertibles, 204 Coronet 500 two-door hardtops and 12 Coronet 500 convertibles.

NOTE 4: Two Coronet four-door sedans have also been authenticated as being produced with 426 Hemi power, but more may exist.

NOTE 5: One Coronet 440 two-door hardtop is known to have been built with the 426-cid Wedge V-8.

NOTE 6: During model-year 1966 Chrysler built only 3,360 426-cid Street Hemi V-8s in all divisions.

ENGINES

OPTIONAL V-8: Overhead valve with hemispherical segment combustion chambers. Cast-iron block. Displacement: 426 cid. Bore and stroke: 4.25 x 3.75 inches. Compression ratio: 10.25:1. Brake hp: 425 at 5000 rpm. Taxable hp: 57.80. Torque: 490 at 4000 rpm. Five main bearings. Hydraulic valve lifters. Carburetor: Two Carter AFB 3084-S four-barrel. Engine code: B-426. VIN code: H.

OPTIONAL V-8: Overhead valve with hemispherical segment combustion chambers. Cast-iron block. Displacement: 426 cid. Bore and stroke: 4.25 x 3.75 inches. Compression ratio: 10.25:1. Compression ratio: 12.0:1. Brake hp: 425 at 5600 rpm. Taxable hp: 57.80. Torque: 480 at 4600 rpm. Five main bearings. Solid valve lifters. Carburetor: Two Carter AFB 3084-S four-barrel. Engine code: B-426. VIN code: K.

OPTIONS

426-cid Hemi V-8. Automatic transmission, Four-speed manual transmission.

Power brakes. Power steering, Sure Grip differential. Heavy-duty suspension package with heavy duty springs and shocks in front and rear. Trailer towing package. Air conditioning (integral with heater). Remote-control, outside rear view mirror. Inside, glare-resistant mirror. Electric window lifts. Tinted windshield.

Tinted windshield and windows. Retractable seat belts (front and rear). Transistorized radio. Trunk compartment light. Emergency flasher. Parking brake warning light. Electric clock mounted on center console. White sidewall tires. Front and rear bumper guards.

1967 CORONET R/T MAGNUM 440/HEMI

PHIL KUNZ

1967 Hemi Coronet R/T

The Coronet was again Dodge's mid-sized car for 1967. Using the same basic body shell used in 1966, Dodge designers adapted the Charger grille to it and slightly changed the rear end treatment. The Coronet R/T was the high-performance model of the Coronet series. Its standard equipment included the 440-cid Magnum V-8 with four-barrel carburetor and dual exhaust and other muscle car stuff.

One 440-powered R/T did 0-to-60 mph in 7.2 seconds and the quarter-mile in 15.4 at 94 mph. *Motor Trend* drove the same car with racing slicks mounted and did the 0-to-60 test in 6.5 seconds. The fat-tired car required 14.7 seconds for the quarter-mile with a 96-mph terminal speed.

It was on January 23, 1967 that Dodge announced it was going to build Hemi-powered Coronet 440 two-door hardtops on a production-line basis to meet National Hot Rod Association's (NHRA) Super Stock B rules. These "WO23" cars were the latest in the Mopar tradition of special lightweight models built for drag racing. The lightweight body had standard sheet metal and the big fresh-air hood scoop that was common to

earlier S/S Dodges. Sound deadeners and body sealers were deleted and the battery was mounted in the trunk. The usual sway bar up front was also axed, since quick travel around corners was not in the job description for the S/S-B cars. There were two versions of these drag-racing-only Dodges. One came with a modified TorqueFlite automatic using a 2,300 to 2,500-rpm-stall-speed torque converter and 4.86:1 Sure-Grip Chrysler-built 8 3/4-inch differential. The second had a four-speed manual transmission with Hurst linkage, reinforced gearing and clutch and an explosion-proof clutch housing.

Motor Trend's stock-tired Hemi-powered Coronet went 0-to-60 mph in 6.8 seconds and ran the quarter-mile in 15.0 seconds at 96 mph. When shod with racing slicks, it went 0-to-60 in 6.6 seconds and did the quarter-mile in 14.8 seconds at 99 mph.

To meet the rules, Dodge had to build at least 50 of the cars and when 55 went out the door, enough was enough. At least the availability of S/S-B Dodge Coronets was of some consolation to those who missed the Coronet 500 and other lesser-model Hemis. Prices for nice survivors are in the stratosphere today.

DODGE

Model Number	Body/Style Number	Body Type & Seating	Factory Price	Shipping Weight	Production Total
CORONET R/T (MAGNUM 440) — SERIES CW2P — V-8					
CW2P	23	2d HT-6P	$3,199	3,545 lbs.	10,109
CW2P	27	2d Conv-6P	$3,438	3,640 lbs.	628

NOTE 1: Prices and weights include 440 Magnum V-8.

NOTE 2: Production totals are for all Coronet R/Ts.

NOTE 3: 9,826 of the above Coronet R/Ts (no body style breakout available) had the 440 Magnum V-8.

NOTE 4: 1,355 of the Coronet R/Ts with the 440 Magnum V-8 had a four-speed manual transmission.

Model Number	Body/Style Number	Body Type & Seating	Factory Price	Shipping Weight	Production Total
CORONET DELUXE (HEMI) — SERIES WL — V-8					
WL	21	2d Sed-6P	$2,948	3,655 lbs.	1*
CORONET 440 SUPER/STOCK (HEMI) — SERIES WO — V-8					
WO	23	2d HT-6P	$3,051	3,680 lbs.	55*
CORNET 500 (HEMI) — SERIES WP — V-8					
WP	23	2d HT-6P	$3,230	3,715 lbs.	N/A
CORNET R/T (HEMI) — SERIES WS — V-8					
WS	23	2d HT-6P	$3,656	3,990 lbs.	Note 3
WS	27	2d Conv-6P	$3,895	4,085 lbs.	Note 3

* Production totals are for Hemis.

NOTE 1: Prices include the 426 Hemi V-8 but no other extras.

NOTE 2: Weights are calculated based on the known weight of 3,680 lbs. for the WO23 two-door hardtop.

NOTE 3: Acccording to Mopar authority Galen V. Govier the known Hemi production. totals include 55 Coronet 440 S/S two-door hardtops and 283 Coronet R/T two-door

hardtops and convertibles combined (body style breakout not available). In addition, one Coronet Deluxe 426 Hemi two-door sedan has been authenticated and production of Coronet 500 two-door hardtops with the 426 Hemi has been authenticated, but the total number equipped this way is unknown.

NOTE 4: Other sources verify that a total of 283 Coronet R/T Hemi cars were built, of which 121 had the four-speed manual transmission.

ENGINES

BASE V-8: Overhead valve. Cast-iron block. Bore and stroke: 4.32 x 3.75 inches. Displacement: 440 cid. Compression ratio: 10.10:1. Brake hp: 375 at 4600 rpm. Taxable hp: 59.70. Torque: 480 at 3200 rpm. Five main bearings. Hydraulic valve lifters. Carburetor: Carter AFB 3959-S four-barrel. Engine code: C-440. VIN code: L.

OPTIONAL V-8: Overhead valve with hemispherical segment combustion chambers. Cast-iron block. Displacement: 426 cid. Bore and stroke: 4.25 x 3.75 inches. Compression ratio: 10.25:1. Brake hp: 425 at 5000 rpm. Taxable hp: 57.80. Torque: 490 at 4000 rpm. Five main bearings. Hydraulic valve lifters. Carburetor: Two Carter AFB 3084-S four-barrel. Engine code: C-426. VIN code: J.

OPTIONS

426-cid "Hemi" V-8 ($457). TorqueFlite automatic transmission ($183). Four-speed manual transmission ($145-$175). Air conditioning ($274). Auto Pilot cruise control ($64). Power steering ($73). Power brakes ($16). Power front disc brakes ($54). Electric clock ($11). Console ($20). Sure-Grip differential ($29-$37). Heavy-duty differential ($107). Power door locks ($42). Buffed paint ($16). Music Master AM radio ($44). Tilt & Telescope steering wheel ($67). Woodgrained steering wheel ($20). Tachometer ($38). Vinyl top on hardtop ($70). Simulated "mag" wheel covers ($41-$57). Road wheels ($59-$75). Three-speed windshield wipers ($4).

1967 440 MAGNUM/HEMI CHARGER

PHIL KUNZ

1967 Hemi Charger

The 1967 Dodge Charger had few changes from the 1966 model. Like the first car to carry the Charger nameplate, the latest one was aimed at the sporty-car buyer who didn't want to give up room and comfort. Right from the start, Chrysler product planners assumed that the type of man (or woman) interested in such a car would want a V-8. A six-cylinder engine was not offered for the Charger. However, at the opposite end of the equipment choices presented to buyers was a wide variety of powerful overhead valve V-8s.

With its slant towards competition in NASCAR and USAC, Dodge wanted the Charger to reflect its racing image and again made available a very large selection of V-8s. The top dog was the 426-cid/425-hp Hemi. The Hemi was an $877.55 option in the Charger. With the Hemi, the three-speed TorqueFlite automatic came with a high-upshift speed governor. If you ordered a four-speed manual transmission, the Sure-Grip no-slip rear axle was mandatory. A good idea for the Hemi Charger was 11-inch front disc brakes, which could slow the car down from

60 mph in an amazing 133 feet. With this engine the Charger went 0 to 60 mph in 7.6 seconds and did the quarter mile in 14.4 seconds at 100 mph!

The 440-cid/375-hp "Magnum V-8" was new to the Charger lineup in 1967. It put out 375 hp and was the base engine in the R/T. For a "second banana" on the engine list, it was a pretty impressive power plant. Chargers equipped with the 440 Magnum could go from for 0-to-60 in 8 seconds and post a 15.5-second quarter-mile at 93 mph.

The 1967 Chargers were much rarer than '66s and only 15,788 were built. This included 118 cars with the Hemi, of which half were four-speeds. If you're considering buying a 1967 Hemi Charger today, you might appreciate knowing that it got 11.7 mpg in city driving and about 14.4 mpg on the open highway. Don't tell that to the people who set CAFE standards. One of them might have a heart attack!

Model Number	Body/Style Number	Body Type & Seating	Factory Price	Shipping Weight	Production Total
CHARGER — SERIES CW2P — V-8 (440)					
CW2P	29	2d HT-6P	$3,442	3,480 lbs.	660

NOTE 1: The price above is for the Charger with the 440-cid V-8 and no other options.
NOTE 2: The production total above is Chargers with a 440-cid V-8. Includes both 350- and 375-hp version of the 440-cid V-8.

Model Number	Body/Style Number	Body Type & Seating	Factory Price	Shipping Weight	Production Total
HEMI CHARGER — SERIES CW2P — V-8 (HEMI)					
CW2P	29	2d HT-6P	$4,006	3,480 lbs.	117

NOTE 1: The price above is for the Charger with the 426-cid Hemi V-8 and no other options.
NOTE 2: The production total above is for 1967 Chargers with the 426-cid Hemi V-8.

ENGINE

CHARGER OPTIONAL V-8: Overhead valve with hemispherical segment combustion chambers. Cast-iron block. Displacement: 426 cid. Bore and stroke: 4.25 x 3.75 inches. Compression ratio: 10.25:1. Brake hp: 425 at 5000 rpm. Taxable hp: 57.80. Torque: 490 at 4000 rpm. Five main bearings. Hydraulic valve lifters. Carburetor: Two Carter AFB 3084-S four-barrel. Engine code: C-426. VIN code. J.

OPTIONS

Hemi V-8 engine ($878). TorqueFlite automatic transmission ($183-$176). Four-speed manual transmission ($145-$175). Air conditioning ($274). Auto Pilot cruise control ($64). Power steering ($73). Power brakes ($16). Power front disc brakes ($54). Electric clock ($11). Console ($20). Sure-Grip differential ($29-$37). Heavy-duty differential ($107). Power door locks ($42). Dual exhaust ($24). Buffed paint ($16). Music Master AM radio ($44). Tilt & Telescope steering wheel ($67). Woodgrained steering wheel ($16). Tachometer ($38). Vinyl top ($70). Bucket seats ($75). Wheel covers ($14-$22). Simulated "mag" wheel covers ($41-$57). Road wheels ($59-$75). Three-speed windshield wipers ($4).

1968 DART GTS 340/383/HEMI

PHIL KUNZ

1968 Dart GTS

The 1968 Darts continued to use the same body as introduced in 1967 with only minor trim updating.

GTS meant GT Sport. It was the name of a sexy new-for-'68 "sawed-off shotgun" that was a whole bunch more than a sporty compact car. "Not to take the edge off the Road Runner, the GTS might be a more sensible package," said *Hot Rod* magazines's Steve Kelly in the publication's April 1968 issue. "The base price is higher, but you get things like carpet on the floor, fat tires, bucket seats and a few other niceties that can make Saturday night roaming more comfortable. The engine's

smaller, but that could prove an advantage for drag racing classes." Two hefty V-8s were available. A special version of the 383-cid big-block V-8 with a four-barrel carburetor and 300 hp was an option. The 383 added 89 lbs. to the car if you got a four-speed gear box and 136 lbs. if you got an automatic transmission.

GT was the top trim level Dart for 1968 and added 14- or 15-inch wheels and tires with deluxe wheel covers. GT hardtops came standard with bucket seats. GT convertibles had power tops and full-width all-vinyl bench seats. The GTS was a special high-performance version of the GT and was equipped with a new 340-cid small-block V-8 derived from the 273/318-cid Chrysler family of engines. The 1968 Dart GTS hardtop with the 340-cid/275-hp V-8 tested out with a 0-to-60 time of 6 seconds. It did the quarter-mile in a "Scat Pack" time of 15.2 seconds.

Approximately 80 special lightweight Dodge Darts were built for racing purposes. These "S/S" (Super Stock) Darts had 426-cid Hemi V-8s installed. They came with a fiberglass hood and fiberglass front fenders. The front bumper and doors were made out of lightweight steel. They were true "stripper" cars and wore a sticker that stated, "This vehicle was not manufactured for use on Public Streets, Roads or Highways, and does not conform to Motor Vehicle Safety Standards." The Hemi Darts would run the quarter-mile in the 10-second bracket. They were among the fastest factory-built muscle cars in history.

Model Number	Body/Style Number	Body Type & Seating	Factory Price	Shipping Weight	Production Total
DART GTS 340 — SERIES CL2 — V-8					
CL2	23	2-dr HT Cpe-5P	$3,189	3,065 lbs.	8,293
CL2	27	2-dr Conv-6P	$3,383	3,150 lbs.	452

NOTE 1: Prices and weights above are for Dart GTS with 340-cid/275-hp V-8.
NOTE 2: Production totals above are for GTS models with all engines.

Model Number	Body/Style Number	Body Type & Seating	Factory Price	Shipping Weight	Production Total
DART GTS 383 — SERIES CL2 — V-8					
CL2	23	2-dr HT Cpe-5P	3,310	3,154 lbs.	8,293
CL2	27	2-dr Conv-6P	3,504	3,239 lbs.	452

NOTE 1: Prices above are for Dart GTS with 383-cid/300-hp V-8.
NOTE 2: Weights above are for 383-powered GTS with stick shift.
NOTE 3: Production totals above are for GTS models with all engines.

Model Number	Body/Style Number	Body Type & Seating	Factory Price	Shipping Weight	Production Total
DART GTS — SERIES CL2 — V-8					
CL2	23	2-dr HT Cpe-5P	$4,500	—	80

NOTE 1: The price about is the approximate price for a typical Hemi Dart S/S.
NOTE 2: Production total is for Hemi Darts.
NOTE 3: According to Mopar authority Galen V. Govier all 80 Dart S/S cars were two-door hardtops. They were not GTS models.

ENGINES

BASE V-8: Overhead valve. Cast-iron block. Bore and stroke: 4.04 x 3.31 inches. Displacement: 340 cid. Compression ratio: 10.5:1. Brake hp: 275 at 5000 rpm. Taxable hp: 52.20. Torque: 340 at 3200 rpm. Five main bearings. Hydraulic valve lifters. Carburetor: Carter Thermo-Quad AVS-4424-S four-barrel. Engine code: PT-340. VIN code: H.

OPTIONAL V-8: Overhead valve. Cast iron block. Displacement: 383 cid. Bore and stroke: 4.25 x 3.38 inches. Compression ratio: 10.00:1. Brake hp: 300 at 4400 rpm. Taxable hp: 57.80. Torque: 400 at 2400 rpm. Five main bearings. Hydraulic valve lifters. Carburetor: Carter BBD-4422-S two-barrel. Engine code: PT-383. VIN code: H.

OPTIONAL STREET HEMI V-8: Overhead valve with hemispherical segment combustion chambers. Cast iron block. Cast iron heads. Displacement: 426 cid. Bore and stroke: 4.25 x 3.75 inches. Compression ratio: 10.25:1. Brake hp: 425 at 5000 rpm. Taxable hp: 57.80. Torque: 490 at 4000 rpm. Five main bearings. Hydraulic valve lifters. Header type exhaust system. Two Holley four-barrel carburetors on a magnesium cross-ram intake manifold. Engine code: PT-426. VIN code: J.

OPTIONS

Power brakes ($16). Power steering ($80). Air conditioning ($335). Torque-Flite transmission ($181). Four-speed transmission ($179). Music Master AM radio ($44). Tachometer ($38). Mag-styled wheel covers ($55).

1968 GRAND SPAULDING DART GTS 440

1968 Grand Spaulding Dart GTS 440

Dodge offered 68 Mopar lovers the opportunity to own very special Dodge Darts. These cars had the same chassis and hardware upgrades as a 383-powered Dart GTS, but they were built without the engine and other drivetrain components. The cars were shipped directly to Hurst-Campbell, Inc., an aftermarket company that had a facility in Michigan. Hurst added factory-prepped 440 Magnum V-8s to the cars.

After the conversions, the cars were inspected by Dodge factory reps and sent to Grand Spaulding Auto Sales in Chicago, a performance-oriented factory dealer. The cars had VIN numbers, but they were not eligible for factory warranty service. They lacked power steering, because the power steering gear no longer fit. The cars were purpose-built for drag racing.

The 440-cid/375-hp Dodge Darts did 0-to-60 mph in 5.0 seconds and covered the quarter-mile in 13.3 seconds at 107 mph.

Model Number	Body/Style Number	Body Type & Seating	Factory Price	Shipping Weight	Production Total
DART GTS — SERIES CL2 — V-8					
CL2	232-dr	HT Cpe-5P	NA	NA	NOTE 1
CL2	27	2-dr Conv-6P	NA	NA	NOTE 1

NOTE 1: A total of 68 Dodge Darts were fitted with the 440-cid V-8.

ENGINE

OPTIONAL V-8: Overhead valve. Cast-iron block. Bore and stroke: 4.32 x 3.75 inches. Displacement: 440 cid. Compression ratio: 10.10:1. Brake hp: 375 at 4600 rpm. Taxable hp: 59.70. Torque: 480 at 3200 rpm. Five main bearings. Hydraulic valve lifters. Carburetor: Carter AFB 3959-S four-barrel. Engine code: C-440. VIN code: L.

OPTIONS

Most of the modified 440-powered Darts also carried high-performance parts such as aftermarket headers, ignition kits, special hoses, specials wiring and a special air cleaner, that were sourced from the aftermarket.

1968 CORONET R/T 440 MAGNUM/HEMI

ROBERT SEROKA

1968 Coronet R/T

The mid-size Dodge Coronet underwent a transformation for model-year 1968. It was completely restyled from stem to stearn. This was a high-volume series for Dodge and production rose from 159,781 units in 1967 to 189,500 in 1968. In the Coronet R/T line, 10,849 cars were turned out — up from 10,433 the year before. Two body styles were available in R/T format. R/T equipment included bucket seats, dual exhausts, a stiff suspension, heavy-duty brakes and other goodies including a 150-mph speedometer. TorqueFlite automatic transmission was the standard setup. Bumblebee stripes — or alternatively no-cost optional body side stripes — were provided to set off the 1968 model's appearance. There were R/T emblems on the grille and R/T medallions on the fenders and rear trunk latch panel. Coronet R/Ts used the same interior as Coronet 500s, but had a special "power bulge" hood with simulated air vents.

In a Motor Trend comparison of eight 1968 muscle cars (Plymouth Road Runner, Dodge Charger R/T, Pontiac GTO, Buick GS 400, Chevelle SS 396, Olds 4-4-2, Ford Torino and Dodge Coronet R/T) the Coronet was said to have a "good engine" and "easily the best in comfort and in room." It's quality of construction was rated "surprisingly good" and the magazine liked its comfort, roominess, engine and boulevard ride. Buyers again got a choice betwee a four-speed manual transmission or an automatic transmission as standard equipment. High-performance tires and bucket seats were also standard.

The optional Street Hemi V-8 cost $604.75. A four-speed manual transmission or TorqueFlite automatic was mandatory. The Hemi V-8 was installed in 101 Coronet R/Ts with a four-speed and 127 with TorqueFlite. One stick-shift car and eight TorqueFlite cars were convertibles. Hemi cars came with a special heavy-duty suspension and air conditioning couldn't be ordered.

With the hair-raising Hemi engine a Coronet R/T could sprint from 0-to-60 mph in 6.1 seconds and run the quarter-mile in 14.5 seconds. With a 440 Magnum V-8, the Coronet R/T took 6.9 seconds for the 0 to 60-mph test and 15.1 seconds for the quarter-mile at 94 mph. The 440-motivated Coronet R/T got 9.6 to 12.1 mpg.

DODGE

At Daytona, the "Coke bottle"-shaped Coronets were capable of lapping the NASCAR oval at speeds up to 185 mph.

Model Number	Body/Style Number	Body Type & Seating	Factory Price	Shipping Weight	Production Total
CORONET R/T (MAGNUM 440) — SERIES WS — V-8					
WS	23	2d HT-6P	$3,379	3,455 lbs.	9,734
WS	27	2d Conv-6P	$3,438	3,640 lbs.	519

NOTE 1: Prices and weights include 440 Magnum V-8.
NOTE 2: Production totals are for Coronet R/Ts with the 440 Magnum V-8.
NOTE 3: Of the 440 Magum cars listed above 1,983 two-door hardtops and one convertible had the four-speed manual transmission.

Model Number	Body/Style Number	Body Type & Seating	Factory Price	Shipping Weight	Production Total
CORONET R/T (HEMI) — SERIES WS — V-8					
WS	23	2d HT-6P	$3,984	3,555 lbs.	Note 3
WS	27	2d Conv-6P	$4,218	3,640 lbs.	Note 3

NOTE 1: Prices above include the Hemi V-8 and no other options.
NOTE 2: The weights above are an estimate.
NOTE 3: Total production of Hemis was 283 with no body style breakout available.
NOTE 4: Of the 283 Hemi cars 121 had the four-speed manual transmission.

ENGINE

BASE V-8: Overhead valve. Cast-iron block. Bore and stroke: 4.32 x 3.75 inches. Displacement: 440 cid. Compression ratio: 10.10:1. Brake hp: 375 at 4600 rpm. Taxable hp: 59.70. Torque: 480 at 3200 rpm. Five main bearings. Hydraulic valve lifters. Carburetor: Carter AVS-4428-S four-barrel. Engine code: PT-440. VIN code: L.

OPTIONS

426-cid Hemi V-8 ($604.75). 440-cid Magnum V-8 engine ($88-$133). Torque-Flite automatic transmission ($163-$176). Four-speed manual transmission ($145-$175). Air conditioning ($274). Auto Pilot cruise control ($64). Power steering ($73). Power brakes ($16). Power front disc brakes ($54). Electric clock ($11). Console ($20). Heavy-duty differential ($107). Power door locks ($42). Dual exhaust ($24). Buffed paint ($16). Music Master AM radio ($44). Tilt & Telescope steering wheel ($87). Woodgrained steering wheel ($20). Tachometer ($38). Vinyl top on hardtop ($70). Simulated "mag" wheel covers ($41-$57). Road wheels ($59-$75). Three-speed windshield wipers ($4). Limited-slip differential for ($42). Custom wheels ($97). Front disc brakes ($72.95). Front seat console ($52.85).

1968 CORONET SUPER BEE 383/HEMI

DOUG MITCHEL

1968 Coronet Super Bee

Mopar invented the bargain-basement muscle car in the late '60s. When the GTO started the muscle car craze some pricey performance options were standard, but the car itself was pretty basic. It even came with "bottle cap"-style wheel covers. As muscle car mania caught on, the emphasis switched to bucket seats, consoles, mag wheels and even luxury features like air conditioning. This sent the prices of many muscle cars beyond the budgets of the young drivers who were most interested in the breed. Plymouth introduced the Road Runner as a reaction to rising prices. It wasn't a cheap car, but it was a car that gave you great value for the price and emphasized muscle over chrome and convenience options. The "Beep-Beep!"car was designed to fit a young man's budget, if he wanted to spend money on go-fast equipment, rather than tinsel.

Dodge Division's corresponding entry was the Coronet Super Bee, which was introduced in February 1968 with a price tag in the $3,395 range. It was based on the Coronet 440 two-door sedan. This was done because a "post coupe" was needed to accommodate the non-lowering rear windows that swung open on hinges mounted to the center pillar. Base Super Bee engine was the big-block 383-cid V-8 in 335-hp format. It came linked to a heavy-duty four-speed gear box with a Hurst "Competition-Plus" floor shifter. Fat dual exhausts, fat F40 x 14 tires and a heavy-duty suspension with fat torsion bars were included. Everything was fat except the price tag. Also part of the Super Bee look was a dummy hood "power bulge," bench seat interior, wide wheels and rear bumblebee striping with a bee inside a circular decal emblem.

You couldn't get a vinyl roof on your '68 Super Bee, but for $712, you could add the legendary Hemi engine. A total of 166 Hemi Super Bees were produced — 92 had four-speed transmissions and 74 had TorqueFlite attachments. Cars equipped with the standard engine went from 0-to-60 mph in 6.8 seconds while the Hemi Super Bees made the same speed in 6.6. Quarter-mile times were 15 seconds and 14 seconds for the two engines, respectively.

Model Number	Body/Style Number	Body Type & Seating	Factory Price	Shipping Weight	Production Total
CORONET SUPER BEE (383) — SERIES WM — V-8					
WM	21	2d Sedan-6P	$3,027	3,395 lbs.	7,716

NOTE 1: Prices and weights include 383-cid/335-hp V-8.
NOTE 2: Production totals are for Coronet R/Ts with the 383-cid/335-hp V-8.
NOTE 3: Of the cars listed above, 2,933 had the four-speed manual transmission..

Model Number	Body/Style Number	Body Type & Seating	Factory Price	Shipping Weight	Production Total
CORONET SUPER BEE (HEMI) — SERIES WM — V-8					
WM	21	2d Sedan-6P	$3,739	3,495 lbs.	125

NOTE 1: Price includes 426-cid/425-hp V-8 and no other options.
NOTE 2: Of the cars listed above, 31 had the four-speed manual transmission.
NOTE 3: Three additional Hemi Super Bees were sold in Canada.

ENGINE

BASE V-8: Overhead valve. Cast-iron block. Displacement: 383 cid. Bore and stroke: 4.25 x 3.38 inches. Compression ratio: 10.00:1. Brake hp: 335 at 5000 rpm. Taxable hp: 57.80. Torque: 425 at 3400 rpm. Five main bearings. Hydraulic valve lifters. Carburetor: Carter Thermo-Quad AVS-4615-S four-barrel. Engine code: PT-383. VIN code: H.

OPTIONAL V-8: Overhead valve with hemispherical segment combustion chambers. Cast-iron block. Displacement: 426 cid. Bore and stroke: 4.25 x 3.75 inches. Compression ratio: 10.25:1. Brake hp: 425 at 5000 rpm. Taxable hp: 57.80. Torque: 490 at 4000 rpm. Five main bearings. Hydraulic valve lifters. Carburetor: Two Carter AFB 3084-S four-barrel. Engine code: C-426. VIN code: J.

OPTIONS

426-cid Hemi V-8 ($712). TorqueFlite automatic transmission ($163-$176). Four-speed manual transmission ($145-$175). Air conditioning ($274). Auto Pilot cruise control ($64). Power steering ($73). Power brakes ($16). Power front disc brakes ($54). Electric clock ($11). Console ($20). Heavy-duty differential ($107). Power door locks ($42). Dual exhaust ($24). Buffed paint ($16). Music Master AM radio ($44). Tilt & Telescope steering wheel ($87). Woodgrained steering wheel ($20). Tachometer ($38). Vinyl top on hardtop ($70). Simulated "mag"-wheel covers ($41-$57). Road wheels ($59-$75). Three-speed windshield wipers ($4). Limited-slip differential for ($42). Custom wheels ($97). Front disc brakes ($72.95). Front seat console ($52.85).

1968 CHARGER R/T 440 MAGNUM/HEMI

DOUG MITCHEL

1968 Charger R/T Hemi

Dodge's R/T designation meant "Road/Track. "The '60s was a time when youthful car enthusiasts drove their car to work at the grocery store five days a week just to earn enough to pay the loan they took out to by a muscle car. Then, on Saturday, they took their supercar to the drag strip for some "track time." The Charger R/T was pushed as a machine that was well suited for both purposes.

Motor Trend magazine summed up the look of the R/T model as "a Charger with a set of mag wheels, wide oval tires and a bumblebee stripe around its rear end." Appropriate name badges, heavy-duty underpinnings and a 440-cid/375-hp Mag-num V-8 put extra emphasis on the car's split personality. The engine had a 4.32 x 3.75-inch bore and stroke, a 10.1:1 compression ratio and a single four-barrel carburetor. All Charger models underwent a vast amount of change in 1968, giving up the flat, wide fastback roof of 1966-1967 that resembled a jumping ramp for Jake Kochman's Dodge-loving "Helldrivers." Dodge stylists did a great job of adopting the popular late-1960s "Coke-bottle" shape to the more smoothly rounded 1968 Charger body, which was shared by the R/T version. Neat details styling details of the R/T version of the Charger included an integral rear deck lid spoiler and a competition-

DODGE

type gas filler cap. Chargers retained a 117-inch wheelbase, but the rear track was widened from 58.5 inches to 59.2 inches in 1968. Bucket seats and high-performance tires were standard.

Merchandised as a separate model, the standard Charger R/T with the 440-cid V-8 could move from 0-to-60 mph in 6.5 seconds and zip down a drag strip in 15 seconds at 93 mph.

The Charger R/T was the only Charger model that you could get a Hemi in during 1968. The move up to the Hemi option cost $604.75 in 1968 dollars, which might explain why only 475 such cars were put together. Of the total, 211 had the four-speed manual gearbox, which was a no-cost option.

Muscle Car Review reported a 6.0-second 0-to-60 time for the Hemi Charger R/T and said it could do the quarter-mile in 13.54 seconds at 101 mph.

ENGINE

BASE V-8: Overhead valve. Cast-iron block. Bore and stroke: 4.32 x 3.75 inches. Displacement: 440 cid. Compression ratio: 10.10:1. Brake hp: 375 at 4600 rpm. Taxable hp: 59.70. Torque: 480 at 3200 rpm. Five main bearings. Hydraulic valve lifters. Carburetor: Carter AVS-4428-S four-barrel. Engine code: PT-440. VIN code: L.

OPTIONAL V-8: Overhead valve with hemispherical segment combustion chambers. Cast-iron block. Displacement: 426 cid. Bore and stroke: 4.25 x 3.75 inches. Compression ratio: 10.25:1. Brake hp: 425 at 5000 rpm. Taxable hp: 57.80. Torque: 490 at 4000 rpm. Five main bearings. Hydraulic valve lifters. Carburetor: Two Carter AFB 3084-S four-barrel. Engine code: C-426. VIN code. J.

Model Number	Body/Style Number	Body Type & Seating	Factory Price	Shipping Weight	Production Total
CHARGER R/T 440 — SERIES XS — V-8					
XS	29	2d HT-5P	$3,613	3,750 lbs.	17,109

NOTE 1: The price above includes the 440 Magnum V-8 and no other options.
NOTE 2: The weight above is an estimate.
NOTE 3: The production above is for Chargers with the 440 Magnum V-8 only.
NOTE 4: 2,743 of the cars above had the four-speed manual transmission.

Model Number	Body/Style Number	Body Type & Seating	Factory Price	Shipping Weight	Production Total
HEMI CHARGER R/T (HEMI) — SERIES XS — V-8					
XS	29	2d HT-5P	$4,085	3,900 lbs.	475

NOTE 1: The price above includes the 426 Hemi V-8 and no other options.
NOTE 2: The weight above is an estimate.
NOTE 3: The production above is for Chargers with the 426 Hemi V-8 only.
NOTE 4: 211 of the cars above had the four-speed manual transmission.
NOTE 5: 22 additional Hemi Chargers were built for Canadian buyers.

OPTIONS

426 Hemi engine ($630). 440-cid Magnum V-8 engine $133). TorqueFlite automatic transmission ($163-$176). Four-speed manual transmission ($145-$175). Air conditioning ($274). Auto Pilot cruise control ($64). Power steering ($73). Power brakes ($16). Power front disc brakes ($54). Electric clock ($11). Console ($20). Sure-Grip differential ($29-$37). Heavy-duty differential ($107). Power door locks ($42). Dual exhaust ($24). Buffed paint ($16). Music Master AM radio on Coronets and Chargers ($44). Tilt & Telescope steering wheel ($87). Woodgrained steering wheel ($16). Tachometer ($38). Vinyl top ($70). Simulated "mag" wheel covers ($41-$57). Road wheels ($59-$75). Three-speed windshield wipers ($4).

1969 DART GTS 340/383/440

1969 Dart GTS

PHIL KUNZ

The GTS always had that Spanky McFarland tough-little-guy look when it rumbled into the drive-in. *Car Life* said, "All-around performance that outdoes its bigger cousins and most other rivals."

The 1969 Darts featured new grilles, headlights, tail lights and other exterior trim mounted on the same basic body shell as used in 1968. All Darts featured chrome windshield and rear window moldings, the Dodge name in block letters, across the vertical section of the trunk lid and on the left front corner of the hood, all mandatory safety equipment, and a heater and defroster. The high-performance version of the Dodge Dart,

came with a power bulge hood and GTS identification emblems on the hood, front fenders and trunk lid. The GTS was available only as a two-door hardtop or convertible. The GTS came with up-level interior trim. A bench seat was standard in the convertible (bucket seats were optional). Bucket seats were standard in the two-door hardtop.

The base engine was the Mopar 340-cid small block attached to a TorqueFlite automatic transmission. The 383-cid/330-hp big-block V-8 was an extra. Both of these engines could be ordered with a four-speed manual transmission at no extra cost. Late in the year, a small number of GTS Darts had

440 Magnum V-8s installed. The GTS had a special suspension including heavy-duty torsion bars, heavy-duty springs, heavy-duty shocks and a front sway bar. The GTS power bulge hood had simulated scoops that faced the fenders and carried badges indicating engine size. Rear "bumblebee" stripes were optional. The GTS-style stripe was a unique single-band design.

The 383-powered version did 0-to-60 in 6 seconds flat and the quarter-mile in 14.40 seconds at 99 mph.

Model Number	Body/Style Number	Body Type & Seating	Factory Price	Shipping Weight	Production Total
DART GTS — SERIES LS — V-8					
LS	23	2d HT-6P	$3,226	3,105 lbs.	5,717
LS	27	2d Conv-6P	$3,419	3,210 lbs.	360

NOTE 1: Prices and weights above are for the GTS with the base 340-cid V-8.
NOTE 2: Production total above are for all GTS models including all engines.

ENGINES

BASE V-8: Overhead valve. Cast-iron block. Bore and stroke: 4.04 x 3.31 inches. Displacement: 340 cid. Compression ratio: 10.5:1. Brake hp: 275 at 5000 rpm.

Taxable hp: 52.20. Torque: 340 at 3200 rpm. Five main bearings. Hydraulic valve lifters. Carburetor: Carter Thermo-Quad AVS-4611-S four-barrel. Engine code: PT-340. VIN code: P.

OPTIONAL V-8: Overhead valve. Cast-iron block. Displacement: 383 cid. Bore and stroke: 4.25 x 3.38 inches. Compression ratio: 10.00:1. Brake hp: 330 at 5200 rpm. Taxable hp: 57.80. Torque: 425 at 3200 rpm. Five main bearings. Hydraulic valve lifters. Carburetor: Carter four-barrel. Engine code: PT-383. VIN code: H.

OPTIONAL (LATE) V-8: Overhead valve. Cast-iron block. Bore and stroke: 4.32 x 3.75 inches. Displacement: 440 cid. Compression ratio: 10.10:1. Brake hp: 375 at 4600 rpm. Taxable hp: 59.70. Torque: 480 at 3200 rpm. Five main bearings. Hydraulic valve lifters. Carburetor: Carter AVS-4617-S four-barrel. Engine code: PT-440. VIN code: L.

OPTIONS

Four-speed manual transmission, in place of TorqueFlite (No cost). Power steering ($85, except not available with 383- or 440-cid big-block V-8s). Power brakes ($43). Console ($53). Tinted glass ($33). Air conditioning ($361). Two-tone paint ($23). Music Master AM radio ($62). AM/FM radio ($135). AM/FM 8-Track stereo ($196). Custom steering wheel with full horn ring ($15). Simulated woodgrain Sport steering wheel ($32). White sidewall tires ($34).

1969 DART SWINGER 340

PHIL KUNZ

1969 Dart Swinger 340

Not every Mopar muscle machine that came down the pike was a fire-breathing, Hemi-powered, big-engine-in-small-body bomber that fit in better at the drag strip than at the strip mall. There were also some compact Dodges fitted with hi-po small-block V-8s that provided enough sizzle for the masses without going overboard on the "high-end" high-performance hardware. The 1969 Dodge Swinger 340 was one example of such a car.

This model qualified as a member of the hot Dodge "Scat Pack" and proudly wore its bumblebee stripes, even though it was really more of a swinger than a stinger. Designed to give muscle car fans more bang for the buck by emphasizing performance over luxury, the Swinger fit right into the "budget muscle car" trend that produced cars like the Plymouth Road Runner and Pontiac GTO Judge. It was like a small-scale counterpart to such models. "The Swinger 340 isn't a supercar, it's just faster than a Swinger," said *Car Life* magazine in its January 1969 edition. "For once the ad men picked the

right name; the Swinger does." The idea was that a small car really doesn't need a big-block to go fast.

As muscle cars went, the Swinger 340 was a bargain and collector's today can still swing a pretty good deal on one of these cars. "Play your cards right and three bills can put you in a whole lot of car this year," said an ad showing a red Swinger two-door hardtop with a black vinyl roof. "Dart Swinger 340. Newest member of the Dodge Scat Pack. You get 340 cubes of high-winding, four-barrel V-8. A four-speed Hurst shifter on the floor to keep things moving. All the other credentials are in order."

Standard equipment for 1969 included the 340-cid/275-hp V-8 engine, four-speed full-synchro manual transmission with Hurst shifter, a three-spoke steering wheel with a padded hub, a heavy-duty Rallye suspension, "Swinger" bumblebee stripes, D70 x 14 wide-tread tires, dual exhausts, a performance hood with die-cast louvers and fat 14-inch wheels. Seven colors were

DODGE

available for the car and four colors for vinyl roofs. All-vinyl upholstery (with full-carpeting on four-speed cars only) was included. Two axle options — a 3.55:1 and a 3.91:1 — gave better drag strip performance. A total of 20,000 were built.

Even today, muscle car collectors can find bargains in the Swinger 340 market, since these cars don't look as flashy as a GTS, although they are equally fast.

Model Number	Body/Style Number	Body Type & Seating	Factory Price	Shipping Weight	Production Total
DART SWINGER 340 — SERIES LM — V-8					
LM	23	2d HT-6P	$2,836	3,097 lbs.	20,000

NOTE 1: Price and weight are for the base Swinger 340; with typical options these cars cost around $3,600.
NOTE 2: Most sources show production of 20,000, but it is not clear if this includes the LL23 Swinger six.

ENGINE

BASE V-8: Overhead valve. Cast-iron block. Bore and stroke: 4.04 x 3.31 inches. Displacement: 340 cid. Compression ratio: 10.5:1. Brake hp: 275 at 5000 rpm. Taxable hp: 52.20. Torque: 340 at 3200 rpm. Five main bearings. Hydraulic valve lifters. Carburetor: Carter Thermo-Quad AVS-4611-S four-barrel. Engine code: PT-340. VIN code: P.

OPTIONS

Four-speed manual transmission, in place of TorqueFlite (No cost). Power steering ($85). Power brakes ($43). Console ($53). Tinted glass ($33). Air conditioning ($361). Two-tone paint ($23). Music Master AM radio ($62). AM/FM radio ($135). AM/FM 8-Track stereo ($196). Custom steering wheel with full horn ring ($15). Simulated woodgrain Sport steering wheel ($32). White sidewall tires ($34).

1969 CORONET R/T 440 MAGNUM/HEMI

1969 Coronet R/T

Back in the '60s, thousands of young car enthusiasts looked forward to weekends at the drag strip — and they didn't go there to watch other muscle car owners run. Instead, they spent Saturday night in the garage, tuning the engine of the car they had driven all week for a couple of quick runs on Sunday afternoon. After that, it was re-tuned for additional street use until the following weekend. The "Dodge Boys" were well aware of how the car world worked, so they used the R/T designation to identify the cars best suited for dual-purpose use. The mid-sized Coronet was one of the favorites.

In 1969, the Coronet R/T continued to play its traditional role as the high-performance model in the Coronet series. It included all of the features of the upscale Coronet 500 model, plus the Magnum 440-cid V-8, TorqueFlite automatic transmission, a light group option, body sill moldings and R/T bumblebee stripes across the trunk lid and down the fender sides. Two simulated hood air scoops located on the rear fenders, just ahead of the rear wheel openings, were optional

equipment. There was also a wider choice of rear axle ratios. Standard equipment was a 3.23:1 unit but 3.54:1, 3.55:1, 3.91:1 and 4.10:1 performance axle packages were also available. Obviously, Dodge was placing additional emphasis on the "Track" portion of the Road and Track model designation by adding more performance to its Coronet muscle car. Overall styling was similar to 1968, except that the previous front fender medallion became a large decal that appeared as part of the rear bumblebee stripe. The four-barrel high-performance 440-cid V-8 was the standard motor.

The Hemi V-8 engine was an additional $418 option for 1969 Coronet R/Ts. A Ramcharger fresh-air induction system was standard on Hemi-powered cars. It included twin air scoops on the hood that fed cold air into a fiberglass plenum bolted to the underside of the hood. Only about 107 of these Hemi cars were produced. The lucky few that own them today would have no trouble finding buyers if they ever wanted to part with them.

Model Number	Body/Style Number	Body Type & Seating	Factory Price	Shipping Weight	Production Total
CORONET R/T (440-4 HIGH-PERFORMANCE) — SERIES WS — V-8					
WS	23	2d HT-6P	$3,442	3,601 lbs.	6,351
WS	27	2d Conv-6P	$3,660	3,721 lbs.	416

NOTE 1: Prices and weights above are for Coronet R/T with base Magnum 440 four-barrel V-8.

NOTE 2: Production totals are for Coronet R/Ts with the 440 Magnum four-barrel V-8.

NOTE 3: Of the cars above, 1,541 two-door hardtops and 99 convertibles had the four-speed manual transmission.

Model Number	Body/Style Number	Body Type & Seating	Factory Price	Shipping Weight	Production Total
Coronet R/T (HEMI) — SERIES WS — V-8					
WS	23	2d HT-6P	$3,860	3,601 lbs.	97
WS	27	2d Conv-6P	$4,139	3,721 lbs.	10

NOTE 1: The prices above include the Hemi V-8 and no other options.

NOTE 2: The weights above are estimates.

NOTE 3: The production totals above are for Hemi-powered Coronet R/Ts.

NOTE 4: Of the Hemi-powered cars above, the four-speed manual transmission was installed in 58 hardtops and four convertibles.

ENGINES

CORONET R/T BASE V-8: Overhead valve. Cast-iron block. Bore and stroke: 4.32 x 3.75 inches. Displacement: 440 cid. Compression ratio: 10.10:1. Brake hp: 375 at 4600 rpm. Taxable hp: 59.70. Torque: 480 at 3200 rpm. Five main bearings. Hydraulic valve lifters. Carburetor: Carter AVS-4617-S four-barrel. Engine code: PT-440. VIN code: L.

CORONET R/T OPTIONAL "STREET HEMI" V-8: Overhead valve with hemispherical segment combustion chambers. Cast-iron block. Displacement: 426 cid. Bore and stroke: 4.25 x 3.75 inches. Compression ratio: 10.25:1. Brake hp: 425 at 5000 rpm. Taxable hp: 57.80. Torque: 490 at 4000 rpm. Five main bearings. Hydraulic valve lifters. Carburetor: Two Carter AFB 3084-S four-barrel. Engine code: PT-426. VIN code: J.

OPTIONS

426-cid Hemi V-8 ($418). TorqueFlite automatic transmission (standard). Four-speed manual transmission (no charge substitution on R/T models). Air conditioning ($358). Power steering ($100). Power brakes ($43). Power front disc brakes ($49). Power seats ($100). Power windows ($105). Electric clock ($18). Con¬sole ($54). Sure-Grip differential ($42). Two-tone paint ($23). Music Master AM radio ($62). AM/FM radio ($135). AM/8-track stereo ($196). Automatic speed control ($58). Rallye suspension ($23). Woodgrain steering wheel ($27). Vinyl top ($89). Chrome stamped 14-inch wheels ($86). White sidewall tires ($34).

1969 SUPER BEE 440 SIX-PACK/HEMI

DON BOWSER

1969 Coronet Super Bee

A two-door hardtop joined the Coronet Super Bee line in 1969, the sport coupe returned, and there were few changes in appearance or standard equipment. New items included a single, wider rear bumblebee stripe and a Dodge "Scat Pack" badge on the grille and trunk, plus front fender engine callouts. Three two-barrel Holley carbs on an aluminum Edelbrock manifold were the heart of the new "Six-Pack" performance option. Cars so equipped generated 390 hp and 490 lbs.-ft. of torque. The Six-Pack option included a flat black fiberglass hood that locked in place with four chrome pins so that it could be entirely removed for access to the engine. There was also a new Ramcharger cold-air induction system that featured two large hood-mounted air scoops, an under hood air plenum and a switch to select between warm and cold air. The Super Bee

Six-Pack came with a choice of a four-speed manual gearbox or a TorqueFlite automatic transmission linked to a 9 3/4-inch Dana 60 Sure-Grip axle with 4.10:1 gears.

The new Ramcharger cold-air induction system was standard on Coronet Super Bees having the optional Street Hemi V-8. Counting cars with the base 383-cid V-8, a total of 27,800 Super Bees were built. This included 166 Hemi-powered cars, 92 of them with four-speeds.

In a January 1969 comparison of six "econo-racers" _Car and Driver_ magazine got its hands on a new Super Bee with the base 383-cid/335-hp V-8. The car, which listed for $3,858 fully equipped and weighed 3,765 lbs., could go from 0-to-60 in 5.6 seconds. It did the quarter-mile in 14.04 seconds at 99.55 mph. However, the magazine found the car to have a

DODGE

dual-point distributor and large-diameter exhaust pipes, which seemed at first to be "stock" but later proved to be tweaks made by Chrysler. "We can't consider our test car's performance to be representative of a 383 Super Bee you would buy," said the editors. "From our experience, we would estimate a production car in good tune to run about 98.5 mph in the 14.20-second range." Even that's not too shabby! *Car Life* reported a 0-to-60 time of 6.3 seconds and its test car did the quarter-mile in 13.8 seconds at 104.2 mph.

Hemi Super Bee performance numbers did not show up in our research, but these lightweight Dodges should be a bit faster than the Hemi Coronet R/T hardtop.

Model Number	Body/Style Number	Body Type & Seating	Factory Price	Shipping Weight	Production Total
CORONET SUPER BEE — SERIES WM — V-8 (440-6)					
WM	21	2d Cpe-6P	$3,545	3,480 lbs.	420
WM	23	2d HT-6P	$3,607	3,510 lbs.	1,487

NOTE 1: Prices above include the 440 Six-Pack option and no other extrras.
NOTE 2: The weights above are estimates.
NOTE 3: Production totals above are for Coronet Super Bees with the 440 "Six-Pack" V-8.
NOTE 4: Of the cars above, 267 coupes and 826 hardtops had the four-speed manual transmission.

CORONET SUPER BEE — SERIES WM — HEMI V-8 (426)					
WM	21	2d Cpe-6P	3907	3540	91
WM	23	2d HT-6P	3969	3570	10

NOTE 1: Prices above include the Hemi V-8 and no other option.
NOTE 2: The weights above are estimates.
NOTE 3: Production totals above are for Coronet Super Bees with the Hemi V-8.
NOTE 4: Of the cars above, 38 coupes and 92 hardtops had the four-speed manual transmission.
NOTE 5: In addition, 12 coupes and 12 convertibles were built for Canada.

ENGINES

OPTIONAL V-8: Overhead valve. Cast-iron block. Bore and stroke: 4.32 x 3.75 inches. Displacement: 440 cid. Compression ratio: 10.50:1. Brake hp: 390 at 4700 rpm. Taxable hp: 59.70. Torque: 490 at 3200 rpm. Five main bearings. Hydraulic valve lifters. Carburetor: three Holley two-barrel. Engine code: PT-440. VIN code: M.

OPTIONAL V-8: Overhead valve with hemispherical segment combustion chambers. Cast-iron block. Displacement: 426 cid. Bore and stroke: 4.25 x 3.75 inches. Compression ratio: 10.25:1. Brake hp: 425 at 5000 rpm. Taxable hp: 57.80. Torque: 490 at 4000 rpm. Five main bearings. Hydraulic valve lifters. Carburetor: Two Carter AFB 3084-S four-barrel. Engine code: PT-426. VIN code: J.

OPTIONS

426-cid Hemi V-8 ($831). 440-cid Six-Pack V-8 ($469). TorqueFlite automatic transmission (standard). Four-speed manual transmission (no charge substitution on R/T models). Air conditioning ($358). Power steering ($100). Power brakes ($43). Power front disc brakes ($49). Power seats ($100). Power windows ($105). Electric clock ($18). Console ($54). Sure-Grip differential ($42). Two-tone paint ($23). Music Master AM radio ($62). AM/FM radio ($135). AM/8-track stereo ($196). Automatic speed control ($58). Rallye suspension ($23). Woodgrain steering wheel ($27). Vinyl top ($89). Chrome stamped 14-inch wheels ($86). White sidewall tires ($34).

1969 CHARGER R/T 440 MAGNUM/HEMI

The 1969 Dodge Charger didn't change much from the 1968 model. As *Motor Trend* magazine put it, "That brute Charger styling, that symbol of masculine virility, was still intact." (Of course, those were the good old days when you could say things like that — which would be considered "politically incorrect" today — in the pages of a national magazine!)

For 1969, the Charger grille was divided into two sections and the taillights were modified a bit. However, the fastback Dodge was basically the same good-looking beast as before on the outside. Amazingly, you could get the big fastback with a six-cylinder engine, but only about 500 of those were made. The balance of the cars carried some type of V-8, usually a muscular version.

The R/T was the high-performance version of the Charger. The name once again implied its reliability as a street car and its adaptability to weekend dragstrip use. The Charger R/T included the 440-cid Magnum V-8, with a four-barrel carburetor, hooked to a three-speed TorqueFlite automatic transmission. Also included as part of the R/T package were low-restriction dual exhausts with chrome tips, heavy-duty manually adjusted drum brakes, F70-14 Red Line tires, the R/T heavy-duty handling package and bumblebee stripes. A new option package for Chargers that was also available on the R/T models was the

SE (or Special Edition) interior with leather bucket seats, lots of extra lights and wood-grained trim pieces.

With a 3.55:1 rear axle, the standard-equipped 440-powered Charger R/T, which came with a column-mounted gear shift lever, was found capable of running down the quarter-mile in 13.9 seconds at 101.4 mph.

Sinking in popularity to 400 production units was the Hemi Charger R/T. Around 192 of the Hemi-powered cars had four-speed manual transmissions in 1969. The R/T was the only Charger available with the Hemi V-8 engine again this year.

The 426-cid/425-hp powerhouse had a $648 price tag in 1969. You probably wouldn't trade a Hemi Charger for your rich neighbor's Ferrari today.

Model Number	Body/Style Number	Body Type & Seating	Factory Price	Shipping Weight	Production Total
CHARGER R/T — SERIES XS — V-8 (440)					
XS	29	2d HT-5P	3,592	3,646 lbs.	18,344

NOTE 1: The price and weight above include the 440 Magnum V-8 and no other options.
NOTE 2: The production above is for Charger R/Ts with the 440 Magnum four-barrel V-8.
NOTE 3: 3,605 of the cars above had the four-speed manual transmission.

Model Number	Body/Style Number	Body Type & Seating	Factory Price	Shipping Weight	Production Total
CHARGER R/T — SERIES XS — V-8 (HEMI)					
XS	29	2d HT-5P	$4,244	3,746 lbs.	432

JERRY HEASLEY

1969 Charger R/T 440 Magnum

ENGINES

BASE V-8: Overhead valve. Cast-iron block. Bore and stroke: 4.32 x 3.75 inches. Displacement: 440 cid. Compression ratio: 10.10:1. Brake hp: 375 at 4600 rpm. Taxable hp: 59.70. Torque: 480 at 3200 rpm. Five main bearings. Hydraulic valve lifters. Carburetor: Carter AVS-4617-S four-barrel. Engine code: PT-440. VIN code: L.

OPTIONAL V-8: Overhead valve with hemispherical segment combustion chambers. Cast-iron block. Displacement: 426 cid. Bore and stroke: 4.25 x 3.75 inches. Compression ratio: 10.25:1. Brake hp: 425 at 5000 rpm. Taxable hp: 57.80. Torque: 490 at 4000 rpm. Five main bearings. Hydraulic valve lifters. Carburetor: Two Carter AFB 3084-S four-barrel. Engine code: PT-426. VIN code: J.

OPTIONS

426-cid Hemi V-8 ($648). TorqueFlite automatic transmission (standard). Four-speed manual transmission (no charge substitution on R/T models). Air conditioning ($358). Power steering ($100). Power brakes ($43). Power front disc brakes ($49). Power seats ($100). Power windows ($105). Electric clock ($18). Console ($54). Sure-Grip differential ($42). Two-tone paint ($23). Music Master AM radio ($62). AM/FM radio ($135). AM/8-track stereo ($196). Automatic speed control ($58). Rallye suspension ($23). Woodgrain steering wheel ($27). Vinyl top ($89). Chrome stamped 14-inch wheels ($86). White sidewall tires ($34).

1969 CHARGER 500

Sleek, beautiful new styling had characterized the '68 Dodge Charger and had helped to boost the model's sales to 96,100 units — from only 15,800 in 1967. Wind-tunnel testing revealed that the good-looking body's recessed grille and tunneled-in rear window created wind turbulence on the high-speed NASCAR superspeedways. Dodge engineers figured out that a flush grille and flush-mounted rear glass could reduce this wind resistance. Some say that a prototype car with these changes — which was actually the first Charger 500 — was really a modified 1968 model. The production-type 1969 Charger 500 was issued as a special limited-production model based on the style of the Charger 500 prototype. It was released to the public on September 1, 1968, but as a 1969 model. Dodge Division literature said it was offered specifically for high-performance racing tracks and available only to qualified race drivers.

In reality, that was a great promotion, as muscle car lovers flocked to Dodge dealerships trying to buy one of the cars.

Chances are pretty good that, if they didn't get one, they at least drove away in another Charger or a jazzy Coronet.

The Charger 500's handcrafted body modifications were actually the workmanship of a company called Creative Industries, which was an aftermarket firm from Detroit. A minimum of 500 such cars had to be sold to the public to authorize the changes and make the Charger legal for racing under NASCAR rules. The Charger 500 model designation was based on the number of cars that was scheduled to be made. Even though some books say Hemi engines were standard in the Charger 500, at least 392 of these cars have been researched and only about nine percent have turned out to have Hemis. Officially, 32 Hemi-powered Charger 500s were built, though experts have tracked down serial numbers for 35 such vehicles. About 15 cars had four-speed manual gear boxes.

Two different Hemi-powered Charger 500 were tested by both *Hot Rod* (February 1969) and *Car Life* (April 1969). The first car tested by Hot Rod had automatic transmission

DODGE

JERRY HEASLEY

1969 Charger 500

and 3.23:1 gearing. It did the quarter-mile in 13.80 seconds at 105.01 mph. The second car tested by *Hot Rod* had a four-speed manual transmission and 4.10:1 gearing. It did the quarter-mile in 13.48 seconds at 109 mph.

Model Number	Body/Style Number	Body Type & Seating	Factory Price	Shipping Weight	Production Total
CHARGER 500 — SERIES XS — V-8 (440-4)					
XS	29	2d HT-5P	$3,843	3,671 lbs.	140
CHARGER 500 — SERIES XS — V-8 (HEMI)					
XS	29	2d HT-5P	$4,491	3,701 lbs.	84

NOTE 1: The weight above for the Charger 500 with the 440-4 V-8 is actual, the weight for the Hemi V-8 is an estimate.

NOTE 2: The production numbers above are known production numbers for Charger 500s built for the public.

NOTE 3: 26 of the 440-4 cars and 27 Hemi cars are reported to have four-speed manual transmissions.

NOTE 4: 103 of the 440-4 cars and 32 Hemi cars are reported to have TorqueFlite.

NOTE 5: At least two additional Hemi cars were made for Canada.

ENGINES

BASE V-8: Overhead valve. Cast-iron block. Bore and stroke: 4.32 x 3.75 inches. Displacement: 440 cid. Compression ratio: 10.10:1. Brake hp: 375 at 4600 rpm. Taxable hp: 59.70. Torque: 480 at 3200 rpm. Five main bearings. Hydraulic valve lifters. Carburetor: Carter AVS-4617-S four-barrel. Engine code: PT-440. VIN code: L.

OPTIONAL V-8: Overhead valve with hemispherical segment combustion chambers. Cast-iron block. Displacement: 426 cid. Bore and stroke: 4.25 x 3.75 inches. Compression ratio: 10.25:1. Brake hp: 425 at 5000 rpm. Taxable hp: 57.80. Torque: 490 at 4000 rpm. Five main bearings. Hydraulic valve lifters. Carburetor: Two Carter AFB 3084-S four-barrel. Engine code: PT-426. VIN code: J.

CHASSIS

Wheelbase: 117 inches. Overall length: 208 inches. Overall width: 77 in. Tires: F70-14.

OPTIONS

TorqueFlite automatic transmission (standard). Four-speed manual transmission (no-charge substitution on R/T models). Air conditioning ($358). Power steering ($100). Power brakes ($43). Power front disc brakes ($49). Power seats ($100). Power windows ($105). Electric clock ($18). Console ($54). Sure-Grip differential ($42). Two-tone paint ($23). Music Master AM radio ($62). AM/FM radio ($135). AM/8-track stereo ($196). Automatic speed control ($58). Rallye suspension ($23). Woodgrain steering wheel ($27). Vinyl top ($89). Chrome stamped 14-inch wheels ($86). White sidewall tires ($34).

1969 CHARGER DAYTONA

JERRY HEASLEY

1969 Charger Daytona

One of Chrysler's famous "winged warriors" was the Dodge Charger Daytona — the ultimate expression of the Charger 500's built-for-racing inspiration. Shortly after the Dodge Charger 500 bowed in 1969, Ford launched the Torino Talladega and Mercury Cyclone Spoiler models. Both FoMoCo products had superior aerodynamics, which helped them to outrun the slippery Charger 500s in enough races (including the Daytona 500) to take the National Association of Stock Car Automobile Racing title. The '69 Charger Daytona was designed to get the NASCAR championship back.

A company called Creative Industries received the contract to build 500 Daytonas to legalize the 200-mph body modifications for stock car competition. The rear window was flush, rather than tunneled. The front fenders and hood were lengthened and dipped lower in front. The front air intake was lower. Reinforced-plastic parts were used on the front-end extension and hood parts. The concealed headlights popped up like bug eyes. The hood featured a fresh air intake similar to the NASA inlets employed on aircraft. The hood and fenders had cooling vents. At the rear was an airfoil/spoiler of fin-and-wing that provided greater aerodynamic stability. Dodge press releases noted the modifications had been submitted to NASCAR for approval.

The winged cars won so many races that NASCAR outlawed the Hemi as well as wedge engines with piston displacements over 305 cubic inches. A 440-powered Daytona was tested in the December 1969 issue of *Road Test* magazine. It did the quarter-mile in 14,48 seconds at 96.15 mph. A Hemi-powered Daytona was tested in the December 1969 issue of *Car and Driver*. It did 0-to-60 mph in 6 seconds and the quarter-mile in 13.9 seconds at 101 mph.

Model Number	Body/Style Number	Body Type & Seating	Factory Price	Shipping Weight	Production Total
CHARGER DAYTONA — SERIES XS — V-8 (440-4)					
XS	29	2d HT-5P	$3,993	—	433
CHARGER DAYTONA — SERIES XS — V-8 (HEMI)					
XS	29	2d HT-5P	$4,641	—	70

NOTE 1: The price for the Hemi Daytona includes the 426-cid Hemi V-8 and no other options.

NOTE 2: 139 of the 440-4 cars and 22 Hemi cars are reported to have four-speed manual transmissions

NOTE 3: 294 of the 440-4 cars and 48 Hemi cars are reported to have TorqueFlite.

NOTE 4: At least five additional Hemi cars were made for Canada.

NOTE 5: One yellow Daytona, with 5,000 original miles, has been documented to be a car with a dealer-installed 440 Six-Pack V-8. Dodge did not, however, offer this set up as a factory-installed option.

ENGINES

BASE V-8: Overhead valve. Cast-iron block. Bore and stroke: 4.32 x 3.75 inches. Displacement: 440 cid. Compression ratio: 10.10:1. Brake hp: 375 at 4600 rpm. Taxable hp: 59.70. Torque: 480 at 3200 rpm. Five main bearings. Hydraulic valve lifters. Carburetor: Carter AVS-4617-S four-barrel. Engine code: PT-440. VIN code: L.

DEALER-INSTALLED V-8: Overhead valve. Cast-iron block. Bore and stroke: 4.32 x 3.75 inches. Displacement: 440 cid. Compression ratio: 10.50:1. Brake hp: 390 at 4700 rpm. Taxable hp: 59.70. Torque: 490 at 3200 rpm. Five main bearings. Hydraulic valve lifters. Carburetor: three Holley two-barrel. Engine code: PT-440. VIN code: M.

OPTIONAL V-8: Overhead valve with hemispherical segment combustion chambers. Cast-iron block. Displacement: 426 cid. Bore and stroke: 4.25 x 3.75 inches. Compression ratio: 10.25:1. Brake hp: 425 at 5000 rpm. Taxable hp: 57.80. Torque: 490 at 4000 rpm. Five main bearings. Hydraulic valve lifters. Carburetor: Two Carter AFB 3084-S four-barrel. Engine code: PT-426. VIN code: J.

OPTIONS

TorqueFlite automatic transmission (standard). Four-speed manual transmission (no charge substitution on R/T models). Air conditioning ($358). Power steering ($100). Power brakes ($43). Power front disc brakes ($49). Power seats ($100). Power windows ($105). Electric clock ($18). Console ($54). Sure-Grip differential ($42). Two-tone paint ($23). Music Master AM radio ($62). AM/FM radio ($135). AM/8-track stereo ($196). Automatic speed control ($58). Rallye suspension ($23). Woodgrain steering wheel ($27). Vinyl top ($89). Chrome stamped 14-inch wheels ($86). White sidewall tires ($34).

DODGE

1970 DART SWINGER 340

JERRY HEASLEY

1970 Dart Swinger 340

The Swinger 340 two-door hardtop was a member of the "Scat Pack" that returned to Dodge dealerships in 1969. As our ace photographer Jerry Heasley once wrote in *Car Review*, way back in 1986, "If the Road Runner was the first econo-supercar, then the Dart was very much its counterpart in the compact lineup. Nobody built this car better than the 'Good Guys' in the white hats from Dodge."

When it came to the Swinger 340, the Good Guys advertised the car as "6000 rpm for under $3,000." With a short 97-inch wheelbase and overall length of just 178 inches, the Swinger 340 was a small, light car that used hot versions of the small-block V-8 to the best advantage. The 1970 Dodge Darts shared revised front and rear cosmetics and the Swinger 340 version even got a slightly reduced $2,631 price tag. A three-speed manual gear box was on the standard equipment list. Instead of small power vents, the mini Mopar muscle machine now carried two long, narrow hood scoops.

The Swinger 340 was as fast — or perhaps even slightly faster than — the 340-powered Dart GT Sport. It accomplished 0-to-60 mph in about 6.5 seconds and did the quarter-mile in around 14.5 seconds with a 98-mph terminal speed. At 3,179 lbs., the '70 Swinger carried about 11.4 lbs. per horsepower and proved to be highly motivated by the 340-cid V-8's "herd" of 275 horses.

Despite the introduction of the all-new Challenger "pony car" in 1970, the Swinger 340 remained popular enough to generate 13,785 assemblies. One reason for its popularity was that insurance companies considered it a "compact" car. As a result, the insurers charged lower premiums for a Swinger 340 than for other more obvious muscle cars. Today, in-the-know muscle car collectors find tremendous bargains in the Swinger 340 market. These cars just don't share the flashy looks of the Dodge Dart GTS, although they are equally as fast. And you know that some people will pay silly money just to get a little flashiness.

Model Number	Body/Style Number	Body Type & Seating	Factory Price	Shipping Weight	Production Total
DART SWINGER 340 — SERIES LM — V-8					
LM	23	2d HT-6P	$2,631	3,130 lbs.	13,785

NOTE 1: Price and weight are for the base Swinger 340.

ENGINE

BASE V-8 : Overhead valve. Cast-iron block. Bore and stroke: 4.04 x 3.31 inches. Displacement: 340 cid. Compression ratio: 8.80:1. Brake hp: 275 at 5000 rpm. Taxable hp: 52.20. Torque: 340 at 3200 rpm. Five main bearings. Hydraulic valve lifters. Carburetor: Carter Thermo-Quad AVS-4933-S four-barrel. VIN code: H.

OPTIONS

Four-speed manual transmission ($188). Power steering ($85). Power brakes ($43). Tinted glass ($33). Air conditioning ($361). Two-tone paint ($23). Music Master AM radio ($62). AM/FM radio ($135). AM radio with 8-track tape ($196). Simulated woodgrain Sport steering wheel ($32). White sidewall tires ($34).

1970 CHALLENGER R/T 440/HEMI

1970 Challenger R/T Hemi

In writing about the '70 Challenger R/T, *Car Life* magazine posed the unusual question, "What do you call a car with a 440 Six-Pack, four on the floor, purple metallic paint and an urge to challenge the world? Genghis Grape?" The new-for-1970 Challenger was Dodge's answer to the Mustang, Camaro, Cougar, Firebird, Camaro and Barracuda. The sports compact model was offered in three body styles: two-door hardtop, Special Edition coupe (with a formal roof) and convertible.

For high-performance buffs, Dodge offered all three models in the Challenger R/T format. The R/T package included everything on the base Challenger's equipment list, plus a 383-cid V-8 with a four-barrel carburetor and a bunch of other muscle car stuff. The 440-cid Magnum V-8 was one of the real high-performance options for the R/T. The 375-hp four-barrel version of this overhead-valve V-8 was $250 extra. A dual exhaust was standard. A 390-hp version of the 440-cid V-8 with the "Six-Pack" option (three Holley two-barrel carburetors) was another extra.

The Hemi option included several heavy-duty upgrades as well and cost an additional $1,228, due to the huge price hike, it was only chosen by 356 buyers in 1970. The Hemi came standard with a 727 TorqueFlite automatic transmission, but could be ordered with a four-speed manual transmission with a Hurst pistol-grip style shifter. With the 440 or Hemi V-8s, buyers got 15-inch wheels and fat 60-series tires. Hemi R/Ts came with a dual hood scoop setup. The scoops did not force air directly into the engine. However, for only $97, a "Shaker" hood scoop option could be ordered. It mounted to the engine

itself and stuck up through a large hole in the hood to force air into the carburetors.

The Challenger convertible with the 440-cid/375-hp V-8 could move from 0-to-60 mph in 7.1 seconds according to *Muscle Car Field Guide*. The quarter-mile got covered in 14.64 seconds with a terminal speed of 97.82 mph. The Challenger with Hemi power did the quarter-mile in 14 seconds at 104 mph.

Model Number	Body/Style Number	Body Type & Seating	Factory Price	Shipping Weight	Production Total
CHALLENGER R/T 440-4 — SERIES JS — V-8					
JS	23	2d HT-6P	$3,516	3,405 lbs.	2,802
JS	29	2d SE HT-6P	$3,748	3,440 lbs.	87
JS	23	2d Conv-6P	$3,785	3,470 lbs.	163
CHALLENGER R/T 440-6 — SERIES JS — V-8					
JS	23	2d HT-6P	$3,516	3,405 lbs.	1,640
JS	29	2d SE HT-6P	$3,748	3,440 lbs.	296
JS	23	2d Conv-6P	$3,785	3,470 lbs.	99

NOTE 1: Weights are for the base 440-4 Challenger.

NOTE 2: Production is for Challenfgers with 440-cid V-8s only.

Model Number	Body/Style Number	Body Type & Seating	Factory Price	Shipping Weight	Production Total
CHALLENGER R/T HEMI — SERIES JS — V-8					
JS	23	2d HT-6P	$4,056	3,505 lbs.	287
JS	29	2d SE HT-6P	$4,288	3,540 lbs.	60
JS	23	2d Conv-6P	$4,325	3,570 lbs.	9

NOTE 1: Prices above include the cost of the Hemi engine and no other extras.

NOTE 2: Weights are estimated.

NOTE 3: Production is for Hemi Challenger R/Ts only.

ENGINES

OPTIONAL V-8: Overhead valve. Cast-iron block. Bore and stroke: 4.32 x 3.75 inches. Displacement: 440 cid. Compression ratio: 9.70:1. Brake hp: 375 at 4600 rpm. Taxable hp: 59.70. Torque: 480 at 2800 rpm. Five main bearings. Hydraulic valve lifters. Carburetor: Carter AVS-4737-S four-barrel. VIN code: U.

PHIL KUNZ

DODGE

OPTIONAL V-8: Overhead valve. Cast-iron block. Bore and stroke: 4.32 x 3.75 inches. Displacement: 440 cid. Compression ratio: 10.50:1. Brake hp: 390 at 4700 rpm. Taxable hp: 59.70. Torque: 490 at 3200 rpm. Five main bearings. Hydraulic valve lifters. Carburetor: three Holley two-barrel. VIN code: V.

OPTIONAL V-8: Overhead valve with hemispherical segment combustion chambers. Cast-iron block. Displacement: 426 cid. Bore and stroke: 4.25 x 3.75 inches. Compression ratio: 10.20:1. Brake hp: 425 at 5000 rpm. Taxable hp: 57.80. Torque: 490 at 4000 rpm. Five main bearings. Hydraulic valve lifters. Carburetor: Two Carter AFB 3084-S four-barrel. VIN code: R.

OPTIONS

Hemi V-8 ($1,228). Four-speed manual transmission ($188). Power steering ($85). Power brakes ($43). Tinted glass ($33). Music Master AM radio ($62). AM/FM radio ($135). AM radio with 8-track tape ($196). Simulated woodgrain Sport steering wheel ($32). Vinyl roof for hardtop (All Special Edition hardtops came with a vinyl roof due to the rear window modifications). M51 power sunroof (vailable in conjunction with vinyl roof; operates by switch or hand. A01

light group. A04 basic group: includes AM radio (upgrades could be ordered at differential price), power steering, left-hand remote-control outside rearview mirror, variable speed wipers and electric washers. A05 protection group. A32 Super Performance axle package.. A33 Track Pack package includes four-speed manual transmission, 3.54 gears with Sure Grip in a Dana 9.75-inch axle, seven-blade fan, high-cool radiator and dual-point distributor. A34 Super Track Pack package: Same as Track Pack but with 4.10 gears and power front disc brakes. A35 trailer tow package. A36 performance axle package: available on cars with four-barrel or multiple carburetors. A44 backlite louver group. A45 aerodynamic spoiler package, includes front chin spoiler and T/A type aerodynamic rear spoiler. A63 moulding group. C15 seat belt group. C16 floor console group. H31 rear window defroster (hardtop only). H51 air conditioning, includes belt-driven R12 freon system (not available with 440 Six-Pack). W23 14 x 5.5-inch chrome Road Wheel ("Magum 500"). W21 14 x 5.5 or 15 x 7-inch slotted Rallye Wheel (with separate polished center cap in 1970). 440 R/T models came standard with F70 x 14 Goodyear Polyglas GT tires. E60x15 Goodyear Polyglas GT tires were optional.

1970 CHALLENGER T/A

PHIL KUNZ

1970 Challenger T/A

The Challenger T/A package was offered to comply with the rules of the Sports Car Club of America's Trans-American Sedan Championship. The Challenger T/A featured a hot 340-cid "small-block" V-8 with a Six-Pack carburetor setup. Though rated somewhat lower, this engine actually put out about 350 hp.

The T/A had a matte-black-finished fiberglass hood with a huge oval-shaped air filter over its triple two-barrel carburetors. It also had a special high-flow dual exhaust system that ran to the rear axle, then doubled back to exit ahead of the rear wheel. Two large-diameter chrome-plated exhaust tips were included. The T/A came equipped with either the 727 Torque-Flite automatic or a four-speed gearbox with a Hurst shifter. Buyers got a choice of 3.55:1 or 3.90:1 gears and manual or power steering. Front-disc brakes and a heavy duty "Rallye Suspension" were standard.

The Challenger T/A was one of the first American regular-production automobiles to use different-size tires in front and back.. Dodge engineers increased the camber of the springs to elevate the rear end enough to clear the fat rear tires. A wide, black trim stripe ran the length of the body and a subtle, molded-wing spoiler was featured.

The 1970 Challenger T/As were good for 0-to-60 mph in a flat 6 seconds. They could hit 100 mph in 14 seconds and do the quarter-mile in 14.5 seconds. T/As were not very competitive in the SCCA T/A series, and the street model understeered badly at high speeds, so it did not make for a very popular car from that aspect, although it did turn out mid-14 second quarter-mile time, which was very good for that era, especially from a small block car. But even with the fine quarter-mile time, and mean appearance, Dodge removed itself from the SCCA series after 1970, and dropped the T/A option.

Model Number	Body/Style Number	Body Type & Seating	Factory Price	Shipping Weight	Production Total
CHALLENGER T/A — SERIES JH — V-8					
JH	23	2d HT-6P	$4,643	3,500 lbs.	2,399

NOTE 1: The prices above was the actual price for a Challenger T/A with the following equipment: 340–6 V-8, four-speed manual transmission, power disc brakes, heavy-duty shocks, fiberglass hood, fresh air package, 3.91 Sure Grip differential, tinted windshield, racing mirrors, rear spoiler and fast-ratio power steering.

NOTE 2: Weight is estimated.

NOTE 3: Production is for Challenger T/A only.

ENGINE

BASE V-8: Overhead valve. Cast-iron block. Bore and stroke: 4.04 x 3.31 inches. Displacement: 340 cid. Compression ratio: 8.80:1. Brake hp: 275 at 5000 rpm. Taxable hp: 52.20. Torque: 340 at 3200 rpm. Five main bearings. Hydraulic valve lifters. Carburetor: Carter Thermo-Quad AVS-4933-S four-barrel. VIN code: J.

OPTIONS

Four-speed manual transmission ($188). Power steering ($85). Power brakes ($43). Tinted glass ($33). Music Master AM radio ($62). AM/FM radio ($135). AM radio with 8-track tape ($196). Simulated woodgrain Sport steering wheel ($32). Black, White, Green or Gator Grain vinyl roof. A01 light group. A04 ba- sic group: includes AM radio (upgrades could be ordered at differential price), power steering, left-hand remote-control outside rearview mirror, variable speed wipers and electric washers. A05 protection group. A32 Super Performance axle package. A33 Track Pack package includes 4-speed manual transmission, 3.54 gears with Sure Grip in a Dana 9.75-inch axle, 7-blade fan, high-cool radiator and dual-point distributor. A34 Super Track Pack package: Same as Track Pack but with 4.10 gears and power front disc brakes. A36 performance axle package: available on cars with four-barrel or multiple carburetors, includes 3.55:1 axle gears with Sure Grip in a 8.75-inch axle, heavy-duty cooling and heavy-duty suspension. A44 backlite louver group. A63 moulding group. C15 seat belt group. C16 floor console group: offered different (but very similar) center consoles for manual-shift or automatic transmission cars. H31 rear window defroster (hardtop only): includes an electric heater and blower motor mounted under the rear shelf panel, air duct and vent. Challenger standard steel wheels came two ways: 1) painted to match the body color with a small "doggie-dish" hubcaps or 2) painted black with a full rim cover. Full wheel covers came three ways: 1) a simulated wire wheel (code W15), 2) deep dish (code W13), 3) deluxe (code W11). Hemi T/As came with the 15 x 7- inch steel wheel standard. W23 14 x 5.5-inch chrome Road Wheel ("Magnum 500"). W21 14 x 5.5 or 15 x 7-inch slotted Rallye Wheel (with separate polished center cap in 1970).

1970 CORONET R/T 440-4/440 SIX-PACK/HEMI

DOUG MITCHELL

1970 Coronet R/T 440

Like most automakers, Dodge offered several flavors of muscle in its mid-size cars and the basis for the hotter models was the Coronet, which was facelifted with a new grille and new delta-shaped tail lights. It was the last year for the Coronet convertible body style and also the last year for the Coronet R/T model. Standard R/T equipment included all Coronet 500 features plus the 440-cid Magnum four-barrel V-8 engine. Buyers could substitute a four-speed manual gearbox for the TorqueFlite if they preferred to shift for themselves. Engines were essentially the same as before with the "440 Six-Pack" installed in 210 cars this year. The R/T continued to come in an outrageous assortment of colors, like Plum Crazy, Sublime, Go-Mango, Hemi Orange and Banana.

The Coronet R/T with the 440 Magnum four-barrel V-8 could do 0-to-60 mph in 6.5 seconds and covered the quarter-mile in 14 seconds at 102.2 mph.

In 1970 the 426-cid/425-hp Hemi was priced at $718 and only 14 Hemi R/Ts were built. There are probably more than that around today! We have not found performance test figures for the '70 Coronet R/T Hemi but if someone has a time slip on one of these puppies, send it in and we'll put it in the next edition of this book.

ENGINES

BASE V-8: Overhead valve. Cast-iron block. Bore and stroke: 4.32 x 3.75 inches. Displacement: 440 cid. Compression ratio: 10.10:1. Brake hp: 375 at 4600 rpm. Taxable hp: 59.70. Torque: 480 at 3200 rpm. Five main bearings. Hydraulic valve lifters. Carburetor: Carter AVS-4617-S four-barrel. Engine code: PT-440. VIN code: U.

OPTIONAL V-8: Overhead valve. Cast-iron block. Bore and stroke: 4.32 x 3.75 inches. Displacement: 440 cid. Compression ratio: 10.50:1. Brake hp: 390 at 4700 rpm. Taxable hp: 59.70. Torque: 490 at 3200 rpm. Five main bearings. Hydraulic valve lifters. Carburetor: three Holley two-barrel. VIN code: V.

OPTIONAL V-8: Overhead valve with hemispherical segment combustion chambers. Cast-iron block. Displacement: 426 cid. Bore and stroke: 4.25 x 3.75

DODGE

inches. Compression ratio: 10.20:1. Brake hp: 425 at 5000 rpm. Taxable hp: 57.80. Torque: 490 at 4000 rpm. Five main bearings. Hydraulic valve lifters. Carburetor: Two Carter AFB 3084-S four-barrel. VIN code: R.

OPTIONS (PARTIAL LIST)

E74 426 Hemi V-8 with dual four-barrel carburetors ($718.05, but not available with three-speed manual transmission, air conditioning, trailer towing group or automatic speed control). H51 Air conditioning ($357.65, but not available with four-speed, 440-6 V-8, hood air scoop or performance axle groups). N96 Ramcharger air scoop hood ($73.30 forcars without air conditioning or speed control). F11 50-amp alternator ($11, but standard on V-8s with air conditioning). D56 3.55:1 ratio rear axle ($10.35). B41 front disc brakes ($27.90 and B51 required). B11 heavy-duty auto-adjusting brakes ($22.65). A48 front bumper guards with front stone shield ($16). M83 rear bumper guards ($16). J21 electric clock ($18.45). C16 console ($53.35). H31 rear window defogger, except convertible ($26.25). D91 Sure Grip differential ($42.35, but standard with high-performance axle equipment). E87 440 Six-Pack V-8 ($119.05, but not available with air conditioning, trailer towing group or automatic speed control). V21 thin longitudinal dual-stripe bumblebee stripe (no charge). J41 pedal dress-up kit ($5.45). A32 Super Performance axle ($250.65, but not available with air conditioning or trailer towing package, TorqueFlite required). A33 Track Pak performance axle ($142.85, but not available with air conditioning, four-speed manual transmission required). A34 Super Track Pak performance axle ($235.65, but not available with air conditioning, four-speed manual transmission required). A36 performance axle, D34 required, with 440-cid V-8 ($92.25). B51 power brakes, disc brakes required ($42.95). S77 power steering ($105.20). P31 power windows ($105.20). N85 tachometer ($50.15 and not available with clock). A35 trailer towing package ($14.05, but not availablw with 440-6 V-8). D34 Torque-Flite automatic transmission (standard). D21 four-speed manual transmission with floor shift (no charge option, but Track Pak required). J59 undercoating and hood insulator pad ($16.60). Vinyl roof for hardtop ($95.70). W13 14-inch deep-dish wheel covers ($36.25). W15 14-inch wire wheel covers ($64.10). Wheel covers without Group A04: W13 deep-dish 14-inch wheels for Coronet ($36.25). W15 14-inch wire wheels for Coronet ($64.10). Wheel covers with Group A04: W13 14-inch deep-dish ($15.00). W15 14-inch wire wheels ($42.85). Wheels without Group A04: W23 14-inch Road Wheels with trim rings ($86.15). Wheels with Group A04: W23 14-inch Road Wheels with trim rings ($64.95). Wheels without Group A04: W23 14-inch Road Wheels with trim rings ($86.15). Wheels with Group A04: W23 14-inch Road Wheels with trim rings ($64.95). T87 F70-14 blackwall raised-white-lletter tires, replacing standard F70-14 whitewall tires (no charge). U84 F60-14 blackwall raised-white-letter tires in place of standard F70-14 whitewalls ($63.25).

Model Number	Body/Style Number	Body Type & Seating	Factory Price	Shipping Weight	Production Total
CORONET R/T — SERIES WS — V-8 (440-4 HIGH-PERFORMANCE)					
WS	23	2d HT-6P	$3,569	3,545 lbs.	1,948
WS	27	2d Conv-6P	$3,785	3,610 lbs.	219
CORONET R/T — SERIES WS — V-8 (440-6 Six-Pack)					
WS	23	2d HT-6P	$3,442	3,601 lbs.	194
WS	27	2d Conv-6P	$3,660	3,721 lbs.	16

NOTE 1: Prices and weights are for Coronet R/T with indicated version of 440-cid V-8.

NOTE 2: Production totals are for Coronet R/Ts with indicated version of 440-cid V-8.

NOTE 3: Of the 440-4 cars above, 405 two-door hardtops and 16 convertibles had the four-speed manual transmission.

NOTE 4: Of the 440-6 cars above, 97 two-door hardtops and seven convertibles had the four-speed manual transmission.

Model Number	Body/Style Number	Body Type & Seating	Factory Price	Shipping Weight	Production Total
CORONET R/T — SERIES WS — V-8 (HEMI)					
WS	23	2d HT-6P	$4,287	3,645 lbs.	13
WS	27	2d Conv-6P	$4,503	3,710 lbs.	1

NOTE 1: Prices above include the cost of the Hemi and no other options.

NOTE 2: The weights above are estimates.

NOTE 3: Production totals are for Coronet R/Ts with the 426 Hemi V-8.

NOTE 4: Of the Hemi cars above, four two-door hardtops and one convertible had the four-speed manual transmission.

NOTE 5: One hardtop and one convertible were built for Canada.

1970 CORONET SUPER BEE 440 SIX-PACK/HEMI

The Dodge Super Bee was a genuine muscle car created with an emphasis on keeping the price down as low as possible, while still delivering some serious go-fast hardware. The Super Bee was not a "cheap" car. The hardtop version was in the same bracket as a top-of-the line Coronet 500 hardtop — in fact it was $26 more expensive. In the fancy 500 model, the buyer was getting more chrome, richer upholstery, carpets and a cigar lighter. In the Super Bee, the buyer got less of the comfort and convenience items and more muscle for the money.

Also available for an even lower price was the Super Bee coupe or two-door sedan. It cost less than a Coronet 440 Deluxe coupe, but you got a whole lot more under the hood. So the Super Bee was more of a "good value" car than it was cheap. You were just buying hardware, rather than tinsel. Restyled for 1970 along the lines of the Coronet R/T, the Super Bee did not get the dummy rear fender scoops, at least as standard equipment. Standard ingredients were the 383-cid magnum V-8, a heavy-duty torsion-bar suspension and a three-speed manual transmission (last year's four-speed manual gear box was optional). Despite a price reduction for 1970, production dropped. That made the '70 Super Bee rare, as well as fast. Wouldn't you love to own one?

Hemis were installed in just 36 cars. The Hemi 426-cid/425-hp Super Bee did 0-to-60 in 5.3 seconds and the quarter-mile in 13.49 seconds at 105 mph.

Model Number	Body/Style Number	Body Type & Seating	Factory Price	Shipping Weight	Production Total
CORONET SUPER BEE — SERIES WM –V-8 (440-6)					
WM	21	2d Cpe-6P	$3,262	3,525 lbs.	196
WM	23	2d HT-6P	$3,324	3,560 lbs.	1,072

NOTE 1: Prices above include the 440 Six-Pack option and no other extras

NOTE 2: The weights above are estimates.

NOTE 3: Production totals above are for Coronet Super Bees with the 440 "Six-Pack" V-8.

NOTE 4: Of the cars above, 109 coupes and 599 hardtops had the four-speed manual transmission.

Model Number	Body/Style Number	Body Type & Seating	Factory Price	Shipping Weight	Production Total
CORONET SUPER BEE — SERIES WM — V-8 (HEMI)					
WM	21	2d Cpe-6P	$3,860	3,625 lbs.	4
WM	23	2d HT-6P	$3,922	3,660 lbs.	32

NOTE 1: Prices above include the 426 Hemi option and no other extras

NOTE 2: The weights above are estimates.

NOTE 3: Production totals above are for Coronet Super Bees with the 426 Hemi V-8

NOTE 4: Of the cars above, the four coupes and 21 hardtops had the four-speed manual transmission.

NOTE 5: Four coupes and two hardtops were built for Canada.

JERRY HEASLEY

1970 Coronet Super Bee

ENGINE

OPTIONAL V-8: Overhead valve. Cast-iron block. Bore and stroke: 4.32 x 3.75 inches. Displacement: 440 cid. Compression ratio: 10.50:1. Brake hp: 390 at 4700 rpm. Taxable hp: 59.70. Torque: 490 at 3200 rpm. Five main bearings. Hydraulic valve lifters. Carburetor: three Holley two-barrel. VIN code: M.

OPTIONAL V-8: Overhead valve with hemispherical segment combustion chambers. Cast-iron block. Displacement: 426 cid. Bore and stroke: 4.25 x 3.75 inches. Compression ratio: 10.20:1. Brake hp: 425 at 5000 rpm. Taxable hp: 57.80. Torque: 490 at 4000 rpm. Five main bearings. Hydraulic valve lifters. Carburetor: Two Carter AFB 3084-S four-barrel. VIN code: R.

OPTIONS (PARTIAL LIST)

E74 426 Hemi V-8 with dual four-barrel carburetors ($848.50, but not available with three-speed manual transmission, air conditioning, trailer towing group or automatic speed control). H51 Air conditioning (not available with four-speed, 440-6 V-8, hood air scoop or performance axle groups). N96 Ramcharger air scoop hood ($73.30 forcars without air conditioning or speed control). E87 440 Six-Pack V-8 ($249.55, but not available with air conditioning, trailer towing group or automatic speed control). N95 evaporative control system, California cars only ($37.85). C92 protective rubber floor mats ($13.60). G11 all tinted glass, except convertible backlite ($40.70). G15 tinted windshield only ($25.90). L41 headlight time delay with lamp-on reminder ($13). J45 hood tie-down pins ($15.40). G33 remote-ontrol left-hand rearview mirror ($10.45). G31 manual right-hand rearview mirror ($6.85). M31 belt moldings ($13.60). M33 vinyl body side molding ($14.80). M05 door edge guards, ($4.65). High-Impact paint colors ($14.05). Two-tone paint, except convertible ($23.30). V21 thin longitudinal dual-stripe bumblebee stripe (no charge). V21 single longitudinal stripe (no charge). A32 Super Performance axle ($250.65, but not avail-

able with air conditioning or trailer towing package, TorqueFlite required). A33 Track Pak performance axle ($142.85, but not available with air conditioning, four-speed manual transmission required). A34 Super Track Pak performance axle ($235.65, but not available with air conditioning, four-speed manual transmission required). A36 performance axle, D34 required, with 440-cid V-8 ($92.25). B51 power brakes, disc brakes required ($42.95). S77 power steering ($105.20). P31 power windows ($105.20). Radios without group A04: R11 Music Master AM radio ($61.55). R21 solid state AM/FM radio ($134.95). R22 stereo tape with AM radio ($196.25). Radios withgroup A04: R21 solid state AM/FM radio ($73.50). R22 stereo tape with AM radio ($134.75). R31 single rear speaker ($15.15). C21 center armrest with cushion, optional for all with bucket seats and without console ($54.45). C62 manual 6-way seat aduster ($33.30). C65 vinyl bucket seats ($100.85). N88 automatic speed control, requires TorqueFlite($57.95, but not avaialable with 440 Six-Pack or N96). D34 TorqueFlite automatic transmission (standard). D21 four-speed manual transmission with floor shift ($197.25, but not available with Track Pak, Super Track Pak or trailer towing package). J59 undercoating and hood insulator pad ($16.60). Vinyl roof for hardtop ($95.70). Wheel covers without Group A04: W13 deep-dish 14-inch wheels for Coronet ($36.25). W15 14-inch wire wheels for Coronet ($64.10). Wheel covers with Group A04: W13 14-inch deep-dish ($15.00). W15 14-inch wire wheels ($42.85). Wheels without Group A04: W23 14-inch Road Wheels with trim rings ($86.15). Wheels with Group A04: W23 14-inch Road Wheels with trim rings ($64.95). T87 F70-14 blackwall raised-white-lletter tires, replacing standard F70-14 whitewall tires (no charge). U84 F60-14 blackwall raised-white-letter tires in place of standard F70-14 whitewalls ($63.25). A04 radio group ($177.20). A01 light group ($26.55). C15 seat belt group ($13.75).

1970 CHARGER R/T 440-4/440 SIX-PACK/HEMI

The 1970 Dodge Charger continued to use the same semi fastback body that it had employed in 1969. Naturally, there were several minor trim changes to set cars of both years apart. The R/T (Road/Track) edition was again marketed as a higher-performance version of the basic Charger. It had a newly designed grille, a new loop-style front bumper, two hood scoops (one near each outside edge of the hood), big bolt-on side scoops (with R/T badges) on the rear quarter panels and a choice of longitudinal or bumblebee racing stripes on the rear.

A new interior design and some wild new exterior body colors like Plum Crazy, Sublime, Go Mango, Hemi Orange and Banana Yellow were also featured. The 440-cid Magnum V-8 engine was standard equipment, along with Mopar's sturdy TorqueFlite automatic transmission.

The 426-cid "Street Hemi" V-8 with twin four-barrel carburetors was optional. The Hemi Charger could do 0-to-60 mph in six seconds and the quarter-mile took a scant 13.54 seconds at 101 mph.

DODGE

CLIFF GROMER

1970 Charger R/T Hemi

Motor Trend did a comparison test between a 440-powered Charger R/T, a Mercury Cyclone GT and an Oldsmobile Cutlass SX in its April 1970 issue. The Charger test car had the standard equipment V-8, which produced 375 hp at 4600 rpm and 480 lbs.-ft. of torque at 3200 rpm. It also had a 3.55:1 rear axle. The car did 0-to-60 mph in 6.4 seconds and covered the quarter-mile in 14.9 seconds at 98 mph. It also averaged 14.9 to 15.7 mpg, which was much better fuel mileage than the two other cars. The magazine liked the Charger R/T's image and its race-bred heritage.

Car Life reported, "They keep making the Charger go like stink and handle better than a lot of so-called sportsters." For a big car, the Charger R/T packed a big wallop when it came to high-speed performance.

Model Number	Body/Style Number	Body Type & Seating	Factory Price	Shipping Weight	Production Total
CHARGER R/T (440-4) — SERIES XS — V-8					
XS	29	2d HT-5P	$3,711	3,638 lbs.	8,574
CHARGER R/T (440-6) — SERIES XS — V-8					
XS	29	2d HT-5P	$3,830	3,688 lbs.	684

NOTE 1: The prices above includes the indicated 440-cid V-8.
NOTE 2: The weight above for the 440 Six-Pack is an estimate.
NOTE 3: The production above is for Charger R/Ts the indicated 440-cid V-8.
NOTE 4: 1,443 of the 440-4 cars and 347 of the 440 Six-Pack cars had the four-speed manual transmission.

Model Number	Body/Style Number	Body Type & Seating	Factory Price	Shipping Weight	Production Total
CHARGER R/T (HEMI) — SERIES XS — V-8					
XS	29	2d HT-5P	$4,359	3,738 lbs.	112

NOTE 1: The price above includes the 426 Hemi V-8.
NOTE 2: The weight above is an estimate.
NOTE 3: The production above is for Charger R/Ts with the 426 Hemi V-8.
NOTE 4: 56 of the Hemi Charger R/Ts had the four-speed manual transmission.

ENGINES

BASE V-8: Overhead valve. Cast-iron block. Bore and stroke: 4.32 x 3.75 inches. Displacement: 440 cid. Compression ratio: 9.70:1. Brake hp: 375 at 4600 rpm. Taxable hp: 59.70. Torque: 480 at 2800 rpm. Five main bearings. Hydraulic valve lifters. Carburetor: Carter AVS-4737-S four-barrel. VIN code: U

OPTIONAL V-8: Overhead valve. Cast-iron block. Bore and stroke: 4.32 x 3.75 inches. Displacement: 440 cid. Compression ratio: 10.50:1. Brake hp: 390 at 4700 rpm. Taxable hp: 59.70. Torque: 490 at 3200 rpm. Five main bearings.

Hydraulic valve lifters. Carburetor: three Holley two-barrel. VIN code: V.

OPTIONAL V-8: Overhead valve with hemispherical segment combustion chambers. Cast-iron block. Displacement: 426 cid. Bore and stroke: 4.25 x 3.75 inches. Compression ratio: 10.20:1. Brake hp: 425 at 5000 rpm. Taxable hp: 57.80. Torque: 490 at 4000 rpm. Five main bearings. Hydraulic valve lifters. Carburetor: Two Carter AFB 3084-S four-barrel. VIN code: J.

OPTIONS (PARTIAL LIST)

H51 Air conditioning ($357.65, but not available with four-speed, 440-6 V-8, hood air scoop or performance axle groups). B41 front disc brakes ($27.90 and B51 required). B11 heavy-duty auto-adjusting brakes ($22.65). A48 front bumper guards with front stone shield ($16). J21 electric clock ($18.45). C16 console, with bucket seats ($54.45). H31 rear window defogger ($26.25). D91 Sure Grip differential ($42.35, but standard with high-performance axle equipment). E87 440 Six-Pack V-8 ($119.05, but not available with air conditioning, trailer towing group or automatic speed control). J45 hood tie-down pins ($15.40). M91 rear deck lid luggage rack ($33.30). G33 remote-control left-hand rearview mirror ($10.45). G31 manual right-hand rearview mirror ($6.85). M05 door edge guards, ($4.65). M08 lower deck lid sill guard ($21.15). M26 wheel lip moldings ($14.05). High-Impact paint colors ($14.05). V21 hood performance tape ($18.05). V22 Longitudinal thin dual stripe bumble bee stripe (no charge). V23 longitudinsal stripe (no charge). A32 Super Performance axle ($250.65, but not available with air conditioning or trailer towing package, TorqueFlite required). A33 Track Pak performance axle ($142.85, but not available with air conditioning, four-speed manual transmission required). A34 Super Track Pak performance axle ($235.65, but not available with air conditioning, four-speed manual transmission required). Cloth-and-vinyl front bucket seats (no charge) N88 automatic speed control, requires TorqueFlite ($57.95, but not available with 440 Six-Pack or N96). S80 wood-grain sports-type steering wheel ($26.75). S83 rim-blow steering wheel ($19.15). M51 sun roof with vinyl roof ($461.45). N85 tachometer with clock ($68.4, but standard with A62). A35 trailer towing package ($14.05, but not available with 440-6 V-8). D34 TorqueFlite automatic transmission (standard). D21 four-speed manual transmission with floor shift (no charge option, but Track Pak required). J59 undercoating and hood insulator pad ($16.60). Vinyl roof for hardtop ($100, but standard with sun roof). W13 14-inch deep-dish wheel covers ($36.25). W15 14-inch wire wheel covers for Chargers without A04 or A47 ($64.10). Wheel covers without Group A04: W13 deep-dish 14-inch wheels for Charger without A04 or A47 ($36.25). W15 14-inch wire wheels for Charger without A04 or A07 ($64.10). Wheel covers with Group A04: W15 14-inch wire wheels for Charger without A04 or A07 ($28.00). Wheels without Group A04: W21 14- or 15-inch Rallye for Charger without A47 ($43.10). W23 Road wheels with chrome trim rings for Charger without A04 or A47 ($86.15). Wheels with Group A04: W21 14- or 15-inch Rallte for Charger without A04 or A47 ($7.05). W23 14-inch Road wheels with chrome trim rings for Charger without A04 or A47 ($50.10). T87 F70-14 blackwall raised-white-lletter tires, replacing standard F70-14 whitewall tires (no charge). U84 F60-14 blackwall raised-white-letter tires in place of standard F70-14 whitewalls ($63.25). A47 Charger Special Edition package.

1970 CHARGER 500

1970 Charger 500

The Dodge Charger 500 made a return appearance for 1970. In the second season, it did not have aerodynamic enhancements like the '69 model, which featured a flush-mounted grille and flush rear window glass. The second 500 — at least in its standard format — was a regular Charger with "500" badges, new vinyl front bucket seats, an electric clock and front and rear wheel lip moldings. New options included a pistol-grip gear shifter and an electrically operated sun roof.

The biggest regular-production engine option for the '70 Charger 500 was the 383-cid V-8. This E63 engine, with a single four-barrel carburetor, added $137.55 to the price. One Charger 500 was ordered with a Hemi V-8, but this wasn't listed as a regular production option. In addition to 13 standard exterior colors, Charger 500 buyers could special order Plum Crazy (purple), Sublime (green), Go Mango, Hemi Orange and Banana Yellow paint.

The '70 Charger 500 wasn't as much a muscle car as the '69 edition, except for the one Hemi, but it was still a hot Dodge in its own right. Writing about the Charger 500 with the 383-cid big-block V-8 in the December 1970 issue of *Motor Trend*, A.B. Shuman noted, "The engine is flexible; the transmission is easy to work. Shuman could sense that this "383" Charger was an outstanding drive-it-daily muscle car that combined above-average street performance with a fairly affordable window sticker and decent road manners."

Model Number	Body/Style Number	Body Type & Seating	Factory Price	Shipping Weight	Production Total
CHARGER 500 (383) — SERIES XH — V-8					
XH	29	2d HT-5P	$3,384	3,413 lbs.	7,027
CHARGER 500 (HEMI)) — SERIES XH — V-8					
XH	29	2d HT-5P	$3,894	3,513 lbs.	1

NOTE 1: The price above includes the the indicated V-8.

NOTE 2: The weights above are estimates.

NOTE 3: The production for 383-4 powered Charger 500 is 7,027.

NOTE 4: 109 of the 383-powered cars had a three-speed manual transmission and 1,335 had a four-speed manual transmission.

NOTE 5: Only a single Hemi-powered car was built

ENGINE

OPTIONAL V-8: Overhead valve. Cast-iron block. Displacement: 383 cid. Bore and stroke: 4.25 x 3.38 inches. Compression ratio: 9.50:1. Brake hp: 330 at 5000 rpm. Taxable hp: 57.80. Torque: 425 at 3200 rpm. Five main bearings. Hydraulic valve lifters. Carburetor: Carter AVS-4376-S four-barrel. VIN code: G.

OPTIONS

H51 Air conditioning ($357.65), but not available with four-speed, 440-6 V-8, hood air scoop, performance axle groups or Hemi V-8). F11 50-amp alternator ($11, but standard on V-8s with air conditioning). C14 rear shoulder belts ($26.45). B11 heavy-duty self-adjusting brakes ($22.65). B41 front disc brakes ($27.90 and B51 required). B11 heavy-duty auto-adjusting brakes ($22.65). A48 front bumper guards with front stone shield ($16). J21 electric clock ($18.45). C16 console, with bucket seats ($54.45). H31 rear window defogger ($26.25). D91 Sure Grip differential ($42.35, but standard with high-performance axle equipment). E87 440 Six-Pack V-8 ($119.05, but not available with air conditioning, trailer towing group or automatic speed control). N95 evaporative control system, California cars only ($37.85). N42 bright exhaust tips, except not available in California ($20.80). C92 protective rubber floor mats ($13.60). G11 all tinted glass, except convertible backlite (($40.70). G15 tinted windshield only ($25.90). J45 hood tie-down pins ($15.40). M91 rear deck lid luggage rack ($33.30). G33 remote-control left-hand rearview mirror ($10.45). G31 manual right-hand rearview mirror ($6.85). M05 door edge guards, ($4.65). M08 lower deck lid sill guard ($21.15). M26 wheel lip moldings ($14.05). High-Impact paint colors ($14.05). V21 hood performance tape ($18.05). V22 Longitudinal thin dual stripe bumble bee stripe (no charge). V23 longitudinal stripe (no charge). A32 Super Performance axle ($250.65, but not available with air conditioning or trailer towing package, TorqueFlite required). A33 Track Pak performance axle ($142.85, but not available with air conditioning, four-speed manual transmission required). A34 Super Track Pak performance axle ($235.65, but not available with air conditioning, four-speed manual transmission required). A36 performance axle, D34 required, with 440-cid V-8 ($92.25). B51 power brakes, disc brakes required ($42.95). S77 power steering ($105.20). P31 power windows ($105.20). Radios without group A04: R11 Music Master AM radio ($61.55). R21 solid state AM/FM radio ($134.95). R22 stereo tape with AM radio ($196.25). Radios with group A04: R21 solid state AM/FM radio ($73.50). R22 stereo tape with AM radio ($134.75). R31 single rear speaker ($15.15). C21 center armrest with cushion, optional for all with bucket seats and without console ($54.45). Cloth-and-vinyl front bucket seats (no charge) N88 automatic speed control, requires TorqueFlite ($57.95, but not avaialable with 440 Six-Pack or N96). S80 wood-grain sports-type steering wheel ($26.75). S83 rim-blow steering wheel ($19.15). M51 sun roof with vinyl roof ($461.45). N85 tachometer with clock ($68.4, but standard with A62). A35 trailer towing package ($14.05, but not availablw with 440-6 V-8). D34 TorqueFlite automatic transmission (standard). D21 four-speed manual transmission with floor shift (no charge option, but Track Pak required). J59 undercoating and hood insulator pad ($16.60). Vinyl roof for hardtop ($100, but standard with sun roof). W13 14-inch deep-dish wheel covers ($36.25).

DODGE

W15 14-inch wire wheel covers for Chargers without A04 or A47 ($64.10). Wheel covers without Group A04: W13 deep-dish 14-inch wheels for Charger without A04 or A47 ($36.25). W15 14-inch wire wheels for Charger without A04 or A07 ($64.10). Wheel covers with Group A04: W15 14-inch wire wheels for Charger without A04 or A07 ($28.00). Wheels without Group A04: W21 14- or 15-inch Rallte for Charger without A47 ($43.10). W23 Road wheels with chrome trim rings for Charger without A04 or A47 ($86.15). Wheels with Group A04: W21 14- or 15-inch Rallye for Charger without A04 or A47 ($7.05). W23 14-inch Road wheels with chrome trim rings for Charger without A04 or

A47 ($50.10). T87 F70-14 blackwall raised-white-lletter tires, replacing standard F70-14 whitewall tires (no charge). U84 F60-14 blackwall raised-white-letter tires in place of standard F70-14 whitewalls ($63.25). A04 radio group for models without A47 S.E. package ($256.40). A04 radio group for models with A47 S.E. package ($220.15). A01 light group ($34.70, but standard with A47 S.E. package). A47 Special Edition package for Charger 500 adds leather-and-vinyl front bucket seats, a simulated walnut sports steering wheel, a pedal dress-up kit, the light group, deep-dish wheel covers, vinyl map and utility pockets in the right- and left-hand door panels.

1971 DEMON 340

JERRY HEASLEY

1971 Demon 340

After Plymouth experienced a runaway sales success with its 1970 Valiant Duster, the Dodge Division of Chrysler Corp. couldn't wait to get its hands on the platform. It became the base for a new mini muscle car. Things started really cooking that fall, when the Dart Demon was added to the 1971 model range. It was the first Dart, since the model's 1963 inception, with a true compact wheelbase. Like the Duster, the Demon came in two models. The base version had a 198-cid "Slant Six" and minimal standard equipment. It listed for $2,343, only $30 over the cost of a base Duster.

More interesting was the Demon 340, which at $2,721 was a mere $18 upstream from the Duster 340. It came standard with a well-balanced small-block V-8. A three-speed, fully synchronized floor shifter was included, along with a Rallye instrument cluster, a heavy-duty suspension, E70-14 rubber, racing stripes and dual exhaust. Playing the option list was the name of the game with domestic compacts and the Demon 340 had some interesting extras. They included a dual-scoop hood complete with hood pins, a rear deck lid spoiler and a "Tuff" steering wheel. You could also order a four-speed manual gearbox, TorqueFlite automatic transmission or an upgraded interior. The 340 was a card-carrying member of the 1971 Dodge "Scat Pack," which boasted many performance

cars. *Motor Trend* tested the Dodge Dart Demon 340 in its April 1971 issue. The car turned 0-to-60 mph in 7.8 seconds and did the quarter-mile in 14.56 seconds at 96 mph.

It would be the final year for the Scat Pack, however. At midyear, the Demon Sizzler option package became available. It was on the base Demon and started with the base six, but it added some of the 340's pieces and stripes to the base model. Demons also became the vehicles of choice for Pro Stock Dodge-mounted drag racers. Though the basic body was used, the cars were highly modified.

All the tricks worked and the Demon was a success, with 69,861 base models built and the 340 adding 10,098 more. While cousin Duster produced 173,592 base models, the 340 sales race was surprisingly close, as the Plymouth version came in at 12,886. The Dodge Demon returned for 1972, but the name was scrapped after that, in part because the religious community was less than thrilled by it. Dart Sport nomenclature sufficed from 1973 models through the end of production after the 1976 model year.

Model Number	Body/Style Number	Body Type & Seating	Factory Price	Shipping Weight	Production Total
DEMON 340 — SERIES LM29 — V-8					
LM29	29	2d Cpe-6P	$2,721	3,165 lbs.	10,098

ENGINE

BASE V-8: Overhead valve. Cast-iron block. Bore and stroke: 4.04 x 3.31 inches. Displacement: 340 cid. Compression ratio: 10.20:1. Brake hp: 275 at 5000 rpm. Taxable hp: 52.20. Torque: 340 at 3200 rpm. Five main bearings. Hydraulic valve lifters. Carburetor: Carter Thermo-Quad TQ-4972-S four-barrel. VIN code: H.

OPTIONS

Airtemp air conditioner. AM radio. AM/FM radio. Single rear seat speaker. Front bucket seats. Center console with TorqueFlite automatic transmission (requires bucket seats). Power brakes. Power steering. Tinted glass all windows. Deluxe wheel covers. Rallye wheels with chrome trim ring. Vinyl roof. Folding sun roof. Inside day/night mirror. Dual outside racing mirrors. Rear window defogger. Bumper guards. Vinyl body side molding. Sure Grip differential. Undercoating and hood insulator pad. Variable-speed windshield wipers and electric windshield washers. "Tuff" steering wheel, requires power steering. Hood scoops and hood black-out treatment. Four-speed manual transmission. TorqueFlite automatic transmission, Interior Decor Group, includes simulated wood-grained door trim panels, instrument panel with additional simulated wood-grained applique, rear armrests with ashtrays and carpeting. Custom Package, includes Interior Decor Group, 3-spoke steering wheel with spoke-mounted horn bars, cigarette lighter, dual horns and Exterior Decor Group. Exterior Decor Group, includes drip rail molding, grille surround molding and wheel lip moldings. Light Group, includes fender-mounted turn signal indicators, map and courtesy light, glove box light, ashtray light, trunk light and ignition switch light with time delay. Protection Group includes glove box lock, door-edge protectors and inside hood release.

1971 "MR NORM" DEMON 340 SIX-PACK

CLIFF GROMER

1971 "Mr. Norm" Demon 340 Six-Pack

The famous Mr. Norm's high-performance dealership in Chicago built a limited number of 1971 Dodge Dart Demons with a Six-Pack version of the 340-cid small-block V-8 under the hood. This was a factory option in Challengers, but not Demons. At least one of these cars even used a three-speed manual gearbox. Built primarily for drag racing (whether on the track or on the street), the cars carried stickers, stripes and decals indicating their association with Dodge Super salesman Norm Krauss. Some of these stickers will sell for over $1,000 today.

The cars also had special drag racing features such as battery boxes located in the trunk and special Mr. Norm's gauges and under-dash gauge clusters. Another item seen on some cars was a Mr. Norm's "wired down" clutch pedal. On some cars the inner fenders were modified to allow the use of headers.

ENGINE

SPECIAL V-8: Overhead valve. Cast-iron block. Bore and stroke: 4.04 x 3.31 inches. Displacement: 340 cid. Compression ratio: 10.20:1. Brake hp: 290 at 5000 rpm. Taxable hp: 52.20. Torque: 340 at 3200 rpm. Five main bearings. Hydraulic valve lifters. Carburetor: three Holley two-barrel. VIN code: J.

OPTIONS

Airtemp air conditioner. AM radio. AM/FM radio. Single rear seat speaker. Front bucket seats. Center console with TorqueFlite automatic transmission (requires bucket seats). Power brakes. Power steering. Tinted glass all windows. Deluxe wheel covers. Rallye wheels with chrome trim ring. Vinyl roof. Folding sun roof. Inside day/night mirror. Dual outside racing mirrors. Rear window defogger. Bumper guards. Vinyl body side molding. Sure Grip differential. Undercoating and hood insulator pad. Variable-speed windshield wipers and electric windshield washers. "Tuff" steering wheel, requires power steering. Hood scoops and hood black-out treatment. Four-speed manual transmission. TorqueFlite automatic transmission, Interior Decor Group, includes simulated wood-grained door trim panels, instrument panel with additional simulated wood-grained applique, rear armrests with ashtrays and carpeting. Custom Package, includes Interior Decor Group, Three-spoke steering wheel with spoke-mounted horn bars, cigarette lighter, dual horns and Exterior Decor Group. Exterior Decor Group, includes drip rail molding, grille surround molding and wheel lip moldings. Light Group, includes fender-mounted turn signal indicators, map and courtesy light, glove box light, ashtray light, trunk light and ignition switch light with time delay. Protection Group includes glove box lock, door-edge protectors and inside hood release.

Model Number	Body/Style Number	Body Type & Seating	Factory Price	Shipping Weight	Production Total
DEMON 340 — SERIES LM29 — V-8					
LM29	29	2d Cpe-6P	$4,000	3,200 lbs.	—

NOTE 1: Prices and weights are estimates.
NOTE 2: Production unknown.

DODGE

1971 CHALLENGER R/T 440 SIX-PACK/HEMI

CLIFF GROMER

1971 Challenger R/T 440

The R/T ("road/track") was Dodge's high-performance Challenger. The R/T package included a Rallye suspension, an instrument cluster with an 8,000-rpm tachometer, a 150-mph speedometer, heavy-duty drum brakes, chrome exhaust tips and distinctive graphic stripes. The R/T now had dummy air duct scoops in front of the rear wheel arches. All Six-Pack cars used the "power bulge" hood as standard and a "shaker" hood was optional. A total of 102 R/T big-block cars were fitted with the shaker hood.

The 426-cid-powered Hemi Challenger R/T made a return visit in 1971. The monster mill again carried two four-barrel carburetors and made 425 hp. It was only available in the Challenger R/T model. Hemi cars came with 15 x 7-inch steel wheels and F70x14 Goodyear Polyglas GT tires as standard equipment. Hemi models with a manual transmission came with a 9.75-inch Dana 60 "SureGrip" axle offering buyers a choice of 3.54:1 or 4.10:1 gearing. In Hemis with TorqueFlite, this rear end was optional, in place of the standard 8.75-inch housing.

ENGINE

OPTIONAL V-8: Overhead valve. Cast-iron block. Bore and stroke: 4.32 x 3.75 inches. Displacement: 440 cid. Compression ratio: 10.50:1. Brake hp: 390 at 4700 rpm. Taxable hp: 59.70. Torque: 490 at 3200 rpm. Five main bearings. Hydraulic valve lifters. Carburetor: three Holley two-barrel. VIN code: V.

OPTIONAL HEMI V-8: Overhead valve with hemispherical segment combustion chambers. Cast-iron block. Displacement: 426 cid. Bore and stroke: 4.25 x 3.75 inches. Compression ratio: 10.20:1. Brake hp: 425 at 5000 rpm. Taxable hp: 57.80. Torque: 490 at 4000 rpm. Five main bearings. Hydraulic valve lifters. Carburetor: Two Carter AFB 3084-S four-barrel. VIN code: R.

OPTIONS (PARTIAL LIST)

E74 426-cid Hemi V-8, requires W34; A33 or A34 required with four-speed floor shift ($789.95, but not available with air conditioning, N88 or A35). H51 air conditioning (usually $370.15 but not available with 440-cid V-8). D54 3.23:1 rear axle ($12.55, but no extra cost with B41 and D91). C16 center console, bucket seats required ($53.05). D91 Sure-Grip differential ($41.70, but

The Challenger with Hemi power did the quarter-mile in 14 seconds at 104 mph. The 440 Six-Pack Challenger was good for 0-to-60 mph in six seconds and a 13.62-second quarter mile at 104 mph. Those are the numbers *Car Craft* printed for the '70 model in November 1969, but the performance of the '71 should be in the same general bracket.

Model Number	Body/Style Number	Body Type & Seating	Factory Price	Shipping Weight	Production Total
CHALLENGER R/T — SERIES JS — V-8 (440-6)					
JS	23	2d HT-6P	$3,533	3,945 lbs.	250

NOTE 1: Weight is for the base Challenger R/T.
NOTE 2: Production is for Challengers with 440-6 V-8 only.
NOTE 3: 129 cars had the four-speed manual transmission.

Model Number	Body/Style Number	Body Type & Seating	Factory Price	Shipping Weight	Production Total
CHALLENGER R/T — SERIES JS — V-8 (HEMI)					
JS	23	2d HT-6P	$4,063	3,505 lbs.	71

NOTE 1: Prices above include the cost of the Hemi engine and no other extras.
NOTE 2: Weights are estimated.
NOTE 3: Production is for Hemi Challenger R/Ts only.
NOTE 4: 59 of the above cars had the four-speed manual transmission.

standard with A31). N25 engine block heater ($14.30). E87 440-cid Six-Pack V-8, reqires A33 or A34 with four-speed floor shift ($253.20, but not available with air conditioning. J46 locking flip-top gas cap ($7.75). G11 all-tinted windows ($36.85). G15 tinted windshield only ($25.05). N94 fiberglass hood with fresh air pack ($152.95, but not available with A46). V21 performance hood tape treatment ($23.50). N96 "shaker" hood scoop ($94). J45 hood tie-down pins ($15.20, but not available with N94 fiberglass hood with fresh air pack). A62 Rallye instrument panel cluster (standard Challenger R/T). M91 rear deck lid luggage rack ($31.10, but not available with A44 or J81). G33 remote-control chrome left-hand outside rearview mirror ($14.95). High-Impact paint colors ($13.85). Body side performance tape striopes (standard on R/T). B51 power brakes ($41.55). S77 power steering ($96.55). P31 power windows ($101.30). R11 Music Master radio ($61.10). R26 AM radio with stereo tape cassette ($201.60). R35 AM/FM stereo multiplex radio ($196.60). R36 AM/FM stereo multiplex radio with cassette ($337.05). R33 microphone, casette radio required ($10.75). R31 single rear speaker, not available with stereo radios ($13.85). R32 dual rear speakers, stereo required ($25.05). C62 Six-way manual adjuster for left-hand front bucket seat ($32.20, bucket seats required). Split-back vinyl bench seat with center armrest, D34 required ($16). Cloth-and-vinyl bucket seat (no charge in R/T). J81 rear spoiler ($34.35, but not with A78). A45 front and rear spoiler ($54.65, but not on cars with A78). M51 full vinyl top with sun roof ($445.85, but not available with A78). S13 Rallye suspension with sway bar (standard oin R/T or with 440). D34 TorqueFlite automatic transmission ($229.35). D21 four-speed manual gearbox with floor shift ($198.10, but not available with A33 or A34). L31 fender-mounted turn signal indicators ($11.60). Full vinyl roof ($82.40, but standard with A78 or M51). W11 deluxe 14-inch wheel covers ($27.35). W15 wire wheel covers ($64.55). W12 14- or 15-inch wheel trim rings with hubcaps ($25.15). W21 Rallye type wheels with standard spare for cars without G70 tires ($54.25). W23 14- or 15-inch road wheels for cars without E78 or G70 tires ($83.30). J25 variable-speed windshield wipers and electric washers (standard on R/T). T87 F70-14 raised-white-letter bias-belted tires ($11.50). U82 E60-15 raised-white-letter bias-belted tires, W34 required ($51.65). W34 E78 x 14 black sidewall rayon collapsible spare tires ($12.55).

1971 CHARGER SUPER BEE 440/440 SIX-PACK/HEMI

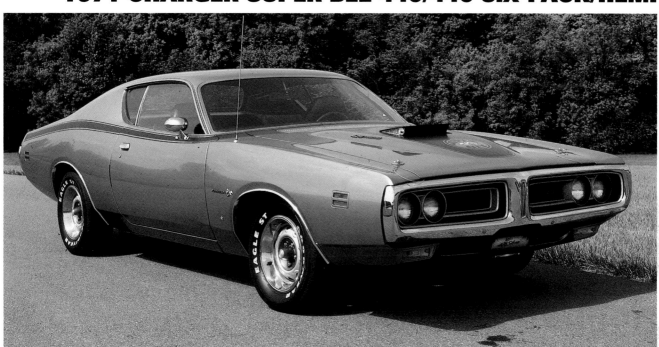

JERRY HEASLEY

1971 Charger Super Bee Hemi

In 1971, the Coronet name was used only on four-door models in the mid-sized Dodge car lines. Two-door models were renamed Super Bees. The Super Bee used the same "W" code as Coronets, but it was called a Charger. Chargers were completely restyled and had a semi-fastback roofline with a flush rear window and an integral rear deck lid spoiler.

The Charger Super Bee was unusual in several ways. It was the only car in the Mopar Scat Pack lineup to offer five different engines. It was manufactured only one year. It offered the 440-cid four-barrel V-8 for a short time, although its cousin the Plymouth Road Runner did not. (Note: This engine does not appear on some price sheets). The Charger Super Bee was aimed at the same market niche as the Coronet Super Bee and represented a value-priced serious high-performance package. Standard equipment included a 383-cid Magnum V-8 that cranked out 300 hp. The "power bulge" hood came with flat black finish. There were tape stripes and bumblebee decals. The interior was similar to that of the Charger 500, but substituted a standard bench seat for bucket seats. The Charger Super Bee's optional equipment list included a first-for-the-Charger functional Ramcharger hood scoop, color-keyed bumpers, a Super Trak-Pack performance axle (with up to

4.10:1 gearing), a four-speed gear box with Hurst "pistol grip" shifter, a dual-point distributor, heavy-duty cooling aids and bucket seats.

The 1971 Charger Super Bee with the 440 "Six-Pack" engine blasted 0-to-60 in 6.9 seconds. The quarter-mile required 14.74 seconds with a terminal speed of 97.3 mph. The Charger Hemi Super Bee did 0-to-60 mph in 5.8 seconds and the quarter-mile took 13.73 seconds at 104 mph.

Not too many 1971 Charger Hemi Super Bees were built. In *Motor Trend*, A. B. Shuman wrote, "If the Super Bee SE was interesting, the Hemi car was remarkable. It was a Hemi and you knew it!"

Model Number	Body/Style Number	Body Type & Seating	Factory Price	Shipping Weight	Production Total
CHARGER SUPER BEE — SERIES WM — V-8 (440-4)					
WH23	23	2d HT-6P	$3,408	3,740 lbs.	26
CHARGER SUPER BEE — SERIES WM — V-8 (440-6)					
WH23	23	2d HT-6P	$3,533	3,790 lbs.	99

NOTE 1: The 440-4 price is an estimate; this option is not on a Jan. 8, 1971 price sheet.
NOTE 2: Weights are estimated.
NOTE 3: Production is for cars with the indicated engine only.
NOTE 4: 30 of the 440-6 cars had a four-speed manual transmission; no transmission breakout available for 440-4 cars.

DODGE

Model Number	Body/Style Number	Body Type & Seating	Factory Price	Shipping Weight	Production Total
CHARGER SUPER BEE — SERIES WM — V-8 (HEMI)					
WH23	23	2d HT-6P	$4,154	3,850 lbs.	22

NOTE 1: Price includes the Hemi V-8 and no other options.
NOTE 2: The weight above is estimated.
NOTE 3: Nine Hemi cars had a four-speed manual transmission.
NOTE 4: One additional Hemi was built for Canada.

ENGINES

LIMITED AVAILABILITY OPTIONAL V-8: Overhead valve. Cast-iron block. Bore and stroke: 4.32 x 3.75 inches. Displacement: 440 cid. Compression ratio: 9.70:1. Brake hp: 370 at 4600 rpm. Taxable hp: 59.70. Torque: 480 at 3200 rpm. Five main bearings. Hydraulic valve lifters. Crankcase capacity: 4 qt. Carburetor: Carter AVS-4967-S four-barrel. VIN code: U.

REGULAR PRODUCTION OPTIONAL V-8 (RARE): Overhead valve. Cast-iron block. Bore and stroke: 4.32 x 3.75 inches. Displacement: 440 cid. Compression ratio: 10.30:1. Brake hp: 385 at 4700 rpm. Taxable hp: 59.70. Torque: 490 at 3200 rpm. Five main bearings. Hydraulic valve lifters. Carburetor: three Holley two-barrel. VIN code: V.

OPTIONAL V-8: Overhead valve with hemispherical segment combustion chambers. Cast-iron block. Displacement: 426 cid. Bore and stroke: 4.25 x 3.75 inches. Compression ratio: 10.20:1. Brake hp: 425 at 5000 rpm. Taxable hp: 57.80. Torque: 490 at 4000 rpm. Five main bearings. Hydraulic valve lifters. Carburetor: Two Carter AFB 3084-S four-barrel. VIN code: R.

OPTIONS (PARTIAL LIST)

E86 426-cid two four-barrel V-8 with TorqueFlite or four-speed manual transmission ($883.55). H51 Air conditioning (not available with four-speed, 440-4 V-8 or Ramcharger hood air scoop; tinted glass recommended $382). N88 automatic speed control, V-8s only, automatic transmission required with 383 and 440-4 engines ($50.50, but not available with 340, 440-6 or Ramcharger hood). Vinyl bucket seats ($105.95). Cloth-and-vinyl bucket seats ($105.95). A81 front bumper guards ($16.85). M83 rear bumper guards ($16.85). M85 front and rear bumper guards ($33.70). Center front seat with armrest, not with bucket seats and center console ($57.65). C16 center console, bucket seats required ($57.65, but not available with three-speed manual transmission or center front seat with armrest). D91 Sure Grip differential ($45.35, but standard with high-performance axle equipment). B41 front disc brakes ($24.45). N25 engine block heater ($15.55). E86 440-cid four-barrel V-8 with TorqueFlite or four-speed manual transmission (price not listed). E87 440-cid Six-Pack V-8 with Torque-Flite or four-speed manual transmission ($262.15, but not available with trailer tow package or automatic speed control). J45 hood tie-down pins ($16.55). J52 inside hood release ($10.55). N96 Ramcharger air scoop hood ($68.90 forcars without air conditioning or speed control). High-impact paint colors ($15.05). B51 power brakes ($45.15, but required with disc brakes). S77 power steering ($115.25). P31 power windows ($121.75). M91 rear deck luggage rack ($35.00, but not available on cars with spoiler). R11 Music Master AM radio ($66.40). R26 AM radio with cassette ($219.15). R35 multiplex AM/FM stereo radio ($213.70). R36 multiplex AM/FM stereo radio with cassette ($366.40). A08 radio group, includes Music Master radio, power steering, deluxe windshield wipers and chrome left-hand remote-control outside rearview mirror ($204.75). A01 light group ($25.90). A33 Track Pak performance axle ($149.80, but not available with air conditioning, four-speed manual transmission required). A34 Super Track Pak performance axle ($219.30, but not available with air conditioning, four-speed manual transmission required). A36 performance axle, D34 required, with 440-cid V-8 ($81.80). A85 Charger "Topper" package, includes landau vinyl top, chrome left-hand remote-control outside rearview mirror, fender-mounted turn signals, sill moldings, belt moldings, front and rear bumper guards, F70-14 white sidewall tires and deluxe wheel covers ($187.75) A02 Driver Aid group, includes low-fuel warning light, lock-doors reminder light and fasten seat belt light ($14.20). A54 colored bumper group, includes front-and-rear colored bumpers and louvered tail lights ($21.40). W15 wire wheel covers ($42.90). W21 Rallye type road wheels 14- or 15-inch ($51.60). W23 14-inch road wheels with chrome trim rings ($63.20). T87 F70-14 raised-white-letter tires ($31.30). T53 G70-14 raised-white-letter tires with heavy-duty drum or disc brakes required ($52) L85 G60-15 raised white-letter tires, disc or heavy-duty drum brakes and heavy-duty suspension required ($115.10).

1971 CHARGER R/T 440-4/440 SIX-PACK/HEMI

The Dodge Charger started life in 1966 as a semi-limited-production specialty car, but it caught on and grew to become an important part of the Chrysler division's line. In 1969, more than 70,000 Chargers were sold. For 1971, management decided that it was time to give the Charger an image of its own—one quite separate from that of the mid-sized Coronet.

The re-sized Charger was two inches shorter in wheelbase than the 1970 model and more than 3 inches shorter at 205.4 inches. However, it had nearly 3 more inches of front overhang and 3 1/2 inches more width. The R/T model was the quintessential "muscle" model and technically represented a sub-series of the middle-priced Charger 500 series. It included all of the many features of the Charger 500, plus hot stuff like heavy-duty underpinnings and the 440-cid Magnum V-8. The 440 Six-Pack Charger was good for 0-to-60 mph in under 7 seconds. Getting to the end of a drag strip took under 15 seconds. By that time you were moving almost 100 mph.

The Hemi was optional in a handful of 1971 Dodge Charger R/Ts. The Hemi came only with TorqueFlite automatic transmission or four-speed manual transmission. A Ramcharger hood scoop was standard. Air conditioning, the trailer towing package and automatic speed control were not available in Hemi cars.

*Motor Trend r*oad tested a Hemi Charger with automatic transmission and a 4.10:1 ratio rear axle. The car did 0-to-60 mph in 5.7 seconds. The quarter-mile was covered in an elapsed time of 13.73 seconds at 104 mph.

Model Number	Body/Style Number	Body Type & Seating	Factory Price	Shipping Weight	Production Total
CHARGER R/T — SERIES WS — V-8 (440-4)					
WH23	23	2d HT-6P	$3,777	3,795 lbs.	Note 4
CHARGER R/T — SERIES WS — V-8 (440-6)					
WH23	23	2d HT-6P	$3,902	3,850 lbs.	Note 4

NOTE 1: The 440-4 V-8 was standard.
NOTE 2: The 440 Six-Pack price includes theE87 engine and no other options.
NOTE 3: The 440 Six-Pack weight is estimated.
NOTE 4: Total production (all engines) was 2,659 R/Ts. Since a 440-cid V-8 was standard and 63 cars are known to have Hemis, it is likely that 2,596 cars had 440-cid V-8s, but there is no breakout of four-barrel and Six-Pack cars available.

Model Number	Body/Style Number	Body Type & Seating	Factory Price	Shipping Weight	Production Total
HEMI CHARGER R/T— SERIES WS — V-8					
WH23	23	2d HT-6P	$4,524	3,900 lbs.	63

NOTE 1: The price above includes the 426-cid Hemi V-8 and no other options.
NOTE 2: The weight is estimated.
NOTE 3: Production is for all Hemi cars only.
NOTE 4: Thirty Hemi cars had a four-speed manual transmission.

ENGINES

BASE V-8: Overhead valve. Cast-iron block. Bore and stroke: 4.32 x 3.75 inches. Displacement: 440 cid. Compression ratio: 9.70:1. Brake hp: 370 at 4600 rpm. Taxable hp: 59.70. Torque: 480 at 3200 rpm. Five main bearings. Hydraulic valve lifters. Carburetor: Carter AVS-4967-S four-barrel. VIN code: U.

JERRY HEASLEY

1971 Charger R/T

OPTIONAL V-8: Overhead valve. Cast-iron block. Bore and stroke: 4.32 x 3.75 inches. Displacement: 440 cid. Compression ratio: 10.30:1. Brake hp: 385 at 4700 rpm. Taxable hp: 59.70. Torque: 490 at 3200 rpm. Five main bearings. Hydraulic valve lifters. Carburetor: three Holley two-barrel. VIN code: V.

OPTIONAL V-8: Overhead valve with hemispherical segment combustion chambers. Cast-iron block. Displacement: 426 cid. Bore and stroke: 4.25 x 3.75 inches. Compression ratio: 10.20:1. Brake hp: 425 at 5000 rpm. Taxable hp: 57.80. Torque: 490 at 4000 rpm. Five main bearings. Hydraulic valve lifters. Carburetor: Two Carter AFB 3084-S four-barrel. VIN code: R.

OPTIONS (PARTIAL LIST)

E86 426-cid Hemi two four-barrel V-8 with TorqueFlite or four-speed manual transmission ($746.50). H51 Air conditioning (not available with four-speed, 440-4 V-8 or Ramcharger hood air scoop; tinted glass recommended $382). N88 automatic speed control, V-8s only, automatic transmission required with 383 and 440-4 engines ($50.50, but not available with 440-6 or Ramcharger hood). Cloth-and-vinyl bucket seats (no charge). Center front seat with armrest, not with bucket seats and center console ($57.65). J21 electric clock ($18.45, but not available with tachometer). C16 center console, bucket seats required ($57.65, but not available with three-speed manual transmission or center front seat with armrest). H31 rear window defogger ($31.45). D91 Sure Grip differential ($45.35, but standard with high-performance axle equipment). B41 front disc brakes ($24.45). N25 engine block heater ($15.55). E86 440-cid four-barrel V-8 with TorqueFlite or four-speed manual transmission (standard in R/T). E87 440-cid Six-Pack V-8 with TorqueFlite or four-speed manual transmission ($125.00, but not available with trailer tow package or automatic speed control). N42

bright exhaust tips, except in California ($21.90). L31 fender-mounted turn signals ($11.00). C92 protective rubber floor mats ($14.25). G15 tinted windshield only ($29.80). L41 headlight time delay with lamp-on reminder ($19.45 for cars without light group). L41 headlight time delay with lamp-on reminder ($13.90 for cars with light group). A09 concealed headlights, includes inside hood release ($85.60). J24 headlight washer, concealed headlights required ($29.30). J45 hood tie-down pins ($16.55). J52 inside hood release ($10.55). N96 Ramcharger air scoop hood ($68.90 for cars without air conditioning or speed control). High-impact paint colors ($15.05). B51 power brakes ($45.15, but required with disc brakes). S77 power steering ($115.25). P31 power windows ($121.75). M91 rear deck luggage rack ($35.00, but not available on cars with spoiler). R11 Music Master AM radio ($66.40). R26 AM radio with cassette ($219.15). R35 multiplex AM/FM stereo radio ($213.70). R36 multiplex AM/FM stereo radio with cassette ($366.40). A08 radio group ($204.75). A33 Track Pak performance axle ($149.80, but not available with air conditioning, four-speed manual transmission required). A34 Super Track Pak performance axle ($219.30, but not available with air conditioning, four-speed manual transmission required). A36 performance axle, D34 required, with 440-cid V-8 ($81.80). A85 Charger "Topper" package ($187.75) Light group ($17.00). A02 Driver Aid group ($14.20). A54 colored bumper group ($21.40). W15 wire wheel covers ($42.90). W21 Rallye type road wheels 14- or 15-inch ($51.60). W23 14-inch road wheels with chrome trim rings ($63.20). T87 F70-14 raised-white-letter tires ($31.30). T53 G70-14 raised-white-letter tires with heavy-duty drum or disc brakes required ($52) L85 G60-15 raised white-letter tires, disc or heavy-duty drum brakes and heavy-duty suspension required ($115.10).

DODGE

1972 DEMON 340

PHIL KUNZ

1972 Demon 340

In January 1971, *Motor Trend* writer Jim Brokaw described the Dodge Demon 340 as a "reasonable alternative" for buyers who wanted an insurable muscle car with just enough extra spice to make it interesting. The Demon was essentially a clone of the popular Plymouth Duster with different paint options, different striping options, a little more styling flair and tougher quality control.

The 340-cid small-block V-8 came as standard equipment in the Demon 340. It carried a single four-barrel carburetor and ran a 10.0:1 compression ratio. A three-speed manual floor-mounted "stick shift" was standard equipment in the Demon 340, but a four-speed was optional. Such an option was actually rather rare in 1972 and most direct competitors did not offer one. Dodge used a 3.91:1 rear axle. The '72 Demon had only minor trim and taillight changes. It remained on the same wheelbase utilized the year before. If you ordered a 1972 Demon 340, Dodge would add a Rallye suspension with heavy-duty shock absorbers front and rear, a front sway bar and heavy-duty torsion bars. The 1972 version of the 340-cid engine was set up for unleaded gas. It had a lower 8.5:1 compression ratio and carried an output rating of 240 net horsepower. Other standard equipment included all Dodge Dart group features plus (or substituted for) swing-out rear quarter windows, ventless side windows, E70-14 black sidewall tires, grille surround moldings and body side and rear deck lid performance tape stripes.

The Demon 340 was very affordable and it still did the quarter-mile in 14.49 seconds at 98.25 mph. It also went from a standing start to 60 mph in 6.5 seconds.

Model Number	Body/Style Number	Body Type & Seating	Factory Price	Shipping Weight	Production Total
DEMON 340 — SERIES LM29 — V-8					
LM29	29	2d Cpe-6P	$2,656	3,125 lbs.	8,700

NOTE 1: Production is estimated and rounded off, U.S. only.

ENGINE

BASE V-8: Overhead valve. Cast-iron block. Bore and stroke: 4.04 x 3.31 inches. Displacement: 340 cid. Compression ratio: 10.20:1. Brake hp: 275 at 5000 rpm. Taxable hp: 52.20. Torque: 340 at 3200 rpm. Five main bearings. Hydraulic valve lifters. Carburetor: Carter Thermo-Quad TQ-4972-S four-barrel. VIN code: H.

OPTIONS

Airtemp air conditioning ($353.80). D53 3.23:1 rear axle ($12.20). F23 59-amp battery ($13.30). M85 front and rear bumper guards ($24.20). C93 carpets ($17.45). J15 cigar lighter ($3.80). H31 rear window defogger ($26.55). D91 Sure-Grip differential ($40.65). N95 exhaust emissions control system, required in California ($25.55). G11 tinted glass, all windows ($35.85). G15 tinted windshield only ($24.35). J54 hood scoops ($43.15). J31 dual horns ($4.95). N23 electronic ignition system ($30.75). G41 inside day/night ($6.85). G33 remote-control left-hand outside rearview mirror ($11.60). G31 dual chrome racing-style outside rearview mirrors, left-hand remote-controlled ($13.50 with A06 or $25.10 without it). M31 belt moldings ($14.30). M25 Custom sill moldings ($10.85). M15 vinyl body side moldings ($13.90). M26 wheel opening moldings ($7.25). V21 hood performance paint ($17.30). High Impact paint colors ($14.70). Body side stripes (standard Demon 340). Tu-tone paint ($27.70). B41 front disc brakes ($62.30). B51 power drum brakes ($40.45). S77 power steering ($92.25). R11 AM radio ($59.40). R21 AM/FM radio ($64.15 with A06 and $124.55 without it). R31 rear seat speaker ($13.45). Full vinyl roof ($75.45). Vinyl seat trim ($34.20). S84 "Tuff" steering wheel ($28.00). S81 deluxe steering wheel ($9.80). M51 sun roof with vinyl top ($223.40). D13 three-speed manual transmission with floor shift (standard). D21 four-speed manual transmission with floor shift ($184.50). D34 TorqueFlite automatic transmission ($208.40). J55 undercoating and hood insulation pad ($20.25). W11 deluxe wheel covers ($24.50). W21 Rally road wheels on cars without A06 ($52.80). J25 variable-speed windshield wipers ($10.35). A68 Custom interior package ($46.50-$82.65). A21 exterior decor group ($28.15). A88 interior decor package ($36.15). A01 light group ($28.80). A15 protection group ($17.85). E70-14 raised-white-letter tires ($37.30).

FORD MUSCLE 1960-1971

The big-block Ford V-8s that tore up drag strips in the '60s had their beginnings with the 332- and 352-cid blocks of 1958, which shared the same bore with 3.3- and 3.5-inch strokes, respectively. By 1960, a big-bore 390-cid version evolved. This was bored to 406 cid in 1962. The hot 406 was then displaced by the 427, which retained the same 3.78 stroke with a new 4.23-inch bore. This engine was offered in awesome 410- and 425-hp versions.

Another famous Ford V-8 of the '60s was the compact, lightweight 289-cid type that made history in the Mustang. It was originally a 221-cid V-8 designed for the compact Falcon and mid-size Fairlane, then grew to 260 cid. Both of these configurations were dropped when the 289 appeared in 1965. It did not have the Y-block layout of earlier Ford V-8s, which gave it a stronger "bottom end" that racing enthusiasts appreciated.

By 1968, the 289 Ford small-block V-8 was replaced by the 302-cid V-8 and a 351-cid version was also offered. The high-performance "Boss 302" made its debut in mid-1969 and a new 351C followed shortly thereafter. The "C" stood for Cleveland, where the engine was built. Although it had the same displacement and horsepower rating as the standard 351W (for Windsor engine plant) Ford motor, the low-deck "Cleveland" V-8 was actually related to the Boss 302 and Boss 429 high-performance engines. Its canted valves improved engine "breathing" characteristics by permitting the large head valves to open away from each other. The heads from the two 351-cid engines are not interchangeable. The base two-barrel version of the 351C produced 250 hp and a four-barrel version gave 300 hp.

A 428-cid big-block V-8 bowed in the 1966 Thunderbird. It was a bored-and-stroked 390 and was offered in 340- and 360-hp editions. Also available in this series of V-8s was the 427-cid racing engine, which retained the 390's 3.784-inch stroke but had a larger 4.23-inch bore. It generated 390 hp. All of these were 90-degree V-8s with high-performance features. On the other hand, the Thunderjet 429 V-8 that bowed in the 1969 Thunderbird was not a true performance engine like the Cobra-Jet V-8s of the same era. It was based on the 460-cid Lincoln engine, which was also used in later Fords. The base version of the 429 generated just 320 hp. However, the hotter Cobra-Jet and "Boss 429" editions were available with up to 375 hp. Ford brought out a 400-cid V-8 with 4.00 x 4.00-in. bore and stroke dimensions in 1971. It was not a performance engine, but it was a sign that the muscle car era was winding to its close.

JERRY HEASLEY

FORD

GALAXIE 352/360 SPECIAL

1960 Galaxie

PHIL KUNZ

"We like the way it looks, we like the way it rides, we like the way it corners, we like the way it stops and we especially like how it goes when equipped with the 360-horsepower engine." That's what *Hot Rod* magazine's technical editor Ray Brock said after road testing the 1960 Ford Galaxie 352/360 special. Styling departed radically from the popular and conservative 1959 Fords. Grille-mounted headlights and gull-wing fins gave deep meaning to the often-used term "all-new." Arranged in a separate Galaxie Special line were the sleek Starliner two-door hardtop and its convertible counterpart the Sunliner. They came with six-cylinder engines or a variety of V-8s.

The 360-hp Thunderbird Super V-8, which was based on the 352. It was also called the "Interceptor" or "Super Interceptor" and carried an "R" code. This engine was not initially available with Cruise-O-Matic, but only with a Borg-Warner T-85 three-speed manual gearbox, with or without overdrive. A Holley 540-cfm four-barrel carburetor, an aluminum intake manifold, new cast-iron exhaust headers, a cast nodular crank, solid valve lifters, a 10.6:1 compression ratio and a dual-point ignition system all helped. The muscular combination was available on any full-sized 1960 model. The most desirable combination for the 360-hp 352 is with a Starliner two-door hardtop or a Sunliner convertible.

Motor Life magazine got hold of a pre-production example and found it capable of going from 0-to-60 mph in 7.5 seconds with a top speed of 152 mph. Obviously, it had been modified a bit over the production version.

Model Number	Body/Style Number	Body Type & Seating	Factory Price	Shipping Weight	Production Total
GALAXIE SPECIAL — SERIES 27 — V-8					
53	53	2d HT-6P	$2,723	3,667 lbs.	68,641
55	55	2d Conv-6P	$2,973	3,841 lbs.	44,762

NOTE 1: Prices and weights for base V-8 model.
NOTE 2: Production is for cars with all engines combined

ENGINE

OPTIONAL V-8: Overhead valve. Cast-iron block. Bore and stroke: 4.00 x 3.50 inches. Displacement: 352 cid. Compression ratio: 10.60:1. Brake hp: 360. Taxable hp: 51.2. Five main bearings. Hydraulic valve lifters. Dual exhaust with special header-type exhaust manifolds. Aluminum intake manifold. Dual point distributor. Carburetor: Holley four-barrel. Code Y.

OPTIONS

Polar Air conditioning, including tinted glass and V-8 ($271). Select Air air conditioning, including tinted glass and V-8 ($404). Back-up lights ($11). Heavy-duty 70-amp battery ($8). Equa-lock differential ($39). Electric clock ($15). Fresh Air heater/defroster ($75). Recirculating heater/defroster ($47). Four-way manual seat ($11). Rocker panel molding ($14). Two-tone paint ($19). Power brakes ($43). Power seat ($64). Power steering ($77). Front and rear power windows ($102). Push-button radio with antenna ($59). Front seat belts ($21). Tinted glass ($43). Cruise-O-Matic ($211). Ford-O-Matic with V-8 ($190). Overdrive ($108). Wheel covers ($17). Windshield washer ($14). Two-speed windshield wipers ($10). Numerous tire options including whitewalls and oversize.

1961 GALAXIE STARLINER 390

PHIL KUNZ

1961 Galaxie Starliner 390

The year 1961 was a big one for Ford performance. Inspired by the "win-on-Sunday-sell-on-Monday" marketing mentality, the company released a 390-cid V-8 at the start of the year and a four-speed manual transmission near the end of the season. Both performance add-ons were hot options for the steamy Starliner hardtop. In 1960, Ford had advised the Automobile Manufacturers Association (AMA) that it was suspending its support of the trade organization's 4-year-old ban on stock car racing. The company then showed up at the Daytona Motor Speedway with a 360-engined Starliner that ran 40 laps at an average of 142 mph.

By fall, similar cars had been put into the hands of racing car drivers and racked up 15 checkered flags in Grand National stock car competition. At the same time, a re-entry into factory-backed drag racing was made and a "three deuces" carburetor setup was legalized by the National Hot Rod Association.

The new-for-'61 Starliner was smaller, but had a bigger engine. Three versions of the 390-cid V-8 were offered. The standard rating was 300 hp. A police car variant was rated for 330 hp. Tops on the list was the 375-hp Thunderbird Super edition with a four-barrel carburetor. At midyear, when the triple two-barrel carburetor system was released, it pushed the big engine up to 401 hp. After it was approved for NHRA racing, Fords dominated their classes.

Despite its spaceship name and looks, the '61 Galaxie had the underhood stuff to make a drag strip competitor sweat. "In base form, the Ford 390 V-8 was nothing to write home about," admitted *Car Review* magazine in December 1985. "But by using some components from the earlier 352 Interceptor, Ford came up with the 375-hp 390 Thunderbird Special. Put that in your Galaxie and smoke the tires." Performance-wise, the

6V (six venturi) engine was capable of 7-second 0-to-60 mph runs and quarter-miles with ETs just over 15 seconds. This definitely put it into the "muscle car" category.

Model Number	Body/Style Number	Body Type & Seating	Factory Price	Shipping Weight	Production Total
GALAXIE — SERIES 53 — V-8					
53	53	2d HT-6P	$2,713	3,615 lbs.	29,669

NOTE 1: Prices and weights for base V-8 model.
NOTE 2: The number of 390-cid/401-hp and 390-cid/375-hp cars built was a fraction of the total production listed above.

ENGINE

OPTIONAL V-8: Overhead valve. Cast-iron block. Bore and stroke: 4.05 x 3.78 inches. Displacement: 390 cid. Compression ratio: 10.60:1. Brake hp: 375 at 6000 rpm. Taxable hp: 52.49. Torque: 427 at 3400 rpm. Five main bearings. Solid valve lifters. Carburetor: Ford four-barrel Model CIAE-9510-AG with standard transmission or CIAE-9510-AH with automatic transmission. Code Q (Early versions may use code Z and export models used code R).

(NOTE: Some cars were delivered with the intake manifold and carburetors in the trunk.)

OPTIONAL V-8: Overhead valve. Cast-iron block. Bore and stroke: 4.05 x 3.78 inches. Displacement: 390 cid. Compression ratio: 10.60:1. Brake hp: 401 at 6000 rpm. Taxable hp: 52.49. Torque: 430 at 3500 rpm. Five main bearings. Solid valve lifters. Carburetor: Three two-barrel carburetors. Code Q (Early versions may use code Z).

OPTIONS

Polar Air conditioning, including tinted glass and V-8 ($271). Select Air air conditioning, including tinted glass and V-8 ($436). Back-up lights ($11). Heavy-duty 70-amp battery ($8). Crankcase vent system ($6). Equa-lock differential ($39). Electric clock ($15). Magic-Aire heater/defroster ($75). Recirculating heater/defroster ($47). Four-way manual seat ($17). Rocker panel molding ($16). Padded dash and visors ($24). Two-tone paint ($22). Power brakes ($43). Power seat ($64). Power steering ($82). Front and rear power windows ($102). Push-button radio with antenna ($59). Front seat belts ($21). Tinted glass ($43). Cruise-O-Matic ($212). Ford-O-Matic with V-8 ($190). Overdrive ($108). Wheel covers ($19). Windshield washer ($14). Two-speed windshield wipers ($10). Numerous tire options including whitewalls and oversize.

FORD

1962 GALAXIE 500 XL "406"

PHIL KUNZ

1962 Galaxie 500 XL

Certainly not the least significant attraction of the 1962 Fords was their appearance. They stand out as one of the best examples of Ford's competence level in car design. With a 209-inch overall length they were large automobiles, but their clean lines — now totally free of fender fins and devoid of any overtones of General Motors influence — gave them a handsome appearance.

Shortly after New Year's celebrations ended in 1962, Ford introduced a new 406-cid V-8 packing 405 hp at 5800 rpm. This "Thunderbird Special 406" carried over the triple carbs, special cam, valve gear, ignition, bearings and exhaust system of the 390-cid/401-hp engine. A 385-hp version with a single four-barrel carburetor was also available.

Despite the similarity to previous engines, there were some changes that reflected Ford's growing expertise in developing modern, high-performance automobiles. The 406-cid engine block, with its larger 3.78-inch bore, used a totally different casting that provided thicker cylinder walls. To cope with the 406's added power, stronger pistons and connecting rods were installed and the oil relief valve was set at 60 psi instead of 45 psi. Dual valve springs with greater maximum load were also used on the 406. Included in the $379.70 price tag of the 406 engine (one of which was Ford's 30,000,000th V-8) was a comprehensive performance package. Its most obvious feature was an excellent Borg-Warner four-speed transmission with ratios of 2.36:1, 1.78:1, 1.41:1 and 1.0:1. Less apparent — until the 406 Ford got into motion — were its stiffer (by 20 percent) springs and shocks.

In *Hot Rod* magazine, Ray Brock opined, "Anyway you look at it, this is a bargain-priced hi-po automobile. Ford

should not have any trouble selling 10,000 of these items." With Ford's standard 3.56:1 ratio rear axle, the typical 405-hp Galaxie was capable of 0-to-60-mph runs in 7 seconds and of doing the quarter-mile in 15.5 seconds at 92 mph.

Model Number	Body/Style Number	Body Type & Seating	Factory Price	Shipping Weight	Production Total
GALAXIE 500XL — SERIES 65B/76B — V-8					
63	65B	2d HT-6P	$3,268	3,672 lbs.	28,412
65	76B	2d Conv-6P	$3,518	3,831 lbs.	13,183

NOTE 1: Prices and weights for base V-8 model.

NOTE 2: Production above is for all engines.

NOTE 3: A total of 8,384 of the 406-cid V-8s were installed in all FoMoCo cars in model-year 1962.

ENGINE

OPTIONAL V-8: Overhead valve. Cast-iron block. Displacement: 406 cid. Bore and stroke: 4.13 x 3.78 inches. Compression ratio: 11.40:1. Brake hp: 385 at 5800 rpm. Torque: 444 at 3400 rpm. Five main bearings. Solid valve lifters. Carburetor: Ford four-barrel Model CIAE-9510-AG with standard transmission or CIAE-9510-AH with automatic transmission. Dual exhaust. Code B.

OPTIONAL V-8: Overhead valve. Cast-iron block. Displacement: 406 cid. Bore and stroke: 4.13 x 3.78 inches. Compression ratio: 11.40:1. Brake hp: 405 at 5800 rpm. Torque: 448 at 3500 rpm. Five main bearings. Solid valve lifters. Carburetor: Holley three two-barrel. Dual exhaust. Code G.

OPTIONS

Polar Air conditioning, including tinted glass and V-8 ($271). Select Air air conditioning, including tinted glass and V-8 ($361). Back-up lights ($11, but standard on Galaxie 500 XL). Heavy-duty 70-amp battery ($8). Crankcase vent system ($6). Equa-lock differential ($39). Electric clock ($15, but standard in Galaxie 500 XL). Recirculating heater/defroster ($28 credit if deleted). Four-way manual seat ($17). Rocker panel molding ($16). Padded dash and visors ($24). Two-tone paint ($22). Power brakes ($43). Power seat ($64). Power steering ($82). Front and rear power windows ($102). Push-button radio with antenna ($59). Front seat belts ($21). Tinted glass ($40). Tinted windshield ($22). Cruise-O-Matic ($212). Ford-O-Matic with V-8 ($190). Overdrive ($108). Four-speed manual transmission, 385 or 405-hp V-8 required ($188). Wheel covers ($19). Deluxe wheel covers ($26). Two-speed windshield wipers and washers ($20). Numerous tire options including whitewalls and oversize.

1963 GALAXIE "427"

FORD

1963 Galaxie 427

Ford really got its act into gear around the middle of 1963. Its first step was the release of the good-looking 1963 1/2 Galaxie fastback. Then came a new 427-cid V-8 with massive muscle for the street, the drag strip and the NASCAR superspeedways. To promote the 427-powered 1963 Galaxie, Ford manufactured 50 special cars at its factory in Atlanta, Georgia. These cars were "factory lightweights" made exclusively for going down the quarter mile faster than the competition. They had fiberglass doors, hoods, trunks and front-end components. The bumpers and other parts were made of aluminum. Virtually everything that wasn't needed for racing was left off the cars.

For motivation, the Galaxie lightweights got a 427-cid V-8 with two Holley 600-cfm four-barrel carburetors advertised at 425 hp at 6000 rpm. The actual output was much higher. The engine was attached to a special version of Ford's "top-loader" four-speed manual gearbox that had an aluminum case to cut even more weight off. These cars tipped the scales at below 3,500 lbs. and ran the quarter-mile in the low-12-second bracket at just under 120 mph!

In addition to the just-for-racing cars, FoMoCo produced 4,978 big Fords with one of two versions of the 427-cid V-8. One was the 425-hp engine tuned for the street. It had dual Holley 540-cfm carburetors on top of a cast-aluminum intake manifold and most owners who took these cars racing on weekends felt that the power rating was very conservative.

The second street engine was a 427-cid V-8 with a single four-barrel carburetor. It produced 410 hp. Both of the big engines were available in Galaxie 500 or Galaxie 500 XL two-door hardtops. The dual-quad engine was a $461.60 option.

ENGINES

OPTIONAL V-8: Overhead valve. Cast-iron block. Displacement: 427 cid. Bore and stroke: 4.23 x 3.78 inches. Compression ratio: 11.50:1. Brake hp: 410 at 5600 rpm. Torque: 476 at 3400 rpm. Five main bearings. Solid valve lifters. Carburetor: Holley four-barrel. Dual exhaust. Code Q.

Model Number	Body/Style Number	Body Type & Seating	Factory Price	Shipping Weight	Production Total
GALAXIE 500 — SERIES 60 — V-8					
63	65A	2d HT-6P	$3,245	3,615 lbs.	97,939
66	63B	2d FSBK-6P	$3,245	3,615 lbs.	48,488
GALAXIE 500XL — SERIES 60 — V-8					
67	65B	2d HT-6P	$3,730	3,670 lbs.	33,870
68	63C	2d FSBK-6P	$3,730	3,670 lbs.	29,713

NOTE 1: Prices and weights for base V-8 model plus cost of 427-cid four-barrel V-8.
NOTE 2: Production totals above are for model with V-8 engine (not just 427-cid V-8).
NOTE 3: 4,978 full-size Fords were built with the 427-cid V-8 (all body styles and both versions of 427).
NOTE 4: 50 additional lightweight just-for-racing cars were built.
NOTE 5: A total of 4,715 of the 406-cid V-8s and 4,978 of the 427-cid V-8s were installed in all FoMoCo cars in model-year 1963.

OPTIONAL V-8: Overhead valve. Cast-iron block. Displacement: 427 cid. Bore and stroke: 4.23 x 3.78 inches. Compression ratio: 11.50:1. Brake hp: 425 at 6000 rpm. Torque: 480 at 3700 rpm. Five main bearings. Solid valve lifters. Carburetor: Two Holley four-barrel. Dual exhaust. Code R.

OPTIONS

Polar Air conditioning, including tinted glass and V-8 ($231.70). Select Air air conditioning, including tinted glass and V-8 ($360.90. but standard on Galaxie 500 and Galaxie 500XL). Back-up lights ($10.70, but standard with 385- or 405-hp V-8s). Heavy-duty 70-amp battery ($7.60). Equa-lock differential ($42.50). Electric clock in base Galaxie only ($14.60). Remote-control outside rearview mirror ($12.00). Rocker panel molding ($16.10). Padded dash and visors, except convertible ($24.30). Padded dash in convertible ($18.60). Tu-tone paint ($22). Power brakes ($43.20). Full-width power seat ($63.80). Power driver's seat only in Galaxie 500 and Galaxie 500XL ($92.10). Power steering ($81.70). Front and rear power windows ($102.10). Push-button radio with antenna ($58.50). AM/FM radio and antenna ($129.30). Front seat belts ($16.80). Front bucket seats with console in Galaxie, Squires ($141.60 and standard in Galaxie 500XL). Movable steering column ($50). Tinted glass ($40.30). Tinted windshield ($21.55). Cruise-O-Matic ($212.30). Ford-O-Matic with V-8 ($189.60). Overdrive ($108.40). Four-speed manual transmission ($34.80 credit when order for Galaxie 500 and Galaxie 500XL). Vinyl trim in Galaxie 500 ($32.20). Wire design wheel covers for Galaxie 500 or Galaxie 500XL ($27.40). Deluxe wheel covers ($18.60). Deluxe wheel covers ($26). Two-speed windshield wipers and washers ($20.10). Whitewall tires ($33.90). 427-cid four-barrel V-8 ($462).

FORD

1963 GALAXIE LIGHTWEIGHT "427"

PHIL KUNZ

1963 Galaxie Lightweight

Although some people regarded 1963 Ford styling changes as "minor," it wasn't hard to identify the new models. For those interested in how the new Ford would "go," the car shined on race tracks early in the year, showing off both of Ford's new 427-cid V-8 and 1963 1/2 fastback body. The 427-cid engine was based on the 406-cid V-8, but had a 4.23-inch bore and 3.78-inch stroke. It encompassed design improvements outlined in Ford's "Total Performance" program.

Beginning with cross-bolted mains (numbers two, three and four), lighter-weight impact-extruding aluminum pistons and stronger connecting rods, the 427 had many advantages over the 406. Since NASCAR did not allow multi-carb setups to run on its superspeedways, Ford also offered a single four-barrel 427-cid. Although some questioned the use of the term "fastback" for Ford's 1963 1/2 model, there was good reason for its existence. By adopting the "sportsroof" for NASCAR competition, Ford had a car that could maintain 160 mph with 100 less hp.

The lightweight fastbacks were made to let it all hang out on the drag strip. Ford offered these hardtops only in a white-and-red exterior/interior color combination. Although the drag model's steel body was identical to that of a stock Galaxie, all bolt-on items, such as the doors, trunk lid, hood and front fenders, were constructed of fiberglass. Aluminum was used for the bumpers. The interiors offered only the basics: skinny front buckets, cheap floor mats and absolutely no sound deadening.

The tremendous performance of the 427-cid NASCAR Ford was demonstrated in a road test of a car that stock-car builders Holman & Moody had prepared. It was conducted by *Car Life* magazine. Although rated at 410 hp, the true output

of the 427, after the Holman & Moody treatment, was closer to 500 hp. With a 3.50:1 rear axle, the Ford's top speed was approximately 155 mph. Even with this gearing, however, the Ford was a strong sprinter with *Car Life* (February 1964) reporting the following acceleration times: 0-to-30 mph in 2.3 seconds; 0-to-60 mph in 6.3 seconds and 0-to-100 mph in 13.2 seconds. The same car did the quarter mile in 14.2 seconds at 105 mph. With special race tuning, these Galaxies — which the NHRA declared eligible for both super stock and stock eliminator competitions — were capable of quarter-mile marks of 12 seconds and 118 mph." Before the competition season came to a close, Ford offered a "Mark II" version of the 427-cid V-8 with new cylinder heads. It had larger ports and valves, an aluminum high-rise manifold, stronger connecting rods, a forged-steel crankshaft and a 10-quart oil pan.

Model Number	Body/Style Number	Body Type & Seating	Factory Price	Shipping Weight	Production Total
GALAXIE — SPECIAL RACING SERIES — V-8					
66	63	2d FSBK-6P	—	—	50

NOTE 5: A total of 4,715 of the 406-cid V-8s and 4,978 of the 427-cid V-8s were installed in all FoMoCo cars in model-year 1963.

ENGINES

OPTIONAL V-8: Overhead valve. Cast-iron block. Displacement: 427 cid. Bore and stroke: 4.23 x 3.78 inches. Compression ratio: 11.50:1. Brake hp: 410 at 5600 rpm. Torque: 476 at 3400 rpm. Five main bearings. Solid valve lifters. Carburetor: Holley four-barrel. Dual exhaust. Code Q.

OPTIONAL V-8: Overhead valve. Cast-iron block. Displacement: 427 cid. Bore and stroke: 4.23 x 3.78 inches. Compression ratio: 11.50:1. Brake hp: 425 at 6000 rpm. Torque: 480 at 3700 rpm. Five main bearings. Solid valve lifters. Carburetor: Two Holley four-barrel. Dual exhaust. Code R.

OPTIONS

Some regular options may have been used, plus specialized competition options.

1964 FAIRLANE HI-PO "K" CODE

JERRY HEASLEY

1965 Fairlane "K" Code

Along with new styling, the 1964 Ford Fairlane offered some neat engine options based on he 289-cid small-block V-8. In 1964, the basic "C" code version of the Challenger 289 had a 9.0:1 compression ratio and a two-barrel carburetor. It generated 195 hp at 4400 rpm and there was nothing "muscular" about that. There was an "A" code edition with a four-barrel carburetor and a 9.8:1 compression ratio, which generated 225 hp — acceptable for keeping up with traffic on the freeway. But for muscle car fans, the only way to order it was as a "K" code or "Hi-Po" version. This meant that you got a 10.5:1 compression ratio and 271 horses at 6000 rpm with a single Holley four-barrel carb.

Starting with such an engine, Fairlane owners who wanted more performance could add one of Ford's Cobra kits, which were being heavily advertised in enthusiast magazines. The

kits included a wide combination of hot cams, solid valve lifters, special manifolds, special cylinder heads with larger valves, dual-point distributors with a centrifugal advance mechanism and other go-fast goodies. With these factory-issued bolt-on items they could raise the output of the 289-cid V-8 to over 300 hp.

Model Number	Body/Style Number	Body Type & Seating	Factory Price	Shipping Weight	Production Total
FAIRLANE — SERIES 31 — V-8					
31	62A	2d Sedan-6P	$2,294	2,997 lbs.	5,644
FAIRLANE 500 — SERIES 31 — V-8					
41	62B	2d Sedan-6P	$2,376	3,012 lbs.	14,687
43	65A	2d HT-6P	$2,441	3,072 lbs.	38,266
47	65B	2d FSBK-6P	$2,602	3,096 lbs.	20,485

NOTE 1: Prices and weights for base V-8 model plus cost of 289-cid four-barrel V-8.
NOTE 2: Production totals above are for model with V-8 engine (not just 289-cid V-8).
NOTE 3: No breakout available for 289.

ENGINE

OPTIONAL V-8: Overhead valve. Cast-iron block. Displacement: 289 cid. Bore and stroke: 4.00 x 2.87 inches. Compression ratio: 10.50:1. Brake hp: 271 at 6000 rpm. Torque: 312 at 3400 rpm. Five main bearings. Solid valve lifters. Carburetor: Four-barrel. Code K.

OPTIONS

Polar Air conditioning, including tinted glass and V-8 ($231.70 and 7.00 x 14 tires required on Fairlanes). Select Air air conditioning, including tinted glass and V-8 ($360.90). Back-up lights ($10.70). Heavy-duty 70-amp battery ($7.60). Equa-lock differential ($42.50). Electric clock ($14.60). Rocker panel molding ($16.10). Padded dash and visors ($24.30). Tu-tone paint ($22). Power brakes ($43.20). Power steering ($86.30). Front and rear power windows ($102.10). Push-button radio with antenna ($58.50). Front seat belts ($16.80). Movable steering column ($50). Tinted glass ($40.30). Tinted windshield ($21.55). Cruise-O-Matic ($212.30). Ford-O-Matic with V-8 ($189.60). Overdrive ($108.40). Select-Shift four-speed transmission with V-8 ($188.00). Vinyl trim in Fairlane 500 ($25.00). Wire design wheel covers ($45.10). Deluxe wheel covers ($18.60). Deluxe wheel covers ($18.60). Two-speed windshield wipers and washers ($20.10). Whitewall tires ($33.90). 289-cid/271-hp V-8 ($421.80). Vinyl roof on two-door hardtop ($75).

1964 FAIRLANE 500 THUNDERBOLT

PHIL KUNZ

1965 Fairlaine 500 Thunderbolt

In 1963, Ford's special vehicle department joined with Tasca Ford, of East Providence, Rhode Island, to create the Fairlane Thunderbolt racing cars. Tasca Ford had built a '62 Fairlane drag racer powered by a 406-cid V-8. Since Ford was on a "Total Performance" kick, the automaker and Tasca Ford joined forces to build a test "mule" car to determine how the Fairlane would perform on drag strips with big-block V-8 power. The Fairlane's unit-body was lighter than the full-size Galaxie, which used conventional body-on-frame construction. A '63 Fairlane 500 hardtop was used. It was painted Ford Blue and equipped with a 427-cid/425-hp engine and a four-speed transmission. The test mule is thought to have been scrapped afterwards.

Reactions to the car's performance by Ford were positive. The special vehicle department saw it as a way to compete with the soon-to-be-released Chrysler Hemi race cars. Dearborn Steel Tubing Co. was contracted to build similarl -equipped '64 Fairlane two-door sedans made expressly for racing and these were the cars that became famous as Thunderbolts. The name was a take-off on the Thunderbird's longstanding performance image. The cars were built at Ford's home plant in Dearborn, Michigan. They started as Fairlane 500 Tudor sedans without the normal sound-deadening materials, sealers and body insulation. These cars also came without radios, heaters or rear-window cranks. They had Plexiglas side windows. They were built as K-code cars so that they got the nine-inch rear end and larger-diameter brakes that came with the K-code 289 V-8.

The first batch of Thunderbolts was constructed late in 1963. All of these cars were painted Vintage Burgundy and had tan interiors. Eleven cars were sent to nearby Dearborn Steel Tubing Co., where they were hand-converted into awesome drag racers. It is thought that nine of these cars (eight with stick shift and one with automatic transmission) were initially put together for professional drag racing teams. Driver Paul Harvey, who was sponsored by Bob Ford in Dearborn,

raced the one-of-a-kind automatic transmission car. A deadly racing accident in 1965 wiped out this car and killed the driver. Two additional batches of Thunderbolts were built later — and differently. Instead of starting with factory-built K-Code Fairlanes, Dearborn Steel Tubing built the entire cars from pieces that Ford shipped to them. In addition to the first 11 cars built in October of 1963, there were two other batches made.

The cars in the second group were constructed between December 1963 and February 1964. A total of 39 White cars were constructed and 30 had automatic transmissions.

The third group consisted of 50 cars made between March 1964 and May of the same year. These were also painted White and 28 of them got the automatic transmission.

The Thunderbolts are not identical cars. For example, some have fiberglass bumpers and others have fiberglass doors to save weight. The cars were also modified, both during their racing careers and later. The 427 V-8 used in the cars (except for one with "hemi" type heads) was a "center-oiler" type with a high-rise intake designed for twin for-barrel carbs. Special four-speed gearboxes with an aluminum case were used in stick-shift cars. The other cars used a beefed-up Lincoln automatic.

Model Number	Body/Style Number	Body Type & Seating	Factory Price	Shipping Weight	Production Total
SPECIAL THUNDERBOLT FAIRLANE 500 — SERIES 41 — V-8					
41	62B	2d Sedan-6P	$3,900	—	100

NOTE 1: Weights varied.
NOTE 2: Price was $4,000 with automatic transmission.

ENGINE

THUNDERBOLT V-8: Overhead valve. Cast-iron block. Displacement: 427 cid. Bore and stroke: 4.23 x 3.78 inches. Compression ratio: 11.50:1. Brake hp: 425 at 6000 rpm. Torque: 480 at 3700 rpm. Five main bearings. Solid valve lifters. Carburetor: Two Holley four-barrel. Dual exhaust. Code R.

OPTIONS

Some regular options may have been used, plus specialized competition options. Automatic transmission was $100 extra.

1964 FALCON FUTURA SPORT + SPRINT

JERRY HEASLEY

1965 Falcon Futura Sprint

New, squared-off styling from the belt line down marked the Falcon's fifth year in the automotive marketplace. The new Falcon used the same unitized chassis it had since its introduction as a 1960 model. The '64 Sports Futura hardtop listed for $2,314 and the Sprint package added $275 extra. The Sports Futura convertible started at $2,586 and $238 more bought the Sprint setup. Sports models started with front bucket-type seats and a center console, although not all Sprints had these items. The Sprint option added a standard 260-cid V-8 engine (complete with a chrome dress-up kit), wire wheel covers, a sports-type steering wheel, a tachometer and appropriate model badging. For $188 more, a four-speed manual floor shift was available.

The introduction of the Mustang diminished the impact of the Sprint option package. Had it not been for the "pony car," the Sprint would likely have gone down in automotive history as one of the year's sportiest and best high-performance offerings. With much other competition as well, the Falcon Sprint returned for model year 1965, but it was even more overshadowed by its Mustang stable mate. Today, the most collectable Falcon Sprints are into five-figure prices, which is getting respectable, but not as high as Mustang prices.

Car Life tested a four-speed equipped Falcon Sprint convertible and found it did 0-to-60 mph in 12.1 seconds and had a top speed of 105 mph. By the time the road test appeared in print, in the magazine's June 1964 issue, the Mustang legend was already approaching full gallop.

Model Number	Body/Style Number	Body Type & Seating	Factory Price	Shipping Weight	Production Total
FALCON FURURA SPORT + SPRINT — SERIES 12/14 — V-8					
12	63D/E	2d HT-6P	$2,436	2,803 lbs.	13,830
14	76D/E	2d Conv-6P	$2,671	2,976 lbs.	4,278

NOTE 1: Prices and weights for Falcon Futura Sports with Sprint package and base 260-cid two-barrel V-8.

NOTE 2: Production totals above are for all Sprint-optioned cars (not just 260-cid V-8).

NOTE 3: No breakout available for 289s.

NOTE4: Body style suffixes: D indicated bucket seats; E indicated front bench seat.

ENGINES

BASE V-8: Optional in Fairlane and full-size Fords Overhead valve. Cast-iron block. Displacement: 260 cid. Bore and stroke: 3.80 x 2.87 inches. Compression ratio: 8.8:1. Brake hp: 164 at 4400 rpm. Torque: 258 at 2200 rpm. Five main bearings. Hydraulic valve lifters. Carburetor: Two-barrel. Code F.

OPTIONAL V-8: Overhead valve. Cast-iron block. Displacement: 289 cid. Bore and stroke: 4.00 x 2.87 inches. Compression ratio: 9.00:1. Brake hp: 195 at 4400 rpm. Torque: 282 at 2200 rpm. Five main bearings. Hydraulic valve lifters. Carburetor: Ford two-barrel C30F-9510. Code C.

OPTIONAL V-8: Overhead valve. Cast-iron block. Displacement: 289 cid. Bore and stroke: 4.00 x 2.87 inches. Compression ratio: 9.0:1. Brake hp: 210 at 4400 rpm. Torque: 300 at 2800 rpm. Five main bearings. Hydraulic valve lifters. Carburetor: Four-barrel. Code A.

OPTIONAL HI-PO V-8 (K-CODE): Overhead valve. Cast-iron block. Displacement: 289 cid. Bore and stroke: 4.00 x 2.87 inches. Compression ratio: 10.50:1. Brake hp: 271 at 6000 rpm. Torque: 312 at 3400 rpm. Five main bearings. Solid valve lifters. Carburetor: Four-barrel. Code K.

OPTIONS

Ford-O-Matic with V-8 ($177.00). Select-Shift four-speed transmission with V-8 ($188.00). Push-button radio with antenna ($58.50). Tu-tone paint ($19). Whitewall tires ($30.00). Back-up lights ($10.70). Deluxe wheel covers ($18.60).

1964 GALAXIE 500/500XL "427"

JERRY HEASLEY

1964 Galaxie 427 (with dragstrip option)

After their 1-2-3-4-5 finish at the '63 Daytona 500, 427-powered Ford Galaxies became a legend in NASCAR-land. But, despite their best-ever-for-Ford performances on drag strips and racetracks, the 1963 Galaxie lightweights had not dominated quarter-mile competition the way Ford hoped they would.

At first the hot Fords competed with Pontiac's powerful 421 Super-Duty V-8 and later the Chrysler Hemi V-8 came along. To keep up with the Joneses, Ford changed its focus to mid-size muscle by launching its fleet of Fairlane-based Thunderbolts that could run down a drag strip in less than 12 seconds at close to 125 mph. However, the 427-powered full-sized Fords were still the hot ticket for stock car racing and to get them sanctioned for NASCAR competition the company kept producing big muscle cars. The new Galaxie was offered with big-car-based lightweight drag package as well. The 1964 Galaxie A/ Stock dragster package was offered for two-door models. Also available was a B/Stock Dragster package with added a low-riser manifold for the monstrous 427-cid V-8 engine. These cars came in white with red interiors. Body sealer, sound deadening insulation and heaters were deleted. Added were lightweight seats and a fiberglass "power bubble" hood. The grilles were modified with fiberglass air induction vents.

The 427-cid V-8 was also offered in two versions for production-type full-sized 1964 Fords. The "Thunderbird High-Performance" option carried code "Q" and was the 410-hp (at 5600 rpm) version. The specifications for this power plant included a 4.23 x 3.78-inch bore and stroke, an 11.5:1 compression ratio and a single Holley four-barrel carburetor. The "Thunderbird Super High-Performance" engine carried code "R" and added two larger Holley carburetors to boost output to 425 hp at 6000 rpm.

A 427-powered stock-bodied Galaxie was basically good for a 0-to-60 time of just over 6 seconds and a quarter-mile time of just under 15 seconds.

Model Number	Body/Style Number	Body Type & Seating	Factory Price	Shipping Weight	Production Total
GALAXIE 500 — SERIES 60 — V-8					
61	62A	2d Sedan-6P	$2,733	3,597 lbs.	13,830
65	76A	2d Conv-6P	$3,056	3,779 lbs.	36,277
66	63B	2d FSBK-6P	$2,794	3,608 lbs.	201,963
GALAXIE 500XL — SERIES 60 — V-8					
69	76B	2d Conv-6P	$3,495	3,801 lbs.	15,169
68	63C	2d FSBK-6P	$3,233	3,633 lbs.	58,306

NOTE 1: Prices and weights for Galaxie 500 and Galaxie 500XL with base V-8
NOTE 2: Production totals above are for all Galaxie 500 and Galaxie 500XL V-8s
NOTE 3: No breakout available for 427s.
NOTE 4: According to Carlisle Productions, a total of 50 Galaxie 427 lightweight racing cars were built in 1964.
NOTE 5: A total of 3,168 of the 427-cid V-8s were installed in all FoMoCo cars in model-year 1964.

ENGINES

OPTIONAL V-8: Overhead valve. Cast-iron block. Displacement: 427 cid. Bore and stroke: 4.23 x 3.78 inches. Compression ratio: 11.50:1. Brake hp: 410 at 5600 rpm. Torque: 476 at 3400 rpm. Five main bearings. Solid valve lifters. Carburetor: Holley four-barrel. Dual exhaust. Code Q.

OPTIONAL V-8: Overhead valve. Cast-iron block. Displacement: 427 cid. Bore and stroke: 4.23 x 3.78 inches. Compression ratio: 11.50:1. Brake hp: 425 at 6000 rpm. Torque: 480 at 3700 rpm. Five main bearings. Solid valve lifters. Carburetor: Two Holley four-barrel. Dual exhaust. Code R.

OPTIONS

Polar Air conditioning, including tinted glass and V-8 ($231.70). Select Air air conditioning, including tinted glass and V-8 ($360.90. but standard on Galaxie 500 and Galaxie 500XL). Back-up lights ($10.70), but standard with 385- or 405-hp V-8s). Heavy-duty 70-amp battery ($7.60). Equa-lock differential ($42.50). Electric clock in base Galaxie only ($14.60). Remote-control outside rearview mirror ($12.00). Rocker panel molding ($16.10). Padded dash and visors, except convertible ($24.30). Padded dash in convertible ($18.60). Tu-tone paint ($22). Power brakes ($43.20). Full-width power seat ($96.80). Power driver's seat only in Galaxie 500 and Galaxie 500XL ($92.10). Power steering ($96.00). Front and rear power windows ($102.10). Push-button radio with antenna ($58.50). AM/FM radio and antenna ($129.30). Front seat belts ($16.80). Front bucket seats with console in Galaxie, Squires ($141.60 and standard in Galaxie 500XL). Movable steering column ($50). Tinted glass ($40.30). Tinted windshield ($21.55). Cruise-O-Matic ($212.30). Ford-O-Matic with V-8 ($189.60). Overdrive ($108.40). Four-speed manual transmission ($34.80 credit when order for Galaxie 500 and Galaxie 500XL). Vinyl trim in Galaxie 500 ($32.20). Wire design wheel covers for Galaxie 500 or Galaxie 500XL ($27.40). Deluxe wheel covers ($18.60). Two-speed windshield wipers and washers ($20.10). Whitewall tires (add $33.90). 427-cid four-barrel V-8 ($462).

1965 FALCON FUTURA SPORT + SPRINT

1965 was the final year for the Sprint, and not many were made: 2,806 hardtops and 300 convertibles. With the new Mustang on the block, production of Falcons fell to 233,641. The big news was that the Sprint now included the new 289-cid, 200 horsepower V-8. Alternators replaced generators in Falcons this year.

A horizontal-bars grille made the '65 Falcon look wider. New 14-inch tires were used on all models but the cheapest Falcon and created a lower profile. The standard equipment started off with a heater and defroster (which could be deleted for an $73.50 credit), directional signals, front seat belts (which could also be deleted for a smaller $11.00 credit), dual inside sun visors and five tubeless black sidewall tires. Futura models added foam seat cushions, carpeting, a deluxe steering wheel and bright exterior body moldings. Hardtops and convertibles came only in the Futura model range.

The Sprint package — including the 289-cid/200-hp V-8, front bucket seats and Sprint identification features — could be added to the Futura two-door hardtop or convertible. A console was a required extra in Sprint convertibles.

Model Number	Body/Style Number	Body Type & Seating	Factory Price	Shipping Weight	Production Total
FALCON FURURA SPORT + SPRINT — SERIES 12/14 — V-8					
12	63H	2d HT-6P	$2,545	2,746 lbs.	2,806
14	76B	2d Conv-6P	$2,856	3,022 lbs.	300

NOTE 1: Price for hardtop includes Sprint package; price for convertible includes Sprint package and required console.

NOTE 2: Weights are estimated.

NOTE 3: Production totals are for cars with the Sprint option only.

NOTE4: Body style suffixes: D indicated bucket seats; E indicated front bench seat.

ENGINES

BASE V-8: Overhead valve. Cast-iron block. Displacement: 289 cid. Bore and stroke: 4.00 x 2.87 inches. Compression ratio: 9.30:1. Brake hp: 200 at 4400 rpm. Torque: 282 at 2400 rpm. Five main bearings. Hydraulic valve lifters. Carburetor: Two-barrel. Code C.

OPTIONAL V-8: Overhead valve. Cast-iron block. Displacement: 289 cid. Bore and stroke: 4.00 x 2.87 inches. Compression ratio: 10.0:1. Brake hp: 225 at 4800 rpm. Torque: 305 at 3200 rpm. Five main bearings. Hydraulic valve lifters. Carburetor: Four-barrel. Code A.

OPTIONAL V-8: Overhead valve. Cast-iron block. Displacement: 289 cid. Bore and stroke: 4.00 x 2.87 inches. Compression ratio: 10.5:1. Brake hp: 271 at 6000 rpm. Torque: 312 at 3400 rpm. Five main bearings. Solid valve lifters. Carburetor: Four-barrel. Code K.

OPTIONS

Ford Air conditioning ($231.70). Heavy-duty battery ($7.60). Bucket seats for two-door hardtop and convertible, console required with convertible ($68.90). Console, with bucket seats or Sprint option ($51.60). Convenience package including hood ornament, body side molding, cigar lighter, deluxe steering wheel, front door courtesy light switch, rear armrests, rear ash tray and bright drip moldings ($43.50). Courtesy light group including ash tray light, glove box light, trunk light, map light, back-up lights, front door courtesy light switches ($25.10). Limited-slip differential for 289-cid hardtop only ($38.00). California type closed emissions system ($5.30). Tinted glass with banded windshield ($27.00). Tinted and banded windshield only ($12.95.) Rocker panel molding ($16.10). Padded dash ($17.30). Padded dash and visors in hardxtop ($21.80). Tu-tone paint ($19.40). Power steering ($86.30). Push-button radio with antenna ($58.50). Deluxe front seat belts with retractors ($7.55). Sprint package with 289-cid 200-hp V-8, front bucket seats and Sprint identification features for Futura two-door hardtop or convertible, console required in convertible ($226.00). Cruise-O-Matic transmission ($182.20). Four-speed manual transmission with V-8 ($188.00). Vinyl roof on two-door hardtop ($75.80). Visibility group including remote-control mirror, day/nite inside rearview mirror and two-speed electric wipers and washers ($36.60). Wheel covers ($16). Wire wheel design covers ($45.10). Fresh air heater delete ($73.50 credit). Front seat belts delete ($11.00 credit). 6.50 x 13 four-ply white sidewall tires for models with standard 6.50 x 13 tires (add $33.00). 6.45 x 14 four-ply black sidewall tires for models with standard 6.50 x 13 tires (add $7.40). 6.45 x 14 four-ply white sidewall tires for models with standard 6.50 x 13 tires (add $41.30).

1965 GALAXIE 500/500XL/LTD "427"

Though the Mustangs and Malibus of the world were better suited to the budgets of the young car buyers most interested in muscle cars, there was always a substantial number of young-at-heart car enthusiasts who needed roomier cars and wanted them to go fast. They were "money-is-no-object" type buyers and Detroit had the hardware available to build what they wanted, as long as they were quite willing to pay for it.

The Galaxie 500XL two-door fastback hardtop with the 427-cid/425-hp Thunderbird Super High-Performance V-8 could be purchased for as little as $3,233 in 1965. Even though it was a big car with a 119-inch wheelbase, a 210-inch overall length and a curb weight of about 3,507 lbs., it still carried only 9.6 pounds per horsepower with the big-block V-8 installed. It could fly from 0-to-60 mph in 4.8 seconds and do the quarter-mile in only 14.9 seconds.

FORD

JERRY HEASLEY

1965 Galaxie 500

Ford continued offering the 427-cid V-8 for the big cars to help maintain Ford's "total performance" image. It didn't fit into other models like the Falcon, Mustang and Fairlane without extensive modifications, but it was a drop-in for the big Galaxie. Fortunately for Ford, NASCAR had kicked the Chrysler Hemi V-8 out of stock car racing, so FoMoCo's 427-powered stock cars took a record of 48 Grand National wins.

Ford only put 327 of the 427-cid V-8s in all of its passenger cars during 1965 and it's a good guess that nearly all went in two-door body styles in the Galaxie 500XL line.

Model Number	Body/Style Number	Body Type & Seating	Factory Price	Shipping Weight	Production Total
GALAXIE 500 — SERIES 60 — V-8					
65	76A	2d Conv-6P	$2,996	3,634 lbs.	30,896
66	63B	2d FSBK-6P	$2,737	3,395 lbs.	150,185
GALAXIE 500XL — SERIES 60 — V-8					
69	76B	2d Conv-6P	$3,426	3,704 lbs.	9,849
68	63C	2d FSBK-6P	$3,167	3,556 lbs.	28,141
GALAXIE 500 LTD — SERIES 60 — V-8					
67	63F	2d FSBK-6P	$3,167	3,516 lbs.	37,691

NOTE 1: Prices and weights for Galaxie 500, Galaxie 500XL and Galaxie 500 LTD with base V-8.

NOTE 2: Production totals above are for all Galaxie 500, Galaxie 500XL and Galaxie 500 LTD V-8s.

NOTE 3: No breakout available for 427s other than corporate total below.

NOTE 4: A total of only 327 of the 427-cid V-8s installed in all FoMoCo cars in model-year 1965.

ENGINE

OPTIONAL V-8: Overhead valve. Cast-iron block. Displacement: 427 cid. Bore and stroke: 4.23 x 3.78 inches. Compression ratio: 11.50:1. Brake hp: 410 at 5600 rpm. Torque: 476 at 3400 rpm. Five main bearings. Solid valve lifters. Carburetor: Holley four-barrel. Dual exhaust. Code Q.

OPTIONAL V-8: Overhead valve. Cast-iron block. Displacement: 427 cid. Bore and stroke: 4.23 x 3.78 inches. Compression ratio: 11.50:1. Brake hp: 425 at 6000 rpm. Torque: 480 at 3700 rpm. Five main bearings. Solid valve lifters. Carburetor: Two Holley four-barrel. Dual exhaust. Code R.

OPTIONS

Select Air air conditioning, including tinted glass and V-8 ($363.80). Heavy-duty 70-amp battery ($7.60, but standard with 427-cid V-8). Courtesy light group ($14.80). Limited-slip differential ($42.50). California type closed emissions system ($5.03). Electric clock in base Galaxie and LTD ($14.60). Tinted glass ($40.30). Tinted windshield only ($21.55). Transistorized ignition system, optional with 427-cid V-8 only ($76.00). Parking brake light ($5.20). Padded dash and visors ($24.30). Padded dash ($18.60). Tu-tone paint ($22). Power brakes ($43.20). Full-width power seat ($96.80). Power driver's seat only ($92.10). Power steering ($97.00). Front and rear power windows ($102.10). Push-button radio with antenna ($58.50). AM/FM radio and antenna, except Galaxie 500 LTD ($129.30). Push-button radio with front antenna and rear speaker in Galaxie 500 LTD ($72.00). Push-button AM/FM radio with front antenna and rear speaker in Galaxie 500 LTD ($142.80). Rear speaker, except Galaxie 500 LTD ($13.50). Deluxe front seat belts with retractors ($7.35). Reclining seat with head rest in Galaxie 50 and Galaxie 500XL only ($45.10). Speed control system with V-8 and Cruise-O-Matic transmission ($63.40). Movable steering column ($43.00). Cruise-O-Matic with 427-cid V-8 ($108.40). Vinyl roof on Galaxie 500 XL or Galaie 500 LTD fastback ($75.80). Vinyl trim in Galaxie 500 ($25.00). Wire design wheel covers for Galaxie 500, Galaxie 500XL and Galaxie 500 LTD ($42.60). Safety convenience package ($51.50). Visibility group ($36.60). Fresh Air/Magic Air heater delete ($75.10 credit, but not available if Select Aire conditioning was ordered). Seat belts delete ($11.00 credit). Whitewall tires (add $37.00). Oversize tires (add $15.70-$52.60 depending on type of tire and standard equipment). 427-cid four-barrel V-8 (approximately $462).

1965 MUSTANG GT

FORD

JERRY HEASLEY

1965 Mustang GT

Mustang initiated the "pony car" segment. There is argument among purists over whether the Mustangs produced prior to September 1964 are 1964 1/2 or 1965 models. However, when it comes to the interesting and collectible GT equipment group, there can be no question, as it was introduced for the first anniversary of the Mustang's introduction on April 17, 1965.

The Mustang had already become a desirable commodity. Its standard equipment included bucket seats. It had the immediately popular long hood, short deck look. At first it came as a Sport Coupe (two-door hardtop) and a sporty-looking convertible. In the fall of 1964, a fastback model called the 2+2 was added to the lineup. From the outset, the options list was important in marketing the Mustang. Buyers could add lots of appearance and convenience extras, plus some bolt-on high-performance hardware. However, being based on the low-priced compact Falcon, there was some room for improvement in the go-fast department. Combining available mechanical features with new visual pieces made the GT package a fairly thorough upgrade. First, the buyer had to order an optional V-8 engine, which at the time included the 225-hp Challenger Special 289 at $157, or the high-performance 271-hp/289-cid engine for $430. The GT option included quick-ratio steering, disc front brakes, chromed dual exhaust tips that exited through the rear valance panel, a new grille bar with fog lights built in and GT instrumentation — which replaced the Falcon-based instrument panel with five round dials. Throw in GT badging and lower body striping and you had a bargain for around $150.

Although the exact number of Mustangs built with GT equipment is not available, they had a massive following and the installation rate for this option increased even more when Ford later released the appearance items separately for dealer installation.

The 1965 Mustang GT with the 289-cid Hi-Po V-8 and 4.11:1 gearing could do 0-to-60 mph in 7.5 seconds, according to the August 1964 issue of *Sports Car Graphic* magazine. The quarter-mile took 15.7 seconds at 89 mph.

Model Number	Body/Style Number	Body Type & Seating	Factory Price	Shipping Weight	Production Total
MUSTANG GT — SERIES 07/08/09 — V-8					
07	65	2d HT-6P	$2,728	2,735 lbs.	242,235
08	76	2d Conv-6P	$2,964	2,920 lbs.	53,517
09	63	2d FSBK-6P	$3,086	3,395 lbs.	64,808

NOTE 1: Prices and weights for base Mustang, plus GT package plus 225-hp Challenger Special 289-cid V-8.

NOTE 2: Production totals above are for all Mustang V-8s; just over 15,000 cars of all styles were built with the GT package.

NOTE 3: No breakout available between A code and K code V-8s.

ENGINES

BASE V-8: Overhead valve. Cast-iron block. Displacement: 289 cid. Bore and stroke: 4.00 x 2.87 inches. Compression ratio: 9.0:1. Brake hp: 210 at 4400 rpm. Torque: 300 at 2800 rpm. Five main bearings. Hydraulic valve lifters. Carburetor: Four-barrel. Code A.

OPTIONAL HI-PO V-8 (K-CODE): Overhead valve. Cast-iron block. Displacement: 289 cid. Bore and stroke: 4.00 x 2.87 inches. Compression ratio: 10.50:1. Brake hp: 271 at 6000 rpm. Torque: 312 at 3400 rpm. Five main bearings. Solid valve lifters. Carburetor: Four-barrel. Code K.

OPTIONS

Accent group for hardtop and convertible ($27.70). Accent group for fastback ($14.20). Heavy-duty battery ($7.60). Front disc brakes for V-8s, requires power brakes ($58.00). Full-length console ($51.50). Console for use with air conditioning ($32.20) Equa-Lock limited-slip differential ($42.50). California-type closed emissions system ($5.30). Challenger four-barrel 225-hp V-8 ($162). Challenger 271-hp high-performance V-8 including Special Handling Package and 6.95 x 14 nylon tires ($442.60). Emergency flashers ($19.60). Tinted glass with banded windshield ($30.90). Tinted-banded windshield glass ($21.55). Back-up lights ($10.70). Rocker panel moldings, except fastback coupe ($16.10). Power brakes ($43.20). Power steering ($86.30). Power convertible top ($54.10). Push-button radio with antenna ($58.50). Rally-Pac instrumentation with clock and tachometer ($70.80). Deluxe retractable front seat safety belts ($7.55). Special Handling package, with 225-hp V-8s ($31.30). Padded sun visors ($5.70). Cruise-O-Matic transmission, with 225-hp V-8 ($189.60). Four-speed manual transmission with V-8 ($188). Vinyl roof, on two-door hardtop only ($75.80). Visibility group, includes remote-control outside rearview mirror; day/nite inside rearview mirror, two-speed electric wipers and windshield washers ($36). Wheel covers with knock-off hubs ($18.20). Fourteen-inch wire wheel covers ($45.80). Fourteen-inch styled steel wheels ($122.30). MagicAire heater

FORD

delete ($32.20 credit). Front seat belts delete ($11.00 credit). 6.95 x 14 4-ply white sidewall tires, except with K code V-8 ($33.90). 6.95 x 14 4-ply black sidewall nylon tires, except with K code V-8 ($15.80). 6.95 x 14 4-ply red band tires, except with K code V-8 ($49.60). 6.95 x 14 4-ply white sidewall tires with K code V-8 (no charge). 6.95 x 14 4-ply black sidewall nylon tires with K code V-8 (no charge).

1965 SHELBY MUSTANG GT 350 "R" CODE

JERRY HEASLEY

1965 Shelby Mustang GT-350 "R" Code

The "R" is for race, no joke. After serial number 34, Shelby-American began inserting an R as the second digit of the vehicle identification number (VIN). But in the early days, both Ford and Shelby-American were not entirely clear on the direction of this new high-performance Mustang.

Two things were certain. First, Ford wanted a higher-performance, specialty version of the Mustang. Second, it wanted a car that could compete with Chevy's Corvette. The latter suggested a two-seat car and this could be achieved by removing the back seat from a Mustang 2+2 fastback. Higher performance meant hopping up the 289-cid V-8, since Ford's big-block engines would not fit in the Mustang and because the small-block worked best for road racing. Both jobs were turned over to Shelby-American of Los Angeles, which had taken the AC-based Cobra roadster and thrashed Corvettes in USRRC (United States Road Race of Champions) racing. At the same time, the Cobra completely overpowered the Corvette in SCCA A-production racing and beat out Ferrari for the World Manufacturer's Championship. Ford felt that it made a lot of sense to hire Shelby to turn the Mustang into a car that could beat the Corvette in SCCA B-production racing. The automaker knew this would further reinforce the muscular image of Ford's new pony car.

Shelby-American proceeded to build a street version of a new GT Mustang, which Carroll Shelby himself named the GT 350. It was a rather obvious reference to the 350-cid small-block engine from Chevrolet, although Shelby gave the press some story about walking off 350 steps. With racing victories a major goal, Shelby-American also built a race-ready competition model that was not meant for street use. It was called the R-model. To satisfy SCCA regulations at least 100 cars (race and street versions) had to be built. Therefore, 100 white fastbacks—each fitted with 289-cid high-performance K-code V-8s with solid valve lifters and 271 hp — were lifted off an assembly line at the Ford plant in San Jose, California. The R-model came with the high-performance features of the street GT 350 — the 289-cid 306-hp small-block with a hi-rise aluminum intake manifold, four-speed transmission, No-Spin differential, lowered suspension and lots more—plus special R-model features.

The GT 350 R code Mustang was so specialized that a mere 36 were sold. However, they were available to anyone willing to pay the base price of $5,950 to buy an out-of-the-box race winner. The 1965 GT 350 R was the SCCA B-production national champion in 1965, 1966 and 1967.

Car & Driver tested a Shelby Mustang GT 350R in its May 1965 issue. The car moved from 0-to-60 mph in 6.5 seconds. It traveled the quarter-mile in 14.9 seconds at 95 mph. Not bad for a small-block V-8!

Model Number	Body/Style Number	Body Type & Seating	Factory Price	Shipping Weight	Production Total
SHELBY MUSTANG GT 350 — SERIES R — V-8					
SFM	63( )	2d FSBK-6P	$5,995	—	36

ENGINE
BASE V-8: Overhead valve. Cast-iron block. Displacement: 289 cid. Bore and stroke: 4.00 x 2.87 inches. Compression ratio: 10.50:1. Brake hp: 306. Torque: 312 at 3400 rpm. Solid valve lifters. Carburetor: Holley 3259 four-barrel. Code K.

OPTIONS
Crager mag wheels. LeMans stripes. Axle ratios (3.89:1 was standard).

1966 FAIRLANE 500XL GT/GTA "390"

JERRY HEASLEY

1966 Fairlane GTA 390

The Fairlane GT/GTA was Ford's "Tiger," and brand loyalty dictated that it would hit the streets to prove itself. *Car Life's* Gene Booth said, "The GTA (do you suppose it will be called 'GeeTAw') plants Ford firmly in the performance market." The first production Fairlanes able to carry a big-block V-8 were the totally redesigned 1966 models. The size of the Fairlane body didn't change much on the outside, but the increased dimensions under the hood became important in the muscle car era.

These cars served as Ford's factory hot rods when they were equipped with the monster V-8s. They competed head to head with the GTO and a Ford advertisement for the high-performance model was titled "How to cook a tiger!" Both cars sported special GT and GTA identification and shared luxurious interior appointments with the Fairlane 500XL models. Standard equipment highlights included the 335-hp Thunderbird Special V-8, a Synchro-Smooth Drive three-speed manual transmission in the GT or a Sport Shift Cruise-O-Matic transmission in the GTA, bucket seats and a console, full carpeting, a padded instrument panel and sun visors, front and rear seat belts, a heater-defroster, a choice of 15 colors of Super Diamond Lustre enamel, seven all-vinyl XL-level interior trims, 7.75 x 14 nylon white sidewall tires, full wheel covers, suspended accelerator pedals, back-up lights, an outside rearview mirror, stiffer springs, stiffer shock absorbers, a heavy-duty stabilizer bar, and emergency flashers. The convertible also included a five-ply vinyl convertible top with a glass rear window.

A GTA two-door hardtop with the 390-cid/335-hp V-8 carried only about 10.5 lbs. per horsepower. It could move from 0-to-60 mph in a mere 6.8 seconds and did the quarter-mile in 15.2 seconds.

Model Number	Body/Style Number	Body Type & Seating	Factory Price	Shipping Weight	Production Total
FAIRLANE 500 GT — SERIES 40 — V-8					
40	63D	2d HT-6P	$2,843	3,335 lbs.	33,015
44	76D	2d Conv-6P	$3,680	3,500 lbs.	4,327

NOTE 1: Prices and weights are for Fairlane GT/GTA models with base 390-cid V-8.

NOTE 2: Production above is for all V-8 versions of the indicated Fairlane models.

ENGINE

BASE V-8: Overhead valve. Cast-iron block. Displacement: 390 cid. Bore and stroke: 4.05 x 3.78 inches. Compression ratio: 11.0:1. Brake hp: 335 at 4800 rpm. Torque: 427 at 3200 rpm. Five main bearings. Hydraulic valve lifters. Carburetor: Holley four-barrel. Dual exhaust. Code S.

OPTIONS

Three-speed Cruise-O-Matic drive. Four-speed manual transmission. Power steering. Power brakes. SelectAire conditioner. Push-buttom AM radio. Deluxe seat belts front and rear. Visibility group including remote-control outside rearview mirror, day/night inside rearview mirror and two-speed electric wipers. Electric clock. Tinted windshield. Tinted glass. Courtesy light group, including lights for instrument panel, lighted ash tray, glove box light, trunk light, map light and door courtesy light switches. Power convertible top. Two-tone paint. Dual accent paint stripe for Fairlane 500 and 500XL. White sidewall tires. Sports steering wheel. All-vinyl trim for Fairlane 500 hardtop. Deluxe wheel covers. Heavy-duty battery. Limited-slip differential. Heater/defroster. Styled steel wheels. Deluxe wheel covers.

1966 FAIRLANE 500/ FAIRLANE 500XL "427"

1966 Fairlane 427

The 427 Fairlane was the product of corporate thinking; an attempt to salvage some commercial benefit from the 1963 Thunderbolt drag-racing program. While the T-Bolts had been built for racing only, the later big-block Fairlanes were meant to excite showroom shoppers seeking the ultimate in street performance machines. Ford did a total redesign of the Fairlane for 1966. The engineers specifically left enough room in the engine compartment so the 427 could be shoehorned under the hood. Nothing was held back because of the sales theme Ford wanted to push at the time.

Ford's "Total Performance" program was aimed at taking the wind out of the sails of Mopar and General Motors. FoMoCo's 390 V-8 was eating the dust generated by Hemis, GTOs, 4-4-2s and SS-396 Chevelles. The fact that the 427 out-cubed Mopar's various 426s was no coincidence. It was an engine designed to turn on the hot rodders who wanted a Ford that could smoke the competition.

Identified by a big, long lift-off fiberglass hood with a huge scoop taking in air just above the grille, the Fairlane 500s and 500XLs equipped with the big-block came in 410 hp (single four-barrel) and 425 hp (with twin Holley four-barrel carburetors) configurations. The cars also featured NASCAR-style hood locking pins, chrome engine parts, 11.2-inch diameter disc brakes, a 2 1/4-inch diameter exhaust system, a heavy-duty suspension and a tachometer. Only 57 two-door Fairlanes

with fiberglass hoods and 427 race engines have been documented as built. This may well be the total production and it is very possible that none of the cars were convertibles.

Hot Rod did not do a full road test of the 1966 Fairlane 427, but reported some figures quoted by "some of the mechanics on the project" which indicated quarter-mile runs in 14.5 to 14.6 seconds at 100 mph. Later, on drag strips with some tuning and racing slicks, the cars were found capable of doing the distance in just under 13 seconds at nearly 114 mph. Only about 57 such cars were produced in 1966, but they gave the midsize Fords a muscle car image that boosted the entire line's market impact.

Model Number	Body/Style Number	Body Type & Seating	Factory Price	Shipping Weight	Production Total
FAIRLANE 500 — SERIES 40 — V-8					
43	63B	2d HT-6P	$2,484	3,025 lbs.	65,343
45	76B	2d Conv-6P	$2,709	3,253 lbs.	8,039
FAIRLANE 500 GT — SERIES 40 — V-8					
40	63D	2d HT-6P	$2,843	3,335 lbs.	33,015
44	76D	2d Conv-6P	$3,680	3,500 lbs.	4,327
FAIRLANE 500XL — SERIES 40 — V-8					
46	63C	2d HT-6P	$2,649	3,053 lbs.	21,315
47	76C	2d Conv-6P	$2,874	3,268 lbs.	4,305

NOTE 1: Prices and weights are for Fairlane models with base 289-cid V-8.

NOTE 2: Production above is for all V-8 versions of the indicated Fairlane models.

NOTE 3: Ford built only 237 of the 427-cid V-8s in model-year 1966 and some were used in full-size Ford models. Very few 427 Fairlanes were built.

NOTE 4: Construction of 57 lightweight drag racing cars with 427s has been documented.

ENGINES

OPTIONAL V-8: Overhead valve. Cast-iron block. Displacement: 427 cid. Bore and stroke: 4.23 x 3.78 inches. Compression ratio: 11.50:1. Brake hp: 410 at 5600 rpm. Torque: 476 at 3400 rpm. Five main bearings. Solid valve lifters. Carburetor: Holley four-barrel. Dual exhaust. Code Q.

OPTIONAL V-8: Overhead valve. Cast-iron block. Displacement: 427 cid. Bore and stroke: 4.23 x 3.78 inches. Compression ratio: 11.50:1. Brake hp: 425 at 6000 rpm. Torque: 480 at 3700 rpm. Five main bearings. Solid valve lifters. Carburetor: Two Holley four-barrel. Dual exhaust. Code R.

OPTIONS

Three-speed Cruise-O-Matic drive. Four-speed manual transmission. Power steering. Power brakes. SelectAire conditioner. Push-buttom AM radio. Deluxe seat belts front and rear. Visibility group including remote-control outside rearview mirror, day/night inside rearview mirror and two-speed electric wipers. Electric clock. Tinted windshield. Tinted glass all-around. Courtesy light group including lights for instrument panel, lighted ash tray, glove box light, trunk light, map light and door courtesy light switches. Power convertible top. Two-tone paint. Dual accent paint stripe for Fairlane 500 and 500XL. White sidewall tires. Sports steering wheel. All-vinyl trim for Fairlane 500 hardtop. Deluxe wheel covers. Heavy-duty battery. Limited-slip differential. Heater defroster. Styled steel wheels. Deluxe wheel covers. And more. (Note: This list is from the 8-65 sales catalog and the 427-cid V-8 was not included at that time. It is believed the cost of this engine option was in the $400-$450 range, but other equipment may have been required).

1966 GALAXIE 500/500XL 7-LITRE

FORD

MIKE MUELLER

1966 Galaxie 500 7-Litre

The Galaxie "7-Litre" was a car that belonged in the muscle car world, despite the fact that it was bigger than most of the other machinery in that universe. While full-size 1965 and 1966 Fords shared a similar overall design character, the hood is the only body panel that can be interchanged between the two years. The 1966 feature lines were a bit more rounded and the Galaxie 500 two-door hardtop, with its semi-fastback roofline, had particular eye appeal.

At this time in the muscle car marketplace, the demand for big cars was declining. The mid-sized models, sporty "senior" compacts and pony cars like the Mustang were offering go-fast options designed to steal high-performance buyers away from full-sized models. In reaction to this, Ford decided to package the big-engine Galaxie as a separate, sporty model aimed at mature muscle car mavens. The Galaxie 500 "7-Litre" series offered high-performance versions of the Galaxie 500 two-door hardtop and convertible with a 428-cid/345-hp V-8 engine as standard equipment. Also included was a Cruise-O-Matic automatic transmission, but a four-speed manual gearbox was optional at no extra cost. The code "Q" 428-cid "Thunderbird Special" V-8 had a 4.13 x 3.98-inch bore and stroke. With a single Holley four-barrel carburetor and a 10.5:1 compression ratio, it developed 345 hp at 4600 rpm. A "Police Interceptor" version (Code "P") with 360 hp at 5400 rpm was optional.

The "7-Litre" hardtop could do 0-to-60 mph in about 8 seconds and the quarter-mile in 16.4 seconds.

ENGINES

BASE V-8: Overhead valve. Cast-iron block. Displacement: 428 cid. Bore and stroke: 4.13 x 3.98 inches. Compression ratio: 10.50:1. Brake hp: 345 at 4600 rpm. Torque: 462 at 2800 rpm. Five main bearings. Hydraulic valve lifters. Carburetor: Four-barrel. Dual exhaust. Code Q.

OPTIONAL V-8: Overhead valve. Cast-iron block. Displacement: 427 cid. Bore and stroke: 4.23 x 3.78 inches. Compression ratio: 11.00:1. Brake hp: 410 at 5600 rpm. Torque: 476 at 3400 rpm. Five main bearings. Solid valve lifters. Carburetor: Holley four-barrel. Dual exhaust. Code W.

OPTIONAL V-8: Overhead valve. Cast-iron block. Displacement: 427 cid. Bore and stroke: 4.23 x 3.78 inches. Compression ratio: 11.50:1. Brake hp: 425 at 6000 rpm. Torque: 480 at 3700 rpm. Five main bearings. Hydraulic valve lifters. Carburetor: Two Holley four-barrel. Dual exhaust. Code R.

OPTIONS

Select Air air conditioning, including tinted glass and V-8 ($363.80). Heavy-duty 70-amp battery ($7.60, but standard with 427-cid V-8). Courtesy light group ($14.80). Limited-slip differential ($42.50). California type closed emissions system ($5.03). Electric clock in base Galaxie and LTD ($14.60). Tinted glass ($40.30). Tinted windshield only ($21.55). Transistorized ignition system, optional with 427-cid V-8 only ($76.00). Parking brake light ($5.20). Padded dash and visors ($24.30). Padded dash ($18.60). Tu-tone paint ($22). Power brakes ($43.20). Full-width power seat ($96.80). Power driver's seat only ($92.10). Power steering ($97.00). Front and rear power windows ($102.10). Push-button radio with antenna ($58.50). AM/FM radio and antenna, except Galaxie 500 LTD ($129.30). Push-button radio with front antenna and rear speaker in Galaxie 500 LTD ($72.00). Push-button AM/FM radio with front antenna and rear speaker in Galaxie 500 LTD ($142,80). Rear speaker, except Galaxie 500 LTD ($13.50). Deluxe front seat belts with retractors ($7.35). Reclining seat with head rest in Galaxie 50 and Galaxie 500XL only ($45.10). Speed control system with V-8 and Cruise-O-Matic transmission ($63.40). Movable steering column ($43.00). Cruise-O-Matic with 427-cid V-8 ($108.40). Vinyl roof on Galaxie 500 XL or Galaxie 500 LTD fastback ($75.80). Vinyl trim in Galaxie 500 ($25.00). Wire design wheel covers for Galaxie 500, Galaxie 500XL and Galaxie 500 LTD ($42.60). Safety convenience package ($51.50). Visibility group ($36.60). Fresh Air/Magic Air heater delete ($75.10 credit, but not available if Select Aire conditioning was ordered). Seat belts delete ($11.00 credit). Whitewall tires (add $37.00). Oversize tires (add $15.70-$52.60 depending on type of tire and standard equipment). 427-cid four-barrel V-8 (approximately $462).

Model Number	Body/Style Number	Body Type & Seating	Factory Price	Shipping Weight	Production Total
GALAXIE 500 7-LITRE — SERIES 60 — V-8					
63	76B	2d Conv-6P	$3,972	4,059 lbs.	2,368
61	63D	2d FSBK-6P	$3,621	3,914 lbs.	8,705

NOTE 1: Prices and weights for regular Galaxie 500 7-Litre with 428-cid base V-8

NOTE 2: Apparently there was an XL version available as an option.

NOTE 3: Production by body style only; no engine breakouts available; most were 428s..

NOTE 4: A total of only 237 of the 427-cid V-8s were installed in all FoMoCo cars in model-year 1966.

NOTE 5: A total of 43,055 of the 428-cid V-8s were installed in all FoMoCo cars in model-year 1966.

1966 MUSTANG GT "289 HI-PO"

1966 Mustang GT

For 1966, little change was made to Ford's hot-selling Mustang. You don't mess with success, so why change a good thing? The GT Equipment Group continued to be available in 1966 as a $152.50 option package for Mustangs with high-performance V-8 power plants. The GT Equipment Group included a dual exhaust system, front fog lamps, special body ornamentation, front disc brakes, GT racing stripes (in place of rocker panel moldings) and handling package components.

The Mustang's base V-8 engine for 1966 was the Code "G" 4.00 x 2.87-inch bore and stroke 289-cid with a 9.3:1 compression ratio and an Autolite two-barrel carburetor. It generated 200 hp at 4400 rpm. The performance options included the Code "A" 289-cid Challenger V-8 with a 10.1:1 compression ratio and four-barrel Autolite carburetor, which produced 225 hp at 4800, and the Code "K" Challenger High-Performance V-8, which featured a 10.5:1 compression ratio, a four-barrel Autolite carburetor and solid valve lifters, which helped it to make 271 hp at 6000 rpm. A Mustang 2+2 with this "Challenger High-Performance V-8" could do 0-to-60 mph in 7.6 seconds and needed about 15.9 seconds to make it down the quarter-mile.

The GT package proved to be twice as popular as it had been in 1965 and its sales increased from about 15,000 the earlier year to approximately 30,000.

Model Number	Body/Style Number	Body Type & Seating	Factory Price	Shipping Weight	Production Total
MUSTANG GT — SERIES 07/08/09 — V-8					
07	65	2d HT-6P	$3,108	2,733 lbs.	274,809
08	76	2d Conv-6P	$3,344	2,895 lbs.	48,252
09	63	2d FSBK-6P	$3,299	2,764 lbs.	31,295

NOTE 1: Prices and weights for base Mustang, plus GT package plus 271-hp Challenger Hi-Po 289-cid V-8

NOTE 2: Production totals above are for all Mustang V-8s; just over 30,000 cars of all styles were built with the GT package.

NOTE 3: No breakout available for K code V-8.

ENGINES

BASE V-8: Overhead valve. Cast-iron block. Displacement: 289 cid. Bore and stroke: 4.00 x 2.87 inches. Compression ratio: 9.0:1. Brake hp: 210 at 4400 rpm. Torque: 300 at 2800 rpm. Five main bearings. Hydraulic valve lifters. Carburetor: Four-barrel. Code A.

OPTIONAL HI-PO V-8 (K-CODE): Overhead valve. Cast-iron block. Displacement: 289 cid. Bore and stroke: 4.00 x 2.87 inches. Compression ratio: 10.50:1. Brake hp: 271 at 6000 rpm. Torque: 312 at 3400 rpm. Five main bearings. Solid valve lifters. Carburetor: Four-barrel. Code K.

OPTIONS

Challenger 289-cid V-8 ($105.63). Challenger four-barrel 289 cid/225 hp V-8 ($158.48). High-performance 289-cid/271-hp V-8, in standard Mustang ($433.55); in Mustang GT ($381.97). NOTE: The total cost of the high-performance engine was $327.92 on regular Mustangs and $276.34 on Mustang GTs, plus the cost of the base V-8 attachment over the six (which was $105.63). Cruise-O-Matic automatic transmission with six ($175.80); with standard V-8s ($185.39); with high-performance V-8 ($216.27). Four-speed manual floor shift transmission, with six ($113.45); with all V-8s ($184.02). Power brakes ($42.29). Power steering ($84.47). Power convertible top ($52.95). Heavy-duty 55-amp battery ($7.44). Manual disc brakes, with V-8 only ($56.77). GT Equipment group, with high-performance V-8 only, includes: dual exhaust; fog lamps; special ornamentation; disc brakes; GT racing stripes (rocker panel moldings deleted); and Handling Package components ($152.20). Limited-slip differential ($41.60). Rally-Pack instrumentation, includes clock and tachometer ($69.30). Special Handling Package, with 200-hp and 225-hp V-8 engines, includes increased rate front and rear springs, larger front and rear shocks; 22:1 overall steering ratio and large diameter stabilizer bar ($30.84). Fourteen-inch styled steel wheels, on V-8 models only ($93.84). Two-speed electric windshield wipers ($12.95). Tinted-banded windshield only ($21.09). All glass tinted with banded windshield ($30.25). Deluxe, retractable front seat safety belts and warning lamp ($14.53). Visibility group, includes remote-control outside rearview mirror; day/nite inside mirror and two-speed electric wipers ($29.81). Ford air condi¬tioner ($310.90). Stereo tape player, AM radio mandatory ($128.49). Full-width front seat with armrest for Styles 65A and 76A only ($24.42). Rear deck luggage rack, except fastback ($32.44). Radio and antenna ($57.51). Accent striping, less rear quarter ornamentation ($13.90). Full-length center console ($50.41). Console for use with air conditioning ($31.52). Deluxe steering wheel with simulated woodgrain rim ($31.52). Interior Decor group, includes special interior trim; Deluxe wood-grain steering wheel; rear window door courtesy lights and pistol grip door handles ($94.13). Vinyl top, on hardtop ($74.36). Simulated wire wheel covers ($58.24). Wheel covers with simulated knock-off hubs ($19.48). Closed crankcase emissions system, except with high-performance V-8 ($519). Exhaust emissions control system, except with high-performance V-8 ($45.45). Tire

options, exchange prices listed indicate cost above base equipment: 6.95 x 14 four-ply rated whitewall ($33.31); nylon blackwall ($15.67); nylon whitewall ($48.89); nylon with dual red band design, on cars with high-performance V-8 (no charge); all other ($48.97).

1966 SHELBY MUSTANG GT 350H (HERTZ)

PHIL KUNZ

1966 Shelby Mustang GT 350H

"Rent-A-Race-Car" may seem like an oxymoron, but then, you might have forgotten about the Shelby GT 350H. The "H" stood for Hertz and it was a special version of Carroll Shelby's legendary conversion of the Mustang pony car into a true muscle car.

The GT 350H was not Hertz's first venture involving rental cars that weren't totally ho-hum. Prior to 1965, Hertz had rented Corvettes. In any case, during 1966 you could walk up to the Hertz counter in many major cities and ask for one of the hottest cars of the era. You did have to be a member of the Hertz Sports Car Club. You also had to be at least 25 years old and able to demonstrate "driving skills." The latter often involved no more than a quick spin around the block.

When Hertz switched its allegiance to Ford products, renting 'Vettes didn't seem appropriate. Carroll Shelby's astute sales manager saw the promotional possibilities in having the Shelby-Mustang replace the Corvette. This would be great advertising, as well as a way to get potential buyers in the driver's seat. While Shelby initially hoped to sell a couple dozen cars to Hertz, the ultimate order was larger. The final tally came to 936 GT 350s out of a total run of 2,380 in 1966.

It came as no surprise—except possibly to Hertz—that these muscular rent-a-cars would create some maintenance headaches after being put into the hands of weekend racers. There are tales of "Rent-A-Racers" showing up at drag strips. When the remnants of a roll bar were found under the carpeting in one car, it was concluded that it had seen some track

time in SCCA competition. At a cost of only $17 dollars a day and 17 cents per mile (still about twice the rate of a regular Hertz rental at the time) the GT 350H offered a cheap car to use for a weekend of racing. After the race, Hertz could take care of any needed repairs. The original Borg-Warner T-10 close-ratio four-speed manual transmissions were a real problem,. especially when used by inexperienced drivers. Hertz later switched to Ford's C-4 automatic, which became an option on all Shelbys for 1966. Although lacking a stickshift, this was still a rental car with over 300 hp. With the automatic, the "Cobra-ized" 289-cid High Performance small-block V-8 was fed by a 595-cfm Autolite carburetor that replaced the regular 715-cfm Holley. Another running change was to Mustang-type front disc brakes and a revised master cylinder. This lowered the pedal pressure a bit with sintered metallic brake pads and linings. A warning that read, "This vehicle is equipped with competition brakes. Heavier than normal pedal pressure required" was displayed on the instrument panel.

Statistics for this car were 0-to-60 in 6.2 seconds, quarter-mile in 14 seconds at 92 mph.

The GT 350H had some visual differences from normal '66 GT 350s. Most were finished in black with gold decals (a color scheme Hertz had used when it built its own taxicabs in the 1920s.) A few GT 350Hs were painted white, red, blue and green. Most of these also got gold striping.

After serving Hertz, the GT 350Hs were returned to Ford for minor refurbishing. Then, they were resold to the general public through selected dealers. Unfortunately, during refurbishing, the high-performance parts sometimes got "lost." While there were no special Hertz models in later years, the company did rent GT 350s through 1969. Today, an excellent GT 350H will bring a couple of thousand dollars more than a "plain" GT 350.

Model Number	Body/Style Number	Body Type & Seating	Factory Price	Shipping Weight	Production Total
SHELBY MUSTANG GT 350H — SERIES S — V-8					
SFM	63( )	2d FSBK-6P	—	—	936

ENGINE

MODIFIED HI-PO V-8 (K-CODE): Overhead valve. Cast-iron block. Displacement: 289 cid. Bore and stroke: 4.00 x 2.87 inches. Compression ratio: 10.50:1. Brake hp: 306. Torque: 312 at 3400 rpm. Solid valve lifters. Carburetor: Holley 3259 four-barrel. Code K.

OPTIONS

Paxton supercharger. LeMans stripes. 15-inch Cragar five-spoke wheels. 14-inch aluminum 10-spoke wheels. Detroit No-Spin rear axle. Rear axle ratios (3.89:1 standard). Koni adjustable shocks (standard on early cars — dealer-installed later. LeMans stripes. AM radio. Rear seat. Ford C-4 automatic transmission (no charge).

1967 FAIRLANE 500/500XL "427"

JERRY HEASLEY

1967 Fairlane 427

There was nothing "middle-of-the-road" about Ford's mid-size muscle machines in 1967. If you wanted to go all the way when it came to building a high-performance Fairlane, your FoMoCo dealer had the vehicles and hardware you needed to create a street racer or a weekend dragster. Ford advertisements made this clear when they stated, "The 427 Fairlane is also available without numbers." They weren't talking about meter rates on the side of a taxicab either — they were talking about the numbers on racing cars that went brutally fast.

The stock 1967 Ford Fairlane continued to use the same body introduced in 1966 with only minor trim changes. The 1967 grille was a single aluminum stamping used in place of the two grilles that graced the previous model. The 1967 tail lights were divided horizontally by the back-up light, instead of vertically, as in 1966. The fire-breathing 427-cid "side-oiler" V-8 was again available on the Fairlane's options list.

The 1967 edition of *Car Fax i*ndicated that it came only on non-GT club coupes (two-door sedans) and sport coupes (two-door hardtops). The milder 410-hp single-four-barrel-carburetor version of the 427 was not the only choice. There was the hairier 425-hp version that carried two four-barrel Holley carburetors. Racing versions of the 427-cid V-8 were offered with goodies

like a new eight-barrel induction system that put about 30 extra horses on tap. A tunnel-port version of the 427 was available as an over-the-counter kit, with a tunnel-port intake on special cylinder heads and a special intake manifold.

Model Number	Body/Style Number	Body Type & Seating	Factory Price	Shipping Weight	Production Total
FAIRLANE — SERIES 30 — V-8					
30	62A	2d Sedan-6P	$2,402	2,916 lbs.	3,680
FAIRLANE 500 — SERIES 30 — V-8					
33	62B	2d Sedan-6P	$2,482	2,924 lbs.	5,539
35	63B	2d HT-6P	$2,545	3,011 lbs.	65,256
FAIRLANE 500XL — SERIES 40 — V-8					
40	63C	2d HT-6P	$2,724	3,039 lbs.	14,541

NOTE 1: Prices and weights are for Fairlane models with base 289-cid V-8 (not for 427).

NOTE 2: Production above is for all V-8 versions of the indicated Fairlane models.

NOTE 3: Ford built only 369 of the 427-cid V-8s in model-year 1966 and some were used in Galaxie 7-Litre models. Very few 427 Fairlnes were built.

ENGINES

BASE V-8: Overhead valve. Cast-iron block. Displacement: 427 cid. Bore and stroke: 4.23 x 3.78 inches. Compression ratio: 11.50:1. Brake hp: 410 at 5600 rpm. Torque: 476 at 3400 rpm. Five main bearings. Solid valve lifters. Carburetor: Holley four-barrel. Dual exhaust. Code Q.

OPTIONAL V-8: Overhead valve. Cast-iron block. Displacement: 427 cid. Bore and stroke: 4.23 x 3.78 inches. Compression ratio: 11.50:1. Brake hp: 425 at 6000 rpm. Torque: 480 at 3700 rpm. Five main bearings. Solid valve lifters. Carburetor: Two Holley four-barrel. Dual exhaust. Code R.

OPTIONS

Body side accent stripe ($13.90). Select Aire conditioner ($356.09). 42-amp alternator, not with air conditioning ($10.42). 55-amp alternator, standard with air conditioning ($21.09). High-ratio rear axle ($2.63). Heavy-duty battery (standard with 427). Limited-slip differential ($37.20). Closed crankcase emissions system, exhaust ECS required ($5.19). Electric clock ($15.59, but standard in 500XLs). 427-cid/410-hp four-barrel V-8 available on Club Coupes and hardtops, except GT, includes transistorized ignition, heavy-duty battery, heavy-duty suspension, extra cooling package and power disc brakes; F70-14 Wide-Oval white sidewall tires and four-speed manual gearbox required at extra cost (price not available in or source but believed to be $647.51 over the cost of the 200-hp 289). 427-cid 425-hp four-barrel V-8 available on Club Coupes and hardtops, except GT, includes transistorized ignition, heavy-duty battery, heavy-duty suspension, extra cooling package and power disc brakes; F70-14 Wide-Oval white sidewall tires and four-speed manual gearbox required at extra cost (price not available in or source but believed to be $647.51 over the cost of the 200-hp 289). Tinted glass ($30.73). Tinted windshield ($21.09). Remote-control left-hand outside rearview mirror ($9.58). Magic Aire heater delete ($73.51 credit). Tu-tone paint Fairlane 30 and 33 models$21.54). Power brakes ($42.49, but not available with 427-cid V-8). 6-Way power driver's bucket seat ($84.25). Power steering ($94.95). Power top ($52.95). Push-button AM radio with front antenna ($57.46). Deluxe seat belts with warning light ($10.42). Front seat shoulder harness ($27.27). Deluxe woodgrain steering wheel ($31.52). Stereosonic tape system ($128.49). Heavy-duty suspension (standard with 427). Tachometer ($47.92). Cruise-O-Matic (this had a special price of $34.63 for Fords with 428s and was probably about that price in Fairlanes with the 427). Four-speed manual transmission ($184.02 and required as a mandatory option with the 427). Vinyl roof ($74.36). Deluxe wheel covers ($19.48 for Fairlane 500 XL and $40.76 for other Fairlanes). Styled steel wheels ($93.84 on Fairlane 500XL and $115.11 on other Fairlanes). Protection group including front and rear floor mats, license plate frames and door edge guards ($25.28). Courtesy light group includes glove box light, ash tray light and trunk light ($14.49, includes map light). Extra-cooling package (standard with 427).

1967 FAIRLANE GT/GTA "390"

1967 Fairlane GTA

In 1967, the Pontiac GTO was still the monarch of the muscle car kingdom, but Ford's rebellious Fairlane GT/GTA was back to try to topple royalty once again. As the "pappy" of supercars, the GTO was starting to get a little fat and fancy, while the muscle-building mid-size Fords were looking leaner and more lethal. The '67 Fairlane continued Ford's trend toward sporty, youthful styling. In appearance, it was clearly moving away from the dowdiness of the model's earlier years. The hotter GT models carried a narrow-wide-narrow side stripe motif on both sides of the body, just above the rocker panels. A new deeply-recessed radiator grille added to the midsize Fairlane's performance image and the vertically-mounted dual headlights created instant Ford family identification.

For '67, standard equipment for the Fairlane GT included all Fairlane, Fairlane 500 and Fairlane 500XL features plus power front disc brakes, Wide-Oval sports white tires, a special GT hood carrying simulated "power domes" with integral turn signal indicators, GT body stripes, GT fender plaques, a GT black-out style grille, deluxe full wheel covers, a 289-cid V-8, a left-hand remote-control outside rearview mirror and deluxe seat belts. The 390-cid V-8 was optional in the hot Fairlane. You could get it with a two-barrel carburetor and 270 hp or a single four-barrel carburetor and 320 hp. When a buyer ordered the more powerful version, an extra-cost transmission was mandatory. The cheapest transmission option was the heavy-duty three-speed manual gearbox, but the buyer could opt for a four-speed manual gearbox or Sport Shift Cruise-O-Matic. When this transmission was ordered, the car became a GTA. A heavy-duty suspension was standard equipment on 1967 Fairlane GTs and GTAs with the big-block 390-cid V-8.

A 289-equipped Fairlane hardtop could go from 0-to-60 mph in 10.6 seconds and do the quarter-mile in 18 seconds at 79 mph. The 390-cid/320-hp version required 8.4 seconds to reach 60 mph and did the quarter/mile in 16.2 seconds at 89 mph.

Model Number	Body/Style Number	Body Type & Seating	Factory Price	Shipping Weight	Production Total
FAIRLANE 500 GT — SERIES 30 — V-8					
42	63D	2d HT-6P	$2,919	3,401 lbs.	Note 3
FAIRLANE 500 GTA — SERIES 30 — V-8					
42	63D	2d HT-6P	$3,137	3,161 lbs.	Note 3

NOTE 1: Prices are for Fairlane GT/GTA models with base 390-cid two-barrel V-8.
NOTE 2: Weights are estimated for 390 models.
NOTE 3: Production was 18,670 for both versions combined (all engines).

ENGINES

OPTIONAL V-8: Overhead valve. Cast-iron block. Displacement: 390 cid. Bore and stroke: 4.05 x 3.78 inches. Compression ratio: 9.5:1. Brake hp: 270 at 4400 rpm. Torque: 403 at 2600 rpm. Five main bearings. Hydraulic valve lifters. Carburetor: Two-barrel. Code Y or H.

FORD

OPTIONAL V-8: Overhead valve. Cast-iron block. Displacement: 390 cid. Bore and stroke: 4.05 x 3.78 inches. Compression ratio: 10.5:1. Brake hp: 320 at 4800 rpm. Torque: 427 at 3200 rpm. Five main bearings. Hydraulic valve lifters. Carburetor: Holley four-barrel. Dual exhaust. Code S.

OPTIONS

Body side accent stripe ($13.90). Select Aire conditioner ($356.09). 42-amp alternator, not with air conditioning ($10.42). 55-amp alternator, standard with air conditioning ($21.09). High-ratio rear axle ($2.63). Heavy-duty battery ($2.63). Limited-slip differential ($37.20). Closed crankcase emissions system, exhaust ECS required ($5.19). Electric clock ($15.59). 390-cid/270-hp two-barrel V-8 ($78.25). 390-cid/320-hp V-8, extra-cost transmission required ($158.08). Tinted glass ($30.73). Tinted windshield ($21.09). Remote-control left-hand outside rearview mirror (standard on GTs). Magic Aire heater delete ($73.51 credit). Power brakes ($42.49, but not available with 427-cid V-8). 6-Way power driver's bucket seat ($84.25). Power steering ($94.95). Power top ($52.95). Push-button AM radio with front antenna ($57.46). Deluxe seat belts with warning light (standard in GTs). Front seat shoulder harness ($27.27). Deluxe wood-grain steering wheel ($31.52). Stereosonic tape system ($128.49). Heavy-duty suspension (standard with 427). Tachometer ($47.92). Three-speed heavy-duty manual transmission ($79.20 and minimum requirement with 390-cid four-barrel V-8). Cruise-O-Matic (this had a special price of $34.63 for Fairlanes with the 390-cid V-8). Four-speed manual transmission ($184.02). Vinyl roof ($74.36). Deluxe wheel covers ($40.76). Styled steel wheels ($74.36 price for GTs only). Protection group including front and rear floor mats, license plate frames and door edge guards ($25.28). Courtesy light group includes glove box light, ash tray light and trunk light ($14.49, includes map light). Extra-cooling package ($13.58 special price for GTs).

1967 GALAXIE 500XL 427/428

1967 Galaxie 500 XL

By 1967, Chevrolet Motor Division had brought the huge, powerful Impala SS 427 on the market. This was not the time for Dearborn to rethink its so-far-futile attempt to sell the muscular "7-Litre" version of its full-size car in big numbers. However, there was no separate Galaxie 500XL "7-Litre" series this year. Instead, the 7-Litre engine and chassis goodies were offered as an option package for the Galaxie 500XL two-door hardtop and ragtop.

After two years of somewhat similar, but not identical styling, the big Fords were completely restyled for model year 1967. This gave the cars a new sense of proportion from stem to stern. The new models had even more rounded feature lines than the previous Fords, with rounder tops and rounder fenders. On the front end, dual stacked headlights were seen once again, but the grille was of a completely new design.

The Galaxie 500XL had a base 289-cid/200-hp V-8 engine and a SelectShift Cruise-O-Matic transmission. Muscle car buffs who wanted to go even faster could order the 360-hp "Police Interceptor" version at additional extra cost. Also continuing to be optional at extra cost was the hotter 427-cid V-8 in both the 410-hp "Thunderbird High-Performance" version and the 425-hp "Thunderbird Super High-Performance" version. There was even a tunnel port version of the 427 that

was made available at Ford dealerships as an over-the-counter dealer kit. It featured a tunnel port intake on special cylinder heads and special manifolds.

Being a bit bigger and a bit slower, the 1967 "7-Litre" hardtop was probably a bit slower than the '66 version, which could do 0-to-60 mph in about 8 seconds and the quarter-mile in 16.4 seconds.

Model Number	Body/Style Number	Body Type & Seating	Factory Price	Shipping Weight	Production Total
GALAXIE 500XL 7-LITRE — SERIES 50 — V-8					
59	76C	2d Conv-6P	$3,243	3,632 lbs.	5,161
58	63C	2d HT-6P	$3,621	3,914 lbs.	18,174

NOTE 1: Prices and weights for the base Galaxie 500XL models with base engine.
NOTE 2: Prices for 427-cid and 428-cid V-8s varied according to whether the 7-Litre package was ordered.
NOTE 3: Ford built only 369 of the 427-cid V-8s for all of its 1967 Ford/Fairlane models.

ENGINES

BASE V-8: Overhead valve. Cast-iron block. Displacement: 428 cid. Bore and stroke: 4.13 x 3.98 inches. Compression ratio: 10.50:1. Brake hp: 345 at 4600 rpm. Torque: 462 at 2800 rpm. Five main bearings. Hydraulic valve lifters. Carburetor: Four-barrel. Dual exhaust. Code Q.

OPTIONAL V-8: Overhead valve. Cast-iron block. Displacement: 427 cid. Bore and stroke: 4.23 x 3.78 inches. Compression ratio: 11.00:1. Brake hp: 410 at 5600 rpm. Torque: 476 at 3400 rpm. Five main bearings. Solid valve lifters. Carburetor: Holley four-barrel. Dual exhaust. Code W.

OPTIONAL V-8: Overhead valve. Cast-iron block. Displacement: 427 cid. Bore and stroke: 4.23 x 3.78 inches. Compression ratio: 11.50:1. Brake hp: 425 at 6000 rpm. Torque: 480 at 3700 rpm. Five main bearings. Hydraulic valve lifters. Carburetor: Two Holley four-barrel. Dual exhaust. Code R.

OPTIONS

Body side accent stripe ($13.90). Select Aire conditioner ($356.09). 55-amp alternator, standard with air conditioning ($21.09). High-ratio rear axle ($2.63). Heavy-duty battery (standard with 427- and 428-cid V-8s). Limited-slip differential ($41.60, but not available with 427-cid V-8). Closed crankcase emissions system, exhaust ECS required ($5.19). Electric clock ($15.59). 428-cid/345-hp V-8 (standard with 7-Litre package. $244.77 otherwise). 427-cid/410-hp four-barrel V-8 on cars without the 7-Litre package ($975.09). 427-cid/410-hp four-barrel V-8 on cars with the 7-Litre package ($647.51). 427-cid/425-hp dual four-barrel V-8 on cars without the 7-Litre package ($975.09). 427-cid/425-hp dual four-barrel V-8 on cars with the 7-Litre package ($647.51). Tinted glass ($39.45). Tinted windshield ($21.09). Manual-adjustable load-leveling system for rear suspension ($42.19). Automatically adjusting load-leveling system for rear suspension ($84.78). Luxury trim for XL, includes electric clock, Comfort Stream ventilation and air conditioning control panel for Ford XL only ($167.11). Remote-control left-hand outside rearview mirror ($9.58). Magic Aire heater delete ($73.51 credit). Tu-tone paint ($21.54, but not available for convertible). Power brakes ($42.49, but not available with 427-cid V-8). 6-Way power driver's bucket seat ($84.25). Power disc brakes ($97.21, but standard with 7-Litre option). Power steering ($94.95). power windows ($99.94). Push-button AM radio with front antenna ($57.51 and rear speaker required at extra cost). AM/FM radio with front antenna ($133.65 and rear speaker required at extra cost). Deluxe seat belts with warning light ($10.42). Reclining seat with passenger headrest ($44.15). Front seat shoulder harness ($27.27). Automatic speed control, requires V-8 and Cruise-O-Matic ($71.30). Stereosonic tape system, AM radio required ($128.49 and not available with AM/FM radio). High-speed handling suspension ($30.64 but standard when 7-Litre package is ordered). Cruise-O-Matic in XL only ($34.63). Four-speed manual transmission ($184.02 and required as a mandatory option with the 427). Vinyl roof ($74.36). Comfort Stream ventilation system ($40.02, but standard in Galaxie 500XL). Protection group ($25.28). Courtesy light group ($5.09 on Galaxie 500XL models). Extra-cooling package (standard with 427). Convenience control panel group ($51.82). 7-Litre Sports ($515.86) and offers four-speed manual transmission as a no-cost option.

1967 MUSTANG GT/GTA "390"

JERRY HEASLEY

1967 Mustang GTA

In order to compete against increasingly stiff competition, the 1967 Mustang got a jazzy new body, a wider tread for better road grip and a wider range of engines. Option choices were widened, too. On the exterior, the 1967 Mustang was heftier and more full fendered. Especially low and sleek was the new 2+2, which featured all-new sheet metal.

All Mustangs had bigger engine bays. This was necessary, because the first "big-block" option was among the many 1967 hardware upgrades. It was a 390-cid V-8 with 315 hp. This small bore-long stroke power plant was related to the Ford "FE" engine, introduced way back in 1958. It provided a good street-performance option with its low price tag, lots of low-end performance and plenty of torque. A new designation used on cars with automatic transmission and GT equipment was "GTA." Other technical changes included front suspension improvements. A competition handling package was released, but it cost quite a bit extra and didn't go into too many cars.

The 1967 Mustang GT 2+2 with the 390-cid/335-hp V-8 could do 0-to-60 mph in 7.4 seconds and the quarter-mile in 15.6 seconds.

Model Number	Body/Style Number	Body Type & Seating	Factory Price	Shipping Weight	Production Total
MUSTANG GT — SERIES 07/08/09 — V-8					
01	65	2d HT-6P	$2,930	2,966 lbs.	229,688
03	76	2d Conv-6P	$3,167	2,993 lbs.	34,026
02	63	2d FSBK-6P	$3,061	2,964 lbs.	66,850

NOTE 1: Prices include GT option, 390-cid V-8 and heavy-duty three-speed transmission (lowest-priced mandatory optional transmission).

NOTE 2: Weights are estimates for models equipped with the 390-cid V-8.

NOTE 3: Body style production totals are for all V-8 powered Mustangs.

NOTE 4: 24,079 Mustangs had the GT Equipment Group option.

NOTE 5: 28,800 Mustangs had the 390-cid/320-hp V-8.

FORD

ENGINE

OPTIONAL GT/GTS V-8: Overhead valve. Cast-iron block. Displacement: 390 cid. Bore and stroke: 4.05 x 3.78 inches. Compression ratio: 10.5:1. Brake hp: 320 at 4600 rpm. Torque: 427 at 3200 rpm. Five main bearings. Hydraulic valve lifters. Carburetor: Holley four-barrel. Dual exhaust. Code S.

OPTIONS

Accent stripe ($13.90). Select Aire conditioner ($356.09). High-ratio rear axle ($2.63). Heavy-duty battery ($7.77, but standard with 390-cid V-8 with Cruise-O-Matic). Electric clock ($14.32). Full-length console, radio required ($50.41). Limited-slip differential ($41.60). Closed crankcase emission system for cars with exhaust emission system required ($5.19). 390-cid/320-hp four-barrel V-8 ($158.98 and extra-cost transmission required). Extra-cooling package, V-8 required ($10.47, but standard with air conditioning). Exhaust emission system, where required ($45.45). Glass backlite for convertible ($32.44). Tinted glass with banded windshield ($30.25). Die-cast grille for lower back panel, exterior decor group required ($19.48). Rear deck lid luggage rack for hardtop or convertible only ($32.44). Magic Aire heater delete ($31.52 credit). Two-tone paint for lower back panel, dark gray only ($12.95). Power disc brakes, V-8 only ($64.77). Power steering ($84.47). Power convertible top ($52.95). Push-button radio with antenna ($57.51). AM/FM radio ($133.65). Rocker panel molding for hardtop or convertible only ($15.59). Full-width front seat with armrest ($24.42, but not in 2+2 or with interior decor group or center console). Deluxe seat belts with warning light ($10.42). Sport Deck rear seat for 2+2 fastback ($64.77). Front shoulder harness ($27.27). Fingertip speed control, V-8 and Cruise-O-Matic required ($71.30). Deluxe steering wheel ($31.52). Tilt-Away steering wheel ($59.93). Stereosonic tape system AM radio required ($128.49). Cruise-O-Matic with 320-hp V-8 ($220.17). Four-speed manual transmission with trip odometer and tachometer for cars with 320-hp V-8 ($233.18). Three-speed heavy-duty transmission ($79.20). 8,000-rpm tachometer and trip odometer with hi-po V-8 ($54.45, but included free in cars with four-speed manual transmission and 320-hp V-8. Comfort Weave vinyl trim for hardtop or 2+2 with bucket seats $24.53). Vinyl roof for two-door hardtop ($74.36). Wheel cover for hardtop and convertible ($21.34) Five wire wheel covers for hardtop and convertible ($79.51). Five wire wheel covers for 2+2 ($58.24). 14-inch styled steel wheels for 2+2 with V-8 ($93.84). 14-inch styled steel wheels for hardtop and convertible ($115.11). Competition Handling package ($388.53 with GT only). Convenience control panel ($14.49). Exterior Decor group ($38.86). GT Equipment group ($108.06). Interior Decor group for convertible ($94.36). Protection group with color-keyed floor mats front and rear, license plate frames and door edge guards ($25.28). Heavy-duty suspension group ($30.64).

1967 SHELBY MUSTANG GT-350

PHIL KUNZ

1967 Shelby Mustang GT-350

For 1967, the Shelby GT-350 began to look noticeably different than the Mustang. At the same time, the Shelby became mechanically more similar to its garden-variety cousin. Shelby dealers liked this change. It created a visually exciting product with as much creature comfort as a basic Mustang, but with no need for specialized maintenance equipment and training.

With the base Mustang redesigned for '67, Shelby created an entirely new appearance that made its fastback look longer and lower than stock Mustangs by the use of more fiberglass than in previous years. A twin-scoop fiberglass hood with racing-style lock-down pins, reached farther than the Mustang's all-steel piece and made the grille appear like a dark, menacing mouth. The grille housed two round high-beam headlights placed side-by-side in the middle. The Mustang front bumper, minus the vertical bumperettes, looked like it was made for the Shelby. In front of each rear wheel well were fiberglass, forward-facing scoops that channeled air into the rear brakes. Stock Mustang rear vents were covered with a rear-facing scoop that helped draw air out of the passenger compartment. (Early 1967 cars had a red running light installed in this scoop, but the accessory was dropped later due to legal concerns.) A three-piece spoiler was applied to the rear of all '67 Shelby-Mustangs and accented by extra-wide tail lights.

The Deluxe Mustang Interior in Black, White or Parchment was the only choice for the more luxurious '67 Shelby. A sporty, two- or four-point roll bar was installed. The bar was a mounting point for an inertia reel shoulder harnesses. A unique wood-rimmed steering wheel had a "GT-350" plastic horn button. Fold-down rear seats, once an option, were standard. Stewart-Warner gauges were housed in a metal bezel under the middle of the dashboard. The Mustang's optional 8000-rpm tach sat next to a 140-mph speedometer. Shelbys came with power steering and brakes. Suspension enhancements were largely stock Mustang, including the special handling package, front disc brakes, thicker front stabilizer bar, export brace, and adjustable Gabriel shock absorbers. The 15-inch stamped steel wheels had '67 Thunderbird hubcaps with Shelby center caps. Sporty Kelsey-Hayes rims were optional.

The 289-cid K-code engine was used again with very few changes. Tubular exhaust headers were dropped at the beginning of the year and Ford's high-performance cast-iron manifold, was used. The factory continued claiming 306 hp.

Options included a Paxton supercharger, SelectAire air conditioning and the high-po C-4 automatic transmission.

In the '67 GT-350, a 0-to-60 mph run took 7.1 seconds. The car could do the quarter-mile in 15.3 seconds with a 91 mph terminal speed. Top speed was 129 mph at 6100 rpm.

Model Number	Body/Style Number	Body Type & Seating	Factory Price	Shipping Weight	Production Total
SHELBY MUSTANG GT-350 — SERIES S — V-8					
SFM	63( )	2d FSBK-6P	$3,995	3,360 lbs.	1,175

ENGINE

BASE: Overhead valve. Cast-iron block. Displacement: 289 cid. Bore and stroke: 4.00 x 2.87 inches. Compression ratio: 10.50:1. Brake hp: 306 at 6000 rpm. Torque: 329 ft.-lbs. at 4200 rpm. Torque: 312 at 3400 rpm. Solid valve lifters. Carburetor: Holley R-3259 715-cfm four-barrel (595 cfm with automatic). An S2ms or S7ms aluminum Cobra intake manifold was fitted. Shelby engine code 1.

OPTIONS

Paxton supercharger. 15 x 7-inch Kelsey-Hayes MagStar wheels. 15 x 7-inch 10-spoke aluminum wheels. AM radio. Folding rear seat. Air conditioning. Tinted glass (mandatory with air conditioning). Automatic transmission (Ford C-4).

1967 SHELBY-MUSTANG GT-500

1967 Shelby Mustang GT-500

JERRY HEASLEY

With the new Shelby looks came a new family member: the GT-500. It had essentially the same changes as the GT-350 in terms of size and character. The plastic horn button said "GT-500."

Shelby installed the 428-cid big-block V-8 in his new top-of-the-line offering. It produced at least 50 more horsepower than the hi-po 289. This "Police Interceptor" engine featured hydraulic lifters and an aluminum, medium-rise intake manifold wearing a pair of 600-cfm four-barrel Holley carburetors. Ford's four-speed "top-loader" transmission was used. The stout "police spec" C-6 automatic was optional.

The GT-500 was available only in fastback format like the GT-350. For $200 more than the GT-350 it was an absolute big-block bargain. The GT-500 could post a 0-to-60 mph run in 4.8 seconds. The car could do the quarter-mile in 13.6

seconds with a 106-mph terminal speed. Top speed was 133 mph at 5100 rpm.

Model Number	Body/Style Number	Body Type & Seating	Factory Price	Shipping Weight	Production Total
SHELBY MUSTANG GT-500 — SERIES S — V-8					
SFM	63( )	2d FSBK-6P	$4,195	—	2,048

ENGINE

BASE V-8: Overhead valve. Cast-iron block. Displacement: 428 cid. Bore and stroke: 4.13 x 3.98 inches. Compression ratio: 10.50:1. Brake hp: 355 at 5400 rpm. Torque: 420 ft.-lbs. at 3200 rpm. Hydraulic valve lifters. Carburetor: Two Holley four-barrel. Front #2804, rear #2805. Shelby engine code 4.

OPTIONS

15 x 7-inch Kelsey-Hayes MagStar wheels. 15 x 7-inch 10-spoke aluminum wheels. AM radio. Folding rear seat. Air conditioning. Tinted glass (mandatory with air conditioning). Automatic transmission (Ford C-6).

FORD

1968 FAIRLANE/ FAIRLANE 500 427/428 CJ

MIKE MUELLER

1967 Fairlane

In the mid-to-late 1960s, Ford was doing all it could to promote the benefits of "Total Performance" throughout all of its car lines. This was largely reflective of the company's success in stock car racing, its European Grand Prix racing experience and the performance of certain FoMoCo products at drag strips across the nation. When you added up the numbers to get Total Performance, the Fairlane 428-CJ was one of the combinations you ended up with.

The Fairlane grew in 1968. It retained a 116-inch wheelbase, but overall length grew by four inches to 201. Some enthusiasts felt that it looked almost like a full-size car, although the big Fords of the day were still a whole foot longer. The new 428 Cobra-Jet engine came in two versions. The 428-CJ had a 4.13 x 3.98-inch bore and stroke, which made it a totally different engine than the 427. It came with 10.7:1 compression heads and a single Holley four-barrel carburetor. A Super Cobra-Jet (SCJ) option was offered. According to the 1968 edition of *Car Fax Retail and Wholesale New Car Prices*, the biggest engine option for early-1968 Fairlanes was the 427-cid four-barrel engine in 390-hp format. It was listed as being available on Fairlane two-door hardtops (as well as all standard size Fords). Some Fairlane sources say that no such cars were built and there are no production figures listed for the 427 in *Ward's 1969 Automotive Yearbook*. However, it is very possible that any 427s built early in the model run used engines manufactured in model-year 1967. According to Fairlane experts, the 428-cid V-8 — in Cobra-Jet and Super-Cobra-Jet versions — became the only big-block option in February 1968.

Model Number	Body/Style Number	Body Type & Seating	Factory Price	Shipping Weight	Production Total
FAIRLANE — SERIES 30 — V-8					
30	65A	2d HT-6P	$2,544	3,170 lbs.	28,930
FAIRLANE 500 (BENCH SEAT) — SERIES 30 — V-8					
33	65B	2d HT-6P	$2,679	3,181 lbs.	28,738
35	63B	2d FSBK-6P	$2,653	3,193 lbs.	27,899
FAIRLANE 500 (BUCKET SEATS) — SERIES 30 — V-8					
33	65E	2d HT-6P	$3,789	3,181 lbs.	1,721
35	63E	2d FSBK-6P	$2,763	3,193 lbs.	3,204

NOTE 1: Prices and weights are for Fairlane/Fairlane 500 models with base 302-cid two-barrel V-8.

NOTE 2: Production is for all V-8 Fairlanes (all engines included).

NOTE 3: Ford built 20,600 of the 428-cid V-8s for all of its cars in 1968.

ENGINES

OPTIONAL V-8: Overhead valve. Cast-iron block. Displacement: 428 cid. Bore and stroke: 4.13 x 3.98 inches. Compression ratio: 10.70:1. Brake hp: 335 at 5600 rpm. Torque: 445 at 3400 rpm. Five main bearings. Hydraulic valve lifters. Carburetor: Holley four-barrel. Dual exhaust. Code Q (Cobra-Jet).

OPTIONAL V-8: Overhead valve. Cast-iron block. Displacement: 428 cid. Bore and stroke: 4.13 x 3.98 inches. Compression ratio: 10.70:1. Brake hp: 335 at 5600 rpm. Torque: 445 at 3400 rpm. Five main bearings. Hydraulic valve lifters. Carburetor: Holley four-barrel. Dual exhaust. Code R (Super Cobra-Jet).

OPTIONAL V-8: Overhead valve. Cast-iron block. Displacement: 427 cid. Bore and stroke: 4.23 x 3.78 inches. Compression ratio: 10.90:1. Brake hp: 390 at 4600 rpm. Torque: 460 at 3200 rpm. Five main bearings. Hydraulic valve lifters. Carburetor: Holley four-barrel. Dual exhaust. Code W.

OPTIONS

Body side accent stripe ($13.90). Select Aire conditioner ($360.30). 42-amp alternator, not with air conditioning or 427 four-barrel V-8 ($21.09). High-ratio rear axle ($6.53). Heavy-duty battery ($7.44, but standard with 427- or 428-cid V-8s)). Limited-slip differential ($41.60, but not available with 427-cid V-8). Console, bucket seats required ($50.66). Rear window defogger for hardtops and fastbacks ($21.27). Electric clock ($15.59, but standard in XL). 427-cid/390-hp four-barrel V-8 available for all Fairlane two-door hardtops, except cars with Select Aire conditioning, power steering, 55-amp. Alternator, heavy-duty suspension or optional tires; the Fairlane 427 package included a heavy-duty battery, the 42-amp. Alternator, a GT Handling suspension, the extra-cooling package and FR70-14 Wide-Oval white sidewall tires ($622.97 plus power disc brakes required at extra cost). 428-cid/335-hp Cobra-Jet V-

8 ($287.53). 428-cid/335-hp Super-Cobra-Jet Ram-Air V-8 ($420.96). Tinted glass ($34.97). Adjustable front seat headrests ($42.02). Remote-control left-hand outside rearview mirror ($9.58). Body side moldings on base Fairlane two-door hardtop ($20.75). Tu-Tone paint, except convertibles ($26.85). Power disc brakes ($64.77 and required with big-block V-8). Power steering ($94.95). Power windows ($99.94). Push-button AM radio with front antenna ($61.40). AM/FM stereo radio with two speakers ($181.36). Dual rear speakers ($25.91). Bucket seats ($110.16). Deluxe seat belts with warning light ($12.95). Front seat shoulder harness ($23.38). Rear shoulder belts ($23.38). Seat belts with front or rear shoulder belts ($15.59). Seat belts with front and rear shoulder belts ($18.22). 6,000-rpm tachometer ($47.92). Cruise-O-Matic for Fairlanes with 427- or 428-cid V-8 ($233.17). Heavy-duty three-speed manual transmission ($79.20). Four-speed manual transmission ($184.02, but not available with 427-cid V-8). Vinyl roof for formal hardtop models only ($84.99). Vinyl seat trim in Fairlane 500 hardtop and fastback ($16.85). Comfort Stream ventilation system ($15.59, but not available with air conditioning.) Wheel covers ($21.34). Deluxe or Sport wheel covers ($78.35). Argent Silver styled steel wheels ($38.86). Chrome styled wheels ($116.59). Convenience group ($47.92). Extra-cooling package includes viscous drive or flex-blade fan, fan shroud, extra-cooling radiator ($25.25, but standard with air conditioning and 427- or 428-cid V-8s). GT Handling suspension ($30.64, but standard with 427-cid V-8). Towing package ($30.93). Visibility group ($24.01).

1968 TORINO GT 427/428 CJ

TIM CALVERT

1968 Torino GT

Torino was the new name for up-level 1968 Ford intermediates. These Fairlane-like cars came in Torino six and Torino V-8 lines, as well as a V-8-only Torino GT upper series. In addition to standard Fairlane 500 features, the base Torino models came with full wheel covers and an electric clock. Torino GTs added a 303-cid two-barrel V-8, the GT Handling suspension, Argent Silver styled wheels with chrome trim rings, F70-14 Wide-Oval white sidewall tires, GT stripes, a Gray grille and GT nameplates. If you ordered a 390-cid or larger V-8 power brakes were required.

According to the 1968 edition of *Car Fax Retail and Wholesale New Car Prices* the biggest engine option for early-1968 Torinos was the 427-cid four-barrel engine in 390-hp format. It was available in two-door hardtops and fastbacks. Some experts say that no such cars were built and there are no production figures listed for the 427 in *Ward's 1969 Automotive Yearbook*. However, it is very possible that any 427s built early in the model run used engines manufactured in model-year 1967. According to Fairlane experts, the 428-cid V-8 — in Cobra-Jet and Super-Cobra-Jet versions — became the only big-block option in February 1968. At least 35 R-Code Torino GTs with 428-cid V-8s are known to exist.

Torinos and Torino GTs with a 428 CJ V-8 could run from 0-to-60 mph in just over 6 seconds and do the quarter-mile in 14.5 seconds.

Model Number	Body/Style Number	Body Type & Seating	Factory Price	Shipping Weight	Production Total
TORINO — SERIES 40 — V-8					
42	65C	2d HT-6P	$2,798	3,235 lbs.	35.191
TORINO GT — SERIES 40 — V-8					
44	65D	2d HT-6P	$2,772	3,197 lbs.	74,135
42	63D	2d FSBK-6P	$2,747	3,220 lbs.	23,939

NOTE 1: Prices and weights are for Torino/Torino GT models with base 302-cid two-barrel V-8.

NOTE 2: Production is for all V-8 Torinos (all engines included).

NOTE 3: Ford built 20,600 of the 428-cid V-8s for all of its cars in 1968.

NOTE 4: At least 35 Torino GTs with 428-cid R-code V-8s are known to exist today.

ENGINES

BASE V-8: Overhead valve. Cast-iron block. Displacement: 428 cid. Bore and stroke: 4.13 x 3.98 inches. Compression ratio: 10.70:1. Brake hp: 335 at 5600 rpm. Torque: 445 at 3400 rpm. Five main bearings. Hydraulic valve lifters. Carburetor: Holley four-barrel. Dual exhaust. Code Q (Cobra-Jet).

OPTIONAL V-8: Ram-Air. Overhead valve. Cast-iron block. Displacement: 428 cid. Bore and stroke: 4.13 x 3.98 inches. Compression ratio: 10.70:1. Brake hp: 335 at 5600 rpm. Torque: 445 at 3400 rpm. Five main bearings. Hydraulic valve lifters. Carburetor: Holley four-barrel. Dual exhaust. Code R (Super Cobra-Jet).

FORD

OPTIONAL V-8: Overhead valve. Cast-iron block. Displacement: 427 cid. Bore and stroke: 4.23 x 3.78 inches. Compression ratio: 10.90:1. Brake hp: 390 at 4600 rpm. Torque: 460 at 3200 rpm. Five main bearings. Hydraulic valve lifters. Carburetor: Holley four-barrel. Dual exhaust. Code W.

OPTIONS

Reflective stripes and paint — the stripes were different than the C-stripe used on Fairlanes ($12.95). Select Aire conditioner ($360.30). 42-amp alternator, not with air conditioning or 427 four-barrel V-8 ($21.09). High-ratio rear axle ($6.53). Heavy-duty battery ($7.44, but standard with 427- or 428-cid V-8s)). Limited-slip differential ($41.60, but not available with 427-cid V-8). Console, bucket seats required ($50.66). Rear window defogger for hardtops and fastbacks ($21.27). Electric clock ($15.59, but standard in XL). 427-cid/390-hp four-barrel V-8 available for all Fairlane two-door hardtops, except cars with Select Aire conditioning, power steering, 55-amp. Alternator, heavy-duty suspension or optional tires; the Fairlane 427 package included a heavy-duty battery, the 42-amp alternator, a GT Handling suspension, the extra-cooling package and FR70-14 Wide-Oval white sidewall tires ($622.97 plus power disc brakes required at extra cost). 428-cid/335-hp Cobra-Jet V-8, includes 80-amp alternator, heavy-duty battery, dual exhausts, extra-cooling package, bright engine dress-up kit, cast aluminum rocker arm covers, and 3.25:1 ratio non-locking rear axle ($287.53). 428-cid/335-hp Super-Cobra-Jet Ram-Air V-8, includes 80-amp alternator, heavy-duty battery, dual exhausts, extra-cooling package, bright en-gine dress-up kit, cast aluminum rocker arm covers, functional hood air scoop and 3.50:1 ratio non-locking rear axle ($420.96). Tinted glass ($34.97). Adjustable front seat headrests ($42.02). Remote-control left-hand outsiide rearview mirror ($9.58). Body side moldings on base Fairlane two-door hardtop ($20.75). Tu-Tone paint, except convertibles ($26.85). Power disc brakes ($64.77 and required with big-block V-8). Power steering ($94.95). Power windows ($99.94). Push-button AM radio with front antenna ($61.40). AM/FM stereo radio with two speakers ($181.36). Dual rear speakers ($25.91). Bucket seats ($110.16). Deluxe seat belts with warning light ($12.95). Front seat shoulder harness ($23.38). Rear shoulder belts ($23.38). Seat belts with front or rear shoulder belts ($15.59). Seat belts with front and rear shoulder belts ($18.22). 6,000-rpm tachometer ($47.92). Cruise-O-Matic for Fairlanes with 427- or 428-cid V-8 ($233.17). Heavy-duty three-speed manual transmission ($79.20). Four-speed manual transmission ($184.02, but not available with 427-cid V-8). Vinyl roof for formal hardtop models only ($84.99). Comfort Stream ventilation system ($15.59, but not available with air conditioning.) Wheel covers (standard on Torino). Deluxe or Sport wheel covers ($12.95). Argent Silver styled steel wheels ($17.59, but standard on Torino GT). Chrome styled wheels on Torino ($95.31). Chrome styled wheels on Torino GT ($77.73). Convenience group ($32.44). Extra-cooling package ($25.25, but standard with 427- or 428-cid V-8). GT Handling suspension ($30.64, but standard on Torino GT or with 427- or 428-cid V-8). Towing package ($30.93). Visibility group ($24.01).

1968 MUSTANG GT/GTA "390-4V" & CALIFORNIA SPECIAL

JERRY HEASLEY

1968 Mustang GTA

Ford invited 1968 car shoppers to "Turn yourself on, switch your style and show a new face in the most exciting car on the American road," in its advertising for the 1968 Mustang. Only subtle changes were actually made to the new-in-1967 design. Bucket seats, a floor-mounted stick, a sports steering wheel and rich, loop-pile carpeting remained standard. Minor trim updates included a front end with the Mustang emblem "floating" in the grille, script-style (instead of block letter) Mustang body side nameplates and cleaner-looking bright metal trim on the cove. There was a new two-tone hood. Still, prices rose substantially, averaging about $140 more per model.

The $147 GT option included a choice of stripes. Either the rocker panel type or a reflecting "C" stripe could be specified. The latter widened along the ridge of the front fender and ran across the door, to the upper rear body quarter. From there, it wrapped down, around the sculptured depression ahead of the rear wheel, and tapered forward, along the lower body, to about the midpoint of the door. Other GT goodies included fog lights in the grille, a GT gas cap and GT wheel covers. A total of 17,458 GTs were made in 1968.

A GT equipped with the 390-cid big-block V-8 (four-barrel version, of course) is considered very desirable by muscle car collectors. About 5,000 GT/CS "California Special" Mustangs were produced in 1968. Their features included a Shelby-style deck lid with a spoiler, sequential tail lights and a blacked-out grille. They had no Mustang grille emblem. The wheel covers were the same ones used on 1968 GTs, but without GT identification.

Model Number	Body/Style Number	Body Type & Seating	Factory Price	Shipping Weight	Production Total
MUSTANG — SERIES STANDARD — V-8					
01	65	2d HT-6P	$2,707	2,843 lbs.	155,410
03	76	2d Conv-6P	$2,920	2,953 lbs.	16,796
02	63	2d FSBK-6P	$2,818	2,867 lbs.	32,304
MUSTANG — SERIES DELUXE — V-8					
01	65	2d HT-6P	$2,831	2,843 lbs.	8,992
03	76	2d Conv-6P	$2,942	2,867 lbs.	7,819
02	63	2d FSBK-6P	$3,030	2,953 lbs.	3,194

NOTE 1: Prices and weights above are for all Mustang models with the base 289-cid/195-hp V-8 .

ENGINE

OPTIONAL V-8: Overhead valve. Cast-iron block. Displacement: 390 cid. Bore and stroke: 4.05 x 3.78 inches. Compression ratio: 10.5:1. Brake hp: 325 at 4800 rpm. Torque: 427 at 3200 rpm. Five main bearings. Hydraulic valve lifters. Carburetor: Holley four-barrel. Cooling system capacity: 20.5 qt. with heater. Dual exhaust. Code S.

OPTIONS

Accent stripe ($13.90). Select Aire conditioner ($360.30). High-ratio rear axle ($6.53). Heavy-duty battery ($7.44). Electric clock ($15.59, but standard with Interior Decor group). Center console, radio required ($53.71). Rear window defogger, except convertible ($21.27). Limited-slip differential for V-8 models ($41.60). 390-cid/325-hp V-8, includes 7.35-14 black sidewall tires, 6-inch wheels and dual exhausts ($158.08 and requires minimum of heavy-duty three-speed transmission or four-speed or Cruise-O-Matic). Extra-cooling package for V-8s ($12.95, but standard with air conditioning). Glass convertible backlite ($38.86). Complete tinted glass ($30.25). Adjustable front seat headrests $42.02). remote-control left-hand outside rearview mirror ($9.58). Wheel lip moldings ($15.59). Black paint for top of hood and cowl ($19.48). Power disc brakes ($64.77 and required with GT Equipment group). Power steering

By 1968, the new pony-car competition was getting stiff and Ford was willing to pull out all stops to give the impression that the Mustang was the "500-pound gorilla" in that market niche. Cosmetic changes included a restyled grille, new wheel covers, redesigned gas caps, the introduction of painted or chrome-plated styled steel wheels and upgraded quarter panel trim. The grille was simplified by eliminating the horizontal molding so the "pony" emblem was "floating" again as in 1966. Ford lettering on the front was gone and the fender emblem changed to script, rather than block letters. The "louvered" hood that was optional in 1967 became standard. Front and rear side marker lights and reflectors were added as part of a new government-mandated safety equipment package. Another change was offering only bucket seats in ragtops.

The 427-cid/390-hp big-block "racing" V-8 was optional early in the model year only. It was dubbed the "Cobra V-8." When this engine was installed, the GT Equipment group was a mandatory option. Power disc brakes were also required.

The 427 option was replaced by the 428 option on April 1, 1968. It cost less than half the price of the 427 package.

ENGINE

OPTIONAL V-8: Overhead valve. Cast-iron block. Displacement: 427 cid. Bore and stroke: 4.23 x 3.78 inches. Compression ratio: 10.90:1. Brake hp: 390 at 4600 rpm. Torque: 460 at 3200 rpm. Five main bearings. Hydraulic valve lifters. Carburetor: Holley four-barrel. Dual exhaust. Code W.

($84.47). Power convertible top ($52.95). Push-button AM radio ($61.40). AM/FM stereo radio ($181.39). Stereosonic tape system ($133.86 and AM radio required). Deluxe seat belts with warning light ($12.95). Front seat shoulder harness ($23.38). Rear shoulder belts ($23.38). Seat belts with front or rear shoulder belts ($15.59). Seat belts with front and rear shoulder belts ($18.22). Sport Deck rear seat for 2+2 fastback only ($64.77). Fingertip speed control for Mustang with V-8 and SelectShift automatic transmission ($73.83). Deluxe steering wheel ($31.52, but standard with Interior Decor group). Tilt-away steering wheel ($66.14). Tachometer and trip odometer ($54.45). Select Shift Cruise-O-Matic transmission with 390-cid V-8 ($233.17). Four-speed manual transmission with trip odometer and tachometer ($233.18). Heavy-duty three-speed manual transmission ($79.20). Vinyl roof on hardtop ($74.36). Chrome styled wheels, including trim rings, with E70-14 Wide-Oval white sidewall tires ($160.27). Chrome styled wheels, including trim rings, with F70-14 Wide-Oval white sidewall tires ($174.38). FR70-14 Wide-Oval white sidewall radial tires ($89.11). Collapsible spare tire over Wide-Oval tires ($6.50). Collapsible spare over Wide-Oval radial tires (no charge). Convenience group, including seat belt light, door-ajar light, parking brake light and low-fuel light ($32.44 and console required at extra cost when ordered for cars with air conditioning). GT Equipment group, includes dual exhausts with bright extensions, fog lamps, GT ornamentation, F70-14 Wide-Oval white sidewall nylon tires, heavy-duty suspension, GT-style C-stripe or triple GT stripe, Argent Silver styled wheels with chrome trim rings, poip-open gas cap ($146.71 for Mustangs without Sports Trim group or with optional wheel covers and power disc brakes required). Interior Decor group with bucket seats ($123.86), with full-width seats ($110.16). (Note: Hardtop and fastback only and deleted when ordered with full-width seat, clock, bright pedal pads, woodgrain instrument panel appliques, vinyl-covered "T" shift lever with Cruise-O-Matic and woodgrain knobs with manual transmission, bright buttons in seatback trim, woodgrainsteering wheel rim and insert). Protection group ($25.28). Reflective group including GT tape and paint on Argent Silver styled wheels for all Mustangs with GT Equipment group option ($12.95). Visibility group ($24.01)

1968 MUSTANG 427 COBRA

Model Number	Body/Style Number	Body Type & Seating	Factory Price	Shipping Weight	Production Total
MUSTANG — SERIES STANDARD — V-8					
01	65	2d HT-6P	$2,707	2,843 lbs.	155,410
03	76	2d Conv-6P	$2,920	2,953 lbs.	16,796
02	63	2d FSBK-6P	$2,818	2,867 lbs.	32,304
MUSTANG — SERIES DELUXE — V-8					
01	65	2d HT-6P	$2,831	2,843 lbs.	8,992
03	76	2d Conv-6P	$2,942	2,867 lbs.	7,819
02	63	2d FSBK-6P	$3,030	2,953 lbs.	3,194

NOTE 1: Prices and weights above are for all Mustang models with the base 289-cid/195-hp V-8.
NOTE 2: Production of 427 Mustangs is unavailable.

OPTIONS

Accent stripe ($13.90). Select Aire conditioner ($360.30). High-ratio rear axle ($6.53). Heavy-duty battery ($7.44, but standard with 427-cid V-8 and Cruise-O-Matic). Electric clock ($15.59, but standard with Interior Decor group). Center console, radio required ($53.71). Rear window defogger, except convertible ($21.27). Limited-slip differential for V-8 models ($41.60). 427-cid/390 hp Cobra V-8 including 6-inch wheels, dual exhausts and FR70-14 Wide-Oval white-sidewall radial tires ($622.00 and requires Cruise-O-Matic, power disc brakes and GT Equipment group at additional cost). Extra-cooling package for V-8s ($12.95, but standard with air conditioning). Glass convertible backlite ($38.86). Complete tinted glass ($30.25). Adjustable front seat headrests $42.02). Remote-control left-hand outside rearview mirror ($9.58). Wheel lip moldings ($15.59, but standard with Sports Trim group). Black paint for top of hood and cowl ($19.48). Power disc brakes ($64.77 and required with 427-cid V-8 or GT Equipment group). Power steering ($84.47). Power convertible top ($52.95). Push-button AM radio ($61.40). AM/FM stereo radio ($181.39). Stereosonic tape system ($133.86 and AM radio required). Deluxe seat belts with warning light ($12.95). Front seat shoulder harness ($23.38). Rear shoul-

FORD

der belts ($23.38). Seat belts with front or rear shoulder belts ($15.59). Seat belts with front and rear shoulder belts ($18.22). Sport Deck rear seat for 2+2 fastback only ($64.77). Fingertip speed control for Mustang with V-8 and Se-lectShift automatic transmission ($73.83). Deluxe steering wheel ($31.52, but standard with Interior Decor group). Tilt-away steering wheel ($66.14). Ta-chometer and trip odometer ($54.45). Select Shift Cruise-O-Matic transmission with 427-cid V-8 ($233.17). Four-speed manual transmission with trip odom-eter and tachometer ($233.18). Vinyl roof on hardtop ($74.36). Wheel covers ($21.34, but not available with GT Equipment group or Sports Trim group). Five wire wheel covers ($79.51, but not available with GT Equipment group or Sports Trim group). Deluxe wheel covers ($34.33, but not available with GT Equipment group or Sports Trim group). Argent Silver styled wheels, including trim rings with E70-14 or F70-14 Wide-Oval white sidewall tires ($82.54 and standard on cars with Sports Trim group option). Chrome styled wheels, includ-ing trim rings, with E70-14 Wide-Oval white sidewall tires ($160.27). Chrome

styled wheels, including trim rings, with F70-14 Wide-Oval white sidewall tires ($174.38). FR70-14 Wide-Oval white sidewall radial tires ($89.11). Collaps-ible spare tire over Wide-Oval tires ($6.50). Collapsible spare over Wide-Oval radial tires (no charge). Convenience group ($32.44 and console required at extra cost when ordered for cars with air conditioning). GT Equipment group, includes dual exhausts with bright extensions, fog lamps, GT ornamentation, F70-14 Wide-Oval white sidewall nylon tires, heavy-duty suspension, GT-style C-stripe or triple GT stripe, Argent Silver styled wheels with chrome trim rings, pop-open gas cap, chrome engine trim on 427 ($146.71 for Mustangs without Sports Trim group or with optional wheel covers and power disc brakes re-quired). Interior Decor group with bucket seats ($123.86), with full-width seats ($110.16). Protection group ($25.28). Reflective group ($12.95). Sports Trim group ($98.47 and not available with optional tires, chrome styled wheels, 427-cid V-8 or GT Equipment group). Heavy-duty suspension ($30.64, but not avail-able with GT Equipment group.) Visibility group ($24.01).

1968 MUSTANG 428 COBRA-JET

JERRY HEASLEY

1968 Mustang 428 Cobra Jet

The compact Mustang became a really fast car when Ford decided to shoehorn the 428-cid Cobra-Jet V-8 under its hood. Such a machine could move from 0 to 60 miles per hour in a mere 6.9 seconds. The quarter-mile took only 15.57 to do and the car's terminal speed at the end of such a run was about 99.5 miles per hour. After one test drive at a drag strip, *Hot Rod* magazine declared the Mustang 428 CJ to be "the fastest running pure stock in the history of man."

Ford introduced the 428 Cobra-Jet engine option on April 1, 1968. The new motor was the automaker's big-block per-formance leader. Production of the 428 CJ engine continued through 1970. Rated conservatively for 335 hp at 5200 rpm, the 1968 Mustang 428 CJ put out a lot more like 375 to 400 gross horsepower.

A high-performance variant of the basic 428-cid V-8, the main features of the Cobra-Jet V-8 included revised cylinder heads. They were of a design that was similar to the Ford 427 "low-riser" type, but with bigger valve ports. No 428 SCJ (Su-per Cobra Jet) V-8s were installed in 1968 Mustangs.

Model Number	Body/Style Number	Body Type & Seating	Factory Price	Shipping Weight	Production Total
MUSTANG — SERIES STANDARD — V-8					
01	65	2d HT-6P	$2,707	2,843 lbs.	155,410
03	76	2d Conv-6P	$2,920	2,953 lbs.	16,796
02	63	2d FSBK-6P	$2,818	2,867 lbs.	32,304
MUSTANG — SERIES DELUXE — V-8					
01	65	2d HT-6P	$2,831	2,843 lbs.	8,992
03	76	2d Conv-6P	$2,942	2,867 lbs.	7,819
02	63	2d FSBK-6P	$3,030	2,953 lbs.	3,194

NOTE 1: Prices and weights above are for all Mustang models with the base 289-cid/195-hp V-8.

NOTE 2: 1,299 of the 1968 models were built with 428 CJ V-8s.

NOTE 3: 428 CJ V-8s were installed in 221 Mustang hardtops, 34 convertibles and 1,044 fastbacks.

ENGINE

OPTIONAL V-8: Overhead valve. Cast-iron block. Displacement: 428 cid. Bore and stroke: 4.13 x 3.98 inches. Compression ratio: 10.70:1. Brake hp: 335 at 5600 rpm. Torque: 445 at 3400 rpm. Five main bearings. Hydraulic valve lift-ers. Carburetor: Holley four-barrel. Dual exhaust. Code R.

OPTIONS

Accent stripe ($13.90). Select Aire conditioner ($360.30). High-ratio rear axle ($6.53). Heavy-duty battery ($7.44, but standard with 428-cid V-8 and Cruise-

O-Matic). Electric clock ($15.59, but standard with Interior Decor group). Center console, radio required ($53.71). Rear window defogger, except convertible ($21.27). Limited-slip differential for V-8 models ($41.60). 428-cid 335-hp Cobra-Jet V-8 ($434.00 after April 1, 1968). Extra-cooling package for V-8s ($12.95, but standard with air conditioning). Glass convertible backlite ($38.86). Complete tinted glass ($30.25). Adjustable front seat headrests $42.02). remote-control left-hand outside rearview mirror ($9.58). Wheel lip moldings ($15.59, but standard with Sports Trim group). Black paint for top of hood and cowl ($19.48). Power disc brakes ($64.77 and required with 428-cid V-8 or GT Equipment group). Power steering ($84.47). Power convertible top ($52.95). Push-button AM radio ($61.40). AM/FM stereo radio ($181.39). Stereosonic tape system ($133.86 and AM radio required). Deluxe seat belts with warning light ($12.95). Front seat shoulder harness ($23.38). Rear shoulder belts ($23.38). Seat belts with front or rear shoulder belts ($15.59). Seat belts with front and rear shoulder belts ($18.22). Sport Deck rear seat for 2+2 fastback only ($64.77). Fingertip speed control for Mustang with V-8 and SelectShift automatic transmission ($73.83). Deluxe steering wheel ($31.52, but standard with Interior Decor group). Tilt-away steering wheel ($66.14). Tachometer and trip odometer ($54.45). Select Shift Cruise-O-Matic transmission with 428-cid V-8 ($233.17). Four-speed manual transmission with trip odometer and tachometer ($233.18). Heavy-duty three-speed manual transmission ($79.20). Vinyl roof on hardtop ($74.36). Wheel covers ($21.34, but not available with GT Equipment group or Sports Trim group). Five wire wheel covers ($79.51, but not available with GT Equipment group or Sports Trim group). Deluxe wheel covers ($34.33,

but not available with GT Equipment group or Sports Trim group). Argent Silver styled wheels, including trim rings with E70-14 or F70-14 Wide-Oval white sidewall tires ($82.54 and standard on cars with Sports Trim group option). Chrome styled wheels, including trim rings, with E70-14 Wide-Oval white sidewall tires ($160.27). Chrome styled wheels, including trim rings, with F70-14 Wide-Oval white sidewall tires ($174.38). FR70-14 Wide-Oval white sidewall radial tires ($89.11). Collapsible spare tire over Wide-Oval tires ($6.50). Collapsible spare over Wide-Oval radial tires (no charge). Convenience group, including seat belt light, door-ajar light, parking brake light and low-fuel light ($32.44 and console required at extra cost when ordered for cars with air conditioning). GT Equipment group, includes dual exhausts with bright extensions, fog lamps, GT ornamentation, F70-14 Wide-Oval white sidewall nylon tires, heavy-duty suspension, GT-style C-stripe or triple GT stripe, Argent Silver styled wheels with chrome trim rings, poip-open gas cap ($146.71 for Mustangs without Sports Trim group or with optional wheel covers and power disc brakes required). Interior Decor group with bucket seats ($123.86), with full-width seats ($110.16). (Note: Hardtop and fastback only and deleted when ordered with full-width seat, clock, bright pedal pads, woodgrain instrument panel appliques, vinyl-covered "T" shift lever with Cruise-O-Matic and woodgrain knobs with manual transmission, bright buttons in seatback trim, woodgrainsteering wheel rim and insert). Protection group ($25.28). Reflective group ($12.95). Sports Trim group ($98.47 and not available with optional tires, chrome styled wheels or GT Equipment group). Heavy-duty suspension ($30.64, but not available with GT Equipment group.) Visibility group ($24.01).

1968 SHELBY-MUSTANG GT-350

JERRY HEASLEY

1968 Shelby Mustang GT-350

Starting in 1968, all Shelby-Mustangs were constructed in Michigan from New Jersey-built cars. A.O. Smith did the Shelby conversions in Ionia, Michigan. This brought the operation closer to Canada, from where many Shelby parts were sourced. The 1968 GT-350 moved up from the 289-cid small-block V-8 to the 302-cid small-block.

Style-wise, changes for 1968 included replacement of the high-beam lights in the grille opening by widely spaced rectangular Marchal fog lights. A new hood had twin air scoops way up front. Shelby retained the stock Mustang hood latch, but added extra turn-to-lock fasteners. A new front valance panel made of fiberglass created a wider, "fish-mouth" grille

opening. The tail lights were still the same shape, but the sequential lenses were segmented into a strip of squares.

In the '68 Shelby-Mustang GT-350 a 0-to-60 mph run took less time than in the previous 289-powered version — 6.3 seconds to be specific. The car could do the quarter-mile in 14.9 seconds with a 94 mph terminal speed. Top speed was 119 mph at 6100 rpm.

Model Number	Body/Style Number	Body Type & Seating	Factory Price	Shipping Weight	Production Total
SHELBY MUSTANG GT-350 — SERIES S — V-8					
02	63( )	2d FSBK-6P	$4,116	—	1,227
03	76( )	2d Conv-6P	$4,238	—	404

FORD

ENGINES

BASE V-8: Overhead valve. Cast-iron block. Displacement: 302 cid. Bore and stroke: 4.00 x 3.00 inches. Compression ratio: 10.50:1. Brake hp: 250 at 6000 rpm. Torque: 318 at 3200 rpm. Solid valve lifters. Carburetor: Holley R-4069 600-cfm four-barrel. Cobra aluminum high-rise intake. Dual exhausts. Code J.

OPTIONAL SUPERCHARGED V-8: Overhead valve. Cast-iron block. Displacement: 302 cid. Bore and stroke: 4.00 x 3.00 inches. Compression ratio: 10.50:1. Brake hp: 325 at 5200 rpm. Torque: 325 at 3200 rpm. Solid valve lifters. Carburetor: Holley R-4069 600-cfm four-barrel. Paxton supercharger. Cobra aluminum high-rise intake. Dual exhausts. Code J.

OPTIONS

Paxton supercharger. 15 x 7-inch 10-spoke aluminum wheels. AM radio. Functional Ram-Air hood. AM radio. AM/FM radio. AM radio with 8-track tape player. Ford C-4 automatic transmission. Tilt-Away steering wheel. Shelby performance and dress-up accessories. (Note: Cars were randomly built with and without tilt steering, but this option could not be ordered. You either got it or didn't.)

1968 SHELBY-MUSTANG GT-500

JERRY HEASLEY

1968 Shelby Mustang GT-500

With a slight power boost over 1967, the GT-500 used a 428-cid Police Interceptor engine package with a single four-barrel carburetor and a special oil cooler. A few GT-500s were built with 390-cid V-8s when the supply of 428s ran out. Also, a relative handful of cars with automatic transmission had low-riser intake manifolds instead of the normal Cobra high-riser type.

The 0-to-60 performance of the base GT-500 was slower than that of the GT-350 at 6.5 seconds. However, it was quicker in the quarter-mile and had a higher top speed. The car could get down a drag strip in 14.75 seconds at 98 mph. Its top speed was 129 mph at 5100 rpm.

Model Number	Body/Style Number	Body Type & Seating	Factory Price	Shipping Weight	Production Total
SHELBY MUSTANG GT-500 — SERIES S — V-8					
02	63( )	2d FSBK-6P	$4,317	—	1,046
03	76( )	2d Conv-6P	$4,472	—	1,053

ENGINE

BASE V-8: Overhead valve. Cast-iron block. Displacement: 428 cid. Bore and stroke: 4.13 x 3.98 inches. Compression ratio: 10.50:1. Brake hp: 355 at 5400 rpm. Torque: 420 at 3200 rpm. Hydraulic valve lifters. Carburetor: Single Holley Model R-4129 715-cfm four-barrel.

OPTIONS

15 x 7-inch Kelsey-Hayes MagStar wheels. 15 x 7-inch 10-spoke aluminum wheels. AM radio. Folding rear seat. Air conditioning. Tinted glass (mandatory with air conditioning). Automatic transmission (Ford Toploader or C-6 automatic).

1968 SHELBY MUSTANG GT-500KR

JERRY HEASLEY

1968 Shelby Mustang GT500KR

Somebody stole the Shelby GT-500KR that *Car Life* magazine was going to test drive. You couldn't blame them — the under-$5,000 fastback had a lot of appeal. With its 428-cid Cobra Jet engine, it was a big temptation to any car-loving cat burglar. After a rough three-day break-in, the LAPD recovered the car, but a Ford public relations guy had to call *Car Life* and admit it was in no shape for a national article. The magazine wound up with a replacement car and a good lead-in to introduce it.

Actually, the hot Mustang didn't need too much of an introduction. Everyone knew what Cobra meant and the GT-500 designation was well understood by 1968. As for "KR," the folks at Ford and Shelby said it stood for "King of the Road." The GT-500KR wasn't the undisputed king of drag racing. "But, there's more to life than the quarter-mile," *Car Life's* editors maintained. Tucked below the hood was a 428-cid Cobra Jet V-8 with 4.13 x 3.98-inch bore and stroke, 10.6:1 compression, special hydraulic lifters, dual branched headers and one extra-big Holley four-barrel. True horsepower, however, was in the 400 bracket. The Shelby KR package, for the coupe or convertible, also included a fiberglass hood and front panels, functional air scoops and hot-air extractors. A big speedometer and tachometer were added to the instrument panel and other gauges were moved to the console. Vinyl buckets and thick carpeting were standard. There was wood-look dash trim, suspension upgrades (including staggered shocks), E70-15 Goodyear Polyglas tires, a limited-slip differential, engine dress-up items and special stripes and badges. Large, but ineffective air scoops were attached to the body sides to cool the

disc/drum power brakes. During a test drive, the binders got so hot that they started pouring smoke out of the scoops. No wonder *Car Life* rated overall braking performance poor.

Although it was not the fastest car ever made, the GT 500KR was the fastest Shelby-Mustang made up to its time. Some racers registered ETs below 13 seconds and top speed was around 130 mph. The car was tested for 0-to-60 mph in 6.9 seconds and ran the quarter-mile in 14.04 seconds at 102.73 mph.

Production counts were 933 units for the fastback and 318 for the convertible.

Model Number	Body/Style Number	Body Type & Seating	Factory Price	Shipping Weight	Production Total
SHELBY MUSTANG GT-500KR — SERIES S — V-8					
02	63( )	2d FSBK-6P	$4,317	—	1.046
03	76( )	2d Conv-6P	$4,472	—	1,053

ENGINE

BASE V-8: Overhead valve. Cast-iron block. Displacement: 428 cid. Bore and stroke: 4.13 x 3.98 inches. Compression ratio: 10.60:1. Brake hp: 335 at 5200 rpm. (actual horsepower was close to or above 400). Torque: 440 ft.-lbs. at 3400 rpm. Hydraulic valve lifters. Carburetor: Single Holley Model R-4168 735-cfm four-barrel with manual transmission or single Holley Model R-4174 735-cfm four-barrel with automatic transmission. Cast-iron Cobra high-riser intake manifold. (Note: Some low-riser cars were built and some 428 CJs were fitted with optional drag racing pistons that upped the compression ratio to 12.5:1.)

OPTIONS

15 x 7-inch Kelsey-Hayes MagStar wheels. 15 x 7-inch 10-spoke aluminum wheels. AM radio. Folding rear seat. Air conditioning. Tinted glass (mandatory with air conditioning). Automatic transmission (Ford Toploader or C-6 automatic).

FORD

1969 FAIRLANE/500 428 CJ/SCJ

JERRY HEASLEY

1969 Fairlane 500 428 Cobra Jet

Performance was the key word in the Fairlane lineup for 1969. Virtually all models except four-door sedans looked fast and even the stodgy sedan — as well as the station wagon — could be had with a 428 CJ engine. When equipped with this "Cobra-Jet" V-8 the Fairlanes were awesome as well as beautiful. They shared the same body as 1968 models with only minor trim updating. The tail lights were revised slightly and were squarer in shape than the 1968 type. The grille was revised slightly, with a more prominent center dividing bar than in 1968. The Fairlane 500 was the intermediate trim level and include all Fairlane features plus special 500 trim and moldings, color-keyed front-and-rear carpeting, a choice of four nylon-and-vinyl upholstery trims, an aluminum trim panel between the tail lights and the Fairlane 500 name, in script, on the sides of the rear fenders.

These cars would take 7.3 seconds to go 0-to-60 mph and did the quarter-mile in 14.9 seconds at 95.2 mph.

Model Number	Body/Style Number	Body Type & Seating	Factory Price	Shipping Weight	Production Total
FAIRLANE — SERIES 30 — V-8					
30	65A	2d HT-6P	$2,544	3,170 lbs.	85,630
FAIRLANE 500 — SERIES 30 — V-8					
33	65B/E	2d HT-6P	$2,679	3,181 lbs.	28,179
35	63B/E	2d FSBK-6P	$2,653	3,193 lbs.	29,849
36	76B/E	2d Conv-6P	$2,924	3,523 lbs.	2,264

NOTE 1: Prices and weights are for Fairlane/Fairlane 500 with base 302-cid V-8.
NOTE 2: Production is for Fairlane/Fairlane 500 models; no V-8 breakouts are available for 1969.
NOTE 3: Ford Motor Company built 43,477 of the 428-cid V-8s for all of its cars in 1969.

ENGINES

OPTIONAL 428 V-8: Overhead valve. Cast-iron block. Displacement: 428 cid. Bore and stroke: 4.13 x 3.98 inches. Compression ratio: 10.70:1. Brake hp: 335 at 5200 rpm. Torque: 440 at 3400 rpm. Five main bearings. Hydraulic valve lifters. Carburetor: Holley four-barrel. Dual exhaust. Code Q (Cobra Jet).

OPTIONAL V-8: Overhead valve. Cast-iron block. Displacement: 428 cid. Bore and stroke: 4.13 x 3.98 inches. Compression ratio: 10.70:1. Brake hp: 335 at 5200 rpm. Torque: 440 at 3400 rpm. Five main bearings. Hydraulic valve lifters. Carburetor: Holley four-barrel. Dual exhaust. Code R (Super Cobra Jet).

OPTIONS

Body side accent stripe ($13.90). Select Aire conditioner, tinted glass recommended ($380.41 and not available with non-Ram-Air 428 with four-speed manual transmission). Heavy-duty battery (standard with 428-cid V-8s). Console, bucket seats required ($53.82). Rear window defogger for hardtops and fastbacks ($21.27). Electric clock ($15.59). 428-cid/335-hp Cobra-Jet V-8, includes 55-amp alternator, 80-amp heavy-duty battery, dual exhausts, extra-cooling package, bright engine dress-up kit, cast aluminum rocker arm covers, and 3.25:1 ratio non-locking rear axle ($287.53). 428-cid/335-hp Super-Cobra-Jet Ram-Air V-8, includes 55-amp alternator, 80-amp heavy-duty battery, dual exhausts, extra-cooling package, bright engine dress-up kit, cast aluminum rocker arm covers, and 3.25:1 ratio non-locking rear axle ($420.96). Tinted glass ($36.86). Adjustable front seat headrests ($17.00 and mandatory after January 1, 1969). Dual-note horn ($6.53). Remote-control left-hand outside rearview mirror ($12.95). Color-keyed dual racing-style outside mirrors — left-hand remote-control type — and including chrome exhaust exits with 428s ($19.48). Body side moldings on base Fairlane two-door hardtop ($20.75). Tu-Tone paint, except convertibles and fastbacks ($26.85). Power disc brakes ($64.77). 6-Way power front bench seat in Fairlane 500 ($100.15). Power steering ($100.26). Power ventilation ($15.50, but not available for cars with air conditioning). Power windows ($105.11). Push-button AM radio with front antenna ($61.40). AM/FM stereo radio with two speakers ($181.36). Dual rear speakers ($25.91). Bucket seats in Fairlane 500 hardtop or convertible ($120.59). Deluxe rim-blow steering wheel ($35.70). GT Handling suspension ($30.64). 6,000-rpm tachometer ($47.92). Select Shift Cruise-O-Matic ($222.08). Four-speed manual transmission ($194.31, but not available for four-door sedans with 428-cid V-8). Vinyl roof for formal hardtop models only ($90.15). Vinyl seat trim in Fairlane 500 hardtop and fastback ($19.48). Knit-vinyl seat trim in Fairlane 500 hardtop and fastback ($24.53). Deluxe wheel covers ($40.75). Argent Silver styled steel wheels with chrome trim rings ($38.86). Chrome styled wheels with chrome trim rings ($116.59). Intermittent windshield wipers ($16.85). Towing package ($110.16 and requires Cruise-O-Matic, power steering, 8.55 x 15 tires and 3.25:1 rear axle). Visibility group ($24.01 or $11.06 if car has the color-keyed racing mirrors option). FR70-14 white sidewall Wide-Oval radial tires ($6.29 extra). F70-14 Wide-Oval belted tires with raised white lettering ($13.05). Options added on May 1, 1969 included the following: Blazer stripes for Fairlane 500 hardtop and fastback ($19.48). Drag-Pack package including traction-lok differential, 3.91:1 or 4.30:1 high-ratio rear axle, engine oil cooler, cap-screw connecting rods, modified crankshaft, modified flywheel and modified damper for cars with 428-cid four-barrel V-8 ($155.45).

1969 TORINO GT 428 CJ/SCJ

1969 Torino GT

The Torino was the top Fairlane trim level and included all of the Fairlane 500 trim plus a polished aluminum rocker panel molding, special emblems and special Torino trim inside and out. The Fairlane Torino GT was the sporty version of the Fairlane 500 and included all 500 features plus a standard V-8, bucket seats, a center console, special name plaques, special interior trim. Styled steel wheels, lower body side striping (on hardtops and convertibles) and a C-stripe on fastbacks.

The GT was definitely the "image" machine for muscle car fans, although big-engined base Torinos weighed less and may have been faster. Both are great automobiles and awesome performers capable of going 0-to-60 mph in 6.8 seconds and racing the quarter-mile in 14.2 seconds at 101 mph.

Model Number	Body/Style Number	Body Type & Seating	Factory Price	Shipping Weight	Production Total
TORINO– SERIES 40 — V-8					
30	65C	2d HT-6P	$2,827	3,195 lbs.	20,789
TORINO GT — SERIES 40 — V-8					
33	65F/D	2d HT-6P	$2,848	3,173 lbs.	17,951
35	63F/D	2d FSBK-6P	$2,823	3,220 lbs.	61,319
36	76F/D	2d Conv-6P	$3,073	3,356 lbs.	2,552

NOTE 1: Prices and weights are for Torino/Torino GT models with base 302-cid V-8.

NOTE 2: Production is for all Torino/Torino GT models; no V-8 breakouts are available base Torino, but all GTs were V-8s.

NOTE 3: Ford Motor Company built 43,477 of the 428-cid V-8s for all of its cars in 1969.

ENGINES

OPTIONAL V-8: Overhead valve. Cast-iron block. Displacement: 428 cid. Bore and stroke: 4.13 x 3.98 inches. Compression ratio: 10.70:1. Brake hp: 335 at 5200 rpm. Torque: 440 at 3400 rpm. Five main bearings. Hydraulic valve lifters. Carburetor: Holley four-barrel. Dual exhaust. Code Q (Cobra Jet).

OPTIONAL V-8: Overhead valve. Cast-iron block. Displacement: 428 cid. Bore and stroke: 4.13 x 3.98 inches. Compression ratio: 10.70:1. Brake hp: 335 at 5200 rpm. Torque: 440 at 3400 rpm. Five main bearings. Hydraulic valve lifters. Carburetor: Holley four-barrel. Crankcase capacity: 5 qt. (add 1 qt. with new oil filter). Dual exhaust. Code R (Super Cobra Jet).

OPTIONS

Body side accent stripe ($13.90). Select Aire conditioner, tinted glass recommended ($380.41 and not available with non-Ram-Air 428 with four-speed manual transmission). Heavy-duty battery (standard with 428-cid V-8s). Console, bucket seats required for Torino hardtop ($53.82, but standard in Torino GTs). Rear window defogger for hardtops and fastbacks ($21.27). Electric clock ($15.59). 428-cid/335-hp Cobra-Jet V-8, includes 55-amp alternator, 80-amp heavy-duty battery, dual exhausts, extra-cooling package, bright engine dress-up kit, cast aluminum rocker arm covers, and 3.25:1 ratio non-locking rear axle ($287.53). 428-cid/335-hp Super-Cobra-Jet Ram-Air V-8, includes 55-amp alternator, 80-amp heavy-duty battery, dual exhausts, extra-cooling package, bright engine dress-up kit, cast aluminum rocker arm covers, and 3.25:1 ratio non-locking rear axle ($420.96). Tinted glass ($36.86). Adjustable front seat headrests ($17.00 and mandatory after January 1, 1969). Dual-note horn ($6.53). Remote-control left-hand outside rearview mirror ($12.95). Color-keyed dual racing-style outside mirrors — left-hand remote-control type — and including chrome exhaust exits with 428s ($19.48). Tu-Tone paint, except convertibles and fastbacks ($26.85). Power disc brakes ($64.77). 6-Way power front bench seat ($100.15). Power steering ($100.26). Power ventilation ($15.50, but not available for cars with air conditioning). Power windows ($105.11). Push-button AM radio with front antenna ($61.40). AM/FM stereo radio with two speakers ($181.36). Dual rear speakers ($25.91). Bucket seats in base Torino ($120.59, but standard in GTs). Deluxe rim-blow steering wheel ($35.70). GT Handling Suspension ($30.64). 6,000-rpm tachometer ($47.92). Select Shift Cruise-O-Matic ($222.08). Four-speed manual transmission ($194.31, but not available for four-door sedans with 428-cid V-8). Vinyl roof for formal hardtop models only ($90.15). Knit-vinyl seat trim in Torino GT hardtop and fastback ($24.53). Deluxe wheel covers ($40.75). Argent Silver styled steel wheels with chrome trim rings ($17.69 for base Torino, but standard for Torino GTs). Chrome styled wheels with chrome trim rings ($116.59 for base Torion and $77.73 for Torino GT). Intermittent windshield wipers ($16.85). Towing package ($110.16 and requires Cruise-O-Matic, power steering, 8.55 x 15 tires and 3.25:1 rear axle). Visibility group ($24.01 or $11.06 if car has the color-keyed racing mirrors option. FR70-14 white sidewall Wide-Oval radial tires ($6.29 extra). F70-14 Wide-Oval belted tires with raised white lettering ($13.05). Options added on May 1, 1969 included the following: Blazer stripes for Torino GT hardtop and fastback ($19.48). Drag-Pack package including traction-lok differential, 3.91:1 or 4.30:1 high-ratio rear axle, engine oil cooler, cap-screw connecting rods, modified crankshaft, modified flywheel and modified damper for cars with 428-cid four-barrel V-8 ($155.45).

FORD

1969 COBRA 428 CJ/SCJ

JERRY HEASLEY

1969 Cobra

Ford's sexy-looking Torino Cobra had an Italian-sounding first name that meant "fast" plus looks that meant "muscle car" in any language. "Torque gives rubber big bite for fast acceleration," *Motor Trend* said to sum up the car in a few words. "Four speed helps and Ford has many hop up parts for the 428."

A new sub-series in the Torino GT lineup, the Cobra models included a formal hardtop and Sportsroof fastback. The emphasis was on performance and standard equipment included a 428-cid/335-hp Cobra Jet V-8, a four-speed manual transmission, competition suspension, Wide-Oval belted black sidewall tires and 6-inch-wide wheels with hub caps.

While most people think that Detroit is really a place where they make cars, the truth is it's a giant genetic engineering laboratory. The Torino Cobra was Ford's answer to the Plymouth Road Runner. At least it was a good answer. Ford people say the standard 428 CJ actually trumped the Road Runner, which came only with 383 cubic inches. The Torino Cobra even included campy coiled-snake cartoon character of its own.

One of the buff books tested a 1969 Torino Cobra two-door hardtop with the 428-cid/335-hp engine option. It gave the price of the car as $3,139. The hot Torino had the base 428 CJ V-8 and moved from 0-to-60 mph in 7.8 seconds. It needed 14.9 seconds for the quarter-mile at 95.2 mph. *Motor Trend* road tested a Cobra with the Ram Air engine and liked the car. The magazine charted 0-to-60 mph performance at 6.3 seconds and the quarter-mile at 14.5 seconds and 100 mph.

ENGINES

OPTIONAL V-8: Overhead valve. Cast-iron block. Displacement: 428 cid. Bore and stroke: 4.13 x 3.98 inches. Compression ratio: 10.70:1. Brake hp: 335 at 5200 rpm. Torque: 440 at 3400 rpm. Five main bearings. Hydraulic valve lifters. Carburetor: Holley four-barrel. Dual exhaust. Code Q (Cobra Jet).

OPTIONAL V-8: Overhead valve. Cast-iron block. Displacement: 428 cid. Bore and stroke: 4.13 x 3.98 inches. Compression ratio: 10.70:1. Brake hp: 335 at 5200 rpm. Torque: 440 at 3400 rpm. Five main bearings. Hydraulic valve lifters. Carburetor: Holley four-barrel. Dual exhaust. Code R (Super Cobra Jet).

OPTIONS

Body side accent stripe ($13.90). Select Aire conditioner, tinted glass recommended ($380.41 and not available with non-Ram-Air 428 with four-speed manual transmission). Heavy-duty battery (standard with 428-cid V-8s). Console, bucket seats required for Torino hardtop ($53.82, but standard in Torino GTs). Rear window defogger for hardtops and fastbacks ($21.27). Electric clock ($15.59). 428-cid/335-hp Cobra-Jet V-8, includes 55-amp alternator, 80-amp heavy-duty battery, dual exhausts, extra-cooling package, bright engine dress-up kit, cast aluminum rocker arm covers, and 3.25:1 ratio non-locking rear axle ($287.53). Dual-note horn ($6.53). Remote-control left-hand outside rearview mirror ($12.95). Color-keyed dual racing-style outside mirrors — left-hand remote-control type — and including chrome exhaust exits with 428s ($19.48). Tu-Tone paint, except convertibles and fastbacks ($26.85). Power disc brakes ($64.77). 6-Way power front bench seat ($100.15). Power steering ($100.26). Power ventilation ($15.50, but not available for cars with air conditioning). Power windows ($105.11). Push-button AM radio with front antenna ($61.40). AM/FM stereo radio with two speakers ($181.36). Dual rear speakers ($25.91). Deluxe rim-blow steering wheel ($35.70). GT Handling suspension including extra-high-rate front and rear springs, extra-heavy-duty front and rear shock absorbers and large-diameter heavy-duty stabilizer bar ($30.64). 6,000-rpm tachometer ($47.92). Select Shift Cruise-O-Matic ($222.08). Four-speed manual transmission ($194.31, but not available for four-door sedans with 428-cid V-8). Vinyl roof for formal hardtop models only ($90.15). Knit-vinyl seat trim in hardtop and fastback ($24.53). Deluxe wheel covers ($40.75). Argent Silver styled steel wheels with chrome trim rings ($17.69). Chrome styled wheels with chrome trim rings ($77.73). Intermittent windshield wipers ($16.85). Towing package including extra-cooling package, heavy-duty suspension, power disc brakes, heavy-duty alternator, heavy-duty battery and trailer towing identification ($110.16 and requires Cruise-O-Matic, power steering, 8.55 x 15 tires and 3,25 rear axle). Visibility group including ash tray light, glove box light, trunk light and remote-control outside rearview mirror ($24.01 or $11.06 if car has the color-keyed racing mirrors option. FR70-14 white sidewall Wide-Oval radial tires ($6.29 extra). F70-14 Wide-Oval belted tires with raised white lettering ($13.05). Options added on May 1, 1969 included the following: Blazer stripes for hardtop and fastback ($19.48). Drag-Pack package including traction-lok differential, 3.91:1 or 4.30:1 high-ratio rear axle, engine oil cooler, cap-screw connecting rods, modified crankshaft, modified flywheel and modified damper for cars with 428-cid four-barrel V-8 ($155.45).

Model Number	Body/Style Number	Body Type & Seating	Factory Price	Shipping Weight	Production Total
TORINO COBRA — SERIES 40 — V-8					
45	65B/E	2d HT-6P	$3,208	3,490 lbs.	Note 1
46	63B/E	2d FSBK-6P	$3,183	3,537 lbs.	Note 1

NOTE 1: Prices and weights are for Torino/Torino GT models with base 302-cid V-8
NOTE 2: Production not available.
NOTE 3: Ford Motor Company built 43,477 of the 428-cid V-8s for all of its cars in 1969.

1969 TALLADEGA 428 CJ/SCJ

JERRY HEASLEY

1969 Talladega

This fastback Ford is the perfect quarter-mile machine for the FoMoCo fan who wants to go drag racing against Starsky & Hutch rather than John Force. Though the Talladega was a bit heftier and weightier than other Torinos, the 428 CJ still pushed it to mid-14-second quarter-miles. However, it was much better suited to left hand turns on an oval-shaped racetrack. At the time they were built, the fastback cars that became combatants in the "aerodynamic wars" on the 1969-1970 NASCAR Grand National superspeedways were more of a headache to their manufacturers than the worshipped treasures they are today.

Requirements to "legalize" them for racing meant at least 500 examples had to be produced during the 1969 model year. That minimum production level was raised to one car per dealer for 1970. Ford's hopes rode on the sloped-nosed 1969 Torino Talladega, which was part of the midsized Fairlane model lineup. Standard features and options found on all "street" version Talladegas included: a factory-custom wind-cheating front end with flush grill and reinforcements, a rear bumper mounted up front after being narrowed, veed and re-welded, re-rolled side rocker panels to lower the cars by one inch, the 335-hp/428-cid Cobra Jet (Q code) V-8, C6 automatic transmission, staggered rear shock absorbers, an open 9-inch rear axle with 3.25:1 gearing, an engine oil cooler, power front disk brakes, power steering and other good stuff. All Talladegas were finished in either Burgundy, Blue or White. They had full-length white body side striping.

A similar, but not identical, Mercury Montego counterpart was produced and called the Cyclone Spoiler II.

Counting prototypes, Talladega production easily passed the required 500 units and wound up at 754. The cars came in Wimbleton White, Royal Maroon or Presidential Blue. The idea behind the Talladega was to get the production work over with as quickly as possible and let the racers create a performance image for the Torino series. They did this, too. David Pearson won his second straight NASCAR Grand National championship. The 1969 Talladegas proved very adept at racing. In fact, test drivers found that their 1970 replacements were some 5 mph slower on the big tracks. As a result, Ford's factory-backed teams ran year-old models at many tracks during the 1970 racing season.

Model Number	Body/Style Number	Body Type & Seating	Factory Price	Shipping Weight	Production Total
TORINO TALLADEGA — SERIES 40 — V-8					
46	63B	2d FSBK-6P	NA	NA	754

NOTE 1: Production total includes prototype units.

ENGINE

OPTIONAL V-8: Overhead valve. Cast-iron block. Displacement: 428 cid. Bore and stroke: 4.13 x 3.98 inches. Compression ratio: 10.70:1. Brake hp: 335 at 5200 rpm. Torque: 440 at 3400 rpm. Five main bearings. Hydraulic valve lifters. Carburetor: Holley four-barrel. Dual exhaust. Code Q (Cobra Jet).

OPTIONAL V-8: Overhead valve. Cast-iron block. Displacement: 428 cid. Bore and stroke: 4.13 x 3.98 inches. Compression ratio: 10.70:1. Brake hp: 335 at 5200 rpm. Torque: 440 at 3400 rpm. Five main bearings. Hydraulic valve lifters. Carburetor: Holley four-barrel. Dual exhaust. Code R (Super Cobra Jet).

OPTIONS

Select Aire conditioner, tinted glass recommended ($380.41 and not available with non-Ram-Air 428 with four-speed manual transmission). Rear window defogger for hardtops and fastbacks ($21.27). Electric clock ($15.59). Dual-note horn ($6.53). 6-Way power front bench seat ($100.15). Power ventilation ($15.50, but not available for cars with air conditioning). Power windows ($105.11). AM/FM stereo radio with two speakers ($181.36). Dual rear speakers ($25.91). Deluxe rim-blow steering wheel ($35.70). 6,000-rpm tachometer ($47.92). Select Shift Cruise-O-Matic ($222.08). Argent Silver styled steel wheels with chrome trim rings ($17.69). Chrome styled wheels with chrome trim rings ($77.73). Intermittent windshield wipers ($16.85). Visibility group including ash tray light, glove box light, trunk light and remote-control outside rearview mirror ($24.01 or $11.06 if car has the color-keyed racing mirrors option.) FR70-14 white sidewall Wide-Oval radial tires ($6.29 extra). F70-14 Wide-Oval belted tires with raised white lettering ($13.05). Options added on May 1, 1969 included the following: Drag-Pack package including traction-lok differential, 3.91:1 or 4.30:1 high-ratio rear axle, engine oil cooler, cap-screw connecting rods, modified crankshaft, modified flywheel and modified damper for cars with 428-cid four-barrel V-8 ($155.45). (NOTE: Our reference gives option information only through May 1 and the Talladega apparently arrived after that. The above list is a "best guess" estimate of what the Talladega options list might have looked like.)

FORD

1969 MUSTANG BOSS 302

1969 Mustang Boss 302

JERRY HEASLEY

In the slang of the '60s, the word "boss" had a bundle of connotations. It meant "tough" or "awesome" (in the sense kids use the word today) and something that was "boss" was something every right-minded person aspired to. So, Ford picked it as a good name for its hot Mustang with the new 302-cid V-8. Actually there were two Bosses. The first was a race-ready Boss 429 with Ford's NASCAR racing engine and completely redesigned front suspension. Then came the Boss 302, which was intended for high-performance street use.

What made the Boss special was a beefed-up 302-cid V-8 with four-bolt main bearing caps, a stronger crankshaft and — most important of all — redesigned cylinder heads that allowed dramatically better breathing. These "Cleveland" heads (as they are called) were also designed to sit atop Ford's 351 Cleveland V-8. While a Boss 302 in the hands of a collector is likely to be driven a little more gingerly than the paces original owners put these cars through, Ford built an rpm limiter to keep lead-footed types from blowing up the engine.

Besides the special 302 engine, a Boss can be recognized by the matte black paint on its hood and trunk, Boss 302 name swatches on its sides, a front spoiler and styled steel wheels. Its performance equipment includes front disc brakes and a four-speed manual transmission. The optional rear spoiler was obviously decorative.

In stock tune, a Boss 302 could turn in 0 to 60-mph times of under 7 seconds and nudge the century mark in a standing-start quarter-mile. Unlike other performance cars of the period, however, the Boss 302 had exceptionally good street manners — although the firm suspension did broadcast tar strips and other pavement irregularities.

Model Number	Body/Style Number	Body Type & Seating	Factory Price	Shipping Weight	Production Total
MUSTANG BOSS 302 — SERIES 02 — V-8					
02	63	2d FSBK-6P	$3,669	3,250 lbs.	1,628

NOTE 1: Price includes Boss 302 package plus cost of required wide-ratio four-speed transmission and power disc brakes

ENGINE

BASE V-8: Overhead valve. Cast-iron block. Displacement: 302 cid. Bore and stroke: 4.00 x 3.00 inches. Compression ratio: 10.50:1. Brake hp: 290 at 5000 rpm. Torque: 290 at 4300 rpm. Five main bearings. Solid valve lifters. Carburetor: Holley 780-cfm four-barrel. Dual exhaust. Dual-plane aluminum intake manifold. Code G.

OPTIONS

Select Aire conditioner, tinted glass recommended ($376.20). Optional axle ratio ($6.53). Heavy-duty battery ($8.43). Front bumper guards ($12.95). Electric clock ($15.59, but standard with Interior Decor group). Center console ($53.82). Limited-slip differential ($41.60). Traction-Lok differential ($63.51). 302-cid/290-hp Boss 302 V-8 includes black hood, black headlight casting, black rear deck lid, black lower back panel, four F60-15 belted black sidewall tires with raised white lettering, 15 x 7 five-bolt Magnum 500 styled wheels with Argent Silver painted finish, collapsible spare, C-stripes, dual exhausts, quick-ratio 16:1 steering, special handling suspension, staggered rear shocks, special cooling package, 3.50:1 non-locking rear axle, electronic rpm limiter, functional front spoiler shipped knocked-down and 45-amp battery, for Sportsroof after May 1, 1969 ($676.15 and requires power disc brakes and wide-ratio four-speed transmission). Extra-cooling package for V-8s ($12.95, but standard with air conditioning). Complete tinted glass ($38.86). Adjustable front seat headrests $17.00 and mandatory after January 1, 1969. Color-keyed dual racing-style mirrors, left-hand remote-control right-hand manual ($19.48). Rocker panel molding ($12.95, but standard with exterior decor group). Power disc brakes ($64.77 and required with Boss 302 option after May 1, 1969). Power steering ($94.95). Power ventilation ($40.02, but not available with air conditioning). Push-button AM radio ($61.40). AM/FM stereo radio ($181.39). Stereosonic tape system ($133.84 and AM radio required). Rear seat speaker ($12.95). High-back bucket seats ($84.25). Sport Deck rear seat ($97.21). Full-width front seat with armrest ($32.44). Fingertip speed control for Mustang with V-8 and SelectShift automatic transmission ($73.83). Tilt-away steering wheel ($66.14). Deluxe Rim-Blow steering wheel ($35.70, but standard with interior decor group). Tachometer and trip odometer ($54.45). Select Shift Cruise-O-Matic transmission ($200.85). Wide-ratio four-speed manual transmission ($204.64). FR70-14 Wide-Oval white sidewall radial tires ($89.11). Interior Decor group ($88.15). Deluxe interior Decor group ($120.48). Other

options added on May 1, 1969 included the following: Functional and adjustable rear spoiler ($19.48 for Boss only). Sport slats with functional rear window louvers, dual racing-style outside mirror required ($128.28 for Boss only). Chrome Magnum 500 styled wheels for Boss only ($77.73).

1969 MUSTANG GT 428 CJ/SCJ

JERRY HEASLEY

1969 Mustang GT

For model year 1969, the Mustang got its third major restyling. Its new body wasn't drastically changed, but it grew 3.8 inches. Missing for the first time was a side scoop (or cove) on the body. This styling gimmick was replaced with a feature line that ran from the tip of the front fender to just behind the rear-most door seam, at a level just above the front wheel opening. On convertibles and hardtops there was a rear-facing, simulated air vent in front of the rear wheel opening on both sides. On fastbacks, this feature line lead to a backwards C-shaped air scoop above the main feature line. The fastback was now referred to as the SportsRoof or Sports Roof (various Ford ads spelled the term differently). It had a 0.9-inch lower roofline than earlier fastbacks.

One nice performance option was the Mustang GT with the 428 Cobra-Jet engine. This motor was Ford's big-block performance leader. It also came in a Super-Cobra-Jet versions. The former was called the "standard Cobra engine" in the *1969 Performance Buyer's Guide.* It generated 335 hp at 5200 rpm and 440 lbs.-ft. of torque at 3400 rpm. The latter was the same engine with Ram Air induction, a hardened steel cast crankshaft, special "LeMans" connecting rods and improved balancing for drag racing. It had the same advertised horsepower.

A Mustang two-door hardtop with the 428-cid/335-hp engine carried just 9.6 lbs. per hp. It could do 0-to-60 mph in 5.5 seconds and cover the quarter-mile in 13.9 seconds according to one road test.

Model Number	Body/Style Number	Body Type & Seating	Factory Price	Shipping Weight	Production Total
MUSTANG GT — SERIES 01/02/03 — V-8					
01	65	2d HT-6P	$3,542	3,248 lbs.	127,954
02	63	2d FSBK-6P	$3,542	3,272 lbs.	61,980
03	76	2d Conv-6P	$3,761	3,358 lbs.	1,628

NOTE 1: Prices estimates include GT equipment package, 428 CJ V-8, four-speed transmission and F70-14 tires.

NOTE 2: Weights are estimates including options.

NOTE 3: Only 5,396 Mustangs got the GT Equipment package in model-year 1969.

ENGINES

OPTIONAL V-8: Overhead valve. Cast-iron block. Displacement: 428 cid. Bore and stroke: 4.13 x 3.98 inches. Compression ratio: 10.70:1. Brake hp: 335 at 5200 rpm. Torque: 440 at 3400 rpm. Five main bearings. Hydraulic valve lifters. Carburetor: Holley four-barrel. Dual exhaust. Code Q (Cobra Jet).

OPTIONAL V-8: Overhead valve. Cast-iron block. Displacement: 428 cid. Bore and stroke: 4.13 x 3.98 inches. Compression ratio: 10.70:1. Brake hp: 335 at 5200 rpm. Torque: 440 at 3400 rpm. Five main bearings. Hydraulic valve lifters. Carburetor: Holley four-barrel. Dual exhaust. Code R (Super Cobra Jet).

OPTIONS (PARTIAL LIST):

Select Aire conditioner, tinted glass recommended ($376.20). Optional axle ratio ($6.53). Heavy-duty battery standard with 428 CJ V-8. Front bumper guards ($12.95). Electric clock ($15.59, but standard with Interior Decor group. Center console, bucket seats required ($53.82). Limited-slip differential ($41.60). Traction-Lok differential ($63.51). 428-cid 335-hp non-Ram-Air V-8, includes 80-amp heavy-duty battery, 55-amp. alternator, dual exhausts, extra-cooling package, bright engine dress-up kit, cast-aluminum rocker covers, 3.25:1 non-locking axle and requires E70-14 Wide-Oval belted white sidewall tires and Cruise-O-Matic or four-speed manual transmission ($287.53, but not available with limited-slip axle, air conditioning with four-speed transmission or with handling suspension). 428-cid/335-hp Ram-Air V-8, includes ram-air induction system, 80-amp heavy-duty battery, 55-amp alternator, dual exhausts, extra-cooling package, bright engine dress-up kit, cast-aluminum rocker covers, 3.50:1 non-locking rear axle and requires F70-14 Wide-Oval belted white sidewall tires and Cruise-O-Matic or four-speed manual transmission ($420.96, but not available with limited-slip axle, air conditioning with four-speed transmission or with handling suspension). Extra-cooling package for V-8s ($12.95, but standard with air conditioning). Complete tinted glass ($38.86). Power

FORD

disc brakes ($64.77 and required with Boss 302 option after May 1, 1969). Power steering ($94.95). Power ventilation ($40.02, but not available with air conditioning). Push-button AM radio ($61.40). AM/FM stereo radio ($181.39). Stereosonic tape system ($133.84 and AM radio required). Rear seat speaker ($12.95). High-back bucket seats ($84.25). Sport Deck rear seat ($97.21). Full-width front seat with armrest ($32.44). Fingertip speed control for Mustang with V-8 and SelectShift automatic transmission ($73.83). Tilt-away steering wheel ($66.14). Deluxe Rim-Blow steering wheel ($35.70, but standard with interior decor group). Tachometer and trip odometer ($54.45). Select Shift Cruise-O-Matic transmission ($222.08). Wide-ratio four-speed manual transmission ($253.92). Vinyl roof on hardtop ($84.25). Argent Silver styled steel wheels with chrome trim rings for Mustang V-8 without exterior décor group ($38.86). Argent Silver styled steel wheels with chrome trim rings for Mustang V-8 with exterior décor group (standard on GT). Color-keyed styled steel wheels with

chrome trim rings for Mustang GT, includes GT logo on hubcaps ($77.73). Chromed styled steel wheels with chrome trim rings for Mustang GT, includes GT logo on hubcaps ($77.73). FR70-14 Wide-Oval white sidewall radial tires ($14.29 extra on non-Ram-Air model). Interior Decor group with full-width seats ($88.15). Deluxe interior Decor group with full-width seats ($120.48). Mustang GT Equipment Group includes GT ornamentation, GT rocker panel tape stripe, Argent Silver styled wheels package, pop-open gas cap, exposed hood lock pins, dual exhausts with bright extensions, competition suspension, F70-14 Wide-Oval belted white sidewall tires, non-functional on 428 CJ or functional hood scoop on 428 SCJ with integral turn signals and GT letters on hubcaps. Options added on May 1, 1969 included the following: Drag-Pack package including traction-lok differential, 3.91:1 or 4.30:1 high-ratio rear axle, engine oil cooler, cap-screw connecting rods, modified crankshaft, modified flywheel and modified damper for cars with 428-cid four-barrel V-8 ($155.45).

1969 MUSTANG MACH 1

JERRY HEASLEY

1969 Mustang Mach 1

The Mustang Mach 1 was Dearborn's budget-basement version of a racing car that Carroll Shelby whipped up on the Left Coast. *Car Life* magazine's March 1969 issue said, "Greatness makes its own demands. An enthusiast will find the Mach 1 a rewarding car. Best Mustang yet and quickest ever."

The Mach 1 was based on the SportsRoof body style. Standard on all Mach 1's was a spoiler, a matte black hood, a simulated hood scoop and exposed NASCAR-style hood lock pins, which could be deleted. A two-tone reflective side stripe and rear stripes carried the model designation just behind the front wheel arches and above the chrome pop-up gas cap.

The Mach 1's base engine was a 351-cid two-barrel Windsor V-8. This was essentially a stroked 302-cid Ford V-8 with raised deck height, which created a great street performance engine. The basic version cranked up 250 horses. Options included the 351-cid/290-hp four-barrel V-8 and a 390-cid/320-hp V-8. Another option available to enthusiast buyers was a Mustang GT or Mach 1 with a Cobra Jet 428 or Super Cobra Jet 428 engine. The big 428s put out 335 hp.

When fitted with the optional 428 SCJ V-8, the Mach 1 went 0-to-60 mph in 5.5 seconds and ate up the quarter in 13.9 seconds at 103.32 mph.

Model Number	Body/Style Number	Body Type & Seating	Factory Price	Shipping Weight	Production Total
MUSTANG MACH 1 — SERIES 02 — (BASE) V-8					
02	63	2d FSBK-6P	$3,122	3,253 lbs.	72,458

NOTE 1: Price and weight for base model.

ENGINES

BASE V-8: Overhead valve. Cast-iron block. Displacement: 351 cid. Bore and stroke: 4.00 x 3.50 inches. Compression ratio: 9.50:1. Brake hp: 250 at 4600 rpm. Torque: 355 at 2600 rpm. Five main bearings. Hydraulic valve lifters. Carburetor: Motorcraft two-barrel. Serial number code H.

OPTIONAL V-8: Overhead valve. Cast-iron block. Displacement: 351 cid. Bore and stroke: 4.00 x 3.50 inches. Compression ratio: 10.70:1. Brake hp: 290 at 4800 rpm. Torque: 385 at 3200 rpm. Five main bearings. Hydraulic valve lifters. Carburetor: Motorcraft four-barrel. Serial number code M.

OPTIONAL V-8: Overhead valve. Cast-iron block. Displacement: 390 cid. Bore and stroke: 4.05 x 3.78 inches. Compression ratio: 10.5:1. Brake hp: 320 at 4600 rpm. Torque: 427 at 3200 rpm. Five main bearings. Hydraulic valve lifters. Carburetor: Four-barrel. Dual exhaust. Code S.

OPTIONAL V-8: Overhead valve. Cast-iron block. Displacement: 428 cid. Bore and stroke: 4.13 x 3.98 inches. Compression ratio: 10.70:1. Brake hp: 335 at 5200 rpm. Torque: 440 at 3400 rpm. Five main bearings. Hydraulic valve lifters. Carburetor: Holley four-barrel. Dual exhaust. Code Q (Cobra Jet).

OPTIONAL V-8: Overhead valve. Cast-iron block. Displacement: 428 cid. Bore and stroke: 4.13 x 3.98 inches. Compression ratio: 10.70:1. Brake hp: 335 at 5200 rpm. Torque: 440 at 3400 rpm. Five main bearings. Hydraulic valve lifters. Carburetor: Holley four-barrel. Dual exhaust. Code R (Super Cobra Jet).

FORD

OPTIONS

Select Aire conditioner, tinted glass recommended ($376.20). Optional axle ratio ($6.53). Heavy-duty battery standard with 428 CJ V-8). Front bumper guards ($12.95). Center console, bucket seats required ($53.82). Limited-slip differential ($41.60). Traction-Lok differential ($63.51). Heavy-duty 80-amp battery with 351-cid V-8s ($16.85). 351-cid/250-hp two-barrel V-8 (standard). 351-cid/290-hp four-barrel V-8 ($84.25). 390-cid/320-hp V-8 requires F70-14 Wide-Oval belted tires with raised white letters and Traction-Lok differential with 3.91 or 4.30 axle, plus eith Cruise-O-Matic or four-speed manual transmission ($99.74). 428-cid/335-hp non-Ram-Air V-8, includes 80-amp. heavy-duty battery, 55-amp. alternator, dual exhausts, extra-cooling package, bright engine dress-up kit, cast-aluminum rocker covers, 3.25:1 non-locking axle and requires E70-14 Wide-Oval belted white sidewall tires and Cruise-O-Matic or four-speed manual transmission ($224.12, but not available with limited-slip axle, air conditioning with four-speed transmission or with handling suspension). 428-cid/335-hp Ram-Air V-8, includes ram-air induction system, 80-amp heavy-duty battery, 55-amp alternator, dual exhausts, extra-cooling package, bright engine dress-up kit, cast-aluminum rocker covers, 3.50:1 non-locking rear axle and requires F70-14 Wide-Oval belted white sidewall tires and Cruise-O-Matic or four-speed manual transmission ($357.46, but not available with limited-slip axle, air conditioning with four-speed transmis-

sion or with handling suspension). Extra-cooling package for V-8s ($12.95, but standard with air conditioning). Complete tinted glass ($38.86). Rocker panel molding ($12.95, but standard with exterior decor group). Power disc brakes ($64.77). Power steering ($94.95). Power ventilation ($40.02, but not available with air conditioning). Push-button AM radio ($61.40). AM/FM stereo radio ($181.39). Stereosonic tape system ($133.84 and AM radio required). Rear seat speaker ($12.95). High-back bucket seats ($84.25). Sport Deck rear seat ($97.21). Full-width front seat with armrest for hardtop ($32.44). Fingertip speed control for Mustang with V-8 and SelectShift automatic transmission ($73.83). Tilt-away steering wheel ($66.14). Tachometer and trip odometer ($54.45, but standard in big-block cars with four-speed manual transmission). Select Shift Cruise-O-Matic transmission ($200.85 with small-block V-8s and $222.08 with big-block V-8s). Wide-ratio four-speed manual transmission ($204.64 with 351-cid V-8, $253.92 with 390- or 428-cid V-8). Chromed styled steel wheels with chrome trim rings (standard Mach 1). FR70-14 Wide-Oval white sidewall radial tires ($14.29 extra on non-Ram-Air models). Options added on May 1, 1969 included the following: Drag-Pack package including traction-lok differential, 3.91:1 or 4.30:1 high-ratio rear axle, engine oil cooler, cap-screw connecting rods, modified crankshaft, modified flywheel and modified damper for cars with 428-cid four-barrel V-8 ($155.45).

1969 MUSTANG BOSS 429

JERRY HEASLEY

1969 Mustang Boss 429

Boss models were basic Mustangs in layout. They had the same exterior styling and an interior with circular gauges, dash lights to monitor oil pressure and electrical systems and a tachometer. The Boss 429 was born because Ford had a big-block V-8 that it wanted to get approved for racing. The Boss 302 had been designed to compete with the Camaro in Trans-Am racing. The Boss 429 was created to legalize the 429-cid V-8 for use on the NASCAR circuit.

Ford considered doing a 429-powered Torino, but decided to offer the new-for-1969 429-cid "semi-hemi" big-block in the popular Mustang platform instead. Marketing experts felt that it would be easier to sell 500 big-block Mustangs than the same number of Torino-based supercars. Kar Kraft, an aftermarket firm in Brighton, Michigan, was contracted to build Boss 429s. Since the Mustang's engine compartment was not designed to house such a wide power plant, the job required

a big shoehorn and a lot of suspension changes and chassis modifications. Body alterations included engine bay bracing, inner wheel well sheet metal work and flared wheel housings (to accommodate a widened track and the use of seven-inch Magnum 500 rims). The hood received a huge, functional scoop, and a special spoiler underlined the front bumper. Power steering and brakes, a Traction-Lok axle with 3.91 gears and the Boss 302's rear spoiler were also included.

All Boss 429s had the fancy Decor Group interior option, high-back bucket seats, deluxe seat belts, wood-trimmed dash and console treatment and Visibility Group option. Automatic transmission and air conditioning were not available. Two very desirable Boss options were an adjustable rear deck lid spoiler and rear window SportSlats. Horsepower for the Boss 429 was advertised as 375, although real ratings were rumored to be much higher.

At least two contemporary road tests were published on Boss 429 Mustangs. *Car Life* (July 1969) gave the 0-to-60 mph time as 7.1 seconds and the quarter-mile numbers of 14.09 seconds at 102.85 mph. *High Performance Cars* (September 1969) did not print a 0-to-60 mph time but pegged quarter-mile performance at 13.34 seconds at 107.5 mph. Both cars had the four-speed, of course, and both also ran a 3.91:1 rear axle.

Model Number	Body/Style Number	Body Type & Seating	Factory Price	Shipping Weight	Production Total
MUSTANG BOSS 429 — SERIES 02 — V-8					
02	63	2d FSBK-6P	$3,826	3,250 lbs.	859

ENGINE

BASE V-8: Overhead valve. Cast-iron block. Displacement: 429 cid. Bore and stroke: 4.36 x 3.59 inches. Compression ratio: 11.30:1. Brake hp: 375 at 5600 rpm. Torque: 450 at 3400 rpm. Five main bearings. Solid or hydraulic valve lifters. Carburetor: Holley four-barrel. Dual exhaust. Code Z.

OPTIONS

Optional axle ratio ($6.53). Heavy-duty battery ($8.43). Front bumper guards ($12.95). Electric clock ($15.59, but standard with Interior Decor group). Center console ($53.82). Limited-slip differential ($41.60). Traction-Lok differential ($63.51). Boss 429 V-8 includes black hood, black headlight casting, black rear deck lid, black lower back panel, four F60-15 belted black sidewall tires with raised white lettering, 15 x 7 five-bolt Magnum 500 styled wheels with Argent Silver painted finish, collapsible spare, C-stripes, dual exhausts, quick-ratio 16:1 steering, special handling suspension, staggered rear shocks, special cooling package, 3.50:1 non-locking rear axle, electronic rpm limiter, functional front spoiler shipped knocked-down and 45-amp battery, for Sportsroof ($833.15 and requires power disc brakes and wide-ratio four-speed transmission). Extra-cooling package for V-8s ($12.95). Complete tinted glass ($38.86). Adjustable front seat headrests ($17.00 and mandatory after January 1, 1969). Color-keyed dual racing-style mirrors, left-hand remote-control right-hand manual ($19.48). Rocker panel molding ($12.95, but standard with exterior decor group). Power disc brakes ($64.77 and required). Power steering ($94.95). Power ventilation ($40.02). Push-button AM radio ($61.40). AM/FM stereo radio ($181.39). Stereosonic tape system ($133.84 and AM radio required). Rear seat speaker ($12.95). High-back bucket seats ($84.25). Sport Deck rear seat ($97.21). Full-width front seat with armrest ($32.44). Tilt-away steering wheel ($66.14). Deluxe Rim-Blow steering wheel ($35.70, but standard with interior decor group). Tachometer and trip odometer ($54.45). Wide-ratio four-speed manual transmission ($204.64). FR70-14 Wide-Oval white sidewall radial tires ($89.11). Interior Decor group ($88.15). Deluxe interior Decor group ($120.48). Other options added on May 1, 1969 included the following: Functional and adjustable rear spoiler ($19.48 for Boss only). Sport slats with functional rear window louvers, dual racing-style outside mirror required ($128.28 for Boss only). Chrome Magnum 500 styled wheels for Boss only ($77.73).

1969 SHELBY MUSTANG GT-350

JERRY HEASLEY

1969 Shelby Mustang GT-350

The '69 Shelby's cosmetic camouflage relied on the extensive use of fiberglass. The use of this material for fender, hood, and rear cap panels allowed Shelby designers to make the GT-350 three inches longer than the factory-stretched Mustang. The Shelby hood had five recessed NASA-type hood scoops, The leading edge was trimmed with a chrome strip that curved around and down to meet the unique Shelby bumper. A chrome strip formed a wide rectangle as it ran around the outside of the flat-black grille. Lucas driving lights that added a degree of nighttime safety were attached to the underside of the bumper. The Shelby side stripes in the middle of the body were larger and ran the entire length of the car. The rear brakes were cooled through a scoop mounted just ahead of the wheel well. On convertibles it was in line with the body stripe, on fastbacks it sat just behind the door handle. A set of 1965 T-Bird sequential tail lights further removed the cars from their Mustang roots. Directly between the two tail light lenses sat a spring-mounted frame that displayed the license plate and concealed the fuel filler cap. A pair of rectangular exhaust tips, separated from the fuel filler only by the width of the rear bumper, were part of a fire-hazard recall later in the year. Early in the year, Blue, Green, Yellow and Orange "Grabber" colors and Competition Orange were added to Black Jade, Acapulco Blue, Gulfstream Aqua, Pastel Gray, Candy Apple Red and Royal Maroon. Interiors came in Black, White and Red (less than 80) with high-back bucket seats, a vinyl-covered "Rim Blow" steering wheel and a center console appearing as part of the deluxe Mustang equipment. The door panels and dashboard had many fake wood inserts.

The '69 Shelby used heavy-duty Mustang components straight from the Ford factory. No longer was the Shelby Mustang a car that could be ordered as a Plain-Jane racing car. Instead of stamped steel wheels, Shelby buyers got 15 x 7-inch five-spoke rims shod with Goodyear E-70 x 15 wide oval tires (F-60 x 15 tires were optional).

Some Shelbys wound up with Boss 302 "Magnum 500" wheels when a defect in the stock rim forced a recall. Every GT-350 built in 1969 received Ford's new 351-cid/290-hp Windsor V-8 with a 470-cfm Autolite four-barrel carburetor. It came attached to Ford's four-speed manual transmission. Optional gearboxes included a close-ratio four-speed manual and the FMX automatic. A limited number of GT-350H editions were made for Hertz Rent-A-Car Company.

The '69 Shelby-Mustang GT-350 with the 351-cid V-8 and 2.90:1 gearing did 0-to-60 mph in 8 seconds flat and the quarter-mile in 15.59 seconds with an 89.09-mph terminal speed.

Model Number	Body/Style Number	Body Type & Seating	Factory Price	Shipping Weight	Production Total
SHELBY MUSTANG GT-350 — SERIES S — V-8					
02	63( )	2d FSBK-6P	$4,434	—	935
03	76( )	2d Conv-6P	4,753 lbs.	—	404
SHELBY MUSTANG GT-350H — SERIES S — V-8					
02	63( )	2d FSBK-6P	$4,434	—	152

NOTE 1: 789 of the cars originally built as 1969s were sold as 1970 Shelbys. No body style breakout available.

ENGINE

BASE V-8: Overhead valve. Cast-iron block. Displacement: 351 cid. Bore and stroke: 4.00 x 3.50 inches. Compression ratio: 10.70:1. Brake hp: 290. Hydraulic valve lifters. Carburetor: Ford four-barrel. Dual exhausts. Code M.

OPTIONS

Power ventilation. AM radio. AM/FM stereo. Stereo tape player (requires AM radio). Folding rear seat (Sportsroof only). Automatic transmission. Tilt-away steering wheel. Tinted glass. Drag pack. Extra-heavy-duty suspension package including F70-15 Goodyear tires.

1969 SHELBY MUSTANG GT-500

JERRY HEASLEY

1969 Shelby Mustang GT-500

1969 was the last year for the first generation of the Shelby Mustangs, although some of the 1969s were held over and sold as 1970 models. A total of 3,153 cars were built for the model year, with some sources indicating that 789 were sold as 1970 models. Regardless, the last GT-500s were still awesome cars and remain beloved collector cars today.

Staggered shocks were standard on the 1969 GT-500. It retained the fire-breathing 428-cid Cobra Jet V-8. A close-ratio four-speed was standard, with the C-6 back as an optional automatic. Sales were brisk with more GT-500s going to new owners than GT-350s.

A GT-500 with 3.91:1 gearing did 0-to-60 mph in 5.5 seconds and the quarter-mile in 13.9 seconds with a 103.32 mph terminal speed.

Model Number	Body/Style Number	Body Type & Seating	Factory Price	Shipping Weight	Production Total
SHELBY MUSTANG GT-500 — SERIES S — V-8					
02	63( )	2d FSBK-6P	$4,709	—	1,534
03	76( )	2d Conv-6P	$5,027	—	335

NOTE 1: 789 of the cars originally built as 1969s were sold as 1970 Shelbys. No body style breakout available.

ENGINE

BASE V-8: Overhead valve. Cast-iron block. Displacement: 428 cid. Bore and stroke: 4.13 x 3.98 inches. Compression ratio: 10.50:1. Brake hp: 335 at 5400 rpm. Torque: 420 at 3200 rpm. Hydraulic valve lifters. Carburetor: Single Holley four-barrel.

OPTIONS

Power ventilation. AM radio. AM/FM stereo. Stereo tape player (requires AM radio). Folding rear seat (Sportsroof only). Automatic transmission. Tilt-away steering wheel. Tinted glass. Drag pack. Extra-heavy-duty suspension package including F70-15 Goodyear tires.

1970 MUSTANG 428CJ/428SCJ

FORD

JERRY HEASLEY

1970 Mustang Mach 1 Super Cobra Jet

In Mustang enthusiast circles, the 428 CJ/428 SCJ Mustang is legendary for grabbing the Stock Eliminator title at the 1970 National Hot Rod Association's (NHRA) Winternationals. This was the race of the year for high-performance buffs and the Mustang was the monarch that season. In his book *Fast Mustangs*, marque expert Alex Gabbard observed, "The 428 Cobra Jet engine has been called the fastest running pure stock in the history of man."

The 1970 Mustang had some distinctions to set it apart from the 1969 edition. The biggest change was a return to single headlights up front. The new headlights were located inside a larger new grille opening. Simulated air intakes were seen where the outboard headlights were on the 1969 Mustang models. The 1970 rear end appearance was also slightly restyled. Among the many muscle car options were power front disc brakes, a functional hood scoop, louvered sport slats for the rear window (which were very popular at the time), a Hurst shifter, a tachometer and a Drag Pack racing kit.

While the pre-packaged Boss models were the hit of the enthusiast magazines this season, the 428-cid performance engines were both available in any base Mustang. A 2.32:1

close-ratio four-speed manual gearbox ($205) or a Cruise-O-Matic automatic transmission ($222) was required with Cobra-Jet engines. In addition, on base Mustangs F70-14 whitewall tires were required over E78-14 black sidewall tires when a 428-cid V-8 was ordered.

A Mustang two-door hardtop with the 428-cid/335-hp engine carried just 9.6 lbs. per hp. It could do 0-to-60 mph in 5.5 seconds and cover the quarter-mile in 13.9 seconds according to one road test.

Model Number	Body/Style Number	Body Type & Seating	Factory Price	Shipping Weight	Production Total
MUSTANG — SERIES 01/02/03 — V-8					
01	65	2d HT-6P	$2,822	3,145 lbs.	82,569
02	63	2d FSBK-6P	$2,872	3,145 lbs.	38,421
03	76	2d Conv-6P	$3,126	3,267 lbs.	7,673
MUSTANG GRANDE — SERIES 01/02/03 — V-8					
01	65	2d HT-6P	$3,028	3,190 lbs.	22,182

NOTE 1: Prices estimates include 428 CJ V-8, four-speed transmission and F70-14 tires.
NOTE 2: Weights are estimates including options.
NOTE 3: Production totals are for all Mustang engines, not just 428 CJ/SCJs.
NOTE 4: Fastback production total above does not include Boss 302 or Boss 429 models.
NOTE 5: Ford Motor Company built 13,116 428-cid V-8s for all of its 1970 cars.
NOTE 6: 428 CJ/SCJ V-8s were installed in 3,489 non-Shelby Mustangs.

ENGINES

OPTIONAL V-8: Overhead valve. Cast-iron block. Displacement: 428 cid. Bore and stroke: 4.13 x 3.98 inches. Compression ratio: 10.70:1. Brake hp: 335 at 5200 rpm. Torque: 440 at 3400 rpm. Five main bearings. Hydraulic valve lifters. Carburetor: Holley four-barrel. Dual exhaust. Code Q (Cobra Jet).

OPTIONAL V-8: Overhead valve. Cast-iron block. Displacement: 428 cid. Bore and stroke: 4.13 x 3.98 inches. Compression ratio: 10.70:1. Brake hp: 335 at 5200 rpm. Torque: 440 at 3400 rpm. Five main bearings. Hydraulic valve lifters. Carburetor: Holley four-barrel. Dual exhaust. Code R (Super Cobra Jet).

OPTIONS

Select Aire conditioner, tinted glass recommended ($389.00). Optional axle ratio ($13.00). Drag-Pack with 3.91:1 axle ($155.00). Drag-Pack with 4.30:1 axle ($155.00). Traction-Lok differential ($43.00). Heavy-duty 70-amp battery ($13.00). Heavy-duty 55-amp battery ($13.00). Front bumper guards ($13.00). Electric clock, round or rectangular ($16.00, but standard in Grande

hardtop). Center console, bucket seats required ($54.00). Convenience group for Grande ($32.00). Convenience group for base Mustangs ($45.00). Decor group ($78.00). Decor group for base Mustang convertible ($97.00). Evaporative emissions control system ($37.00). 428-cid/335-hp non-Ram-Air V-8, requires close-ratio four-speed manual or Cruise-O-Matic transmission ($356.00 for Mustangs other than Mach 1). 428-cid/335-hp non-Ram-Air V-8, requires close-ratio four-speed manual or Cruise-O-Matic transmission ($421.00 for Mustangs other than Mach 1). Extra-cooling package for V-8s ($13.00). Complete tinted glass ($32.00). Heater and froster delete ($17 credit). Rocker panel molding for Mustangs without décor group ($16). Color-keyed dual racing-style mirrors, left-hand remote-control right-hand manual ($26.00). Power steering ($94.95). Power front disc brakes ($65.00). Push-button AM radio ($61.00). AM/FM stereo radio ($214.00). Stereosonic tape system ($134.00). Vinyl roof on base hardtop ($84.00). Vinyl roof on Grande hardtop ($26.00). Rear sport deck on Sportsroof model ($97.00). Rear deck lid spoiler on Sportsroof ($20.00). Sport slats "venetian blind" rear window treatment on Sportsroof ($65.00). Quick-Ratio power steering ($16). Deluxe Rim-Blow steering wheel ($39.00). Tilt steering, requires power steering and automatic transmission ($45.00). Competition suspension (standard with 428 CJ/SCJ). 8,000-rpm tachometer and trip odometer ($54.00). Select Shift Cruise-O-Matic transmission ($222). Four-speed manual transmission with Hurst shifter ($205.00). Trim rings with hubcaps ($26.00 but no charge on Grande hardtop). Standard type wheel covers ($26.00, but not available on Grande hardtop). Wire wheel covers on base Mustang ($79.00). Wire wheel covers on Grande ($53.00). Argent Silver styled wheels on base Mustangs ($58.00 extra). Argent Silver styled wheels on Grande hardtop ($32.00 extra). Magnum 500 chrome styled wheels on base Mustangs ($129.00 extra). Intermittent windshield wipers ($26.00). Five F70-14 raised white letter tires over F70-14 white sidewall ($13.00). Space Saver spare ($7.00 extra).

1970 MUSTANG BOSS 302

JERRY HEASLEY

1970 Mustang Boss 302

The Boss 302 made a return appearance for 1970 after making big waves with its debut in '69. Its standard features included vinyl-upholstered bucket seats, a four-speed manual gearbox, power front disc brakes, dual color-keyed racing-style outside rearview mirrors, a Space-Saver spare tire, quick-ratio steering, a competition suspension system, a functional front spoiler, floor carpeting, a Boss 302-cid four-barrel V-8 and four F60-15 glass-belted tires with raised white letters. The Boss 302 package was offered only on the Sportsroof body style.

Four of the most visible add-ads associated with the cars — rear window slats, Magnum 500 wheels, shaker hood scoop and rear spoiler — are often mistakenly believed to be standard items. They were, in fact, extra-cost options.

A pair of 1970 Boss 302s earned contemporary road test exposure. *Car Life* (September 1969) reported 6.5 seconds for 0-to-60 mph and 14.85 seconds at 96.15 mph for the quarter-miles run. *Motor Trend (*April 1970), tested a virtually identical car and reported 8.1 seconds for 0-to-60 mph and 15.8 seconds at 90 mph for the drag strip run.

ENGINE
BASE V-8: Overhead valve. Cast-iron block. Displacement: 302 cid. Bore and stroke: 4.00 x 3.00 inches. Compression ratio: 10.50:1. Brake hp: 290 at 5000 rpm. Torque: 290 at 4300 rpm. Five main bearings. Solid valve lifters. Carburetor: Holley 780-cfm four-barrel. Dual exhaust. Dual-plane aluminum intake manifold. Code G.

OPTIONS
Optional axle ratio ($13.00). Drag-Pack with 3.91:1 axle ($155.00). Drag-Pack with 4.30:1 axle ($155.00). Traction-Lok differential ($43.00). Heavy-duty 70-amp battery ($13.00). Heavy-duty 55-amp battery ($13.00). Front bumper guards ($13.00). Electric clock, round or rectangular ($16.00). Center console, bucket seats required ($54.00). Convenience group for Boss 302 including trunk light, glove box light, parking brake light, headlights-on warning buzzer, dash panel courtesy light in hardtop, automatic seat back latch and left-hand remote-control mirror ($32.00). Decor group for Boss 302 includes knitted vinyl or cloth-and-vinyl décor seats, wood-grained dash panel applique, deluxe two-spoke steering wheel, dual color-keyed racing mirrors, rocker panel moldings and wheel lip moldings ($78.00). Evaporative emissions control system ($37.00). 302-cid/290-hop Boss four-barrel V-8 (included in model option). Complete tinted glass ($32.00). Heater and defroster delete ($17 credit). Shaker hood scoop ($65.00). Rocker panel molding for Mustangs without Decor group ($16). Power steering ($94.95). Push-button AM radio ($61.00). AM/FM stereo radio ($214.00). Stereosonic tape system ($134.00). Paint on shaker hood scoop ($13.00). Rear sport deck on Sportsroof model ($97.00). Rear deck lid spoiler on Boss 302 ($20.00). Sport slats "venetian blind" rear window treatment ($65.00). Quick-Ratio power steering ($16). Deluxe Rim-Blow steering wheel ($39.00). Tilt steering, requires power steering and automatic transmission ($45.00). 8,000-rpm tachometer and trip odometer ($54.00). Select Shift Cruise-O-Matic transmission ($201). Trim rings with hub caps ($26.00). Standard type wheel covers ($26.00). Wire wheel covers ($79.00). Argent Silver styled wheels ($58.00 extra). Argent Silver styled wheels ($32.00 extra). Magnum 500 chrome styled wheels ($129.00 extra). Intermittent windshield wipers ($26.00). Five F70-14 raised white letter tires over F70-14 white sidewall ($13.00). Space Saver spare ($7.00 extra).

Model Number	Body/Style Number	Body Type & Seating	Factory Price	Shipping Weight	Production Total
MUSTANG BOSS 302 — SERIES 02 — V-8					
02	63	2d FSBK-6P	$3,720	3,169 lbs.	7,014

FORD

1970 MUSTANG BOSS 429

1970 Mustang Boss 429

JERRY HEASLEY

The Boss 429 also made a return appearance for 1970. Its standard features were about the same as those for the Boss 302, but a close-ratio four-speed or Cruise-O-Matic were required options with the 429 Cobra-Jet V-8 version of the Mustang. All of these cars were actually built in calendar year 1969.

In February of 1970, *Autodriver* magazine tested a 1970 Boss 429 with four-speed and the 3.91:1 rear axle. The car did the quarter-mile in 14.45 seconds at 99 mph.

Model Number	Body/Style Number	Body Type & Seating	Factory Price	Shipping Weight	Production Total
MUSTANG BOSS 429 — SERIES 02 — V-8					
02	63	2d FSBK-6P	$3,826	3,250 lbs.	499

ENGINE

BASE V-8: Overhead valve. Cast-iron block. Displacement: 429 cid. Bore and stroke: 4.36 x 3.59 inches. Compression ratio: 11.30:1. Brake hp: 375 at 5600 rpm. Torque: 450 at 3400 rpm. Five main bearings. Solid or hydraulic valve lifters. Carburetor: Holley four-barrel. Dual exhaust. Code Z.

OPTIONS

Optional axle ratio ($13.00). Drag-Pack with 3.91:1 axle ($155.00). Drag-Pack with 4.30:1 axle ($155.00). Traction-Lok differential ($43.00). Heavy-duty 70-amp. battery ($13.00). Heavy-duty 55-amp. battery ($13.00). Front bumper guards ($13.00). Electric clock, round or rectangular ($16.00). Center console, bucket seats required ($54.00). Convenience group for Boss 429 including trunk light, glove box light, parking brake light, headlights-on warning buzzer, dash panel courtesy light in hardtop, automatic seat back latch and left-hand remote-control mirror ($32.00). Decor group for Boss 429 includes knitted vinyl or cloth-and-vinyl decor seats, wood-grained dash panel applique, deluxe two-spoke steering wheel, dual color-keyed racing mirrors, rocker panel moldings and wheel lip moldings ($78.00). Evaporative emissions control system ($37.00). 429-cid/375-hp Boss four-barrel V-8 (included in model option). Complete tinted glass ($32.00). Heater and defroster delete ($17 credit). Shaker hood scoop ($65.00). Rocker panel molding for Mustangs without décor group ($16). Power steering ($94.95). Push-button AM radio ($61.00). AM/FM stereo radio ($214.00). Stereosonic tape system ($134.00). Paint on shaker hood scoop ($13.00). Rear sport deck on Sportsroof model ($97.00). Rear deck lid spoiler on Boss 429 ($20.00). Sport slats "Venetian blind" rear window treatment ($65.00). Quick-Ratio power steering ($16). Deluxe Rim-Blow steering wheel ($39.00). Tilt steering, requires power steering and automatic transmission ($45.00). 8,000-rpm tachometer and trip odometer ($54.00). Select Shift Cruise-O-Matic transmission ($222). Vinyl seat ($19). Trim rings with hub caps ($26.00). Standard type wheel covers ($26.00). Sports type wheel covers ($32.00). Wire wheel covers ($79.00). Argent Silver styled wheels ($58.00 extra). Magnum 500 chrome styled wheels ($129.00 extra). Intermittent windshield wipers ($26.00). Five F70-14 raised white letter tires over F70-14 white sidewall ($13.00). Space Saver spare ($7,00 extra).

1970 MUSTANG MACH 1

The 1970 Mach 1 featured the new year's front end styling and had its tail lights recessed in a flat panel with honeycomb trim between them. Ribbed aluminum rocker panel moldings with big Mach 1 call-outs and a cleaner upper rear quarter treatment without simulated air scoops at the end of the main feature line were seen. A black-striped hood with a standard fake scoop replaced the completely matte-black hood. New twist-in hood pins held the hood down. You could also get a shaker hood scoop on Mach 1's with the standard 351-cid V-8. A redesigned steering wheel was the big interior change. A larger rear stripe, larger rear call-out, mag-type hubcaps, wide 14 x 7-inch wheels and bright oval exhaust tips were also new. Black-painted styled wheels were a no-cost option.

Motor Trend tested a 1970 Mustang Mach 1 with the 351-cid four-barrel V-8. With automatic transmission and a 3.00:1 axle the car turned 0-to-60 mph in 8.2 seconds and did the quarter-mile in 16 seconds at 86.2 mph.

PHIL KUNZ

1970 Mustang Mach 1

Model Number	Body/Style Number	Body Type & Seating	Factory Price	Shipping Weight	Production Total
MUSTANG MACH 1 — SERIES 02 — V-8 (351-2V)					
02	63	2d FSBK-6P	$3,271	3,240 lbs.	Note 3
MUSTANG MACH 1 — SERIES 02 — V-8 (351-4V)					
02	63	2d FSBK-6P	$3,364	—	Note 3
MUSTANG MACH 1 — SERIES 02 — V-8 (428 CJ)					
02	63	2d FSBK-6P	$3,787	—	Note 3
MUSTANG MACH 1 — SERIES 02 — V-8 (428 SCJ)					
02	63	2d FSBK-6P	$3,852	—	Note 3

NOTE 1: Calculated prices include engine options and base mandatory options.

NOTE 2: Weights are estimates.

NOTE 3: 40,970 Mach 1s were built; no Mach 1 engine breakouts are available.

NOTE 4: 428 CJ/SCJ V-8s were installed in 3,489 non-Shelby Mustangs.

ENGINES

BASE V-8: Overhead valve. Cast-iron block. Displacement: 351 cid. Bore and stroke: 4.00 x 3.50 inches. Compression ratio: 9.50:1. Brake hp: 250 at 4600 rpm. Torque: 355 at 2600 rpm. Five main bearings. Hydraulic valve lifters. Carburetor: Motorcraft two-barrel. Serial number code H.

OPTIONAL V-8: Overhead valve. Cast-iron block. Displacement: 351 cid. Bore and stroke: 4.00 x 3.50 inches. Compression ratio: 11.0:1. Brake hp: 300 at 5400 rpm. Torque: 380 at 3400 rpm. Five main bearings. Hydraulic valve lifters. Carburetor: Motorcraft four-barrel. Serial number code M.

OPTIONAL V-8: Overhead valve. Cast-iron block. Displacement: 428 cid. Bore and stroke: 4.13 x 3.98 inches. Compression ratio: 10.60:1. Brake hp: 335 at 5200 rpm. Torque: 440 at 3400 rpm. Five main bearings. Hydraulic valve lifters. Carburetor: Holley four-barrel. Dual exhaust. Code Q (Cobra Jet).

OPTIONAL V-8: Overhead valve. Cast-iron block. Displacement: 428 cid. Bore and stroke: 4.13 x 3.98 inches. Compression ratio: 10.60:1. Brake hp: 335 at 5200 rpm. Torque: 440 at 3400 rpm. Five main bearings. Hydraulic valve lifters. Carburetor: Holley four-barrel. Dual exhaust. Code R (Super Cobra Jet).

OPTIONS

Selectaire conditioner ($380.00) Optional axle ratio ($13.00). Drag-Pack with 3.91:1 axle ($155.00). Drag-Pack with 4.30:1 axle ($155.00). Traction-Lok differential ($43.00). Heavy-duty 70-amp battery ($13.00). Heavy-duty 55-amp. battery ($13.00). Front bumper guards ($13.00). Electric clock, round or rectangular ($16.00). Center console, bucket seats required (standard in Mach 1). Convenience group for Mach 1 including trunk light, glove box light, parking brake light, headlights-on warning buzzer, dash panel courtesy light in hardtop, automatic seat back latch and left-hand remote-control mirror ($32.00). Decor group for Mach 1 includes knitted vinyl or cloth-and-vinyl décor seats, wood-grained dash panel applique, deluxe two-spoke steering wheel, dual color-keyed racing mirrors, rocker panel moldings and wheel lip moldings ($78.00). Evaporative emissions control system ($37.00). 351-cid two-barrel V-8 (standard in Mach 1). 351-cid/300-hp four-barrel V-8 (special price of $48 over cost of base V-8 in Mach 1). 428 CJ V-8 (special price of $311 over base V-8 in Mach 1). 428 SCJ V-8 (special price of $376 over base V-8 in Mach 1). Complete tinted glass ($32.00). Heater and defroster delete ($17 credit). Shaker hood scoop with 351-cid V-8 ($65.00). Rocker panel molding for Mustangs without décor group ($16). Power front disc brakes ($65.00). Power steering ($94.95). Push-button AM radio ($61.00). AM/FM stereo radio ($214.00). Stereosonic tape system ($134.00). Paint on shaker hood scoop ($13.00). Rear sport deck on Sportsroof model ($97.00). Rear deck lid spoiler ($20.00). Sport slats "Venetian blind" rear window treatment ($65.00). Quick-Ratio power steering ($16). Deluxe Rim-Blow steering wheel (standard on Mach 1). Tilt steering, requires power steering and automatic transmission ($45.00). 8,000-rpm tachometer and trip odometer ($54.00). Competition suspension (standard for Mach 1). Select Shift Cruise-O-Matic transmission with 351-cid V-8 ($201). Select Shift Cruise-O-Matic transmission with 428-cid V-8 ($222). Four-speed manual transmission with Hurst shifter for cars with 351-cid V-8s ($205.00). Four-speed manual transmission with Hurst shifter for cars with 428 CJ/SCJ V-8s ($205.00). Vinyl seat ($19). Trim rings with hub caps (no charge for Mach 1). Standard type wheel covers ($26.00). Sports type wheel covers ($58.00). Wire wheel covers ($79.00). Argent Silver styled wheels (no charge for Mach 1). Magnum 500 chrome styled wheels ($129.00 extra). Intermittent windshield wipers ($26.00). Five F70-14 raised white letter tires over F70-14 white sidewall ($13.00). Space Saver spare ($7.00 extra).

FORD

1970 SHELBY-MUSTANG GT-350

In the fall of 1969, Carroll Shelby convinced Ford to end the Shelby GT program. Shelby could see that the American auto industry and federal government were tightening the screws on performance cars and that there would soon be no market for the type of vehicles he wanted to produce. Also, Ford was mass-producing cars that competed directly with the GT-350 and GT-500, such as the Mach 1, Boss 302, and Boss 429.

With several hundred cars still in the pipeline, Shelby agreed to update 1969 leftovers into 1970 models with new vehicle identification numbers, a set of black hood stripes, a chin spoiler, and a mandatory emissions control unit. The hands-on work of converting from one year to the next was handled directly by the factory, under the watchful eyes of representatives from the Federal Bureau of Investigation.

There is no definitive count of how many 1970 Shelbys were created, but some reports say it was 789 units.

Model Number	Body/Style Number	Body Type & Seating	Factory Price	Shipping Weight	Production Total
SHELBY MUSTANG GT-350 — SERIES S — V-8					
02	63( )	2d FSBK-6P	$4,434	—	Note 1
03	76( )	2d Conv-6P	$4,753	—	Note 1

NOTE 1: 789 of the cars originally built as 1969s were sold as 1970 Shelbys. No body style breakout available.

ENGINE

BASE V-8: Overhead valve. Cast-iron block. Displacement: 351 cid. Bore and stroke: 4.00 x 3.50 inches. Compression ratio: 10.70:1. Brake hp: 290. Hydraulic valve lifters. Carburetor: Ford four-barrel. Dual exhausts. Code M.

OPTIONS

Power ventilation. AM radio. AM/FM stereo. Stereo tape player (requires AM radio). Folding rear seat (Sportsroof only). Automatic transmission. Tilt-away steering wheel. Tinted glass. Drag pack. Extra-heavy-duty suspension package including F70-15 Goodyear tires.

1970 SHELBY-MUSTANG GT-500

JERRY HEASLEY

1970 Shelby Mustang GT-500

A direct carryover of the 1969-spec car retitled as a 1970 model with government approval. Possibly a bit more valuable for being the last of the series and one of just a few hundred made, but virtually the same cars as a '69 in all respects except VIN.

Model Number	Body/Style Number	Body Type & Seating	Factory Price	Shipping Weight	Production Total
SHELBY MUSTANG GT-500 — SERIES S — V-8					
02	63( )	2d FSBK-6P	$4,709	—	1,534
03	76( )	2d Conv-6P	$5,027	—	335

NOTE 1: 789 of the cars originally built as 1969s were sold as 1970 Shelbys. No body style breakout available.

ENGINE

BASE V-8: Overhead valve. Cast-iron block. Displacement: 428 cid. Bore and stroke: 4.13 x 3.98 inches. Compression ratio: 10.50:1. Brake hp: 335 at 5400 rpm. Torque: 420 at 3200 rpm. Hydraulic valve lifters. Carburetor: Single Holley four-barrel.

OPTIONS

Power ventilation. AM radio. AM/FM stereo. Stereo tape player (requires AM radio). Folding rear seat (Sportsroof only). Automatic transmission. Tilt-away steering wheel. Tinted glass. Drag pack. Extra-heavy-duty suspension package including F70-15 Goodyear tires.

1970 FAIRLANE 500 429 CJ/SCJ

The Fairlane series was completely restyled with a sleeker body shell and more rounded fender contours. The Fairlane 500 became the base mid-sized Ford in 1970. Standard features included chrome windshield and rear window moldings, chrome rain gutter moldings, front and rear door arm rests, a cigarette lighter, nylon carpeting, the Fairlane 500 name in script on the rear fenders above the sidemarker lights, two chrome has marks on the front fenders behind the wheel openings and the Ford name in block letters on the driver's side of the hood and rear panel.

The series included a formal two-door hardtop with some muscle appeal, plus a sedan and a wagon. All models were available with a six-cylinder engine and a small-block 302 was the base V-8. Other options included two-and four-barrel versions of the 351, plus a Thunderbird 429, but the two "429 Cobra" options were the engines that muscle car mavens drooled for. The Cobra-Jet version was officially rated 370 hp. The Super-Cobra-Jet version carried a 375-hp rating. The more expensive version featured Ram Air induction, athough both carried the same torque ratings. These cars would take 7.3 seconds to go 0-to-60 mph and did the quarter-mile in 14.9 seconds at 95.2 mph.

According to some sources, the Boss 429 V-8 was made available briefly in these cars and also put out 375 hp. We should note that there is a bit if conflicting information about the engines used in these cars in various sources and it is hard to sort out some fine details 36 years later. A Drag-Pack option was mandatory.

Model Number	Body/Style Number	Body Type & Seating	Factory Price	Shipping Weight	Production Total
FAIRLANE 500 — SERIES 29 — V-8					
29	65B	2d HT-6P	$2,750	3,211 lbs.	70,636

NOTE 1: Prices and weights are for Fairlane 500 hardtop with base 302-cid V-8.

NOTE 2: Production is for Fairlane 500 hardtop with all engines; no 429-cid V-8 breakouts are available for 1970.

NOTE 3: Ford Motor Company built 186, 815 of its 429-cid V-8s of all types for all of its cars in 1970.

ENGINES

OPTIONAL V-8: Overhead valve. Cast-iron block. Displacement: 429 cid. Bore and stroke: 4.36 x 3.59 inches. Compression ratio: 11.30:1. Brake hp: 370 at 54200 rpm. Torque: 450 at 3400 rpm. Five main bearings. Hydraulic valve lifters. Carburetor: Holley 700-cfm four-barrel. Dual exhaust. Special heads. High-lift camshaft. High-rise intake manifold. Code C.

OPTIONAL V-8: Overhead valve. Cast-iron block. Displacement: 429 cid. Bore and stroke: 4.36 x 3.59 inches. Compression ratio: 11.30:1. Brake hp: 375 at 5600 rpm. Torque: 450 at 3400 rpm. Five main bearings. Hydraulic valve lifters. Carburetor: Holley 700-cfm four-barrel. Dual exhaust. Special heads. High-lift camshaft. High-rise intake manifold. Code J.

OPTIONS

Selectaire conditioner, tinted glass recommended ($389.00) Optional axle ratio ($13.00). Drag-Pack with 3.91:1 axle ($155.00). Drag-Pack with 4.30:1 axle ($155.00). Traction-Lok differential ($43.00). Heavy-duty 70-amp. battery ($13.00). Deluxe seat belts with warning light ($39.00). Electric clock, round or rectangular ($16.00). Center console, bucket seats required ($54.00). Rear window defogger ($26.00). Evaporative emissions control system ($37.00). 429-cid/370-hp Cobra-Jet V-8 ($356.00). 429-cid/370-hp Super-Cobra-Jet V-8 ($421.00). Complete tinted glass ($36.00). Heater and defroster delete, Hawaii only ($17 credit). Shaker hood scoop (with 351-cid four-barrel V-8 only). Remote-control left-hand outside rearview mirror ($13.00). Body side moldings with color-keyed vinyl insert ($26). Two-tone roof paint ($27.00). Power front disc brakes ($65.00). Four-way power full-width seat ($74.00). Power steering ($105.00). Power side windows ($105.00). AM radio ($61.00). Push-button AM/FM stereo radio ($214.00). Dual rear seat speakers ($26.00). Vinyl roof ($95.00). High-back bucket seats ($133.00). Deluxe Rim-Blow steering wheel ($39.00). Heavy-duty suspension ($23.00). 8,000-rpm tachometer ($49.00 for V-8s and not available with electric clock). Trailer towing package, including power disc brakes, heavy-duty battery, heavy-duty suspension, 70-amp. heavy-duty battery and extra-cooling package ($115.00). Select Shift Cruise-O-Matic transmission with 429-cid V-8 ($222). Four-speed manual transmission with Hurst shifter ($194.00). Knitted vinyl or plaid seat ($32.00). Trim rings with hub caps ($26.00). Standard type wheel covers ($26.00). Deluxe hubcaps ($78.00). Sports type wheel covers ($58.00). Argent Silver styled wheels ($58.00). Magnum 500 chrome styled wheels ($155.00 extra). Intermittent windshield wipers ($26.00). Optional tires replacing standard E78-14 black sidewall belted tires on Fairlane with engines other than 429-cid V-8: E78-14 white sidewall tires ($30.00 extra). F78-14 F-78-14 black sidewall tires ($16.00 extra). F78-14 white sidewall tires ($46.00 extra). F70-14 white sidewall tires ($64.00 extra). F70-14 raised white letter tires ($77.00 extra). G70-14 white sidewall tires ($80.00 extra) G70-14 raised white letter tires ($93.00). Optional tires replacing standard F78-14 black sidewall belted tires on Fairlane with 429-cid V-8: E78-14 white sidewall tires ($30.00 extra). F78-14 F-78-14 black sidewall tires ($16.00 extra). F78-14 white sidewall tires ($46.00 extra). F70-14 white sidewall tires ($48.00 extra). F70-14 raised white letter tires ($61.00 extra). G70-14 white sidewall tires ($64.00 extra) G70-14 raised white letter tires ($77.00).

1970 TORINO GT 429 CJ/SCJ

The Torino was the bottom trim level for the intermediate-size Torino series, which now stood apart from the Fairlane lineup. The Torino line offered five body styles, but only the two-door hardtop and fastback had real muscle-car appeal. The Torino Brougham was the mid-range version of the Torino stressing extra luxury, but still available with big, powerful V-8s. Broughams had bright exterior moldings, hideaway headlights and full wheel covers and a base V-8 was standard. With optional engines the Brougham two-door hardtop might qualify as an upscale muscle car. There was also a four-door hardtop and station wagon which were family cars.

The Torino GT was the sport/performance version of the Torino came only in the sportier fastback and convertible models. The Torino GT convertible had a power top and larger F-70-15 tires of the same type.

A 302-cid engine with a two-barrel carburetor was the base V-8 in both models, but buyers could opt for two- or four-barrel versions of a 351-cid V-8, a Thunderbird 429, the 429 Cobra-Jet or the 429 Super-Cobra-Jet. Some sources say the Boss 429 was also offered for a brief time.

Different models had different weights, but a typical 429 Cobra-Jet Torino required 7.3 seconds to go 0-to-60 mph and did the quarter-mile in 14.9 seconds at 95.2 mph.

FORD

JERRY HEASLEY

1970 Torino GT Super Cobra Jet

Model Number	Body/Style Number	Body Type & Seating	Factory Price	Shipping Weight	Production Total
TORINO– SERIES 30 — V-8					
30	65C	2d HT-6P	$2,812	3,273 lbs.	49,826
34	63C	2d FSBK-6P	$2,899	3,311 lbs.	12,490
TORINO BROUGHAM — SERIES 30 — V-8					
33	65E	2d HT-6P	$3,006	3,293 lbs.	16,911
TORINO GT — SERIES 30 — V-8					
35	63F	2d FSBK-6P	$2,848	3,173 lbs.	17,951
37	76F	2d Conv-6P	$3,212	3,490 lbs.	3,939

NOTE 1: Prices and weights are for Torino/Torino Brougham/Torino GT models with base 302-cid V-8.

NOTE 2: Production is for Torino/Torino Brougham/Torino GT models; no V-8 breakouts are available for the base Torino, but all Broughams and GTs were V-8s.

NOTE 3: Ford built 186,815 of its 429-cid V-8s of all types for all of its cars in 1970.

ENGINES

OPTIONAL V-8: Overhead valve. Cast-iron block. Displacement: 429 cid. Bore and stroke: 4.36 x 3.59 inches. Compression ratio: 11.30:1. Brake hp: 370 at 54200 rpm. Torque: 450 at 3400 rpm. Five main bearings. Hydraulic valve lifters. Carburetor: Holley 700-cfm four-barrel. Dual exhaust. Special heads. High-lift camshaft. High-rise intake manifold. Code C.

OPTIONAL V-8: Overhead valve. Cast-iron block. Displacement: 429 cid. Bore and stroke: 4.36 x 3.59 inches. Compression ratio: 11.30:1. Brake hp: 375 at 5600 rpm. Torque: 450 at 3400 rpm. Five main bearings. Hydraulic valve lifters. Carburetor: Holley 700-cfm four-barrel. Dual exhaust. Special heads. High-lift camshaft. High-rise intake manifold. Code J.

OPTIONS

Selectaire conditioner, tinted glass recommended ($389.00) Optional axle ratio ($13.00). Drag-Pack with 3.91:1 axle ($155.00). Drag-Pack with 4.30:1 axle ($155.00). Traction-Lok differential ($43.00). Heavy-duty 70-amp battery ($13.00). Deluxe seat belts with warning light for Torino two-door hardtop ($39.00). Deluxe seat belts with warning light for Torino models other than two-door hardtop ($15.00). Electric clock, round or rectangular ($16.00). Center console, bucket seats required ($54.00). Rear window defogger ($26.00). Evaporative emissions control system ($37.00). 429-cid/370-hp Cobra-Jet V-8 ($356.00). 429-cid/370-hp Super-Cobra-Jet V-8 ($421.00). Complete tinted glass ($36.00). Hide-away headlights ($53.00, but standard for Brougham hardtop). Laser stripe for Torino GT ($39.00, but not available if car has body mold-

ing). Heater and defroster delete, Hawaii only ($17 credit). Shaker hood scoop (with 351-cid four-barrel V-8 only). Remote-control left-hand outside rearview mirror ($13.00). Body side moldings with color-keyed vinyl insert ($26). Two-tone roof paint ($27.00, but not available for Torino GT). Power front disc brakes ($65.00). Four-way power full-width seat ($74.00). Power steering ($105.00). Power side windows ($105.00). AM radio ($61.00). Push-button AM/FM stereo radio ($214.00). Dual rear seat speakers ($26.00). Vinyl roof ($95.00, but not available for Torino GT). High-back bucket seats ($133.00). Sports slats rear window, racing mirrors required ($65.00). Deluxe Rim-Blow steering wheel ($39.00). Heavy-duty suspension ($23.00). 8,000-rpm tachometer ($49.00 for V-8s and not available with electric clock). Trailer towing package ($115.00). Select Shift Cruise-O-Matic transmission with 429-cid V-8 ($222.00). Four-speed manual transmission with Hurst shifter ($194.00). Blazer stripe seat for Torino GT fastback ($32.00). Blazer stripe seat for Torino two-door hardtops ($52.00). Knitted vinyl or plaid seat ($32.00, except Brougham or GT). Trim rings with hubcaps ($26.00, but no charge for Brougham). Deluxe hubcaps for Torino Brougham or GT ($52.00). Deluxe hubcaps for other Torinos ($78.00). Standard type wheel covers ($26.00). Sports type wheel covers for Torino Brougham and GT ($32.00). Sports type wheel covers for other Torinos ($58.00). Argent Silver styled wheels for Torino Brougham or GT ($32.00). Argent Silver styled wheels for other Torinos ($58.00). Magnum 500 chrome styled wheels for Torino Brougham or GT ($129.00). Magnum 500 chrome styled wheels for other Torinos ($155.00). Intermittent windshield wipers ($26.00). Optional tires replacing standard E78-14 black sidewall belted tires on Torinos, except GT with engines other than 429-cid V-8: E78-14 white sidewall tires ($30.00 extra). F78-14 F-78-14 black sidewall tires ($16.00 extra). F78-14 white sidewall tires ($46.00 extra). F70-14 white sidewall tires ($64.00 extra). F70-14 raised white letter tires ($77.00 extra). G70-14 white sidewall tires ($80.00 extra) G70-14 raised white letter tires ($93.00). Optional tires replacing standard F78-14 black sidewall belted tires on Torinos, except GT with 429-cid V-8: E78-14 white sidewall tires ($30.00 extra). F78-14 F-78-14 black sidewall tires ($16.00 extra). F78-14 white sidewall tires ($46.00 extra). F70-14 white sidewall tires ($48.00 extra). F70-14 raised white letter tires ($61.00 extra). G70-14 white sidewall tires ($64.00 extra) G70-14 raised white letter tires ($77.00). Optional tires replacing standard E70-14 white sidewall belted tires on Torino GT fastback with 429-cid V-8: F70-14 raised white letter ($13.00 extra). F60-14 raised white letter tires ($31.00 extra). G70-14 white sidewall with raised white letter tires ($16.00 extra). G70-14 black sidewall with raised white letter tires ($29.00). Optional tires replacing standard F70-14 white sidewall belted tires on Torino GT convertible with 429-cid V-8: G70-14 black sidewall with raised white letter tires ($13.00).

1970 TORINO COBRA 429/429 CJ/429 SCJ

1970 Torino Cobra

With the Super-Cobra-Jet version of the 429 under its hood, the '70 Torino Cobra was good for 6.4 seconds 0-to-60 and did the quarter-mile in 14.5 seconds at 99 mph. "Maybe this shaped for the wind thing is real," said A.B. Shuman in *Motor Trend*.

Based on the fastback-styled Torino GT Sportsroof model, the Cobra added a four-speed manual gearbox, padded seats, competition suspension, seven-inch wheels with hub caps, a black two-toned hood, hood lock pins, bright exterior moldings, carpeting, courtesy lights, Cobra emblems, F70-15 fiberglass-belted black side wall tires and the 360-hp Thunderbird 429 V-8 as standard equipment. The 370-hp Cobra-Jet and 375-hp Super-Cobra-Jet engines were optional at prices nearly $200 under what they cost to add to other Torino models.

Model Number	Body/Style Number	Body Type & Seating	Factory Price	Shipping Weight	Production Total
TORINO COBRA — SERIES 38 — V-8					
38	63H	2d FSBK-6P	$3,270	3,774 lbs.	7,675

NOTE 1: Prices and weights are for Torino Cobra with Thunderjet 429 V-8.
NOTE 2: Production is for all Torino Cobras.
NOTE 3: Ford Motor Company built 186, 815 of its 429-cid V-8s of all types for all of its cars in 1970.

ENGINES

BASE V-8: Overhead valve. Cast-iron block. Displacement: 429 cid. Bore and stroke: 4.36 x 3.59 inches. Compression ratio: 10.50:1. Brake hp: 360 at 4600 rpm. Torque: 480 at 3400 rpm. Five main bearings. Hydraulic valve lifters. Carburetor: Motorcraft four-barrel. Dual exhaust. Code N.

(NOTE: We have included this engine for the Cobra only because it is the base V-8 for this model.)

OPTIONAL V-8: Overhead valve. Cast-iron block. Displacement: 429 cid. Bore and stroke: 4.36 x 3.59 inches. Compression ratio: 11.30:1. Brake hp: 370 at 54200 rpm. Torque: 450 at 3400 rpm. Five main bearings. Hydraulic valve lifters. Carburetor: Holley 700-cfm four-barrel. Dual exhaust. Special heads. High-lift camshaft. High-rise intake manifold. Code C.

OPTIONAL V-8: Overhead valve. Cast-iron block. Displacement: 429 cid. Bore and stroke: 4.36 x 3.59 inches. Compression ratio: 11.30:1. Brake hp: 370 at 5400 rpm. Torque: 450 at 3400 rpm. Five main bearings. Hydraulic valve lifters. Carburetor: Holley 700-cfm four-barrel. Dual exhaust. Special heads. High-lift camshaft. High-rise intake manifold. Code J.

OPTIONAL V-8 (WITH DRAG PACK): Overhead valve. Cast-iron block. Displacement: 429 cid. Bore and stroke: 4.36 x 3.59 inches. Compression ratio: 11.30:1. Brake hp: 375 at 5600 rpm. Torque: 450 at 3400 rpm. Five main bearings. Solid valve lifters. Carburetor: Holley 780-cfm four-barrel. Dual exhaust. Special heads. High-lift camshaft. High-rise intake manifold. 4-bolt main bearings. Aluminum pistons. Code C.

OPTIONAL V-8 (WITH DRAG PACK): Overhead valve. Cast-iron block. Displacement: 429 cid. Bore and stroke: 4.36 x 3.59 inches. Compression ratio: 11.30:1. Brake hp: 375 at 5600 rpm. Torque: 450 at 3400 rpm. Five main bearings. Solid valve lifters. Carburetor: Holley 780-cfm four-barrel. Dual exhaust. Special heads. High-lift camshaft. High-rise intake manifold. 4-bolt main bearings. Aluminum pistons. Code J.

OPTIONS

Selectaire conditioner, tinted glass recommended ($389.00) Optional axle ratio ($13.00). Drag-Pack with 3.91:1 axle ($155.00). Drag-Pack with 4.30:1 axle ($155.00). Traction-Lok differential ($43.00). Heavy-duty 70-amp battery ($13.00). Deluxe seat belts with warning light ($15.00). Electric clock, round or rectangular ($16.00). Center console, bucket seats required ($54.00). Rear window defogger ($26.00). Evaporative emissions control system ($37.00). 429-cid/370-hp Cobra-Jet V-8 ($164.00). 429-cid/370-hp Super-Cobra-Jet V-8 ($229.00). Complete tinted glass ($36.00). Laser stripe for Torino GT ($39.00, but not available if car has body molding). Heater and defroster delete, Hawaii only ($17 credit). Remote-control left-hand outside rearview mirror ($13.00). Body side moldings with color-keyed vinyl insert ($26). Two-tone roof paint ($27.00, but not available for Torino GT). Power front disc brakes ($65.00). 4-way power full-width seat ($74.00). Power steering ($105.00). Power side windows ($105.00). AM radio ($61.00). Push-button AM/FM stereo radio ($214.00). Dual rear seat speakers

($26.00). High-back bucket seats ($133.00). Deluxe Rim-Blow steering wheel ($39.00). Heavy-duty suspension ($23.00). 8,000-rpm tachometer ($49.00 for V-8s and not available with electric clock). Sports slats rear window, racing mirrors required ($65.00). Trailer towing package, including power disc brakes, heavy-duty battery, heavy-duty suspension, 70-amp heavy-duty battery and extra-cooling package ($115.00). Select Shift Cruise-O-Matic transmission with 429-cid V-8 ($222). Four-speed manual transmission with Hurst shifter ($194.00). Blazer

stripe seat ($32.00). Knitted vinyl or plaid seat ($32.00, except Brougham or GT). Deluxe hubcaps ($52.00). Standard type wheel covers ($26.00). Sports type wheel covers for Torino ($32.00).). Argent Silver styled wheels ($32.00). Magnum 500 chrome styled wheels ($129.00). Optional tires replacing standard F70-14 black sidewall glass-belted tires with raised white letters on Torino Cobra: F60-15 black sidewall with raised white letters ($18.00). G70-14 white sidewall ($3.00). G70-14 black sidewall with raised white letter tires ($16.00).

1971 MUSTANG 429 CJ/429 SCJ

BRAD BOWLING

1971 Mustang Mach 1 SCJ

1971 Mustangs were completely restyled. They were over two inches longer and had a new hood and concealed windshield wipers. The styling left little doubt that the cars were Mustangs, but they were lower, wider and heavier than any previous models. A full-width grille, incorporating the headlights within its opening, was used. The fastback- styled "Sportsroof" was now available dressed in a vinyl top. Sadly, two of the most exotic engines were gone.

The base engines were a 250-cid/145-hp six or a 302-cid/210-hp V-8 with a two-barrel carburetor. However, V-8 options included a 351-cid/240-hp four-barrel V-8, a 351-cid/285-hp four-barrel V-8 with dual exhausts and both the CJ and SCJ Ram-Air versions of the 429-cid V-8, which we are focusing on here. Theoretically, the Cobra V-8s were available in any model, although we cannot confirm that hardtop or convertible versions were actually built. The 429 engine packages also included a competition suspension, a Mach 1-style hood, an 80-amp battery, a 55-amp alternator, dual exhausts, the extra-cooling pack-

age, a bright engine dress-up kit with cast aluminum rocker arm covers and a 3.25:1 non-locking rear axle. The 429 CJ and SCJ V-8s were not available with air conditioning if the car had the Drag Pack or dual Ram-Air induction options. On other cars, you could get A/C, but then you had to add power steering. If the buyer wanted a Drag-Pak option a 3.91:1 or 4.11:1 rear axle was required at extra cost.

Model Number	Body/Style Number	Body Type & Seating	Factory Price	Shipping Weight	Production Total
MUSTANG — SERIES 01/02/03 — V-8					
01	65D	2d HT-6P	$3,006	3,026 lbs.	65,696
02	63D	2d FSBK-6P	$3,068	2,993 lbs.	23,956
03	63R	2d Conv-6P	$3,322	3,145 lbs.	6,121

NOTE 1: Prices and weights for base V-8 model.

NOTE 2: Production includes all engines; a total of 1,250 429 CJ and 429 SCJ V-8s were installed in 1971 Mustangs.

ENGINES

OPTIONAL V-8: Overhead valve. Cast-iron block. Displacement: 429 cid. Bore and stroke: 4.36 x 3.59 inches. Compression ratio: 11.30:1. Brake hp: 370 at 54200 rpm. Torque: 450 at 3400 rpm. Five main bearings. Hydraulic valve lifters. Carburetor: Holley 700-cfm four-barrel. Dual exhaust. Special heads. High-lift camshaft. High-rise intake manifold. Code C.

OPTIONAL V-8: Overhead valve. Cast-iron block. Displacement: 429 cid. Bore and stroke: 4.36 x 3.59 inches. Compression ratio: 11.30:1. Brake hp: 375 at 5600 rpm. Torque: 450 at 3400 rpm. Five main bearings. Solid valve lifters. Carburetor: Holley 780-cfm four-barrel. Dual exhaust. Special heads. High-lift camshaft. High-rise intake manifold. Four-bolt main bearings. Aluminum pistons. Code J.

OPTIONS

Selectaire conditioner, includes 55-amp alternator and extra-cooling package and requires power steering ($412, but not available on cars with both 429 CJ/ SCJ V-8 and Drag Pack option). Optional axle ratio ($13.00). Drag Pak, includes the following 429-four-barrel modifications: four-bolt mains, forged pistons, cap screw connecting rods and modified crankshaft, flywheel and dampener ($155.00). Traction-Lok differential ($48.00), but not available when 3.91:1 or 4.11:1 axle is combined with 429-cid V-8). Heavy-duty 70-amp. battery ($16.00). Deluxe seat belts with warning light ($17.00). Front and rear bumper guards (not available on Mach 1). Center console with electric clock with Sports interior ($76.00). Electric rear window defogger, except convertibles ($48.00). NOX emissions system, required in California (no charge). 429-cid/370-hp 429 CJ V-8 ($372.00). 429-cid/375-hp 429 SCJ Ram-Air V-8 ($436.00). Extra-cooling package (standard with 429-cid V-8s). Complete tinted glass, except convertible ($40.00). Complete tinted glass, except convertible ($15.00). Dual racing-style outside rearview mirrors ($26.00). Body side protection molding package

($34.00). Power disc brakes ($70.00 and required with 429 V-8s). Power side windows ($127.00). Power steering ($115.00 and includes variable ratio on models with competition suspension). Push-button AM radio ($66.00). AM/FM stereo radio. Including two front-door-mounted speakers ($214.00). Rear sport deck on Sportsroof model, includes Spacer-Saver spare tire, folding rear seat and load floor ($97.00). Rear deck lid spoiler ($32.00). Deluxe Rim-Blow steering wheel ($39.00). Tilt steering, requires power steering ($45.00). Stereophonic tape system ($134.00). Competition suspension includes extra-heavy-duty front and rear springs, front and rear shock absorbers, front stabilizer bar and rear stabilizer bar (standard with 429-cid V-8). Body side tape stripes ($26.00). Trim rings and hubcaps ($35.00). SelectShift Cruise-O-Matic transmission with 429-cid V-8s ($238.00). Four-speed manual transmission with Hurst shifter in cars with 429-cid V-8 ($217.00). Deluxe wheel covers ($78.00). Sports type wheel covers ($58.00). Magnum 500 chrome styled wheels ($155.00). Intermittent windshield wipers ($26.00). Decor group includes choice of knitted vinyl or cloth-and-vinyl high-back bucket seats, rear ashtray, deluxe right-and left-hand Black instrument panel appliqués and a deluxe two-spoke steering wheel for hardtop or fastback ($78.00). Decor group includes knitted vinyl high-back bucket seats, rear ashtray, deluxe right- and left-hand Black instrument panel appliques, a deluxe two-spoke steering wheel and molded door trim panels for convertible ($97.00). Instrumentation group including tachometer, trip odometer and triple instrument pod gauges ($79.00). Protection package ($34.00). Protection package for Mustangs without front and rear bumper guards ($45.00). Sports interior option for fastback only ($130.00). Five F60-15 raised white letter tires over E78-14 base tires for Mustangs with 429-cid V0-8 ($99.00).

1971 MUSTANG BOSS 351

JERRY HEASLEY

1971 Mustang Boss 351

The Boss 302 and Boss 429 power plants bit the dust in 1971. Although rumors persist that five cars were assembled with the "Boss 429," they are unconfirmed. There was a new Boss 351 Mustang that provided a more refined package, with a better weight distribution layout than the front-heavy Boss 429.

The Boss 351 had more extras than regular Mustangs. In addition to the basic equipment, this model featured a func-

tional NASA hood scoop, a Black or Argent Silver painted hood, hood lock pins, Ram-Air engine call-outs, color-keyed racing-style outside rearview mirrors (left remote-controlled), a unique grille with Sportslamps, hubcaps with trim rings, body side tape stripes in Black or Argent Silver, color-keyed hood and front fender moldings, Boss 351 call-outs, a Space-Saver spare tire, a competition suspension with staggered rear shocks, a 3.91:1 rear axle gear ratio with Traction-Lok differential, an electronic rpm limiter, a functional front spoiler (finished in black and shipped "knocked-down"), an 80-ampere battery, the Instrumentation Group, F60-15 raised-white-letter tires and a High-Output 351-cid/330-hp V-8 with four-barrel carburetion. When you were "working for the man" back in 1971, a car like this could make you look forward to the weekend — especially your Sunday afternoon trip to the drag strip. *Road Test* magazine observed in March 1971 that the Boss 351 was the "Sophisticated Mustang." The magazine said, "The '71 Boss is 40 hp bossier than last year's 302 (and) still gives fine handling coupled to straightaway performance."

The 351 "Cleveland" V-8 featured four-bolt main bearings, solid valve lifters and a four-barrel carburetor. The 1971 models were the last for Ford high-compression engines and the last for gross advertised horsepower numbers, which were 330 hp for the Boss 351. Other mechanical features included a four-speed "top-loader" manual transmission with a Hurst gear shifter and dual exhausts with non-exposed tips. Only about 1,800 Boss 351s were made, which adds up to rarity today. There was no 1972 Boss Mustang of any kind, but by playing with the options list, you could come close to "building" one. The last year for the "big" Mustang was 1973.

With the base 330-hp V-8, the Boss 351 did 0-to-60 mph in 5.9 seconds and the quarter-mile in 13.98 seconds at 104 mph according to one contemporary road test. But *Car & Driver*, in February 1971, tested the 370-hp version and published the 0-to-60 time as 5.8 seconds and the quarter-mile performance as 14.1 seconds at 100.6 mph.

Model Number	Body/Style Number	Body Type & Seating	Factory Price	Shipping Weight	Production Total
MUSTANG BOSS 351 — SERIES 02 — V-8					
02	63R	2d FSBK-6P	$4,124	3,281 lbs.	1,800

ENGINE

BASE V-8: Overhead valve. Cast-iron block. Displacement: 351 cid. Bore and stroke: 4.00 x 3.50 inches. Compression ratio: 11.7:1. Brake hp: 330 at 5400 rpm. Torque: 370 at 4000 rpm. Five main bearings. Hydraulic valve lifters. Carburetor: Holley four-barrel. Cooling system capacity: (Mid-size/Mustang) 14.6 with heater; (Full-size) 16.5 with heater. Serial number code R.

OPTIONS

Selectaire conditioner (not available on Boss 351). Optional axle ratio ($13.00). Traction-Lok differential (standard on Boss 351). Heavy-duty 70-amp. battery (standard with 351-cid V-8s). Deluxe seat belts with warning light ($17.00). Front and rear bumper guards ($31.00). Center console with electric clock without Sports interior ($76.00). Center console with electric clock with Sports interior ($60.00). Electric rear window defogger ($48.00). NOX emissions system, required in California (no charge). Extra-cooling package (not available with Boss). Complete tinted glass ($40.00). NASA style hood scoops (no charge with 351-cid V-8). Dual racing-style outside rearview mirrors (standard on Boss 351). Power disc brakes (standard with Boss 351). Power side windows ($127.00). Power steering ($115.00 and includes variable ratio on models with competition suspension such as Boss 351). Push-button AM radio ($66.00). AM/FM stereo radio. Including two front-door-mounted speakers ($214.00). Rear sport deck on Sportsroof model, includes Spacer-Saver spare tire, folding rear seat and load floor ($97.00). Rear deck lid spoiler ($32.00). Deluxe Rim-Blow steering wheel ($39.00). Tilt steering, requires power steering ($45.00). Stereophonic tape system ($134.00). Body side tape stripes (standard on Boss 351). Competition suspension includes extra-heavy-duty front and rear springs, front and rear shock absorbers, front stabilizer bar and rear stabilizer bar (standard on Boss 351, but requires F60-15 black sidewall tires with raised white letters). SelectShift Cruise-O-Matic transmission ($217.00). Four-speed manual transmission with Hurst shifter (standard in Boss 351). Sports type wheel covers ($23.00). Magnum 500 chrome styled wheels ($120.00 extra). Intermittent windshield wipers ($26.00). Decor group includes choice of knitted vinyl or cloth-and-vinyl high-back bucket seats, rear ashtray, deluxe right- and left-hand Black instrument panel appliques, a deluxe two-spoke steering wheel and molded door trim panels ($97.00). Dual Ram-Air induction includes functional NASA type hood scoop with Black or Argent two-tone paint, hood lock pins and Ram-Air decals ($65.00). Sports interior ($88.00). Instrumentation group (standard on Boss 351). Five F70-14 raised white letter tires over F70-14 white sidewall ($13.00).

1971 MUSTANG MACH 1 429 CJ/429 SCJ

You may not be able to break Mach 1 in a Mustang Mach 1, but it's the kind of car that looks — and feels — like it could do just that if you pushed it real hard. "For those interested in owning a sporty car which reflects up-to-the-minute design, Mustang (Mach 1), an all-around vehicle without a significant flaw, can't be a bad choice," opined *Road Test* magazine in September 1970. The Mach I had all of the basic Mustang equipment, plus a color-keyed spoiler, hood moldings, fender moldings, racing mirrors, a unique grille with Sportlamps, a competition suspension, trim rings and hubcaps, high-back bucket seats, a honeycomb texture back panel appliqué, a pop-open gas cap, a deck lid paint stripe, Black or Argent Silver finish on lower body sides (with bright molding at upper edge), E70-14 whitewalls and the two-barrel 302-cid V-8. A NASA-styled hood scoop treatment was a no-cost option.

Available for the last time was a 429-cid big-block engine, which came in Cobra-Jet Ram-Air and Super-Cobra-Jet Ram-Air versions. Ford put together 1,255 of the CJ-R equipped Mach 1's and 610 of the SCJ-Rs. Basically a de-stroked Thunderbird/Lincoln 460-cid V-8, the 429 had a wedge-head-shaped combustion chamber derived from up-to-date performance technology. The CJ-R version utilized large valves, a hydraulic camshaft, reworked porting and a 715-cfm Quadrajet carburetor (sourced from General Motors). A Ram Air induction system was included. Advertised horsepower for the 429 CJ-R was 370 at 5400 rpm. The 429 SCJ-R had a 780-cfm Holley carburetor and was rated at 475 hp. Both Cobra Jet engines had 11.3:1 compression and produced 450 lbs.-ft. of torque at 3400 rpm. The SCJ-R had a bit more camshaft duration (200/300 degree versus 282/296 degrees).

JERRY HEASLEY

1971 Mustang Mach 1 Super Cobra Jet

A Drag Pack option with either a 3.91:1 Traction-Lok differential or a 4.11:1 Detroit Locker axle was a required option with the 429-cid V-8s. This option also included an oil cooler for when things really got hot at the drag strip. Its other performance features included four-bolt main bearing caps, cap-screw connecting rods, drop-forged pistons, a modified crankshaft, a modified flywheel and a modified damper.

Road Test magazine (September 1970) said, "For those interested in owning such a sporty car which reflects up-to-the-minute design, Mustang Mach 1, an all-around solid vehicle without a significant flaw, can't be a bad choice." The magazine's car had the SCJ Ram-Air V-8 with 375 hp and it did 0-to-60 in 7.1 seconds. The quarter-mile took 14.09 seconds at 102.85 mph.

Model Number	Body/Style Number	Body Type & Seating	Factory Price	Shipping Weight	Production Total
MUSTANG MACH 1 — SERIES 02 — V-8					
02	63R	2d FSBK-6P	$3,268	3,220 lbs.	36,449

NOTE 1: Prices and weights for base model.
NOTE 2: Production includes all engines; a total of 1,250 429 CJ and 429 SCJ V-8s were installed in 1971 Mustangs.

ENGINES

OPTIONAL V-8: Overhead valve. Cast-iron block. Displacement: 429 cid. Bore and stroke: 4.36 x 3.59 inches. Compression ratio: 11.30:1. Brake hp: 370 at 54200 rpm. Torque: 450 at 3400 rpm. Five main bearings. Hydraulic valve lifters. Carburetor: Holley 700-cfm four-barrel. Dual exhaust. Special heads. High-lift camshaft. High-rise intake manifold. Code C.

OPTIONAL V-8: Overhead valve. Cast-iron block. Displacement: 429 cid. Bore and stroke: 4.36 x 3.59 inches. Compression ratio: 11.30:1. Brake hp: 375 at 5600 rpm. Torque: 450 at 3400 rpm. Five main bearings. Solid valve lifters. Carburetor: Holley 780-cfm four-barrel. Dual exhaust. Special heads. High-lift camshaft. High-rise intake manifold. Four-bolt main bearings. Aluminum pistons. Code J.

OPTIONS

Selectaire conditioner, includes 55-amp alternator and extra-cooling package and requires power steering ($412, but not available on cars with both 429 CJ/SCJ V-8 and Drag Pack option). Optional axle ratio ($13.00). Drag Pak, includes the following 429-four-barrel modifications: four-bolt mains, forged pistons, cap screw connecting rods and modified crankshaft, flywheel and dampener ($155.00). Traction-Lok differential ($48.00, but not available when 3.91:1 or 4.11:1 axle is combined with 429-cid V-8). Heavy-duty 70-amp. battery ($16.00). Deluxe seat belts with warning light ($17.00). Front and rear bumper guards (not available on Mach 1). Center console with electric clock with Sports interior ($60.00). Electric rear window defogger ($48.00). NOX emissions system, required in California (no charge). 429-cid/370-hp 429 CJ V-8 ($372.00). 429-cid/375-hp 429 SCJ Ram-Air V-8 ($436.00). Extra-cooling package (standard with 429-cid V-8s). Complete tinted glass ($40.00). Dual racing-style outside rearview mirrors ($26.00). Power disc brakes ($70.00). Power side windows ($127.00). Power steering ($115.00 and includes variable ratio on models with competition suspension such as Boss 351). Push-button AM radio ($66.00). AM/FM stereo radio. Including two front-door-mounted speakers ($214.00).

Rear sport deck on Sportsroof model, includes Spacer-Saver spare tire, folding rear seat and load floor ($97.00). Rear deck lid spoiler ($32.00). Deluxe Rim-Blow steering wheel ($39.00). Tilt steering, requires power steering ($45.00). Stereophonic tape system ($134.00). Competition suspension includes extra-heavy-duty front and rear springs, front and rear shock absorbers, front stabilizer bar and rear stabilizer bar (standard on Mach 1, but requires F60-15 black sidewall tires with raised white letters). Body side tape stripes ($26.00). Trim rings and hubcaps (standard on Mach 1). SelectShift Cruise-O-Matic transmission with 429-cid V-8s ($238.00). Four-speed manual transmission with Hurst shifter in cars with 429-cid V-8 ($217.00). Sports type wheel covers ($23.00). Magnum 500 chrome styled wheels ($120.00 extra). Intermittent windshield wipers ($26.00). Decor group includes choice of knitted vinyl or cloth-and-vinyl high-back bucket seats, rear ashtray, deluxe right- and left-hand Black instrument panel appliques, a deluxe two-spoke steering wheel and molded door trim panels ($78.00). Instrumentation group including tachometer, trip odometer and triple instrument pod gauges on Mach 1 with sports interior and console ($54.00). Instrumentation group including tachometer, trip odometer and triple instrument pod gauges on Mach 1 without sports interior ($79.00). Instrumentation group including tachometer, trip odometer and triple instrument pod gauges on Mach 1 with sports interior without console ($37.00). Sports interior option includes knitted vinyl high-back bucket seats with accent stripes, deluxe two-spoke steering wheel with woodtone insert, electric clock, bright pedal trim pads, molded door trim panels with integral pull handle and armrest, color-accented embossed carpet runners, deluxe instrument panel with black applique and woodtone center section, triple instrument pod gauges for oil pressure, amps and temperature and rear ash tray ($88.00). Five F70-14 raised white letter tires over F70-14 white sidewall ($13.00 for Mach 1 with 429 CJ V-8). Five F60-15 raised white letter tires over F70-14 white sidewall ($31.00 for Mach 1 with 429 CJ V-8). Five F60-15 raised white letter tires over F70-14 white sidewall ($18.00 for Mach 1 with 429 SCJ V-8).

1971 TORINO/TORINO 500 429 CJ/SCJ

The '71 Ford Torino was picked as *Motor Trend's* "Car of the Year" in 1971 and it could turn out to be one of the muscle cars of the century if its star keeps rising among the ranks of today's collectors. In reviewing the car in February 1971, the magazine stated, "To have had it, 16 years ago, on Main St. in Lockport, N.Y., with all its shuttered-back-lite, fat-tired, shaker-hood, chopped-top magnificence would have equated with having the Bean Bandit's fuel dragster." In other words, a pretty cool car for a car guy!

Standard equipment included a 250-cid/145-hp six or a 302-cid/210-hp V-8. Torinos came in a range of body styles, all available with muscular engines, but the serious muscle car interest is in the two-door styles.

These cars would take 7.3 seconds to go 0-to-60 mph and did the quarter-mile in 14.9 seconds at 95.2 mph.

Model Number	Body/Style Number	Body Type & Seating	Factory Price	Shipping Weight	Production Total
TORINO — SERIES 20 — V-8					
25	65A	2d HT-6P	$2,801	3,230 lbs.	37,518
TORINO 500 — SERIES 30 — V-8					
30	65C	2d HT-6P	$2,982	3,235 lbs.	89,966
34	63C	2d FSBK-6P	$3,038	3,291 lbs.	11,150

NOTE 1: Prices and weights are for cars with base 302-cid V-8.
NOTE 2: Production is for cars with all engines; no 429-cid V-8 breakouts are available for 1971.
NOTE 3: Ford built 172,185 of its 429-cid V-8s of all types for all of its cars in 1971.

ENGINES

OPTIONAL V-8: Overhead valve. Cast-iron block. Displacement: 429 cid. Bore and stroke: 4.36 x 3.59 inches. Compression ratio: 11.30:1. Brake hp: 370 at 5400 rpm. Torque: 450 at 3400 rpm. Five main bearings. Hydraulic valve lifters. Carburetor: Holley 700-cfm four-barrel. Dual exhaust. Special heads. High-lift camshaft. High-rise intake manifold. Code C.

OPTIONAL V-8: Overhead valve. Cast-iron block. Displacement: 429 cid. Bore and stroke: 4.36 x 3.59 inches. Compression ratio: 11.30:1. Brake hp: 375 at 5600 rpm. Torque: 450 at 3400 rpm. Five main bearings. Hydraulic valve lifters. Carburetor: Holley 700-cfm four-barrel. Dual exhaust. Special heads. High-lift camshaft. High-rise intake manifold. Code J.

OPTIONS

Selectaire conditioner, tinted glass recommended, required with 429-cid V-8 ($412.00) Optional axle ratio ($13.00). Traction-Lok differential ($48.00). Heavy-duty 70-amp battery ($16.00). Deluxe seat belts with warning light for Torino two-door models, includes automatic seatback release ($43.00). Electric clock ($17.00, but not available in Torinos with tachometer). Bumper guards ($31.00). Center console, bucket seats required for Torino 500 two-door hardtop only ($60.00). Electric rear window defroster ($48.00, but not available for air-conditioned cars with a 429-cid V-8). Evaporative emissions control system, all required in California (no charge). 429-cid/370-hp Cobra-Jet V-8, includes competition suspension, 80-amp heavy-duty battery, 55-amp alternator, dual exhausts, extra-cooling package, bright engine dress-up kit with cast aluminum rocker covers and 3.25:1 ratio non-locking rear axle ($372.00). 429-cid/370-hp Super-Cobra-Jet V-8, includes competition suspension, 80-amp heavy-duty battery, 55-amp alternator, dual exhausts, extra-cooling package, bright engine dress-up kit with cast aluminum rocker covers and 3.25:1 ratio non-locking rear axle ($436.00). Complete tinted glass ($43.00). Hideaway headlights, Torino 500 ($53.00). Laser stripe for Torino 500 ($39.00). Dual racing-style outside rearview mirrors for two-door hardtops, left-hand remote-control ($26.00). Body side protection molding ($34.00). Power front disc brakes ($70.00). Four-way power full-width seat for two-door hardtop ($74.00). Power side windows ($127.00, but not available on two-door hardtop). Power steering ($115.00 and required on air-conditioned cars with 429-cid V-8). AM radio ($66.00). Push-button AM/FM stereo radio ($214.00). Vinyl roof for formal two-door hardtop ($95.00). High-back bucket seats for Torino 500 two-door hardtop ($150.00). Dual rear seat speakers ($33.00). Sports slats rear window louvers for fastback ($65.00 and racing mirrors required). Deluxe Rim-Blow steering wheel ($39.00). Heavy-duty suspension, includes heavy-duty springs and shocks front and rear and heavy-duty stabilizer ($23.00). 8,000-rpm tachometer ($49.00 for V-8s and not available with electric clock). Knitted vinyl seat in Torino ($32.00). Knitted vinyl seat in Torino 500, two-tone bench seat required ($32.00). Vinyl seat trim in Torino 500 ($19.00). Trim rings with hubcaps ($35.00). SelectShift Cruise-O-Matic transmission ($238.00). Four-speed manual with Hurst shifter ($205.00). DirectAire ventilation ($16.00 for cars without air conditioning). Standard type wheel covers ($26.00). Deluxe hubcaps ($78.00). Sporty type wheel covers ($58.00 and Wide-Oval tires required at extra cost). Argent Silver styled wheels ($58.00). Magnum 500 chrome styled wheels ($155.00 extra). Intermittant windshield wipers ($26.00). Trailer towing package ($120.00 and requires Cruise-O-Matic, power steering, power front disc brakes, H78-15 belted black sidewall tires, 3.25:1 optional rear axle ratio and engine of 390-cid or larger). Visibility group on cars without racing mirrors, ($38), with racing mirrors ($25). Optional tires replacing standard F78-14 black sidewall belted tires on Torino with engines other than 429-cid V-8: F78-14 white sidewall tires ($32.00 extra). G78-14 F-78-14 black sidewall tires ($18.00 extra). G78-14 white sidewall tires ($50.00 extra). F70-14 white sidewall tires ($50.00 extra). F70-14 raised white letter tires ($63.00 extra). G70-14 white sidewall tires ($68.00 extra). G60-14 black sidewall raised white-letter tires ($81.00). F60-15 black sidewall raised white-letter tires ($81.00). Optional tires replacing standard G78-14 black sidewall belted tires on Torino with 429-cid V-8: G78-14 white sidewall tires ($32.00 extra). G70-14 white sidewall tires ($50.00 extra) G70-14 raised white letter tires ($63.00 extra).

FORD

1971 TORINO COBRA 429/429 CJ/429 SCJ

PHIL KUNZ

1971 Torino Cobra SCJ

The 1971 Torino was virtually identical to the 1970 model, although with only 3,054 cars produced for the model year, they were less than half as popular with buyers.

The Torino Cobra included a wide-ratio four-speed manual transmission with Hurst shifter, unique front, side and rear Cobra identification, a heavy-duty load suspension, 7-inch-wide Argent Silver wheels with bright hubcaps, a black two-tone hood, wheel lip moldings, color-keyed carpets, a 55-amp heavy-duty battery, pleated vinyl seat trim, a sporty dual exhaust system, a 351-cid/285-hp V-8 and F70-14 glass-belted Wide-Oval white sidewall tires. The standard grille had black finish, but the optional hidden headlight front end treatment was also available. The lower back panel was also finished in black.

Different models had different weights, but a typical 429 Cobra-Jet Torino required 7.3 seconds to go 0-to-60 mph and did the quarter-mile in 14.9 seconds at 95.2 mph.

Model Number	Body/Style Number	Body Type & Seating	Factory Price	Shipping Weight	Production Total
TORINO COBRA — SERIES 38 — V-8					
38	63H	2d FSBK-6P	$3,295	3,594 lbs.	3,054

NOTE 1: Prices and weights are for Torino Cobra with 351-cid V-8.

NOTE 2: Production is for all Torino Cobras.

NOTE 3: Ford Motor Company built 172,185 of its 429-cid V-8s of all types for all of its cars in 1971.

ENGINES

OPTIONAL V-8: Overhead valve. Cast-iron block. Displacement: 429 cid. Bore and stroke: 4.36 x 3.59 inches. Compression ratio: 11.30:1. Brake hp: 370 at 54200 rpm. Torque: 450 at 3400 rpm. Five main bearings. Hydraulic valve lifters. Carburetor: Holley 700-cfm four-barrel. Dual exhaust. Special heads. High-lift camshaft. High-rise intake manifold. Code C.

OPTIONAL V-8: Overhead valve. Cast-iron block. Displacement: 429 cid. Bore and stroke: 4.36 x 3.59 inches. Compression ratio: 11.30:1. Brake hp: 375 at 5600 rpm. Torque: 450 at 3400 rpm. Five main bearings. Hydraulic valve lifters. Carburetor: Holley 700-cfm four-barrel. Dual exhaust. Special heads. High-lift camshaft. High-rise intake manifold. Code J.

OPTIONS

Selectaire conditioner, tinted glass recommended, required with 429-cid V-8 ($412.00) Optional axle ratio ($13.00). Traction-Lok differential ($48.00). Heavy-duty 70-amp battery ($16.00). Deluxe seat belts with warning light for Torino two-door models, includes automatic seatback release ($43.00). Electric clock ($17.00, but not available in Torinos with tachometer). Bumper guards ($31.00). Center console, bucket seats required for Torino Cobra two-door hardtop only ($60.00). Electric rear window defroster ($48.00, but not available for air-conditioned cars with a 429-cid V-8). Evaporative emissions control system, all required in California (no charge). 429-cid/370-hp Cobra-Jet V-8, includes competition suspension, 80-amp heavy-duty battery, 55-amp alternator, dual exhausts, extra-cooling package, bright engine dress-up kit with cast aluminum rocker covers and 3.25:1 ratio non-locking rear axle ($279.00). 429-cid/370-hp Super-Cobra-Jet V-8, includes competition suspension, 80-amp heavy-duty battery, 55-amp. alternator, dual exhausts, extra-cooling package, bright engine dress-up kit with cast aluminum rocker covers and 3.25:1 ratio non-locking rear axle ($343.00). Complete tinted glass ($43.00). Hideaway headlights ($53.00). Laser stripe ($39.00). Dual racing-style outside rearview mirrors for two-door hardtops, left-hand remote-control ($26.00). Body side protection molding ($34.00). Power front disc brakes ($70.00 and required on GT convertible with 429-cid V-8). Power side windows ($127.00). Power steering ($115.00 and required on air-conditioned cars with 429-cid V-8). AM radio ($66.00). Push-button AM/FM stereo radio ($214.00). Vinyl roof for formal two-door hardtop ($95.00). High-back bucket seats for Torino Cobra two-door fastback ($150.00). Dual rear seat speakers ($33.00). Sports slats rear window louvers for fastback ($65.00 and racing mirrors required). Deluxe Rim-Blow steering wheel ($39.00). Heavy-duty suspension, includes heavy-duty springs and shocks front and rear and heavy-duty stabilizer ($23.00). 8,000-rpm tachometer ($49.00 for V-8s and not available with electric clock). Knitted vinyl seat in Torino GT, two-tone bench seat required ($32.00). Trim rings with hubcaps on Torino Brougham ($9.00). SelectShift Cruise-O-Matic transmission for Cobra with 429-cid V-8 ($43.00). Four-speed manual with Hurst shifter (standard). DirectAire ventilation ($16.00 for cars without air conditioning). Argent Silver styled wheels (standard). Magnum 500 chrome styled wheels ($120.00 extra). Intermittant windshield wipers ($26.00). Trailer towing package ($120.00 and requires Cruise-O-Matic, power steering, power front disc brakes, H78-15 belted black sidewall tires, 3.25:1 optional rear axle ratio and engine of 390-cid or larger). Visibility group for Torino without dual racing-style outside rearview mirrors ($38) on cars with racing mirrors ($25). Optional tires replacing standard F70-14 white sidewall belted tires on Torino Cobra with 429-cid V-8: F70-14 white letter tires ($13.00 extra). G70-14 white sidewall tires ($18.00 extra) G70-14 raised white letter tires ($31.00). F60-14 raised white letter tires ($31.00).

MERCURY

MERCURY MUSCLE 1964-1972

Mercury had long been highly regarded as a "factory hot rod" version of the Ford, but its image was always keyed to hot full-size vehicles. In fact, in the mid-'50s the cars carried the maker's first initial in their grille and were promoted as "Big M" models. By the early '60s, Mercurys were bigger and more powerful than ever, but that wasn't what the booming "youth market" wanted in a car. Big engines in a smaller body were the trend. In 1964, Lincoln Mercury Division decided to bring out a real muscle car carrying the Mercury Comet nameplate.

The new Comet Cyclone high-performance model arrived in showrooms in the middle of the 1964 model year. It used the compact, lightweight 289-cid V-8 that evolved from the 221-/260-cid V-8s, both of which were dropped when the 289 appeared in the '64 Comet Cyclone. The 289 did not have the Y-block layout of earlier Mercury V-8s and featured a stronger "bottom end" that racing enthusiasts appreciated. The 289 became base engine in the '67 Cougar.

In 1968, only one 289 (200 hp) was offered. However, this "small" V-8 was stroked to 302 cid and offered in 210- and 230-hp formats. This made the engine competitive and "legal" for use in SCCA Trans-Am series sedan racing. The 302 was basically stroked again, in 1969, to 351 cid, This provided a compact and lightweight V-8 that came in factory 250- and 290-hp versions and made a great platform for aftermarket performance hardware

In 1968, the 427-cid/390-hp racing engine was offered in some Mercurys. It retained the 390's 3.784-inch stroke, but had a larger 4.23-inch bore. The 428-cid big-block V-8 replaced the 427. It was a bored-and-stroked 390 and was offered in 345- and 360-hp editions. The Thunderjet 429 was not a true performance engine. It was based on the 460-cid Lincoln engine. However, the hotter versions with 360- and 375-hp were available, too. Mercury brought out a 400-cid V-8 with 4.00 x 4.00-inch bore and stroke dimensions in 1971, but it was not a performance engine, either.

PHIL KUNZ

1964 COMET CYCLONE

1964 Comet Cyclone

This two-door hardtop was the first macho Comet. Literature told of "under the hood, a whiplash of surging power" and of the "masculine feel of black vinyl in the instrument panel." As a safety feature the "bucket seats are contoured to hold you more securely in turns." Fender nameplates, full-length lower body moldings, vinyl roof coverings and "chrome wheel look" wheel covers distinguished the Cyclone.

The Cyclone went for a "serious street performance" image and featured less chrome than other Comets. There were thin moldings over the wheel wells and under the doors and "C-O-M-E-T" lettering appeared only on the rear fins. "Cyclone" front fender badges, done in the same style used on the full-size Marauder, sat low on the fenders. A three-spoke steering wheel, a center console and a tachometer were standard. The engine came with special chromed parts, including air cleaner, dipstick, oil filter, radiator cap and rocker arm covers. Camera-case-grained black vinyl replaced wood trim on the instrument panel. A special option was a "convertible" style vinyl roof covering. Cyclones offered a three- or four-speed manual transmission, plus Merc-O-Matic. Promotions for the car were tied into the 100,000-mile endurance run at Daytona.

As tested in _Car Life_ (April 1964), the Cyclone priced-out at $3,027 with a typical array of options. The magazine listed 0-to-60-mph times of 11.8 seconds with automatic transmis-sion and 10.2 seconds with a four-speed gear box. The quarter-mile was covered in 16.5 seconds at 73.8 mph by the Merc-O-Matic-equipped Cyclone and 16.4 seconds at 77 mph by the four-speed Cyclone. The car with automatic averaged 12 to 15 mpg in normal driving, while the stick-shift car did a bit better at 13 to 16 mpg. Top speed was listed as 109 mph.

Model Number	Body/Style Number	Body Type & Seating	Factory Price	Shipping Weight	Production Total
CYCLONE — SERIES 27 — V-8					
27	63E	2d HT-6P	$2,655	3,044 lbs.	7,454

ENGINE

BASE V-8: 90 degree, overhead valve. Cast-iron block. Bore and stroke: 4.00 x 2.875 in. Displacement: 289 cid. Compression ratio: 9.00:1. Brake hp: 210 at 4400 rpm. Taxable hp: 51.20. Torque: 300 at 2800 rpm. Five main bearings. Hydraulic valve lifters. Carburetor: Ford C4GF-9510-D four-barrel. Engine code: D.

OPTIONS

Power steering ($86). Air conditioning ($232). Heavy-duty battery ($7.60). Tinted glass ($27.10). Tinted windshield ($18.10). Station wagon luggage rack ($64.35). Outside remote-control rearview mirror ($12). Padded instrument panel ($18.40). Padded visors ($4.50). Two-tone paint ($19.40). Power brakes ($43.20). Push-button AM radio ($58.50). Tachometer ($43.10). Wheel covers ($19.20). Windshield washer and wipers ($21.80). A three-speed manual transmission was standard. Four-speed manual, Merc-O-Matic and Multi-Drive automatic transmissions were optional. A 289 cid/271-hp four-barrel V-8 was available. A limited number of Comets with 427-cid/425-hp engines were built as lightweight factory drag racing cars.

MERCURY

1965 COMET CYCLONE

1965 Comet Cyclone

Mercury's 1965 Comet Cyclone was as whiplashingly fast as the Coney Island roller coaster that it shared the Cyclone name with. The Cyclone series consisted of a single two-door hardtop that was the second-most expensive Comet next to the Villager station wagon. The Cyclone had a special grille with only two groups of horizontal blades and blacked-out finish around its perimeter. Cyclones had all the equipment that came on Calientes, plus bucket seats in front, a center console, a tachometer, unique deluxe wheel covers, curb moldings and a 289-cid "Cyclone" V-8. A distinctive twin-air-scoop fiberglass hood was optional.

In addition to the 200-hp Cyclone, there was a 225-hp Super Cyclone 289. A three-speed manual gearbox was standard. A four-speed manual transmission or Multi-Drive Merc-O-Matic transmission were optional. The latter was a three-speed automatic comparable to Ford's Cruise-O-Matic.

Auto writer John Ethridge said, "The Cyclone's 225-hp engine had what you'd consider a healthy feeling at any speed between idle and 3000 rpm. Then it felt like four more cylinders were added and came on very strongly." In May 1965, *Motor Trend* printed a road test titled "2 Comets: Hot & Cool" that compared the Caliente and Cyclone two-door hardtops. The tested Caliente had the 289-cid, 200-hp engine and Merc-O-Matic transmission. It did 0-to-60 mph in 11 seconds and ran down the drag strip in 18.1 seconds with a 76-mph terminal speed. Its top speed was 96 mph. The tested Cyclone had the 225-hp version of the 289 and a four-speed gearbox. It trimmed 2.2 seconds off the other car's 0-to-60-mph time and the quarter-mile took 17.1 seconds at 82 mph. Its top speed was 108 mph.

ENGINES

BASE V-8: 90 degree, overhead valve. Cast-iron block. Bore and stroke: 4.00 x 2.875 in. Displacement: 289 cid. Compression ratio: 9.30:1. Brake hp: 200 at 4400 rpm. Taxable hp: 51.20. Torque: 282 at 2400 rpm. Five main bearings. Hydraulic valve lifters. Carburetor: Ford C5MF-9510-A two-barrel. Engine code: C.

OPTIONAL V-8: 90 degree, overhead valve. Cast-iron block. Bore and stroke: 4.00 x 2.875 in. Displacement: 289 cid. Compression ratio: 10.9:1. Brake hp: 225 at 4800 rpm. Taxable hp: 46.20. Torque: 305 at 3200 rpm. Five main bearings. Hydraulic valve lifters. Carburetor: Ford C4GF-9510-D four-barrel. Engine code: A.

OPTIONAL V-8: 90 degree, overhead valve. Cast-iron block. Bore and stroke: 4.00 x 2.875 in. Displacement: 289 cid. Compression ratio: 10.50:1. Brake hp: 271 at 6000 rpm. Taxable hp: 46.20. Torque: 312 at 3400 rpm. Five main bearings. Solid valve lifters. Carburetor: Ford C4GF-9510-D four-barrel. Engine code: K. (The Hi-Po 289 wasn't officially an option, but it has been documented that some cars were built with it).

SPECIAL-PRODUCTION OPTIONAL V-8: 90 degree, overhead valve. Cast-iron block. Bore and stroke: 4.23 x 3.781 in. Displacement: 427 cid. Compression ratio: 11.2:1. Brake hp: 425 at 6000 rpm. Taxable hp: 54.58. Torque: 480 at 3700 rpm. Five main bearings. Solid valve lifters. Carburetor: Two Holley four-barrel carburetors. Engine code: R. (The 427 wasn't officially an option, but it has been documented that some cars were built with it).

OPTIONS

Air conditioning ($257.50, but not available with four-speed manual transmission). Power transfer axle ($38.00). Heavy-duty battery ($7.60). Elapsed time clock ($20.00). Courtesy light group ($14.80). Remote-control deck lid release ($11.00). Closed crankcase emissions system for California cars only ($5.30). Power booster fan ($16.10). Emergency flasher ($12.80). All tinted glass ($27.10). Tinted windshield ($18.10). Heater delete ($74.30). Back-up lights ($10.70). Inside non-glare mirror ($4.30). Remote-control outside rearview mirror ($12.00). Curb molding ($16.10). Padded instrument panel ($18.40). Padded sun visors ($4.50). Two-tone paint ($19.40). Performance handling package ($20.80). Power brakes ($43.20). Power steering ($86.30). AM push-button radio ($58.50). AM/FM radio ($129.30). Rally Pac ($40). Front rubber floor mats ($5.80). Front and rear rubber floor mats ($9.00). Retractable front seat belts ($7.10). Front seat belts delete ($11.00 credit). Oversize 7.35 x 14 white sidewall tires ($37.00). Merc-O-Multi-Drive automatic transmission ($189.60). Four-speed manual transmission ($188.60). Vacuum gauge ($20.00). Vinyl roof ($75.80). Wire wheel covers ($43.20). Windshield washers and wipers ($21.80). Super Cyclone 289 V-8 ($45.20).

Model Number	Body/Style Number	Body Type & Seating	Factory Price	Shipping Weight	Production Total
CYCLONE — SERIES 27 — V-8					
27	63E	2d HT-6P	$2,625	3,283 lb.	12,347

1966 COMET CYCLONE GT

DOUG MITCHEL

1966 Comet Cyclone GT

"This one will start a glow in any red-blooded American driver," Mercury promised car buyers in 1966. *Car Life* said that the newly redesigned '66 Cyclone provided "Supercar status for Lincoln's little brother." The base Cyclone version of the mid-sized Comet had premiered in mid-1965. The high-performance '66 Cyclone GT came out in the fall of 1965, along with the rest of the new Comet line. From its inception, the Comet/Cyclone body had grown almost every year. The 1966 version was based on Ford's Fairlane. It rode on a 116-inch wheelbase. This moved it out of the compact category and into the intermediate size class.

For performance buffs, this change made the Cyclone a viable contender against the small-bodied, big-engined muscle cars of the period. For 1966, Mercury went full blast and brought out the Cyclone GT. Powered by Ford's popular 390 V-8, the Cyclone GT had an optional handling package, front disc brakes and optional four-speed manual or automatic transmission. (A three-speed manual was standard.) Also standard were dual exhausts, a fiberglass hood with twin non-functional scoops and GT identification and stripes. The optional Merc-O-Matic transmission only came with a GT Sport Shift enabling manual inter-range control via a floor-mounted lever. The '66 Cyclone GTs were rare models. Only 13,812 hardtops and 2,158 convertibles were built.

The 390-cid/335-hp Cyclone GT was capable of 0-to-60 mph in 7 seconds and quarter-mile runs in the high 14s. This was in spite of the fact that the 390-cid engine added some 430 lbs. to the standard six-cylinder Comet.

Model Number	Body/Style Number	Body Type & Seating	Factory Price	Shipping Weight	Production Total
CYCLONE GT — SERIES 27 — V-8					
27	63H	2dr HT-5P	$2,891	3,315 lbs.	13,812
29	76H	2dr Conv-5P	$3,152	3,595 lbs.	2,158

ENGINE

BASE V-8: 90 degree, overhead valve. Cast-iron block. Bore and stroke: 4.047 x 3.781 in. Displacement: 390 cid. Compression ratio: 10.50:1. Brake hp: 335 at 4800 rpm. Taxable hp: 52.49. Torque: 427 at 3200 rpm. Five main bearings. Hydraulic valve lifters. Carburetor: Ford four-barrel. Engine code: S.

OPTIONS

Air conditioning ($355.95). High-performance axle ($2.95). Power transfer axle ($37.20). Heavy-duty battery ($7.44). Electric clock, except cars with tachometer ($15.75). Remote-control deck lid release ($12.65). Closed crankcase emissions system where required ($5.19). Exhaust emission control where required ($45.45). All tinted glass ($28.50). Tinted windshield ($19.50). Heater delete ($72.73 credit). Right-hand OSRV mirror ($6.95). Remote-control outside rearview mirror (standard on Cyclone). Curb molding ($15.76). Oxford roof ($84.25). Two-tone paint ($27.06). Power disc brakes (standard with GT). Power front seata ($62.45). Power steering ($95.00). Power windows ($100.10). AM push-button radio ($60.05). AM/FM radio with antenna ($133.65). Rear seat speaker ($15.60). Deluxe front and rear seat belts with rear warning light ($10.40). Shoulder belts ($27.06). Sports console ($46.65). Stereo-Sonic tape system ($128.50). Tachometer ($47.30). Heavy-duty three-speed transmission with GT Performance Group ($79). SelectShift Merc-O-Matic transmission ($215.99). Four-speed manual transmission ($184.02). Cyclone wheel covers ($34.97). Wire wheel covers ($50.75). Styled steel wheels ($96.36). Interval selector windshield wipers ($11.59). 7.75 x 14 black sidewall tires ($33.45). Courtersy light group ($19.69).

1967 "COMET" CYCLONE GT

PHIL KUNZ

1967 Comet Cyclone GT

Mercury had a hard time attaining a presence in the booming intermediate market in the 1960s. Its cars were always in the shadows of other Ford products. In 1966, the Comet became a mid-sized car. Just when people were starting to get used to it, the mildly facelifted 1967 models came along and the Comet name was only applied to the lowest-priced series. Other "Comets" like the Capri, Calient and Cyclone were simply referred to as "Mercury Intermediates." So, the '67 models lacked a common name and promotional backing as well.

For the performance buyer, Mercury continued its Cyclone series. The GT was no longer a series, but a GT option was available. The base Cyclone line offered two-door hardtop and convertible models. Standard equipment included a 289-cid V-8. The Cyclone GT Performance Group of options added the 390-cid/320-hp GT V-8, an engine dress-up kit, unique GT exterior and interior ornamentation, console-mounted transmission controls (except with three-speed manual gearbox or Select-Shift automatic without optional console), a racing stripe, Wide-Oval nylon whitewall tires, 5 1/4 x 14-inch wheels, a heavy-duty suspension, a 3.25:1 rear axle ratio, a Power Booster fan, a twin-scoop GT hood and power front disc brakes.

The GT's horsepower was down 15 from the 1966 version, but it was still fairly hot. The recession of 1967 was not kind to car sales and the Mercury intermediates took a beating. As a result 1967 Cyclone GTs are quite rare today — especially the convertible.

Racing promotion for the 1967 Cyclone was limited to its body lines being used atop funny cars for drag racing, but better things were ahead for Cyclones. They would become the NASCAR superspeedway stars of 1968 and beyond, fi-

nally helping Mercury's intermediate-sized models to establish a name for themselves. The 427-cid racing engine was available in mid-size Mercury two-door sedans and hardtops, but was not offered for cars with the GT equipment group. A factory-modified Mercury Cyclone GT with the 390-cid V-8 did the quarter-mile in 13.98 seconds at 103.8 mph in a *Car & Driver* test.

Model Number	Body/Style Number	Body Type & Seating	Factory Price	Shipping Weight	Production Total
CYCLONE GT — SERIES 27 — V-8					
15	63E	2dr HT-5P	$2,891	3,315 lbs.	3,419
16	76C	2dr Conv-5P	$3,152	3,595 lbs.	378

NOTE: Production for Cyclone GT models only.

ENGINES

OPTIONAL-FOR-CREDIT V-8: 90-degree, overhead valve. Cast-iron block. Bore and stroke: 4.047 x 3.781 in. Displacement: 390 cid. Compression ratio: 9.50:1. Brake hp: 270 at 4400 rpm. Taxable hp: 52.49. Torque: 403 at 2600 rpm. Five main bearings. Hydraulic valve lifters. Carburetor: Holley two-barrel. Engine code: H.

BASE V-8: 90 degree, overhead valve. Cast-iron block. Bore and stroke: 4.047 x 3.781 in. Displacement: 390 cid. Compression ratio: 10.50:1. Brake hp: 320 at 4800 rpm. Taxable hp: 52.49. Torque: 427 at 3200 rpm. Five main bearings. Hydraulic valve lifters. Carburetor: Holley C7AF-9510-AE four-barrel. Engine code: S.

OPTIONS

Air conditioning ($355.95). High-performance axle ($2.65). Power transfer axle ($37.20). Heavy-duty battery ($7.44). Electric clock, except cars with tachometer ($15.75). Remote-control deck lid release ($12.65). Closed crankcase emissions system where required ($5.19). Exhaust emission control where required ($45.45). All tinted glass ($28.50). Tinted windshield ($19.50). Heater delete ($72.73 credit and not available when air conditioning was ordered). Right-hand OSRV mirror ($6.95). Remote-control outside rearview mirror (standard on Cyclones including GTs). Curb molding ($15.76). Oxford roof for hardtop ($84.25). Two-tone paint, except convertible($27.06). Power disc brakes (standard with GT equipment group). Four-way power left bucket seat ($62.45). Power frone bench seat for bench seat cars ($62.45). Power steering ($95.00). Power windows ($100.10). AM push-button radio ($60.05). AM/FM radio with antenna ($133.65). Rear seat speaker ($15.60). Deluxe front and rear seat belts with rear warning light (standard in Cyclones). Shoulder belts ($27.06). Sports console, Cyclones only ($46.65). Stereo-Sonic tape system ($128.50). Tachometer ($47.30 and not available with clock). Heavy-duty three-speed transmission with GT Performance Group only ($79). SelectShift Merc-O-Matic transmission with 289-cid two-barrel V-8 ($197.45). SelectShift Merc-O-Matic transmission with 390 two-barrel V-8 and GT performance group ($215.99). Four-speed manual transmission ($184.02). Cyclone wheel covers ($34.97). Wire wheel covers ($50.75). Styled steel wheels ($96.36). Interval selector windshield

wipers ($11.59). 7.75 x 14 black sidewall tires ($33.45). Appearance protection group (price not available). Courtesy light group ($19.69). Cyclone GT Performance Group including 390-cid/320-hp GT V-8, an engine dress-up kit, unique GT exterior and interior ornamentation, console-mounted transmission controls (except with three-speed manual gearbox or Select-Shift automatic without optional console), a racing stripe, Wide-Oval nylon whitewall tires, 5-1/4 x 14-inch wheels, a heavy-duty suspension, a 3.25:1 rear axle ratio, a Power Booster fan, a twin-scoop GT hood and power front disc brakes ($296.60 and extra-cost transmission required). Performance handling package ($15.60 for cars with 390-cid two-barrel V-8 only). F70-14 nylon whitewall Wide-Oval tires ($70.35).

1967 COMET "427"

ENGINES

OPTIONAL V-8: Overhead valve. Cast-iron block. Displacement: 427 cid. Bore and stroke: 4.23 x 3.78 inches. Compression ratio: 11.00:1. Brake hp: 410 at 5600 rpm. Torque: 476 at 3400 rpm. Five main bearings. Solid valve lifters. Carburetor: Holley four-barrel. Dual exhaust. Code W.

OPTIONAL V-8: Overhead valve. Cast-iron block. Displacement: 427 cid. Bore and stroke: 4.23 x 3.78 inches. Compression ratio: 11.50:1. Brake hp: 425 at 6000 rpm. Torque: 480 at 3700 rpm. Five main bearings. Solid valve lifters. Carburetor: Two Holley four-barrel. Dual exhaust. Code R.

OPTIONS

Air conditioning ($355.95). High-performance axle ($2.65). Power transfer axle ($37.20). Heavy-duty battery (standard). Electric clock, except cars with tachometer ($15.75). Remote-control deck lid release ($12.65). Closed crankcase emissions system where required ($5.19). Exhaust emission control where required ($45.45). All tinted glass ($28.50). Tinted windshield ($19.50). Heater delete ($72.73 credit and not available when air conditioning was ordered). Right-hand OSRV mirror ($6.95). Remote-control outside rearview mirror. Curb molding ($15.76). Oxford roof for hardtop ($84.25). Two-tone paint, except convertible ($27.06). Power disc brakes. Four-way power left bucket seat ($62.45). Power front bench seat for bench seat cars ($62.45). Power steering ($95.00). Power windows ($100.10). AM push-button radio ($60.05). AM/FM radio with antenna ($133.65). Rear seat speaker ($15.60). Deluxe front and rear seat belts with rear warning light (standard in Cyclones). Shoulder belts ($27.06). Sports console, Cyclones only ($46.65). Stereo-Sonic tape system ($128.50). Tachometer ($47.30 and not available with clock). SelectShift Merc-O-Matic transmission ($215.99). Four-speed manual transmission ($184.02). Cyclone wheel covers ($34.97). Wire wheel covers ($50.75). Styled steel wheels ($96.36). Interval selector windshield wipers ($11.59). 7.75 x 14 black sidewall tires ($33.45). Appearance protection group (price not available). Courtersy light group includes two panel lights, glove box light, ash tray light, luggage compartment light and parking brake light($19.69). F70-14 nylon whitewall Wide-Oval tires ($70.35).

Although the Comet name was used only on the lowest-priced mid-sized Mercurys in 1967, all of the various lines — Comet, Capri, Caliente and Cyclone — were "Commets" to the rest of the world (at least until they became Montegos in 1968). A CAR FAX factory options list indicated that the 427-cid Ford big-block V-8 was optional in all Mercury intermediate two-door sedans and hardtops, except cars with the GT Equipment Option. Unfortunately, the publication noted that the prices for the two versions of the 427 were "not available at time of publication." The prices for the 427 in the Fairlane was $975.09. This prices was used to estimate the car prices below. Without a doubt, the offering of the 427 was aimed at serious racers, but it could also be ordered in cars produced for street driving.

There are no documented performance firgures for these cars, but the similar 427/425 Fairlane did the quarter-mile in 14 seconds at 102 mph in a *Hot Rod* magazine test.

Model Number	Body/Style Number	Body Type & Seating	Factory Price	Shipping Weight	Production Total
COMET 202 — SERIES 01 — 427 V-8					
01	62A	2dr Sed-5P	$3,364	—	22
CAPRI — SERIES 07 — 427 V-8					
07	63E	2dr HT-5P	$3,539	—	7
CALIENTE — SERIES 11 — V-8					
11	63D	2dr HT-5P	$3,638	—	4
CYCLONE — SERIES 15 — V-8					
15	63E	2dr HT-5P	$3,712	—	27

NOTE 1: Production for 427 models only.

NOTE 2: Prices are estimates only, based on Fairlane 427-cid/425-hp engine cost, with no other options.

1967 COUGAR/XR7 GT 390

The '67 Mercury Cougar with the optional big-block 390 V-8 was a muscle car for the enthusiast on his or her way to a Thunderbird. "The Mercury Cougar's fascination is in finesse in fabrication," *Car Life* said of this well-built Merc. Although this power plant was equipped with hydraulic lifters, a fairly mild cam and street-type valve timing, it produced a 1:10 power-to-weight ratio that was good for some driving excitement.

Car Life also called the Cougar a "Mustang with class." It had a shapely, graceful appearance and jewel-like trimmings. Only a two-door hardtop was available the first year. While based on the Mustang platform, the Cougar received some

upgrades to its suspension including a hook-and-eye joint in the lower front A-frames to dampen ride harshness, 6-inch-longer rear leaf springs and better-rated rear spring and axle attachments. The GT, however, came more firmly sprung with solid rear bushings, stiffer springs all around, bigger 1.1875-inch shocks and a fatter .84-inch anti-roll bar, power front disc brakes, 8.95 x 14 wide oval tires, a low-restriction exhaust system and special identification features.

A Holley C70F carburetor with four 1.562-inch venturis and vacuum-operated secondaries sat on the 390-cid engine. With a 10.5:1 compression ratio, it required premium fuel.

MERCURY

1967 Cougar GT 390

Transmission choices included three- or four-speed synchro-mesh gearboxes or a three-speed Merc-O-Matic with manual shift capabilities for downshifting to second below 71 mph or to first below 20 mph. The manual gearboxes used with the 390 were different from those used with the 289. The three-speed with the big-block had ratios of 2.42:1 and 1.61:1. For the four-speed attachment, 2.32:1, 1.69:1 and 1.29:1 ratios were provided. Smaller-engined "stick" cars used numerically higher gear ratios. In the rear axle department, the 390 came standard with a 3.00 axle. A 3.25 unit was optional. They called this the "power transfer" axle. After the XR7 model arrive, it could also be had with the GT 390 performance group.

The Cougar GT 390 was good for 0-to-60-mph in 8.1 seconds and 16 second-quarter miles.

Model Number	Body/Style Number	Body Type & Seating	Factory Price	Shipping Weight	Production Total
COUGAR GT 390 — SERIES 91 — V-8					
91	65A	2d HT-5P	$3,175	3,005 lbs.	2,653
COUGAR XR7 GT 390 — SERIES 91 — V-8					
93	65B	2d HT-5P	$3,405	3,005 lbs.	5,791

ENGINES
BASE V-8: 90 degree, overhead valve. Cast-iron block. Bore and stroke: 4.047 x 3.781 in. Displacement: 390 cid. Compression ratio: 10.50:1. Brake hp: 320 at 4800 rpm. Taxable hp: 52.49. Torque: 427 at 3200 rpm. Five main bearings. Hydraulic valve lifters. Carburetor: Holley C7AF-9510-AE four-barrel. Engine code: S.

OPTIONS
Air conditioner ($355.95). Power transfer axle ($41.60). 55-amp heavy-duty battery ($7.44, but standard with 390 Select-Shift). Rear bumper guards ($12.95). Electric clock ($15.76). Closed crankcase emissions system, where required ($5.19). Cougar GT Performance group, includes 390-cid GT engine, performance handling package, F70-14 Wide-Oval whitewall tires, low-back-pressure exhausts, power disc brakes and exterior ornamentation ($323.85, plus extra-cost transmission required). Courtesy light group, includes parking brake warning lamp, luggage comparttment light and rear roof pillar courtesy lights ($16.85). Door edge guards ($4.40). Exhaust emission controls, where required ($45.45). Tinted glass ($30.25). Tinted windshield ($21.09). Heater and defroster delete ($31.52 credit). Deck lid luggage carrier ($32.45). Oxford roof ($84.25). Two-tone paint ($27.06). Performance handling package with GT 390 four-barrel engine, includeds higher-rate front and rear springs, larger diameter stabilizer bar, heavy-duty front-and-rear shock absorbers, 6-inch-wide wheels and, if specified, faster steering ratio ($30.64, but included with Cougar GT Performance group). Power disc brakes ($64.25, but standard with GT Performance Group). Power steering ($95). AM radio with antenna ($60.05). AM/FM radio with antenna ($133.65). AM radio with Stereo-sonic tape system ($188.50). Deluxe front and rear seat belts, including reminder light ($10.40). Front bench seat with center armrest ($24.42). Shoulder belts ($27.06). Speed control, Select-Shift Merc-O-Matic transmission required ($71.30). Sports console. Requires AM, AM/FM or AM stereo radio ($57, but not available with bench seat). Tilt-Away steering wheel ($60.05). Comfort-weave vinyl interior for cars with bucket front seats only ($33.05). Heavy-duty three-speed manual transmission with GT Performance group ($79.00). Four-speed manual transmission ($184.02). Merc-O-Matic Select-Shift automatic transmission with 390-cid V-8 ($215.99). Deluxe wheel covers ($16.79). Wire wheel covers ($69.51, but not availble on Pennsylvania cars). Five styled steel wheels ($115.15). Visual check panel, includes door-ajar warning lamp, low-fuel warning lamp, seat belt reminder light and parking brake warning light. ($39.50). A three-speed manual transmission was standard except in the XR7, which came with a four-speed manual transmission. The four-speed was optional in the standard Cougar. Merc-O-Matic SelectShift automatic transmission was optional in both series. A 289-cid/225-hp V-8 (four-barrel) and a 390-cid/320-hp V-8 (four-barrel) were available.

1968 COUGAR/XR7 GT-E

MERCURY

PHIL KUNZ

1968 Cougar GT-E

The first Cougar had enough room under the hood to accommodate big-block V-8s. In model year 1968, the Cougar got its first real high-performance package with the 7.0-liter GT-E. The "E" kit became an option for both the base Cougar and the fancier XR7. The option included the mild 390-hp E-code version of Ford's 427-cid engine, plus a SelectShift Merc-O-Matic transmission, a performance handling package, styled steel wheels, power disc brakes and a non-functional "power dome" hood air scoop. The mating of the 427-cid V-8 to the Cougar was a short-term offering because the 427-cid option was discontinued late in 1967.

Later in the model year the Cougar — like Ford's other sporty and mid-sized cars — received an injection of Cobra Jet 428 power. To keep insurance agents and bean counters happy, the 428-cid big-block V-8 carried a rating of 335 advertised horsepower. Strangely enough, because it had a longer stroke, the 428-cid engine had an easier time with emission requirements. However, its actual power output was estimated to be closer to the choked-down 427E it replaced. When the nose-heavy 427-cid V-8 was installed in the Cougar, which had a 111-inch wheelbase (3 inches longer than the Mustang), it produced average performance for the muscle cars of that era. A 7.1 second 0-to-60 time was published in the enthusiast magazines.

Model Number	Body/Style Number	Body Type & Seating	Factory Price	Shipping Weight	Production Total
COUGAR GT-E — SERIES 91 — 427 V-8					
91	65A	2d HT-5P	$3,336	3,117 lbs.	101
COUGAR XR7 GT-E — SERIES 91 — 427 V-8					
93	65B	2d HT-5P	$3,232	3,157 lbs.	256
COUGAR GT-E — SERIES 91 — 428 V-8					
91	65A	2d HT-5P	$3,336	3,117 lbs.	14
COUGAR XR7 GT-E — SERIES 91 — 428 V-8					
93	65B	2d HT-5P	$3,232	3,157 lbs.	23

NOTE 1: Production is for cars with indicated engine.

NOTE 2: Tthree of the XR7 versions with the 428-cid V-8 had a four-speed manual transmission.

ENGINES

(EARLY) BASE V-8: 90 degree, overhead valve. Cast-iron block. Bore and stroke: 4.23 x 3.78 in. Displacement: 427 cid. Compression ratio: 10.90:1. Brake hp: 390 at 5600 rpm. Torque: 460 at 3200 rpm. Five main bearings. Hydraulic valve lifters. Carburetor: Holley C7AF-9510-AE four-barrel. Engine code: W. (NOTE: The 427-cid V-8 was only available for a short time before replacement by the 428-CJ V-8.)

(LATE) BASE V-8: 90 degree, overhead valve. Cast-iron block. Bore and stroke: 4.13 x 3.98 in. Displacement: 428 cid. Compression ratio: 10.6:1. Brake hp: 335 at 5200 rpm. Taxable hp: 54.50. Torque: 440 at 3400 rpm. Five main bearings. Hydraulic valve lifters. Carburetor: Holley C8AF-9510-B four-barrel. Engine code: Q.

OPTIONS (PARTIAL LIST)

Air conditioner ($360.40, but not available in GT-E). Power transfer axle ($41.60). 55-amp heavy-duty battery ($7.44, but standard with 390- or 427-cid engines with Select-Shift). Rear bumper guards ($12.95, but not available for

GT-E). Electric clock ($15.76, but standard in XR7). Cougar GT Performance group, includes Marauder 390-cid GT engine, performance handling package, F70-14 Wide-Oval whitewall tires, low-back-pressure exhausts, power disc brakes, heavy-duty three-speed manual transmission and exterior ornamentation ($402.85, listed as available for "all"). Courtesy light group ($16.85). Decor Group ($84.25, except XR7). Rear window defogger ($21.25). Door edge guards, except GT-E ($4.40). Tinted glass ($30.25). Tinted windshield ($21.09). Adjustable front headrests ($42.75). High-performance axle ($6.50). Remote-control left-hand OSRV mirror, standard XR7 ($9.60). Oxford roof ($84.25). Two-tone paint ($30.96). Performance handling package with GT 390 four-barrel engine ($30.64, but included with Cougar GT Performance group). Power disc brakes ($64.85, but standard with GT Performance Group and on GT-E). Power steering ($95, but standard with GT-E). AM radio with antenna ($61.40). AM/FM stereo radio with antenna ($184.95). AM radio with Stereo-sonic tape system and two speakers ($195.15). Speed control, Select-Shift Merc-O-Matic

transmission required ($71.30). Sports console. Requires AM, AM/FM or AM stereo radio ($57, but not available with 427-cid V-8). Tilt-Away steering wheel ($66.00). FR70 x 14 wide tread radial-ply red-band tires (no extra cost on GT-E). Space-Saver spare tire ($6.50). Four-speed manual transmission (standard with GT-E). Merc-O-Matic Select-Shift automatic transmission ($147.00). Comfort-Weave vinyl interior in XR7, replacing leather-with-vinyl interior ($64.00 credit). Five styled steel wheels (standard with GT-E). GT-E 7.0-Litre package for all models except Cougar GT, includes Cougar 427-cid four-barrel V-8, heavy-duty battery, engine dress-up kit, Aelect-Shift Merc-O-Matic transmission, FR70-14 wide-tread white sidewall tires, styled steel wheels, power steering, power disc brakes, unique two-tone paint, super competition handling packager and unique exterior ornamentation ($1,311 and had to be ordered on a DSO special-order basis). (NOTE: This options list is from early in the year when the GT-E package was based on the 427-cid V-8. Later in the year the package was changed and the 428-cid V-8 was substituted.)

1968 COUGAR/XR7-G (+ HERTZ 390 GT)

1968 Cougar XR-7G

In 1968, the Shelby facility at Los Angeles Airport fell victim to an airport expansion program. Carroll Shelby still had contracts to build Shelby Mustangs and a new Cougar XR7-G model (named for race driver Dan Gurney). Shelby had to subcontract with car-frame-maker A.O. Smith Inc. to do the "pony car" conversions and with American Sunroof Corp. for the addition of sunroofs (which most Cougar XR7-Gs had). The base cars were built at Ford, Dearborn, rail-shipped to A.O. Smith for conversion, then rail-shipped to ASC to have the sun roof installed (along with trim like the headliner and vinyl top).

According to a *CAR FAX* supplement, the XR7-G package included: XR7-G badges on the right headlight cover, badges onboth roof pillars, a trunk lock cover badge, Lucas fog lamps (mounted in a special front valance panel), a hood scoop made of fiberglass, hood-locking pins with cables, three horns (including one extra-loud type), a bullet-shaped remote-control racing-style left-hand OSRV mirror, a specially-wrapped steering wheel with "leaping cat" hub logo, a leather-trimmed center console with AM radio, rally clock and control switches, a genuine wood gear shift knob with "leaping cat" logo, a gold XR7-G instrument panel logo, leather-trimmed door-pull straps, special wheels (early cars had Rader spokes and later cars had styled-steel wheels), special XR7-G hubcaps and a

special dual exhaust system with chrome tips. The XR7-G came with the 302-cid two-barrel, 302-cid four-barrel, 390-cid two-barrel, 390-cid four-barrel or 428-cid Cobra-Jet V-8s. For muscle car fans, the 428 was the one to buy and a handful of enthusiasts did. Some of the earliest XR7-Gs produced were delivered to Hertz Rent-A-Car as specialized rental vehicles similar to the Shelby GT-500H cars. A total of 188 cars were leased to Hertz. Apparently, all of these used the 390-cid four-barrel GT engine.

The 428 CJ-powered Cougar could race down the quarter-mile in 13.16 seconds at 108.14 mph.

Model Number	Body/Style Number	Body Type & Seating	Factory Price	Shipping Weight	Production Total
COUGAR XR7-G — SERIES 93 — 428CJ V-8					
93	65B	2d HT-5P	$3,500	3,300 lbs.	14

NOTE 1: Price and weights are "ballpark" estimates as the cars were available with different equipment and prices varied accordingly.

NOTE 2: The production total above is for 428-powered cars only. Of these, three had a four-speed manual transmission.

NOTE 3: Total production of the XR7-G with all engines was 619

ENGINES

OPTIONAL V-8: 90 degree, overhead valve. Cast-iron block. Bore and stroke: 4.047 x 3.781 in. Displacement: 390 cid. Compression ratio: 10.50:1. Brake hp: 320 at 4800 rpm. Taxable hp: 52.49. Torque: 427 at 3200 rpm. Five main bearings. Hydraulic valve lifters. Carburetor: Holley C7AF-9510-AE four-barrel. Engine code: S.

OPTIONAL V-8: 90 degree, overhead valve. Cast-iron block. Bore and stroke: 4.13 x 3.98 in. Displacement: 428 cid. Compression ratio: 10.6:1. Brake hp: 335 at 5200 rpm. Taxable hp: 54.50. Torque: 440 at 3400 rpm. Five main bearings. Hydraulic valve lifters. Carburetor: Holley C8AF-9510-B four-barrel. Engine code: Q.

OPTIONS

Air conditioner ($360.40). Power transfer axle ($41.60). 55-amp heavy-duty battery ($7.44, but standard with 427-cid engine with Select-Shift). Rear bumper guards ($12.95). Electric clock ($15.76, but standard in XR7). Cougar GT Performance group, includes Marauder 390-cid GT engine, performance handling package, F70-14 Wide-Oval whitewall tires, low-back-pressure exhausts, power disc brakes, heavy-duty three-speed manual transmission and exterior ornamentation ($402.85, listed as available for "all"). Courtesy light group, includes parking brake warning lamp, luggage compartment light and rear roof pillar courtesy lights ($16.85). Decor Group ($84.25, except XR7). Rear window defogger ($21.25).

Door edge guards ($4.40). Tinted glass ($30.25). Tinted windshield ($21.09). Adjustable front headrests ($42.75). High-performance axle ($6.50). Remote-control left-hand OSRV mirror, standard XR7 ($9.60). Oxford roof ($84.25). Two-tone paint ($30.96). Performance handling package ($30.64, but included with Cougar GT Performance group). Power disc brakes ($64.85, but standard with GT Performance Group). Power steering ($95). AM radio with antenna ($61.40). AM/FM stereo radio with antenna ($184.95). AM radio with Stereo-sonic tape system and two speakers ($195.15). Front bench seat with center armrest ($24.42). Deluxe front shoulder belts ($29.60 and deluxe seat belts required). Deluxe rear shoulder belts ($29.60 and deluxe seat belts required). Deluxe seat belts with reminder light ($13.00, but standard in XR7s). Speed control, Select-Shift Merc-O-Matic transmission required ($71.30). Tilt-Away steering wheel ($66.00). FR70 x 14 wide tread radial-ply red-band tires. Space-Saver spare tire ($6.50). Four-speed manual transmission. Merc-O-Matic Select-Shift automatic transmission standard). Comfort-Weave vinyl interior in XR7, replacing leather-with-vinyl interior ($64.00 credit). Five styled steel wheels. Visual check panel, includes door-ajar warning lamp, low-fuel warning lamp, seat belt reminder light and parking brake warning light. ($39.50, but standard in XR7).

1968 CYCLONE GT

1968 Cyclone GT

The mid-size Mercurys were restyled for '68 and looked like full-size Mercurys that went on a diet. The Comet name was used only on the entry-level sports coupe. Eight other models were offered in three series: Montego, Montego MX and Cyclone.

A two-barrel 302-cid V-8 rated at 210 horses was standard in Cyclones. The GT option included bucket seats and trim changes. Big-block V-8s included a mild 265-hp version of the 390-cid V-8, a stronger 325-hp 390 and a 427-cid/390-hp V-8. It would be the only official time that the 427 was offered and it was available only a short while. This engine was axed a couple of months into production and replaced in sparse numbers by the 428 Cobra Jet V-8, rated at 335 insurance-pleasing horses.

Cars with the GT option had an upper-body racing stripe, bucket seats, wide tread whitewalls, special wheel covers, an all-vinyl interior and a special handling package. Cyclones were offered in two-door hardtop and two-door fastback models and both had the same base price. Total output included 6,105 GT-optioned Cyclone fastbacks and 334 notchbacks.

When *Car Life* magazine tested the '68 Cyclone GT with the 428 CJ V-8, it found it pretty impressive, reporting performance figures like 6.2 seconds for 0-to-60 and a 14.4-second quarter-mile at 99.4 miles per hour.

Model Number	Body/Style Number	Body Type & Seating	Factory Price	Shipping Weight	Production Total
CYCLONE GT — SERIES 27 — V-8					
17	65H	2dr HT-5P	$2,936	3,479 lbs.	334
15	63H	2dr FSBK-5P	$2,936	3,525 lbs.	6,105

NOTE 1: Production for Cyclone GT models only — all engines included

ENGINES

BASE V-8: 90 degree, overhead valve. Cast-iron block. Bore and stroke: 4.047 x 3.781 in. Displacement: 390 cid. Compression ratio: 10.50:1. Brake hp: 320 at 4800 rpm. Taxable hp: 52.49. Torque: 427 at 3200 rpm. Five main bearings. Hydraulic valve lifters. Carburetor: Holley C7AF-9510-AE four-barrel. Engine code: S.

OPTIONAL V-8: 90 degree, overhead valve. Cast-iron block. Bore and stroke: 4.23 x 3.78 in. Displacement: 427 cid. Compression ratio: 10.90:1. Brake hp: 390 at 5600 rpm. Torque: 460 at 3200 rpm. Five main bearings. Hydraulic valve lifters. Carburetor: Holley C7AF-9510-AE four-barrel. Engine code: W.

OPTIONAL V-8: 90 degree, overhead valve. Cast-iron block. Bore and stroke:

4.13 x 3.98 in. Displacement: 428 cid. Compression ratio: 10.6:1. Brake hp: 335 at 5200 rpm. Taxable hp: 54.50. Torque: 440 at 3400 rpm. Five main bearings. Hydraulic valve lifters. Carburetor: Holley C8AF-9510-B four-barrel. Engine code: Q.

OPTIONS

Air conditioning ($360.40, not avaialble with 427-cid V-8). Comfort Stream ventilation system ($15.60, but not available with air conditioning). High-performance axle ($6.55). Power transfer axle ($42.15). Heavy-duty battery ($7.44, but standard with 427-cid V-8). Electric clock, except cars with tachometer ($15.76). Rear window defogger ($21.25). 302-cid four-barrel V-8 over Cyclone 302 ($57.61). Marauder 390 two-barrel V-8 over Cyclone 302 ($7.25). Marauder 390 four-barrel V-8 over Cyclone 302 ($158.00). Cyclone 427-cid V-8 for Cyclone GT with Select-Shift automatic transmission ($621.57 and not available with Brougham, air conditioning or power steering). All tinted glass ($35.05). Pair of adjustable headrests ($42.75). Left-hand remote-control mirror ($9.60). Oxford roof for hardtop ($94.55). Two-tone paint, except fastback($30.96). Power front disc brakes ($64.85). Power windows ($100.10). Power steering ($95.00). 4-way power front bench seat ($62.45). Four-way power bucket seats ($62.45, but standard on GT). AM push-button radio ($61.40). AM/FM stereo radio with an-

tenna ($184.95). Rear seat speaker ($26.00). Reflective tape stripe for Cyclone GT only ($16.85). Deluxe front shoulder belts ($29.61 and deluxe seat belts required). Deluxe rear shoulder belts ($29.61 and deluxe seat belts required). Deluxe seat belts with reminder light ($13.05). Front shoulder belts ($27.06, but not available with deluxe seat belts). Rear shoulder belts ($27.06, but not available with deluxe seat belts). Sports console, Cyclones ($50.65). Deluxe steering wheel ($13.90, but standard on Cyclone and Cyclone GT). Tachometer ($48.00 and not available with clock). Heavy-duty three-speed manual transmission with 390 GT engine only ($79). SelectShift Merc-O-Matic transmission with 302-cid V-8s ($198.00). SelectShift Merc-O-Matic transmission with 390- and 427-cid V-8s ($226.10). Four-speed manual transmission — close-ratio with 390 GT at same price ($184.02). Wire wheel covers ($50.75). Styled steel wheels ($96.36). Interval selector windshield wipers ($14.19). FR70 x 14 white sidewall radials ($38.95). Cyclone GT Performance Group including tape stripe, GT nameplates, F70 x 14 white sidewall tires, unique turbine wheel covers, special handling package and bucket seats ($168.40). GT Engine group includes power booster fan and bright engine dress-up kit ($34.35). Special handling package ($15.60 for V-8s only). Appearance protection group ($25.28). Courtesy light group ($19.69). Visual check group ($432.15).

1969 COUGAR ELIMINATOR 428 CJ

PHIL KUNZ

1969 Cougar Eliminator

The 1969 Mercury Cougar was completely restyled. It was a larger car with sculptured side panels that swept from the front fenders to the rear wheel openings. A new horizontal grille hid the concealed headlights and the sequential taillights had a new concave shape that culminated with wraparound back-up lights.

An "Eliminator" package was added to the options list in the spring. This name was based on the 427 SOHC-powered Eliminator funny cars driven by famed drag racer "Dyno" Don Nicholson. The package was based on the lowest-priced Cougar hardtop with the standard interior in a choice of three trims: (5A) Black, (EA) White or (5B) Blue. It then added specific exterior appearance upgrades, performance hardware and a couple of interior features. The exterior add-ons included a blacked-out grille with the bars painted flat black, except on the center section, which was left in bright metal. A large body-color scoop sat in the center of the hood and was functional when mated with the 428 CG V-8.

Four engines were available in early versions of the Eliminator package: the code M 351-cid 290-hp "Windsor" V-8 with a four-barrel carburetor, the code S 390-cid/320-hp Marauder/GT V-8, the code Q 428-cid 335-hp CJ V-8 and the 428-cid 335-hp SCG ram-air V-8 (also code Q). Later in year, the Boss 302-cid/290-hp V-8 was added to the list (for Eliminators only). Since the Cougar was a relatively heavy pony car, the 428-cid options were the ones that made it into a real muscle machine. The Boss 429 is said to be on some option lists, but it is believed it was used only in the drag racing cars built for Don Nicholson and Eddie Schartman. With the 428 CJ engine option you also got a hood scoop, hood hold-down pins, a competition handling package and hood striping.

The Cougar Eliminator with the 428-cid/335-hp Super Cobra Jet V-8 did 0-to-60 mph in an amazing 5.6 seconds and the quarter-mile in 14.10 seconds and 103 mph.

Model Number	Body/Style Number	Body Type & Seating	Factory Price	Shipping Weight	Production Total
COUGAR ELIMINATOR — SERIES 91 — 428 CJ V-8					
91	65A	2d HT-5P	$4,300	3,780 lbs.	Note 1
COUGAR ELIMINATOR — SERIES 91 — 428 SCJ V-8					
91	65B	2d HT-5P	$4,439	3,790 lbs.	Note 1

NOTE 1: A total of 2,250 Cougars (all engines) got the Eliminator package.

ENGINES

OPTIONAL V-8: 90 degree, overhead valve. Cast-iron block. Bore and stroke: 4.13 x 3.98 in. Displacement: 428 cid. Compression ratio: 10.6:1. Brake hp: 335 at 5200 rpm. Taxable hp: 54.50. Torque: 440 at 3400 rpm. Five main bearings. Hydraulic valve lifters. Carburetor: Holley C8AF-9510-B four-barrel. Engine code: Q.

OPTIONAL V-8: 90 degree, overhead valve. Cast-iron block. Bore and stroke: 4.13 x 3.98 in. Displacement: 428 cid. Compression ratio: 10.6:1. Brake hp: 335. Taxable hp: 54.50. Five main bearings. Hydraulic valve lifters. Carburetor: Holley four-barrel. Engine code: R.

OPTIONS

Air conditioner, requires Select-Shift automatic transmission, Traction-Lok differential, 3.25:1 axle and F70 belted or FR70 steel-belted tires ($375.70). Comfort Stream ventilation for cars without A/C ($25.90). High-performance axle ($6.50). Traction-Lok differential, 3.25:1 ratio required ($42.80). Heavy-duty Traction-Lok differential, 3.25:1, 3.91:1 or 4.30:1 ratio required ($42.80). Heavy-duty battery ($7.80). Front bumper guards ($13.00). Electric clock ($15.60). Courtesy light group, including rear roof pillar light, trunk light, underhood light and map light ($16.90). Rear window defogger ($22.10). Door edge guards ($5.20). 428-cid CJ four-barrel V-8 ($336.80). Complete tinted glass ($29.80). Front head restraints ($17.00). Hood lock pins ($7.80; included with 428-cid V-8). Front-and-rear rubber floor mats ($13). Two-tone paint ($31.10). Power disc brakes ($64.80). Power steering ($99.80). Sunroof with vinyl roof (no Eliminators had a vinyl roof so apparently none had the sun roof, a $459.80 option). Power windows ($104.90). AM radio with antenna ($60.90). AM/FM stereo radio with twin speakers ($185.30). AM radio with Stereo-sonic tape system ($195.60). Rear seat speaker, AM radio required ($15.60, but not available in combination with AM/Tape system). Ram-air induction, requires 428 CJ V-8 and includes ram-air induction system, functional hood scoop and F70-14 belted traction tires ($138.60). Front bench seat with center armrest ($24.70). Deluxe front shoulder belts ($15.60). Speed control, Select-Shift Merc-O-Matic transmission required ($71.30 and not available witrh 428 CJ). Sports console. Requires AM, AM/FM or AM stereo radio ($57.10). Tilt-Away steering wheel ($68.70). F70 fiberglass-belted traction tires ($35.00 on cars with 428 CJ V-8). FR70 x 14 wide tread steel-belted-radial-ply red-band tires (35.00). Space-Saver spare tire ($6.50). Four-speed manual transmission ($204.70). Merc-O-Matic Select-Shift automatic transmission ($227.00 with 428-cid V-8s).

(NOTE: Option information based on regular Cougar options list with Eliminator standard features removed or noted above.)

1969 CYCLONE CJ 428/SCJ 428

PHIL KUNZ

1969 Cyclone SCJ 428

Only the Cyclone fastback, in slightly re-trimmed format, returned in 1969 and the GT package became an appearance group option. There was an all-new Cyclone CJ model and it was hot. The CJ included a trendy blacked-out grille insert that was framed with bright metal. There was a single chrome piece in the middle, running from each end of the grille. A Cyclone emblem in the center of the grille highlighted the CJ model's front end. Additional features included front and rear wheel opening moldings, a dual exhaust system, a 3.50:1 ratio rear axle, an engine dress-up kit, a hood tape stripe and a competition-type handling package. A Sports Appearance option group was optional .

The Cyclone CJ was kind of a fastback Charger and bargain-basement Road Runner wrapped in one package. It came with Ford's big-block 428-cid Cobra Jet V-8 as standard equipment. Also included were an engine dress-up kit, a four-speed manual gear box, a 3.50:1 rear axle, a competition handling package, a front bench seat, fiberglass-belted 7.75-14 black sdewall tires and a hood tape stripe. The Cyclone CG sold for just a tad more than a regular Mercury Cyclone V-8 with the 302-cid base engine. It was aimed at the budget-priced super car niche.

A Cyclone CJ with a 435-hp version of the 428-cid V-6 carried only 11.6 lbs. per horsepower. It could do 0-to-60 mph in 6.1 seconds and fly down the quarter-mile in 13.9 seconds.

Model Number	Body/Style Number	Body Type & Seating	Factory Price	Shipping Weight	Production Total
CYCLONE CJ — SERIES 27 — V-8					
16	63H	2d FSBK-5P	$3,224	3,634 lbs.	3,261

NOTE 1: Production for Cyclone CJ/SCJ models only — both engines included.

ENGINES

BASE V-8: 90 degree, overhead valve. Cast-iron block. Bore and stroke: 4.13 x 3.98 in. Displacement: 428 cid. Compression ratio: 10.6:1. Brake hp: 335 at 5200 rpm. Taxable hp: 54.50. Torque: 440 at 3400 rpm. Five main bearings. Hydraulic valve lifters. Carburetor: Holley C8AF-9510-B four-barrel. Engine code: Q.

OPTIONAL V-8: 90 degree, overhead valve. Cast-iron block. Bore and stroke: 4.13 x 3.98 in. Displacement: 428 cid. Compression ratio: 10.6:1. Brake hp: 335. Taxable hp: 54.50. Five main bearings. Hydraulic valve lifters. Carburetor: Holley four-barrel. Engine code: R.

OPTIONS

Whisper-Aire air conditioner, requires Select-Shift automatic transmission, Traction-Lok differential, and 3.00:1 rear axle ($375.70). Comfort Stream ventilation for cars without A/C ($15.60). High-performance axle ($6.50). Traction-Lok differential, 3.00:1 or 3.25:1 ratio required ($42.80). Heavy-duty Traction-Lok differential, 3.25:1, 3.91:1 or 4.30:1 ratio required ($42.80). Heavy-duty battery ($7.80, but available as LPO with CJ 428). Electric clock ($15.60). Courtesy light group, including two dash panel lights, glove box light, ash tray light and luggage compartment light ($19.50). Curb moldings ($15.60). Decor group, ($42.80 with Special Appearance group or $60.90 without it). All tinted glass ($35.00). GT Appeartance Group ($168.40). Front head restraints ($17.00). Hood lock pins ($7.80, butincluded with 428 SCJ V-8). Remote-control left-hand racing mirror ($10.40). Two-tone paint ($31.10). Dual paint-and-tape stripes, replacing standard Cyclone stripes ($31.10). 4-way power bench seat ($73.90). Power disc brakes ($64.80). Power steering ($94.60). Power windows ($104.90). AM radio with antenna ($60.90). AM/FM stereo radio with twin speakers ($185.30). Dual rear seat speakers ($25.90), AM radio required ($15.60, but not available in combination with AM/Tape system). Ram-air induction, requires 428 CJ V-8 and includes ram-air induction system, functional hood scoop and F70-14 belted traction tires ($138.60). Deluxe front shoulder belts ($15.60). Speed control, Select-Shift Merc-O-Matic transmission required ($71.30 and not available witrh 428 CJ). Sports console. Requires AM, AM/FM or AM stereo radio ($55.70). Special Appearance Group ($64.80, but not available withoptional size tires or GT Appearance Group). Sports Appearance Group ($149.00). Rim-blow steering wheel ($35.00). Tachometer ($48.00 and not available with clock). F70 fiberglass-belted traction tires ($22.10 on cars with 428 CJ V-8). FR70 x 14 fiberglass belted traction tires with raised white lettering ($13.00, but standard with Ram Air ($13.00). Four-speed manual transmission (standard in Cyclone CJ). Merc-O-Matic Select-Shift automatic transmission ($42.00 in Cyclone CJ only). Comfort-Weave interior with bucket seats ($24.70).

1969 CYCLONE SPOILER II

DOUG MITCHEL

1969 Cyclone Spoiler II

Cars like the Cyclone Spoiler II were designed to put some Viagra into Mercury's high-performance image in the muscle car era. When NASCAR Grand National stock car racing teams tested the new 1968 body styles, they found the Mercury Cyclone fastback to be a bit faster than its Ford Fairlane fastback counterpart. A more aerodynamic nose design was said to be the reason. When Cale Yarborough drove the Wood Brothers Cyclone to victory in the Daytona 500 in February 1968, the battle of the NASCAR noses was on. Dodge countered with the Charger 500 for 1969. Ford forces fought back with the Torino Talladega and Mercury Cyclone Spoiler II. Both featured flush grilles and extended noses.

The Talladega was fairly simple, but the Cyclone Spoiler was not. Mercury announced the Spoiler as a midyear model to go on sale in January 1969. The main feature in early information was a spoiler bolted on the trunk deck. It was nice, but the device was not legal in NASCAR at the time. Originally, an extended nose similar to the Talladega was to

be an option. After considerable confusion, the long-nosed Spoiler came to be known as the Cyclone Spoiler II. All the cars came with the 351-cid four-barrel V-8 despite an announcement that there also would be a 428-cid Cobra-Jet Ram-Air option. At least 500 needed to be produced to qualify the car as a production model so it could be raced. Cyclone Spoilers came in two trim versions. A "Dan Gurney" Spoiler had dark blue roof and striping and a signature decal on the white lower portion. A "Cale Yarborough" edition featured red trim similar to his Wood Brothers stock car. It, too, had a signature decal.

As it turned out, the Spoiler wasn't declared legal in NASCAR until the Atlanta 500 on March 30. This put Cyclone pilots in Talladegas for the Daytona 500 race, which was won by Lee Roy Yarbrough in Junior Johnson's Talladega.

The Cyclone II Spoiler was good for 0-to-60 mph in 7.4 seconds or a 14.4-second quarter-mile at 99 mph. Mercurys won four NASCAR Grand National races in 1969.

Model Number	Body/Style Number	Body Type & Seating	Factory Price	Shipping Weight	Production Total
CYCLONE SPOILER II — SERIES 27 — V-8					
15	63H	2d FSBK-5P	$3,700	3,700 lbs.	519

NOTE 1: Production for Cyclone Spoiler II model-option only — both engines included.
NOTE 2: Factory price and shipping weight are estimated.

ENGINE

BASE V-8: 90 degree, overhead valve. Cast-iron block. Bore and stroke: 4.00 x 3.50 in. Displacement: 351 cid. Compression ratio: 10.7:1. Brake hp: 290 at 4800 rpm. Taxable hp: 51.20. Torque: 385 at 3200 rpm. Five main bearings. Hydraulic valve lifters. Carburetor: Four-barrel. Engine code M.

OPTIONS

Whisper-Aire air conditioner, requires Select-Shift automatic transmission, Traction-Lok differential, and 3.00:1 rear axle ($375.70). Comfort Stream ventilation for cars without A/C ($15.60). High-performance axle ($6.50). Traction-Lok differential, 3.00:1 or 3.25:1 ratio required ($42.80). Heavy-duty Traction-Lok differential, 3.25:1, 3.91:1 or 4.30:1 ratio required ($42.80). Heavy-duty battery ($7.80). Electric clock ($15.60). Courtesy light group ($19.50). Curb moldings ($15.60). Decor group ($42.80 with Special Appearance group or $60.90 without it). All tinted glass ($35.00). GT Appeartance Group ($168.40). Front head restraints ($17.00). Hood lock pins ($7.80). Remote-control left-hand racing mirror ($10.40). Two-tone paint ($31.10). Dual paint-and-tape stripes, replacing standard Cyclone stripes ($31.10). 4-way power bench seat ($73.90). Power disc brakes ($64.80). Power steering ($94.60). Power windows ($104.90). AM radio with antenna ($60.90). AM/FM stereo radio with twin speakers ($185.30). Dual rear seat speakers ($25.90), AM radio required ($15.60, but not available in combination with AM/Tape system). Deluxe front shoulder belts ($15.60). Speed control, Select-Shift Merc-O-Matic transmission required ($71.30 and not available witrh 428 CJ). Sports console. Requires AM, AM/FM or AM stereo radio ($55.70). Special Appearance Group ($64.80, but not available withoptional size tires or GT Appearance Group). Sports Appearance Group ($149.00). Rim-blow steering wheel ($35.00). Tachometer ($48.00 and not available with clock). F70 fiberglass-belted traction tires ($99.80). FR70 x 14 fiberglass belted traction tires with raised white lettering ($13.00). Four-speed manual transmission ($194.30). Merc-O-Matic Select-Shift automatic transmission ($206.10). Comfort-Weave interior with bucket seats ($24.70).

1970 COUGAR ELIMINATOR 428 CJ

JERRY HEASLEY

1970 Cougar Eliminator

The 1970 Mercury Cougar Eliminator was again based on the standard Cougar, but had a few changes from the '69 model. Six body colors were standard: (M) Pastel Blue, (U) Competition Gold, (D) Competition Yellow, (J) Competition Blue, (Z) Competition Green and (1) Competition Orange. Other colors could again be special ordered at extra cost. An upgraded version of the standard Cougar interior was available.

Exterior details for 1970 included a blacked-out grille with vertical bars painted flat black, including the bars in the center section, which had a new design. The same large air scoop sat in the center of the hood, but it was now finished in flat black. It was functional when mated with the 428 CG V-8. Racing-style OSRV mirrors were used on both sides of the car, but only the driver's was a remote-control type. There was again a flat black fiberglass front spoiler and a body-color full-width wing-type rear deck lid spoiler (which now had striping with the Eliminator name).

Four engines were available: the code G Boss 302-cid/290-hp V-8, the code M 351-cid/290-hp "Windsor" V-8 with a four-barrel carburetor, the code Q 428-cid/335-hp CJ V-8 and the 428-cid/335-hp SCG ram-air V-8 (also code Q). The package also included a 3.25:1 ratio rear axle, the performance handling package and F70-14 glass-belted traction tires with raised white lettering.

The Cougar Eliminator with the 428-cid/335-hp Super Cobra Jet V-8 did 0-to-60 mph in an amazing 5.6 seconds and the quarter-mile in 14.10 seconds and 103 mph.

Model Number	Body/Style Number	Body Type & Seating	Factory Price	Shipping Weight	Production Total
COUGAR ELIMINATOR— SERIES 91 — 428 CJ V-8					
91	65A	2d HT-5P	$3,568	3,285 lbs.	Note 1
COUGAR ELIMINATOR— SERIES 91 — 428 CJ V-8					
91	65A	2d HT-5P	$3,633	3,295 lbs.	Note 1
COUGAR XR7 ELIMINATOR— SERIES 93 — 428 SCJ RAM-AIR V-8					
93	65B	2d HT-5P	$3,867	3,311 lbs.	Note 1
COUGAR XR7 ELIMINATOR — SERIES 93 — 428 SCJ RAM-AIR V-8					
93	65B	2d HT-5P	$3,932	3,321 lbs.	Note 1

NOTE 1: Estimated prices above include base price, price of Eliminator package, price of 428 CJ or 428 SCJ V-8 and added cost of required F70-14 white-letter tures.
NOTE 2: Total production was 2,267.
NOTE 3: Best information indicates 469 Eliminators had the Boss 302, 1,424 had the 351 Cleveland and 374 had one of the 428 CJ.SCJ V-8s.

ENGINES

OPTIONAL V-8: 90 degree, overhead valve. Cast-iron block. Bore and stroke: 4.13 x 3.98 in. Displacement: 428 cid. Compression ratio: 10.6:1. Brake hp: 335 at 5200 rpm. Taxable hp: 54.50. Torque: 440 at 3400 rpm. Five main bearings. Hydraulic valve lifters. Carburetor: Holley C8AF-9510-B four-barrel. Engine code: Q.

OPTIONAL V-8: 90 degree, overhead valve. Cast-iron block. Bore and stroke: 4.13 x 3.98 in. Displacement: 428 cid. Compression ratio: 10.6:1. Brake hp: 335. Taxable hp: 54.50. Five main bearings. Hydraulic valve lifters. Carburetor: Holley four-barrel. Engine code: R.

OPTIONS

Air conditioner, requires Select-Shift automatic transmission with 428 V-8 ($375.70). Higher-ratio rear axle axle ($6.50). Traction-Lok differential, 3.00:1 or 3.25:1 ratio required ($42.80). Heavy-duty Traction-Lok differential, 3.50:1 ($46.70). Heavy-duty battery ($7.80). Front bumper guards ($13.00). Electric clock ($15.60, but standard in XR7). Sports console ($57.10). Rear window defogger ($25.90). 428 CJ four-barrel V-8 over 351-cid two-barrel V-8, available only with four-speed manual or Select-Shift automatic transmission (includes engine, dual exhausts, competition handling package, F70-14 whitewall tires,

3.50:1 rear axle, power dome hood, Black or Argent stripes and engine call-out badge $310.90). Complete tinted glass ($32.40). Heater and defroster delete ($22.10 credit). Left-hand remote-control mirror ($10.40). Left-hand remote-control racing style mirror ($13.00). Two-tone paint ($31.10, but not available with Eliminator). Power disc brakes ($64.80). Automatic seat back release ($25.90). Power steering ($104.90). Power windows ($104.90). AM radio with antenna ($60.90). AM/FM stereo radio ($212.50). AM radio with Stereo-sonic tape system ($195.60). Rear seat speaker, AM radio required ($15.60, but not available in combination with AM/Tape system). Deluxe front and rear seat and front shoulder belts ($15.60). Spoke-type Rim-Blow steering wheel ($35.00). Sunroof with vinyl roof (no Eliminators had a vinyl roof so apparently none had the sun roof — a $459.80 option which required a vinyl top). Select-Shift Merc-O-Matic transmission ($227.00). Four-speed manual transmission with Hurst shifter ($204.70, but included with 428 CJ V-8). Tilt steering wheel ($45.40). Houndstooth cloth-and-vinyl trim for base Cougar hardtop with bucket seats, Decor Group required ($32.40). Houndstooth cloth-and-vinyl trim for XR7 Cougar hardtop with bucket seats replacing leather trim ($51.90 credit). Vinyl top ($89.40, but not available on Eliminator). Deluxe wheel covers ($25.90). Rallye wheels over hubcaps ($41.50). Rallye wheels over other options (($15.60). Wire wheel covers over hubcaps ($73.90). Wire wheel covers over other options ($48.00). Styled wheels over hubcaps ($116.60). Styled wheels over other options ($90.70). Interval windshield wipers ($25.90). F70 fiberglass-belted traction tires ($35.00 on cars with 428 CJ V-8). F70 x 14 Traction-Belted tires replacing F70 whitewalls, white-letter style required with Eliminator option ($13.00 on Eliminator with 428 CJ V-8 and $76.50 on other Eliminators). Space-Saver spare tire ($15.60). Appearance Protection Group ($31.10). Competition Handling Group ($31.10, and required on Eliminator but only available as optional equipment on Eliminators with the 351-cid V-8; otherwise standard). Courtesy Light Group ($19.50). Decor Group ($90.70 for Cougar hardtop, but $70 for Eliminator which comes with curb moldings and different wheel treatment). Drag-Pack option for Cougar with 428 CJ V-8 ($155.50). Super Drag-Pack option for Cougar with 428 CJ or Boss 302 V-8 ($207.30). Elimator option ($129.40, but reqires F70 raise-white-letter tires and competition handling group when ordered with 351-cid V-8). Ram-air induction, requires 428 CJ V-8 and includes ram-air induction system, functional hood scoop in body color, hood stripes and 428 CJ logo ($64.80). Visual Check panel ($25.90, but standard with XR7).

1970 CYCLONE GT 429 CJ/429 SCJ

PHIL KUNZ

1970 Cyclone GT SCJ 429

Mercury Cyclones got all kinds of things when they were restyled for 1970 after a two-season stint with a more radical fastback roofline. Some of the changes made for 1970 were good for muscle car fans. Though the same unitized chassis was used, the Cyclone wheelbase grew by one inch to 117 inches and the overall length of the cars was extended by a hefty 6.7 inches. The latter alteration was due primarily to a protruding nose and fender design that produced somewhat

questionable styling. Cyclones also got a gun sight-type design in the center of their grilles.

While its Ford Torino cousin got new fastback designs, the Mercury intermediate did not. The Cyclone hardtops had trunk lines about halfway between the old notchback hardtop and a true fastback. The GT, which had once been the hottest Cyclone model, was now the mildest. It came standard with only a 351-cid/250-hp V-8 with a two-barrel carburetor. The

351-cid "Cleveland" V-8 was among the available engine options. The 429 CJ and 429 SCJ V-8s were optional for real muscle car maniacs.

Model Number	Body/Style Number	Body Type & Seating	Factory Price	Shipping Weight	Production Total
CYCLONE GT — SERIES 16 — V-8 (429 CJ V-8)					
16	65H	2d FSBK-5P	$3,396	3,700 lbs.	Note 2
CYCLONE GT — SERIES 16 — V-8 (428 SCJ RAM-AIR V-8)					
16	65H	2d FSBK-5P	$3,700	3,700 lbs.	Note 2

NOTE 1: Price above includes base price, 429 CJ and (where applicable) Ram-Air.
NOTE 2: Total production of Cyclone GTs with all engines was 10,170.

ENGINES

OPTIONAL V-8: 90 degree, overhead valve. Cast-iron block. Bore and stroke: 4.36 x 3.59 in. Displacement: 429 cid. Compression ratio: 11.3:1. Brake hp: 370 at 5400 rpm. Taxable hp: 60.83. Torque: 450 at 3400 rpm. Five main bearings. Hydraulic valve lifters. Carburetor: Four-barrel. Engine code: C.

OPTIONAL V-8: 90 degree, overhead valve. Cast-iron block. Bore and stroke: 4.36 x 3.59 in. Displacement: 429 cid. Compression ratio: 10.5:1. Brake hp: 375 at 5200 rpm. Taxable hp: 60.83. Torque: 450 at 3400 rpm. Five main bearings. Solid valve lifters. Carburetor: Four-barrel. Engine code: J.

OPTIONS

Whisper-Aire air conditioner, requires power steering with 429-cid V-8 ($388.60). Heavy-duty 55-amp. Alternator ($20.80). Higher-ratio rear axle ($6.50). Traction-Lok differential, 3.00:1 or 3.25:1 ratio required ($42.80). Heavy-duty Traction-Lok differential, 3.50:1 or 3.91:1 with Boss 429 ratio required ($63.50). Electric

clock ($15.60). Extra cooling ($7.80). Console ($55.70). 429 CJ V-8 includes cast aluminum rocker arm covers, bright dip stick handle, bright oil filler cap, bright radiator cap, bright air cleaner on non-Ram-Air versions and must have power steering when air conditioning is ordered ($169.70 over regular optional 429-cid four-barrel V-8). 429 CJ V-8 includes cast aluminum rocker arm covers, bright dip stick handle, bright oil filler cap, bright radiator cap, bright air cleaner on non-Ram-Air versions and must have power steering when air conditioning is ordered ($310.90 over base 351-cid two-barrel V-8). Evaporative emissions controls for California cars ($37.60). Complete tinted glass ($36.30). Heater and defroster delete($22.10 credit). Left-hand remote-control racing style mirror ($13.00). Power disc brakes ($64.80). Power steering ($104.90). Power windows ($104.90). AM radio with antenna ($60.90). AM/FM stereo radio ($212.50). AM radio with Stereo-sonic tape system ($195.60). Dual rear seat speaker, AM radio required ($27.30, but not available in combination with AM/FM radio or AM/Tape system). Deluxe front and rear seat and front shoulder belts ($15.60). Deluxe seat with automatic seat back release ($38.90). Rim-Blow steering wheel ($35.00). Sun roof ($375.70). Select-Shift Merc-O-Matic transmission ($42 over cost of same car with four-speed manual transmission). Four-speed manual transmission with Hurst shifter (standard). Houndstooth Upbeat interior trim ($32.40). Luxury wheel covers ($15.60 over price of trim rings). Styled steel wheels (over trim rings $13). Interval windshield wipers ($25.90). G70-14 white sidewall tires (no charge over standard equipment). G70-14 Traction tires ($18.20). Drag-Pack option includes 3.91:1 high-performance axle, heavy-duty traction-lok differential, engine oil cooler and unique 429 SCJ V-8 ($155.50). Super Drag-Pack option includes 4.30:1 high-performance axle, Detroit Automotive no-spin locking axle, engine oil cooler and other unique components ($207.30). Ram-air induction, requires 428 CJ V-8 and includes ram-air induction system, functional hood scoop in body color, hood stripes and 428 CJ logo ($64.80).

1970 CYCLONE SPOILER

1970 Cyclone Spoiler

Motor Trend (September 1969) said: "Leader of the leaders is the surly Spoiler. It combines both 'go' and appearance. Base engine is the 429 four-barrel Cobra Jet with ram-air, backed up by the four-speed Hurst shifter and a Traction-Lok 3.30:1 axle. Mercury's wings take the form of a black front spoiler under the front bumper to help reduce front -end lift and a rear spoiler on the deck to increase rear wheel traction. If you can do 140 mph without getting a ticket you'll find the car stays flat. The Spoiler has, as standard, a special tachom-eter/instrumentation package inset in the instrument panel to the right of the regular instrument cluster. This package consists of four gauges with dial faces angled toward the driver for quick and easy viewing. Gauges included are a three-inch tach calibrated to 8,000 rpm with a manually-adjustable red line, engine oil pressure, engine temperature and ammeter. This package is optional on other models with 429 engines."

The complete list of standard equipment for the Spoiler model included the instrumentation group, G70-14 traction-belted tires, ram-air induction, Comfort-Weave vinyl hi-back bucket seats, a rim-blow sports steering wheel, hub caps with bright trim rings, a remote-control left-hand racing mirror and a manual right-hand racing mirror.

"The Cyclone's racy looks are borne out in the accompanying specs," said *Motor Trend*. "Cyclone has the looks and performance."

Model Number	Body/Style Number & Seating	Body Type Price	Factory Weight	Shipping Total	Production
CYCLONE SPOILER — SERIES 17 — V-8 (428 SCJ RAM-AIR V-8)					
17	65G	2d FSBK-5P	$3,759	3,773 lbs.	1,695

ENGINE

BASE V-8: 90 degree, overhead valve. Cast-iron block. Bore and stroke: 4.36 x 3.59 in. Displacement: 429 cid. Compression ratio: 10.5:1. Brake hp: 375 at 5200 rpm. Taxable hp: 60.83. Torque: 450 at 3400 rpm. Five main bearings. Solid valve lifters. Carburetor: Four-barrel. Engine code: J.

OPTIONS

Whisper-Aire air conditioner, requires power steering with 429-cid V-8 ($388.60). Heavy-duty 55-amp. Alternator ($20.80). Higher-ratio rear axle ($6.50). Electric clock ($15.60). Extra cooling ($7.80). Console ($55.70). 429 CJ V-8 includes cast aluminum rocker arm covers, bright dip stick handle, bright oil filler cap, bright radiator cap, bright air cleaner on non-Ram-Air versions and must have power steering when air conditioning is ordered (standard). Evaporative emissions controls for California cars ($37.60). Complete tinted glass ($36.30). Concealed headlights ($53.20). Heater and defroster delete ($22.10 credit). Left-hand remote-control racing style mirror ($13.00). Power disc brakes ($64.80). Power steering ($104.90). Power windows ($104.90). AM radio with antenna ($60.90). AM/FM stereo radio ($212.50). AM radio with Stereo-sonic tape system ($195.60). Dual rear seat speaker, AM radio required ($27.30, but not available in combination with AM/FM radio or AM/Tape system). Deluxe front and rear seat and front shoulder belts ($15.60). Deluxe seat with automatic seat back release ($38.90). Rim-Blow steering wheel ($35.00). Sun roof ($375.70). Select-Shift Merc-O-Matic transmission ($42 over cost of same car with four-speed manual transmission). Four-speed manual transmission with Hurst shifter (standard). Houndstooth Upbeat interior trim ($32.40). Luxury wheel covers ($15.60 over price of trim rings). Styled steel wheels (over trim rings $13). Interval windshield wipers ($25.90). G70-14 white sidewall tires (no charge over standard equipment). Drag-Pack option includes 3.91:1 high-performance axle, heavy-duty traction-lok differential, engine oil cooler and unique 429 SCJ V-8 ($92.00). Super Drag-Pack option includes 4.30:1 high-performance axle, Detroit Automotive no-spin locking axle, engine oil cooler and other unique components ($143.80).

1971 COUGAR/XR7/GT 429 CJ

1971 Cougar GT CJ 429

The 429 CJ option was released for 1971 Cougars and offered for only one year. So-equipped cars were among the last Mercury muscle cars of the era. Both Cobra-Jet and Cobra-Jet with ram air versions were available. The engine was offered in the all models in the Cougar Group. A four-speed manual transmission with Hurst shifter and rev limiter was standard with the 429 CJ. The Ford C6 Select-Shift automatic transmission was optional. These were special transmissions with extra clutch plates, a Cast-iron tail-shaft and an "R" servo. Both hardtops and convertibles were built with 429s. They are all rare cars, especially ragtops.

The package included ribbed cast-aluminum rocker arm covers, a bright dipstick handle, a bright oil filler cap, a bright radiator cap, a bright air cleaner (on cars without ram air only) and a heavy-duty battery. All 429 CJs had a competition-type suspension with a larger front sway bar, a beefed-up rear sway bar and staggered, heavy-duty rear shocks.

The Ram Air induction package included a functional hood scoop. This should not be confused with the non-functional scoop that the GT package included, although GTs with 429 CJ V-8s got the functional upgrade.

Model Number	Body/Style Number	Body Type & Seating	Factory Price	Shipping Weight	Production Total
COUGAR — SERIES 91/92 — 429 CJ V-8					
91	65D	2d HT-5P	$3,600	3,331 lbs.	Note 3
92	76D	2d Conv-5P	$3,992	3,461 lbs.	Note 3

COUGAR — SERIES 91/92 — 429 CJ RAM-AIR V-8					
91	65D	2d HT-5P	$3,665	3,341 lbs.	Note 3
92	76D	2d Conv-5P	$4,057	3,471 lbs.	Note 3
COUGAR GT — SERIES 91 — 429 CJ V-8					
91	65D	2d HT-5P	$3,730	3,381 lbs.	Note 3
COUGAR GT — SERIES 91 — 429 CJ RAM-AIR V-8					
91	65D	2d HT-5P	$3,795	3,391 lbs.	Note 3
COUGAR XR7 — SERIES 93/94 — 429 CJ V-8					
93	65F	2d HT-5P	$3,940	3,391 lbs.	Note 3
94	76F	2d Conv-5P	$4,188	3,511 lbs.	Note 3
COUGAR XR7 — SERIES 93/94 — 429 CJ RAM-AIR V-8					
93	65F	2d HT-5P	$4005	3,401 lbs.	Note 3
94	76F	2d Conv-5P	$4,253	3,521 lbs.	Note 3

NOTE 1: Estimated prices above include base price, for GTs price of GT package, price of 429 CJ or 429 CJ RAM-AIR V-8, but no other mandatory options.

NOTE 2: The weights are estimates.

NOTE 3: 429 CJ cars totaled 448 units (47 convertibles and 401 hardtops).

ENGINES

OPTIONAL V-8: 90 degree, overhead valves. Cast-iron block. Displacement: 429 cid. Bore and stroke: 4.36 x 3.59 inches. Compression ratio: 11.30:1. Brake hp: 370 at 5400 rpm. Torque: 450 at 3400 rpm. Five main bearings. Hydraulic valve lifters. Carburetor: Holley four-barrel. Dual exhaust. Code C.

OPTIONAL V-8: 90 degree, overhead valves. Cast-iron block. Displacement: 429 cid. Bore and stroke: 4.36 x 3.59 inches. Compression ratio: 11.30:1. Brake hp: 375 at 5600 rpm. Torque: 450 at 3400 rpm. Five main bearings. Solid valve lifters. Carburetor: Holley four-barrel. Dual exhaust. Code J.

OPTIONS (PARTIAL LIST)

Air conditioner with 429-cid V-8, requires 3.25:1 or higher rear axle ratio, includes heavy-duty alterrnator and not available in convertible ($408.00). Traction-Lok differential ($48.00). Heavy-duty battery (80-amp standard with 429 CJ V-8). Sports console with clock ($76.50). Electric rear window defroster in hasrdtop only ($48.00). 429 CJ four-barrel V-8 over 351-cid two-barrel V-8, with four-speed manual transmission standard, includes cast-aluminum rocker arm covers, bright dip stick handle, bright oil filler cap, bright radiator cap, bright non Ram-Air air cleaner and heavy-duty battery ($310.90 and requires power disc brakes and F70-14 or larger tires). Complete tinted glass, convertible ($15.60). Complete tinted glass, hardtop ($37.60). Tinted windshield, fleet cars only ($22.10). Remote-control left-hand OSRV mirror ($14.30, but not available on XR7). Remote-control left-hand racing-style OSRV mirror ($15.60, but standard on XR7 or with GT package). Power front disc brakes, includes power rear drum brakes ($70.00 and required with 429 CJ V-8). 4-Way power driver's seat ($77.80). Power steering, variable-ration of 429 CJs and other cars with competition handling package ($115.30). Vinyl roof with sun roof for base Cougar hardtop ($483.10). Power side windows ($115.30). AM radio ($60.80). AM/FM stereo radio ($218.90). AM radio with Stereo-sonic tape system ($200.80). Vinyl roof for base Cougar hardtop ($89.40). Vinyl roof for XR7 hardtop (vinyl roof delete options of $39.96 and $50.60 available). Up-beat stripe cloth-and-vinyl interior for base Cougar hardtop (no charge). Up-beat stripe cloth-and-vinyl interior for XR7 ($54.50 credit for delete option instead of leather). Special Select-Shift automatic with 429 CJ V-8 ($243.10). Four-speed manual transmission with Hurst shifter ($215.10, but included with 429 CJ V-8). Styled wheels over hubcaps for base Cougar hardtop ($58.30). Styled wheels over other options for all in Cougar Group ($32.40). Interval windshield wipers ($25.90). Appearance Protection Group ($32.40). Competition Handling Group 429 CJ V-8 ($32.40). Convenience Group ($48.00 for hardtops and $32.40 for convertibles because seat belt warning light is standard in convertibles). Courtesy Light Group ($19.50). Decor Group ($70.00 and not available for XR7). GT package for base Cougar hardtop only, includes high-ratio axle, competition suspension, dual racing mirrors, non-functional hood scoop — except with 429 CJ Ram-Air — performance cooling package, tachometer, rim-blow steering wheel, F78-14 white sidewall tires, hub caps with bright trim rings, GT fender ID and black instrument panel ($129.60 with all engines). Ram-Air induction package, with 429 CJ V-8 only ($64.80).

1971 CYCLONE GT AND SPOILER 429 CJ/SCJ

Muscle cars don't come much bigger than the hefty '71 Cyclone GT and Cyclone Spoiler, but with a 429 Cobra-Jet V-8 on board, the big beast turned into a brute. Zero-to-60 took about 6.5 seconds and the quarter-mile could be accomplished in about 14.5 seconds with a terminal speed close to the century mark.

The intermediate-size Mercury Montego continued to be the basis for the high-performance models still offered by Lincoln Mercury Division in 1971. The new models were again actually based on the mid-sized Ford Falcon-Torino series that was first launched in 1968. Muscle car models included the Cyclone GT and Montego Cyclone Spoiler. All Cyclones were two-door hardtops.

The Montego Cyclone's standard equipment included a 351-cid/285-hp four-barel V-8 and a four-speed manual transmission with a floor-mounted Hurst gear shifter. The Cyclone GT included the cross-country ride package, a performance hood with integral scoop, concealed headlights and a 351-cid/240-hp V-8 with a two-barrel carburetor and Select-Shift automatic transmission.

With these cars, the longer their model names, the better their collector-car potential is. The Cyclones were tough cars with good reliability, but 1971 was the final year for the Cyclone name. A 429-cid Cobra-Jet V-8 with 370 hp was op- tional in 1971 Cyclones, Cyclone GTs and Cyclone Spoilers. The "429" got less than 10 mpg, but it had some real muscle. The 429 CJ package included cast-aluminum rocker arm covers and a bright dipstick handle, oil filler cap, radiator cap and air cleaner (on non-Ram-Air cars). Power disc brakes were mandatory and, if you wanted air conditioning, you also had to add power steering

Model Number	Body/Style Number	Body Type & Seating	Factory Price	Shipping Weight	Production Total
CYCLONE GT — SERIES 16 — V-8 (429 CJ)					
16	65H	2d FSBK-5P	$3,938	3,542 lbs.	Note 3
CYCLONE GT — SERIES 16 — V-8 (429 CJ RAM-AIR)					
16	65H	2d FSBK-5P	$4,003	3,552 lbs.	Note 3
CYCLONE SPOILER — SERIES 17 — V-8 (428 CJ)					
17	65G	2d FSBK-5P	$4,059	3,823 lbs.	Note 3
CYCLONE SPOILER — SERIES 17 — V-8 (428 CJ RAM-AIR)					
17	65G	2d FSBK-5P	$4,124	3,833 lbs.	Note 3

NOTE 1: Estimated prices above include base price, for GTs price of GT package, price of 429 CJ or 429 CJ RAM-AIRV-8, but no other mandatory options.

NOTE 2: The weights are close estimates.

NOTE 3: In 1971 Mercury built 444 Cyclones, 2,287 Cyclone GTs and 353 Cyclone Spoilers. No engine breakouts are available.

ENGINES

OPTIONAL V-8: 90 degree, overhead valves. Cast-iron block. Displacement: 429 cid. Bore and stroke: 4.36 x 3.59 inches. Compression ratio: 11.30:1. Brake hp: 370 at 5400 rpm. Torque: 450 at 3400 rpm. Five main bearings. Hydraulic valve lifters. Carburetor: Holley four-barrel. Dual exhaust. Code C.

MERCURY

1971 Montego Cyclone GT

OPTIONAL V-8: 90 degree, overhead valves. Cast-iron block. Displacement: 429 cid. Bore and stroke: 4.36 x 3.59 inches. Compression ratio: 11.30:1. Brake hp: 375 at 5600 rpm. Torque: 450 at 3400 rpm. Five main bearings. Solid valve lifters. Carburetor: Holley four-barrel. Dual exhaust. Code J.

OPTIONS

Air conditioner with 429-cid V-8, requires power steering with 429 CJ V-8s ($408.00). Heavy-duty alternator (standard with 429 CJ V-8). Higher-ratio rear axle ($13.00). Traction-Lok differential ($48.00, but standard with Cyclone Spoiler). Heavy-duty Traction-Lok differential ($67.40, but on charge with Cyclone Spoiler). Heavy-duty battery (80-amp standard with 429 CJ V-8). Electric clock ($18.20). Extra-duty cooling package ($7.80). Heavy-duty cooling package ($36.30, but standard with 3.25:1 axle or trailer towing). Concole, bucket seats required ($60.90). Rear window defogger ($31.10). Electric rear window defroster in hasrdtop only ($48.00). 429 CJ four-barrel V-8 over 351-cid two-barrel V-8, in Cyclone GT with automatic transmission, includes cast-aluminum rocker arm covers, bright dip stick handle, bright oil filler cap, bright radiator cap, bright non Ram-Air air cleaner and heavy-duty battery ($332.90 and requires power disc brakes). 429 CJ four-barrel V-8 over 351-cid two-barrel V-8, in Cyclone GT with four-speed manual transmission, includes cast-aluminum rocker arm covers, bright dip stick handle, bright oil filler cap, bright radiator cap, bright non Ram-Air air cleaner and heavy-duty battery ($310.90 and requires power disc brakes). 429 CJ four-barrel V-8 over 351-cid four-barrel V-8, in Cyclone

or Cyclone Spoiler, includes cast-aluminum rocker arm covers, bright dip stick handle, bright oil filler cap, bright radiator cap, bright non Ram-Air air cleaner and heavy-duty battery ($257.80 and requires power disc brakes). Complete tinted glass, fastback hardtop ($42.80). Tinted windshield, fleet cars only ($25.90). Power front disc brakes, includes power rear drum brakes ($70.00 and required with 429 CJ V-8). Four-way power driver's seat ($77.80, except GT and Spoiler with bench seat). Power steering, variable-ration in 429 CJs and other cars with competition handling package ($115.30). Power side windows ($115.30). AM radio ($66.10). AM/FM stereo radio ($239.60). AM radio with Stereo-sonic tape system ($200.80). Dual rear radio speakers ($31.10). Vinyl roof ($99.80). High-back bucket seats Cyclone, standard in GT and Spoiler ($132.20). Houndstooth upholstery, high-back bucket seats required ($32.40). Rim-blow steering wheel ($35.00 over standard, but included in GT and Spoiler). Tilt steering wheel ($45.40). Special Select-Shift automatic with 429 CJ V-8 ($48.20). Four-speed manual transmission with Hurst shifter ($04.70, but standard in GT or Spoiler with 429 CJ V-8). Deluxe wheel covers over hubcaps ($25.90, but standard on GT and not available for Spoiler). Luxury wheel covers over hubcaps on Cyclone GT ($18.20). Luxury wheel covers over trim rings on Cyclone Spoiler ($13.00). Courtesy Light Group ($20.80). Ram-Air induction package, with 429 CJ V-8 only ($64.80). Trailer towing package ($103.70). Tire options replacing standard F70-14 traction for cars with 429 CJ V-8 and air conditioning: G70-14 traction tires.

OLDSMOBILE MUSCLE 1964-1971

OLDSMOBILE

By the early 1960s, Oldsmobile was on the move upwards on many sales and engineering fronts. An innovative chief engineer named John Beltz would move into the general manager's chair in this era. A lot of great automotive concepts were advanced by this executive, who was a genuine auto enthusiast. The Cutlass had once seen a brief fling with high-performance in its turbocharged Jetfire models in 1962 and 1963. Now more was on the way.

Until 1964, all of the Rocket V-8 engines had a strong "family resemblance." The main differences were in compression ratios, carburetion, ignition, air cleaners, intake and exhaust manifolds, cylinder heads and piston design. Late in 1964, Oldsmobile made a bold move back into the high- performance field with its 4-4-2 package. First as an F-85/Cutlass option, later as a full-fledged series, this Oldsmobile intermediate package was a real hit with the performance crowd. The 330-cid Olds V-8 used in the first 4-4-2 was a blend of old and new. It traced its ancestry to the first Rocket V-8 in terms of dimensions, like the distance between cylinder bores and the crankshaft-to-camshaft span. This meant that old tooling could be re-used to save money. At the same time, the 330 was a more compact engine with entirely new cylinder head, block and manifold castings, new internal parts and new valve gears. The options list was also expanded.

In 1965, there was a new 400-cid/345-hp Olds V-8 for the year-old 4-4-2 high-performance model. With muscle car fever in full swing, there were many different compression ratios, valve setups and carburetion options available.

The biggest ever Rocket V-8 was a bored-out 400 that arrived in 1968 with 455 cubic inches of displacement. It offered five horsepower ratings from 310 to 400 that year.

For those seeking a bit more zing, the potent W-cars were offered in the late 1960s. Finally, buyers who wanted to taste more luxury with their high-performance Cutlass were tempted by the limited-production Hurst/Olds. By the 1970s, the Cutlass had grown into a powerful market force thanks to the image established by the muscular W-cars, the Hurst/Olds and the 4-4-2.

EDITOR'S NOTES:

— GM muscle cars were not made in all GM factories, but the codes for all factories are shown.

— Because of the way that factory options were listed in our sources, it is not always clear if certain options were avaiable only on specific models.

JERRY HEASLEY

1964 F-85/CUTLASS 4-4-2

OLDSMOBILE

1964 4-4-2

PHIL KUNZ

The first Oldsmobile 4-4-2 was a 1964 3/4 offering for drivers who wanted just a bit more performance and handling than the standard mid-size Oldsmobile delivered. The package was available for any V-8 powered mid-size Olds except the station wagon. On the official price sticker attached to the window, this $136.00 package was described as "Option number B-09 Police Apprehender Pursuit."

One piece of Oldsmobile factory literature called Product Selling Information for Oldsmobile Salesmen explained the 4-4-2 like this, "police needed it—Olds built it—pursuit proved it." This literature clearly pointed out the original meaning of the 4-4-2 designation was as follows: "4-BARREL CARBU-RETION—plus high-lift cams boost the power of the "4-4-2" Ultra High-Compression V-8 to 310 hp—up 20 hp over Cutlass V-8. 4-ON-THE-FLOOR—stick shift synchromesh transmission captures every power advantage both up and down the entire gear range. 2 DUAL EXHAUSTS—complete dual exhaust system features less back pressure for better performance ... aluminized for longer life." Other Olds 4-4-2 features included heavy-duty shocks and springs, a rear stabilizer bar, a dual-snorkel air cleaner, a higher-lift camshaft and extra-high-quality rod bearings and main bearings.

Motor Trend tested an Oldsmobile F-85 Cutlass 4-4-2 two-door hardtop in its September 1964 issue. The car had a base price of $2,784 and an as-tested price of $3,658.74. Options on the test vehicle included power steering, two-speed windshield wipers, an electric deck-lid release, back-up lights, a crankcase ventilation system, an outside rear view mirror, a power front seat, simulated wire wheel covers and the Police Apprehender Pursuit package. The car had a 3.55:1 non-Positraction rear axle. In another piece of factory sales literature, Oldsmobile pointed out what a bargain the first 4-4-2 was by making a direct comparison between the F-85 Club Coupe with 4-4-2 equipment and a similarly equipped Mustang and GTO. The Oldsmobile sold for $2,734.57 compared to $3,120 for the Mustang and $3,161.31 for the GTO LeMans. Even the fancier Cutlass Holiday Coupe with the 4-4-2 package was only $3,144.46 — a tad more than the optioned Mustang and a tad less than the GTO hardtop.

The 4-4-2 accelerated from 0 to 30 mph in 3.1 seconds and from 0 to 60 mph in 7.5 seconds. It could do the standing-start quarter mile in 15.5 seconds at 90 mph. *Car Life* (August 1964) reported a 7.4-second 0 to 60-mph time and a 15.6-second quarter mile. "What Olds engineers have done, in the final analysis, is produce a car which at long last lives up to the claims of the company's advertising copywriters and top-level spokesmen," said *Car Life*. "The 4-4-2 is indeed 'where the action is.' No better Oldsmobile has rolled off the Lansing assembly line in many a year and though it isn't quite the sports car that corporate brass likes to think, it doesn't miss by much."

Series Number	Body/Style Number	Body Type & Seating	Factory Price	Shipping Weight	Production Total
F-85 + 4-4-2 — SERIES 3000 — V-8					
30	27	2d Coupe-6P	$2,551	2,875 lbs.	148
30	69	4d Sedan-6P	$2,605	2,980 lbs.	3
F-85 DELUXE + 4-4-2 — SERIES 3100 — V-8					
31	69	4d Sedan-6P	$2,713	3,140 lbs.	7
CUTLASS + 4-4-2 — SERIES 3200 — V-8					
32	27	2d Coupe-6P	$2,780	3,140 lbs.	563
32	37	2d HT-6P	$2,920	3,155 lbs.	1,842
32	67	2d Conv-6P	$3,120	3,307 lbs.	436

NOTE 1: Prices include basic cost of 4-4-2 package.

ENGINE

BASE V-8: Overhead valves. Cast-iron block. Bore and stroke: 3.938 x 3.385 inches. Displacement: 330.0 cid. Compression ratio: 10.25:1. Brake hp: 310 at 5200 rpm. Taxable hp: 49.60. Torque: 355 at 3600 rpm. Hydraulic valve lifters. Five main bearings. Carburetor: Rochester 2GC two-barrel. Engine painted metallic gold. Dual-snorkel air cleaner with red, orange and yellow bands carrying 4-4-2 lettering.

OPTIONS

Power brakes ($43). Power steering ($107). Air conditioning ($430). Power seats ($71). Clock ($16). Convenience lamps ($8). Outside mirror ($4). Tow-tone paint ($17). AM/FM radio ($150). Deluxe push-button radio ($88). Super Deluxe signal-seeking radio ($124). Power antenna ($26). Rear speaker ($16). Cruise control ($91). Tilt steering ($43). Trunk release ($10). Rear window defroster ($21). Tinted glass ($43). 4-4-2 package ($285.14).

1965 F-85/CUTLASS 4-4-2

DOUG MITCHEL

1965 4-4-2

If you wanted to buy a muscle car that gave you the thrill of a GTO or an SS 396 without the headline-high pricing, the 4-dash-4-dash-2 was the way to go in 1965. A new engine was the year's big news. As _Car Life_ put it, "Olds joins the bigger-inch crowd with another meaning for that first "4" — 400 cubic inches."

The F-85 Cutlass line was mildly face lifted for 1965 and the 4-4-2 performance and handling package gained in popularity. Noting the runaway success of the Pontiac GTO with its 389-cid engine, Oldsmobile engineers saw the need to cram more cubes into their creation. Reducing the bore of the new Olds 425-cid engine from 4.125 inches to an even 4.0 produced an engine ideally sized for the 4-4-2 at 400 cid. This year the 4-4-2 package was offered with an optional Hydra-Matic transmission. Since the second "4" in the 1964 model designation had stood for "four-speed manual transmission," Oldsmobile had to explain the 4-4-2 name a different way. The company now said that the first four (4) stood for the new 400-cid V-8, the second four (4) meant four-barrel carburetor and the two (2) meant dual exhaust. This sounded a little awkward, since "4" and "400" aren't the same, but who cared? With the 400-cid engine, power rose by 35 horses to a total of 345 hp at 4800 rpm and torque increased by 85 lbs.-ft. to

440 at 3200 rpm. A total of 25,003 cars had the 4-4-2 package installed this year.

Car and Driver magazine test drove a 1965 Olds 4-4-2 convertible with a four-speed manual gearbox and a 3.55:1 axle in May 1965. Its 0-to-60-mph time was recorded as 5.5 seconds and the quarter-mile run took 15.0 seconds at 98 mph.

Series Number	Body/Style Number	Body Type & Seating	Factory Price	Shipping Weight	Production Total
F-85 + 4-4-2 — SERIES 3400 — V-8					
34	27	2d Coupe-6P	$2,553	3,146 lbs.	1,087
CUTLASS + 4-4-2 — SERIES 3800 — V-8					
38	27	2d Coupe-6P	$2,742	3,221 lbs.	287
38	37	2d HT-6P	$2,880	3,245 lbs.	14,735
38	67	2d Conv-6P	$3,074	3,338 lbs.	3,468

NOTE 1: Prices include basic cost of 4-4-2 package.

NOTE 2: Base F-85 production included 109 with three-speed, 736 with four-speed and 242 with automatic transmission.

NOTE 3: Cutlass coupe production includes 287 with three-speed, 3,164 with four-speed and 2,262 with automatic transmission

NOTE 4: Cutlass hardtop production includes 204 with three-speed, 8,140 with four-speed and 6,391 with automatic transmission

NOTE 5: Cutlass convertible production includes 90 with three-speed, 1,695 with four-speed and 1,683 with automatic transmission

ENGINE

BASE V-8: Overhead valves. Cast-iron block. Bore and stroke: 4.00 x 3.975 inches. Displacement: 400.0 cid. Compression ratio: 10.25:1. Brake hp: 345 at 4800 rpm. Taxable hp: 51.20. Torque: 400 at 3200 rpm. Hydraulic valve lifters. Five

OLDSMOBILE

main bearings. Carburetor: Rochester 4GC four-barrel. Engine code: V.

OPTIONS (PARTIAL LIST)

Air conditioning ($351). Carpets in standard model ($19.37). Electric clock ($16.14). Heavy-duty clutch ($5.38). Front compartment console for sports coupe and Cutlass ($75.32 and requires optional transmission). Closed circuit crankcase ventilation ($5.38). Cruise control ($91.46). Rear window defroster in coupes ($21.52). Deluxe interior option for standard model $20.17). Anti-spin differential ($43.04). Door guards ($3.77). Chrome door window frames for standard model ($21.52). Special-duty engine cooling with air conditioning ($33.36). Front auxiliary floor mats ($6.36). Rear auxiliary floor mats ($5.85). All tinted glass ($31.20). Tinted windshield ($19.91). Heavy-duty guard-beam frame for standard coupe and closed Cutlass models ($11.90). Heater and defroster delete ($73.00 credit). Back-up lights ($9.68). Courtesy lights ($4.52, but standard in convertible). Parking brake signal light $3.98). Glareproof inside rearview mirror ($4.51). Outside rearview mirror ($4.51). Remote-control outside rearview mirror ($11.78) . Body and fender moldings ($21.52). Roof drip moldings for standard coupe ($8.61 and dtandard on Cutlass models). Deluxe exterior moldings for standard coupe ($32.28). Side window sill moldings ($18.83). Padded instrument panel in standard coupe ($19.37). Two-tone paint ($16.46). 4-4-2 performance package for standard coupe ($190.45). 4-4-2 performance package for Cutlass ($156.02). Power antenna ($26.09). Power brakes ($42.50). 4-Way power driver's bucket seat for Sports Coupe and Cutlass ($66.71). Power trunk lock ($10.22). Power windows in Cutlass 4-4-2s only ($102.22). Power steering ($96.84). Radio ($65.64). Rear speaker, except Cutlass convertible ($16.14). Instrument panel safety pad in standard models ($19.37). Front seat belts with retractorsa ($7.53). Rear seat belt ($10.76). Standard seat belt delete ($11.00 credit). Front and rear seat belts with retractors ($21.52). Super-Lift rear shock absorbers (standard 4-4-2). Spare wheel and tire lock ($5.38). Heavy-duty rear springs (standard on 4-4-2). Custom Deluxe steering wheel in standard F-85 4-4-2 ($34.97). Custom Deluxe steering wheel in Cutlass 4-4-2 ($21.52). Deluxe Safety V steering wheel in standard F-85 with 4-4-2 ($13.45). Tilt-Away steering wheel, optional transmission required ($43.04). Special-duty Jetaway automatic transmission ($209.82 and mandatory with 4-4-2 option). Four-speed manual transmission ($188.30). Wheel discs ($17.22). Deluxe wheel discs ($36.15). Chrome wheel rings for all except convertible, 15-inch wheels and tires required ($11.30). Simulated wire wheels ($64.56). Two-speed windshield washer wipers ($16.46).

1966 F-85/CUTLASS 4-4-2

JERRY HEASLEY

1966 4-4-2

When it was restyled for 1966, the Oldsmobile Cutlass F-85 took on a more massive, creased-edge look. The 4-4-2 high-performance option package now included seat belts, an instrument panel with a padded dashboard, a windshield washer system, two-speed windshield wipers, a left-hand manual outside rear view mirror, foam padded seat cushions, carpeting on the floor front and rear, chrome roof bow moldings, a deluxe steering wheel, front bucket or custom seats, deluxe armrests, a courtesy lamp package, 7.35 x 14 tires and seat upholstery in either all vinyl or cloth.

Under the hood of the 4-4-2 model, the 400-cid V-8 had been tweaked by another five horsepower (to 350 hp) thanks to a slight increase in compression ratio. Late in the model year,

the 4-4-2 received another adrenalin injection (to 360 hp) with the one-year-only triple two-barrel carburetor setup. From the standpoints of both performance and rarity, the 1966 Olds Cutlass 4-4-2 equipped with the 360-hp factory Tri-Power installation is the most desirable example of these production years to a real muscle-car enthusiast.

Car Life magazine took one of the Tri-Power screamers from 0-to-60 mph in a mere 6.3 seconds and called it the "civilized supercar." Quarter-mile runs were made in as little as 14.8 seconds with a terminalspeed of 97 miles per hour. Car and Driver magazine test drove a 1965 Olds 4-4-2 convertible with a four-speed manual gearbox and a 3.55:1 axle in May 1965. Its 0-to-60 time was recorded as 5.5 seconds and the quarter-mile run took 15.0 seconds at 98 mph. Motor Trend also got its hands on a tri-power 4-4-2 anmd reported in covered the drag strip in 15.16 seconds at 95.56 mph.

Series Number	Body/Style Number	Body Type & Seating	Factory Price	Shipping Weight	Production Total
F-85 + 4-4-2 — SERIES 3400 — V-8					
34	07	2d Coupe-6P	$2,570	3,153 lbs.	647
F-85 DELUXE + 4-4-2 — SERIES 3600 — V-8					
36	17	2d Coupe-6P	$2,735	3,196 lbs.	1,217
CUTLASS + 4-4-2 — SERIES 3800 — V-8					
38	07	2d Coupe-6P	$2,785	3,219 lbs.	3,787
38	17	2d HT-6P	$2,922	3,243 lbs.	13,493
38	67	2d Conv-6P	$3,117	3,349 lbs.	2,853

NOTE 1: Prices include basic cost of 4-4-2 package.

NOTE 2: Base F-85 production included 103 with three-speed, 456 with four-speed and 88 with automatic transmission.

NOTE 3: Deluxe F-85 production included 88 with three-speed, 798 with four-speed and 331 with automatic transmission.

NOTE 4: Cutlass coupe production includes 221 with three-speed, 2,422 with four-speed and 1,144 with automatic transmission.

NOTE 5: Cutlass hardtop production includes 297 with three-speed, 8,025 with four-speed and 5,171 with automatic transmission.

NOTE 6: Cutlass convertible production includes 62 with three-speed, 1,448 with four-speed and 1,343 with automatic transmission.

ENGINES

BASE V-8: Overhead valves. Cast-iron block. Bore and stroke: 4.00 x 3.975 inches. Displacement: 400.0 cid. Compression ratio: 10.50:1. Brake hp: 350 at 4400 rpm. Taxable hp: 51.20. Torque: 440 at 3600. Hydraulic valve lifters. Five main bearings. Carburetor: Rochester 4MV four-barrel. Engine code: V.

OPTIONAL V-8: Overhead valves. Cast-iron block. Bore and stroke: 4.00 x 3.975 inches. Displacement: 400.0 cid. Compression ratio: 10.50:1. Brake hp: 360 at 5000 rpm. Taxable hp: 51.20. Torque: 440 at 3600. Hydraulic valve lifters. Five main bearings. Carburetion: Three Rochester two-barrel. Engine code: V. (NOTE: This rare engine was installed in the foillowing cars with the 4-4-2 package:157 standard F-85s, 178 Deluxe F-85 s, 383 Cutlass coupes, 1,171 Cutlass hardtops and 240 Cutlass c onvertibles.)

OPTIONS

Power brakes ($41). Power steering ($94). Air conditioning ($343). Tinted windows ($30). Power seat ($69). Head rests ($52). Power trunk ($12). Floor mats ($7). Vinyl roof ($74). Sports console ($68). Cruise control ($41). Tilt steering column ($41). Wire wheel discs ($61). Tachometer ($52). Electric clock ($15). Radio ($64). Power antenna ($29). Rear radio speaker ($15). AM/FM radio ($147). Power door locks ($68). Rear defroster ($21). 4-4-2 package fror F-85 and Cutlass two-door models ($152). Automatic transmission ($230). Four-speed manual transmission with Hurst shifter ($184). Close-ratio four-speed manual transmission with floor shift ($184). Positive traction rear axle ($46). Heavy-duty clutch ($5).

1967 F-85/CUTLASS 4-4-2

JERRY HEASLEY

1967 4-4-2

The 1967 Cutlass 4-4-2 option was available for the top-of-the-line Cutlass Supreme series, which grew from a single four-door hardtop in 1966 to a full model range for 1967. You could add the 4-4-2 package to all Cutlass Supreme two-door models, which came with a standard 330-cid/320-hp V-8. Checking option box L78 added the 4-4-2 option and cost only $184.

While a standard rating of 350 hp was good for openers in 1967, it was necessary to have a trick setup a step beyond that. General Motors bureaucracy had undergone another of its periodic soul cleansings and banned Tri-Power in all cars except the Corvette. Oldsmobile's reaction was the W-30 option. The flush hood louvers over the air cleaner were functional on the 4-4-2, but they did not have any ram-effect needed for added horses. Using factory ducting from the front of the car, the 1967 W-30-optioned version was advertised at 360 hp, the same as the 1966 Tri-Power Cutlass 4-4-2.

Car & Driver road tested a '67 Oldsmobile 4-4-2 with the 400-cid/350-hp V-8 and a 3.08:1 rear axle in its December 1966 issue. The car knocked off a 0-60-mph run in 7.8 seconds and did the quarter-mile in 15.8 seconds at 91 mph.

OLDSMOBILE

Series Number	Body/Style Number	Body Type & Seating	Factory Price	Shipping Weight	Production Total
CUTLASS SUPREME + 4-4-2 — SERIES 3800 — V-8					
38	07	2d Coupe-6P	$2,878	3,219 lbs.	4,751
38	17	2d HT-6P	$3,015	3,243 lbs.	16,998
38	67	2d Conv-6P	$3,084	3,349 lbs.	3,080

NOTE 1: Prices include basic cost of 4-4-2 package.

NOTE 2: Cutlass coupe production includes 422 with three-speed, 2,535 with four-speed and 1,793 with automatic transmission

NOTE 3: Cutlass hardtop production includes 409 with three-speed, 7,661 with four-speed and 8,928 with automatic transmission

NOTE 4: Cutlass convertible production includes 87 with three-speed, 1,185 with four-speed and 1,807 with automatic transmission

ENGINES

BASE V-8: Overhead valves. Cast-iron block. Bore and stroke: 4.00 x 3.975 inches. Displacement: 400.0 cid. Compression ratio: 10.50:1. Brake hp: 350 at 5000 rpm. Taxable hp: 51.20. Torque: 440 at 3600. Hydraulic valve lifters. Five main bearings. Carburetor: Rochester 4MV four-barrel. Engine code: VG.

OPTIONAL RAM-AIR V-8: V-8. Overhead valves. Cast-iron block. Bore and stroke: 4.00 x 3.975 inches. Displacement: 400.0 cid. Compression ratio: 10.50:1. Brake hp: 360 at 5000 rpm. Taxable hp: 51.20. Torque: 440 at 3600. Hydraulic valve lifters. Five main bearings. Carburetor: Rochester 4MV four-barrel. Ram-air induction. Engine code: VG.

OPTIONAL TURNPIKE CRUISER V-8: Overhead valves. Cast-iron block. Bore and stroke: 4.00 x 3.975 inches. Displacement: 400.0 cid. Compression ratio: 10.50:1. Brake hp: 300 at 4600 rpm. Taxable hp: 51.20. Torque: 425 at 3000. Hydraulic valve lifters. Five main bearings. Carburetor: Rochester two-barrel. Engine code: VG.

OPTIONS (PARTIAL LIST)

C60 Four Seasons air conditioning ($343.20). K50 Air induction system, Climate Comb. Cont. ($33.70 and mandatory with L66 package). Y73 automatic transmission control for V-8 ($5.27 and standard with M34 transmission). T60 special battery for all V-8s, but standard with 4-4-2 and L78 ($7.37). J56 heavy-duty brakes ($25.80). Electric clock ($15.80). M01 heavy-duty clutch, except with L78 ($5.27). D55 front sports console for Cutlass two-doors, bucket seats required ($57.93, but not available with three-speed manual transmission with column-mounted gearshifter). K20 closed crankcase ventilation system ($5.27). K30 automatic cruise control, requires automatic transmission and power brakes ($44.23). B52 foam rear seat cushion ($10.53). C51 rear window air deflector ($14.11). C50 rear window defogger, except convertible ($21.06).

G80 anti-spin differential ($19.75). Y76 heavy-duty engine cooling, standard with air conditioning ($32.65). B35 heavy-duty rear floor covering ($4.21 and requires A52 on coupe and A65 on hardtop and convertible). B34 heavy-duty front floor covering ($6.32 and requires A52 on coupe and A65 on hardtop and convertible). B32 auxiliary front floor mats ($6.32). B33 auxiliary rear floor mats ($6.77). A01 all windows tinted glass ($30.54). A02 tinted windshield only ($21.06). F35 heavy-duty Guard-Beam frame ($12.53). A82 dual headrests for conventional front seat ($42.13 and requires A52 on coupe and A65 on hardtop and convertible). A81 dual headrests for Strato Bench or bucket front seats ($52.66 and requires Strato Bench or Bucket seats at extra cost). D99 two-tone paint ($31.07). G90-1 performance axle with 3.08:1 or 3.23:1 gear ratios (no cost). G95 2.78:1 expressway axle (no cost). G96 2.56:1 expressway axle (no cost). L78 4-4-2 performance package including 350-hp four-barrel V-8, heavy-duty high-performance axle, heavy-duty front suspension, heavy-duty rear suspension, heavy-duty wheels, bucket front seats and Red Line tires ($184.31). U75 rear-mounted power antenna ($29.12). J50 power brakes ($41.60). J52 power front disc brakes ($104.79, but not available with three-speed manual transmission or heavy-duty brakes option). A46 four-way power left-hand bucket seat ($69.51). A41 four-way power bench seat ($69.51). A91 power trunk lid latch ($12.64, but not available on cars with heater and defroster deleted). A31 power windows ($100.05). N40 power steering ($94.79). U63 Deluxe push-button radio ($64.25). U69 AM/FM radio ($133.76). V01 heavy-duty radiator ($21.06). K19 Air Injection reactor system, mandatory on California cars ($44.73). U80 bi-phonic rear seat radio speaker, except convertible ($16.85). U21 Rocket Rally Pac ($84.26). U22 Rocket Rally Pac with Safety Sentinel ($94.79). A65 Custon sport front seat for Cutlass Supreme convertible with 4-4-2 (no cost). G66 rear Superlift shock absorbers (standard on 4-4-2). AS1 standard front shoulder belts ($23.17). A85 Deluxe front shoulder belts ($26.33 and option A39 deluxe seat belts required). G51 heavy-duty rear springs (standard). N33 tilt-away steering column ($42.13, but not available in cars with column-mounted manual gearshift). U89 trailer electrical wiring harness ($10,53). M40 Turbo Hydra-Matic transmission ($236.97 and mandatory on 4-4-2 if automatic transmission was ordered). M14 heavy-duty three-speed transmission with floor shift (standard on 4-4-2 with stick shift). M21 close-ratio four-speed manual transmission, heavy-duty radiator required ($184.31). M34 heavy-duty Jetway transmission, 4-4-2 package required ($215.91). M20 wide-ratio four-speed manual transmission ($184.31). G97 Turnpike 2.41:1 axle ratio (no cost). L66 Turnpike Cruising package ($142.18 and M40 Turbo Hydra-Matic required). K66 ultra-high-voltage ignition system ($100.05). C08 vinyl roof covering on coupes ($84.26). P01 14-inch wheel discs ($16.85). P02 deluxe 14-in. wheel discs ($46.34). N95 simulated wire wheel discs ($69.51). P05 14-inch Super stock wheels ($88.47). U69 AM/FM radio with accessory groups No. 1 and No. 2 (add $69.51).

1968 4-4-2

Oldsmobile deserved congratulations for the '68 Olds 4-4-2. As one astute writer of the day noted in *Car Life*, "The 4-4-2 Holiday Coupe looked every bit as quick and strong as it really is. A true hi-po car and the best handling of today's supercars." Along with the car's all-new General Motors A-car body, the 4-4-2 also had separate model status for the first time in 1968—it was no longer a Cutlass add-on.

There were three models: Holiday hardtop, sports coupe (post sedan) and convertible in this first 4-4-2 series. The new 4-4-2 had more curves than ever on its long hood and short deck body with razor edge fenders and a swoopy rear.

As in 1967, a 400-cid V-8 was standard, but it was a totally new one with 3.87 x 4.25-inch bore and stroke (4 x 3.975-inch bore and stroke in 1967). There were three basic four-barrel versions of this 10.5:1 compression engine, the hottest with the W-30 Force Air package added. They gave 325 hp (au-

tomatic), 350 hp (stick) and 360 hp, respectively. However, a milder two-barrel "turnpike cruiser" economy engine with 9.0:1 compression and 290 hp (including Turbo Hydra-Matic) could be had, too.

Car Life's 4-4-2 Holiday listed for $3,127 f.o.b. in Lansing, Michigan, but went out the showroom door at $4,059. It had the 350-hp engine and took 15.13 seconds to do the quarter mile at 92.2 mph.

Series Number	Body/Style Number	Body Type & Seating	Factory Price	Shipping Weight	Production Total
4-4-2 — SERIES 4400 — V-8					
44	77	2d Coupe-6P	$3,087	3,450 lbs.	4,282
44	87	2d HT-6P	$3,150	3,470 lbs.	24,183
44	67	2d Conv-6P	$3,084	3,349 lbs.	5,142

ENGINES

OPTIONAL V-8: Overhead valves. Cast-iron block. Bore and stroke: 4.00 x 3.975 inches. Displacement: 400.0 cid. Compression ratio: 9.00:1. Brake hp: 290 at

PHIL KUNZ

1968 4-4-2

4600 rpm. Torque: 425 at 2400. Hydraulic valve lifters. Five main bearings. Carburetor: Rochester two-barrel model 7028251. Engine code: QL.

BASE V-8 (AUTOMATIC): Overhead valves. Cast-iron block. Bore and stroke: 4.00 x 3.975 inches. Displacement: 400.0 cid. Compression ratio: 10.50:1. Brake hp: 325 at 4600 rpm. Torque: (Vista Cruiser) 440 at 3200 rpm; (4-4-2) 440 at 3000 rpm. Hydraulic valve lifters. Five main bearings. Carburetor: Rochester 4MV four-barrel. Engine code: QR, QS or QT.

BASE V-8 (MANUAL): Overhead valves. Cast-iron block. Bore and stroke: 4.00 x 3.975 inches. Displacement: 400.0 cid. Compression ratio: 10.50:1. Brake hp: 350 at 4800 rpm. Torque: 440 at 3200. Hydraulic valve lifters. Five main bearings. Carburetor: Rochester 4MV four-barrel. Engine code: QW or QU.

OPTIONAL FORCE-AIR V-8: Overhead valves. Cast-iron block. Bore and stroke: 4.00 x 3.975 inches. Displacement: 400.0 cid. Compression ratio: 10.50:1. Brake hp: 360 at 5400 rpm. Torque: 440 at 3600. Hydraulic valve lifters. Five main bearings. Carburetor: Rochester 4MV four-barrel. Engine code: (W-30 package).

OPTIONS (PARTIAL LIST)

C60 Four Seasons air conditioning ($360.19). G80 anti-spin differential ($42.13 and required with Force Air package with 4.33:1 axle). G88/92 heavy-duty performance axle with 3.42:1 or 3.91:1 ratio (no cost on 4-4-2). G90-1 performance axle with 3.08:1 or 3.23:1 gear ratios (no cost). G93-4 heavy-duty performance axle with 3.55 or 3.90 ratio. G95 2.78:1 express-way axle (no cost). G96 2.56:1 expressway axle (no cost). U35 electric clock ($16.85). D55 front sports console, bucket seats required ($57.93). K30 automatic cruise control, requires automatic transmission and power brakes ($50.56). C50 rear window defogger, except convertible ($21.06). 400-cid two-barrel Rocket V-8 ($236.97). Y72 engine cooling equipment, for cars without air conditioning ($57.93). Y72 engine cooling equipment, for cars with air conditioning ($21.06). A82 dual head restraints for conven-

tional front seats ($42.13 and A52 front bench seat or A65 Custom Sport front seat required in 4-4-2). A81 dual head restraints with Strato Bench or Strato Bucket seats ($52.66). W30 Force-Air induction system for 4-4-2 ($263.30), but not available with air conditioner, Pedal Ease brakes, front disc brakes or engine-cooling equipment; V01 heavy-duty radiator and M40 or M21 transmission are mandatory options). U29 panel courtesy lights for coupes ($6.32). D33 remote-control left-hand outside rearview mirror ($9.48). M55 automatic transmission auxiliary oil cooler ($15.80). D99 two-tone paint ($31.07). U75 rear-mounted power antenna ($29.12). J50 power brakes ($41.60). J52 power front disc brakes ($104.79, but not available with three-speed manual transmission). A46 four-way power left-hand bucket seat ($69.51). A41 four-way power bench seat ($69.51). N40 power steering ($94.79). A31 power windows ($100.05). U63 Deluxe push-button radio ($69.51). U69 AM/FM radio ($133.76). V01 heavy-duty radiator ($21.06). A39 Deluxe seat belts front and rear for 4-4-2 with A52 front bench seat or A65 Custom Sport front seat ($9.48). A65 Custon sport front seat (no cost). A70 Strato Bucket seat with right-hand reclining backrest ($31.60). A52 front bench seat ($68.46 credit). G66 rear Superlift shock absorbers ($42.13). N33 tilt-away steering column ($42.13, but not available in cars with column-mounted manual gearshift). N34 woodgrain finish steering wheel ($31.60). N38 heavy-duty manual steering ($6.32). N63 7.75-14 White Line nylon cord tires no charge. M40 Turbo Hydra-Matic transmission ($236.97 and mandatory on 4-4-2 if automatic transmission was ordered). M21 close-ratio four-speed manual transmission, heavy-duty radiator required ($184.31). M20 wide-ratio four-speed manual transmission ($184.31). K66 ultra-high-voltage ignition system for 4-4-2 without two-barrel V-8 ($100.05). C08 vinyl roof covering on coupes ($94.79). P01 14-inch wheel discs ($21.06). P02 deluxe 14-in. wheel discs ($42.13). N95 simulated wire wheel discs ($73.20). P05 14-inch Super stock wheels ($88.47). PA1 special 14-inch wheel discs ($31.60).

OLDSMOBILE

1968 HURST/OLDS

TOM GLATCH

1968 Hurst/Olds

"These executive supercars won't last very long," said *Super Stock* magazine's Jim McCraw about the '68 Hurst/Olds. He was right, too. Back then, Oldsmobile had a quality-car image that couldn't be beat and Hurst had a high-performance image that other aftermarket firms would kill for. Teaming up these two companies was a marriage made in heaven and produced one of the legendary muscle machines. For 1968, what had formerly been the largest Olds engine offering, at 425 cid, was punched out to a full 455 cid. GM brass would not permit the cramming of the new 455 into the 4-4-2 platform, but this didn't stop George Hurst, of Hurst Performance Products, from trying it on his own.

So successful was his effort that he—along with Olds officials—got entrepreneur and Oldsmobile supplier John Demmer, of Lansing, Michigan, to assemble clones of Hurst's car in his own facility on a limited basis. This is how the first Hurst/Olds was born!

To power the Hurst/Olds, the 4-4-2's standard 400-cid engine was replaced with a Force Air 455 with a 10.5:1 compression ratio that was beefed-up internally to develop 390 hp at 5000 rpm and 500 lbs.-ft. of torque at 3600 rpm.

The big W45 motor was based on the Toronado engine, but built with a special crankshaft, a custom-curved distributor, special carburetor jets, a 308-degree camshaft with a .474-inch lift and hand-assembled Ram-Air cylinder heads. The power plant was hooked to a modified Turbo Hydra-Matic with a Hurst Dual-Gate shifter that could be shifted like a manual transmission or used like an automatic. A heavy-duty

rear end incorporated a standard 3.91:1 rear axle. The entire car was dressed up in a special Silver-and-Black trim package that looked very distinctive. A total of 515 Hurst/Olds were built for 1968. Of these, 451 were based on the 4-4-2 Holiday two-door hardtop while the remaining 64 were originally 4-4-2 coupes. No Hurst/Olds were produced in convertible form.

In August 1968, Super Stock magazine road tested the Hurst/Olds and reported a top run of 12.90 seconds for the quarter-mile at 109 mph. Another magazine testing a similar car with air conditioning reported a 5.9-second 0-to-60 run and a 13.77-second quarter mile at 103.91 mph.

Series Number	Body/Style Number	Body Type & Seating	Factory Price	Shipping Weight	Production Total
HURST/OLDS — SERIES 4400 — V-8					
44	77	2d Coupe-6P	—	3,850 lbs.	64
44	87	2d HT-6P	—	3,870 lbs.	451

ENGINE

BASE V-8: Overhead valves. Cast-iron block. Bore and stroke: 4.126 x 4.250 inches. Displacement: 455.0 cid. Compression ratio: 10.50:1. Brake hp: 390 at 5000 rpm. Torque: 500 at 3600. Hydraulic valve lifters. Five main bearings. Carburetor: Rochester 4MV four-barrel. Engine code: W35. (NOTE: This motor was based on the Toronado engine, but built with a special crankshaft, a custom-curved distributor, special carburetor jets, a 308-degree camshaft with a .474-inch lift and hand-assembled Force-Air cylinder heads.)

OPTIONS

C60 Four Seasons air conditioning ($360.19). G80 anti-spin differential ($42.13). G88/92 heavy-duty performance axle with 3.42:1 or 3.91:1 ratio (no cost). U35 electric clock ($16.85). D55 front sports console, bucket seats required ($57.93). K30 automatic cruise control, requires automatic transmission and power brakes ($50.56). C50 rear window defogger ($21.06).. BG1 heavy-duty vinyl front and rear floor covering ($10.53 for cars with bench seat). B32 auxiliary front floor mats ($7.37). B33 auxiliary rear floor mats ($7.16). A01 all windows tinted glass ($36.86). A02 tinted windshield only ($25.27). A81 dual head restraints with Strato Bench or Strato Bucket seats ($52.66). U29 panel courtesy lights for coupes ($6.32). D33 remote-control left-hand outside rearview mirror ($9.48). B93 door edge guards ($5.27). M55 automatic transmission auxiliary oil cooler ($15.80). U75 rear-mounted power antenna ($29.12). J50 power brakes ($41.60). J52 power front disc brakes ($104.79, but not available with three-speed manual transmission). A46 four-way power left-hand bucket seat ($69.51). A41 four-way power bench seat ($69.51). N40 power steering ($94.79). A31 power windows ($100.05). U63 Deluxe push-button radio ($69.51). U69 AM/FM radio ($133.76). V01 heavy-duty radiator ($21.06). A39 Deluxe seat belts front and rear for 4-4-2 with A52 front bench seat or A65 Custom Sport front seat ($9.48). A65 Custon sport front seat (no cost).

A70 Strato Bucket seat with right-hand reclining backrest ($31.60). A52 front bench seat ($68.46 credit). AS4 deluxe rear shoulder belts ($26.33 and deluxe seat belts required). AS1 standard front shoulder belts ($23.17). A85 deluxe front shoulder belts, requires A39 deluxe seat belts ($26.33). G51 heavy-duty rear springs ($3.69). N33 tilt-away steering column ($42.13). N34 woodgrain finish steering wheel ($31.60). N38 heavy-duty manual steering ($6.32).. U89 trailer electrical wiring harness ($10.53). M40 Turbo Hydra-Matic transmission ($236.97). M21 close-ratio four-speed manual transmission, heavy-duty radiator required ($184.31). M20 wide-ratio four-speed manual transmission ($184.31). K66 ultra-high-voltage ignition system ($100.05). C08 vinyl roof covering on coupes ($94.79). P01 14-inch wheel discs ($21.06). P02 deluxe 14-in. wheel discs ($42.13). N95 simulated wire wheel discs ($73.20). P05 14-inch Super stock wheels ($88.47). PA1 special 14-inch wheel discs ($31.60).

1969 F-85/CUTLASS W-MACHINE

The W-31 package was a performance option for the F-85 and two-door Cutlass models. The package included a small-block Olds V-8 with a distinctive dual-snorkle air cleaner that had a chrome cover. The Force-Air option was included and the black-finished inner fenders had holes drilled to mount the ram-air hardware. induction system, along with brackets on the inner fenders for the hoses and scoops. To save weight, the cars came with less insulation materials. Only manual brakes were available. The suspension featured sway bars front and rear with boxed lower rear control arms.

All of these cars were manufactured at the home factory in Lansing, Mich. Dual sport-type outside rearview mirrors were part of the package.

Series Number	Body/Style Number	Body Type & Seating	Factory Price	Shipping Weight	Production Total
F-85 — SERIES 3200 — V-8					
32	77	2d Coupe-6P	$2,983	3,521 lbs.	5,541
Cutlass — SERIES 3600 — V-8					
36	77	2d Coupe-6P	$3,103	3,537 lbs.	10,682
36	87	2d HT-6P	$3,166	3,585 lbs.	66,495
36	67	2d ConvT-6P	$3,420	3,634 lbs.	13,498

NOTE 1: Production total is for all F-85/Cutlass two-door models; no W-31 breakout available.
NOTE 2: Price includes base cost of W31 package with no other options.
NOTE 3: Weights are estimated.

ENGINE

F-85, CUTLASS OPTIONAL V-8: Overhead valves. Cast-iron block. Bore and stroke: 4.06 x 3.39 inches. Displacement: 350.0 cid. Compression ratio: 10.50:1. Brake hp: 325 at 5400 rpm. Torque: 360 at 3600 rpm. Hydraulic valve lifters. Five main bearings. Carburetor: Rochester 4MV four-barrel. Engine code: QX.

OPTIONS

C60 Four Seasons air conditioning ($375.99). G80 anti-spin differential ($42.13). M55 automatic transmission oil cooler ($15.80). T60 heavy-duty battery ($7.37 and required with W31). VE1 Rear bumper ($7.37). U35 electric clock ($16.85). D55 Sports console for Cutlass versions only. Bucket seats required ($61.09, but not availailable with column-shifted manual transmission and includes U29 courtesy lights). C50 rear window defogger, except convertible ($22.12). Y72 engine cooling equipment, for cars without air conditioning ($57.93). Y72 engine cooling equipment, for cars with air conditioning ($21.06). B30 wall-to-wall floor carpeting in F-85 models ($18.96). A01 all windows tinted glass ($38.97). A02 tinted windshield only ($26.33). A82 dual front seat head restraints ($16.85). W31 Force-Air induction system special order for 4-4-2 (($310.69). D15 deluxe interior decor with front door and rear quarter armrests and moldings ($20.80). U29 panel courtesy lights for coupes ($6.32). D33 remote-control left-hand outside

rearview mirror ($10.53). B90 chrome side window frames on Cutlass sport coupe ($21.06). B93 door edge guards ($5.27). B96 chrome wheel opening moldings ($15.80). D99 two-tone Magic Mirror paint for coupes ($31.07). Y62 special solid color paint ($83.26). Y66 special two-tone paint, except convertible ($114.28). W40 special Firemist paint ($158.53). W42 dual hood paint stripe ($18.90, but included with W31 at no cost). Y73 hood paint stripe on Cutlass two-door models ($10.53). U75 rear-mounted power antenna ($31.60). J50 Pedal Ease power brakes ($41.60 but not available with J50 front disc brakes or J55). JL2 power front disc brakes ($64.25, but not available with three-speed manual transmission). A93 power door locks ($44.76). A41 four-way power bench seat ($73.72). A46 four-way power left-hand bucket seat for Cutlass versions($73.72). N40 Roto-Matic power steering ($100.05). A31 power windows in Cutlass versions ($105.32). V01 heavy-duty radiator with W-31($21.06). U63 Deluxe push-button radio ($69.51). U69 AM/FM radio ($133.76). U578 AM/FM stereophonic radio with rear seat speaker ($238.03). U57 stereo tape player, includes rear seat speaker with U58 ($116.91). U57 stereo tape player, includes rear seat speaker without U58 ($133.76). U80 bi-phonic rear seat speaker ($16.85, but included in U57 and U58 orptions). U21 Rocket Rally pac ($84.26). U15 Safety Sentinel ($11.59). A39 Deluxe seat belts front and rear for convertible with bucket seats ($8.96). A85 deluxe front shoulder belts for convertibles, A39 deluxe seat belts required ($26.33). AS1 standard front shoulder belts for convertibles without A39 or AS4 ($23.17). AS4 deluxe rear shoulder belts with A39 or W39 required ($26.33). AS5 standard rear shoulder belts ($23.17). W39 deluxe front and rear seat belts and front shoul;der belts for coupes ($12.11). W39 deluxe front and rear seat belts and front shoul;der belts for convertibles ($13.69). A52 bench seat delete option for Cutlass convertible ($68.46 credit). A51 Strato bucket seat for Cutlass versions ($68.46). B50 foam-padded front seat cushion ($9.48). FG2 Firm Ride front and rear suspension ($5.27). G66 Super lift rear shocks ($42.13 but not available with FG2 option). G51 heavy-duty rear springs ($3.69). N34 Custom Sport finish steering wheel ($15.80). N33 tilt-away steering column ($45.29, but not available in cars with column-mounted manual gearshift). N42 deluxe instant horn ($31.60). P26 7.75 x 14 white sidewall tires replacing 7.75 x 14 black sidewall ($31.60). P80 7.75 x14 fiberglass-belted white sidewall tires replacing 7.75 x 14 black sidewall tires ($80.05). P81 F70-7.75 x 14 fiberglass-belted Red Stripe tire replacing 7.75 x 14 black sidewall ($89.52). PL5 Wide-Oval raised white letter tires replacing F70-7.75 X 14 black sidewall tires ($89.52). PQ9 custom polyester white sidewall tires replacing 7.75 x 14 black sidewall ($49.50). U89 trailer electrical wiring harness ($10.53). M14 heavy-duty three-speed manual transmission with floor shift ($84.26). M20 wide-ratio four-speed manual transmission ($184.80). M21 close-ratio four-speed manual transmission ($184.80). M38 Turbo Hydra-Matic 350 transmission ($205.92). C56 Flo-Thru body ventilation for coupe without air conditioning ($15.80). C08 vinyl roof covering on coupes and hardtops ($100.05). P01 14-inch wheel discs ($21.06). P02 deluxe 14-in. wheel discs ($47.39). N95 simulated wire wheel discs ($73.72). P05 14-inch Super stock wheels ($90.58). N66 Super stock II wheels ($73.72). BC1 woodgrain vinyl dashboard trim ($10.53). Y60 accessory package including ashtray, luggage compartment, underhood and glove box lights and visor-vanity mirrort ($14.32-16.43 depending on body style). U58 stereo radio ($168.52).

OLDSMOBILE

1969 4-4-2

PHIL KUNZ

1969 4-4-2

"Built like a 1 3/4-ton watch" is how Oldsmobile described its 4-4-2 for 1969. The 4-4-2 was hotter than just about anything other than the Hurst model and it was a whole lot less money than that type of conversion.

A new pitchman named Dr. Oldsmobile prescribed image enhancements for the 4-4-2 in 1969. They included a bolder split grille, fat hood stripes and bright, new name badges. Also, the two-barrel "turnpike cruiser" option was eliminated to purify Oldsmobile's muscle car reputation. Transmission options were unchanged. Hurst shifters again came with stick-shift cars. A divider between the halves of the grille, finished in body color, carried big 4-4-2 identifiers. W-30s had special hood stripes and front fender decal cutouts.

With the standard 350-hp engine the 1969 olds 4-4-2 took 15.13 seconds to do the quarter-mile at 92.2 mph. It clicked off 60 mph from a standing start in a flat 7 seconds.

Series Number	Body/Style Number	Body Type & Seating	Factory Price	Shipping Weight	Production Total
4-4-2 — SERIES 4400 — V-8					
44	77	2d Coupe-6P	$3,141	3,502 lbs.	2,475
44	87	2d HT-6P	$3,204	3,512 lbs.	19,587
44	67	2d Conv-6P	$3,395	3,580 lbs.	4,295

ENGINES

BASE V-8 (AUTOMATIC): Overhead valves. Cast-iron block. Bore and stroke: 4.00 x 3.975 inches. Displacement: 400.0 cid. Compression ratio: 10.50:1. Brake hp: 325 at 4600 rpm. Torque: 440 at 3000 rpm. Hydraulic valve lifters. Five main bearings. Carburetor: Rochester 4MV four-barrel. Engine code: QR and QS.

BASE V-8 (MANUAL): Overhead valves. Cast-iron block. Bore and stroke: 4.00 x 3.975 inches. Displacement: 400.0 cid. Compression ratio: 10.50:1. Brake hp: 350 at 4800 rpm. Torque: 440 at 3200. Hydraulic valve lifters. Five main bearings. Carburetor: Rochester 4MV four-barrel. Engine code: QW.

4-4-2 OPTIONAL V-8: Overhead valves. Cast-iron block. Bore and stroke: 4.00 x 3.975 inches. Displacement: 400.0 cid. Compression ratio: 10.50:1. Brake hp: 360 at 5400 rpm. Torque: 400 at 3600. Hydraulic valve lifters. Five main bearings. Carburetor: Rochester 4MV four-barrel. Engine code: QU and QT.

OPTIONS

C60 Four Seasons air conditioning ($375.99). G80 anti-spin differential ($42.13). K30 automatic cruise control, requires Pedal Ease power brakes ($57.93 and not available with W30 Force Air package). M55 automatic transmission oil cooler ($15.80). VE1 rear bumper guard insert ($7.37). D55 Sports console, Bucket seats required ($61.09, but not availaible with column-shifted manual transmission and includes U29 courtesy lights). C50 rear window defogger, except convertible ($22.12). Y72 engine cooling equipment, for cars without air conditioning ($57.93). B30 wall-to-wall floor carpeting ($18.96). A01 all windows tinted glass ($38.97). A02 tinted windshield only ($26.33). A82 dual front seat head restraints ($16.85). W30 Force-Air induction system special order for 4-4-2 ($263.30). D15 deluxe interior decor with front door and rear quarter armrests and moldings ($20.80). U29 panel courtesy lights for coupes ($6.32). D33 remote-control left-hand outside rearview mirror ($10.53). B93 door edge guards ($5.27). B96 chrome wheel opening moldings ($15.80). D99 two-tone Magic Mirror paint for coupes ($31.07). Y62 special solid color paint ($83.26). Y66 special two-tone paint, except convertible ($114.28). W40 special Firemist paint ($158.53). W42 dual hood paint stripe ($18.90, but included with W30 or W31 at no cost). U75 rear-mounted power antenna ($31.60). J50 Pedal Ease power brakes ($41.60 but not available with J50 front disc brakes or J55). JL2 power front disc brakes ($64.25, but not available with three-speed manual transmission). A93 power door locks ($44.76).). A41 four-way power bench seat ($73.72). A46 four-way power left-hand bucket seat ($73.72). N40 Roto-Matic power steering ($100.05). A31 power windows ($105.32). V01 heavy-duty radiator for 4-4-2 with W30 ($21.06). V01 heavy-duty radiator for 4-4-2 without W30 ($36.86). U59 AM/FM signal-seeking radio ($133.76). U63 Deluxe push-button radio ($69.51). U69 AM/FM radio ($133.76). U578 AM/FM stereophonic radio with rear seat speaker ($238.03). U57 stereo tape player, includes rear seat speaker with U58 ($116.91). U57 stereo tape player, includes rear seat speaker without U58 ($133.76). U80 bi-phonic rear seat speaker ($16.85, but included in U57 and U58 optrions). U21 Rocket Rally pac ($84.26). U15 Safety Sentinel ($11.59). A39 Deluxe seat belts front and rear for convertible with bucket seats ($8.96). A85 deluxe front shoulder belts for convertibles, A39 deluxe seat belts required ($26.33). AS1 standard front shoulder belts for convertibles without A39 or AS4 ($23.17). AS4 deluxe rear shoulder belts with A39 or W39 required ($26.33). AS5 standard rear shoulder belts ($23.17). A52 bench seat delete option ($68.46 credit). G66 Super lift rear shocks ($42.13 but not available with FG2 option). G51 heavy-duty rear springs ($3.69). N34 woodgrain Custom Sport finish steering wheel ($15.80). N33 tilt-away steering column ($45.29, but not available in cars with column-mounted manual gearshift). N42 deluxe instant horn ($31.60). P26 G78 x 14 white sidewall tires replacing F70-7.75 x 14 Red Stripe (no cost). P81 F70-7.75 x 14 fiberglass-belted Red Stripe tire replacing 7.75 x 14 Red Stripe ($26.33). PL5 Wide-Oval raised white letter tires replacing F70-7.75 X 14 Red Stripe ($26.33). U89 trailer electrical wiring harness ($10.53). M40 Turbo Hydra-Matic transmission ($227.04). M20 wide-ratio four-speed manual transmission ($184.80). M21

close-ratio four-speed manual transmission ($184.80). C56 Flo-Thru body ventilation ($15.80). C57 Forced-Air body ventilation (no cost). C08 vinyl roof covering on coupes ($100.05). P01 14-inch wheel discs ($21.06). P02 deluxe 14-in. wheel discs ($47.39). N95 simulated wire wheel discs ($73.72). P05 14-inch Super stock wheels ($90.58). N66 Super stock II wheels ($73.72). BC1 woodgrain vinyl dashboard trim ($10.53). Y60 accessory package including ashtray, luggage compartment, underhood and glove box lights and visor-vanity mirrort ($14.32-16.43 depending on body style).

1969 HURST/OLDS

JERRY HEASLEY

1969 Hurst/Olds

In George Hurst's "magic kingdom" the 4-4-2 that he built for Dr. Oldsmobile sat on the golden chair in the musclecar throne room. The famous red-and-black H/O badge reflected high-performance perfection. "Ah yes friends, there really is a supercar without lumps in it," advised *Super Stock* magazine in July of 1969.

Olds 4-4-2 styling was basid on the mid-sized Cutlass and it was altered only slightly for the 1969 model year. Essentially, each pair of lenses in the quad headlight system was brought closer together. This, along with some modification of the central grille and bumper area contributed to an overall smoother, less-cluttered frontal appearance. This year the Cutlass taillights were recessed and took on a more vertical theme, as opposed to the horizontal orientation of the 1968 model. For this year, all Hurst/Olds were based on the 4-4-2 Holiday two-door hardtop body style.

Stimulated by a special 455-cid 380-hp "Rocket" V-8, this year's Hurst/Olds was slightly lighter (3,715 lbs.) than its '68 counterpart (3,870 lbs.) and therefore bettered the original version's 0 to 60-mph acceleration times (5.9 seconds versus

6.7 seconds). However, it took slightly longer to cover the quarter-mile (14.0 seconds versus 13.9 seconds). At least, that's what one publication said. A second car magazine had different numbers — 6.0 seconds for 0-to-60 mph and 13.9 seconds at 102.27 mph for the quarter. Pick the ones you like best — the point is it was a fast car!

Series Number	Body/Style Number	Body Type & Seating	Factory Price	Shipping Weight	Production Total
HURST/OLDS — SERIES 4400 — V-8					
44	87	2d HT-6P	$4,500	3,716 lbs.	906

ENGINE
BASE V-8: Overhead valves. Cast-iron block. Bore and stroke: 4.126 x 4.250 inches. Displacement: 455.0 cid. Compression ratio: 10.50:1. Brake hp: 380 at 5000 rpm. Torque: 500 at 3200. Hydraulic valve lifters. Five main bearings. Carburetor: Rochester 4MV four-barrel. Engine code: W35. (NOTE: This motor was based on the Toronado engine, but built with a special crankshaft, a custom-curved distributor, special carburetor jets, a 308-degree camshaft with a .474-inch lift and hand-assembled Force-Air cylinder heads.)

OPTIONS
C60 Four Seasons air conditioning ($375.99). K30 automatic cruise control, requires M55 automatic transmission oil cooler ($15.80). VE1 rear bumper guard insert ($7.37). D55 Sports console. Bucket seats required ($61.09). C50 rear window defogger ($22.12). Y72 engine cooling equipment, for cars without air

conditioning ($57.93). B30 wall-to-wall floor carpeting ($18.96). A01 all windows tinted glass ($38.97). A02 tinted windshield only ($26.33). A82 dual front seat head restraints ($16.85). D33 remote-control left-hand outside rearview mirror ($10.53). B93 door edge guards ($5.27). B96 chrome wheel opening moldings ($15.80). D99 two-tone Magic Mirror paint for coupes ($31.07). Y62 special solid color paint ($83.26). Y66 special two-tone paint ($114.28). W40 special Firemist paint ($158.53). U75 rear-mounted power antenna ($31.60). J50 Pedal Ease power brakes ($41.60). JL2 power front disc brakes ($64.25). A93 power door locks ($44.76).). A41 four-way power bench seat ($73.72). A46 four-way power left-hand bucket seat ($73.72). N40 Roto-Matic power steering ($100.05). A31 power windows ($105.32). U59 AM/FM signal-seeking radio ($133.76). U63 Deluxe push-button radio ($69.51). U69 AM/FM radio ($133.76). U578 AM/FM stereophonic radio with rear seat speaker ($238.03). U57 stereo tape player, includes rear seat speaker with U58 ($116.91). U57 stereo tape player, includes rear seat speaker without U58 ($133.76). U80 bi-phonic rear seat speaker ($16.85, but included in U57 and U58 optrions). U15 Safety Sentinel ($11.59). A39 Deluxe seat belts front and rear for convertible with bucket seats ($8.96). A85 deluxe front shoulder belts for convertibles, A39 deluxe seat belts required ($26.33). AS1 standard front shoulder belts for convertibles without A39 or AS4

($23.17). AS4 deluxe rear shoulder belts with A39 or W39 required ($26.33). AS5 standard rear shoulder belts ($23.17). A52 bench seat delete option ($68.46 credit). G66 Super lift rear shocks ($42.13 but not available with FG2 option). G51 heavy-duty rear springs ($3.69). N34 woodgrain Custom Sport finish steering wheel ($15.80). N33 tilt-away steering column ($45.29, but not available in cars with column-mounted manual gearshift). N42 deluxe instant horn ($31.60). P26 G78 x 14 white sidewall tires replacing F70-7.75 x 14 Red Stripe (no cost). P81 F70-7.75 x 14 fiberglass-belted Red Stripe tire replacing 7.75 x 14 Red Stripe ($26.33). PL5 Wide-Oval raised white letter tires replacing F70-7.75 x 14 Red Stripe ($26.33). U89 trailer electrical wiring harness ($10.53). M40 Turbo Hydra-Matic transmission ($227.04). M20 wide-ratio four-speed manual transmission ($184.80). M21 close-ratio four-speed manual transmission ($184.80). C56 Flo-Thru body ventilation ($15.80). C57 Forced-Air body ventilation (no cost). C08 vinyl roof covering on coupes ($100.05). P01 14-inch wheel discs ($21.06). P02 deluxe 14-inch wheel discs ($47.39). N95 simulated wire wheel discs ($73.72). P05 14-inch Super stock wheels ($90.58). N66 Super stock II wheels ($73.72). BC1 woodgrain vinyl dashboard trim ($10.53). Y60 accessory package including ashtray, luggage compartment, underhood and glove box lights and visor-vanity mirror ($14.32-16.43 depending on body style).

1970 F-85/CUTLASS "S" W-MACHINE

The 1970 Oldsmobile W-31 option for the lower-priced lines was Oldsmobile's answer to value-priced muscle cars like the Road Runner, Super Bee and GTO Judge. Using the cheap, lightweight F-85 and Cutless "S" coupes as a base, Oldsmobile turned them into "W-Machines" with this all-in-one package of performance equipment. The engine used was a high-performance 350-cid V-8 with special features and a full dual exhaust system. The F-85 version had the lowest level of trim and equipment — just the basics. The Cutlass "S" added chrome hood louver grilles, a front bench seat with bright moldings, foam-padded front and rear seat cushions and Flo-Thru ventilation on hardtop coupes.

Hot Rod magazine's test car with the W-31 engine took 14.92 seconds to do the quarter mile at 96.05 mph. It had the tall G88 group 3.91:1 rear axle.

Series Number	Body/Style Number	Body Type & Seating	Factory Price	Shipping Weight	Production Total
F-85 — SERIES 3200 — V-8					
32	77	2d Coupe-6P	$3,155	3,511 lbs.	8,274
Cutlass "S" — SERIES 3600 — V-8					
36	77	2d Coupe-6P	$3,275	3,540 lbs.	10,677
36	87	2d HT-6P	$3,338	3,551 lbs.	88,578

NOTE 1: Production total is for all F-85/Cutlass "S" two-door models; no W-31 breakout available.
NOTE 2: Price includes base cost of W31 package without G88 or G92 axles.
NOTE 3: Weights are estimated.

ENGINE

OPTIONAL V-8: Overhead valves. Cast-iron block. Bore and stroke: 4.06 x 3.39 inches. Displacement: 350.0 cid. Compression ratio: 10.50:1. Brake hp: 325 at 5400 rpm. Torque: 360 at 3600 rpm. Hydraulic valve lifters. Five main bearings. Carburetor: Rochester 4MV four-barrel. Engine code: QD and QX.

OPTIONS

C60 Four Seasons air conditioning ($375.99). G80 anti-spin differential ($42.13, but included in G88 and G92 performance rear axle options). M55 automatic transmission auxiliary oil cooler ($15.80). W27 aluminum rear axle carrier and cover for cars with W31 Force Air package ($157.98). U35 electric clock ($16.85, but included with option U21). D55 Sports console for Cutlass "S" only. ($61.09). W26 console with dual-gate sports shifter for Cutlass "S" ($76.88, but not available with front bench or Custom Sport seats). C50 rear window

defogger ($26.33). B30 wall-to-wall carpeting for F-85 with W31 ($18.96). B32 front auxiliary floor mats ($7.37). B33 rear auxiliary floor mats ($7.16). A01 all windows tinted glass ($38.97). A02 tinted windshield only ($26.33). T81 Night watch headlight-off delay control ($10.53). W25 Force-Air dual-intake hood ($157.98, but not available with GT hood stripes and included with W31). T44 inside hood release ($10.53). D15 interior decor package for coupe ($12.64), for hardtop ($6.32). D35 sports-styled dual outside rearview mirrors, left-hand remote-controlled (included in W31 package). B93 door edge guards ($5.27). B80 chrome roof drip moldings for Cutlass "S" with W31 ($13.69). B85 chrome window frames ($12.64). D99 two-tone Magic Mirror paint for F-85 and Cutlass "S" coupes ($31.07). Y73 GT hood stripes ($10.53, but not available with W31). Y66 special two-tone paint, except convertible ($114.28). W40 special Firemist paint ($158.53). Y62 special solid color paint ($83.20). AU3 power door locks ($44.75). AU5 power door locks and front seatback back release ($68.46). A41 four-way power bench seat ($73.72). A46 four-way power left-hand bucket seat ($73.72). N47 variable-ratio power steering ($105.32). A90 power trunk lid release ($14.74). A31 power windows ($105.32). V01 heavy-duty radiator ($21.06). U63 Deluxe push-button radio ($69.51). U58 AM/FM stereophonic radio with rear seat speaker ($238.03). U57 stereo tape player, includes rear seat speaker with U58 ($116.91). U57 stereo tape player, includes rear seat speaker without U58 ($133.76). U80 bi-phonic rear seat speaker ($16.85, but included in U57 and U58 optrions). U21 Rocket Rally pac ($84.26). U15 Safety Sentinel ($11.59). AS4 deluxe rear shoulder belts with A39 or W39 required ($26.33). AS5 standard rear shoulder belts ($23.17). AK1 deluxe front and rear seat belts and front shoulder belts ($13.69). A51 Strato bucket seats in Cutlass "S" ($68.46). N34 Custom Sport finish steering wheel in F-85 ($31.60). N34 Custom Sport finish steering wheel in F-85 ($15.80). N30 deluxe steering wheel in F-85s ($15.80). N42 deluxe Instant Horn for F-85 ($31.60). N33 tilt-away steering column ($45.29, but not available in cars with column-mounted manual gearshift). FG2 front and rear firm ride suspension ($5.27, but included in F41 option and not available with G66 option). G66 Super lift rear shocks, requires M40 option ($42.13). F41 heavy-duty suspension including front and rear heavy-duty springs, front stabilizer bar and firm ride suspension ($42.13). FE2 Rallye suspension ($18.54). P26 G78-14 dual white-stripe fiberglass-belted tires ($30.54). PK5 G70-14 Wide-Oval raised white letter tires ($88.47). PX8 G70-14 Wide-Oval raised white letter white stripe tires ($62.14). U89 trailer electrical wiring harness ($10.53). M14 heavy-duty three-speed manual transmission ($84.26). M15 three-speed manual transmission with column shift (no charge). M38 Turbo Hydra-Matic 350 transmission ($205.92). M20 close-ratio four-speed manual transmission ($184.80). M21 close-ratio four-speed manual transmission ($184.80). C08 vinyl roof covering on coupes ($102.16). P01 14-inch wheel discs ($21.06). P02 deluxe 14-inch wheel discs ($47.39). N95 simulated wire wheel discs ($73.72). P05 14-inch Super stock wheels ($90.58). N66 Super stock II wheels ($73.72). P06 chrome trim rings ($21.06). BC1 woodgrain vinyl dashboard trim ($10.53). Y60 accessory group in coupes includes trunk light, underhood light, courtesy lights, map light, dash panel control lighting and dash panel ashtray light ($28.02). W31 W-Machine package includes high-compression 350-cid/325-hp Rocket V-8, Force-Air induction, aluminum intake manifold, heavy-duty clutch, manual front disc brakes, lightweight body insulation, dual-scoop fiberglass hood, body paint stripes and "W" emblems with G88 axle ($591.17), with G92 axle ($585.91), without G88 or G92 axles ($368.62).

G88 performance rear axle package ($63.19 and other options required). G92 performance rear axle package ($63.19 and other options required). G90 3.08:1 rear axle, recommended for trailer towing (no charge). G91 rear axle with 3.08:1 gearing (no charge). G95 Expressway rear axle with 2.78:1 gearing (no charge). G96 rear axle with 2.56:1 gearing (no charge).

1970 4-4-2

JERRY HEASLEY

1970 4-4-2

The ultra-cool Oldsmobile 4-4-2 continued as a separate series in 1970. Three two-door models were now available: Sports coupe, hardtop coupe and convertible. The new 4-4-2s had few exterior changes from the 1969 versions, but wore a distinctive grille formed of black, vertical rectangles. The fenders, rear quarters, trunk lid and both bumpers were also unique to the 4-4-2. All three models were based on the Cutlass Supreme.

Standard equipment included full dual exhaust system, chrome hood louver grilles, body side paint stripes, trunk lid paint stripes, Rally Sports heavy-duty suspension, a power top on the convertible, a heavy-duty three-speed manual transmission with floor-mounted Hurst gearshift, chrome hubcaps, G70-14 single white stripe Wide-Oval tires and a 455-cid/365-hp V-8.

Hot Rod magazine's test car with the W-30 engine took 13.98 seconds to do the quarter-mile at 100.78 mph. It had the tall G88 group 3.91:1 rear axle.

Series Number	Body/Style Number	Body Type & Seating	Factory Price	Shipping Weight	Production Total
4-4-2 — SERIES 4400 — V-8					
44	77	2d Coupe-6P	$3,312	3,667 lbs.	1,688
44	87	2d HT-6P	$3,376	3,713 lbs.	14,709
44	67	2d Conv-6P	$3,567	3,740 lbs.	2,933

ENGINE

BASE V-8: V-8. Overhead valves. Cast-iron block. Bore and stroke: 4.126 x 4.250 inches. Displacement: 455 cid. Compression ratio: 10.25:1. Brake hp: 365 at 4600 rpm. Torque: 510 at 3000 rpm. Five main bearings. Hydraulic valve lifters. Carburetor: Rochester 4MV four-barrel. Engine code: TP, TQ, TU, TV, TW, UN and UO.

OPTIONAL V-8: Overhead valves. Cast-iron block. Bore and stroke: 4.126 x 4.250 inches. Displacement: 455 cid. Compression ratio: 10.50:1. Brake hp: 370 at 5200 rpm. Torque: 500 at 3600 rpm. Five main bearings. Hydraulic valve lifters. Carburetor: Rochester 4MV four-barrel. Engine code: TS and TT.

OPTIONS

C60 Four Seasons air conditioning ($375.99). G80 anti-spin differential ($42.13, but included in G88 and G92 performance rear axle options). K30 automatic cruise control, requires Pedal Ease power brakes or power front disc brakes ($57.93 and not available with W30 Force Air package). M55 automatic transmission auxiliary oil cooler ($15.80). W27 aluminum rear axle carrier and cover for 4-4-2 with W30 Force Air package ($157.98). U35 electric clock ($16.85, but included with option U21). D55 Sports console ($61.09). W26 console with dual-gate sports shifter ($76.88, but not available for 4-4-2 with front bench or Custom Sport seats). C50 rear window defogger, except convertible ($26.33). B32 front auxiliary floor mats ($7.37). B33 rear auxiliary floor mats ($7.16). T44 hinside hood release ($10.53). A01 all windows tinted glass ($38.97). A02 tinted windshield only ($26.33). T81 Night watch headlight-off delay control ($10.53). W25 Force-Air dual-intake hood ($157.98, but not available with GT hood stripes and included with W30). D33 remote-control left-hand outside rearview mirror ($10.53). B93 door edge guards ($5.27). B85 chrome window frames for 4-4-2 coupes ($12.64). D99 two-tone Magic Mirror paint for coupes ($31.07). Y73 GT hood stripes ($10.53, but not available with W30). Y66 special two-tone paint, except convertible ($114.28). W40 special Firemist paint ($158.53). Y62 special solid color paint ($83.20). AU3 power door locks ($44.75). AU5 power door locks and front seatback back release ($68.46). A41 four-way power bench seat ($73.72). A46 four-way power left-hand bucket seat ($73.72). N47 variable-ratio power steering ($105.32). A90 power trunk lid release ($14.74). A31 power windows ($105.32). V01 heavy-duty radiator for 4-4-2 with W30 ($21.06). V01 heavy-duty radiator for 4-4-2 without W30 ($36.86). U63 Deluxe push-button radio ($69.51). U58 AM/FM stereophonic radio with rear seat speaker ($238.03). U57 stereo tape player, includes rear seat speaker with U58 ($116.91). U57 stereo tape player, includes rear seat speaker without U58 ($133.76). U80 bi-phonic rear seat speaker ($16.85, but included in U57 and U58 optrions). U21 Rocket Rally pac ($84.26). U15 Safety Sentinel ($11.59). A39 Deluxe seat belts front and rear for convertible with bucket seats

OLDSMOBILE

($8.95). A39 Deluxe seat belts front and rear for convertible without bucket seats ($10.53). A85 deluxe front shoulder belts for convertibles, A39 deluxe seat belts required ($26.33). AS1 standard front shoulder belts for convertibles without A39 or AS4 ($23.17). AS4 deluxe rear shoulder belts with A39 or W39 required ($26.33). AS5 standard rear shoulder belts ($23.17). AK1 deluxe front and rear seat belts and front shoulder belts ($12.11). A52 bench seat delete option ($68.46 credit). A65 Custom Sport seat in 4-4-2 convertible (no charge). N34 Custom Sport finish steering wheel ($15.80). N33 tilt-away steering column ($45.29, but not available in cars with column-mounted manual gearshift). G66 Super lift rear shocks, requires M40 option ($42.13). G51 heavy-duty rear springs ($3.69). PK5 Wide-Oval raised white letter tires replacing F70-7.75 X 14 Red Stripe ($26.33, but included in W30 option). U89 trailer electrical wiring harness ($10.53). M40 Turbo Hydra-Matic 400 transmission ($227.04). M21 close-ratio four-speed manual transmission ($184.80). C08 vinyl roof covering on coupes ($100.05). P01 14-inch wheel discs ($21.06). P02 deluxe 14-in. wheel discs ($47.39). N95 simulated wire wheel discs ($73.72). P05 14-inch

Super stock wheels ($90.58). N66 Super stock II wheels ($73.72). P06 chrome trim rings ($21.06). BC1 woodgrain vinyl dashboard trim ($10.53). Y60 accessory group in coupes ($28.02) in convertible ($14.32). W30 W-Machine package includes high-compression 455-cid/370-hp Rocket V-8, Force-Air induction, special air cleaner, special four-barrel carburetor, aluminum intakje manifold, dual-intake Force-Air fiberglass hood with special paint, wide body side paint stripe, "W" emblems, lightweight body insulation, manual front disc brakes and G92 axle at extra cost — except C60 with has G91 axle at no cost ($321.23 for 4-4-2 with M40 transmission or M21 transmission with G88 or G92 axles), ($369.68 for 4-4-2 with D35 or PK5 options). G88 performance rear axle package with 3.91:1 anti-spin axle and heavy-duty radiator ($63.19 and other options required). G92 performance rear axle package with 3.42:1 anti-spin axle and heavy-duty radiator ($63.19 and other options required). G91 rear axle with 3.08:1 gearing (no charge). G95 Expressway rear axle with 2.78:1 gearing (no charge). G96 rear axle with 2.56:1 gearing (no charge). G90 3.08:1 rear axle, recommended for trailer towing (no charge).

1970 RALLYE 350

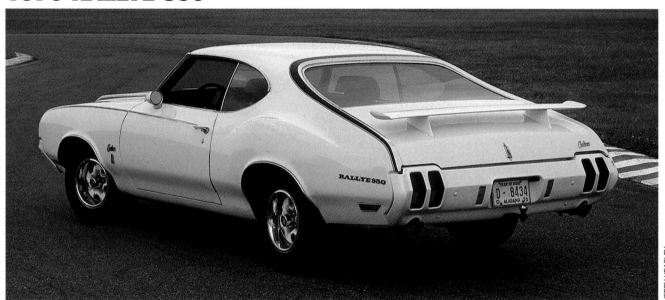

JERRY HEASLEY

1970 Rallye 350

While not the brawniest muscle car ever built, the Oldsmobile Rallye 350 was surely one of the brightest. Its smart Sebring Yellow paint makes it stand out wherever it's seen. So does the fact that its urethane-clad Sebring Yellow front and rear bumpers and Rallye spoke wheels are done in the same color. Other standard equipment on these cars included custom-painted Super Stock II wheels, G70-14 Wide-Oval black sidewall tires, bold Rallye 350 fender decals, sports styled dual outside rearview mirrors, a Rallye suspension, a Custom Sport steering wheel, a dual-intake Force Air hood and a high-compression 350-cid/310-hp four-barrel V-8 with dual exhausts.

Introduced in February 1970, the car was initially planned as a Hurst/Olds, but Lansing wound up marketing it as a new option that combined the looks of a limited-edition muscle car with a more "streetable" power-train package. It could be added to either the F-85 sport coupe or the Cutlass "S" sport coupe or Holiday hardtop. Like the GTO "Judge," this trendy-looking Olds was aimed at a market niche that proved to be smaller than sales projections forecasted.

In February 1970, *Motor Trend* tested a Rallye 350 with the 310-hp engine, three-speed manual transmission and 3.23:1 rear axle. It did 0-to-60 mph in 7.7 seconds and covered the quarter-mile in 15.4 seconds at 89 mph.

Series Number	Body/Style Number	Body Type & Seating	Factory Price	Shipping Weight	Production Total
F-85 — SERIES 3200 — V-8					
32	77	2d Coupe-6P	$3,253	3,511 lbs.	1,020
Cutlass "S" — SERIES 3600 — V-8					
36	77	2d Coupe-6P	$3,373	3,540 lbs.	Note 1
36	87	2d HT-6P	$3,436	3,551 lbs.	Note 1

NOTE 1: Production total of Cutlass "S" versions was 2,527 combined.

NOTE 2: Weights are estimated.

ENGINE

BASE V-8: Overhead valves. Cast-iron block. Bore and stroke: 4.06 x 3.39 inches. Displacement: 350.0 cid. Compression ratio: 10.25:1. Brake hp: 310 at 4800 rpm. Torque: 390 at 3200 rpm. Hydraulic valve lifters. Five main bearings. Carburetor: Rochester 4MV four-barrel. Engine code: QM, QP and QV.

OPTIONAL FORCED-AIR V-8: Overhead valves. Cast-iron block. Bore and stroke: 4.06 x 3.39 inches. Displacement: 350.0 cid. Compression ratio: 10.50:1. Brake hp: 325 at 5400 rpm. Torque: 360 at 3600 rpm. Hydraulic valve

OLDSMOBILE

lifters. Five main bearings. Carburetor: Rochester 4MV four-barrel. Engine code: QD and QX.

OPTIONS (PARTIAL LIST)

C60 Four Seasons air conditioning ($375.99). G80 anti-spin differential ($42.13, but included in G88 and G92 performance rear axle options). M55 automatic transmission auxiliary oil cooler ($15.80). W27 aluminum rear axle carrier and cover for cars with W31 Force Air package ($157.98). U35 electric clock ($16.85, but included with option U21). D55 Sports console for Cutlass "S" only. Bucket seats required. Includes lockable map case with manual transmission or floor shift, map case lamp and rear console lamp with automatic transmission. ($61.09). W26 console with dual-gate sports shifter for Cutlass "S" only, includes lockable map case with light and rear console light. Automatic transmission required ($76.88, but not available with front bench or Custom Sport seats). C50 rear window defogger ($26.33). B30 wall-to-wall carpeting for F-85 with W31 ($18.96). B32 front auxiliary floor mats ($7.37). B33 rear auxiliary floor mats ($7.16). A01 all windows tinted glass ($38.97). A02 tinted windshield only ($26.33). T81 Night watch headlight-off delay control ($10.53). W25 Force-Air dual-intake hood ($157.98, but not available with GT hood stripes and included with W31). T44 inside hood release ($10.53). N47 variable-ratio power steering ($105.32). A90 power trunk lid release ($14.74). A31 power windows ($105.32). V01 heavy-duty radiator ($21.06). U63 Deluxe push-button radio ($69.51). U58 AM/FM stereophonic radio with rear seat speaker ($238.03). U57 stereo tape player, includes rear seat speaker with U58 ($116.91). U57 stereo tape player, includes rear seat speaker without U58

($133.76). U80 bi-phonic rear seat speaker ($16.85, but included in U57 and U58 options). U21 Rocket Rally pac ($84.26). U15 Safety Sentinel ($11.59). AS4 deluxe rear shoulder belts with A39 or W39 required ($26.33). AS5 standard rear shoulder belts ($23.17). AK1 deluxe front and rear seat belts and front shoulder belts ($13.69). A51 Strato bucket seats in Cutlass "S" ($68.46). N34 Custom Sport finish steering wheel in F-85 ($31.60). N34 Custom Sport finish steering wheel in F-85 ($15.80). N30 deluxe steering wheel in F-85s ($15.80). N42 deluxe Instant Horn for F-85 ($31.60). N33 tilt-away steering column ($45.29, but not available in cars with column-mounted manual gearshift). FG2 front and rear firm ride suspension ($5.27, but included in F41 option and not available with G66 option). G66 Super lift rear shocks, requires M40 option ($42.13). F41 heavy-duty suspension including front and rear heavy-duty springs, front stabilizer bar and firm ride suspension ($42.13). FE2 Rallye suspension ($18.54). W45 Rallye 350 appearance package including Sebring Yellow exterior with black-and-orange decals, urethane-coated Sebring Yellow front and rear bumpers, a blacked-out grille, custom-painted Super Stock II wheels, G70-14 Wide-Oval black sidewall tires, bold Rallye 350 fender decals, sports styled dual outside rearview mirrors, a Rallye suspension, a Custom Sport steering wheel, a dual-intake Force Air hood and a high-compression 350-cid/310-hp four-barrel V-8 with dual exhausts. PK5 G70-14 Wide-Oval tires with white lettering on Rallye 350s ($56.87). PX8 G70-14 Wide-Oval tires with single white stripe on Rallye 350 ($30.54). U89 trailer wiring harness ($10.53). M14 heavy-duty three-speed manual transmission ($84.26). M15 three-speed manual transmission with column shift (no charge). M38 Turbo Hydra-Matic 350 transmission ($205.92).

1971 4-4-2

1971 4-4-2

This was the last year that Oldsmobile would have the 4-4-2 as a separate model. In 1972, the 4-4-2 would become an appearance and handling option for the Cutlass "S." For its last year as a separate series, the 4-4-2's standard equipment included a special 455-cid engine, a dual exhaust system, carpeting, special springs, stabilizer bars, special engine mounts, Strato bucket seats, heavy-duty wheels, special emblems and a deluxe steering wheel. Oldsmobile offered a choice of vinyl or cloth upholstery.

To ensure that the calibrated settings on the Rochester 4MC four-barrel carburetor stayed constant, plastic caps were snapped over the idle mixture screws. Because the lowered compression ratio used in 1971 generated more heat than previous 4-4-2 high-compression engines, the fan speed was increased. To counter the resultant increase in fan noise, Oldsmobile used a new clutch designed to release the fan be-

fore an objectionable noise level was reached. It was used with fans set up to increase speed faster from idle.

On balance, *Hot Rod* concluded that the 1971 version of the 4-4-2 and its W-30 variant represented no appreciable performance sacrifice. As the last of the special series, the '71 4-4-2 is worth collecting.

Series Number	Body/Style Number	Body Type & Seating	Factory Price	Shipping Weight	Production Total
4-4-2 — SERIES 4400 — V-8					
44	87	2d HT-6P	$3,552	3,835 lbs.	6,285
44	67	2d Conv-6P	$3,743	3,792 lbs.	1,304

ENGINES

BASE V-8: Overhead valves. Cast-iron block. Bore and stroke: 4.126 x 4.250 inches. Displacement: 455 cid. Compression ratio: 8.50:1. Brake hp: 340 at 4600 rpm. Net hp: 270 at 4400 rpm. Torque: 460 at 3200 rpm. Net torque: 370 at 3200 rpm. Hydraulic valve lifters. Carburetor: Rochester 4MV four-barrel. Engine code: TT, TL, TS and TB.

OPTIONAL W30 V-8: Overhead valves. Cast-iron block. Bore and stroke: 4.126 x 4.250 inches. Displacement: 455 cid. Compression ratio: 8.50:1. Brake hp: 280 at 4700 rpm (net). Torque: 3700 at 3200 rpm (net). Five main bearings. Hydraulic valve lifters. Carburetor: Rochester 4MV four-barrel. Engine code: US, UT.

OPTIONS

C60 Four Seasons air conditioning ($407.59). W27 aluminum rear axle housing cover ($26.33). G80 anti-spin differential, required with 3.73:1 ratio ($44.23). G89 heavy-duty performance axle for 4-4-2 with W30 required ($68.46 and not available with C60 or Y72). G92 heavy-duty performance axle with 3.42:1 ratio ($21.06). A39 Deluxe seat belts front and rear for convertible without A65 ($11.06). A39 Deluxe seat belts front and rear for convertible with A65 ($12.64). AK1 deluxe front and rear seat belts and front shoulder belts ($38.97). AS4 deluxe rear shoulder belts with A39 or W39 required ($26.33). U35 electric clock ($18.96, but included with option U21). D55 Sports console. ($61.09). W26 console with dual-gate sports shifter ($76.88, but not available for 4-4-2 with front bench or Custom Sport seats). C49 electric rear window defogger, except convertible ($63.19). B32 front auxiliary floor mats ($7.37). B33 rear auxiliary floor mats ($7.37). A01 all windows tinted glass ($43.18). A02 tinted windshield only ($30.54). V36 bumper guards with vinyl inserts ($31.60). T44 hinside hood release ($10.53). W25 Force-Air dual-intake fiberglass hood ($157.98, but not available with Y73 and included with W30). B93 door edge guards ($6.32). B85 chrome window frames for 4-4-2 hardtop ($21.06). D99 two-tone Magic Mirror paint for hardtops ($36.86). Y73 GT hood stripes ($47.39). Y66 special two-tone paint, except convertible ($152.84). Y76 special Firemist paint ($200.11). Y62 special Oldsmobile solid color paint ($115.85). WM6 special non-Oldsmobile solid color paint ($157.98). JL2 power front disc brakes ($69.51 and required on cars with W30 and C60). AU3 power door locks ($47.39). A41 four-way power bench seat ($70.56 and requires A52 or A65 options). A46 four-way power left-hand bucket seat ($78.99). N47 variable-ratio power steering ($115.85). A90 power trunk lid latch ($14.74). A31 power windows ($115.85). U63 Deluxe push-button radio ($74.78). U58 AM/FM stereophonic radio with rear seat speaker ($239.08). UM1 AM radio with stereo tape player ($221.17). UM2 AM/FM stereo with tape player ($372.83). U57 stereo tape player, includes rear seat speaker with U58 ($116.91). U57 stereo tape player, includes rear seat speaker without U58 ($133.76). U80 bi-phonic rear seat speaker ($18.96, but included in U57 and U58 oprtions). U21 Rocket Rally pac ($84.26). C08 vinyl roof covering on coupes ($102.16). A52 bench seat delete option ($68.46 credit). A65 Custom Sport seat in 4-4-2 convertible (no charge). G66 Super lift rear shocks, requires M40 option ($42.13). FE2 rally suspension package includes F41 heavy-duty suspension, heavy-duty spprings, shocks, stabilizer shafts, rear lower control arm and PC2 wheels ($18.54 for cars without N66, N67 or P05). FE2 rally suspension package includes F41 heavy-duty suspension, heavy-duty spprings, shocks, stabilizer shafts, rear lower control arm and PC2 wheels ($13.27 for cars with N66, N67 or P05). W35 rear deck lid spoiler ($73.72). N34 Custom Sport steering wheel ($31.60). N33 tilt-away steering column ($45.29, but not available in cars with column-mounted manual gearshift). PK5 G70-14 Wide-Oval raised white letter tires for 4-4-2 ($26.33 and C60, FE2 or Y79 option required). M40 Turbo Hydra-Matic 400 transmission ($242.88). M22 close-ratio four-speed manual transmission ($237.60). P01 wheel discs ($26.33). P02 deluxe wheel discs ($47.39). P05 Super Stock I wheels ($90.58). N66 Super Stock II wheels ($73.72). N67 Custom Sport color-keyed wheels with steel trim rings ($73.72). CD3 shift-lever-controlled windshield wiper-washer for cars with automatic transmission and column-mounted gear shift ($21.06). BC1 woodgrain vinyl dashboard trim ($10.53). U89 trailering wiring harness ($10.53). Y60 accessory group in hardtop ($30.12), in convertible ($16.43). W30 W-Machine package includes Sports-style outside rearview mirrors, G70-14 Wide-Oval raised-white-letter tires, a 455-cid/370-hp four-barrel Force-Air induction engine, a dual-intake Force-Air fiberglass hood, wide body side paint stripes, lightweight body insulation and "W" emblems for 4-4-2 without power disc brakes ($369.67 and M21, M22 or M40 transmission and G80, G89 or G92 rear axle required). W30 W-Machine package includes Sports-style outside rearview mirrors, G70-14 Wide-Oval raised-white-letter tires, a 455-cid/370-hp four-barrel Force-Air induction engine, a dual-intake Force-Air fiberglass hood, wide body side paint stripes, lightweight body insulation and "W" emblems for 4-4-2 with power disc brakes ($347.96 and M21, M22 or M40 transmission and G80, G89 or G92 rear axle required).

1972 4-4-2

PHIL KUNZ

1972 4-4-2

Mid-size 1972 Oldsmobiles looked pretty much the same as the 1971 models, but there was a consolidation of models and only V-8 engines were used. The base F-85 series offered just a four-door sedan. There were a coupe, sedan and two-door hardtop in the next-step-up Cutlass line. The hardtop had an "F" series code like an F-85, but was considered part of the Cutlass "G" series, which is an unusual fact.

The Cutlass "S" line offered a sport coupe and a two-door hardtop. Both used the same "G" series code as the four-door Cutlass models. In the "J" series were three Cutlass Supremes: two- and four-door hardtops and a convertible. The "K" series contained the Vista Cruiser wagons. A 4-4-2 Appearance & Handling package (code W29) was offered for the Cutlass F87 hardtop, all Cutlass "S" models and the Cutlass Supreme convertible. The package retailed for $147.00.

Series Number	Body/Style Number	Body Type & Seating	Factory Price	Shipping Weight	Production Total
CUTLASS F-87 + W29 — SERIES F — V-8					
F	87	2d HT-6P	$2,973	3,509 lbs.	751
CUTLASS "S" + W29 — SERIES G — V-8					
G	77	2d Cpe-6P	$3,027	3,503 lbs.	123
G	87	2d HT-6P	$3,087	3,509 lbs.	7,800
CUTLASS SUPREME + W29 — SERIES G — V-8					
J	67	2d HT-6P	$3,433	3,614 lbs.	1,041

NOTE 1: Base prices shown; cost of 4-4-2 option varied by series and other options on car. See options list below.

ENGINES

BASE V-8: Overhead valves. Cast-iron block. Bore and stroke: 4.06 x 3.39 inches. Displacement: 350.0 cid. Compression ratio: 8.50:1. Net hp: 160 at 4000 rpm. Net torque: 275 at 2400 rpm. Hydraulic valve lifters. Five main bearings. Carburetor: Rochester 2GC two-barrel. IN code: H.

OPTIONAL V-8: Overhead valves. Cast-iron block. Bore and stroke: 4.06 x 3.39 inches. Displacement: 350.0 cid. Compression ratio: 8.50:1. Net hp: 175 at 4000 rpm. Net torque: 295 at 2600 rpm. Hydraulic valve lifters. Five main bearings. Carburetor: Rochester 4MV four-barrel. VIN code: J.

OPTIONAL V-8: Overhead valves. Cast-iron block. Bore and stroke: 4.06 x 3.39 inches. Displacement: 350.0 cid. Compression ratio: 8.50:1. Net hp: 180 at 4000 rpm. Net torque: 275 at 2800 rpm. Hydraulic valve lifters. Five main bearings. Carburetor: Rochester 4MV four-barrel. VIN code: K.

OPTIONAL V-8: Overhead valves. Cast-iron block. Bore and stroke: 4.06 x 3.39 inches. Displacement: 350.0 cid. Compression ratio: 8.50:1. Net hp: 200 at 4400 rpm. Net torque: 300 at 3200 rpm. Hydraulic valve lifters. Five main bearings. Carburetor: Rochester 4MC four-barrel. VIN code: M.

OPTIONAL V-8: Overhead valves. Cast-iron block. Bore and stroke: 4.126 x 4.250 inches. Displacement: 455 cid. Compression ratio: 8.50:1. Net hp: 250 at 4200 rpm. Net torque: 370 at 2800 rpm. Hydraulic valve lifters. Carburetor: Rochester 4MC four-barrel. VIN code: U.

OPTIONAL V-8: Overhead valves. Cast-iron block. Bore and stroke: 4.126 x 4.250 inches. Displacement: 455 cid. Compression ratio: 8.50:1. Net hp: 300 at 4700 rpm. Net torque: 410 at 3200 rpm. Hydraulic valve lifters. Carburetor: Rochester 4MC four-barrel. VIN code: X.

OPTIONS (PARTIAL LIST)

C60 Four Seasons air conditioning ($397). G80 anti-spin differential, required with 3.73:1 ratio ($43). G89 heavy-duty performance axle for 4-4-2 with 3.73:1 rear, W30 required (no charge). G92 heavy-duty performance axle with 3.42:1 ratio, W30 required (no charge). D55 Sports console ($59). W26 console with dual-gate sports shifte ($75). K30 cruise control ($62). C49 electric rear window defogger, except convertible ($62). N10 dual exhaust system ($29.70). U63 Deluxe push-button radio ($73). U69 AM/FM monaural push-button radio ($135). U56 AM/FM stereophonic radio with rear seat speaker ($233). UM1 AM radio with stereo tape player ($215). UM2 AM/FM stereo with tape player ($363). U57 stereo tape player, includes rear seat speaker with U58 ($114). U57 stereo tape player, includes rear seat speaker without U58 ($130). U80 bi-phonic rear seat speaker ($18). U21 Rocket Rally pac ($82). C08 vinyl roof covering on coupes ($99). A65 Custom Sport seat in 4-4-2 convertible (no charge). B50 extra foam-padded seat on front seat of base Cutlass (9). A51 Strato bucket seats in Cutlass "S" hardtop ($67). FG2 Firm Ride shock absorbers ($5). G66 Super lift rear shocks, requires M40 option ($41). FE2 rally suspension package includes F41 heavy-duty suspension, heavy-duty spprings, shocks, stabilizer shafts, rear lower control arm and PC2 wheels ($12.60-$17.60). Y75 Sport Equipment exterior package for F-87 hardtop ($51). N34 Custom Sport steering wheel ($31). N33 tilt-away steering column ($44). PK2 G78-14 white-striped glass-belted tires ($32). PK5 G70-14 Wide-Oval tires with raised white lettering ($86.00-100.00 depending on series and body stylee). PX6 F78-14 white stripe glass-belted tires ($30). PX8 G70-14 white stripe Wide Oval tires ($63.00-$77.00 depending on series and body style). M20 wide-ratio four-speed manual transmission ($190). M38 Turbo Hydra-Matic 350 transmission ($215). M40 Turbo Hydra-Matic 400 transmission for cars with L75 or W30 options only ($236). W39 three-speed manual transmission with Hurst floor shifter ($41). BC1 woodgrained dashboard trim ($10). W37 heavy-duty two-plate clutch ($96). P01 wheel discs ($26). P02 deluxe wheel discs ($46). N95 simulated wire wheel covers ($113). N66 Super Stock II wheels ($72). N67 Custom Sport color-keyed wheels with steel trim rings ($72). U89 trailering wiring harness ($10). Y60 accessory group in hardtop ($15.60-$35.60 depending on series and body style). W29 Olds 4-4-2 appearance and handling package for Cutlass F87 without W39 ($147). W29 Olds 4-4-2 appearance and handling package for Cutlass F87 with W39 ($106). W29 Olds 4-4-2 appearance and handling package for Cutlass "S" and Cutlass Supreme models without W39 ($70). W29 Olds 4-4-2 appearance and handling package for Cutlass "S" and Cutlass Supreme models with W39 ($29). W30 W-Machine package includes Sports-style outside rearview mirrors, G70-14 Wide-Oval raised-white-letter tires, a 455-cid/370-hp four-barrel Force-Air induction engine, a dual-intake Force-Air fiberglass hood, wide body side paint stripes, lightweight body insulation and "W" emblems for F87 4-4-2 without power disc brakes with specific qualifications ($722). W30 W-Machine package includes Sports-style outside rearview mirrors, G70-14 Wide-Oval raised-white-letter tires, a 455-cid/370-hp four-barrel Force-Air induction engine, a dual-intake Force-Air fiberglass hood, wide body side paint stripes, lightweight body insulation and "W" emblems for F87 4-4-2 with power disc brakes with specific qualifications ($700). without power disc brakes with specific qualifications ($645), without power disc brakes with specific qualifications ($599), with power disc brakes with specific qualifications ($577).

1972 HURST/OLDS

Standard equipment included a Rallye Suspension, dual exhausts, power front disc brakes, the W25 fiberglass hood and a 3:23:1 ratio anti-spin rear axle. Only Turbo Hydra-Matic transmissions with a Hurst Dual-Gate shifter were fitted. Hurst also tweaked the standard 455-cid V-8, but buyers could opt for the W-30 high-performance version. V-8 could be specified by the buyer. The W-30 cars came with a 3:42:1 rear axle. A small number of Hurst/Olds Vista Cruiser wagons were built for use as didnitary cars during the Indy 500.

ENGINES

BASE V-8: Overhead valves. Cast-iron block. Bore and stroke: 4.126 x 4.250 inches. Displacement: 455 cid. Compression ratio: 8.50:1. Net hp: 270 at 4400 rpm. Net torque: 370 at 3200 rpm. Hydraulic valve lifters. Carburetor: Rochester 4MC four-barrel. VIN code: U.

OPTIONAL V-8: Overhead valves. Cast-iron block. Bore and stroke: 4.126 x 4.250 inches. Displacement: 455 cid. Compression ratio: 8.50:1. Net hp: 300

All 1972 Hurst Oldsmobiles were patterned after the Hurst/Olds convertible that paced the Indy 500 that year. All of the cars were Cameo White like the actual pace car and had similar gold striping.

Series Number	Body/Style Number	Body Type & Seating	Factory Price	Shipping Weight	Production Total
CUTLASS F-87 + W29 — SERIES F — V-8					
F	87	2d HT-6P	—	—	Note 1
CUTLASS "S" + W29 — SERIES G — V-8					
G	77	2d Cpe-6P	—	—	Note 1
G	87	2d HT-6P	—	—	Note 1
CUTLASS SUPREME + W29 — SERIES G — V-8					
J	67	2d HT-6P	—	—	Note 1

NOTE 1: Base prices shown; cost of 4-4-2 option varied by series and other options on car. See options list below.

NOTE 2: Total production of regular Hurst/Olds model was about 629 cars of which 130 were convertible.

NOTE 3: Indy 500 festival cars included 42 convertibles, 27 coupes, 6 station wagons and 1 four-door sedan.

OLDSMOBILE

1972 Hurst/Olds Indy Pace Car

at 4700 rpm. Net torque: 410 at 3200 rpm. Hydraulic valve lifters. Carburetor: Rochester 4MC four-barrel. VIN code: X.

OPTIONS (PARTIAL LIST)

C60 Four Seasons air conditioning ($397). G80 anti-spin differential, required with 3.73:1 ratio ($43). G89 heavy-duty performance axle for 4-4-2 with 3.73:1 rear, W30 required (no charge). G92 heavy-duty performance axle with 3.42:1 ratio, W30 required (no charge). G90 towing axle with 3.08:1 or 3.07:1 ratio (no charge). G91 axle with 3.23:1 ratio (no charge). A39 Deluxe seat belts front and rear for convertible without A65 ($12). A39 Deluxe seat belts front and rear for convertible with A65 ($13.50). AK1 deluxe front and rear seat belts and front shoulder belts ($12.00-$36.50 depending on model). B30 floor carpeting in Cutlass F-87 hardtop ($21). U35 electric clock ($18). D55 Sports console. Bucket seats required. Includes locckable map case with manual transmission or floor shift, mamp case lamp and rear console lamp with automatic transmission. ($59). W26 console with dual-gate sports shifter, includes lockable map case with light and rear console light. Automatic transmission required ($75). K30 cruise control ($62). C49 electric rear window defogger, except convertible ($62). N10 dual exhaust system ($29.70). VJ9 emissions test required in California ($15). L32 V-8 in Cutlass Supreme ($33.00 credit) L24 V-8 in Cutlass except Supreme ($46). L75 V-8 in Custom group except Supreme ($183). Y72 engine cooling ($21.00 to $56.00 depending on whether car has air conditioning). B32 front auxiliary floor mats ($7). B33 rear auxiliary floor mats ($7). A01 all windows tinted glass ($42). A02 tinted windshield only ($30). V36 bumper guards with vinyl inserts ($31). T44 inside hood release ($10). W25 Force-Air dual-intake fiberglass hood ($155.00, but not available with Y73 and L34 or L75 required). D33 remote-control outside rearview mirror ($12). D35 dual sport style outside rearview mirrors ($22). D99 two-tone Magic Mirror paint for hardtops ($36). Y73 hood stripes ($31). Y66 special two-tone paint, except convertible ($149). Y76 special Firemist paint ($195). Y62 special Oldsmobile solid color paint ($113). WM7 special non-Oldsmobile solid color paint ($190). Y70 body side stripes ($21). JD2 heavy-duty front disc brakes ($28). JL2 power front disc brakes ($68.00. J50 Pedal ease power brakes ($46). AU3 power door locks ($46) A41 four-way power bench seat ($77). A46 four-way power left-hand bucket seat ($77). N47 variable-ratio power steering ($113). A90 power trunk lid latch ($14). A31 power windows ($113). U63 Deluxe push-button radio ($73). U69 AM/FM monaural push-button radio ($135). U56 AM/FM stereophonic radio with rear seat speaker ($233). UM1 AM radio with stereo tape player ($215). UM2 AM/FM stereo with tape player

($363). U57 stereo tape player, includes rear seat speaker with U58 ($114). U57 stereo tape player, includes rear seat speaker without U58 ($130). U80 bi-phonic rear seat speaker ($18) U21 Rocket Rally pac ($82). C08 vinyl roof covering on coupes ($99). A65 Custom Sport seat in 4-4-2 convertible (no charge). B50 extra foam-padded seat on front seat of base Cutlass (9). A51 Strato bucket seats in Cutlass "S" hardtop ($67). FG2 Firm Ride shock absorbers ($5). G66 Super lift rear shocks, requires M40 option ($41). FE2 rally suspension package includes F41 heavy-duty suspension, heavy-duty spprings, shocks, stabilizer shafts, rear lower control arm and PC2 wheels ($12.60-$17.60). Y75 Sport Equipment exterior package for F-87 hardtop ($51). N34 Custom Sport steering wheel ($31). N33 tilt-away steering column ($44). PK2 G78-14 white-striped glass-belted tires ($32). PK5 G70-14 Wide-Oval tires with raised white lettering ($86.00-100.00 depending on series and body stylee). PX6 F78-14 white stripe glass-belted tires ($30). PX8 G70-14 white stripe Wide Oval tires ($63.00-$77.00 depending on series and body style). M20 wide-ratio four-speed manual transmission ($190). M38 Turbo Hydra-Matic 350 transmission ($215). M40 Turbo Hydra-Matic 400 transmission for cars with L75 or W30 options only ($236). W39 three-speed manual transmission with Hurst floor shifter ($41). BC1 woodgrained dashboard trim ($10). W37 heavy-duty two-plate clutch ($96). P01 wheel discs ($26). P02 deluxe wheel discs ($46). N95 simulated wire wheel covers ($113). N66 Super Stock II wheels ($72). N67 Custom Sport color-keyed wheels with steel trim rings ($72). U89 trailering wiring harness ($10). Y60 accessory groupin hardtop includes trunk light, underhood light, courtesy lights, map light, dash panel control lighting and dash panel ashtray light ($15.60-$35.60 depending on series and body style). W29 Olds 4-4-2 appearance and handling package for Cutlass F87 without W39 ($147). W29 Olds 4-4-2 appearance and handling package for Cutlass F87 with W39 ($106). W29 Olds 4-4-2 appearance and handling package for Cutlass "S" and Cutlass Supreme models without W39 ($70). W29 Olds 4-4-2 appearance and handling package for Cutlass "S" and Cutlass Supreme models with W39 ($29). W30 W-Machine package includes Sports-style outside rearview mirrors, G70-14 Wide-Oval raised-white-letter tires, a 455-cid/370-hp four-barrel Force-Air induction engine, a dual-intake Force-Air fiberglass hood, wide body side paint stripes, lightweight body insulation and "W" emblems for F87 4-4-2 without power disc brakes with specific qualifications ($722), with power disc brakes with specific qualifications ($700), without power disc brakes with specific qualifications ($645), with power disc brakes with specific qualifications ($577).

PLYMOUTH MUSCLE 1963-1972

In the Chrysler family, Plymouth was last to get a V-8. This 1955 engine was basically the '54 Dodge Hemi fitted with cheaper-to-make polyspherical cylinder heads for use on the economical Plymouth. With 241 cubic inches. and 157 hp, it was a start. Later, a 259-cid V-8 was offered in standard and "power pack" formats. Three new V-8s arrived in 1956. The hottest was the 303-cid/240-hp Fury motor. By 1957, the hot ticket was a 318-cid/290-hp V-8 with dual four-barrel carburetors. The 350-cid/305-hp "Golden Commando" V-8 arrived a year later.

For the '60s, the "big" 361-cid V-8 bowed. It was the basis for the 383- and 426-cid B-block — or "wedge" — V-8s. In the same family were the 413 and 440 engines. All were 90-degree V-8s with cast-iron blocks and heads and generous bore spacing that made them very suitable for high-performance modifications. Starting in 1964, a 273-cid "small-block" Mopar V-8 was created to give the compact Valiant a high-performance option. It would grow to 318- and 340-cid versions, which also became popular in mid-sized cars like the Belvedere. Richard Petty won the 1964 Daytona 500 driving a Plymouth. With more pleasing styling and racing successes, a remarkable recovery in Plymouth sales took place by 1965.

As the muscle-car era exploded, small and mid-size Mopars were also fitted with big V-8s and during the 1966 model year, a "street" version of the second-generation Chrysler Hemi became a Belvedere option. It had the same 426-cid displacement as the "wedge" V-8 and the same 425 maximum horsepower as the "Super Stock Max Wedge Stage II" V-8.

The Hemi was offered as an option on Plymouth's Belvedere II and Satellite models, first in racing tune, and then in a street-performance edition to qualify it as a production option. The "Street Hemi" package included heavy-duty suspension and oversized brakes. In factory trim it qualified for A/Stock and AA/Stock drag racing and NASCAR's shorter circuits.

Richard Petty's NASCAR version of the Hemi actually put out 550 hp. Petty's electric blue Plymouth won the 1967 NASCAR championship. Other muscular Plymouth V-8s received hot dual four-barrel or "Six-Pack" carburetor setups and a crowning touch on some street racers was an "Air Grabber" hood.

For 1968, Plymouth restyled its intermediates with more rounded lines and introduced its hot Road Runner. Identified by special wheels, a hood scoop, Road Runner emblems and cartoon birds on sides and rear, the new model could be had with either the 383-cid V-8 or the 426-cid Hemi. In addition to the Road Runner, Plymouth's GTX model, introduced in 1967, was continued for 1968. In 1968 and 1969, Plymouth alsoi offered big-block models of its popular Barracuda called the 'Cuda 340 and 'Cuda 383.

JERRY HEASLEY

In 1970, the Barracuda was completely restyled. It shared an all-new body shell with another Chrysler performance compact, the Dodge Challenger. A midyear variation of the Barracuda was the AAR (All-American Racer) 'Cuda 340, identifiable by its bold tape stripes. Fewer than 2,900 AAR models were built. The Valiant became the '70 Duster. A high-performance variation, the Duster 340, used options similar to the AAR 'Cuda's to convert an otherwise mild ride into a skyrocket.

Plymouth's most awesome 1970 newcomer was the high-performance Superbird, which was part of the Road Runner series. With its droop-snout front end, sleek body and outlandishly tall stabilizer wing, the Superbird was capable of over 220 mph in full stock car racing trim. In street form, the four-barrel 440-cid engine with TorqueFlite automatic transmission was standard. A six-barrel 440 engine, a racing 426 Hemi and a four-speed manual transmission were optional. The Superbird accounted for 21 of 38 Chrysler victories on the Grand National stock car circuit. When NASCAR changed its rules in 1971, however, the Superbird's dominance of high-speed ovals was over.

The street Hemi also disappeared after 1971. By 1972, the Barracuda series was severely cut and the optional 383, 440 and 426 Hemi engines were eliminated. A competition Hemi could still be had by professional racers, however, on special order. High insurance rates and government pressure for emission controls were contributors to a decline of the performance car market. The GTX was no longer around. Due to sagging sales, it was dropped in 1971. This change was a hint of things to come as government smog regulations and rising insurance rates teamed up to kill the high-performance car hobby from 1973 on. By 1979, the only Plymouth V-8s remaining were the 318 and the 360 and the top output was 195 net hp.

1962 PLYMOUTH 413 "WEDGE"

My friend Bruce Davis' family car was a White '62 Plymouth sedan. His father used to drive a New York City taxi and that's where his love of Plymouths came from. From the '30s to the '60s, Plymouths were for taxi drivers. But the world was changing and Plymouth had to modernize. Early-1962 Plymouth sales were really hurting, but an announcement in *Motor Trend's* "Spotlight on Detroit" column in May 1962 publicized a new engine option that would help turn things around. It said, "A new 410-hp, 413-cubic-inch V-8 engine with ram-tube manifolding will be available as a factory-installed option on many Plymouths and Dodge Darts beginning this month. The big power plant will have an 11-to-1 compression ratio, a newly designed short ram-tube intake manifold, two four-barrel carburetors and high-velocity exhausts."

A closer look at the 413-cid V-8 written up in *Motor Trend's* August 1962 issue was described as "the first report on the Plymouth-Dodge Super Stock engine." Technical editor Roger Huntington got his hands on a Super Stock Dodge Dart two-door sedan with the Ramcharger V-8. In his story, he explained that this engine was the same as the Plymouth version. Amazingly, the big monster motor cost only $374.40 more than a base 230-hp V-8. With the SS option you got a big-block V-8 with a 4.19 x 3.75-inch bore and stroke, an 11.0:1 compression ratio and two 650-cfm Carter AFB four-barrel carburetors mounted on a newly designed cross-ram intake manifold. The Max Wedge V-8 was linked to a three-speed TorqueFlite automatic transmission. In the 3,440-lb. car, this combination was good for 5.8-second 0-to-60 times and a standing-start quarter mile in 14.4 seconds at 101 mph. Talk about a quick change in image!

After this crucial year in its history, Plymouth was never quite the taxicab-only car it had been before. Muscle car fans preferred the Max Wedge V-8 in two-door models, though it was possible to get it in any type of Plymouth. Following are the styling features of the various models. Many of the racing cars were based on the low-priced Savoy to take advantage of its low weight.

SAVOY — SERIES SP2L — V-8:

For 1962, full-size Plymouths took on a Valiant-like look and were scaled down by two inches in wheelbase and 7 1/2 inches in overall length. The rear side feature line stopped short of the Valiant's around-the-wheelhouse sweep, so the rear of the cars looked like the mating a Valiant with a regular '61 Plymouth. A low, thin center dorsal fin remained atop the rear deck. The grille was not a Valiant inspiration either. It was concave, with a series of concave, vertically segmented fins. Dual horizontal headlights were seen. The inner lenses were set into the grille and looked smaller than the outer lenses, which were positioned in large, tunneled, circular housings at each corner of the body. Rooflines were a radical departure

from the past, most having wraparound backlights and a more formal look. A long hood/short deck theme was apparent throughout the line. Savoys were the basic models, with their script nameplates high on the front doors and no extraneous trim. Standard equipment included an oil filter, turn signals, sun visors, electric windshield wipers, front armrests, a glovebox lock, five tubeless blackwall tires and small hubcaps. As the lightest-weight models, the Savoy "coupe" (or two-door sedan) had lots of appeal to serious drag racers.

BELVEDERE — SERIES SP2M — V-8:

The Belvedere represented Plymouth's mid-priced full-size nameplate. These cars had a strip of stainless steel running along the fender feature line, from above the headlamps to mid-door, and ending there with a spear tip. Placed above the molding, on the door, were bright Belvedere signatures. Standard equipment was comprised of the Savoy assortment plus armrests, front foam seat cushions and a cigar lighter. Plymouth promoted 32,000-mile intervals between chassis lubrication. The cars had new printed electrical circuits, higher-torque starters, uni-body construction and a new aluminum transmission case to brag about. This automatic transmission was a three-speed TorqueFlite unit, with push-button controls and was available only with V-8s. It allowed a lower transmission tunnel hump and saved a few pounds as well.

FURY — SERIES SP2H — V-8:

High-level appointments and a high level of equipment were standard on Furys. Included were all Belvedere items, plus aluminum exterior trim inserts on the rear door and body top edge), back-up lights and an electric clock. Also available were options such as all-vinyl trim in hardtops, rear foam seat cushions and a Six-Way power seat. Wheel covers, however, were optional — not standard. A Fury signature script, quite large in size, was used for identification. This trim was placed behind the front wheel openings. The front fender feature line was highlighted with a heavy chrome strip, which was fluted at the forward tip. Thin moldings outlined the front and rear wheel openings, too.

SPORT FURY — SERIES SP2P — V-8:

Announced about four months after the rest of the line, the revived Sport Fury became Plymouth's premium (P suffix) offering. It had extras such as bucket seats (which were deleted on some cars), a center front console (in cars with bucket seats), full wheel covers, all-vinyl trim, rear foam seat cushions and a deluxe steering wheel as standard equipment. Even the fanciest 1962 Plymouths looked quite plain. In response to dealer wishes, several tack-on items were added to all Furys and Sport Furys at midyear. They included a third tail light on each side, full-length belt line trim extensions and license plate recess trim. Sport Furys had the signature script placed ahead of the front wheel openings, deck lid license plates and red-white-blue finished trim insert dimples. The grille had a more strongly segmented appearance due to its wider, blacked-out division panels. The Sport Fury came as a two-door hardtop or a convertible. Special engines were optional. The 1962 Sport Fury convertible is quite a rare machine.

Two versions of the "413" V-8 with "short ram" intake manifolds became available in May 1962 and were used mostly for drag racing. Max Wedge racing cars with some aftermarket enhancements and other tweaking could go extremely fast. On July 15, at a drag strip in Fremont, California, Tom Grove became the first Super Stock driver to run the quarter-mile in under 12 seconds. His 413-powered 500-hp "Melrose Missile" ran down the drag strip in 11.93 seconds with a trap speed of 118.57 mph. In August 1962, a specially-equipped Plymouth attained the fastest speed ever recorded for a stock-bodied automobile at this time. Running at the annual Bonneville National Speed Trials, the car reached 190.073 mph over a one-way run.

Model Number	Body/Style Number	Body Type & Seating	Factory Price	Shipping Weight	Production Total
SAVOY — SERIES SP2L — V-8					
SP2L	311	2d Sed-6P	$2,761	3,095 lbs.	3,939
BELVEDERE — SERIES SP2M — V-8					
SP2M	321	2d Sed-6P	$2,898	3,115 lbs.	1,721
SP2M	322	2d HT-6P	$2,986	3,145 lbs.	2,754
FURY — SERIES SP2H — V-8					
SP2H	332	2d HT-6P	$3,141	3,150 lbs.	8,262
SP2H	335	2d Conv-6P	$3,372	3,165 lbs.	4,476
SPORT FURY — SERIES SP2P — V-8					
SP2P	342	2d HT-5P	$3,299	3,195 lbs.	4,131
SP2P	345	2d Conv-5P	$3,530	3,295 lbs.	1,549

NOTE 1: The 413 "Max Wedge" V-8 was available in all models, but used mostly in cars built for racing.
NOTE 2: The prices above include the cost of the base 413 and no other options.
NOTE 3: The weights above are for base V-8 models.
NOTE 4: Production totals are for cars with all V-8s, not just the 413-cid version.

ENGINES

OPTIONAL V-8: Overhead valve. Cast-iron block. Bore and stroke: 4.19 x 3.75 inches. Displacement: 413 cid. Compression ratio: 11.00:1. Brake hp: 365 at 4600 rpm. Taxable hp: 55.90. Torque: 460 at 2800 rpm. Five main bearings. Hydraulic valve lifters. Carburetor: Carter AFB 3251-S four-barrel. Engine code: S-41.

OPTIONAL V-8: Overhead valve. Cast-iron block. Bore and stroke: 4.19 x 3.75 inches. Displacement: 413 cid. Compression ratio: 11.00:1. Brake hp: 385 at 5200 rpm. Taxable hp: 55.90. Torque: 455 at 3600 rpm. Five main bearings. Hydraulic valve lifters. Carburetor: Two Carter AFB four-barrels: (front) 2970-S; (rear) 2971-S. Engine code: S-41.

OPTIONAL V-8: Overhead valve. Cast-iron block. Bore and stroke: 4.19 x 3.75 inches. Displacement: 413 cid. Compression ratio: 11.00:1. Brake hp: 410 at 5200 rpm. Taxable hp: 55.90. Torque: 460 at 4400 rpm. Five main bearings. Solid valve lifters. Carburetor: Two Carter AFB 2903-S four-barrels. Engine code: S-41.

OPTIONS

Power brakes ($43). Power steering ($77). Air conditioning including heater ($446). Air conditioning group ($375). Antifreeze ($5). Front bumper bar ($14). Cigar lighter in Savoy ($4). Front foam seat in Savoy ($11). Clock in Savoy ($16). Tinted glass, all windows ($43). Tinted glass windshield only ($22). Heater and defroster, standard with air conditioning ($75). Back-up lights ($11). Day/Nite inside rearview mirror ($4). Two-tone paint ($17). Six-Way power seat, Fury only ($96). Power windows ($102). Standard push-button radio ($59). Deluxe radio ($84). Seat belts ($19). Padded dashboard ($14). Deluxe steering wheel ($11). All-vinyl trim, Fury hardtop ($30). Four wheel covers, except Sport Fury ($19). Windshield washer ($12). Variable speed windshield wipers ($6). Basic Group, Fury ($104); other models ($114). Basic Radio Group, Fury ($162); other models ($173). Safety Group ($107). Assist Lights Group ($12). Three-speed manual transmission was standard. Aluminum TorqueFlite automatic transmission with V-8 ($211). Short ram V-8 413-cid/410-hp dual four-barrel engine ($545). Short ram V-8 413-cid/420-hp dual four-barrel engine ($612). Sure-Grip positive traction rear axle ($50).

1963 BELVEDERE 426 "WEDGE"

A return to conventionality and more normal size characterized Plymouth's 1963 styling theme. The cars were three inches longer, an inch wider and had a flat roofline that angled into a flatter rear deck. Belvedere was a full-size Plymouth's middle-priced nameplate. This model had a wide, colored molding along the bodyside feature line. Belvedere signatures appeared at mid-fender behind the front wheel cutout. A short molding was placed on the rear roof pillar. Other equipment included rear armrests, front foam seats, and cigar lighter.

Late in 1963, the release of a new 426-cid V-8 made the Plymouth Belvedere a hot muscle car. This "Max Wedge" engine was a reaction to decisions by the National Hot Rod Association (NHRA), the National Association for Stock Car Auto Racing (NASCAR) and several other groups that sanctioned automobile racing to establish an engine displacement limit of 7 liters or 427 cubic inches. As a reaction to this, in June of 1963, Plymouth announced its new V-8 for Super Stock class drag racing. The 426-cid engine block had been introduced only in upper-level Chryslers in 1962 and had not been tuned for drag racing. This changed in 1963. The so-called Stage II version of the motor was intended for sale only to those competing in supervised drag racing and stock car racing. At one cubic inch under the new limit, this engine increased Chrysler's ability to win in both drag and oval-track racing. By the end of the year, a total of 2,130 Plymouths and Dodges with this motor were be built.

PLYMOUTH

JERRY HEASLEY

1963 Belevedere 426 Wedge

The new Max Wedge 426 engine looked identical to the previous Max Wedge 413 V-8 on the outside, but it had a larger bore size of 4.25 inches. The power plant came in three different versions. The first version, fitted with a single four-barrel carburetor, was designed to be "legal" under stock-car racing rules. It put out 400 hp. The second version, with an 11.0:1 compression ratio, was made for dragging. It had dual four-barrel carburetors on a cross-ram manifold and produced 415 hp at 5600 rpm and 470 lbs.-ft. of torque at 4400 rpm. The third version (also for drag racing) had a 13.5:1 compression ratio and dual four-barrel carburetors, also on the cross-ram intake. It produced 425 hp at 5600 rpm and 480 lbs.-ft. of torque at 4400 rpm. Many of the Max Wedge 426s also carried a new Super/Stock package designed for drag racing.

ENGINES

OPTIONAL "NASCAR" WEDGE V-8: Overhead valve. Cast-iron block. Bore and stroke: 4.25 x 3.75 inches. Displacement: 426 cid. Compression ratio: 12.5:1. Brake hp: 400 at 5600 rpm. Five main bearings. Solid valve lifters. Carburetor: Holley four-barrel. Engine code: V-426.

OPTIONAL "MAX WEDGE II SUPER-STOCK" V-8: Overhead valve. Cast-iron block. Bore and stroke: 4.25 x 3.75 inches. Displacement: 426 cid. Compression ratio: 11.0:1. Brake hp: 415 at 5800 rpm. Five main bearings. Solid valve lifters. Carburetor: Dual Carter four-barrel. Engine code: V-426.

OPTIONAL "MAX WEDGE II SUPER-STOCK" V-8: Overhead valve. Cast-iron block. Bore and stroke: 4.25 x 3.75 inches. Displacement: 426 cid. Compression ratio: 13.5:1. Brake hp: 425 at 5600 rpm. Five main bearings. Solid valve lifters. Carburetor: Dual Carter four-barrel. Engine code: V-426.

OPTIONS

Power brakes ($43). Power steering ($77). Air conditioning ($446); as part of accessory group ($375). Front bumper bar ($14). Rear bumper guards ($14). Electric clock ($16). Padded dash ($14). Rear foam seats ($11). Tinted glass, all windows ($40). Tinted glass windshield only ($22). Heater and defroster, without air conditioning ($74). Back-up lights ($11). Left-hand outside rear-view mirror ($6). Standard push-button radio ($59). Deluxe radio ($84). Deluxe steering wheel ($11). Undercoating with hood pad ($14). Tailgate assist handles with rear wind deflector ($21). Four wheel covers, stan¬dard Sport Fury ($19). Windshield washer ($12). Variable speed wipers ($6). Basic Group ($114). Basic Radio Group ($173). Safety Group ($107). Light Group ($12). 7.50 x 14 tires. Four-speed manual floor shift transmission was available in midseason. Super Stock' V-8 426 cid/415 hp four-barrel "Max Wedge Stage II" engine. "Super Stock" V-8 426 cid/425 hp dual four-barrel "Max Wedge Stage II" engine. Sure-Grip positive traction rear axle ($50).

Model Number	Body/Style Number	Body Type & Seating	Factory Price	Shipping Weight	Production Total
BELVEDERE — SERIES TP2M — V-8					
TP2M	321	2d Sed-6P	$3,007	3,200 lbs.	3,666
TP2M	322	2d HT-6P	$3,095	3,210 lbs.	5,865

NOTE 1: The 426 "Max Wedge" V-8 was available in all models, but used mostly in cars built for racing.

NOTE 2: The prices above include the cost of the base 426 and no other options.

NOTE 3: The weights above are for base V-8 models.

NOTE 4: The production totals above are for cars with all V-8s, not just the 426-cid version.

NOTE 5: A total of 2,130 Plymouths, Dodges and Chryslers were equipped with 426-cid wedge engines in 1963.

1964 BARRACUDA

1964 Barracuda

April 1, 1964, was the Barracuda's launch date. The sporty new "glassback" coupe went head-to-head against Ford's new Mustang, but lost in the sales race. It was an adaptation of Valiant sheet metal to a uniquely styled roof, deck and rear window. The roof received a wrapover look mated to an over-size, curved rear backlight with a fastback shape. The deck lid bulged up to meet the glass.

Trim features, front to rear, were distinct for this model. They included a split, negative-space grille with center insert and horizontal outer division bars, wide rocker sill panels and a chrome band across the rear window base housing a center medallion. Plymouth block letters decorated the trunk and Barracuda signatures were positioned on the sides of the cowl. Front fenders with a slimmer V-shaped feature line were seen.

Plymouth's "fish car" was as unique as a Hammerhead Shark or a Manta Ray. There was nothing else like it in 1964. There were other fastbacks of course, but none had the fish bowl-like big piece of curved glass that characterized the Barracudas. It was a love it or leave it type of design aimed at the booming youth market. "We are sure the Plymouth Barracuda is just right for young, sports-minded Americans who want to enjoy the fun of driving a car that also fills their general transportation needs," said Plymouth's general manager P.N.

Buckminster. Like the Valiant, the Barracuda featured front torsion bars and leaf springs at the rear. Power brakes were standard. Tires were size 6.50 x 13.

Barracuda buyers had a choice of three engines, but just one V-8. This 273-cid "small block" produced 180 hp at 4200 rpm. You could settle for the standard three-speed manual transmission, but muscle-car fans usually opted for a new four-speed manual gearbox with a Hurst shift linkage. You could also order a three-speed TorqueFlite automatic at extra cost.

In October 1964, *Car & Driver* reported a 9.1-second 0-to-60-mph figure for the 273-cid/180-hp version of the Barracuda with a 3.23:1 rear axle. The magazine's test car — actually a 1965 edition — did the quarter-mile in 17.5 seconds at 88.5 mph.

Model Number	Body/Style Number	Body Type & Seating	Factory Price	Shipping Weight	Production Total
BARRACUDA — SERIES AV1P — V-8					
AV1P149	2d HT-5P	$2,570	2,927 lbs.		22,300

NOTE 1: All statistics above are for '64 Barracudas with the V-8 engine.

ENGINE

OPTIONAL V-8: Overhead valve. Cast-iron block. Bore and stroke: 3.63 x 3.31 inches. Displacement: 273 cid. Compression ratio: 8.8:1. Brake hp: 180 at 4200 rpm. Taxable hp: 42.20. Torque: 260 at 1600 rpm. Five main bearings. Hydraulic valve lifters. Carburetor: Carter BBD-3767-S two-barrel. Engine code: V-273.

PLYMOUTH

OPTIONS

Power brakes ($43). Power steering ($82). Tinted glass, all windows ($29). Tinted glass, windshield only ($14). Remote-control outside rearview mirror ($12). Barracuda racing stripes ($31). Special bubbled paint ($17). Transaudio radio ($59). Retractable front seat belts ($7). Safety padded instrument panel ($16). Three-spoke steering wheel ($17). Heavy-duty shock ab¬sorbers and suspension package ($17). Custom spinner wheel covers ($13). Bolt-on design sports wheel covers ($34). Variable-speed wipers and washers ($17). Basic Group, includes: left-hand outside rear¬view mirror, windshield washer, variable speed wipers and radio ($84). Sport Group, includes: simulated woodgrain three-spoke steering wheel, bolt-on design wheel covers, whitewalls ($80-$100). Performance Group, includes: suspension package, 273-cid four-barrel V-8 and power brakes ($156). Air conditioning ($364). Four-speed manual floor shift transmission ($180). V-8 273-cid/180-hp two-barrel engine ($131). Heavy-duty 48-amp battery ($8). Sure-Grip positive traction rear axle ($39).

1964 PLYMOUTH 426-R/426-S

JERRY HEASLEY

1964 Sport Fury 426-S

"Motown" stands for Motor City, which stands for Detroit. The term is common to music buffs, but little used by car enthusiasts. Yet in the early '60s, Detroit was really a motor town. The guys who worked at Chrysler got caught up racing Chevys, Fords and Pontiacs on Woodward Ave. and put the pressure on MoPar to build a race car for the streets. And it was a race car. As *Musclecar Review's* Greg Rager said about the Plymouth Max Wedge in February 1989, "The Super Stock was not designed for milk and egg runs to the 7-11."

In 1964, Plymouth continued offering the "Super Stock" Max Wedge Stage III 426-cid engine. Dodge offered the same motor, of course, the only difference being the Plymouth version had a black cooling fan and the Dodge engine had a chrome-plated fan blade. It was a competition-only option and carried the code 426-R, with the "R" indicating "racing." It had an option price in the $500 range. The 426-R engine was again available in 415- and 425-hp versions. The former had the 11.0:1 compression ratio and the latter had the 13.5:1 ratio. The more powerful version also had nifty "Tri-Y" exhaust headers.

New this year was a 426-S "street" version of the 426-cid V-8 that was rated for 365 advertised horsepower, but actually produced around 410 hp. This engine did not include most of the Max Wedge hardware, but because of the similar displacement numbers, many buyers thought it was nearly the same engine. It ran a single four-barrel carburetor on a cast-iron intake and a 10.3:1 compression ratio. It used a standard type exhaust system. With 470 lbs.-ft. of torque at 3200 rpm, it was no slouch and it was far more "streetable" than the race versions of the 426.

Most of 426-R engines went into cheap Savoy two-door sedans because they were the lightest-weight full-size models made by Plymouth and thus went the fastest with the big engine. The NASCAR racing cars carried four-barrel carburetors. The drag racers went for the dual-quad setups and many had the lightweight aluminum front-end sheet metal, large hood scoops, etc. They were plain-Jane machines, but amazingly fast, with performance in the same range as 1963. The street version of the 426 could be had in any model from the Savoy to the Sport Fury hardtop or convertible.

The "Super Stock" Max Wedge Stage III 426-cid (426-R) V-8 was continued as a racing-only option in the $500 price range. Depending on compression ratio, it gave 415 or 425 hp. New was a street-tuned 426-S version of 365 advertised horsepower (about 410 actual horsepower). A 1964 Sport Fury two-door hardtop with the 426-cid 365-hp V-8 carried about 9.5 lbs. per horsepower and could turn in 6.8-second 0-to-60 runs. The same combination was good for a 15.2-second quarter-mile run.

SAVOY — SERIES VP2L — V-8:

Plymouth styling was facelifted for 1964. A bevelled edge feature line was used for the roofs of sedans, while hardtops had a new, cantilevered-type roof pillar. With this design, an extra large, wraparound backlight was employed and the pillars were much wider at the top than the bottom. A full-width grille was seen. It was "veed" to the horizontal plane and featured an insert with six stacks of short horizontal blades, segmented by vertical division bars. There were wider horizontal blade sections at the outboard ends into which the dual headlamps were placed side-by-side. A more massive front bumper, housing the parking lamps, was used. At the rear, the 1963 look was further refined. Savoys had large, rectangular single tail lights. There was just a hint of a dorsal fin remaining. Plymouth block letters decorated the edge of the trunk. Savoy features were comprised of an oil filter, turn signals, electric wipers, glovebox lock, dual sun visors and front armrests. A Savoy identification script was positioned on the sides of front fenders, behind the wheel opening. Any Plymouth from Savoy up, could be ordered with the optional "Commando 426-S" engine. Cars ordered with the special 426 Super Sport "Max-Wedge Stage III" V-8 had unique external telltale signs. Numbers revealing the displacement were set against a black panel bridging the opening of the stand-up hood ornament. This subtle touch was an understated way to let the world know what kind of beast was lurking beneath the hood.

BELVEDERE — SERIES VP2M — V-8:

Plymouth's middle line was again called the Belvedere. This range could be identified by its full-length body side molding that was hook-shaped at the front end. Sedans also earned a horizontal "C" pillar strip. Equipment feature extras were the same as seen the year before. A Belvedere signature script appeared behind the front wheel openings and on the right-hand side of the deck lid latch panel. However, there were no Plymouth letters on the rear edge of the trunk. The company was striving to give the Belvedere its own strong identity. An increased emphasis on performance was evident.

FURY — SERIES VP2H — V-8:

Plymouth's high-priced line was the Fury series. It included four V-8 only models and two cars available with slant sixes. In standard form it came with everything found in Belvederes plus a padded dashboard, back-up lamps and electric clock. Furys included wide bodyside moldings with color inserts that tapered to a single spear on the front fenders. Also seen was Fury block lettering on the rear fender sides; Fury script on the right-hand edge of the trunk; rear deck panel "grille"; dual tail lamps; roof pillar medallions on sedans; and upgraded interior trim.

SPORT FURY — SERIES VP2P — V-8:

The Sport Fury was the year's premium offering. Exterior trim was characterized by a wide bodyside feature line molding with color insert and a red, white and blue cowlside decorative panel. Sport Fury lettering and script were seen in the normal places. Special wheel covers with simulated knock-off hubs were used. Bucket seats were standard equipment, as was V-8 power.

Model Number	Body/Style Number	Body Type & Seating	Factory Price	Shipping Weight	Production Total
SAVOY — SERIES VP2L — V-8					
VP2L	311	2d Sed-6P	$2,889	3,205 lbs.	5,494
BELVEDERE — SERIES VP2M — V-8					
VP2M	21	2d Sed-6P	$2,916	3,000 lbs.	2,198
VP2M	322	2d HT-6P	$3,001	3,010 lbs.	3,296
FURY — SERIES VP2H — V-8					
VP2H	332	2d HT-6P	$3,263	3,215 lbs.	23,348
VP2H	335	2d Conv-6P	$3,494	3,345 lbs.	4,670
SPORT FURY — SERIES VP2P — V-8					
VP2-P	342	2d HT-5P	$3,421	3,270 lbs.	24,173
VP2-P	345	2d Conv-5P	$3,652	3,405 lbs.	3,845

NOTE 1: The 426 "Max Wedge" V-8 was available in all models, but used mostly in cars built for racing.

NOTE 2: The prices above include the cost of the base 426 Wedge V-8 and no other options.

NOTE 3: The weights above are for base V-8 models.

NOTE 4: The production totals above are for cars with all V-8s, not just the 426-cid version.

NOTE 5: Chrysler built 6,088 of its 426-cid Wedge V-8s in 1964 and put them in Plymouths, Dodges and possibly a few Chryslers.

ENGINES

OPTIONAL V-8: Overhead valve. Cast-iron block. Displacement: 426 cid. Bore and stroke: 4.25 x 3.75 inches. Compression ratio: 10.10:1. Brake hp: 365 at 4800 rpm. Taxable hp: 57.80. Torque: 470 at 3200 rpm. Five main bearings. Hydraulic valve lifters. Carburetor: Carter AFB-3859-S four-barrel. Engine code: A-426.

OPTIONAL V-8: Overhead valve. Cast-iron block. Displacement: 426 cid. Bore and stroke: 4.25 x 3.75 inches. Compression ratio: 11.00:1. Brake hp: 415 at 5600 rpm. Taxable hp: 57.80. Torque: 470 at 4400 rpm. Five main bearings. Solid valve lifters. Carburetor: Dual Carter AFB 3859-S four-barrel. Engine code: A-426.

OPTIONAL V-8: Overhead valve with hemispherical segment combustion chambers. Cast-iron block. Displacement: 426 cid. Bore and stroke: 4.25 x 3.75 inches. Compression ratio: 12.0:1. Brake hp: 425 at 5600 rpm. Taxable hp: 57.80. Torque: 480 at 4600 rpm. Five main bearings. Solid valve lifters. Carburetor: Dual Carter AFB 3084-S four-barrel. Engine code: A-426.

OPTIONS

Power brakes ($43). Power steering in Belvedere ($86). Power steering in Fury ($97). Auto-Pilot speed control for Fury/Sport Fury V-8 with automatic/power brakes ($85). Electric clock ($16, but standard in Sport Fury). Rear window defogger in Fury/Sport Fury ($21). Tinted glass, all windows ($40). Tinted glass windshield only ($22). Padded instrument panel ($19). Back-up lights $11, but standard in Sport Fury ($11). Four-Way power left-hand bucket seat, Sport Fury only ($78). Four-Way power left and right bucket seats, Sport Fury only ($156). Four power windows ($102). Transaudio radio ($59). Transaudio AM/FM radio ($129). Front foam seat cushions ($11). Deluxe steering wheel in Belvedere ($11). Adjustable steering wheel, automatic transmission and power steering required ($46). Deluxe steering wheel in Fury ($15). Tachometer for Sport Fury only ($50). Vinyl trim in two-door sedan or hardtop ($25). Wheel covers ($19, but standard on Sport Fury). Front and rear bumper guards for Belvedere ($31). Front and rear bumper guards for Fury or Sport Fury ($34). Retractable seat belts, front and rear compartments ($30). Rear seat speaker with reverberator ($36). Basic Radio Group ($86). Air conditioning ($417). Automatic transmission ($191-$210). Four-speed manual Hurst floor shift transmission ($188). Commando "Street Wedge" V-8 426-cid/365-hp four-barrel engine ($483). Super Stock "Max Wedge Stage III" V-8 426-cid/415-hp engine ($515). Super Stock "Max Wedge Stage III" V-8 426-cid/425-hp engine ($545). Sure-Grip positive traction rear axle ($50). Available rear axle gear ratios: 3.23:1; 3.31:1; 2.93:1 and 2.76:1.

PLYMOUTH

1964 SAVOY/BELVEDERE/FURY 426 RACE HEMI

There's a four-letter word that strikes fear into the hearts of FoMoCo and GM nuts and it isn't a curse or an obsenity. "HEMI" is not only a powerful utterance, it's a legend that you can still buy from Chrysler's parts arm today. That should tell you something about the monster motor's quality, longevity and performance record.

Plymouth's "Super Commando" 426-cid Hemi V-8 was released around February 9, 1964. This wasn't the "Street Hemi" and it was supposedly for competition use only. Its primary role in life was to help Mopar drivers take checkered flags at NASCAR superspeedways and to allow them to dominate Super Stock drag racing classes. It didn't take Plymouth very long to achieve one of those goals. On February 23, 1964, three Hemi-powered Belvederes and one of their Dodge cousins swept the field at the Daytona 500, taking the first four places in order. Taking the checkered flag in the contest was Richard Petty with his Electric Blue No. 43 Plymouth. Running behind him, in order, were Plymouth drivers Jimmy Pardue and Paul Goldsmith.

In order to "legalize" the Hemi engine for use in NASCAR race cars, Chrysler had to build several thousand of the engines and offer them in production cars. In 1964, the corporation made 6,359 (Hemi and Wedge) 426-cid engines and put them in both Plymouths and Dodges. When sold on an in-the-crate basis, the Super Commando 426-cid/415-hp version of the Hemi added $1,800 to the price of a 1964 Plymouth V-8. The Super Commando 426-cid/425-hp Hemi engine was a $2,000 in-the-crate option. The 1964 Hemi had a cylinder head design similar to that used on the famed Chrysler "Firepower" Hemi V-8s of the 1950s. However, in this case the cylinder heads were made of aluminum, rather than cast-iron used in the prior decade.

The official horsepower ratings, advertised as being the same as those for the 426 Wedge V-8, were a figment of someone's vivid imagination. There are rumors that actual dynamometer testing registered Hemi output at over 600 hp. Plymouth's factory dealers sold the Hemi engines over the counter, but they also came in factory-built super stock drag-racing cars.

Depending on the car, the Hemi's 0-to-60 mph performance was in the 5.3-second range and Hemi-powered Belvederes could run the quarter-mile in around 13.8 seconds at about 104 mph.

SAVOY — SERIES VP2L — V-8:

Savoy features were comprised of an oil filter, turn signals, electric wipers, glovebox lock, dual sun visors and front armrests. A Savoy identification script was positioned on the sides of front fenders, behind the wheel opening. Any Plymouth from Savoy up, could be ordered forracing purposes with the optional 426 Hemi and such cars carried special Hemi badges.

BELVEDERE — SERIES VP2M — V-8:

Plymouth's mid-range Belvedere was also available as a Hemi-powered race car.

FURY —SERIES VP2H — V-8:

Plymouth's high-priced line was the Fury series. It is possible that a handful of Hemi Furys were made.

SPORT FURY — SERIES VP2P — V-8:

The Sport Fury added wide bodyside feature line molding with color insert and a red, white and blue cowlside decorative panel. Sport Fury lettering and script were seen in the normal places. Special wheel covers with simulated knock-off hubs were used. Bucket seats were standard equipment. It is possible that a handful of Hemi Sport Furys were made.

Model Number	Body/Style Number & Seating	Body Type Price	Factory Weight	Shipping Total	Production
SAVOY — SERIES VP2L — V-8					
VP2L	311	2d Sed-6P	$4,206	3,205 lbs.	5,494
BELVEDERE — SERIES VP2M — V-8					
VP2M	321	2d Sed-6P	$4,233	3,000 lbs.	2,198
VP2M	322	2d HT-6P	$4,318	3,010 lbs.	3,296
FURY — SERIES VP2H — V-8					
VP2H	332	2d HT-6P	$4,580	3,215 lbs.	23,348
VP2H	335	2d Conv-6P	$4,811	3,345 lbs.	4,670
SPORT FURY — SERIES VP2P — V-8					
VP2-P	342	2d HT-5P	$4,738	3,270 lbs.	24,173
VP2-P	345	2d Conv-5P	$4,969	3,405 lbs.	3,845

NOTE 1: The 426 "Race Hemi" V-8 was available in all models, but used mostly in cars built for racing.

NOTE 2: The prices above include the cost of the base 426 Race Hemi V-8 and no other options.

NOTE 3: The weights above are for base V-8 models.

NOTE 4: Production totals are for cars with all V-8s, not just the 426-cid Race Hemi.

NOTE 5: Chrysler built 271 of its 426-cid Race Hemi V-8s in 1964 and put them in Plymouths and Dodges and possibly a handful of Chryslers.

ENGINES

OPTIONAL "RACE HEMI" V-8: Overhead valve with hemispherical segment combustion chambers. Cast-iron block. Displacement: 426 cid. Bore and stroke: 4.25 x 3.75 inches. Compression ratio: 11.0:1. Brake hp: 415 at 5600 rpm. Taxable hp: 57.80. Torque: 470 at 4400 rpm. Five main bearings. Solid valve lifters. Carburetor: Dual Carter AFB-3859-S four-barrel. Engine code: V-426.

OPTIONAL "RACE HEMI" V-8: Overhead valve with hemispherical segment combustion chambers. Cast-iron block. Displacement: 426 cid. Bore and stroke: 4.25 x 3.75 inches. Compression ratio: 12.5:1. Brake hp: 425 at 5600 rpm. Taxable hp: 57.80. Torque: 480 at 4600 rpm. Five main bearings. Solid valve lifters. Carburetor: Dual Carter AFB-3084-S four-barrel. Engine code: V-426.

OPTIONS

Power brakes ($43). Power steering in Belvedere ($86). Power steering in Fury ($97). Auto-Pilot speed control for Fury/Sport FuryV-8 with automatic/power brakes ($85). Electric clock ($16, but standard in Sport Fury). Rear window defogger in Fury/Sport Fury ($21). Tinted glass, all windows ($40). Tinted glass windshield only ($22). Padded instrument panel ($19). Back-up lights ($11), but standard in Sport Fury ($11). Four-Way power left-hand bucket seat, Sport Fury only ($78). Four-Way power left and right bucket seats, Sport Fury only ($156). Four power windows ($102). Transaudio radio ($59). Transaudio AM/FM radio ($129). Front foam seat cushions ($11). Deluxe steering wheel in Belvedere ($11). Adjustable steering wheel , automatic transmission and power steering required ($46). Deluxe steering wheel in Fury ($15). Tachometer for Sport Fury only ($50). Vinyl trim in two-door sedan or hardtop ($25). Wheel covers ($19, but standard on Sport Fury). Front and rear bumpoer guards for Belvedere ($31). Front and rear bumper guards for Fury or Sport Fury ($34). Retractable seat belts, front and rear compartments ($30). Rear seat speaker with reverberator ($36). Basic Radio Group ($86). Air conditioning ($417). Automatic transmission ($191-$210). Four-speed manual Hurst floor shift transmission ($188). Super Commando V-8 426 cid/415 hp Hemi engine ($1,800). Super Commando V-8 426 cid/425 hp Hemi engine ($2,000). Sure-Grip positive traction rear axle ($50). Available rear axle gear ratios: 3.23:1; 3.31:1; 2.93:1 and 2.76:1.

1965 BARRACUDA FORMULA "S"

PHIL KUNZ

1965 Barracuda Formula "S"

"Infinitely more sporting and a lot more satisfactory," was how *Car Life* magazine compared the '65 Barracuda "Formula S" to the original version of the Plymouth fastback released a year earlier. Although the 1964 1/2 Barracuda had represented a departure in the right direction for Plymouth, it wasn't all that it could have been. *Car and Driver* (May 1964) concluded, "We'd be the first to applaud a product from Chrysler that really puts them into the sports car business, but this car, with nothing but a slick-looking body, seems superfluous." This may explain the Barracuda's return, in 1965, with a hotter engine and a rally-bred suspension package.

While the standard Barracuda had no real changes (other than the elimination of Valiant nameplates on the exterior), the more muscular version inspired *Car and Driver* (October 1964) to change its tune a bit about the car's performance. "Our test Barracuda, with its warmed-up 273 engine, is everything you'd like it to be," wrote the magazine. "In fact, it may well be the most satisfactory enthusiast's car of all three of the sporty compacts."

The hot engine was merchandised as part of the Formula S package, which also included heavy-duty front torsion bars, heavy-duty rear springs, firm-ride shock absorbers, a sway bar, rally stripes, extra-wide wheel rims, Goodyear Blue Streak wide oval tires and "Formula S" medallions ahead of the front wheel openings.

Along with better performance came better sales. By the time the model year ended, a total of 64,596 Barracudas left Plymouth assembly lines.

The new "Golden Commando" version of the 273-cid V-8 was definitely a step towards improving the breed. It upped the compression ratio to 10.5:1 and added a single four-barrel Ball & Ball carburetor. This was enough to produce 235 hp at 5200 rpm and 280 lbs.-ft. of torque at 4000 rpm. In terms of performance, a Barracuda with a 3.23:1 rear axle and four-speed all-synchro manual transmission tested by *Car and Driver* was able to run from 0-to-60 mph in 9.1 seconds and do the quarter-mile in 17.5 seconds at 88.5 mph. *Road & Track* (April 1965) got a like-equipped Barracuda to do 0-to-60 mph in 8.2 seconds and cover the quarter-mile in 15.9 seconds at 85 mph.

Model Number	Body/Style Number	Body Type & Seating	Factory Price	Shipping Weight	Production Total
BARRACUDA — SERIES AV1P — V-8					
AV1P	149	2d HT-5P	$2,793	2,930 lbs.	9,379

NOTE 1: Price shown above is the price of the base V-8 plus the cost of the Formula "S" option package.

NOTE 2: Weight shown above is the weight of the base V-8 model.

NOTE 3: The production total shown above is for all cars with the 235-hp V-8; no Formula "S" total available.

NOTE 4: 4,505 cars with the 235-hp V-8 had manual transmission; 4.874 had automatic transmission.

ENGINE

BASE V-8: Overhead valve. Cast-iron block. Bore and stroke: 3.63 x 3.31 inches. Displacement: 273 cid. Compression ratio: 10.50:1. Brake hp: 235 at 5200 rpm. Taxable hp: 42.20. Torque: 280 at 4000 rpm. Five main bearings. Solid valve lifters. Carburetor: Carter AFB-3853-S four-barrel. Engine code: A-273.

OPTIONS

Power brakes ($43). Power steering ($82). Tinted glass, all windows ($29). Tinted glass, windshield only ($14). Remote-control outside rearview mirror ($12). Barracuda racing stripes ($31). Special buffed paintt ($17). Transaudio radio ($59). Retractable front seat belts ($7). Safety padded instrument panel ($16). Three-spoke steering wheel ($17). Heavy-duty shock absorbers and suspension package ($17). Custom spinner wheel covers ($13). Bolt-on design sports wheel covers ($34). Variable speed wipers and washers ($17). Basic Group, includes: left-hand outside rearview mirror, windshield washer, variable speed wipers and radio ($84). Sport Group, includes: simulated wood-grain three-spoke steering wheel, bolt-on design wheel covers, whitewalls ($80-$100). Performance Group, includes: suspension package, 273-cid four-barrel V-8 and power brakes, except station wagon ($156). Air conditioning

($364). Four-speed manual floor shift transmission ($180). V-8 273-cid/180-hp two-barrel engine ($131). Heavy-duty 48-amp battery ($8). Sure-Grip positive traction rear axle ($39). TorqueFlite automatic transmission with V-8 ($181). Four-speed manual floor shift transmission with V-8 ($179). V-8 273-cid/235-hp four-barrel engine ($230). Crankcase vent system, mandatory for California-built cars ($5). Sure- Grip positive traction rear axle ($39). Available rear axle gear ratios: 2.93:1. Formula S package, includes Commando 273 V-8 engine, rally suspension, heavy-duty shocks, 5.50 x 14 wheels, Goodyear Blue Streak tires, tachometer and open wheel covers ($258).

1965 BELVEDERE I 426 "RACE HEMI"

1965 Belvedere Satellite Race 426 Hemi

Promoted as "the roaring '65s," mid-sized Plymouths boasted new lower body styling, carryover roof lines and a return to single headlights. The Belvedere nameplate was no longer used to designate the level of trim and equipment. It was now used to classify intermediate size ranges. Actually, this was the same platform used for all Plymouths just one year earlier.

There were three kinds of Belvederes. The low-level (L) offerings were in the Belvedere I series and had, as standard equipment, heater and defroster, front seat belts, oil filter, and five blackwall tires. Trim consisted of a straight, three-quarter length side body molding from the front door edge back and with Belvedere I script ahead of it. This basic-transportation model made a great lightweight racing car.

A rare Plymouth engine was the 426-cid "Race Hemi." Introduced in 1964, it was intended for off-road (race) use only. It used a cast-iron block with 4.25 x 3.75-inch bore and stroke, a forged and shotpeened crankshaft, impact extruded pistons, cross-bolted main bearing caps, forged connecting rods and solid valve lifters — all of which would be carried over for the later "Street Hemi." The Race Hemi also had a magnesium dual-four-barrel intake manifold, aluminum cylinder heads, a header-type exhaust system, a 328-degree cam (with 112 degree overlap), bigger valves with stiffer springs and a 12.5:1 compression ratio.

Chrysler built 360 Race Hemi engines in 1965. About 60 percent went into Plymouths. Most likely, the majority of Hemis went into base Belvedere I coupes — the lightest model in the lineup. A '65 Hemi Satellite would have been a rare pos-

sibility, since Chrysler was known to do just about anything to sell a car, but most Hemis — if not all — were low-rung Belvederes built strictrly for race tracks and dragstrips.

A Hemi-powered '65 Plymouth racing car, competing in S/SA drag classes with "Drag-On-Lady" Shirley Shahan behind the wheel, went 129.30 mph in the quarter-mile. While NASCAR issued a temporary ban on the $1,800 engine, Hemi Belvederes won many events in USAC, NHRA and AHRA competition during 1965. Some '65 Plymouths (and Dodges) had an altered wheelbase "drag package" for National Hot Rod Association (NHRA) Factory Experimental class drag racing.

Series Number	Body/Style Number	Body Type & Seating	Factory Price	Shipping Weight	Production Total
BELVEDERE I — SERIES R1 — V-8					
R1	311	2d Cpe-5P	$4,092	3,220 lbs.	3,510

NOTE 1: The price shown above includes the 426-cid Hemi V-8 and no other options.
NOTE 2: The weight shown above is that of the base V-8.
NOTE 3: The production total shown above is for all V-8 powered Belvedere I coupes.
NOTE 4: Only 360 Race Hemis were built (Dodge and Plymouth combined).

OPTIONS

Power brakes ($43). Power steering ($86). Electric clock ($16). Tinted glass, all windows ($40). Tinted glass, windshield only ($22). Padded instrument panel ($19). Back-up lights ($11). Transaudio radio ($59). Transaudio AM/FM radio ($129). Front foam seat cushions ($11). Deluxe steering wheel ($11). Tachometer ($50). Vinyl trim ($25). Wheel covers ($19). Bumper guards, front and rear ($31). Retractable seat belts, front and rear compartments ($30). Rear seat speaker with reverberator, except station wagon ($36). Basic Radio Group ($86). Torque-Flite automatic transmission ($211). Hemi V-8 426-cid/425-hp dual four-barrel engine ($1,800). 426-R Hemi V-8 426-cid/415-hp dual four-barrel engine ($1,150). Crankcase vent system, mandatory on California-built cars ($5). Sure-Grip positive traction rear axle ($39). Available rear axle gear ratios: 3.23:1 or 2.93:1.

1965 SATELLITE 426 "WEDGE"

PLYMOUTH

CLIFF GROMER

1965 Satellite 426 Wedge

In 1965, Plymouth launched a new high-performance line called Satellite. The premium-level (P) Belvedere Satellite was endowed with a rich and sporty character. It had all equipment of the downscale models plus front bucket seats; a center console; full wheel covers and all-vinyl trim on the two-door hardtop. Side trim moldings were deleted, but louvers were seen on the Satellite's rear fenders and rocker panel moldings were used. Wheel opening moldings; Satellite signatures; and a rear horizontal beauty strip were nice accents. The 116-inch wheelbase, Belvedere-based intermediate assumed the muscle car role formerly filled by Sport Furys (which now become sports-luxury cars). A four-section aluminum grille and a crisp, tapering body-side feature line dominated the round-cornered, but mostly square styling.

The Satellite had a glittery, rich look. Sales literature showed the 426-cid/425-hp "Max Wedge" on the options list, as well as the 426-cid/365-hp "Street Wedge." Often confused with the Hemi due to similar displacement and horsepower numbers, the 426 Max Wedge Stage III was a race-bred engine with a different combustion chamber configuration. It had 12.5:1 compression, a NASCAR "Tri-Y" exhaust system, a cam with 320 degrees of overlap, reworked combustion chambers, notched valves and big, twin Carter four-barrels with giant air cleaners. Chrysler did not warranty this engine as it was "not recommended for general driving." The tamer, 426-cid/365-hp Street Wedge, with 10.3:1 compression and a

single four-barrel on a cast-iron intake had better street driveability, due to its lower state of tune.

The Street Wedge was good for a 0-to-60-mph drag in around 7.9 seconds. The quarter-mile would take such a car about 15.4 seconds at 89 mph.

Series Number	Body/Style Number	Body Type & Seating	Factory Price	Shipping Weight	Production Total
BELVEDERE SATELLITE — SERIES R4 — V-8					
AR2-P	R42	2-dr HT Cpe-5P	$2,612	3,220 lbs.	23,452
AR2-P	R45	2-dr Conv-5P	$2,827	3,325 lbs.	1,914

NOTE 1: The price shown above includes the base 426-cid Wedge V-8 and no other options.

NOTE 2: The weight shown above is that of the base V-8.

NOTE 3: The production total shown above is for all V-8 powered Belvedere Satellite hardtops and convertibles.

NOTE 4: 6,569 of the 426 Wedge V-8s were built (Dodge and Plymouth combined).

OPTIONS

Power brakes ($43). Power steering ($86). Air conditioning ($346). Tinted glass, all windows ($40). Tinted glass, windshield only ($22). Padded instrument panel ($19). Back-up lights ($11). Four power windows ($102). Transaudio radio ($59). Transaudio AM/FM radio ($129). Front foam seat cushions ($11). Deluxe steering wheel ($11). Adjustable steering wheel, automatic transmission and power steering required ($46). Tachometer ($50). Bumper guards, front and rear ($31). Retractable seat belts, front and rear compartments ($30). Rear seat speaker with reverberator ($36). Basic Radio Group ($86). TorqueFlite automatic transmission ($211). Four-speed manual floor shift transmission ($188). 426-S V-8 426-cid/365-hp four-barrel engine ($545). Crankcase vent system, mandatory on California- built cars ($5). Sure-Grip positive traction rear axle ($39). Available rear axle gear ratios: (V-8) 3.23:1 or 2.93:1.

1966 BARRACUDA "S"

PLYMOUTH

1966 Barracuda "S"

By 1966, the Plymouth Barracuda "S" fastback had clawed its way to the championship in the Sports Car Club of America's (SCCA) national rallying class. That was not bad for a car that had suffered through its first half year, in 1964, as a "pretty face" without much real performance behind it.

For 1966, the heated-up "Golden Commando" version of the Chrysler 273-cid V-8 was the "hot-ticket" engine option once again. It had a new unsilenced air cleaner, but there were no real serious changes in this power plant's basic specifications. The Barracuda had the Valiant's new split-radiator grille with criss-cross inserts. In addition, the Barracuda got a large, circular center grille medallion with the image of a fish on it. This medallion was also repeated on the rear of the car. A chrome plated "Barracuda" script appeared on the front fenders. When the Barracuda "S" package was added, the presence of this option was noted with small, circular model identification badges below the Barracuda name on each of the front fenders. New pinstriping decorated the body and a vinyl covered roof was a new option. Six types of optional racing stripes were available to Barracuda buyers. Standard equipment for Barracudas included new thin-shell front bucket seats, front fender turn indicators, rocker panel moldings, special full wheel covers and floor carpeting.

In production terms, the 1966 Barracuda's popularity leveled off at 38,029 units for all models.

The Barracuda "S" was featured in the February 1966 edition of *Motor Trend*. It had an as-tested price of $3,616.50. In the test, it achieved 0-to-60 in 8.9 seconds and did the quarter-mile in 16.5 seconds at 84 mph.

Series Number	Body/Style Number	Body Type & Seating	Factory Price	Shipping Weight	Production Total
BARRACUA "S" — SERIES BP — V-8					
BP	29	2d HT-5P	$2,637	2,950 lbs.	5,316

NOTE 1: Price shown above is the price of the base V-8 plus the cost of the "S" option package.

NOTE 2: Weight shown above is the weight of the base V-8 model.

NOTE 3: The production total shown above is for all cars with Formula "S" option.

NOTE 4: A total of 6,295 Barracudas (including Formula "S" models) had the 235-cid four-barrel V-8.

ENGINE

OPTIONAL V-8: Overhead valve. Cast-iron block. Bore and stroke: 3.63 x 3.31 inches. Displacement: 273 cid. Compression ratio: 10.50:1. Brake hp: 235 at 5200 rpm. Taxable hp: 42.20. Torque: 280 at 4000 rpm. Five main bearings. Hydraulic valve lifters. Carburetor: Carter AFB-4119-S four-barrel. Engine code: D.

OPTIONS

Power brakes ($43). Power steering ($82). Tinted glass, all windows ($29). Tinted glass, windshield only ($14). Remote-control outside rearview mirror ($12). Barracuda racing stripes ($31). Special buffed paint ($17). Transaudio radio ($59). Retractable front seat belts ($7). Safety padded instrument panel ($16). Three-spoke steering wheel ($17). Heavy-duty shock absorbers and suspension package ($17). Custom spinner wheel covers ($13). Bolt-on design sports wheel covers ($34). Variable speed wipers and washers ($17). Basic Group, includes: left-hand outside rearview mirror, windshield washer, variable speed wipers and radio ($84). Sport Group, includes: simulated wood-grain three-spoke steering wheel, bolt-on design wheel covers, whitewalls ($80-$100). Performance Group, includes: suspension package, 273-cid four-barrel V-8 and power brakes, except station wagon ($156). Air conditioning ($364). Four-speed manual floor shift transmission ($180). V-8 273-cid/180-hp two-barrel engine ($131). Heavy-duty 48-amp battery ($8). Sure-Grip positive traction rear axle ($39). TorqueFlite automatic transmission with V-8 ($181). Four-speed manual floor shift transmission with V-8 ($179). V-8 273-cid/235-hp four-barrel engine ($230). Crankcase vent system, mandatory for California-built cars ($5). Sure- Grip positive traction rear axle ($39). Available rear axle gear ratios: 2.93:1. Formula "S" package, includes Commando 273 V-8 engine, rally suspension, heavy-duty shocks, 5.50 x 14 wheels, Goodyear Blue Streak tires, tachometer and open wheel covers ($258).

1966 BELVEDERE 426 STREET HEMI

1966 Belvedere 426 Street Hemi

A new powertrain option in 1966 was a "street" version of the 426-cid/425-hp Hemi V-8, which turned any Belvedere into a muscle car. Performance was awesome. Going from 0-to-60 mph took about 6.8 seconds. Racing down the quarter-mile could be accomplished in about 15 seconds at 96 mph.

The Belvedere received a major restyling in 1966. It had a square body. The fenders had a slab-like look, but were also gently sculptured forming a full-length rectangular depression panel above bumper top level. The large front wheel opening curved up into the rectangle, but the feature line passed over the rear wheel cutout. In profile, the edge of the front fender thrusted forward into a wide V-shaped form. Sedans had a square-angular roof with thick rear pillars. Hardtops retained the cantilevered roof treatment with a thicker base. This treatment was now seen at the rear of station wagons as well.

Standard equipment on the Belvedere I included a Belvedere I nameplate behind the front wheelhousing, thin, straight moldings along the lower feature line (from behind front wheel housing to rear bumper), heater and defroster, front seat belts, oil filter, and five blackwall tires. The Belvedere II series had its identification nameplate set a bit higher. It was adorned by a wide, full-length chrome spear placed above the bodyside centerline. The lower trunk lid panel was satin-finished. Carpeting, upgraded upholstery, front foam cushions, and back-up lights were featured.

Series Number	Body/Style Number	Body Type & Seating	Factory Price	Shipping Weight	Production Total
BELVEDERE I — SERIES RL — V-8 Hemi					
RL	21	2d Sed-6P	$3,382	3,190 lbs.	136
BELVEDERE II — SERIES RH — V-8 Hemi					
RH	23	2d HT Cpe-6P	$3,629	3,215 lbs.	531
RH	27	2d Conv-6P	$3,843	3,305 lbs.	10

NOTE 1: Price includes cost of Street Hemi V-8 and no other options.

NOTE 2: Weights are for base cars with the base 273-cid V-8.

NOTE 3: Production is for Hemi-powered cars only.

NOTE 4: Four-speed manual transmission used in79 two-door sedans, 280 two-door hardtops and four (4) convertibles.

ENGINE

OPTIONAL V-8: Overhead valve with hemispherical segment combustion chambers. Cast-iron block. Displacement: 426 cid. Bore and stroke: 4.25 x 3.75 inches. Compression ratio: 10.25:1. Compression ratio: 12.0:1. Brake hp: 425 at 5600 rpm. Taxable hp: 57.80. Torque: 480 at 4600 rpm. Five main bearings. Solid valve lifters. Carburetor: Dual Carter (front) AFB-4139-S; (rear) AFB-4140-S four-barrel. Engine code: H.

OPTIONS

Power brakes ($43). Power steering ($86). Air conditioning ($346). Tinted glass, all windows ($40). Tinted glass, windshield only ($22). Padded instrument panel ($19). Back-up lights ($11). Four power windows ($102). Transaudio radio ($59). Transaudio AM/FM radio ($129). Front foam seat cushions ($11). Deluxe steering wheel ($11). Adjustable steering wheel, automatic transmission and power steering required ($46). Tachometer ($50). Bumper guards, front and rear ($31). Retractable seat belts, front and rear compartments ($30). Rear seat speaker with reverberator ($36). Basic Radio Group ($86). TorqueFlite automatic transmission ($211). Four-speed manual floor shift transmission ($188). 426-cid/425-hp four-barrel Hemi V-8 icluding heavy-duty suspension, larger drum brakes, wide wheels and 7.75 x 14 Goodyear high-speed tires. ($1,105). Crankcase vent system, mandatory on California-built cars ($5). Sure-Grip positive traction rear axle ($39). Available rear axle gear ratios: (V-8) 3.23:1 or 2.93:1.

PLYMOUTH

1966 SATELLITE 426 STREET HEMI

1966 Satellite 426 Street Hemi

"That the Hemi Satellite accelerates in a straight line in astonishing fashion cannot be disputed," *Car Life* magazine gushed in July 1966. Richard Petty's eight NASCAR wins created great demand for the engine — as well as for the Satellite. A USAC championship didn't hurt Plymouth's reputation on the street, either.

Although similar to a race Hemi, this 426-cid engine used a dual four-barrel aluminum intake, milder valve-train specs, different 10.25:1 pistons and a big single air cleaner. A pair of tubes were added to the right-hand exhaust manifold to handle heat riser functions. Chrysler rated the engine for 425 hp at 5,000 rpm and 490 lbs.-ft. of torque at 4,000 rpm. Production of Hemi Belvederes was a bit lower with 136 coupes, 531 hardtops and 10 convertibles recoded.

Like other Plymouth Belvederes, the Satellite featured a major restyling for 1966, highlighted by a slab-sided body with crisper fenders and mild body side sculpturing. Cantilevered rooflines continued on hardtops, with the pillars slightly widened. The windshield was larger and flatter. Up front, parking lamps changed from rectangles in the bumper to circles in the grille. Satellites had bucket seats, consoles, full wheel covers and vinyl trim. Early in the season, the biggest engine for Satellites was the 383-cid big-block V-8 with 325 hp. Use of a new 440-cid/365-hp V-8 was limited to Plymouth Furys. Dodges got the Hemi first, a few months into the season. Then, Plymouth released it. Included in the engine package were heavy-duty suspension, larger drum brakes, wide wheels and 7.75 x 14 Goodyear high-speed tires. Three-on-the-tree couldn't handle the Hemi's torque, so a four-speed or TorqueFlite transmission had to be added, the latter including a transmission fluid cooler. The standard 3.23:1 axle was suitable for the TorqueFlite Hemis, while those with stick shift needed a Dana 60 truck-type axle with identical gear ratio. A

Sure-Grip differential was extra. To announce the Hemi, HP2 badges were placed on the front fenders.

Hemi Satellites were good for 7.4-second 0-to-60 runs and 14.5 second ETs. USAC saw the Hemi-powered cars take its annual championship. In professional drag racing, A/Stock class Belvederes were going 122 mph in 11.6-second quarter-miles, so the Satellites should be in the same bracket.

Series Number	Body/Style Number	Body Type & Seating	Factory Price	Shipping Weight	Production Total
SATELLITE — SERIES RP — V-8 Hemi					
RP	23	2d HT Cpe-6P	$3,800	3,265 lbs.	817
RP	27	2d Conv-6P	$4,015	3,365 lbs.	27

NOTE 1: Price includes cost of Street Hemi V-8 and no other options.
NOTE 2: Weights are for base cars with the base 273-cid V-8.
NOTE 3: Production is for Hemi-powered cars only.
NOTE 4: Four-speed manual transmission used in 503 two-door hardtops.

ENGINE

OPTIONAL V-8: Overhead valve with hemispherical segment combustion chambers. Cast-iron block. Displacement: 426 cid. Bore and stroke: 4.25 x 3.75 inches. Compression ratio: 10.25:1. Compression ratio: 12.0:1. Brake hp: 425 at 5600 rpm. Taxable hp: 57.80. Torque: 480 at 4600 rpm. Five main bearings. Solid valve lifters. Carburetor: Dual Carter (front) AFB-4139-S; (rear) AFB-4140-S four-barrel. Engine code: H.

OPTIONS

Power brakes ($43). Power steering ($86). Air conditioning ($346). Tinted glass, all windows ($40). Tinted glass, windshield only ($22). Padded instrument panel ($19). Back-up lights ($11). Four power windows ($102). Transaudio radio ($59). Transaudio AM/FM radio ($129). Front foam seat cushions ($11). Deluxe steering wheel ($11). Adjustable steering wheel, automatic transmission and power steering required ($46). Tachometer ($50). Bumper guards, front and rear ($31). Retractable seat belts, front and rear compartments ($30). Rear seat speaker with reverberator ($36). Basic Radio Group ($86). TorqueFlite automatic transmission ($211). Four-speed manual floor shift transmission ($188). 426-cid/425-hp four-barrel Hemi V-8 icluding heavy-duty suspension, larger drum brakes, wide wheels and 7.75 x 14 Goodyear high-speed tires. ($1,105). Crankcase vent system, mandatory on California-built cars ($5). Sure-Grip positive traction rear axle ($39). Available rear axle gear ratios: (V-8) 3.23:1 or 2.93:1.

1967 BARRACUDA 383 "S"

1967 Barracuda

Magazines of the era compared the sexy styling of the Gen II Barracuda to that of the classic Buick Riviera. In December 1966, *Car Life* said, "The game is pony car poker and Plymouth raises one — who'll call?"

Plymouth's sports compact really came of age for 1967. It was no longer just a fastback version of the Valiant. It was now a separate sub-make. It grew to three distinct models including a much smoother looking fastback two-door hardtop, a uniquely styled notchback two-door hardtop and a convertible. It officially bowed on November 26, 1966, about two months after the rest of the 1967 Plymouth lineup. In so doing it avoided being buried by the hoopla surrounding two other new sports compacts introduced in early fall, the Chevrolet Camaro and Mercury Cougar.

Barracuda basics were still Valiant-related, like a longer 108-inch wheelbase, but the relationship was far less apparent from the outside package. Curved side glass, mostly its own body panels and unique rooflines, plus a 4.4-inch greater overall length all added to the impression of the Barracuda as its own car line. The fastback (sports) hardtop continued the interior with fold-down rear seats and access to the trunk area. The new notchback hardtop featured a small greenhouse area with a concave rear window.

Power plants were the same used in the earlier models, with one big exception — for the first time you could get a production B-block V-8 in a Barracuda. This was the 383-cid engine, which came with a Carter four-barrel carburetor and a 10:1 compression ratio. It was advertised at 280 hp. The Barracuda 383-"S" was featured in the April 1967 edition of *Car & Driver*. It achieved 0-to-60 in 6.8 seconds and did the quarter-mile in 15.4 seconds at 92 mph.

One way to assure that all the right stuff showed up when you ordered your Barracuda was to order the Formula "S" package. Just as on the earlier Barracudas, it included the Commando 273 engine, wide oval 14-inch tires, heavy-duty suspension, anti-sway bar and appropriate S badges. Actually, there were two Formula S options for 1967, the second coming on stream a bit later and including the 383 — the only way you were supposed to be able to get it. It was the most popular Barracuda model year ever. Today, 1967 Barracuda prices reach into five figures in No. 1 condition, with Formula S models commanding a 10 percent premium and 383s a whopping 40 percent.

Series Number	Body/Style Number	Body Type & Seating	Factory Price	Shipping Weight	Production Total
BARRACUA + "S" — SERIES BH — V-8					
BH	23	2d HT-5P	$2,650	2,865 lbs.	17,151
BH	29	2d FSBK-5P	$2,840	2,940 lbs.	24,090
BH	27	2d CONV-5P	$2,980	2,975 lbs.	3,321

NOTE 1: Prices shown above are the prices of the Barracud 'S' with the 383-cid V-8.
NOTE 2: Weight shown above is the weight of the base 273-cid V-8 model.
NOTE 3: The production total shown above is for all cars with V-8s (no breakouts by body style available).
NOTE 4: A total of 1,784 Barracuda 383-S models were made and 1,036 had a manual transmission.

ENGINE

BASE V-8: Overhead valve. Cast-iron block. Displacement: 383 cid. Bore and stroke: 4.25 x 3.38 inches. Compression ratio: 10.0:1. Brake hp: 280 at 4200 rpm. Taxable hp: 57.80. Torque: 400 at 2400 rpm. Five main bearings. Hydraulic valve lifters. Carburetor: Carter AFB 4326-S four-barrel. Engine code: K.

OPTIONS

Power brakes ($42). Power steering ($80). Air conditioning ($319). Front and rear bumper guards ($22). Tinted glass, all windows ($28). Tinted glass, windshield only ($14). Remote control outside rearview mirror ($7). Special buffed paint ($17). Two-tone paint ($19). Transaudio AM radio ($57). Twin front shoulder belts ($26). Fast manual steering ($13). Deluxe steering wheel ($5). Vinyl roof ($75). Bolt-on design 14-inch wheels ($51). Deluxe 13-inch wheels ($18). Deluxe 14-inch wheels ($21). Heavy-duty suspension package ($14). Decor

PLYMOUTH

group package ($72). Basic group includes: AM radio, wheel covers, power steering and variable speed windshield wipers, with 13-inch wheels ($161); with 14-inch wheels ($164). Disc brakes. Automatic transmission ($181). Four-speed

manual floor shift transmission ($179). Barracuda V-8 383-cid/280-hp four-barrel engine. Heavy-duty battery 70-amp/hour ($8). Sure-Grip positive traction rear axle ($39). Available rear axle gear ratios: 3.23:1; 2.93:1 and various options.

1967 SATELLITE 426 HEMI

Only about eight high-flying Hemi Satellites were reportedly built, so if you have one, don't lose the keys!

Research has found seven hardtops were produced and only one prototype convertible, built for St. Louis plant manger John Berry. The car was recently sold at auction for $135,000.

Satellite models had additional extras including: front bucket seats with console (or center armrest seat), Deluxe wheel covers, glovebox light, fendertop turn signals, upper body accent stripe, courtesy lights, and aluma-plate full-length lower body trim panels.

ENGINE

OPTIONAL V-8: Overhead valve with hemispherical segment combustion chambers. Cast-iron block. Displacement: 426 cid. Bore and stroke: 4.25 x 3.75 inches. Compression ratio: 10.25:1. Compression ratio: 12.0:1. Brake hp: 425 at 5600 rpm. Taxable hp: 57.80. Torque: 480 at 4600 rpm. Five main bearings. Solid valve lifters. Carburetor: Dual Carter (Front) AFB-4139-S; (Rear) AFB-4140-S four-barrel. Engine code: H.

OPTIONS

Power brakes ($42). Power steering ($90). Front and rear bumper guards ($31). Cleaner Air package with ($25). Electric clock ($15). GTX console in Satellite ($53). Disc brakes with V-8 ($70). Tinted glass, all windows ($40). Tinted glass windshield only ($21). Headrests with bucket or individual bench seats, pair ($42). Two-tone paint, except convertible ($22). Special buffed

Car & Driver's road test in April 1966 featured a Hemi Satellite with a 3.54:1 rear axle and registered 5.3 seconds for 0-to-60 and a 13.8-second quarter-mile run at 104 mph. *Car Life*, in July 1966, used a Hemi Satellite with a 3.23:1 axle. It did 0-to-60 mph in 7.1 seconds and the quarter-mile in 14.5 seconds at 95 mph.

Series Number	Body/Style Number	Body Type & Seating	Factory Price	Shipping Weight	Production Total
SATELLITE — SERIES RP — V-8					
RP	23	2dr HT-5P	$3,311	3,245 lbs.	7
RP	27	2dr Conv-5P	$3,550	3,335 lbs.	1

NOTE 1: Price above includes Hemi and no other options.
NOTE 2: Weight is for cars with base V-8.
NOTE 3: Production is for cars with Hemi V-8 only.

paint ($21). Power windows, two-door models ($100). Transaudio AM radio ($57). Transaudio AM/FM radio ($127). GTX front seat with folding center armrest, standard in Satellite (NC). Heavy-duty shock absorbers GTX ($4). Twin front shoulder belts ($26). Full horn ring. Deluxe steering wheel ($5). Woodgrain Deluxe steering wheel ($26). Heavy-duty suspension package ($22). Tachometer ($49). Vinyl roof ($75). Road Wheels ($77). 14-inch sport wheel covers ($18). Variable speed wipers ($5). TorqueFlite automatic transmission ($202. Four-speed manual floor shift transmission ($188). Street Hemi V-8 426-cid/425-hp dual four-barrel engine ($564). Heavy-duty alternator ($11). Heavy-duty battery ($21). Heavy-duty Sure-Grip axle ($139). Sure-Grip positive traction rear axle ($38). Available rear axle gear ratios: 3.23:1; 3.55:1; 2.93:1, and other options.

1967 GTX 440 WEDGE/426 HEMI

Having a big-inch performance model in your lineup was mandatory if you wanted to market your muscle in the mid-'60s. Pontiac started it with its GTO option for the intermediate Tempest in 1964. One by one the competition followed: GT, GTA and so on. One of the last to arrive was the 1967 Plymouth Belvedere GTX.

The mid-size Belvedere already had a hot-car image, thanks to race driver Richard "The King" Petty. The GTX took it one step further as an official factory street machine with all the show-them-off-at-the-drive-in goodies on the outside and under the hood. With its lightweight Super Stock models and its big Wedge and Hemi V-8 engines, Plymouth built limited-production cars that were far faster than the GTO. But the company dragged its feet on doing up an all-inclusive package that put the full range of parts together in one model.

Two vital elements of the Plymouth GTX story resided under the hood. In the middle of the 1966 model year, the company introduced the 426-cid Street Hemi and it then followed up with the release of the 440-cid "Super Commando" Wedge V-8 in 1967. When either of these powerful motors was

combined with the Belvedere's 116-inch wheelbase and lighter weight, you had a potent combination. When you tossed in top-of-the-line front bucket seats, a couple of fake hood scoops and stripes, the GTX was ready to go cruising the boulevard. Also on the GTX model's standard equipment list were TorqueFlite automatic transmission, a heavy-duty suspension and even a pit-stop type gas filler cap. If you plunked down an extra $564, you got the Street Hemi. The monsterous motor was fed by a pair of Carter AFB four-barrel carburetors and carried a conservative 425 hp rating.

Magazine tests proved that the Super Commando GTX was capable of 0-to-60 mph spurts in 7 seconds or less. The exact number of GTXs sold during the model year is not known, since that total was combined with the output of Satellite models. What is known is that the Hemi-optioned GTXs are rare, with only 720 of the approximately 12,500 GTXs that were built being equipped with a Hemi. Of those, 312 had four-speed transmissions and 408 were attached to TorqueFlite automatics. Estimates put the number of Hemi convertibles built at only 17.

JERRRY HEASLEY

1967 GTX

Series Number	Body/Style Number	Body Type & Seating	Factory Price	Shipping Weight	Production Total
GTX — SERIES RS — V-8					
RS	23	2d HT-5P	$3,178	3,535 lbs.	11,429
RS	27	2d Conv-5P	$3,418	3,615 lbs.	680

NOTE 1: Prices above are for 440-powered GTXs.

NOTE 2: Production above is for all GTXs.

NOTE 3: The Hemi V-8 cost $564.

NOTE 4: 720 GTXs (hardtops and convertibles combined) had a Hemi V-8.

NOTE 5: 312 of the Hemi-powered GTXs had a manual tranmission.

ENGINES

BASE V-8: Overhead valve. Cast-iron block. Bore and stroke: 4.32 x 3.75 inches. Displacement: 440 cid. Compression ratio: 10.10:1. Brake hp: 375 at 4600 rpm. Taxable hp: 59.70. Torque: 480 at 3200 rpm. Five main bearings. Hydraulic valve lifters. Carter AFB 4326-S four-barrel. Engine code: L.

OPTIONAL V-8: Overhead valve with hemispherical segment combustion chambers. Cast-iron block. Displacement: 426 cid. Bore and stroke: 4.25 x 3.75 inches. Compression ratio: 10.25:1. Brake hp: 425 at 5000 rpm. Taxable hp: 57.80. Torque: 490 at 4000 rpm. Five main bearings. Hydraulic valve lifters. Carburetor: Dual Carter AFB 3084-S four-barrel. Engine code: J.

OPTIONS

Power brakes ($42). Power steering ($90). Front and rear bumper guards ($31). Cleaner Air package with ($25). Electric clock ($15). Disc brakes with V-8 ($70). Tinted glass, all windows ($40). Tinted glass windshield only ($21). GTX front seat with folding center armrest ($53). Headrests with bucket or individual bench seats, pair ($42). Two-tone paint, except convertible ($22). Special buffed paint ($21). Power windows, two-door models ($100). Transaudio AM radio ($57). Transaudio AM/FM radio ($127). Twin front shoulder belts ($26). Full horn ring. Deluxe steering wheel ($5). Woodgrain Deluxe steering wheel ($26). Heavy-duty suspension package ($22). Tachometer ($49). Vinyl roof ($75). Road Wheels ($77). 14-inch sport wheel covers ($18). Variable speed wipers ($5). TorqueFlite automatic transmission ($202). Four-speed manual floor shift transmission ($188). Street Hemi V-8 426-cid/425-hp dual four-barrel engine ($564). Heavy-duty alternator ($11). Heavy-duty battery ($21). Heavy-duty Sure-Grip axle ($139). Sure-Grip positive traction rear axle ($38). Available rear axle gear ratios: 3.23:1; 3.55:1; 2.93:1, and other options.

1968 BARRACUDA FORMULA S "383"/SS/HEMI

Plymouth's menacing fish car was more lethal than ever in 1967. The 1968 Barracuda received minor styling changes, a wider choice of engines, and the 383 had its power increased by 20 hp.

Regular Barracudas came with all standard safety features, a torsion bar suspension, chromed hood louvers, amber rallye lights, a pit-stop gas cap, carpeting, full instrumentation, D70-14 Red Streak tires and a choice of bucket seats or a front Sportseat with fold-down center armrest. The fastback included belt moldings. The convertible had a locking glove box (for obvious reasons), foam front seat cushions and bucket seats. The Formula S package added either a 340- or a 383-cid high-performance V-8 with dual exhausts, the heavy-duty suspension group, Firm Ride shock absorbers, E70-14 Red Streak tires, 14 x 5.5-in. heavy-duty wheels, Formula medallions and engine call-out plaques.

The 1967 Barracuda 383 S achieved 0-to-60 in 6.8 seconds and did the quarter-mile in 15.4 seconds at 92 mph. With 20 added horsepower, the '68 should be noticeably faster, but no specific documentation of its performance was found.

1968 BARRACUDA FORMULA S "383"/SS/HEMI

PLYMOUTH

1968 Barracuda

For 1968, Chrysler also came up with the idea of stuffing the 426-cid/425-hp Street Hemi into Plymouth Barracudas and Dodge Darts. The purpose was to build the ultimate, big-engined, lightweight, production-based muscle car.

These cars were made with the help of George Hurst and his company. Hemi production totals at the Chrysler Historical Archives do not include the 1968 Hemi Barracudas and Hemi Darts, since they were not considered factory-built vehicles. However, in this case, the Hurst association with the cars increases their collectibility. Former employees of Hurst Performance Products estimate that 70 Hemi Barracudas and 80 Hemi Darts were made. The cars were built by Hurst mainly for professional drag racers, so they did not get a standardized cosmetics package. After all, the pros were only going to decorate them in their own colors and graphics. Hurst did replace some stock steel body panels with fiberglass replicas. The interiors were gutted and fitted with lightweight truck bucket seats. Hurst added headers to the cars. Of course, the company's own shifter kits went in, too. Hefty S/S axles were used, with various gear ratios available. All of the cars had either modified TorqueFlite transmissions or four-speed manual gearboxes.

Series Number	Body/Style Number	Body Type & Seating	Factory Price	Shipping Weight	Production Total
BARRACUA + "S" — SERIES BH — V-8					
BH	23	2d HT-5P	$2,907	2,895 lbs.	12,050
BH	29	2d FSBK-5P	$3,064	2,980 lbs.	18,742
BH	27	2d CONV-5P	$3,235	3,010 lbs.	2,239

NOTE 1: Prices shown include the Formula "S" package and the 383-cid V-8.
NOTE 2: Weight shown above is the weight of the base 318-cid V-8 model.
NOTE 3: The production total shown above is for all cars with V-8s (no breakouts by engine displacement).

Series Number	Body/Style Number	Body Type & Seating	Factory Price	Shipping Weight	Production Total
BARRACUA + "S" — SERIES BO — V-8					
BO	29	2d FSBK-5P	$3,540	2,980 lbs.	70

NOTE 1: Price shown above is an estimate based on the price of the Hemi in the Satellite.
NOTE 2: Weight shown above is the weight of the base 273-cid V-8 model; the SS cars may have been lightened.
NOTE 3: The production total shown above is for Barracuda SS only.

ENGINES

BASE V-8: Overhead valve. Cast-iron block. Displacement: 383 cid. Bore and stroke: 4.25 x 3.38 inches. Compression ratio: 10.0:1. Brake hp: 300 at 4400 rpm. Taxable hp: 57.80. Torque: 400 at 2400 rpm. Five main bearings. Hydraulic valve lifters. Carburetor: Carter AFB 4326-S four-barrel. Engine code: G.

OPTIONAL V-8: Overhead valve with hemispherical segment combustion chambers. Cast-iron block. Displacement: 426 cid. Bore and stroke: 4.25 x 3.75 inches. Compression ratio: 10.25:1. Brake hp: 425 at 5000 rpm. Taxable hp: 57.80. Torque: 490 at 4000 rpm. Five main bearings. Hydraulic valve lifters. Carburetor: Dual Carter AFB 3084-S four-barrel. Engine code: J.

OPTIONS

Power brakes ($44). Power steering ($84). Air conditioning ($335). Front disc brakes ($73). Bumper guards ($23). Console, with bucket seats, except three-speed ($51). Custom sill moldings ($21). Paint accent stripes ($15). Sport paint stripes ($20). Special buffed paint ($18). Wheelhouse liners, except convertible ($47). Deluxe wiper and washer package ($10). Undercoating with hood pad ($16). Vinyl roof, hardtop ($79). Fast manual steering ($14). Full horn ring steering wheel ($9). Woodgrain sport steering wheel ($27). Tachometer, V-8 only ($51). Performance gauge cluster, without clock or tachometer ($16). Deluxe wheel covers ($22). Bolt-on design wheel covers ($45). Wire wheel covers ($67). AM radio ($60). Basic Group: includes AM radio, power steering remote-control outside rearview mirror, variable-speed wipers and electric washers with 383 V-8 ($80), without 383 V-8 ($164). Rally Cluster: includes trip odometer, 150 mph speedometer and woodgrain dash trim ($6). Formula S Group, as described in text, with 383 engine ($251). Automatic transmission ($222). Four-speed manual floor shift transmission ($188). Formula "S" V-8 383-cid/300-hp four-barrel engine ($222). Heavy-duty battery ($6). Heavy-duty alternator ($11 or $15). Positive traction rear axle ($45). Transmissions available with 383-cid engine were four-speed manual or high-performance TorqueFlite with high-speed governor.

1968 GTX 440 WEDGE/426 HEMI

PLYMOUTH

JERRY HEASLEY

1968 GTX

The GTX was more like the GTO than any other member of Plymouth's muscle car fleet. It started out hot and got even hotter as you added more and more extras. Even the Hemi was available under the hood. "The Hemi GTX will appeal to the acceleration enthusiast who wants the ultimate," said _Car Life_ magazine, which also referred to this version as "The fastest standard car on the market."

Plymouth's intermediate-size performance model should have been one of the more popular muscle machines in its market segment as the 1960s waned, but that just didn't turn out to be the case. Instead, the potent high-performance model was forced to play second fiddle in the Plymouth lineup to the Spartan-looking, lower-priced, but more imaginative Road Runner. The Belvedere GTX never wavered from its mission of being a high-content muscle car with a nice assortment of big-block power plant offerings. However, since it was only a year old when the redesigned 1968 Plymouth models were introduced, it didn't have a loyal following to see it through.

It shared the new Belvedere body — including a special high-performance hood — with the Road Runner. The GTX was equipped like a Sport Satellite (with the same grille), but had many standard extras. They included the 440 Super Commando V-8, heavy-duty brakes, suspension, battery and shocks, a dual scoop hood and GTX identification.

Car Life (you can tell what magazines I read in the super '60s) road tested a 440-powered GTX with automatic transmission and reported a 0-to-60 time of 6.8 seconds. It did the quarter-mile in 14.6 seconds with a 96-mph terminal speed. Its top speed was about 121 mph. The Hemi shaved a half a second off the 0-to-60 mph time and shrunk the quarter-mile time to 14 seconds with a 96.5-mph terminal speed.

Series Number	Body/Style Number	Body Type & Seating	Factory Price	Shipping Weight	Production Total
GTX — SERIES RS — V-8					
RS	23	2d HT-5P	$3,355	3,470 lbs.	17,914
RS	27	2d Conv-5P	$3,590	3,595 lbs.	1,027

NOTE 1: Prices above are for 440-powered GTXs.

NOTE 2: Production above is for all GTXs.

NOTE 3: The Hemi V-8 cost $605.

NOTE 4: 450 GTXs (hardtops and convertibles combined) had a Hemi V-8.

NOTE 5: 234 of the Hemi-powered GTXs had a four-speed manual tranmission.

ENGINES

BASE V-8: Overhead valve. Cast-iron block. Bore and stroke: 4.32 x 3.75 inches. Displacement: 440 cid. Compression ratio: 10.10:1. Brake hp: 375 at 4600 rpm. Taxable hp: 59.70. Torque: 480 at 3200 rpm. Five main bearings. Hydraulic valve lifters. Carburetor: Carter AFB 4326-S four-barrel. Engine code: L.

OPTIONAL V-8: Overhead valve with hemispherical segment combustion chambers. Cast-iron block. Displacement: 426 cid. Bore and stroke: 4.25 x 3.75 inches. Compression ratio: 10.25:1. Brake hp: 425 at 5000 rpm. Taxable hp: 57.80. Torque: 490 at 4000 rpm. Five main bearings. Hydraulic valve lifters. Carburetor: Dual Carter AFB 3084-S four-barrel. Engine code: J.

OPTIONS

Power brakes ($44). Power steering ($94). Air conditioning ($355). Automatic speed control ($53). Armrest with ashtray ($8). Bumper guards front and rear ($14). Electric clock ($16). Rear window defogger ($21). Tinted glass, all windows ($42). Tinted glass windshield only ($22). Left and right head restraints ($44). Remote control left outside rearview mirror ($9). Right manual outside rearview mirror ($7). Upper belt moldings, two-door hardtop ($18). Two-tone paint, except convertible ($15). Special buffed paint ($22). Performance black-out hood finish ($18). Solid state AM radio with stereo tape ($195). Solid state AM radio ($60). Tachometer ($51). Vinyl roof ($79). Power windows ($105). Vinyl trim ($26). Road Wheels, except with Street Hemi ($102). Deluxe wheel covers, 14-inch ($22). Deluxe wheel covers, 15-inch ($26). Sport-style wheel covers, except Street Hemi ($38). Automatic transmission ($227). Four-speed manual floor shift transmission, with 426 only ($198). 426-cid/425-hp Street Hemi four-barrel engine ($605). Heavy-duty Sure-Grip axle ($146). Sure-Grip positive traction rear axle ($45).

1968 ROAD RUNNER 383 WEDGE/426 HEMI

PLYMOUTH

JERRY HEASLEY

1968 Hemi Road Runner

The idea of putting a powerful engine in the cheapest, lightest model available was not a new one and wise users of the option list had been ordering "Q-Ships" for years. What Plymouth did with the Road Runner was to do all the work for the customer. The company gave the car a low price that youthful buyers could more easily afford and wrapped it all up in a gimmicky fashion—using a popular Warner Bros. cartoon character as the car's namesake. Using Road Runner identification and a cheap horn that emulated the cartoon bird's well-known "beep-beep" got attention in the marketplace.

The lowest-priced Belvedere two-door sedan was the basis for the Road Runner and came "complete" with such standard fleet items as plain bench seat and rubber floor mats. The first Road Runner's standard engine was a 335-hp version of the 383-cid Chrysler B-block. It was rated at only 5 hp more than the regular 383, but it probably had more power than that due to the use of cylinder heads, intake and exhaust manifolds and a camshaft from the Chrysler 440-cid V-8. Added to the mechanical goodies were a standard four-speed manual transmission, a heavy-duty suspension, 11-inch drum brakes and Red Stripe tires.

The kicker for the Road Runner was its low price. If you wanted some interior niceties such as carpeting and bright trim, you had to invest in the Road Runner Decor Group. If you wanted to kick the toy image, you had to ante up for the Street Hemi. A two-door hardtop was added at midyear. *Car Life* said that the Road Runner "emulates what a young, performance-minded buyer might do on his own if properly experienced and motivated." It was the car you would have had, back in the '60s, if old J.C. Whitney sent you every goodie he had in his catalog.

Even with its base 383-cid/335-hp V-8, the Road Runner turned a 7.3-second 0-to-60 and a 15.37-second quarter-mile at 91.4 mph.

Series Number	Body/Style Number	Body Type & Seating	Factory Price	Shipping Weight	Production Total
ROAD RUNNER — SERIES RM — V-8					
RM	21	2d Coupe-5P	$2,896	3,390 lbs.	30,353
RM	23	2d HT-5P	$3,034	3,425 lbs.	15,701

NOTE 1: Prices above are for 383-powered Road Runners.
NOTE 2: Production above is for all Road Runners.
NOTE 3: The Hemi V-8 cost $714.
NOTE 4: 1,019 Road Runners (hardtops and coupes combined) had a Hemi V-8.
NOTE 5: 576 of the Hemi-powered Road Runnershad a four-speed manual tranmission.

ENGINES

BASE V-8: Overhead valve. Cast-iron block. Displacement: 383 cid. Bore and stroke: 4.25 x 3.38 inches. Compression ratio: 10.00:1. Brake hp: 335 at 5200 rpm. Taxable hp: 57.80. Torque: 425 at 3400 rpm. Five main bearings. Hydraulic valve lifters. Carburetor: Carter four-barrel. Engine code: H.

OPTIONAL V-8: Overhead valve with hemispherical segment combustion chambers. Cast-iron block. Displacement: 426 cid. Bore and stroke: 4.25 x 3.75 inches. Compression ratio: 10.25:1. Brake hp: 425 at 5000 rpm. Taxable hp: 57.80. Torque: 490 at 4000 rpm. Five main bearings. Hydraulic valve lifters. Carburetor: Dual Carter AFB 3084-S four-barrel. Engine code: J.

OPTIONS

Power brakes ($44). Power steering ($94). Air conditioning ($355). Automatic speed control ($53). Armrest with ashtray ($8). Bumper guards front and rear ($14). Electric clock ($16). Rear window defogger ($21). Tinted glass, all windows ($42).Tinted windshield only ($22). Left and right head restraints ($44). Remote control left outside rearview mirror ($9). Right manual outside rearview mirror ($7). Road Runner, Satellite, Sport Wagon custom sill molding ($21). Upper belt moldings, two-door coupe and hardtop ($18). Two-tone paint ($15). Road Runner body accent stripes ($15). Special buffed paint ($22). Performance black-out hood finish ($18). Solid state AM radio with stereo tape ($195). Solid state AM radio ($60). Firm Ride shocks ($4). Tachometer ($51). Vinyl roof ($79). Power windows, hardtop only ($105). Vinyl trim ($26). Road Wheels, except with Street Hemi ($102). Deluxe wheel covers, 14-inch ($22). Deluxe wheel covers, 15-inch ($26). Sport-style wheel covers, except Street Hemi ($38). Automatic transmission ($39). Four-speed manual transmission in Road Runner (standard). Road Runner V-8 426-cid/425-hp Street Hemi dual four-barrel engine ($714). Heavy-duty Sure-Grip axle ($146). Sure-Grip positive traction rear axle ($45).

1969 BARRACUDA 340, 'CUDA & FORMULA "S"

PLYMOUTH

TOM GLATCH

1969 'Cuda S 340

An easy way to tell a 1969 Barracuda from a 1968 edition is by the new side marker lamps, which were now rectangular. The hood and grille was slightly changed, but few other obvious differences were made. Standard equipment included all standard (government required) safety equipment, an all-vinyl interior with bucket seats, a Pit-Stop gas cap, rally lights, front shoulder belts (except convertibles), a belt line molding on the fastback, red or white stripe tires on all V-8 models and an aluminized horizontal rear deck panel with Barracuda block lettering.

A 340-cid V-8 was available as an option in all 1969 Barracuda models: hardtop, fastback and convertible. This engine was also standard in cars with the Formula "S" option or a new 'Cuda option. While all of these cars were in the same ballpark as far as performance, the 'Cuda package definitely fit the muscle car image the best. It included a four-speed manual transmission, hood scoops, tape stripes, black lower body stripes, dual exhausts, chrome exhaust tips, a heavy-duty suspension, heavy-duty front and rear shock absorbers, E70-14 "Wide Boot" tires with red stripes, 14 x 5 1/2-inch wheels, a blacked-out grille, heavy-duty brakes and a front bench seat with vinyl trim. The hardtop was available with an optional yellow flowered vinyl roof.

NOTE 1: Prices shown above include 340-cid V-8.

NOTE 2: Weights shown above are the weights of the base V-8 models.

NOTE 3: The Barracuda production totals are for cars with the 340-cid V-8 only.

NOTE 4: The other production totals are for 340-powered cars with the Formula "S" and 'Cuda packages.

NOTE 5: Four-speed manual transmission used in 1,708 Barracudas, and 470 'Cudas with the 340-cid V-8; no breakout available for Formula "S" models.

ENGINE

BASE V-8: Overhead valve. Cast-iron block. Bore and stroke: 4.04 x 3.31 inches. Displacement: 340 cid. Compression ratio: 10.5:1. Brake hp: 275 at 5000 rpm. Taxable hp: 52.20. Torque: 340 at 3200 rpm. Five main bearings. Hydraulic valve lifters. Carburetor: Carter Thermo-Quad AVS-4611-S four-barrel. Engine code: P.

OPTIONS

Air conditioning ($361). Disc front brakes ($49). Bumper guards, front and rear ($24). Console with bucket seats 'Cuda ($53). Fold-down rear seat in fastback ($65). All-tinted glass ($33). Tinted windshield ($21). Dual head rests ($27). (Note: Head rests standard after Jan. 1, 1969.) Power steering ($85). Sport stripes paint treatment ($26). Performance gauges in Barracuda without clock or tachometer ($17). Power brakes ($43). Solid state AM radio ($62). Solid state AM/FM radio ($135). Tachometer ($50). Floral roof treatment on Barracuda hardtop ($96). Floral interior in Barracuda hardtop with buckets and 'Cuda option ($113). Formula "S" option package for Barracuda convertible with 340-cid V-8 ($162). Formula "S" option package for Barracuda haydtop or fastback with 340-cid V-8 ($186). Rally gauge cluster ($6). Barracuda Sport Group, except cars with 'Cuda package ($51). Barracuda interior Decor Group, including fold-down rear seat (on fastback), woodgrain door and quarter panel trim, door map pouches, bright pedal trim, rear compart¬ment carpet (required fastback), luxury vinyl bucket seats, rear armrests, ashtrays and wheelhouse carpets on fastback ($181 for fastback). 'Cuda 340 package for hardtop or fastback includes: four-speed manual transmission, hood scoops, hood tape stripe, lower black body stripes, dual exhaust with chrome tips, heavy-duty suspension, firm-ride shocks, E70-14 red stripe "Wide-Boot" tires, 14 x 5 1/2-inch wheel rims, black grille, vinyl bench seat and 340-cid V-8 ($309.35). 340-cid four-barrel V-8 for Barraciuda hardtop and fastback ($141, but standard with Formula "S" or 'Cuda packages). 340-cid four-barrel V-8 for Barraciuda convertible ($117 but standard with Formula "S" package).

Series Number	Body/Style Number	Body Type & Seating	Factory Price	Shipping Weight	Production Total
BARRACUA — SERIES BH — V-8					
BH	23	2d HT-5P	$2,921	2,899 lbs.	703
BH	29	2d FsBk-5P	$2,954	2,987 lbs.	2,685
BH	27	2d Conv-5P	$3,199	3,034 lbs.	125
FORMULA "S" — SERIES BH — V-8					
BH	23	2d HT-5P	$3,107	—	325
BH	29	2d FsBk-5P	$3,140	—	1,431
BH	27	2d Conv-5P	$3,199	—	83
'Cuda — SERIES BH — V-8					
BH	23	2d HT-5P	$3,230	—	98
BH	29	2d FsBk-5P	$3,263	—	568

PLYMOUTH

1969 'CUDA & FORMULA "S" 383/440

1969 Cuda "S" 383

In 1969, Plymouth introduced the 'Cuda 383 package to compete with the hotter big-block pony cars that GM and Ford had brought to market. The 'Cuda concept originated as a development car called the "Mopar 340," but the 'Cuda nickname was later adopted for the high-performance production version.

The 'Cuda package was easily characterized by a pair of distinctive-looking black-finished hood scoops and matching hood stripes across the hood. Additional tape strips were applied to the lower portion of the body and incotrporated engine call-out graphics. The 'Cuda package was actually derived from the Plymouth Roadrunner and some enthusiasts described it as a "Pocket Roadrunner." The package was geared to the street-racing fraternity. The 'Cuda shared Formula "S" suspension and drive train components, but had a more Spartan nature without lots of standard accessories. The 383 version carried a 335-hp rating thanks tro its improved exhaust manifolding and a new camshaft.

It took until April of 1969 for Plymouth to realize that if the 383 fit under the 'Cuda's hood, the 440 would fit, too — and widen the car's market appeal. The two models shared the same platform and carried basically the same package of goodies, other than the engine.

The 'Cuda 440 'Cuda was really a car built strictly with quarter-mile performance in mind. With the 440 crammed under the dual-scoop hood, there was no space for some everyday driving conveniences like power drum brakes or power disc brakes and power steering. This was the only year the big monster engine came in the Chrysler A-body platform. So this is an extremely rare Mopar.

Lucky old *Car Life* magazine (one of my favorites) got to test the 'Cuda 440 in June 1969. The car had a 3.55:1 rear end ratio and rather mind-boggling go power, although the big mill in such a small car wasn't the perfect combo for ultimate elapsed times. It zipped from a standing start to 60 mph in 5.6 seconds. The quarter-mile took a whole 14.01 seconds and the car's trap speed was 103.81 mph.

Series Number	Body/Style Number	Body Type & Seating	Factory Price	Shipping Weight	Production Total
FORMULA "S" — SERIES BH — V-8 383					
BH	23	2d HT-5P	—	—	98
BH	29	2d FsBk-5P	—	—	603
BH	27	2d Conv-5P	—	—	17
'Cuda — SERIES BH — V-8 383					
BH	23	2d HT-5P	—	—	84
BH	29	2d FsBk-5P	—	—	378

NOTE 1: Prices not available.
NOTE 2: Weights not avaialble.
NOTE 3: The production totals are for cars with the 383-cid four-barrel V-8 only.
NOTE 4: A total of 391 of the 383-powered Formula "S" Barracudas had a four-speed manual transmission.
NOTE 5: A total of 153 of the 383-powered 'Cudas had a four-speed manual transmission.

Series Number	Body/Style Number	Body Type & Seating	Factory Price	Shipping Weight	Production Total
'Cuda — SERIES BH — V-8 440					
BH	23	2d HT-5P	—	—	Note 3
BH	29	2d FsBk-5P	—	—	Note 3

NOTE 1: Prices not available.
NOTE 2: Weights not available.
NOTE 3: The production totals are for all 'Cuda 440s was 360 with no body style breakout available.
NOTE 4: The Barracuda 440 was available with automatic transmission only.

ENGINE

OPTIONAL V-8: Overhead valve. Cast-iron block. Displacement: 383 cid. Bore and stroke: 4.25 x 3.38 inches. Compression ratio: 10.00:1. Brake hp: 335 at 5000 rpm. Taxable hp: 57.80. Torque: 425 at 3400 rpm. Five main bearings. Hydraulic valve lifters. Carburetor: Carter Thermo-Quad AVS-4615-S four-barrel. Engine code: H.

OPTIONS

Air conditioning ($361). Disc front brakes ($49). Bumper guards, front and rear ($24). Console with bucket seats 'Cuda ($53). Fold-down rear seat in fastback ($65). All-tinted glass ($33). Tinted windshield ($21). Power steering ($85). Sport stripes paint treatment ($26). Performance gauges in Barracuda without clock or tachometer ($17). Power brakes ($43). Solid state AM radio ($62). Solid state AM/FM radio ($135). Tachometer ($50). Floral roof treatment on Barracuda hardtop ($96). Floral interior in Barracuda hardtop with buckets and 'Cuda option ($113). Formula "S" option package for Barracuda convertible with 383-cid V-8 (price not available). Formula "S" option package for Barracuda haydtop or fastback with 383-cid V-8 (price not available). Rally gauge cluster ($6). Barracuda Sport Group, except cars with 'Cuda package ($51). Barracuda interior Decor Group, including fold-down rear seat (on fastback), woodgrain door and quarter panel trim, door map pouches, bright pedal trim, rear compartment carpet (required fastback), luxury vinyl bucket seats, rear armrests, ashtrays and wheelhouse carpets (fastback) ($181 for fastback). 'Cuda 383 package for hardtop or fastback includes: four-speed manual transmission, hood scoops, hood tape stripe, lower black body stripes, dual exhaust with chrome tips, heavy-duty suspension, firm-ride shocks, E70-14 red stripe "Wide-Boot" tires, 14 x 5 1/2-inch wheel rims, black grille, vinyl bench seat and 383-cid V-8 (price not available). 'Cuda 440 package for hardtop or fastback, includes: automatic transmission, hood scoops, hood tape stripe, lower black body stripes, dual exhaust with chrome tips, heavy-duty suspension, firm-ride shocks, E70-14 red stripe "Wide-Boot" tires, 14 x 5 1/2-inch wheel rims, black grille, vinyl bench seat and 440-cid V-8 (price not available).

1969 GTX 440 WEDGE/426 HEMI

1969 GTX 440

"No matter how you may try to camouflage it by loading a car with power and comfort options, when you get down to the nitty gritty of supercar existence, an inescapable, basic fact always remains on the surface," said *Motor Trend's* Bill Sanders in January 1969. "One primary purpose of a super car is to get from here to there, from this light to the next, in the shortest elapsed time. To this end, the Plymouth GTX is the flat out, best qualifier of all."

The GTX two-door hardtop Model RS23 had a dealer cost of $2,710.82 and retailed for $3,329. The convertible, Model RS27, cost dealers $2,924.89 and sold for $3,590. Sanders listed the base price of his test car as $3,433, which included federal excise tax. Standard GTX equipment included a heavy-duty rear suspension, heavy-duty front torsion bars, anti-sway bars, the 440-cid Super Commando V-8, foam padded front bucket seats, simulated woodgrain trim on the doors, simulated woodgrain trim on the instrument panel, floor carpeting, F70 x 14 red streak or F70 x 14 white streak tires, body side accent stripes, heavy-duty brakes, a heavy-duty 70-amp battery, roof drip-rail moldings, firm-ride shocks, custom body sill moldings, front foam seat cushions, arm rests with ash trays and dual horns.

Sander's *Motor Trend* test car had the 440-cid base engine, rather than the Street Hemi. It produced the same 375 hp at 4600 rpm and 480 lbs.-ft. of torque at 3200 rpm that it had in 1968. The test car was also equipped with a TorqueFlite automatic transmission and a 4.10:1 rear axle. Sanders managed to achieve 0-to-60 mph in 5.8 seconds. The car did the quarter-mile in a mere 13.7 seconds at 102.8 mph.

Series Number	Body/Style Number	Body Type & Seating	Factory Price	Shipping Weight	Production Total
GTX — SERIES RS — V-8 440					
RS	23	2d HT-5P	$3,416	3,465 lbs.	17,707
RS	27	2d Conv-5P	$3,635	3,590 lbs.	1,010
GTX — SERIES RS — V-8 HEMI					
RS	23	2d HT-5P	$4,166	—	207
RS	27	2d Conv-5P	$4,291	—	16

NOTE 1: Hemi GTX prices include cost of the engine and no other options.
NOTE 2: Hemi GTX weights unknown.
NOTE 3: Four-speed manual transmission used in 98 Hemi GTX hardtops and five convertibles.

ENGINES

BASE V-8: Overhead valve. Cast-iron block. Bore and stroke: 4.32 x 3.75 inches. Displacement: 440 cid. Compression ratio: 10.10:1. Brake hp: 375 at 4600 rpm. Taxable hp: 59.70. Torque: 480 at 3200 rpm. Five main bearings. Hydraulic valve lifters. Carburetor: Carter AFB 4326-S four-barrel. Engine code: L.

OPTIONAL V-8: Overhead valve with hemispherical segment combustion chambers. Cast-iron block. Displacement: 426 cid. Bore and stroke: 4.25 x 3.75 inches. Compression ratio: 10.25:1. Brake hp: 425 at 5000 rpm. Taxable hp: 57.80. Torque: 490 at 4000 rpm. Five main bearings. Hydraulic valve lifters. Carburetor: Dual Carter AFB 3084-S four-barrel. Engine code: J.

OPTIONS

Air conditioning ($358). Air Grabber hood scoop ($55). Auto speed control ($58). Disc front brakes ($49). Bumper guards, front and rear ($32). Color-keyed carpet mats ($14). Console with bucket seats, Road Runner/Sport Satellite ($54). All-tinted glass ($41). Tinted windshield ($26). Dual head rests ($27). Note: Head rests standard after Jan. 1, 1969. Headlights-on signal ($7). Cornering lamps ($36). Power steering ($100). Performance hood paint ($18). Power brakes ($43). Solid state AM radio ($62). Solid state AM/FM radio ($135). Solid state AM with tape ($196). Tachometer ($50). Chrome-styled wheels 14 inch, except with Hemi ($100). Super performance axle package in GTX with Hemi ($242). Track Pack option, required with four-speed manual transmission ($143). Super Track Pack with four-speed ($256). 426-cid Eight-Barrel Hemi V-8 ($813). 440-cid Six-Pack V-8 ($250).

1969 ROAD RUNNER 440 SIX-PACK/426 HEMI

PHIL KUNZ

1969 Road Runner

Car and Driver magazine included a Hemi Road Runner coupe in its comparison test of six "econo-racers" in January 1969. It showed the list price of the car to be $4,362.05 as tested. *Car and Driver* recorded 0-to-60 mph in 5.1 seconds. The quarter-mile was covered in 13.54 seconds with a trap speed of 105.14 mph. Ithe Hemi Road Runner had an estimated top speed of 142 mph. "To say that the Road Runner scored heavily in the performance part of the test is Anglo Saxon understatement in the best tradition," said the magazine. "It was the quickest in acceleration, stopped in the shortest distance and ranked second in handling. That's a pretty tough record." *Super Stock* magazine gave its own test to the 440-Six-Pack Road Runner — a car with 4.10:1 gearing. It ran the quarter in 13.09 seconds at 111 mph!

New grilles and new rear-end styling characterized the 1969 Plymouth Road Runner models, which were now available in three different body styles. Standard features of the 1969 Road Runner included a heavy-duty suspension, heavy-duty brakes, heavy-duty shocks, a dash nameplate, a deck lid nameplate, door nameplates, top-opening hood scoops, chrome engine parts, an unsilenced air cleaner, Hemi orange paint treatment, red- or white-streak tires, a four-speed manual transmission with a Hurst gear shifter, a fake walnut shift knob, back-up lights and a deluxe steering wheel. Road Runners came in the following factory colors: Performance Red, Bahama Yellow, Rallye Green, Vitamin C Orange and White.

The standard engine was the 383-cid V-8. The 426-cid Street Hemi was optional all year long. A midyear option was the 440 Six-Pack V-8, a choice that was designed to bridge the gap between the 383 Wedge V-8 and the much more costly Hemi. The engine option included a matte black fiberglass hood, hood-locking pins, a four-speed manual transmission, a 9.75-in. Dana Sure-Grip rear axle with 4.10:1 gears, 15 x 6-inch matte black painted wheelswith bright metal lug nuts, G70-15 glass-belted Red Streak tires and the 440-cid V-8 with

triple two-barrel carburetors mounted on an Edelbrock aluminum intake manifold. The carbs moved 1,300 cubic feet of air per minute. For ordinary street use, the cars ran on the center carburetor most of the time, but when the pedal was put to the metal the No. 1 and No. 3 carbs kicked in. The engine was tweaked with specially selected rocker arms and a low-taper cam with longer-lasting flat-faced tappets was fitted. Heavy-service valve springs, chrome-plated valves stems and moly-type upper pistons rings were included as well as a dual-point ignition system, a heavy-duty cooling system and a viscous-drive fan w/heavy duty cooling. Wheels on the Road Runner were plain 15 x 6-inch steel wheels painted flat black with G70x15 fiberglass belted Red Streak tires.

Series Number	Body/Style Number	Body Type & Seating	Factory Price	Shipping Weight	Production Total
ROAD RUNNER — SERIES RM — V-8 440					
RM	21	2d Coupe-5P	$3,195	3,450 lbs.	615
RM	23	2d HT-5P	$3,333	3,435 lbs.	817
ROAD RUNNER — SERIES RM — V-8 HEMI					
RM	21	2d Coupe-5P	$3,758	—	378
RM	23	2d HT-5P	$3,896	—	436
RM	27	2d Conv-5P	$4,126	—	12

NOTE 1: Prices above are include the cost of the indicated engine option.

NOTE 2: Weights are given for Road Runner hardtops and coupes with the base 383-cid V-8; the 383-powered convertible weighed 3790 lbs.

NOTE 3: No 440 Six-Pack convertibles were built.

NOTE 4: Production totals are only for cars with the indicated engines.

NOTE 5: Four-speed manual transmission used in 234 Hemi Road Runner hardtops, 194 Hemi Road Runner coupes and four Hemi Road Runner convertibles.

ENGINES

OPTIONAL V-8: Overhead valve. Cast-iron block. Bore and stroke: 4.32 x 3.75 inches. Displacement: 440 cid. Compression ratio: 10.50:1. Brake hp: 390 at 4700 rpm. Taxable hp: 59.70. Torque: 490 at 3200 rpm. Five main bearings. Hydraulic valve lifters. Carburetor: three Holley two-barrel. Engine code: L.

OPTIONAL V-8: Overhead valve with hemispherical segment combustion chambers. Cast-iron block. Displacement: 426 cid. Bore and stroke: 4.25 x 3.75 inches. Compression ratio: 10.25:1. Brake hp: 425 at 5000 rpm. Taxable hp: 57.80. Torque: 490 at 4000 rpm. Five main bearings. Hydraulic valve lifters. Carburetor: Dual Carter AFB 3084-S four-barrel. Engine code: M.

PLYMOUTH

OPTIONS

Air conditioning ($358). Air Grabber hood scoop ($55). Auto speed control ($58). Disc front brakes ($49). Bumper guards, front and rear($32). Color-keyed carpet mats ($14). Console with bucket seats, Road Runner/Sport Satellite ($54). All-tinted glass ($41). Tinted windshield ($26). Dual head rests ($27). Note: Head rests standard after Jan. 1, 1969. Headlights-on signal ($7). Cornering lamps ($36). Power steering ($100). Performance hood paint ($18). Power brakes ($43). Solid state AM radio ($62). Solid state AM/FM radio ($135). Solid state AM with tape ($196). Tachometer ($50). Chrome-styled wheels 14 inch, except with Hemi ($100). Super performance axle package in GTX with Hemi ($242). Track Pack option, required with four-speed manual transmission ($143). Super Track Pack with four-speed ($256).

1970 DUSTER 340

PHIL KUNZ

1970 Duster 340

New for 1970, the Duster was a derivative of Plymouth's Valiant compact. Both cars were built on the same platform and shared the same front end sheet metal, but they were different from the cowl back. The Duster came only as a two-door sedan or coupe. Plymouth didn't anticipate the public's positive response to redesigned compact. Valiant production increased from 107,218 in 1969 to 268,002 in 1970. Of that number, most of the cars sold were Dusters.

The Duster 340 played a distinct role in Plymouth's "Rapid Transit System" — it was the entry-level muscle car for young enthusiasts. The Duster replaced the rather staid two-door sedan in the Valiant lineup. Its body styling was characterized by a contemporary look, with bulging lines from the firewall back. This was known as the "Coke-bottle" shape. The same 108-inch wheelbase unitized chassis was used for both cars and both were 188.4 inches long.

Doing for compact cars what the Road Runner did for mid-sized cars, the Duster 340 was the low-priced performance machine. It came standard with a 340-cid 275-hp V-8 that had been used in Plymouths since 1968. Other Duster goodies included a three-speed manual gear box with a floor-mounted shifter, a special instrument panel, a heavy-duty suspension with high-rate front torsion bars, and a front anti-sway bar, E70 x 14 fiberglass-belted tires with black sidewalls and raised white letters, styled steel Road Wheels, performance body striping and the obligatory cartoon character — in this case a friendly dust devil. The Duster 340's bottom-line base price was low. Front bucket seats and other dress-up items were optional, as with the Road Runner.

Car Life tested an automatic-equipped Duster 340 and found that it could go from 0-to-60 mph in only 6.2 seconds and that it was a great buy. The buying public felt the same, which made the Duster a success in general and the 340 version a particular hit.

Series Number	Body/Style Number	Body Type & Seating	Factory Price	Shipping Weight	Production Total
DUSTER — SERIES VS — V-8					
BH	29	2d Coupe-5P	$2,547	3,110 lbs.	24,817

ENGINE

BASE V-8: Overhead valve. Cast-iron block. Bore and stroke: 4.04 x 3.31 inches. Displacement: 340 cid. Compression ratio: 10.5:1. Brake hp: 275 at 5000 rpm. Taxable hp: 52.20. Torque: 340 at 3200 rpm. Five main bearings. Hydraulic valve lifters. Carburetor: Carter Thermo-Quad AVS-4611-S four-barrel. Engine code: P.

OPTIONS

Power brakes ($43). Power steering ($85). Air conditioning ($347). Front disc brakes ($28). Rear window defogger ($27). Headlight time delay warning signal ($18). Remote-control left-hand outside rearview mirror ($10). Color-keyed racing mirrors ($26). Solid state AM radio ($62). Solid state AM/FM radio ($135). Four-place style vinyl bench seats, (Duster $13; Duster 340 standard). Bucket seat with vinyl trim ($100). Tachometer, Duster 340 ($50). Vinyl roof ($84). Duster vinyl and cloth trim, includes carpets, Deluxe and '340' models ($39). TorqueFlite automatic transmission with V-8 ($191-$227). Four-speed manual floor shift transmission ($188-$197).). Heavy-duty, 70-amp battery ($13). Heavy-duty, 59-amp battery ($13). Heavy-duty 50-amp alternator ($11-$15). Sure-Grip positive traction rear axle ($42). Evaporative emissions control system ($38). Available rear axle gear ratios: 2.76:1 or 3.55:1 optional ($10).

PLYMOUTH

1970 'CUDA 340

PHIL KUNZ

1970 'Cuda 340

For 1970, Barracudas had an all-new E-body. The E-body was essentially a shortened wheelbase 68-70 B-body. With the styling change, Chrysler dropped the fastback, but retained the hardtop and convertible.

For the "I'll-drive-my-muscle-car-everyday-and-die-with-a-smile-on-my-face" buyer, the 'Cuda 340 returned. Its small-block V-8 was a little more suitable for hops to the 7-11 than a 440 Wedge or a Hemi, but don't get the idea that the 340 was a whimpy car. With the new sheet metal, the distance between the front wheels was upped to comfortably swallow any power plant from a slant-six to a Hemi.

Attracting less media attention than the big-blocks, the 340 package continued as a no-cost 'Cuda option (a 383 Wedge V-8 was actually standard). The 340 was a nice alternative, especially for youthful muscle car buyers who couldn't quite hack the price of a 440 or a Hemi. It delivered a lot of "snort" for the price. For all-around use, the 'Cuda 340 was really a quite nicely-balanced package.

Motor Trend ran a comparison test between 'Cudas with all three available engines. In the 0 to 60-mph category, the 340-powered version needed 6.4 seconds compared to the 440's 5.9 seconds and the Hemi's 5.8 seconds. Its quarter-mile performance was 14.5 seconds (96 mph) compared to 14.4 seconds and 100 mph for the 440 version and 14 seconds and 102 mph for the Hemi 'Cuda. The 440-powered test car had a four-speed manual gear box, while the 'Cuda 340 and the Hemi 'Cuda had automatic transmission.

After driving 'Cudas with three different engines, *Motor Trend's* A.B. Shuman admitted to his readers, "From the foregoing you may have detected a 'slight' preference for the 340 'Cuda. This was intentional. It was the best of the lot!" There are many Mopar maniacs who were glad they listened to A.B. and even more who wished they had! Sometime during the model year, a 340 Six-Pack option with three two-barrel carburetors was released and used in nearly 2,800 hardtops.

Series Number	Body/Style Number	Body Type & Seating	Factory Price	Shipping Weight	Production Total
'CUDA — SERIES BS — V-8					
BS	23	2d HT-5P	$3,164	3,395 lbs.	8,756
BS	27	Conv-5P	$3,433	3,480 lbs.	262

NOTE 1: Weights shown above are the weights of the base 383-cid V-8 models.

NOTE 2: Production of 'Cuda 340 hardtops included 1,872 cars with three-speed manual transmission, 2,372 cars with four-speed manual transmission and 1,788 cars with automatic.

NOTE 3: Production of 'Cuda 340 convertibles included 19 cars with three-speed manual transmission, 88 cars with four-speed manual transmission and 155 cars with automatic.

ENGINE

OPTIONAL V-8: Overhead valve. Cast-iron block. Bore and stroke: 4.04 x 3.31 inches. Displacement: 340 cid. Compression ratio: 10.5:1. Brake hp: 275 at 5000 rpm. Taxable hp: 52.20. Torque: 340 at 3200 rpm. Five main bearings. Hydraulic valve lifters. Carburetor: Carter Thermo-Quad AVS-4611-S four-barrel. Engine code: H.

OPTIONS

Power brakes ($43). Power steering ($90). Air conditioning ($357). Black air scoop, quarter panel and lower body paint ($36). Heavy-duty brakes ($23). Rear window defogger in hardtop only ($27). Headlight time delay warning signal ($18). Racing mirrors, left-hand remote control ($11). Color-keyed racing mirrors, left-hand remote control ($26). Sport striping, 'Cuda without side molding vinyl insert ($26). Power convertible top ($53). Power windows ($105). Solid state AM radio, all models ($62). Solid state AM/FM radio ($135). Multiplex AM/FM stereo system ($214). Vinyl bench seat with armrest and folding cushion ($17). Leather bucket seat with consolette ($119). Leather bucket seat in convertible ($65). Shaker hood fresh air package ($97). Floral vinyl roof ($96). Deluxe wheel covers ($16). Wire wheel covers ($50). Rally Road Wheels ($17). Chrome Road Wheels Barracuda ($50). Super Track Pak racing equipment package ($236). Three-speed manual transmission was standard; with floor shift in some models ($14). TorqueFlite automatic transmission ($191-$227). Four-speed manual floor shift transmission ($188-$197). Heavy-duty, 70-amp battery ($13). Heavy-duty, 59-amp battery ($13). Heavy-duty 50-amp alternator ($11-$15). Sure-Grip positive traction rear axle ($42). Evaporative emissions control system ($38). Available rear axle gear ratios: 2.76:1 or 3.55:1 optional ($10). 340-cid V-8 in place of base 383-cid V-8 (no charge).

1970 AAR 'CUDA

JERRY HEASLEY

1970 AAR 'Cuda

The Plymouth AAR 'Cuda was one very fast small-block muscle car. Though its name evolved from the Trans-Am racing series, the AAR had a split personality. "Everything makes sense if you forget all about Dan Gurney and think of it in terms of the Burbank Blue Bombers," said the July 1970 issue of *Car and Driver*. "The new AAR 'Cuda is every inch a hot rod."

Having a car in the Sports Car Club of America (SCCA) Trans-American sedan racing series was a must for the Detroit purveyors of pony cars in 1970. There were factory-backed efforts from American Motors, Ford, Dodge and Plymouth. Chevrolet and Pontiac had back-door programs. Open Plymouth and Dodge participation was new. It came together because there were new Plymouth Barracuda and Dodge Challenger designs and because rules changed so that the 5.0-liter engines used in the racing cars didn't have to be exactly the same size as the production engines they were derived from. This meant that Chrysler's potent 340-cid small-block could be de-stroked to 303.8 inches to meet the limit. Plymouth could legalize its Trans-Am racing equipment by building 1,900 or more special models. The result was the 1970 AAR 'Cuda.

After pilot model assembly, all production-line AAR 'Cudas were build between March 10 and April 20, 1970. Production of the AAR began on March 10 and continued until April 17. All of the cars used a 340 Six-Pack V-8 and wore unique "Strobe Stripe" graphics that incorporated the AAR 'Cuda logo. The AAR logo featured four white stars surrounded in

blue at the top with "AAR" lettering below the stars. A functional air scoop atop the fiberglass hood, front eyebrow-like spoilers and a rear airfoil were included in the package. A custom exhaust system exited near each rear wheel.

The 340-6 could accelerate the 'Cuda from 0-to-60 mph in 5.8 seconds, 0-to-100 in 14.4 seconds and race a quarter-mile in 14.4 seconds at 100 mph.

Series Number	Body/Style Number	Body Type & Seating	Factory Price	Shipping Weight	Production Total
AAR 'CUDA — SERIES BS — V-8					
BS	23	2d HT-5P	$3,966	3,395 lbs.	2,727

NOTE 1: Production of AAR 'Cudas included 1,120 cars with four-speed manual transmission.

ENGINE
BASE V-8: Overhead valve. Cast-iron block. Bore and stroke: 4.04 x 3.31 inches. Displacement: 340 cid. Compression ratio: 10.20:1. Brake hp: 290 at 5000 rpm. Taxable hp: 52.20. Torque: 340 at 3200 rpm (except Fury is 380 ft.-lbs. at 2400 rpm). Five main bearings. Hydraulic valve lifters. Carburetor: three Holley two-barrel. Engine code: J.

OPTIONS
Power brakes ($43). Power steering ($90). Air conditioning ($357). Rear window defogger ($27). Headlight time delay warning signal ($18). Racing mirrors, left-hand remote control ($11). Color-keyed racing mirrors, left-hand remote control ($26). Power windows ($105). Solid state AM radio, all models ($62). Solid state AM/FM radio ($135). Multiplex AM/FM stereo system ($214). Vinyl bench seat with armrest and folding cushion ($17). Super Track Pak racing equipment package ($236). TorqueFlite automatic transmission ($191-$227). Four-speed manual floor shift transmission ($188-$197). Sure-Grip positive traction rear axle ($42). Evaporative emissions control system ($38).

PLYMOUTH

1970 'CUDA 440/440 SIX-PACK/HEMI

JERRY HEASLEY

1970 Hemi 'Cuda

With Plymouth's 1970 changes, the Formula "S" Barracuda was gone, but the 'Cuda survived. Its base engine was the 335-hp/383-cid big-block V-8 with single four-barrel carb. If you were willing to part with a few more bucks, you could select four other engines. The was the 340-cid high-performance small-block motor for starters. Then a trio of even larger big-blocks. First came the 440 with a four-barrel carb, followed by a Six-Pack version with three two-barrel carbs. Then came "King Kong," the 425-hp/426-cid Hemi. These cars featured beefy suspensions, and Hemis came standard with 15-inch wheel rims.

The 440 Six-Pack was just as fast as a Hemi at the drag strip and could beat a Hemi in the Stoplight Grand Prix. It was torquier than a Hemi, which helped acceleration-wise. The Hemi was also a handful to tune and to drive on the street.

When *Motor Trend* tested the 440 Six-pack 'Cuda in May 1970, it drew a unit with 3.55:1 gearing and reported a 5.9-second 0-to-60 sprint. The quarter-mile took 14.04 seconds at a flat 100 mph. *Musclecar Review* magazine also did a "retro test" on this model (with automatic) in December 1997. Its quarter-mile number was 13 seconds flat at 105.74 mph.

Street Hemis got new hydraulic valve lifters for 1970, but a new cam profile gave the Mopar engineers no reason to alter the 425 advertised hp rating. The Hemi's two Carter AFB four-barrel carburetors breathed through the Air Grabber "shaker" hood scoop. In order to get the horses to the pavement, Hemi-powered 'Cudas and other big-engined Barracudas relied on heavy-duty drive line parts. There was a choice of the New Process A-833 four-speed manual gearbox or the 727 TorqueFlite automatic. A Dana 9-3/4-inch differential was kept in place by a leaf-spring rear suspension with six leafs

on the right and five leafs plus two half-leafs on the left. Fifteen-inch-diameter, 7-inch-wide wheels held F60 x 15 tires. In short, power was the Hemi 'Cuda's long suit. Not long was the list of buyers. By the time the 1970 run came to an end, only 652 hardtops had left the factory with Hemi power and 284 of them had four-speed transmissions. Far more spectacular in terms of rarity was the convertible with only 14 being made, five with a manual gearbox.

Insurance companies did not look kindly on Hemi 'Cudas and did not care if they could do 0-to-60 mph in 5.8 seconds and run down the quarter-mile in 14.1 seconds at 103.2 mph.

Series Number	Body/Style Number	Body Type & Seating	Factory Price	Shipping Weight	Production Total
'Cuda — SERIES BS — V-8 (FOUR-BARREL)					
BS	23	2d HT-5P	$3,295	3,395 lbs.	952
BS	27	2d Conv-5P	$3,564	3,480 lbs.	34
'Cuda — SERIES BS — V-8 (SIX-PACK)					
BS	23	2d HT-5P	$3,410	—	1,755
BS	27	2d Conv-5P	$3,683	—	29

NOTE 1: Prices include indicated engine and no other options.
NOTE 2: Weights are for base 383-cid V-8 models.
NOTE 3: Production of four-barrel 'Cudas included 334 hardtops and six convertibles with four-speed manual transmission.
NOTE 3: Production of Six-Pack 'Cudas included 902 hardtops and 17 convertibles with four-speed manual transmission.

Series Number	Body/Style Number	Body Type & Seating	Factory Price	Shipping Weight	Production Total
HEMI 'Cuda — SERIES BS — V-8 HEMI					
BS	23	2d HT-5P	$4,035	3,395 lbs.	289
BS	27	2d Conv-5P	$4,364	3,480 lbs.	377

NOTE 1: Prices include indicated engine and no other options.
NOTE 2: Weights are for base 383-cid V-8 models.
NOTE 3: Production of Hemi 'Cudas included 284 hardtops and five convertibles with four-speed manual transmission.

ENGINES

OPTIONAL V-8: Overhead valve. Cast-iron block. Bore and stroke: 4.32 x 3.75 inches. Displacement: 440 cid. Compression ratio: 10.10:1. Brake hp: 375 at 4600 rpm. Taxable hp: 59.70. Torque: 480 at 3200 rpm. Five main bearings.

Hydraulic valve lifters. Carburetor: Carter AVS-4617-S four-barrel. Engine code: K.

OPTIONAL V-8: Overhead valve. Cast-iron block. Bore and stroke: 4.32 x 3.75 inches. Displacement: 440 cid. Compression ratio: 10.50:1. Brake hp: 390 at 4700 rpm. Taxable hp: 59.70. Torque: 490 at 3200 rpm. Five main bearings. Hydraulic valve lifters. Carburetor: three Holley two-barrel. Engine code: L.

OPTIONAL V-8: Overhead valve with hemispherical segment combustion chambers. Cast-iron block. Displacement: 426 cid. Bore and stroke: 4.25 x 3.75 inches. Compression ratio: 10.20:1. Brake hp: 425 at 5000 rpm. Taxable hp: 57.80. Torque: 490 at 4000 rpm. Five main bearings. Hydraulic valve lifters. Carburetor: Dual Carter AFB 3084-S four-barrel. Engine code: R.

OPTIONS

Power brakes ($43). Power steering ($90). Air conditioning ($357). Black air scoop, quarter panel and lower body paint ($36). Heavy-duty brakes ($23). Rear window defogger in hardtop only ($27). Headlight time delay warning signal ($18). Hood hold-down pins, Road Runner and GTX only ($15). Racing mirrors, left-hand remote control ($11). Color-keyed racing mirrors, left-hand remote control ($26). Sport striping, 'Cuda without side molding vinyl insert ($26). Power convertible top ($53). Power windows ($105). Solid state AM radio, all models ($62). Solid state AM/FM radio ($135). Multiplex AM/FM stereo system ($214). Vinyl bench seat with armrest and folding cushion ($17). Leather bucket seat with consolette ($119). Leather bucket seat in convertible ($65). Shaker hood fresh air package ($97). Floral vinyl roof ($96). Deluxe wheel covers ($16). Wire wheel covers ($50). Rally Road Wheels ($17). Chrome Road Wheels Barracuda ($50). Super Track Pak racing equipment package ($236). TorqueFlite automatic transmission ($191-$227). Four-speed manual floor shift transmission ($188-$197). Heavy-duty, 70-amp battery ($13). Heavy-duty, 59-ampere battery ($13). Heavy-duty 50-amp alternator ($11-$15). Sure-Grip positive traction rear axle ($42). Evaporative emissions control system ($38). Available rear axle gear ratios: 2.76:1 or 3.55:1 optional ($10).440-cid four-barrel V-8 ($131). 440-cid Six-Pack V-8 ($250).

1970 GTX 440/440 SIX-PACK/426 HEMI

1970 GTX

"The difference between Priority Mail and Parcel Post is a matter of money and speed — kind of like the GTX version of Plymouth's mid-size muscle machinery. Paul Zazarine summed the car up in the November '86 issue of *Musclecar Review*. Said Zazerine, "The Plymouth GTX was always considered an upscale version of the Road Runner — it could still boil the hides, but in a classy sort of way."

A redesigned grille, a new hood and restyled front fenders characterized all of Plymouth's intermediate models in 1970. The Belvedere GTX featured much of the same standard equipment as the Road Runner, including a heavy-duty suspension, heavy-duty brakes, a dual exhaust system, a high-performance hood with the "air grabber" scoop, front and rear bumper guards and a 150-mph speedometer. It also had a standard 440-cid Super Commando V-8, a deluxe vinyl interior, foam seat padding on its new-for-1970 high-back front bucket seats and rear bench seat, body-side reflective tape stripes, side markers, dual (non-beep-beep) horns, a 70-amp battery and bright exhaust trumpets.

The Belvedere GTX lineup lost its convertible for 1970. The only body style left was the two-door hardtop. Belvedere GTX buyers could also get the 440-cid Six-Pack option or a Hemi. "The GTX six-barrel is no slouch in the performance department either," said *Motor Trend* in its fall 1969 review of the hot '70s models. TorqueFlite automatic transmission was standard. A four-speed manual was a no-cost extra.

Series Number	Body/Style Number	Body Type & Seating	Factory Price	Shipping Weight	Production Total
GTX — SERIES RS —V-8 440 (FOUR-BARREL)					
RS	23	2d HT-5P	$3,535	3,515 lbs.	6,398
GTX — SERIES RS — V-8 (SIX-PACK)					
RS	23	2d HT-5P	$3,654	—	678
HEMI GTX — SERIES RS — V-8 HEMI					
RS	23	2d HT-5P	$4,216	—	72

NOTE 1: Prices include cost of the indicated engine and no other options.

NOTE 2: Five additional Hemis were made for Canada.

NOTE 3: Four-speed manual transmission used in 43 Hemi GTX hardtops.

ENGINES

BASE V-8: Overhead valve. Cast-iron block. Bore and stroke: 4.32 x 3.75 inches. Displacement: 440 cid. Compression ratio: 9.70:1. Brake hp: 375 at 4600 rpm. Taxable hp: 59.70. Torque: 480 at 2800 rpm. Five main bearings. Hydraulic valve lifters. Carburetor: Carter AVS-4737-S four-barrel(Federal). Engine code: U.

OPTIONAL V-8: Overhead valve. Cast-iron block. Bore and stroke: 4.32 x 3.75 inches. Displacement: 440 cid. Compression ratio: 10.50:1. Brake hp: 390 at 4700 rpm. Taxable hp: 59.70. Torque: 490 at 3200 rpm. Five main bearings. Hydraulic valve lifters. Carburetor: three Holley two-barrel. Engine code: V.

OPTIONAL V-8: Overhead valve with hemispherical segment combustion chambers. Cast-iron block. Displacement: 426 cid. Bore and stroke: 4.25 x 3.75 inches. Compression ratio: 10.20:1. Brake hp: 425 at 5000 rpm. Taxable hp: 57.80. Torque: 490 at 4000 rpm. Five main bearings. Hydraulic valve lifters. Carburetor: Dual Carter AFB 3084-S four-barrel. Engine code: R.

PLYMOUTH

OPTIONS

A01 light group ($26.55). A04 basic group ($198.50). A31 high-performance axle package ($102.15, but not available with H51). A32 super performance axle package with 440-cid V-8, but not available with H51 or A35 ($250.65). A32 super performance axle package with 426-cid Hemi V-8, but not available with H51 or A35 ($221.40). A36 performance axle package with 440-cid V-8 plus D34 ($92.25). A36 performance axle package with 426-cid Hemi V-8 plus D34 ($64.40). B41 front disc brakes, with B51 required ($27.90). B51 power brakes ($42.95). C13 front shoulder belts ($26.45). C14 rear shoulder belts ($26.45). C15 deluxe seat belts ($13.75). C16 console ($54.45). C21 center seat and folding armrest ($4.60). C62 Comfort position manual six-way seat adjuster ($33.30). C92 Color-keyed carpet protection mats ($13.60). D21 four-speed manual transmission (no charge). D34 Torqueflite 727 automatic trans ($227.05). D91 sure grip differential ($42.35). E74 426 Hemi V-8 ($710.60, but not available with three-speed manual transmission, air conditioning, A35 or N88). E87 440+6 wedge engine ($119.05, but not available with three-speed manual transmission, air conditioning or N88). F11 50-amp alternator ($11). F25 70-amp battery ($12.95, but standard with E74). G11 tinted glass-all ($40.70). G15 tinted windshield ($25.90). G31 manual outside right mirror ($6.85). G33 remote control outside left mirror ($10.45). H31 rear window defogger ($26.25). H51 Air conditioning, D34 required ($357.65). J41 pedal dress-up ($5.45). J45 hood hold-down pins ($15.40). J55 undercoating with underhood pad ($16.60). L42 headlights time delay and warning signal ($18.20). M05 door edge protectors ($4.65). M07 B-pillar mouldings ($4.25). M31 bodyside belt moldings ($13.60). M83 rear bumper guards ($16). N42 bright exhaust trumpets ($20.80, but not available in California and standard with 426 Hemi V-8). N85 tachometer with clock ($68.45). N88 automatic speed control ($57.95, but not available with 440 Six-Pack or 426 Hemi V-8s). N95 California emissions package ($37.85). N96 air grabber hood scoop ($65.55). N97 noise reduction package, required in California (no charge). P31 power windows ($105.20). R11 AM radio ($61.55). R21 AM/FM radio ($134.95). R22 AM/tape ($196.25). R31 rear speakers ($14.05). S77 power steering ($105.20). S81 3-spoke wood grain steering wheel ($26.75). S83 2-spoke rim-blow steering wheel ($19.15). V21 performance hood paint ($18.05). W11 14-inch deluxe wheel covers or 15-inch with 426-cid Hemi V-8 ($24.60). W15 14-inch deep-dish wheel covers ($64.10). W21 rally road wheels ($43.10). W23 14-inch chrome styled road wheels ($86.15, but not available with 426-cid Hemi V-8). Accent stripes ($15.15). High impact paint colors ($14.05). Two-tone paint ($28.30). Vinyl roof ($95.70).

1970 ROAD RUNNER 383/440 SIX-PACK/HEMI

JERRY HEASLEY

1970 Road Runner 440

Plymouth's "beep-beep" bomb still did a great job of kicking its feathers up in the stoplight grand prix in 1970, "It's no longer just a stripped down Belvedere with a big engine and heavy suspension" A. B. Shuman pointed out in *Motor Trend*.

Like the GTO, the Road Runner got a few more creature comforts each year to widen its market niche, but the underhood hardware remained impressive, as did the performance figures. Plymouth's Spartan muscle car did continue its traditional use of the same basic Belvedere body. Standard Road Runner equipment was listed in *Car Fax* as: a three-speed manual transmission with floor-mounted gear shift, front armrests, rear armrests, a cigar lighter, a glove box light, the famous "beep-beep" horn, a high-performance hood, front bumper guards, a 150-mph speedometer, Road Runner emblems, the 383-cid/335-hp Road Runner V-8, F70-14 white-line tires on wide safety rim wheels, three-speed windshield wipers, roof-drip rail and upper door-frame moldings and heavy-duty shock absorbers all around. Power train options included a 440 "Six-Pak" V-8 with 390 hp and a 426-cid/425-hp Hemi. With the optional 440 engine you could nail down 6.6-second 0-to-60 runs and a 14.4-second quarter at 99 mph.

There were again three Road Runner models. To a degree, it seemed as if Plymouth was gradually losing sight of the Road Runner's original concept of being a "real" muscle car with a low price tag. Replacing the four-speed manual transmission with a three-speed gearbox was one sign of this. Another was the use of hydraulic valve lifters on the Hemi.

Series Number	Body/Style Number	Body Type & Seating	Factory Price	Shipping Weight	Production Total
ROAD RUNNER — SERIES RM — 383 V-8					
RM	21	2d Cpe	$2,896	3,450 lbs.	14,018
RM	23	2d HT-5P	$3,034	3,475 lbs.	19,695
RM	23	2d Conv-5P	$3,289	3,550 lbs.	647
ROAD RUNNER — SERIES RM — 440 SIX-PACK V-8					
RM	21	2d Cpe	$3,146	—	651
RM	23	2d HT-5P	$3,284	—	1,130
RM	23	2d Conv-5P	$3,539	—	34
ROAD RUNNER — SERIES RM — 426 HEMI V-8					
RM	21	2d Cpe	$3,737	—	74
RM	23	2d HT-5P	$3,875	—	75
RM	23	2d Conv-5P	$4,130	—	3

NOTE 1: Prices include cost of the indicated engine and no other options.

NOTE 2: U.S. production only; one additional Hemi was made for Canada.

NOTE 3: The 440 Six-Pack cars with four-speed manual transmission included 429 coupes, 697 hardtops and 20 convertibles.

NOTE 4: Hemi Road Runners with four-speed manual transmission included 44 coupes, 59 hardtops and one convertible.

ENGINES

BASE V-8: Overhead valve. Cast-iron block. Displacement: 383 cid. Bore and stroke: 4.25 x 3.38 inches. Compression ratio: 8.70:1. Brake hp: 290 at 4400 rpm. Taxable hp: 57.80. Torque: 390 at 2800 rpm Five main bearings. Hydraulic valve lifters. Carburetor: Carter BBD-4613-S two-barrel (Federal). Engine code: L.

OPTIONAL V-8: Overhead valve. Cast-iron block. Bore and stroke: 4.32 x 3.75 inches. Displacement: 440 cid. Compression ratio: 10.50:1. Brake hp: 390 at 4700 rpm. Taxable hp: 59.70. Torque: 490 at 3200 rpm. Five main bearings. Hydraulic valve lifters. Carburetor: three Holley two-barrel. Engine code: V.

OPTIONAL V-8: Overhead valve with hemispherical segment combustion chambers. Cast-iron block. Displacement: 426 cid. Bore and stroke: 4.25 x 3.75

inches. Compression ratio: 10.20:1. Brake hp: 425 at 5000 rpm. Taxable hp: 57.80. Torque: 490 at 4000 rpm. Five main bearings. Hydraulic valve lifters. Carburetor: Dual Carter AFB 3084-S four-barrel. Engine code: R.

OPTIONS

A01 light group ($26.55). A04 basic group ($198.50). A31 high-performance axle package ($102.15, but not available with H51). A32 super performance axle package with 440-cid V-8, but not available with H51 or A35 ($250.65). A32 super performance axle package with 426-cid Hemi V-8, but not available with H51 or A35 ($221.40). A36 performance axle package with 440-cid V-8 plus D34 ($92.25). A36 performance axle package with 426-cid Hemi V-8 plus D34 ($64.40). B41 front disk brakes, with B51 required ($27.90). B51 power brakes ($42.95). C13 front shoulder belts ($26.45). C14 rear shoulder belts ($26.45). C15 deluxe seat belts ($13.75). C16 console ($54.45). C21 center seat and folding armrest ($4.60). C62 Comfort position manual six-way seat adjuster ($33.30). C92 Color-keyed carpet protection mats ($13.60). D21 four-speed manual transmission (no charge). D34 Torqueflite727 automatic trans ($227.05). D91 sure grip differential ($42.35). E74 426 Hemi V-8 ($841.05, but not available with three-speed manual transmission, air conditioning, A35 or N88). E87 440+6 wedge engine ($249.55, but not available with three-speed manual transmission, air conditioning or N88). F11 50-amp alternator ($11). F25 70-amp battery ($12.95, but standard withE74). G11 tinted glass-all ($40.70). G15 tinted windshield ($25.90). G31 manual outside right mirror ($6.85). G33 remote control outside left mirror ($10.45). H31 rear window defogger ($26.25). H51Air conditioning, D34 required ($357.65). J41 pedal dress-up ($5.45). J45 hood hold-down pins ($15.40). J55 undercoating with underhood pad ($16.60). L42 headlights time delay and warning signal ($18.20). M05 door edge protectors ($4.65). M07 B-pillar mouldings ($4.25). M31 bodyside belt moldings ($13.60). M83 rear bumper guards ($16). N42 bright exhaust trumpets ($20.80, but not available in California and standard with 426 Hemi V-8). N85 tachometer withclock ($68.45). N88 automatic speed control ($57.95, but not available with 440 Six-Pack or 426 Hemi V-8s). N95 California emissions package ($37.85). N96 air grabber hood scoop ($65.55). N97 noise reduction package, required in California (no charge). P31 power windows ($105.20). R11 AM radio($61.55). R21 AM/FM radio ($134.95). R22 AM/tape ($196.25). R31 rear speakers ($14.05). S77 power steering ($105.20). S81 3-spoke wood grain steering wheel ($26.75). S83 2-spoke rim-blow steering wheel ($19.15). V21 performance hood paint ($18.05). W11 14-inch deluxe wheel covers or 15-inch with 426-cid Hemi V-8 ($24.60). W15 14-inch deep-dish wheel covers ($64.10). W21 rally road wheels ($43.10). W23 14-inch chrome styled road wheels ($86.15, but not available with 426-cid Hemi V-8). Accent stripes ($15.15). High impact paint colors ($14.05). Two-tone paint ($28.30). Vinyl roof ($95.70).

1970 SUPERBIRD 383/440/HEMI

"The Superbird in concept is a vehicle for the raw competition of NASCAR tracks," suggested _Road Test_ magazine in 1970. "But in street versions, it is also a fun car when you get used to being stared at." We had a neighbor in 1970 who had a true "street" version of the car. He bought it at a clear-out price and let it sit out on the street all winter. Naturally, it went downhill fast. If only we had known then what the Mopar fans know now.

The 1970 Plymouth Road Runner Superbird was the final volley in the battle of muscle-car aerodynamics. With a 7.0-liter engine-displacement limit, competing automakers armed themselves with more wind-cheating body designs, culminating with the "winged warriors" from Chrysler — the 1969 Dodge Charger Daytona and 1970 Plymouth Road Runner Superbird. Designed for use on the NASCAR Grand National superspeedway oval tracks, these Mopars featured a long, peaked nose and a high airfoil on struts above the rear deck. Though similar in

concept, the 1970 Plymouth Superbird and 1969 Dodge Daytona shared little in the way of specialized parts. The noses, airfoil and the basic sheet metal of the Charger and Road Runner two-door hardtops differed. The nose added 19 inches of length.

Rules in 1969 called for only 500 copies of each model to be made to make it "legal" for racing. For 1970, manufacturers had to build one for each dealer. Experts believe that, when it was all over, a total of 1,935 Superbirds were built.

The most popular engine was the 440-cid Super Commando V-8 with a single four-barrel carburetor. It was rated at 375 hp. The racing cars used the Hemi racing engine. Plymouth intermediates were redesigned for 1971 and, with the performance market shrinking and budgets for racing being shifted to meeting Federal safety and emission standards, there was no follow-up to the Superbird. That made the limited-edition Mopar winged machines among the first muscle cars to start climbing in collector value.

PLYMOUTH

PHIL KUNZ

1970 Superbird

Road Test magazine tested the Superbird with the base 440 four-barrel V-8 in April 1970. It turned a 14.26-second quarter mile at 103.7 mph. The Hemi version was put to the test by *Car & Driver*. It did 0-to-60 in 4.8 seconds and turned in a 13.5-second quarter-mile run at 105 mph.

Series Number	Body/Style Number	Body Type & Seating	Factory Price	Shipping Weight	Production Total
ROAD RUNNER SUPER BIRD — SERIES RM — V-8 440					
RM	23	2d HT-5P	$4,298	3,785 lbs.	1,084
ROAD RUNNER SUPER BIRD — SERIES RM —V-8 440 (SIX-PACK)					
RM	23	2d HT-5P	$4,548	—	716
ROAD RUNNER SUPER BIRD — SERIES RM — V-8 426 HEMI					
RM	23	2d HT-5P	$5,139	—	135

NOTE 1: Prices include cost of the indicated engine and no other options.
NOTE 2: U.S. production only; one additional Hemi was made for Canada.
NOTE 3: 440 four-barrel cars with four-speed manual transmission totaled 466.
NOTE 4: 440 Six-Pack cars with four-speed manual transmission totaled 308.
NOTE 5: 440 four-barrel cars with four-speed manual transmission totaled 58.

ENGINES

BASE V-8: Overhead valve. Cast-iron block. Bore and stroke: 4.32 x 3.75 inches. Displacement: 440 cid. Compression ratio: 9.70:1. Brake hp: 375 at 4600 rpm. Taxable hp: 59.70. Torque: 480 at 2800 rpm. Five main bearings. Hydraulic valve lifters. Carburetor: Carter AVS-4737-S four-barrel (Federal). Engine code: U.

OPTIONAL V-8: Overhead valve. Cast-iron block. Bore and stroke: 4.32 x 3.75 inches. Displacement: 440 cid. Compression ratio: 10.50:1. Brake hp: 390 at 4700 rpm. Taxable hp: 59.70. Torque: 490 at 3200 rpm. Five main bearings. Hydraulic valve lifters. Carburetor: three Holley two-barrel. Engine code: V.

OPTIONAL V-8: Overhead valve with hemispherical segment combustion chambers. Cast-iron block. Displacement: 426 cid. Bore and stroke: 4.25 x 3.75

inches. Compression ratio: 10.20:1. Brake hp: 425 at 5000 rpm. Taxable hp: 57.80. Torque: 490 at 4000 rpm. Five main bearings. Hydraulic valve lifters. Carburetor: Dual Carter AFB 3084-S four-barrel. Engine code: R.

OPTIONS

A01 light group ($26.55). A36 performance axle package with 426-cid Hemi V-8 plus D34 ($64.40). B41 front disk brakes, with B51 required ($27.90). B51 power brakes ($42.95). C13 front shoulder belts ($26.45). C14 rear shoulder belts ($26.45). C15 deluxe seat belts ($13.75). C16 console ($54.45). C21 center seat and folding armrest ($4.60). C62 Comfort position manual six-way seat adjuster ($33.30). C92 Color-keyed carpet protection mats ($13.60). D21 four-speed manual transmission (no charge). D34 Torqueflite 727 automatic transmission ($227.05). D91 sure grip differential ($42.35). E74 426 Hemi V-8 ($841.05, but not available with three-speed manual transmission, air conditioning, A35 or N88). E87 440+6 wedge engine ($249.55, but not available with three-speed manual transmission, air conditioning or N88). F11 50-amp alternator ($11). F25 70-amp battery ($12.95, but standard with E74). G11 tinted glass-all ($40.70). G15 tinted windshield ($25.90). G31 manual outside right mirror ($6.85). G33 remote control outside left mirror ($10.45). H31 rear window defogger ($26.25). J41 pedal dress-up ($5.45). J45 hood hold-down pins ($15.40). J55 undercoating with underhood pad ($16.60). L42 headlights time delay and warning signal ($18.20). M05 door edge protectors ($4.65). M07 B-pillar mouldings ($4.25). M31 bodyside belt mouldings ($13.60). M83 rear bumper guards ($16). N42 bright exhaust trumpets ($20.80, but not available in California and standard with 426 Hemi V-8). N85 tachometer withclock ($68.45). N95 California emissions package ($37.85). N97 noise reduction package, required in California (no charge). P31 power windows ($105.20). R11 AM radio($61.55). R21 AM/FM radio ($134.95). R22 AM/tape ($196.25). R31 rear speakers ($14.05). S77 power steering ($105.20). S8 13-spoke wood grain steering wheel ($26.75). S83 Two-spoke rim-blow steering wheel ($19.15). W15 14-inch deep-dish wheel covers ($64.10). W21 rally road wheels ($43.10). W23 14-inch chrome styled road wheels ($86.15, but not available with 426-cid Hemi V-8). Accent stripes ($15.15). High impact paint colors ($14.05). Two-tone paint ($28.30). Vinyl roof ($95.70).

1971 'CUDA 340

JERRY HEASLEY

1971 'Cuda 340

Some people confuse the term "muscle car" with "race car" and they shouldn't. Race cars have one purpose in life and muscle cars have many. For many enthusiasts in the '60s, a muscle car took them to work all week, to the supermarket on Saturday and to the drag strip on "Sunday . . . Sunday . . . Sunday!" One of the best of these multi-purpose muscle machines was the 'Cuda 340.

"The 'Cuda 340 is the kind of car a person could like," said auto writer Steve Kelly in the January 1971 issue of *Hot Rod* magazine. "It runs low-14 without breathing hard, takes corners without yelling and is big enough to be seen." Kelly admitted that the 'Cuda 340 was not the ultimate Trans-Am racer, but he also pointed out that it could beat a stock Camaro Z/28 or Mustang Boss 302 through the quarter-mile.

Standard equipment on the 'Cuda included all Barracuda features plus a performance hood, chrome wheel lip and body-sill moldings, a color-keyed grille, a black-out-style rear deck panel, a heavy-duty suspension front and rear, heavy-duty brakes, 'Cuda ornamentation and whitewall tires as a no-cost option. The 383-cid V-8 was again standard and the 340-cid four-barrel V-8 was a no charge option.

Hot Rod managed to turn in a best run of 14.18 seconds for the quarter-mile (100.33 mph) with its 1971 'Cuda 340 after emptying the trunk and removing the air cleaner element.

Series Number	Body/Style Number	Body Type & Seating	Factory Price	Shipping Weight	Production Total
'Cuda — SERIES BS — V-8					
BS	23	2d HT-5P	$3,199	3,475 lbs.	3,300
BS	27	Conv-5P	$3,456	3,550 lbs.	140

NOTE 1: Weights shown above are the weights of the base 318-cid V-8 models; prices and production are for 'Cuda 340s.

NOTE 2: Production of 'Cuda 340 hardtops included 151 cars with three-speed manual transmission, 1,141 cars with four-speed manual transmission and 2,008 cars with automatic.

NOTE 3: Production of 'Cuda 340 convertibles included 8 cars with three-speed manual transmission, 30 cars with four-speed manual transmission and 102 cars with automatic.

ENGINE

OPTIONAL V-8: Overhead valve. Cast-iron block. Bore and stroke: 4.04 x 3.31 inches. Displacement: 340 cid. Compression ratio: 10.50:1. Brake hp: 275 at 5000 rpm. Taxable hp: 52.20. Torque: 340 at 3200 rpm. Five main bearings. Hydraulic valve lifters. Carburetor: Carter Thermo-Quad TQ-4972-S four-barrel. Engine code: H.

OPTIONS

Power brakes ($43). Power steering ($90. Air conditioning ($357). Black air scoop, quarter panel and lower body paint ($36). Automatic speed control ($58). Heavy-duty brakes ($23). Front disc brakes ($28). Rear window defogger, all except convertible ($27). Racing mirrors, left-hand remote control ($11). Color-keyed racing mirrors, left-hand remote control ($26). Sport striping, 'Cuda without side molding vinyl insert ($26). Power windows ($105). Solid state AM radio, all models ($62). Multiplex AM/FM stereo system ($214). Vinyl bench seat with armrest and folding cushion ($17). Leather bucket seat with consolette ($119). Leather bucket seat in convertible ($65). Shaker hood fresh air package ($97). Floral vinyl roof ($96). Deluxe wheel covers ($16). Wire wheel covers ($50). Rally Road Wheels ($33). Chrome Road Wheels ($50). Super Track Pak racing equipment package ($236). TorqueFlite automatic transmission ($191-$227). Four-speed manual floor shift transmission, prices vary with model and engine ($188-$197). 340-cid V-8 engine ($44.35). Heavy-duty, 70-amp battery ($13). Heavy-duty, 59-amp ($13). Heavy-duty 50-amp alternator ($11-$15). Sure-Grip positive traction rear axle ($42). Evaporative emissions control system ($38). Available rear axle gear ratios: 2.76:1 or 3.55:1 optional ($10).

1971 'CUDA 440 SIX-PACK/HEMI

PLYMOUTH

1971 Hemi 'Cuda

Drag racers like Sox & Martin and PeeWee Wallace were burning up the drag strips in Barracudas back in 1971 and also helping to generate interest in Plymouth's "fish car." A lot of that interest went to non-Hemi-powered cars, however, as the $884 Hemi option was ordered for very few cars.

Paul Zazarine — a name well known to muscle car lovers — put it this way in *Musclecar Review* magazine, "If you're looking for the ultimate Mopar, look no further than the Hemi 'Cuda."

The 1971 Hemi engine featured a 10.2:1 compression ratio and a single four-barrel carburetor. It came attached to either a four-speed manual gear box or an automatic transmission. The standard rear axle had a 3.23:1 ratio. Sure-Grip-only options included 3.55:1, 3.54:1 and 4.10:1. Plymouth's nifty S15 heavy-duty suspension package was standard with Hemi 'Cudas. After model year 1971, Plymouth continued to offer Barracudas, but Hemi versions and convertibles didn't make the cut after the season came to its end. When the Hemi V-8 was ordered, tires were upgraded to G70-14 raised-white-letter models.

Standard Barracuda equipment included dual headlights, dual horns, hub caps, an inside day/night rearview mirror, a brake-on warning light, a left-hand outside rearview mirror, a fuel gauge, a temperature gauge, an ammeter, bucket seats, a cigar lighter, a heater-and-droster, two-speed electric windsield wipers, a six-cylinder or 318-cid V-8 engine and 7.35 x 14 polyester black sidewall tires. The 'Cuda added chrome wheel lip moldings, chrome sill moldings, a performance-style hood, a color-keyed grille, a black rear deck lid panel, heavy-duty suspension, heavy-duty brakes, a 383-cid four-barrel V-8, F70 x 14 bias-belted black sidewall tires and 'Cuda ornamentation. F78 x 14 tires were a no-cost option.

If you wanted the 340-cid high-performance small-block V-8 in place of the standard (in 'Cudas) 383-cid big-block, it was a no-cost option. Unlike 1970, the 440 four-barrel V-8 was no longer an offical Barracuda option, nor were any such cars built (Chrysler sometimes built cars that didn't appear in sales catalogs.) However, the 440 Six-Pack could still be had. Considering that it gave almost-Hemi-like performance, this engine was an absolute bargain for the go-fast set. When the 440 Six-Pack V-8 was ordered, tires were upgraded to G70-14 raised-white-letter models.

Series Number	Body/Style Number	Body Type & Seating	Factory Price	Shipping Weight	Production Total
'Cuda — SERIES BS — V-8 (SIX-PACK)					
BS	23	2d HT-5P	$3,403	3,475 lbs.	237
BS	27	2d Conv-5P	$3,665	3,550 lbs.	17

NOTE 1: Prices include 440 Six-Pack V-8 and no other options.
NOTE 2: Weights are for base 383-cid V-8 models and should be close to 440 weight.
NOTE 3: Production included 108 hardtops and five convertibles with four-speed manual transmission.

ENGINES

OPTIONAL V-8: Overhead valve. Cast-iron block. Bore and stroke: 4.32 x 3.75 inches. Displacement: 440 cid. Compression ratio: 10.30:1. Brake hp: 385 at 4700 rpm. Taxable hp: 59.70. Torque: 490 at 3200 rpm. Five main bearings. Hydraulic valve lifters. Carburetor: three Holley two-barrel. Engine code: V.

OPTIONAL V-8: Overhead valve with hemispherical segment combustion chambers. Cast-iron block. Displacement: 426 cid. Bore and stroke: 4.25 x 3.75 inches. Compression ratio: 10.20:1. Brake hp: 425 at 5000 rpm. Taxable hp: 57.80. Torque: 490 at 4000 rpm. Five main bearings. Hydraulic valve lifters. Carburetor: Dual Carter AFB 3084-S four-barrel. Engine code: R.

OPTIONS

Hemi V-8 ($883.90 and not available with three-speed manual transmission, air conditioning, automatic speed control or trailer tow package). Power brakes ($43). Power steering ($90). Black air scoop, quarter panel and lower body paint ($36). Heavy-duty brakes ($23). Front disc brakes ($28). Rear window defogger, all except convertible ($27). Racing mirrors, left-hand

PLYMOUTH

remote control ($11). Color-keyed racing mirrors, left-hand remote control ($26). Sport striping for 'Cuda without side molding vinyl insert ($26). Power windows ($105). Solid state AM radio ($62). Multiplex AM/FM stereo system ($214). Vinyl bench seat with armrest and folding cushion ($17). Leather bucket seat with consolette ($119). Leather bucket seat in convertible ($65). Shaker hood fresh air package ($97). Floral vinyl roof ($96). Deluxe wheel covers ($16). Wire wheel covers ($50). Rally Road Wheels ($33). Chrome Road Wheels ($50). Super Track Pak racing equipment package ($236). TorqueFlite automatic transmission ($191-$227). Four-speed manual floor shift transmission, prices vary with model and engine ($188-$197). Heavy-duty, 70-amp battery ($13). Heavy-duty, 59-ampere ($13). Heavy-duty 50-amp alternator ($11-$15). Sure-Grip positive traction rear axle ($42). Evaporative emissions control system ($38). Available rear axle gear ratios: 2.76:1 or 3.55:1 optional ($10).

1971 GTX 440/440 SIX-PACK/426 HEMI

JERRY HEASLEY

1971 GTX

The fancy pants "Road Runner" — the GTX — often went unappreciated in its own era. However, with the same styling, the same engines and a little more bright work, it is starting to attract the attention of collectors today.

A pair of 440s were offered for the hole under the GTX hood and the Hemi could be had, though it rarely was ordered. On paper, the optional Six-Pack version of the 440 lost a few horsepower, but this was nothing to bite your nails about.

The Hemi engine was still available for $746.50. The Air Grabber hood was standard with the Hemi and the four-speed manual gearbox was a no-charge item on Hemi GTXs.

Series Number	Body/Style Number	Body Type & Seating	Factory Price	Shipping Weight	Production Total
GTX — SERIES RS — V-8 440 (FOUR-BARREL)					
RS	23	2d HT-5P	$3,707	3,675 lbs.	2,538
GTX — SERIES RS — V-8 440 (SIX-PACK)					
RS	23	2d HT-5P	$3,832	—	135
HEMI GTX — SERIES RS — V-8 426 HEMI					
RS	23	2d HT-5P	$4,454	—	30

NOTE 1: Prices include cost of the indicated engine and no other options.
NOTE 2: Of the 440 four-barrel cars, 327 had a four-speed manual transmission.
NOTE 3: Of the 440 Six-Pack cars, 62 had a four-speed manual transmission.
NOTE 4: Of the 426 Hemi cars, 11 had a four-speed manual transmission.
NOTE 5: In May 1971 the price of the base 440 four-barrel GTX increased to $3,733.

ENGINES

BASE V-8: Overhead valve. Cast-iron block. Bore and stroke: 4.32 x 3.75 inches. Displacement: 440 cid. Compression ratio: 9.50:1. Brake hp: 370 at 4600 rpm. Taxable hp: 59.70. Torque: 480 at 3200 rpm. Five main bearings. Hydraulic valve lifters. Carburetor: Carter AVS-4967-S four-barrel. Engine code: U.

OPTIONAL V-8: Overhead valve. Cast-iron block. Bore and stroke: 4.32 x 3.75 inches. Displacement: 440 cid. Compression ratio: 10.30:1. Brake hp: 385 at 4700 rpm. Taxable hp: 59.70. Torque: 490 at 3200 rpm. Five main bearings. Hydraulic valve lifters. Carburetor: three Holley two-barrel. Engine code: V.

OPTIONAL V-8: Overhead valve with hemispherical segment combustion chambers. Cast-iron block. Displacement: 426 cid. Bore and stroke: 4.25 x 3.75 inches. Compression ratio: 10.20:1. Brake hp: 425 at 5000 rpm. Taxable hp: 57.80. Torque: 490 at 4000 rpm. Five main bearings. Hydraulic valve lifters. Carburetor: Dual Carter AFB 3084-S four-barrel. Engine code: R.

OPTION

A01 light group ($31.95). A02 driver aid group ($14.20 with A01 only). A04 basic group ($199.90). A28 noise reduction package ($36.50 and required on California cars with the 440 Six-Pack V-8). A31 high-performance axle package ($81.80 and not available with air conditioning or trailer towing package). A33 track package ($149.80 and not available with air conditioning or four-speed manual transmission). A34 super track pack ($219.30 and not available with air conditioning or four-speed manual transmission). A35 trailer towing package, front disk brakes required ($26.30 and not available with Six-Pack V-8). A36 performance axle package for 440 Six-Pack with automatic transmission ($81.80). A36 performance axle package for 426 Hemi V-8 with automatic transmission ($45.35). B41 front disk brakes, requires power brakes ($22.50). B51 power brakes ($41.55). C16 center console ($57.65). C21 center seat and folding armrest ($57.65). C62 Comfort position manual 6-way seat adjuster ($35). C92 Color-keyed carpet protection mats ($14.25). D21 four-speed manual transmission ($206.40). D34 TorqueFlight 727 automatic transmission ($237.50). D91 sure grip differential ($42.35). E74 426-cid Hemi engine ($746.50). E87 440 Six-Pack wedge V-8 ($125). F11 50-amp alternator ($11.80). F25 70-amp battery, standard with 426 Hemi V-8 ($14.80 otherwise). G11 all tinted glass ($43.40). G15 tinted windshield only ($29.80). G31 chrome right-hand outside rearview mirror, requires matching left-hand mirror ($11.75). G33 chrome left-hand outside rearview mirror ($16.25). G36 dual colored-keyed remote-control rearview mirrors ($11.75). H31 rear window defogger ($31.34). H41 strato ventilation ($18.20). H51 Air conditioning ($383.25, but not available with GTX with manual transmission).

PLYMOUTH

J21 electric clock, not available with tachometer ($18.45). J25 Variable speed wiper with electric washer ($5.85). J41 Pedal dress-up kit ($5.85). J45 hood hold-down pins ($16.55). J52 inside hood release ($10.55). J55 undercoating with underhood pad ($22.60). J68 backlight louvers ($68.45). L42 nightwatch time delay and warning signal ($19.45). M05 door edge protectors ($6.50). M07 B-pillar mouldings ($4.25). M26 wheel lip mouldings ($14.05). M31 body side belt moldings ($14.60). M51 power sunroof with canopy-style vinyl roof ($455.95). M51 power sunroof with full vinyl roof ($484.65). M73 painted bumpers ($37.85). M75 rear bumper tape treatment ($16.35). M81 front bumper guards ($16.85). M83 rear bumper guards ($16.85). M85 front and rear bumper guards ($33.70). M91 rear deck lid luggage rack ($35). N25 engine block heater ($15.55). N42 decorative exhaust tips ($21.90, but not available in California and standard with Hemi). N85 tachometer ($52.70, but not available with clock). N88 automatic speed control, requires automatic transmis-sion andnot available with 440 Six-Pack or hemi ($60.90). N95 California emissions package ($12.95). N96 air grabber hood scoop ($68.90). N97 noise reduction package, required in California (no charge). P31 power windows ($101.30). R11 AM radio ($66.40). R26 AM radio and tape player ($147.40). R31 rear speakers ($15.05). R33 tape recorder with microphone ($11.70). R35 AM/FM radio ($135.60). R36 AM/FM radio with tape player ($300.10). S62 tilt steering wheel with rim-blow ($55.70). S77 power steering ($96.55). S83 wood grain rim-blow steering wheel ($20.10). S84 "Tuff" Rallye steer-ing wheel ($20.10). W12 14-inch deluxe wheel covers ($27.35). W15 14-inch wire wheel covers ($70.15). W21 Ralley road wheels ($58.95). W23 14-inch chrome styled road wheels, except with Hemi ($90.55). W34 collapsible spare tire ($13.60). Cloth-and-vinyl bench seat (no charge) Accent stripes ($15.15). Full vinyl roof ($95.75). Hood and fender tranverse stripe, not available with Hemi ($22.50). High-impact colors ($15.05). Two-tone paint ($13.10).

1971 ROAD RUNNER 383/440 SIX-PACK/HEMI

JERRY HEASLEY

1971 Road Runner

By 1971, the Coyote clobberer had bred its own cult of Road Runner owners, but high insurance rates were keeping the buyers at bay. The low sales numbers put several models on the endangered species list.

The only body style returning for 1971 in Plymouth's Road Runner line was the two-door hardtop version. Its new grille looked like a big loop around the front of the car. The Road Runner's totally revised sheet metal was shared with the Se-bring and Sebring Plus coupes. The sedan and convertible did not get translated onto the newly designed Mopar mid-size body shell. With the more expensive GTX still around, the Road Runner again filled its low-priced muscle car niche with its trick "beep-beep" horn, hot graphics and other solid per-formance.

Standard in the Road Runner model was a 300-hp version of the trusty 383-cid V-8. You could add the 440-cid V-8 or the Hemi. Other interesting options included the "Air Grabber" pop-up hood scoop and a bolt-on rear deck spoiler.

Motor Trend tested the 383 and 440 Road Runners in March 1971. The 383 version used had a 3.91:1 rear, while the 440 version used the 4.10:1 axle. The cars turned out to be evenly matched. Both did 0-to-60 in 6.7 seconds. Quarter-mile comparisons were 14.84 seconds at 94.5 mph for the 383 and 15.02 seconds at 96 mph for the 440.

Series Number	Body/Style Number	Body Type & Seating	Factory Price	Shipping Weight	Production Total
ROAD RUNNER — SERIES RM —V-8 383					
RM	23	2d HT-5P	$3,147	3,640 lbs.	7,952
ROAD RUNNER — SERIES RM — V-8 440 (SIX-PACK)					
RM	23	2d HT-5P	$3,409	—	246
ROAD RUNNER — SERIES RM — V-8 426 HEMI					
RM	23	2d HT-5P	$4,031	—	55

NOTE 1: Prices include cost of the indicated engine and no other options.
NOTE 2: U.S. production only; four additional Hemis were made for Canada.
NOTE 3: The 383 cars included 3,730 with three- or four-speed manual transmissions.
NOTE 4: The 440 Six-Pack cars included 137 with four-speed manual transmission.
NOTE 5: The 426 Hemi cars included 28 with four-speed manual transmission.
NOTE 6: An additional 1,681 Road Runners with a 340 V-8 were built (438 with four-speed manual transmission)

ENGINES

BASE V-8: Overhead valve. Cast-iron block. Bore and stroke: 4.04 x 3.31 inches. Displacement: 340 cid. Compression ratio: 10.50:1. Brake hp: 275 at 5000 rpm. Taxable hp: 52.20. Torque: 340 at 3200 rpm. Five main bearings. Hydraulic valve lifters. Carburetor: Carter Thermo-Quad TQ-4972-S four-barrel. Engine code: H.

OPTIONAL V-8: Overhead valve. Cast-iron block. Displacement: 383 cid. Bore and stroke: 4.25 x 3.38 inches. Compression ratio: 8.50:1. Brake hp: 300 at 4800 rpm. Taxable hp: 57.80. Torque: 410 at 3400 rpm. Five main bearings. Hydraulic valve lifters. Carburetor: Holley R-4668A four-barrel. Engine code: N.

OPTIONAL V-8: Overhead valve. Cast-iron block. Bore and stroke: 4.32 x 3.75 inches. Displacement: 440 cid. Compression ratio: 10.30:1. Brake hp: 385 at 4700 rpm. Taxable hp: 59.70. Torque: 490 at 3200 rpm. Five main bearings. Hydraulic valve lifters. Carburetor: three Holley two-barrel. Engine code: V.

OPTIONAL V-8: Overhead valve with hemispherical segment combustion chambers. Cast-iron block. Displacement: 426 cid. Bore and stroke: 4.25 x 3.75 inches. Compression ratio: 10.20:1. Brake hp: 425 at 5000 rpm. Taxable hp: 57.80. Torque: 490 at 4000 rpm. Five main bearings. Hydraulic valve lifters. Carburetor: Dual Carter AFB 3084-S four-barrel. Engine code: R.

OPTIONS

A01 light group ($31.95). A02 driver aid group ($14.20 with A01 only). A04 basic group ($199.90). A28 noise reduction package ($36.50 and required on California cars with the 440 Six-Pack V-8). A31 high-performance axle package ($81.80 and not available with air conditioning or trailer towing package). A33 track package ($149.80 and not available with air conditioning or four-speed manual transmission). A34 super track pack ($219.30 and not available with air conditioning or four-speed manual transmission). A35 trailer towing package, front disk brakes required ($26.30 and not available with Six-Pack V-8). A36 performance axle package for 440 Six-Pack with automatic transmission ($81.80). A36 performance axle package for 426 Hemi V-8 with automatic transmission ($45.35). B41 front disk brakes, requires power brakes ($22.50). B51 power brakes ($41.55). C16 center console ($57.65). C21 center seat and folding armrest ($57.65). C62 Comfort position manual 6-way seat adjuster ($35). C92 Color-keyed carpet protection mats ($14.25). D21four-speed manual transmission ($206.40). D34 TorqueFlight 727 automatic transmission ($237.50). D91 sure grip differential ($42.35). E74 426-cid Hemi engine ($883.55). E87 440 Six-Pack wedge V-8 ($262.15). F11 50-amp alternator ($11.80). F25 70-amp battery, standard with 426 Hemi V-8

($14.80 otherwise). G11 all tinted glass ($43.40). G15 tinted windshield only ($29.80). G31 chrome right-hand outside rearview mirror, requires matching left-hand mirror ($11.75). G33 chrome left-hand outside rearview mirror ($16.25). G36 dual colored-keyed remote-control rearview mirrors ($11.75). H31 rear window defogger ($31.34). H41 strato ventilation ($18.20). H51 Air conditioning ($383.25, but not available with GTX with manual transmission). J21 electric clock, not available with tachometer ($18.45). J25 Variable speed wiper with electric washer ($5.85). J41 Pedal dress-up kit ($5.85). J45 hood hold-down pins ($16.55). J52 inside hood release ($10.55). J55 undercoating with underhood pad ($22.60). J68 backlight louvers ($68.45). L42 night-watch time delay and warning signal ($19.45). M05 door edge protectors ($6.50). M07 B-pillar mouldings ($4.25). M26 wheel lip mouldings ($14.05). M31 body side belt mouldings ($14.60). M51 power sunroof with canopy-style vinyl roof ($455.95). M51 power sunroof with full vinyl roof ($484.65). M73 painted bumpers ($37.85). M75 rear bumper tape treatment ($16.35). M81 front bumper guards ($16.85). M83 rear bumper guards ($16.85). M85 front and rear bumper guards ($33.70). M91 rear deck lid luggage rack ($35). N25 engine block heater ($15.55). N42 decorative exhaust tips ($21.90, but not available in California and standard with Hemi). N85 tachometer ($52.70, but not available with clock). N88 automatic speed control, requires automatic transmission andnot available with 440 Six-Pack or hemi ($60.90). N95 California emissions package ($12.95). N96 (air grabber hood scoop ($68.90). N97 noise reduction package, required in California (no charge). P31 power windows ($101.30). R11 AM radio ($66.40). R26 AM radio and tape player ($147.40). R31 rear speakers ($15.05). R33 tape recorder with microphone ($11.70). R35 AM/FM radio ($135.60). R36 AM/FM radio with tape player ($300.10). S62 tilt steering wheel with rim-blow ($55.70). S77 power steering ($96.55). S83 wood grain rim-blow steering wheel ($20.10). S84 "Tuff" Rallye steering wheel ($20.10). W12 14-inch deluxe wheel covers ($27.35). W15 14-inch wire wheel covers ($70.15). W21 Ralley road wheels ($58.95). W23 14-inch chrome styled road wheels, except with Hemi ($90.55). W34 collapsible spare tire ($13.60). Cloth-and-vinyl bench seat (no charge) Accent stripes ($15.15). Full vinyl roof ($95.75). Hood and fender tranverse stripe, not available with Hemi ($22.50). High-impact colors ($15.05). Two-tone paint ($13.10).

1972 'CUDA 340

The popularity of Plymouth's sporty compact car, the Barracuda, was in a tailspin by model year 1972. Insurance companies had upped the premiums for anything thought of as a high-performance machine and the government watchdogs joined them in ganging up on the muscle car makers from the safety and emissions angles. It was a year in which car salesmen did not get fat selling Barracudas.

As the sales charts turned red, the Barracuda convertible disappeared, as did the optional 383-, 440-, 440-Six-Pack and 426 Hemi engines for 'Cudas. Luckily, the 340-cid V-8 managed to slip by the gatekeepers. The 'Cuda model included a 340-cid V-8 with a two-barrel carburetor, chrome front and rear wheel lip mouldings, chrome body sill mouldings, a performance hood, a color-keyed grille, a black rear deck panel, heavy-duty suspension and brakes, an electronic ignition system and F70 x 14 white sidewall tires. A four-barrel version of the 340 was the only engine option. It was available for a special price in the 'Cuda and cost more for other Barracudas. The A36 performance axle package could be ordered for all cars with 340-cid four-barrel engines. A four-speed manual gearbox was available only for 340-cid four-barrel cars. TorqueFlite was another extra for cars with that engine. Other than stripes, styled chrome rims or rallye road wheels

and front disc brakes, there was little left in the way of high-performance options.

The '72 'Cuda 340 with the four-barrel carburetor was rated for 240 net SAE hp. Weighing in at around 3,625 lbs., it carried about 15.1 lbs. per horsepower and could do 0-to-60 mph in 8.5 seconds. The quarter-mile took 16.3 seconds. Hey, it was 1972!

Series Number	Body/Style Number	Body Type & Seating	Factory Price	Shipping Weight	Production Total
'Cuda — SERIES BS — V-8					
BS	23	2d HT-5P	$3,239	3,195 lbs.	5,864

NOTE 1: Production of 'Cuda 340 hardtops included 4,163 cars with manual transmission and 1,701 cars with automatic.

ENGINE

OPTIONAL V-8: Overhead valve. Cast-iron block. Bore and stroke: 4.04 x 3.31 inches. Displacement: 340 cid. Compression ratio: 8.50:1. Net brake hp: 240 at 4800 rpm. Net torque: 290 at 3600 rpm. Five main bearings. Hydraulic valve lifters. Carburetor: Carter Thermo-Quad TQ-6139-S four-barrel. Engine code: H.

OPTIONS

H51 air conditioner ($364.80). D51 2.76:1 axle ratio ($12.20). D53 3.23:1 axle ratio ($12.20). F25 70-amp battery ($13.30). M85 front and rear bumper guards ($26.65). J21 electric clock ($15.70). C16 console ($51.60). H31 rear window defogger ($28.15). D91 Sure-Grip differential, included with A36 performance axle package ($40.65). E55 340-cid four-barrel V-8 in place of standard V-8 in 'Cuda ($209.70). N95 exhaust emissions control test ($25.55).

G15 tinted windshield glass ($24.35). G11 tinted glass all windows ($35.85). J52 inside hood release ($9.50). N23 electronic ignition (standard in 'Cuda). J11 glove box lock ($3.95). G33 remote-control racing mirror ($14.60). G35 dual color-keyed or chrome racing mirrors, left-hand remote controlled with basic group ($10.50). G35 dual color-keyed or chrome racing mirrors, left-hand remote controlled without basic group ($25.10). M25 Custom sill moldings ($12.70). M05 door edge protection moldings ($5.80). M26 wheel opening moldings ($7.25). High-impact paint colors ($13.45). V21 hood performance paint, 'Cuda only ($17.30). J54 performance hood (standard on 'Cuda). B41 front disc brakes ($68.05). S77 power steering ($104.10). R11 AM radio ($59.40). R26 AM radio with stereo tape and basic group ($136.85). R26 AM radio with stereo tape without basic group ($196.25). R35 AM/FM stereo and basic group ($132). R35 AM/FM radio with stereo tape without basic group ($191.40). R31 rear seat speaker ($13.45). R32 dual rear seat speakers ($24.35). J97 Rallye instrument panel with basic group ($74.70). J97 Rallye instrument panel without basic group ($85.70). Vinyl roof ($80.20).

N51 power sun roof with vinyl roof ($434). D34 Torqueflite automatic transmission ($223.30). Four-speed manual transmission ($192.85). J55 undercoating and underhood pad ($20.25). W11 deluxe wheel covers ($24.50). W23 chrome styled Road Wheels ($81.10). W21 Rallye Road wheels with basic group ($28.35). W21 Rallye Road wheels with basic groupe ($52.80). J25 variable speed windshield wipers ($10.35). A04 basic group including power steering, AM radio, variabler-speed windshield wipers with electric wahers and dual racing mirrors ($188.45). A01 light package includes fender-mounted turn signals, trunk light, glove box light, ash tray light, ignition switch warn ing light with time delay, instrument panel flood lamp with time delay, map light and courtesy light ($35). A36 performance axle package, includes 3.55:1 heavy-duty axle ratio, Sure Grip differential, 26-inch high-performance radiator and fan shroud, with 340-four-barrel V-8 only ($59.90). A51 Sports Decor group,includes sport hood, wheel lip moldings, sill moldings and body side tape stripes with 340 four-barrel V-8 ($47.70). F70-14 whitewalls ($11.25 extra).

1972 ROAD RUNNER 340-4/400-4

JERRY HEASLEY

1972 Road Runner 440

This "momentum muscle car" struggled valiantly to keep alive the dwindling interest in high-performance motoring. For 1972, the Road Runner received minor cosmetic changes. The equipment list started with a 400-cid four-barrel V-8. The Code E86 440-cid V-8 with a single four-barrel carburetor was optional in the Road Runner, but could not be ordered in combination with the three-speed manual transmission. Also available for those wanting small-block muscle was the 340-cid high-performance V-8 with a four-barrel. You had to add either a four-speed manual gearbox or TorqueFlite automatic. Plymouth sales literature did not list the output for this engine,

but other sources put it at 280 net hp at 4800 rpm and 375 net lbs.-ft. of torque at 3200 rpm.

An "Air-Grabber" hood scoop could be substituted for the regular style. In this case, a different optional tape stripe treatment was used. A 3.23:1 axle was standard and options in that department included a 2.76:1 that was available with the 340- and 400-cid four-barrel V-8s only.

Performance numbers were published for the '72 Road Runner with the 340-cid/240-hp V-8. It went from a standing start to 60 mph in 7.8 seconds. The quarter-mile was eaten up in 15.5 seconds at 90 mph.

Series Number	Body/Style Number	Body Type & Seating	Factory Price	Shipping Weight	Production Total
ROAD RUNNER — SERIES RM — V-8					
RM	23	2d HT-5P	$3,095	3,495 lbs.	7,628

NOTE 1: Price and weight are for base 400-cid version.

NOTE 2: Production total is for all Road Runners.

NOTE 3: 672 of these cars had the new GTX-Road Runner option.

ENGINES

BASE V-8: Overhead valve. Cast-iron block. Bore and stroke: 4.04 x 3.31 inches. Displacement: 340 cid. Compression ratio: 8.50:1. Net brake hp: 240 at 4800 rpm. Net torque: 290 at 3600 rpm. Five main bearings. Hydraulic valve lifters. Carburetor: Carter Thermo-Quad TQ-6139-S four-barrel. Engine code: H.

OPTIONAL V-8: Overhead valve. Cast-iron block. Bore and stroke: 4.34 x 3.38 inches. Displacement: 400 cid. Compression ratio: 8.2:1. Net brake hp: 255 at 4800 rpm (250 hp in Fury). Net torque: 340 at 3200 rpm. Five main bearings. Hydraulic valve lifters. Carburetor: Carter Thermo-Quad TQ-6090-S four-barrel. Engine code: P.

OPTIONAL V-8: Overhead valve. Cast-iron block. Bore and stroke: 4.32 x 3.75 inches. Displacement: 440 cid. Compression ratio: 8.20:1. Net brake hp: 280 at 4800 rpm. Net torque: 375 at 3200 rpm. Five main bearings. Hydraulic valve lifters. Carburetor: Holley R-6160A four-barrel. Enging code: U. (NOTE: Some sources do not list the 440 Six-Pack V-8 as available. Other sources say that it was available, but that buyers who ordered a 440 Six-Pack car often, or always, received a 440 four-barrel car instead.)

OPTIONS

H51 air conditioner ($386.45). N96 Air Grabber hood scoop (($67.40, but not available with air conditioning or E68 or E86 in California). D51 2.76:1 axle ratio, for Road Runner with 340-4 or 400-4 with B41 and D34 required ($13.30). F25 70-amp battery ($14.50). M85 front and rear bumper guards ($32.90). J21 electric clock ($18.05 and not with tachometer). C16 console ($56.35). H31 rear window defogger ($30.75). D91 Sure-Grip differential, included with performance axle package ($44.75). E55 340-cid four-barrel V-8 in place of standard V-8 ($63.75, but not with three-speed manual transmission.) E86 440-cid four-barrel V-8 ($1152.70, but not available with three-speed manual transmission). N95 exhaust emissions control G15 tinted windshield glass ($29.10). G11 tinted glass all windows ($42.45). J45 hood pins ($16.20). J52 inside hood release ($10.35). N23 electronic ignition (standard in Road Runner). C92 accessory floor mats($13.95). G35 remote-controlled left-hand racing mirror ($15.95). G36 remote-controlled left-hand and dual racing mirrors ($27.45 without basic group). G36 remote-controlled left-hand and dual racing mirrors ($11.55 with basic group). G41 day/night inside rearview mirror ($6.85, but standard with basic group.) M31 belt molding ($14.30). M25 Custom sill moldings ($21.80). M05 door edge protection moldings ($6.35). Vinyl body side moldings ($15.15). M26 wheel opening moldings ($15.75). High-impact paint colors ($13.45). V21 hood-and-fender tape stripe ($22). V25 rear deck tape treatment ($21.55 and requires N96 and V21). S77 power steering ($113.70). R11 AM radio ($64.90). R26 AM radio with stereo tape and basic group ($149.45). R26 AM radio with stereo tape without basic group ($214.30). R35 AM/FM stereo and basic group ($144.15). R35 AM/FM stereo without basic group ($209.05). R36 AM/FM stereo with stereo tape and basic group ($293.45). R35 AM/FM radio with stereo tape without basic group ($358.30). R31 rear seat speaker ($14.70). R32 dual rear seat speakers ($26.60). Vinyl roof ($93.65). C21 center cushion and folding arm rest ($56.35). N88 automatic speed control ($63.45). M51 power sunroof with canopy vinyl roof ($445.90). M51 power sun roof with full vinyl roof ($474.05). N85 tachometer with clock ($51.55). D34 Torqueflite automatic transmission ($231.65). Four-speed manual transmission ($201.85). J55 undercoating and underhood pad ($22.15). W11 deluxe wheel covers ($24.50). W23 chrome styled Road Wheels ($81.10). W21 Rallye Road wheels with basic group ($28.35). W21 Rallye Road wheels with basic groupe ($52.80). J25 variable speed windshield wipers ($10.35). A04 basic group including power steering, AM radio, variable-speed windshield wipers with electric wahers and dual racing mirrors ($188.45). A01 light package includes fender-mounted turn signals, trunk light, glove box light, ash tray light, ignition switch warning light with time delay, instrument panel flood lamp with time delay, map light and courtesy light ($35). A36 performance axle package, includes 3.55:1 heavy-duty axle ratio, Sure Grip differential, 26-inch high-performance radiator and fan shroud, with 340-four-barrel V-8 only ($59.90). A51 Sports Decor group, includes sport hood, wheel lip moldings, sill moldings and body side tape stripes with 340 four-barrel V-8 ($47.70). F70-14 whitewalls ($11.25 extra)

PONTIAC MUSCLE 1960-1972

Starting with 1959 models, the image of a sporty, youthful car with appeal across the spectrum of new car buyers emerged at Pontiac. The result was six straight years of low-slung, Wide-Track, full-size performance machines that outran the majority of competitors in both sales and racing. In the fall of 1960, following intensive research, development, and testing, Pontiac expanded the bottom of its line with a completely innovative compact model called the Tempest that was destined to sire the GTO — America's first true muscle car.

When "Bunkie" Knudsen moved to Chevrolet in 1961, E.M. "Pete" Estes took over at Pontiac. Under his able direction the division continued to grow in sales volume and facilities. The Tempest moved the company into third place in U.S. sales in 1961. Traditionally the hot spot of the auto market, Pontiac was able to dominate the third rung, during the 1960s, with an endless parade of hot cars.

Factory-backed Pontiac drag racing reached a peak in 1963 and racing activities were officially curtailed shortly afterwards due to a corporate ban. To maintain its edge in the youth car market, the company skirted another GM policy by dropping its most popular big-car engine (the 389) into the Tempest in true hot rod fashion. The result was the first Pontiac GTO. A year later, GTO creator John Z. DeLorean was made manager.

In the middle of the 1967 model year, the Firebird sports/personal car was unveiled. It was offered in a range of model options up to a new 400-cid V-8. Ram Air induction was optional. A milestone was achieved in 1968 when an all-time high of 940,000 cars left the factory. It was also the first time that sales of Pontiac specialty models, such as Tempests, Grand Prix, and Firebirds, exceeded the sales of traditional lines.

The hit of 1969 was a the Grand Prix, but a few months later, the most exciting of all Firebirds was introduced as the semi-race-ready Trans Am. Conceived as a factory sedan racer, the Trans Am had an engine that was too big to qualify for track competition, but just right for stoplight performance. By this time the government was starting to crack down on factory hot rods of the late 1960s, but the Trans Am passed as a sports car and thereby kept the performance image alive for a few more years.

In February 1969, F. James McDonald became Pontiac general manager. He replaced DeLorean who moved to Chevrolet in the same capacity. This was a critical era for car development programs, due to pressures from the government and insurance companies alike. High performance was continually de-emphasized in favor of safety and fuel economy gains combined with engine emissions reductions.

During the 1971 calendar year, Pontiac captured third place in U.S. auto sales for the 10th time 11 years, but the division's image was losing impact at the same time. The low-priced Ventura II compact hit the market; a new, less-powerful 1972 Trans Am appeared and the nearest thing to a full-sized performance car available was the luxurious Bonneville with a massive 455-cid V-8.

On October 1, 1972, Martin J. Caserio became general manager of Pontiac Motor Division. Under him a new regular-fuel Super-Duty V-8 evolved. It became an instant collector's item when ultimately released in late-1973 Trans Ams and Formula Firebirds. Under Caserio the GTO disappeared, and the Firebird came close to meeting a similar fate.

The 1973 Pontiac lineup was highlighted by a totally redesigned intermediate series, topped by the stunning Grand Am. Calendar-year sales of 854,343 cars were the second best in company history. The 1974 models featured new engineering, and offered a true high-performance Super-Duty V-8. But this was the end of the line for Pontiac muscle cars, at least for a time.

PHIL KUNZ

1960 CATALINA TEMPEST 425-A

1960 Catalina

Pontiac's major styling changes for 1960 included undivided horizontal bar grilles, straight full-length side trim moldings and a new deck lid that was nearly flush with the tops of the fenders. Catalinas had plain beltline moldings, Catalina front fender scripts, and Pontiac block letters on the belt latch panel. Standard features included turn signals, oil filter, five tubeless tires and courtesy lamps on convertibles.

A four-speed manual floor mounted transmission became available in midyear, though not as a regular production option (RPO). Most went into professionally driven NASCAR racers. The unit was basically the same one used by Corvettes and Chevrolets and retailed for $188.30 from Chevrolet. The Pontiac price is probably the same. A variety of rear axle ratios were available

Four NASCAR Grand Nationals and three other stock car races were won by Pontiacs. Jim Wangers drove a 1960 Pontiac to the NHRA "Top Eliminator" title. Mickey Thompson installed four Pontiac engines in his Challenger I World Land Speed Record car and drove it 363.67 mph.

The 333-hp Catalina two-door hardtop was timed at 7.8 seconds for 0-to-60 mph and 16 seconds for the quarter-mile.

ENGINES

OPTIONAL V-8: Overhead valve. Cast-iron block. Bore and stroke: 4.06 x 3.75. Displacement: 389 cid. Compression ratio: 10.75:1. Brake hp: 345 at 4800 rpm. Taxable hp: 52.80. Torque: 425 at 3200 rpm. Five main bearings. Performance camshaft. Dual exhausts. Carburetor: Four-barrel. Engine code: M-1 or M-4.

OPTIONAL V-8 (HYDRA-MATIC): Overhead valve. Cast-iron block. Bore and stroke: 4.06 x 3.75. Displacement: 389 cid. Compression ratio: 10.75:1. Brake hp: 348 at 4600 rpm. Taxable hp: 52.80. Torque: 425 at 3200 rpm. Five main bearings. Performance camshaft. Dual exhausts. Carburetion: Three (3) two-barrel Rochester carburetors; (front) 7013063; (center) 7013974; (rear) 7013975. Engine code: K-1 or K-4.

OPTIONS

Air-conditioning ($430). Electric antenna ($30). Aluminum hubs and drums ($107). E-Z-Eye glass ($43). Circ-L-Aire heater defroster ($43) Direct Aire heater defroster ($94). Sportable radio ($129). Wonder Bar radio ($125). Super Deluxe radio ($89). Rear seat speaker ($14). Luggage carrier ($99). Padded dash ($19). Bucket seats ($100). Safeguard speedometer ($15). Magi-Cruise ($13). Custom wheel discs ($17-$32). Deluxe wheel discs ($16). Windshield washer ($13). Continental spare tire and cover ($258). Underhood utility lamp ($7). Remote control mirror ($12). Power windows ($58 or $106). Power steering ($108). Power brakes ($43). Custom steering wheel ($15). Super Hydra-Matic (Strato-Flight) transmission ($231.34). Safe-T-Track differential ($43). Dual exhaust cost ($31). Tri-Power on the Tempest 425 block (NASCAR engine with 10.75:1 compression) gave 348 hp @ 4600 rpm. The price for the option was $316. Four-barrel induction on the Tempest 425 V-8 gave 333 hp @ 4600 rpm. Price was $230.

Model Number	Body/Style Number	Body Type & Seating	Factory Price	Shipping Weight	Production Total
CATALINA — SERIES 21 — V-8					
21	37	2d HT-6P	$3,020	3,680 lbs.	14,524
21	67	2d Conv-6P	$3,402	3,805 lbs.	12,379

NOTE 1: Price includes base cost of Tempest 425 four-barrel V-8.

NOTE 2: Weights are for base model with 389-cid V-8.

NOTE 3: Production by body style is for all Catalinas regardless of engine.

PONTIAC

1960 VENTURA TEMPEST 425-A

The Ventura was a Custom trim level Pontiac on the short wheelbase. Identifying cars in this seies were plain belt moldings, Ventura front fender scripts and the model name, in block letters, on the trunk latch panel. Venturas had a Catalina features plus a custom steering wheel, an electric clock, Deluxe wheel discs, full carpeting, triple-tone Morrokide seats, right-hand ash trays and special decor, moldings.

As with the Catalina, a four-speed manual floor mounted transmission became available in midyear, though not as a regular production option (RPO).

Today, the Catalina-size Ventura is a very desirable Pontiac with the same performance, as well as many special trim accents.

Model Number	Body/Style Number	Body Type & Seating	Factory Price	Shipping Weight	Production Total
VENTURA — SERIES 23 — V-8					
23	2337	2d HT-6P	$3,295	3,685 lbs.	13,297

NOTE 1: Price includes base cost of Tempest 425 four-barrel V-8.
NOTE 2: Weights are for base model with 389-cid V-8.
NOTE 3: Production by body style is for all Ventura two-door hardtops regardless of engine.

ENGINES

OPTIONAL V-8: Overhead valve. Cast-iron block. Bore and stroke: 4.06 x 3.75. Displacement: 389 cid. Compression ratio: 10.75:1. Brake hp: 345 at 4800 rpm. Taxable hp: 52.80. Torque: 425 at 3200 rpm. Five main bearings. Performance camshaft. Dual exhausts. Carburetor: Four-barrel. Engine code: M-1 or M-4.

OPTIONAL V-8 (HYDRA-MATIC): Overhead valve. Cast-iron block. Bore and stroke: 4.06 x 3.75.Displacement: 389 cid. Compression ratio: 10.75:1. Brake hp: 348 at 4600 rpm. Taxable hp: 52.80. Torque: 425 at 3200 rpm. Five main bearings. Performance camshaft. Dual exhausts. Carburetion: Three (3) two-barrel Rochester carburetors; (front) 7013063; (center) 7013974; (rear) 7013975. Engine code: K-1 or K-4.

OPTIONS

Air-conditioning ($430). Electric antenna ($30). Aluminum hubs and drums ($107). E-Z-Eye glass ($43). Circ-L-Aire heater defroster ($43) Direct Aire heater defroster ($94). Sportable radio ($129). Wonder Bar radio ($125). Super Deluxe radio ($89). Rear seat speaker ($14). Luggage carrier ($99). Padded dash ($19). Bucket seats ($100). Safeguard speedometer ($15). Magi-Cruise ($13). Custom wheel discs ($17-$32). Deluxe wheel discs ($16). Windshield washer ($13). Continental spare tire and cover ($258). Underhood utility lamp ($7). Remote control mirror ($12). Power windows ($58 or $106). Power steering ($108). Power brakes ($43). Custom steering wheel ($15). Super Hydra-Matic (Strato-Flight) transmission ($231.34). Safe-T-Track differential ($43). Dual exhaust ($31).

1961 CATALINA "421"

1961 Catalina

Downsizing was seen at Pontiac this year. Thanks to a new perimeter frame design the bodies on standard size cars were smaller and lighter in weight. A radically new compact named the Tempest was introduced as a Pontiac entry in the growing small car market. Major design differences included a return to the twin grille styling theme, sculptured side panels, taller rooflines and squared-off bodies with small tailfins added.

The late Mickey Thompson bored out several 389s to 421

cubic inches for racing, but this displacement was not offered straight from the factory in 1961. However, a number of such cars were built for drag strip use. By using parts sold "under-the-counter" at Pontiac parts departments, you could easily buiild the 389 factory engine into a hot 421.

Pontiac took 21 of 52 NASCAR Grand National stock car races. The stock cars used the special 421-cid V-8.

Model Number	Body/Style Number	Body Type & Seating	Factory Price	Shipping Weight	Production Total
CATALINA — SERIES 23 — V-8					
23	11	2d Sed-6P	$2,725	3,650 lbs.	9,846
23	37	2d HT-6P	$2,860	3,680 lbs.	14,524
23	67	2d Conv-6P	$3,172	3,805 lbs.	12,379

NOTE 1: Prices and weights are for base model with 389-cid/256-hp V-8; precise cost of building a 421 not available.

NOTE 2: Production by body style is for all Catalinas regardless of engine.

ENGINE

OPTIONAL SUPER-DUTY V-8 (TWO-DOOR MODELS ONLY): Overhead valve. Cast-iron block. Bore and stroke: 4.09 x 4.00. Displacement: 421 cid. Compression ratio: 11.0:1. Brake hp: 405 at 5600 rpm. Taxable hp: 53.60. Torque: 425 at 4400. Five main bearings. Hydraulic valve lifters. Carburetor: Two (2) Rochester four-barrels.

OPTIONS

Air-conditioning ($430). Electric antenna ($30). Guide-Matic headlamp control ($43). Power brakes ($43). Six-way power seat ($97). Power windows ($104). Safeguard speedometer ($19). Magic-Cruise ($16). Aluminum hubs and drums ($107). Bucket seats ($116). Heavy-duty springs ($19). E-Z-Eye glass ($43). A three-speed manual transmission was standard. Four-speed Super Hydra-Matic was $231.34 extra. A four-speed manual gearbox with floor shift was $306.66 extra on full-sized cars. Rear axle ratios: (synchromesh) 3.23:1; (Hydra-Matic) 2.87:1. Other ratios were available. Safe-T-Track differential was $43 extra. Price of 421-cid Super-Duty V-8 unknown.

1961 CATALINA 389 SUPER-DUTY

MIKE MUELLER

1961 Catalina 389 Super-Duty

The hottest 1961 factory option — available for all Pontiac models except the new Tempest compact — was the 389-cid Super-Duty V-8. It came in four-barrel and Tri-Power versions. Both were high-compression engines with a long-duration hydraulic camshaft, heavy-duty valve springs, heavy-duty valve lifters, a special dual-point ignition system, header-type exhaust manifolds, forged cranks and four-bolt mains. The Tri-Power version carried a special aluminum intake manifold. Both engines were reasonably priced and could be had with three-speed manual, four-speed manual or Hydra-Matic transmissions.

Various rear axles, including Posi, were available. Pontiac dealer parts departments sold plenty of go-faster equipment for both engines. According to Petersen Publication's *Pontiac Performance Handbook* published in 1963, the horsepower ratings for the Super-Duty motors were purely arbitrary. "They just put the figure at and even 15 hp above the eqivalent 425-A's," this source says. The handbook estimated that true output of the Tri-Power mill was close to 400 hp at 5500 rpm.

Two road tests were done on Pontiacs with the 348-hp V-8. The first featured a Ventura hardtop that went 0-to-60 mph in 8.2 seconds and did the quarter-mile in 15.5 seconds. The second featured a Catalina S/S drag racing car based on the two-door hardtop. It went from 0-to-60 mph in 4.6 seconds and did the quarter-mile in 13.7 seconds. The Super-Duty 389 cars would turn over 100 mph on a drag strip and the NASCAR four-barrel versions ran 155 mph on superspeedways of the era.

Model Number	Body/Style Number	Body Type & Seating	Factory Price	Shipping Weight	Production Total
CATALINA — SERIES 23 — V-8 (FOUR-BARREL)					
23	11	2d Sed-6P	$3,025	3,650 lbs.	Note 3
23	37	2d HT-6P	$3,160	3,680 lbs.	Note 3
23	67	2d Conv-6P	$3,472	3,805 lbs.	Note 3
CATALINA — SERIES 23 — V-8 (TRI-POWER)					
23	11	2d Sed-6P	$3,125	3,650 lbs.	Note 3
23	37	2d HT-6P	$3,260	3,680 lbs.	Note 3
23	67	2d Conv-6P	$3,572	3,805 lbs.	Note 3

NOTE 1: Prices include the cost of the indicated engine, but no other options.

NOTE 2: Weights given are for base models.

NOTE 3: Refer to Catalina 421 entry for body style production: about 25 cars were built with the Super-Duty engine.

PONTIAC

ENGINES

OPTIONAL SUPER-DUTY V-8: Overhead valve. Cast-iron block. Bore and stroke: 4.06 x 3.75. Displacement: 389 cid. Compression ratio: 10.75:1. Brake hp: 348 at 5200 rpm. Taxable hp: 52.80. Five main bearings. Hydraulic valve lifters. Carburetor: Carter AFB-3123-S four-barrel.

OPTIONAL SUPER-DUTY V-8: Overhead valve. Cast-iron block. Bore and stroke: 4.06 x 3.75. Displacement: 389 cid. Compression ratio: 10.75:1. Brake hp: 363 at 5200 rpm. Taxable hp: 52.80. Five main bearings. Hydraulic valve lifters. Carburetion: Three (3) two-barrel Rochester carburetors; (front) 7013063; (center) 7013974; (rear) 7013975.

OPTIONS

Air-conditioning ($430). Electric antenna ($30). Guide-Matic head¬lamp control ($43). Power brakes ($43). Six-way power seat ($97). Power win¬dows ($104). Safeguard speedometer ($19). Magic-Cruise ($16). Aluminum hubs and drums ($107). Bucket seats ($116). Heavy-duty springs ($19). E-Z- Eye glass ($43). A three-speed manual transmission was standard. Four-speed Super Hydra-Matic was $231.34 extra. A four-speed manual gearbox with floor shift was $306.66 extra on full-sized cars. Rear axle ratios: (synchromesh) 3.23:1; (Hydra-Matic) 2.87:1. Other ratios were available. Safe-T-Track differential was $43 extra. 389-cid Super-Duty four-barrel V-8 ($134). 389-cid Super-Duty Tri-Power V-8 ($168).

1961 VENTURA TROPHY 425-A

DOUG MITCHEL

1961 Ventura

The Ventura continued as a Catalina-sized car with Custom level trim inside and out. Identification included chrome outline moldings for side spears, Ventura script inside the spear on the door and bright metal roof drip moldings. Unlike the Catalinas with horizontal oval tail lamps and small hubcaps, Venturas carried two round taillamps and full Deluxe wheel discs. Interiors were trimmed in three-tone Jeweltone Morrokide. Standard equipment included custom steering wheel, electric clock and right-hand ashtray, plus all features seen on Catalinas.

Performance was a little less than the Super-Duty Catalinas, although the "bubble window" styling of the '61 Ventura Sport coupe makes it very desirable to muscle car collectors.

ENGINES

OPTIONAL V-8: Overhead valve. Cast-iron block. Bore and stroke: 4.06 x 3.75. Displacement: 389 cid. Compression ratio: 10.75:1. Brake hp: 333 at 4800 rpm. Taxable hp: 52.80. Torque: 425 at 2800 rpm. Five main bearings. Hydraulic valve lifters. Carburetor: Carter AFB-3123-S four-barrel.

OPTIONAL V-8: Overhead valve. Cast-iron block. Bore and stroke: 4.06 x 3.75. Displacement: 389 cid. Compression ratio: 10.75:1. Brake hp: 348 at 4800 rpm. Taxable hp: 52.80. Torque: 430 at 3200 rpm. Five main bearings. Hydraulic valve lifters. Carburetion: Three two-barrel Rochester carburetors; (front) 7013063; (center) 7013974; (rear) 7013975.

OPTIONS

Air-conditioning ($430). Electric antenna ($30). Guide-Matic headlamp control ($43). Power brakes ($43). Six-way power seat ($97). Power windows ($104). Safeguard speedometer ($19). Magic-Cruise ($16). Aluminum hubs and drums ($107). Bucket seats ($116). Heavy-duty springs ($19). E-Z- Eye glass ($43). A three-speed manual transmission was standard. Four-speed Super Hydra-Matic was $231.34 extra. A four-speed manual gearbox with floor shift was $306.66 extra on full-sized cars. Rear axle ratios: (synchromesh) 3.23:1; (Hydra-Matic) 2.87:1. Other ratios were available. Safe-T-Track differential was $43 extra. 389-cid Super-Duty four-barrel V-8 ($134). 389-cid Super-Duty Tri-Power V-8 ($168).

Model Number	Body/Style Number	Body Type & Seating	Factory Price	Shipping Weight	Production Total
VENTURA — SERIES 25 — V-8 (FOUR-BARREL)					
23	37	2d HT-6P	$3,199	3,685 lbs.	Note 3
VENTURA — SERIES 25 — V-8 (TRI-POWER)					
23	37	2d HT-6P	$3,233	3,685 lbs.	Note 3

NOTE 1: Prices include the cost of the indicated engine, but no other options.

NOTE 2: Weights given are for base models.

NOTE 3: Pontiac built a total of 13,297 Venturas; no engine breakouts available.

1962 CATALINA 421 SUPER-DUTY

JERRY HEASLEY

1962 Catalina 421 Super-Duty

The '62 Catalina lightweight sings precious memories from the pre-GTO performance era," said Jerry Heasley in the December 1985 issue of *Car Review*. Pontiac Motor Division was the first automaker to build factory lightweight drag racing cars. Ever since its NASCAR engine options were issued in mid-1957, the company found that racing on Sunday sold cars on Monday. By 1960, the "Poncho" performance image had made Pontiac the third-most popular American car nameplate for the first time in history.

Chevy's new-for 1962 409-cid engine was a threat, though. Pontiac's best match for a 409-powered Chevy was the 1961 Super-Duty 389 Catalina, which had 368 hp with Tri-Power. Perhaps 25 of these cars were built. More power and less weight was needed to keep the Pontiacs competitive, so Pontiac Motor Division put its lightest, most powerful car on a diet with a horsepower supplement. Extensive use of aluminum body parts and a special 421-cid/405-hp V-8 created the 3,600-lb. 1962 Super-Duty Catalina. The new 421-cid V-8 featured four-bolt main bearing caps, forged pistons and twin Carter four-barrel carburetors on a special intake manifold linked to either a Borg-Warner T-85 three-speed manual transmission or a T-10 four-speed manual gear box. Actual output from this massive motor was over 500 hp. Lightweight parts, in addition to the front-end sheet metal like the fenders, hood and grille sections, included an aluminum back bumper and dealer-optional Plexiglas windows.

Many of the Super-Duty Catalinas used a functional hood scoop that was actually a Ford truck part that Pontiac purchased in quantity and issued a GM parts number for. An unusual Super-Duty option was a set of cast aluminum Tri-Y

exhaust headers. In all, 225 of the 421-cid motors were built in 1962. They went into 162 Catalinas and 16 Grand Prixs. The balance of 63 engines were used as replacement motors. Not all cars that got the 421-cid Super-Duty engines had factory lightweight body parts.

Pontiac promotional expert and racing personality Jim Wangers found the 1962 Super-Duty Catalina to his liking and turned in performances like a 12.38-second quarter-mile at 116.23 mph at Detroit Dragway.

Model Number	Body/Style Number	Body Type & Seating	Factory Price	Shipping Weight	Production Total
CATALINA — SERIES 23 — V-8					
23	11	2d Sed-6P	$4,293	3,650 lbs.	14,263
23	37	2d HT-6P	$4,428	3,680 lbs.	46,024

NOTE 1: Prices include cost of 421 Super-Duty V-8 and mandatory four-speed manual transmission.

NOTE 2: Weights are for base model with 389-cid V-8.

NOTE 3: Production by body style is for all Catalinas regardless of engine; a total of 162 Catalinas had the Super-Duty 421 V-8.

ENGINE

OPTIONAL V-8 (TWO-DOOR MODELS ONLY): Overhead valve. Cast-iron block. Bore and stroke: 4.09 x 4.00. Displacement: 421 cid. Compression ratio: 11.0:1. Brake hp: 405 at 5600 rpm. Taxable hp: 53.60. Torque: 425 at 4400. Five main bearings. Hydraulic valve lifters. Carburetor: Two Rochester four-barrels.

OPTIONS

Guidematic headlamp control ($43). Bucket seats for body style 2867 ($116). Console for Body Style 2867 with bucket seats ($161). Padded dash ($16). Power bench seat ($97). Power bucket seat ($28). Power brakes ($43). Power steering ($108). Magi-Cruise ($16). Ventura trim for body styles 2339 and 2347 ($118). Aluminum hubs and drums ($108-$122). Two-speed wipers ($5). Windshield washers ($13). Power tailgate window ($31). Power windows ($18). Four-speed synchromesh with floor shift was mandatory with the 421 Super-Duty V-8 ($234). 421-cid Super-Duty V-8 ($1,334 for Catalina two-door models only).

1962 GRAND PRIX 421 SUPER-DUTY

PONTIAC

MIKE MUELLER

1962 Grand Prix 421 Super-Duty

The new Grand Prix replaced the Ventura model, although Ventura-Catalinas were still available as a trim option. The "GP" was identified by clean side styling with a checkered flag badge in the concave section of side spears, rocker panel molding, an anodized grille insert and nose piece and special rear end styling.

The from-the-factory equipment list included all Bonneville features (except courtesy lamps), plus solid color Morrokide upholstery, bucket seats and center console with tachometer.

A total of 16 Grand Prixs were fitted with Super-Duty 421 V-8s. These engines were normally reserved for two-door Catalina models, but as Pontiac's new-kid-on-the-block, it made sense to stuff a few Grand prixs with the monster mill to generate some extra publicity. The cars were mainly for professionals like Mickey Thompson to race.

In May 1962, *Motor Trend* got its hands on a Grand Prix with the Super-Duty 421 V-8. It had 4.30:1 gears. The car zipped off 0-to-60 mph in 5.4 seconds and tackled a drag strip in 13.9 seconds at 107 mph.

Model Number	Body/Style Number	Body Type & Seating	Factory Price	Shipping Weight	Production Total
GRAND PRIX — SERIES 29 — SUPER-DUTY V-8					
29	47	2d HT-6P	$5,058	3,835 lbs.	16

NOTE 1: Price includes cost of 421 Super-Duty V-8 and mandatory four-speed manual transmissionb(estimated).

NOTE 2: Weights are for base model with 389-cid/303-hp V-8.

ENGINE

OPTIONAL SUPER-DUTY 421 V-8: Overhead valve. Cast-iron block. Bore and stroke: 4.09 x 4.00. Displacement: 421 cid. Compression ratio: 11.0:1. Brake hp: 405 at 5600 rpm. Taxable hp: 53.60. Torque: 425 at 4400. Five main bearings. Hydraulic valve lifters. Carburetor: Two (2) Rochester four-barrels.

OPTIONS

Guidematic headlamp control ($43). Power bucket seat ($28). Power brakes ($43). Power steering ($108). Magi-Cruise ($16). Aluminum hubs and drums ($108-$122). Two-speed wipers ($5). Windshield washers ($13). Power windows ($18). Four-speed synchromesh with floor shift was mandatory with the 421 Super-Duty V-8 ($234). 421-cid Super-Duty V-8 ($1,334).

1963 CATALINA 421 SUPER-DUTY

TOM GLATCH

1963 Catalina 421 Super-Duty

For 1963, Pontiac Motor Division took the Super-Duty Catalina 421 program a few steps further. The cylinder heads got higher intake ports and oval-shaped exhaust ports, plus larger valves and higher-compression (12.5:1) cylinder heads. A new McKellar No. 10 solid lifter camshaft (named for Pontiac engineer Mac McKellar) was released for use in engines with dual valve springs. A transistorized ignition system was added. A few cars even had 13.0:1 compression ratios.

Official ratings for the hottest setup went to 410 hp, but the actual output of the 421-cid Super-Duty engine was somewhere between 540 hp and 550 hp. The 1963 factory lightweight cars lost about another 100 lbs. through the use of Plexiglas windows and aluminum trunk lids. Also available were aluminum splash pans, radiator core supports and bumper-attaching parts. In addition, some Catalina frames were "Swiss cheesed" by drilling large holes through them. They weighed in at about 3,325 lbs. in ultimate lightweight form.

With their low production numbers, the "Swiss cheese" cars did not qualify for S/S "super stock" drag racing classes. Instead, they competed in the F/SX "factory experimental" class. The late Mickey Thompson dreamed up this combination for A/FX competition. Another pair of A/FX-class 421-powered Tempests — a coupe and a station wagon — were campaigned by Arnie Beswick.

Pontiac had four NASCAR wins and startled the drag racing world with the release of "Swiss Cheese" Catalina factory lightweight racing cars. The name came from the fact that their frames were drilled to decrease the weight. Jim Wangers drove his Royal Pontiac-backed 421 Super-Duty '63 Catalina hardtop down the Detroit Dragway in 12.38 seconds at 116.23 mph.

Model Number	Body/Style Number	Body Type & Seating	Factory Price	Shipping Weight	Production Total
CATALINA — SERIES 23 — V-8					
23	11	2d Sed-6P	$4,293	3,300 lbs.	Note 3
23	37	2d HT-6P	$4,428	3,325 lbs.	Note 3

NOTE 1: Prices include cost of 421 Super-Duty V-8 and mandatory four-speed manual transmission.

NOTE 2: Weight is for Super-Duty 421 "Swiss Cheese" car (estimated).

NOTE 3: A total of 77 Super-Duty Catalinas and Grand Prixs (including "Swiss Cheese" units) was made.

NOTE 4: Of the 77 cars, 13 had a single four-barrel carburetor and 64 had two four-barrel carburetors.

NOTE 5: Five of the cars with two four-barrel carburetors are believed to have had aluminum front end sheet metal.

ENGINES

OPTIONAL V-8: Overhead valve. Cast-iron block. Bore and stroke: 4.09 x 4.00. Displacement: 421 cid. Compression ratio: 11.0:1. Brake hp: 405 at 5600 rpm. Taxable hp: 53.60. Torque: 425 at 4400. Five main bearings. Hydraulic valve lifters. Carburetor: Two Rochester four-barrels.

OPTIONAL V-8: Overhead valve. Cast-iron block. Displacement: 421 cid. Bore and stroke: 4.09 x 4.00. Compression ratio: 13.0:1. Brake hp: 410 at 5600 rpm. Taxable hp: 53.60. Torque: 435 at 4400 rpm. Five main bearings. Hydraulic valve lifters. Carburetor: Two Rochester four-barrels. Engine code: 13-5.

OPTIONS

Guidematic headlamp control ($43). Bucket seats for body style 2867 ($116). Console for Body Style 2867 with bucket seats ($161). Padded dash ($16). Power bench seat ($97). Power bucket seat ($28). Power brakes ($43). Power steering ($108). Magi-Cruise ($16). Ventura trim for Body Styles 2339 and 2347 ($118). Aluminum hubs and drums ($108-$122). Two-speed wipers ($5). Windshield washers ($13). Power tailgate window ($31). Power windows ($18). Four-speed synchromesh with floor shift was mandatory with the 421 Super-Duty V-8 ($234). 421-cid Super-Duty V-8 ($1,334 for Catalina two-door models only).

1964 CATALINA 2+2

PONTIAC

1964 Catalina 2+2

The 1964 Pontiac lineup included seven Catalinas, two Star Chiefs and four Bonnevilles. However, this did not count the various model-options, which were base cars with specific extra-equipment packages. Important new full-size option-created-models introduced that year included the Catalina Ventura and the Catalina 2+2. A more-rounded Pontiac front end kept the split grille and vertical headlights of previous years. The new front fender line was squared off flush with the headlights, instead of being cut back. The tail lights were boomerang-shaped and vertical.

Catalinas were Pontiac's "small" full-sized cars. The sport coupe and convertible body styles could be ordered with the 2+2 sports option package for the first time. Catalina 2+2s had identification badges below the Catalina name on the front fenders. The option included a 389-cid V-8 that generated 267-hp with Hydra-Matic transmission or 283-hp with a four-speed manual gearbox plus bucket seats, a center console with a vacuum gauge, a special Morrokide interior and fender and rear deck identification badges for $291 extra. Picture a big GTO and you've got the 1964 Catalina 2+2. This was a model option designed to give the family a real sports car that was big enough for five passengers.

The 421 HO — a hot street version of the big-block Pontiac V-8 — was also available in Catalina 2+2s. It came in three versions with 320, 350 and 370 hp.

The 1964 Catalina 2+2 with the 370-hp Tri-Power "421" did 0-to-60 mph in 7.2 seconds and covered the quarter-mile in 16.1 seconds.

Model Number	Body/Style Number	Body Type & Seating	Factory Price	Shipping Weight	Production Total
CATALINA 2+2 — SERIES 23 — V-8					
23	47	2d HT-6P	$3,160	3,750 lbs.	Note 3
23	67	2d Conv-6P	$3,472	3,825 lbs.	Note 3

NOTE 1: Prices are for Catalinas with base 389-cid V-8 and 2+2 option.

NOTE 2: Weights are for base Catalina with base 389-cid V-8.

NOTE 3: 7,998 cars had the 2+2 option package.

ENGINES

BASE V-8 (MANUAL): Overhead valve. Cast-iron block. Bore and stroke: 4.06 x 3.75. Displacement: 389 cid. Compression ratio: 10.50:1. Brake hp: 267 at 4200 rpm. Taxable hp: 52.80. Torque: 410 at 2400. Five main bearings. Hydraulic valve lifters. Carburetor: Rochester 2GC two-barrel. Engine code: 11H or 12H.

BASE V-8 (AUTOMATIC): Overhead valve. Cast-iron block. Bore and stroke: 4.06 x 3.75. Displacement: 389 cid. Compression ratio: 10.50:1. Brake hp: 283 at 4400 rpm. Taxable hp: 52.80. Torque: 418 at 2800. Five main bearings. Hydraulic valve lifters. Carburetor: Rochester 2GC two-barrel. Engine code: 10A, 17M or 18M.

OPTIONAL V-8: Overhead valve. Cast-iron block. Bore and stroke: 4.09 x 4.00. Displacement: 421 cid. Compression ratio: 10.75:1. Brake hp: 320 at 4400 rpm. Taxable hp: 53.60. Torque: 455 at 2800 rpm. Five main bearings. Hydraulic valve lifters. Carburetor: Four-barrel. Engine code: 35B, 38S or 43N.

OPTIONAL V-8: Overhead valve. Cast-iron block. Bore and stroke: 4.09 x 4.00. Displacement: 421 cid. Compression ratio: 10.75:1. Brake hp: 350 at 4600 rpm. Taxable hp: 53.60. Torque: 454 at 3200 rpm. Five main bearings. Hydraulic valve lifters. Carburetion: Three Rochester two-barrel carburetors. Engine code: 44B, 47S or 49N.

OPTIONAL V-8: Overhead valve. Cast-iron block. Bore and stroke: 4.09 x 4.00. Displacement: 421 cid. Compression ratio: 10.75:1. Brake hp: 370 at 5200 rpm. Taxable hp: 53.60. Torque: 460 at 3800 rpm. Five main bearings. Hydraulic valve lifters. Carburetion: Three Rochester two-barrel carburetors. Engine code: 45B, 46G or 50Q.

OPTIONS

Air conditioning ($430). Console including tachometer ($161). Instrument gauge cluster ($21-$59). Luggage carrier ($94). Remote control mirror ($12). Power brakes ($57). Power seat ($96). Power tilt left-hand bucket seat ($71). Tachometer ($54). Cordova top ($86). Ventura trim on body styles 2339, 2347 and 2369 ($118). Sports wheelcovers ($30-$46). Aluminum hubs and drums ($122-$138). Catalina 2+2 sports option ($291). Ventura trim option ($118). Three-speed manual transmission was standard. Hydra-Matic was optional. A four-speed manual transmission with floor shift was optional.

1964 LEMANS GTO

PONTIAC

JERRY HEASLEY

1964 GTO

The famous Grand Turisimo Omologato (GTO) option package was released for Le Mans models this year. The Italian term used as the model name actually meant Grand Touring Automobile, although the Pontiac GTO was far from a 2+2 closed-body sports car. The real idea behind this package was to circumvent the corporate racing-and-high-performance ban by providing the 389-cid V-8 as an option in the most luxurious intermediate-size Pontiac. This package turned the Le Mans into a "super car" and the term "muscle car" later became the popular label for this breed.

The 389-cid V-8 was the standard power plant and came in two versions, both of which were fitted with special high-performance goodies. One featured a single four-barrel carburetor and the other substituted three two-barrel carburetors. GTOs also featured special appearance items in place of some regular Le Mans styling touches. They included G-T-O letters in the left-hand grille opening, G-T-O lettering on the rear fender tips and deck lid, tri-colored (red, white and blue) GTO crests behind the front wheel openings, a special hood stamping with air scoops and cast aluminum grilles in the scoop openings, a GTO crest on the dashboard and an engine-turned aluminum trim panel surrounding the instruments.

In January 1964, *Motor Trend* magazine found a four-speed GTO convertible capable of doing the quarter-mile in 15.8 seconds at 93 mph. The same car's 0-to-60-mph performance was 7.7 seconds and it had a 115-mph top speed. The 348-hp GTO hardtop went 0-to-60 mph in 6.6 seconds and did the quarter-mile in 14.8 seconds.

Model Number	Body/Style Number	Body Type & Seating	Factory Price	Shipping Weight	Production Total
TEMPEST LEMANS + GTO OPTION — SERIES 22 — V-8					
22	27	2d Cpe-6P	$2,852	3,106 lbs.	7,384
22	37	2d HT-6P	$2,963	3,126 lbs.	18,422
22	67	2d Conv-6P	$3,081	3,360 lbs.	6,644

ENGINES

GTO BASE V-8: Overhead valve. Cast-iron block. Bore and stroke: 4.06 x 3.75. Displacement: 389 cid. Compression ratio: 10.75:1. Brake hp: 325 at 4800 rpm. Taxable hp: 52.80. Torque: 428 at 3200 rpm. Five main bearings. Hydraulic valve lifters. Carburetor: Four-barrel. Engine code: 78X or 79J. Available with standard three-speed manual transmission and standard 3.23:1 rear axle. Also available with optional four-speed manual transmission and standard 3.23:1 rear axle. Also available with optional automatic transmission and standard 3.23:1 rear axle.

GTO OPTIONAL V-8: Overhead valve. Cast-iron block. Bore and stroke: 4.06 x 3.75. Displacement: 389 cid. Compression ratio: 10.75:1. Brake hp: 348 at 4900 rpm. Taxable hp: 52.80. Torque: 428 at 3600 rpm. Five main bearings. Hydraulic valve lifters. Three Rochester two-barrel carburetors. Engine code: 76X or 77J. Available with standard three-speed manual transmission and standard 3.23:1 rear axle. Also available with optional four-speed manual transmission and standard 3.23:1 rear axle. Also available with optional automatic transmission and standard 3.23:1 rear axle. Special order axle ratios included 3.08:1, 3.36:1, 3.55:1 and 3.90:1. A special radiator, a speedometer adapter, a heavy-duty fan, metallic brake linings and Safe-T-Track were required with some combinations at extra cost. Air conditioning was not available when certain axles were ordered.

OPTIONS

581 Tri-Comfort air conditioner ($319). 411 pair of front seat belts. 604 electric clock. 601 front seat center console. 572 spare wheel and tire cover. 412 Custom front foam cushion. 451 remote-control rear deck lid. 541 electric rear window defogger, except convertible. 701 Safe-T-Track differential ($75). 531 Soft-Ray tinted glass in all windows. 532 Soft-Ray tinted glass in windshield only. 382 GTO option for Le Mans coupe, hardtop or convertible ($295). 512 door edge guards. 612 Ride & Handling package. 492

ashtray and cigarette lighter lamp. 491 courtesy lamp, except convertible. 484 dome and reading lamp, except convertible. 482 glove box lamp. 494 parking brake on lamp. 404 underhood lamp. 471 back-up lamp. 631 front floor mats. 632 rear floor mats. 442 non-glare inside day/night rearview mirror. 602 left-hand outside rearview mirror. 444 remote-control left-hand outside rearview mirror. 441 visor-vanity mirror. 424 instrument panel pad. ($16). 502 power brakes. 561 full-width power seat. 501 power steering. 551 power windows. 399 manual radio and electric antenna. 398 manual radio and manual antenna. 393 push-button radio and electric antenna. 392 push-button radio and manual antenna. 401 Separa-Phonic rear speaker, except convertible. 474 Verbra-Phonic amplifier package, except convertible. 624 Custom retractable front seat belts. 622 Superlift rear shock absorbers. 454 tilt-adjustable steering wheel. 524 Custom Sports steering wheel. 452 ta-chometer, except with transistor ignition ($54); with transistor ignition ($54).

421 dual-speed windshield wipers and washers. 462 deluxe wheel discs. 521 Custom wheel discs. 402 dual-speed electric winshield wipers. 061 Basic Group includes push-button radio and manual antenna, Custom foam front seat cushion, dual-speed windshield wipers and washers, heavy-duty air cleaner and back-up lights. 062 Protection Group, includes instrument panel pad, door edge guards, a rear window defogger, a spare tire wheel cover, Custom retractable front seat belts and front and rear floor mats. 081 Mirror Group, includes visor-vanity mirror, non-glare inside rearview mirror and remote-control left-hand outside rearview mirror. 084 Lamp Group includes underhood lamp, luggage lamp, glove box lamp, dome and reading lamp, courtesy lamp and parking-brake-on lamp. 984330 traffic hazard warning flasher. 984333 right-hand tailpipe extension. 984334 left-hand tail-pipe extension. 984326 vacuum gauge ($48). Power convertible top ($54). Power tilt left bucket seat ($67). Cordova top ($75).

1965 CATALINA 2+2

1965 Catalina 2+2

Modest sales of the originall 2+2 were taken in stride by Pontiac Motor Division, which made it a "sports option" for 1965. This blossoming of the 2+2 coincided with new styling and a chassis redesign for all full-sized Pontiacs. The result was an extremely attractive automobile with outstanding performance. The second 2+2 was available again in either two-door hardtop or convertible body form.

The 2+2's performance was given a strong starting point thanks to the 1965 Pontiac's bold "ship's prow" front end with its stacked headlights and a fresh variation on the neo-classic divided grille. Providing sufficient identification were front fender louvers and 2+2 emblems on the hood, rear fenders and rear deck. The Catalina 2+2 base engine was now Pontiac's 421-cid V-8 with a 10.5:1 compression ratio and four-barrel carburetor. The standard transmission was an all-Synchro-mesh close-ratio four-speed. Pontiac also offered a 421 HO version. *Car Life*, April 1965, quoted one happy 421 HO owner as saying "I will say this is the finest road machine I have ever driven — foreign cars included. It has comfort, performance and, in my opinion, handling that should satisfy anyone but a road course driver." The 421 HO benefited from

its quick-bleed hydraulic valve lifters, which made 5400 rpm a realistic rev limit. It was possible to equip the Catalina 2+2 with a "ride and handling package" consisting of extra-stiff front and rear springs, heavier-duty shock absorbers, a front sway bar, aluminum wheel hubs, quicker-ratio power steering, a tachometer, a gauge package and a close-ratio four-speed manual transmission.

Pontiac specified a 3.42:1 standard axle ratio for the 2+2. It provided excellent all-around performance as reflected in the car's 0-to-60 time of 7.2 seconds, its 0-to-100 time of 20.5 seconds and a standing-start quarter-mile completed in 15.8 seconds at 88 mph. A Catalina 2+2 running a 4.11:1 "Saf-T-Track" limited-slip differential was tested by *Car Life* in April 1965. Although its 0-to-60 performance of 7.2 seconds and its quarter-mile time of 15.5 seconds (at 95 mph) were impressive, *Car Life* said the car fell short of true 2+2 potential.

Along with the GTO, the 2+2 further contributed to Pontiac's mid-1960s performance image that has become a modern day legend. It was exciting to look at, exciting to drive and, most of all, exciting to own.

Model Number	Body/Style Number	Body Type & Seating	Factory Price	Shipping Weight	Production Total
CATALINA 2+2 — SERIES 23 — V-8					
23	47	2d HT-6P	$3,219	3,992 lbs.	9,535
23	67	2d Conv-6P	$3,519	4,039 lbs.	1,984

ENGINES

BASE V-8: Overhead valve. Cast-iron block. Bore and stroke: 4.09 x 4.00. Displacement: 421 cid. Compression ratio: 10.50:1. Brake hp: 338 at 4600 rpm. Taxable hp: 53.60. Torque: 459 at 2800 rpm. Five main bearings. Hydraulic valve lifters. Carburetor: Carter AFB Four-barrel. Engine code: WK, YZ, YT, WG or YH.

OPTIONAL V-8: Overhead valve. Cast-iron block. Bore and stroke: 4.09 x 4.00. Displacement: 421 cid. Compression ratio: 10.75:1. Brake hp: 356 at 4800 rpm. Taxable hp: 53.60. Torque: 459 at 3200 rpm. Five main bearings. Hydraulic valve lifters. Carburetion: Three Rochester two-barrel carburetors. Engine code: YJ, YM or WH.

OPTIONAL V-8: Overhead valve. Cast-iron block. Bore and stroke: 4.09 x 4.00. Displacement: 421 cid. Compression ratio: 10.75:1. Brake hp: 376 at 5000 rpm. Taxable hp: 53.60. Torque: 461 at 3600 rpm. Five main bearings. Hydraulic valve lifters. Carburetion: Three Rochester two-barrel carburetors. Engine code: WJ or YK.

OPTIONS

Console ($108). Remote control deck lid ($11). Electro Cruise and fuel warning ($96). Tinted glass ($43). Tinted windshield ($29). Instrument gauge cluster ($21-$38). Glareproof tilt mirror ($4). Remote control rearview mirror ($12). Power brakes ($43). Power door locks ($46-$70). Six-way power seat ($97). Power windows ($106). Power tilt bucket seats L.H. ($71). AM/FM manual radio ($151). Push-button AM radio ($89). Front bucket seats for Catalina two-door hardtop and convertible with special trims ($204). Super-Lift shock absorbers ($40). Sports option 2+2 package for style number 25237 ($419). Sports option 2+2 package for style number 25267 ($397). Tachometer, except on cars with four-speed and console ($54). Cordova top ($97-$108). Ventura trim package for style numbers 25237, 25239, and 25269 ($118). Wire wheel discs ($20-$71). Aluminum hubs and drums ($120-$138). A three-speed manual transmission was standard. Turbo Hydra-Matic transmission and four-speed manual transmission were $231 extra. A heavy-duty clutch was $9 extra on Catalinas with certain engines. Safe-T-Track differential was $43 extra. Dual exhaust were $31 extra, but standard on Grand Prix. The four-barrel V-8 with heavy-duty clutch was $44 extra for Catalinas and Star Chiefs. Transistor ignition was $75 extra on air conditioned cars and $65 extra on others. A transistorized regulator was $11 extra. Various rear axle ratios were available.

1965 LEMANS GTO

JERRY HEASLEY

1965 GTO

The GTO was not yet in a separate series, although special identification features on GTOs replaced some items regularly seen on Tempest Le Mans models. These included GTO lettering for the left-hand grille, the rear fender sides and the rear deck lid, a single hood scoop and horizontally-elongated V-shaped badges behind the front wheel openings. The GTO's redesigned grille was made of heavy die-cast metal and had an Argent Silver grille surround with a thin stainless steel molding snapped into its leading edge. Black-finished thin horizontal bars filled the cavities and "GTO" letters identical to the 1964 letters were mounted towards the outboard end of the left-hand grille opening.

The standard GTO Trophy V-8 gained 10 hp for 1965. The cylinder heads were re-cored to remove restrictions and abrupt changes in cross section. The engine had a revised camshaft and improved intake manifolds with different runners. The GTO was also available with a 360-hp Tri-Power V-8. Stick-shift cars with the Tri-Power engine now used a mechanical progressive linkage, while cars with the Tri-Power V-8 and automatic transmission retained the vacuum-operated linkage used in 1964. Chrome valve covers and a chrome air cleaner were included. The extra horses went to good use, as the car was 3.1 inch longer and 340 lbs. heavier.

The 335-hp GTO convertible went 0-to-60 mph in 7.2 seconds and did the quarter-mile in 16.1 seconds.

Model Number	Body/Style Number	Body Type & Seating	Factory Price	Shipping Weight	Production Total
TEMPEST LEMANS + GTO OPTION — SERIES 22 — V-8					
22	27	2d Cpe-6P	$2,787	3,478 lbs.	8,319
22	37	2d HT-6P	$2,855	3,478 lbs.	55,722
22	67	2d Conv-6P	$3,093	3,700 lbs.	11,311

PONTIAC

ENGINES

BASE V-8: Overhead valve. Cast-iron block. Bore and stroke: 4.06 x 3.75. Displacement: 389 cid. Compression ratio: 10.75:1. Brake hp: 335 at 5000 rpm. Taxable hp: 52.80. Torque: 431 at 3200 rpm. Five main bearings. Hydraulic valve lifters. Carburetor: Four-barrel. Engine code: WT, WW, YS or XE.

OPTIONAL V-8: Overhead valve. Cast-iron block. Bore and stroke: 4.06 x 3.75. Displacement: 389 cid. Compression ratio: 10.75:1. Brake hp: 360 at 5200 rpm. Taxable hp: 52.80. Torque: 424 at 3600 rpm. Five main bearings. Hydraulic valve lifters. Carburetion: Three Rochester two-barrel carburetors. Engine code: WS, WV. XS or YR.

OPTIONS

591 speedometer gear adapter ($11.30). 431 heavy-duty air cleaner ($4.84). 582 Tri-Comfort air conditioner ($345.60). 471 back-up lights with manual transmission ($12.91). 471 back-up lights with automatic transmission ($10.76). 651 heavy-duty battery, standard with air conditioning or GTO ($3.55). 522 floor carpet with base sports coupe or sedan ($19.37). 604 electric clock, not available in cars with a tachometer ($19.37). 601 center console in Le Mans Sports Coupe, two-door hardtop or convertible ($48.15). 572 spare wheel and tire cover, except Safari station wagon ($2.58). 412 front foam cushion in base or Custom models ($8.07). 451 remote-control rear deck lid, except Safari ($10.76). 541 rear window defogger in coupes and sedans ($21.52). 701 Safe-T-Grip non-slip differential ($37.66). 534 heavy-duty engine fan ($3.12). 389-cid Tri-Power V-8 in Le Mans with GTO option ($115.78). 422 tailpipe extensions all Custom and Le Mans models except Safari station wagon ($21.30). 531 tinted glass in all windows ($31.20). 532 tinted windshield ($19.91). 382 Grand Turisimo Omologato option for Le Mans sports coupe, hardtop and convertible ($295.90). 512 door edge guards for two-door models ($4.84). 621 Ride & Handling package ($16.14). 584 heater deletion, not available in cars with air conditioning ($73 credit). 472 dual horns ($4.30). 671 transistor ignition, with air conditioning ($75.27). 671 transistor ignition, without air conditioning ($64.51). 424 padded instrument panel ($16.14). 482 glove box lamp ($2.85).

491 courtesy lamps ($4.30, except standard in convertibles). 492 ash tray lamp ($3.12). 494 parking-brake-on signal lamp ($4.95). 481 luggage lamp ($3.55). 404 underhood lamp ($3.55). 631 front floor mat ($6.24). 632 rear floor mats ($5.81). 602 outside rearview mirror ($4.25). 441 visor-vanity mirror ($1.45). 442 non-glare inside rearview mirror ($4.25). 444 remote-control outside rearview mirror ($11.78). Standard color two-tone paint, except convertible. Special color two-tone paint, except convertible ($71.93). Special color solid paint ($40.19). 504 Rally gauge cluster with tachometer ($86.08). 391 power antenna ($29.75). 502 power brakes ($42.50). 501 power steering ($96.84). 564 left-hand tilt bucket seat ($71.02). 434 Tempest Custom convertible power top ($53.80). 551 power side windows ($102.22). 398 manual-tune radio and antenna ($53.80). 392 push-button radio and antenna ($62.41). 394 AM/FM push-button radio and manual antenna ($136.65). 401 rear seat radio speaker for coupes and sedans ($14.15). 474 Verbra-Phonic "reverb" type rear radio speaker for coupes and sedans ($53.80). 662 transistorized ignition regulator ($10.76). 624 Custom retractable front seat belts ($7.53). 414 seat belts deletion ($11.00 credit). 622 Superlift rear shock absorbers ($40.35). 634 Safeguard speedometer ($16.14). 654 heavy-duty front and rear springs for base coupe and sedan and Custom sedan ($15.06). 454 tilt-adjustable steering wheel, requires power steering ($43.04). 612 quick-ratio steering, except in cars with power steering ($10.76). 581 automatic temperature control, requires air conditioning ($64.56). Cordova top ($71.93). Four-speed manual synchromesh transmission ($188.30). Automatic transmission with V-8 engine ($199.06). 614 positive crankcase ventilation ($5.38). 411 wire wheel discs with Décor Group or Sports Option ($53.80). 411 wire wheel discs with Décor Group or Sports Option ($71.02). 521 Custom wheel discs with Décor Group or Sports Option ($19.90). 521 Custom wheel discs without Décor Group or Sports Option ($37.12). 462 deluxe wheel discs ($17.22). 691 Rally wheels without Décor Group ($52.72). 691 Rally wheels with Décor Group ($35.50). 421 two-speed windshield wipers and washers ($17.27). 062 Protection Group ($64.66). 062 Protection Group ($43.14). 071 Mirror Group ($17.48). 074 Lamp Group ($22.32).

1966 CATALINA 2+2

PHIL KUNZ

1966 Catalina 2+2

With a weight in the over-2-ton range, the 2+2 with the Tri-Power 421 HO engine and four-speed gearbox could hit an incredible 95 mph in the quarter-mile. This was truly an impressive machine.

The Catalina 2+2 models were in a separate series for 1966. They could be easily identified by appearance items such as a twin lens taillamp treatment, 2+2 badges on the deck lid and rear fenders, vertical air slots behind the doors and "Pontiac 421" front fender emblems.

Standard equipment included a four-barrel 421-cid V-8 with

338 hp, low-restriction exhaust, chromed air cleaner and valve covers and three-speed Hurst linkage transmission. A heavy-duty suspension, carpeting, bucket seats, Sports Custom steering wheel and non-glare inside rearview mirror were standard. Available axle ratios included 3.08:1, 3.23:1, and 3.42:1.

Model Number	Body/Style Number	Body Type & Seating	Factory Price	Shipping Weight	Production Total
CATALINA 2+2 — SERIES 254 — V-8:					
254	37	2d HT-5P	$3,298	4,005 lbs.	4,888
254	67	2d Conv-5P	$3,602	4,030 lbs.	1,495

NOTE 1: 2,208 Catalina 2+2s had synchromesh and 4,175 had Hydra-Matic.

ENGINES

BASE V-8: Overhead valve. Cast-iron block. Bore and stroke: 4.09 x 4.00. Displacement: 421 cid. Compression ratio: 10.5:1. Brake hp: 338 at 4600 rpm. Taxable hp: 53.60. Torque: 459 at 2800 rpm. Five main bearings. Hydraulic valve lifters. Cooling system capacity with heater: 19.5 qt. Crankcase capacity: 5 qt. (add 1 qt. for new filter). Carburetor: Carter AFB four-barrel Model 4033S. Engine code: WK, YZ, YT, WG or YH.

OPTIONAL V-8: Overhead valve. Cast-iron block. Bore and stroke: 4.09 x 4.00. Displacement: 421 cid. Compression ratio: 10.75:1. Brake hp: 356 at 4800 rpm. Taxable hp: 53.60. Torque: 459 at 3200 rpm. Five main bearings. Hydraulic valve lifters. Carburetion: Three Rochester two-barrel carburetors. Engine code: YJ, YM or WH.

OPTIONAL V-8: Overhead valve. Cast-iron block. Bore and stroke: 4.09 x 4.00. Displacement: 421 cid. Compression ratio: 10.75:1. Brake hp: 376 at 5000 rpm. Taxable hp: 53.60. Torque: 461 at 3600 rpm. Five main bearings. Hydraulic valve lifters. Carburetion: Three Rochester two-barrel carburetors. Engine code: WJ or YK.

OPTIONS

Console ($108). Remote control deck lid ($11). Electro Cruise and fuel warning ($96). Tinted glass ($43). Tinted windshield ($29). Instrument gauge cluster ($21-$38). Glareproof tilt mirror ($4). Remote control rearview mirror ($12). Power brakes ($43). Power door locks ($46-$70). Six-way power seat ($97). Power windows ($106). Power tilt bucket seats L.H. ($71). AM/FM manual radio ($151). Push-button AM radio ($89). Front bucket seats for Catalina two-door hardtop and convertible with special trims ($204). Super-Lift shock absorbers ($40). Sports option 2+2 package for style number 25237 ($419). Sports option 2+2 package for style number 25267 ($397). Tachometer, except on cars with four-speed and console ($54). Cordova top ($97-$108). Ventura trim package for style numbers 25237, 25239, and 25269 ($118). Wire wheel discs ($20-$71). Aluminum hubs and drums ($120-$138). A three-speed manual transmission was standard. Turbo Hydra-Matic transmission and four-speed manual transmission were $231 extra. A heavy-duty clutch was $9 extra on Catalinas with certain engines. Safe-T-Track differential was $43 extra. Dual exhaust were $31 extra, but standard on Grand Prix. The four-barrel V-8 with heavy-duty clutch was $44 extra for Catalinas and Star Chiefs. Transistor ignition was $75 extra on air conditioned cars and $65 extra on others. A transistorized regulator was $11 extra. Various rear axle ratios were available.

1966 GTO

PHIL KUNZ

1966 GTO

For 1966, the GTO line was a separate series with distinctive trim on the new Tempest sheet metal. The trademark split grille was of an all-new design and was made of plastic. Pontiac was the first automaker to introduce such a grille on the '66 GTO and Grand Prix models. A wire mesh "egg crate" style grille insert was used. Both grilles incorporated rectangular parking/directional lamps on the outboard side and a GTO nameplate was mounted inboard of the rectangular lamp on the left-hand side. A body-color vertical panel again separated the grilles, but it no longer carried a Pontiac arrowhead badge. Instead, such a badge was mounted above it, on the peak of the hood. Circular Guide T-3 headlights were stacked vertically on each side of the grille. A massive new front bumper was

fitted. The hood, except for the new badge on its nose, was identical with the 1965 hood.

There were few major mechanical changes for the 1966 GTO. When Tri-Power was added, the center carburetor was a larger one than used in the past. It was now the same size as the front and rear carburetors. This required revisions to the Tri-Power intake manifold as well. An Air Scoop package was again optional and at midyear a new Ram Air V-8 (code XS) was introduced.

Car Life magazine (May 1966) tested a loaded sport coupe with the 389-cid/335-hp four-barrel engine. The 3,950-lb. GTO went from 0-to-60 mph in 6.8 seconds and did the quarter-mile in 15.4 seconds at 92 mph.

PONTIAC

Model Number	Body/Style Number	Body Type & Seating	Factory Price	Shipping Weight	Production Total
TEMPEST LEMANS + GTO OPTION — SERIES 22 — V-8					
22	27	2d Cpe-6P	$2,787	3,445 lbs.	10,363
22	37	2d HT-6P	$2,847	3,465 lbs.	73,785
22	67	2d Conv-6P	$3,082	3,555 lbs.	12,798

ENGINES

BASE V-8: Overhead valve. Cast-iron block. Bore and stroke: 4.06 x 3.75. Displacement: 389 cid. Compression ratio: 10.75:1. Brake hp: 335 at 5000 rpm. Taxable hp: 52.80. Torque: 431 at 3200 rpm. Five main bearings. Hydraulic valve lifters. Carburetor: Four-barrel. Engine code: WT, WW, YS or XE.

OPTIONAL V-8: Overhead valve. Cast-iron block. Bore and stroke: 4.06 x 3.75. Displacement: 389 cid. Compression ratio: 10.75:1. Brake hp: 360 at 5200 rpm. Taxable hp: 52.80. Torque: 424 at 3600 rpm. Five main bearings. Hydraulic valve lifters. Carburetion: Three Rochester two-barrel carburetors. Engine code: WS, WV, XS or YR.

OPTIONS

582 Custom air conditioner. 612 Air Injector Reactor (AIR) exhaust control, for California cars only. 674 heavy-duty 55-amp alternator. 631 front and rear Custom seat belts. 651 heavy-duty aluminum front brake drums. 444 electric clock. 472 front seat center console. SVT Cordova top. 372 spare wheel and tire cover. 422 remote control rear deck lid release. 374 rear window defogger. 731 Safe-T-Track differential. 482 tailpipe extensions with dual exhausts. 531 tinted glass in all windows. 532 tinted windshield. 382 door edge guards. 571 right- and left-hand headrests. 584 heater deletion, not available in cars with air conditioning. 514 heavy-duty 7-blade de-clutching fan with air conditioning. Rally gauge instrument panel cluster with tachometer. Walnut four-speed gear shifter knob. 402 glove box lamp. 411 courtesy lamps, except standard in convertible. 412 ashtray lamp. 414 parking-brake-on signal lamp. 401 luggage lamp

($3.55). 421 underhood lamp. 404 roof rail reading lamp, except convertible. 522 red fender liners. 631 front floor mats. 632 rear floor mats. 394 non-glare inside rearview mirror. 392 visor-vanity mirror. 394 remote-control left-hand outside rearview mirror. SPS special solid color paint. STT special two-tone paint, except convertible. RTT standard color two-tone paint except convertible. 614 positive crankcase ventilation. 502 Wonder Touch power brakes. 501 Wonder Touch power steering. 564 left-hand power bucket seat. 551 power side windows. 681 heavy-duty radiator without air conditioning, four-barrel engine only. 349 manual radio with electric antenna. 348 manual-tune radio and manual antenna. 343 push-button radio and electric antenna. 342 push-button radio and manual antenna, 344 AM/FM push-button radio and manual antenna. 345 push-button AM/FM radio and electric antenna. 351 Separa Phonic rear speaker, not available with convertible or reverb. 352 Verbra-Phonic "reverb" type rear radio speaker for coupes and sedans. 664 transistorized ignition regulator. 621 Ride & Handling package. 574 headrests and right-hand reclining seat. 634 Superlift rear shock absorbers. 438 front seat shoulder harness. 628 Soft Ride springs and shocks. 441 Safeguard speedometer. 471 Custom Sports steering wheel. 511 quick-ratio 20:1 steering with power steering. 504 tilt-adjustable steering wheel with power steering and floor shift. 521 hazard warning indicator switch. 642 trailer towing provisions. 671 transistor ignition system. 784 four-speed synchromesh transmission. 782 automatic transmission. 785 heavy-duty three-speed manual transmission with floor shift, 458 Custom wheel discs. 461 deluxe wheel discs. 452 wire wheel discs. 454 Rally wheels with 7.75 x 14 tires. 062 Protection Group includes padded instrument panel, door edge guards, rear window defogger, floor mats, spare tire cover and retractable seat belts in two-door models except convertible ($64.66). 062 Protection Group. 071 Mirror Group. 074 Lamp Group. 622 heavy-load springs and shocks. 642 Trailer Towing Group. 661 heavy-duty frame on convertible. Special order axles. 484 metallic brake linings. 731 Safe-T-Track rear axle. 591 speedometer adapter. Special order close-ratio four-speed manual transmission. Special order Stratobench seats.

1967 CATALINA 2+2

According to *Greatest American Cars* (a giant book available from Krause Publications) the 2+2 was the result of a performance oriented package option that just made it into the realm of the muscle car. "The 2+2 adapted cars were marketed as a sort of a giant five-seat luxury sports car with a long list of technical and luxury choices," says the book, which details how the 2+2 could be orded "as fine as you want — or as fierce."

The market niche for full-sized (read that as "huge") performance cars was a small one by the time the 1967 model year rolled around. One by one the full-sized models dropped their specially trimmed, big-engine variants in favor of the plush, quiet motoring experience sought by luxury-oriented buyers. As a result of such swings in buying trends, the Pontiac Catalina 2+2 reverted to option package status in 1967. In fact, this would be the last year that it was offered as a U.S. model, although a full-sized Canadian version was seen as late as 1970 and a different type of 2+2 (based on a down-sized Grand Prix) would surface in 1986 1/2. Only technically minded Pontiac buyers noticed the change in the automaker's 1967 marketing emphasis, however, since the 2+2 Catalina package gave all the appearance of being a completely integrated package.

A massive 428-cid/360-hp V-8 came as standard equipment, as did a heavy-duty suspension, a floor-mounted three-speed manual transmission and front bucket-type seats. A 428-cid/376-hp V-8 with a four-barrel carburetor cost $119 extra. An additional $226 bought you a four-speed manual gear box.

You could also add the usual Pontiac goodies like eight-lug aluminum wheels for $135 and Rally II steel wheels for $56. Of course, you had to start by checking the 2+2 option box on the order form. That added $410 to the $2,951 two-door hardtop and $389 to the $3,276 convertible.

When the model year was over, only 1,768 2+2-equipped Catalinas were built. No hardtop and convertible production breakout is available. Low sales then sealed the fate of the Catalina 2+2 option, ending its much too short four-year production run.

Model Number	Body/Style Number	Body Type & Seating	Factory Price	Shipping Weight	Production Total
CATALINA 2+2 — SERIES 254 — V-8:					
254	37	2d HT-5P	$3,371	3,988 lbs.	1,488
254	67	2d Conv-5P	$3,675	4,038 lbs.	280

ENGINES

OPTIONAL ECONOMY V-8: Overhead valve. Cast-iron block. Bore and stroke: 4.12 x 3.75. Displacement: 400 cid. Compression ratio: 8.6:1. Brake hp: 265 at 4600 rpm. Taxable hp: 54.3. Torque: 397 at 2400 rpm. Five main bearings. Hydraulic valve lifters. Carburetor: Two-barrel. Engine code: WA, YA, YB and WB.

BASE V-8: Overhead valve. Cast-iron block. Bore and stroke: 4.12 x 4.00. Displacement: 428 cid. Compression ratio: 10.5:1. Brake hp: 360 at 4600 rpm. Taxable hp: 54.3. Torque: 472 at 3200 rpm. Five main bearings. Hydraulic valve lifters. Carburetor: Four-barrel. Engine code: WG, WK, XD, Y2, YH, YY, YZ and YT.

OPTION H.O. V-8: Overhead valve. Cast-iron block. Bore and stroke: 4.12 x 4.000. Displacement: 428 cid. Compression ratio: 10.75:1. Brake hp: 376 at 5100 rpm.

Taxable hp: 54.3. Torque: 462 at 3400 rpm. Five main bearings. Hydraulic valve lifters. Carburetor: Four-barrel. Engine code: WJ, WL, XK and YK.

OPTIONS

Custom air conditioner ($421). Air injector exhaust control ($44). Console ($105). Cruise control ($63). Front disc brakes ($105). Rear window defogger ($21). Headrests ($42-$52). Capacitor ignition ($104-$115). Cornering lamps ($34). Low-fuel lamp ($6). Custom gauge panel cluster ($21-$36). Power antenna ($29). Power steering ($95-$105). AM/FM stereo ($239). Safeguard speedometer ($16). Reclining right-hand seat ($84). Super-Lift shock absorbers ($40). Front shoulder belts ($23-$26). Fender skirts ($26). Ride and handling package ($9). Strato Bucket seats on Bonneville coupe and convertible only ($114). Cordova top ($105-$132). Turbo Hydra-Matic ($226). Four-speed

manual transmission ($226). Three-speed manual transmission with floor shift ($42). Ventura Custom option with bench seats ($134). Ventura Custom convertible option with bucket seats ($206). Ventura Custom hardtop option with bucket seats ($248). Aluminum hubs and drums ($118-$135). Rally II wheels ($65-$73). 2+2 Sport Option ($389-$410). (Note: The 2+2 Sport Option included deluxe wheel discs and steering wheel, decor moldings, bucket seats, four-barrel 428-cid V-8, three-speed manual floor shift, dual exhaust and heavy-duty stabilizer bar. The 428-cid V-8 with 10.5:1 compression and four-barrel carburetor was optional in all full-sized Pontiacs at $79-$114 extra, with prices depending upon model, transmission and use of air injector exhaust control. A 428-cid HO (high-output) V-8 was available in all full-sized Pontiacs for $119-$263 extra, with prices depending on model, transmission and use of air injector exhaust control.

1967 FIREBIRD 400

1967 Firebird 400

There was a new Pontiac muscle car on the block on 1967. The first Firebird was made at Lordstown, Ohio, in early January of that year and the new car line was officially released Feb. 23, 1967. External features included sculptured body styling, twin grilles of a bumper-integral design, front vent windows and three vertical air slots on the leading edge of rear body panels. .

Two body styles were offered and came with any of the Tempest or GTO power trains. However, the two body styles were marketed in five "models" created by adding regular production options (UPCs) in specific combinations. The models were the base Firebird, Firebird Sprint, Firebird 326, Firebird 326 H.O. and Firebird 400. The Firebird 400s used a 325-hp version of the GTO V-8 with a four-barrel carburetor.

Standard equipment included a dual scoop hood, chrome engine parts, a three-speed heavy-duty floor shifter and a sport-type suspension. The letters "400" appeared on the right-hand side of the deck lid. Options included a Ram Air induction setup that gave 325 hp at a higher rpm peak and cost over $600 extra.

With the 325-hp Firebird 400 option, 0-to-60 mph took 6.4 seconds and the quarter-mile took 14.3 seconds. The Firebird 400 sport coupe with the 325-hp engine was clocked by a second test driver at 14.7 seconds and 98 mph in the quarter-mile.

Model Number	Body/Style Number	Body Type & Seating	Factory Price	Shipping Weight	Production Total
FIREBIRD 400 — SERIES 223 — V-8:					
223	37	2d HT-5P	$2,777	3,549 lbs.	52,005
223	67	2d Conv-5P	$3,177	3,855 lbs.	12,884

NOTE 1: Production is for all Firebird V-8s; no breakout for "400" model available.

NOTE 2: 18,635 cars had the base 400-cid/325-hp V-8.

NOTE 3: 65 cars had the optional 400-cid/335-hp Ram Air V-8.

ENGINES

BASE V-8: Overhead valves. Cast-iron block. Displacement: 400 cu. in. Bore & stroke: 4.125 x 3.75 in. Compression ratio: 10.75:1. Brake hp: 325 at 4800 rpm. Torque: 410 lbs.-ft. at 3400 rpm. Five main bearings. Hydraulic valve lifters. Carburetor: Four-barrel. Engine codes: WI-WQ-WU-WZ with manual transmission; XN-YT with automatic transmission. UPC W66.

OPTIONAL V-8: Overhead valves. Cast-iron block. Displacement: 400 cu. in. Bore & stroke: 4.125 x 3.75 in. Compression ratio: 10.75:1. Brake hp: 335 at 5200 rpm. Torque: 410 lbs.-ft. at 3600 rpm. Five main bearings. Hydraulic valve lifters. Carburetor: Rochester model 7027071 four-barrel. UPC L67.

PONTIAC

OPTIONS

382 door edge guards (price unavailable). 631 front floor mats (price unavailable). 632 rear floor mats (price unavailable). 502 power brakes with pedal trim ($41.60). 501 17.5:1 ratio power steering ($94.79). 551 power windows ($100.05). 401 luggage lamp (price unavailable). 402 ignition switch lamp (price unavailable). 421 underhood lamp (price unavailable). 582 custom air conditioning ($355.98). 374 rear window defogger/blower ($21.06). 531 all Soft-Ray glass ($30.54). 532 Soft-Ray windshield ($21.06). 441 cruise control with automatic transmission only ($52.66). 442 Safeguard speedometer (price unavailable). 654 carpet-back rear fold-down seat ($36.86). 544 power convertible top ($52.66). 474 electric clock ($15.80). 394 remote-control outside rearview mirror (price unavailable). 391 visor vanity mirror (price unavailable). 572 bench or bucket seat headrest ($52.66) 342 push-button radio with manual antenna ($61.09). manual rear antenna instead of regular front antenna ($9.48). 344 push-button AM/FM radio with manual antenna ($133.76). 351 rear radio speaker ($15.80). 354 Delco stereo tape player ($128.49). unknown stereo multiplex adaptor (price unavailable). 462 deluxe steering wheel (price unavailable). 471 custom sports steering wheel (price unavailable). 504 tilt steering wheel, not available with standard steering, three-speed column shift or Turbo Hydra-Matic transmission without console (price unavailable). 731

Saf-T-Track differential (price unavailable). 491 rally stripes (price unavailable). 444 rally stripes ($31.60). 704 hood-mounted tachometer ($63.19). 524 custom shift knob (price unavailable). 472 console with bucket seats and floor shift ($47.39). 481 tailpipe extensions (price unavailable). 431 front and rear custom seat belts (price unavailable). 434 front seat shoulder belts (price unavailable). 521 front disc brakes, 502 recommended ($63.19). unknown, hood retainer pins (price unavailable). 494 dual horns, standard with custom trim (price unavailable). 738 rear axle options (no cost). OBC-SVT vinyl roof for sport coupe ($84.26). OBC custom trim option ($108.48). OBC Strato-Bench front seat ($31.60). 674 heavy-duty alternator, standard with air conditioning ($15.80). 681 heavy-duty radiator, standard with air conditioning ($14.74). 361 heavy-duty dual-stage air cleaner ($9.43). 678 heavy-duty battery, included with 674 ($3.48). 453 Rally II wheels, available with 521 (with custom trim $55.81; with standard trim $72.67). 454 Rally I wheels, available with 521 (with custom trim $40.02; with standard trim $56.87). 461 deluxe wheel discs (price unavailable). 458 custom wheel discs (price unavailable). 452 wire wheel discs (69.51). Tu-tone paint in standard colors ($31.07). Tu-tone paint in custom colors ($114.27). 185R-14 radial whitewall tires ($10.53).1 E70-14 redline or white sidewall tires (no cost).

1967 GTO

JERRY HEASLEY

1967 GTO

The GTO's new wire mesh grille and four-lens tail light treatment were distinguishing marks of the 1967 model. The rocker panel moldings were made wider and now covered the body sides as well as the lower edge of the doors, the front fenders and the rear quarters. The trim along the center grille divider now went from one side of the car to the other, with a dip around the center divider. V-shaped fender badges behind the front wheel opening were eliminated. Like the Grand Prix, the GTO had twin pinstripes along the upper beltline and bright metal wheel opening moldings. Rectangular front grille parking lamps were still used in front and the new taillights now took the form of four thin rectangles at each side.

All Le Mans features were standard, plus the new 335-hp four-barrel 400-cid V-8. This engine featured new cylinder heads that were reworked for improved volumetric flow. They

carried push rod guides, screw-in studs and larger diameter valves. GM's corporate de-emphasis of performance banned multi-carburetor setups, so Tri-Power carburetion was no longer available. However, there was an H.O. (high-output) 400 using the Rochester Quadrajet four-barrel carburetor.

The 1967 GTO Ram Air 400 with automatic and 3.90:1 gearing did the quarter-mile in 13.37 seconds at 103.40 mph according to the February/March 1996 issue of *Muscle Car Review*.

Model Number	Body/Style Number	Body Type & Seating	Factory Price	Shipping Weight	Production Total
GTO — SERIES 242 — V-8					
22	27	2d Cpe-6P	$2,871	3,425 lbs.	7,029
22	37	2d HT-6P	$2,935	3,430 lbs.	65,176
22	67	2d Conv-6P	$3,165	3,515 lbs.	9517

PONTIAC

ENGINES

OPTIONAL "ECONOMY" V-8 (AUTOMATIC TRANSMISSION): Overhead valve. Cast-iron block. Bore and stroke: 4.12 x 3.75. Displacement: 400 cid. Compression ratio: 8.6:1. Brake hp: 255 at 4400 rpm. Taxable hp: 54.3. Torque: 397 at 2400 rpm. Five main bearings. Hydraulic valve lifters. Carburetor: Two-barrel. Engine code: YB.

BASE V-8: Overhead valve. Cast-iron block. Bore and stroke: 4.12 x 3.75. Displacement: 400 cid. Compression ratio: 10.75:1. Brake hp: 335 at 5000 rpm. Taxable hp: 54.3. Torque: 441 at 3400 rpm. Five main bearings. Hydraulic valve lifters. Chrome air cleaner. Chrome rocker covers. Chrome oil filler cap. Carburetor: Four-barrel. Engine code: WT, WW and YS.

OPTIONAL V-8: Overhead valve. Cast-iron block. Bore and stroke: 4.12 x 3.75. Displacement: 400 cid. Compression ratio: 10.75:1. Brake hp: 360 at 5100 rpm. Taxable hp: 54.3. Torque: 438 at 3600 rpm. Five main bearings. Hydraulic valve lifters. Chrome low-restriction air cleaner. Chrome rocker covers. Chrome oil filler cap. Special dual exhausts. High-output camshaft and valve train. De-clutching fan. Carburetor: Four-barrel. Engine code: WS, WV, XP, XS, YR and YZ.

OPTIONAL V-8: Overhead valve. Cast-iron block. Bore and stroke: 4.12 x 3.75. Displacement: 400 cid. Compression ratio: 10.75:1. Brake hp: 360 at 5400 rpm. Taxable hp: 54.3. Torque: 438 at 3800 rpm. Five main bearings. Hydraulic valve lifters. Chrome low-restriction air cleaner. Chrome rocker covers. Chrome oil filler cap. Special dual exhausts. High-output camshaft and valve train. De-clutching fan. Carburetor: Four-barrel. Engine code: WS, WV, XP, XS, YR and YZ.

OPTIONS (PARTIAL LIST)

472 console in GTO with Hydra-Matic transmission ($68.46). 441 cruise control ($52.66). 371 front foam seat cushions ($7.90). 492 remote-control deck lid, except Safari ($12.64). 374 rear window defogger, all models except convertible ($21.06). 731 Safe-T-Track differential ($42.13). 731 heavy-duty Safe-T-Track differential, in all cars with 74H, 74K, 74P or 74S axles ($63.19). 521 front disc brakes ($104.79). [Engines for manual transmission cars]: 400-cid four-barrel H.O. V-8 with A.I.R. option 612, in GTO ($76.89). 400-cid four-barrel V-8 with A.I.R. option 612, in GTO series (no cost). [Engines for automatic transmission cars]: Code XL-M 400-cid two-barrel V-8 with or without A.I.R. option 612, GTO only (no cost). Code YS 400-cid four-barrel V-8 in GTO (no cost). Code XP 400-cid four-barrel "Ram Air" V-8 in GTO series only ($263.30). Code YZ 400-cid four-barrel H.O. V-8 in GTO only ($76.89). 524 Custom gearshift knob for all with three- or four-speed floor shift ($3.69). 394 remote-control outside rearview mirror ($7.37). SPS special color solid paint ($83.20). STT special color two-tone paint, except convertibles ($114.27). 444 Rally Gauge Cluster with tachometer ($84.26), 341 power antenna ($29.12). 502 power brakes ($41.60). 561 4-Way power bench seat ($69.51). 501 power steering ($94.79). 564 4-Way left-hand power bucket seat in all models with bucket seats ($69.51). 551 power windows ($100.05). 681 heavy-duty radiator without air conditioning ($14.74). 348 manual radio and antenna ($52.66). 342 push-button radio and antenna ($61.09). 344 AM/FM push-button radio and antenna ($133.76). 621 Ride & Handling package ($3.74). 622 heavy load springs and shocks ($3.74). 471 Custom Sports steering wheel ($30.02). 504 tilt steering wheel, power steering required ($42.13). 662 quick steering, all except with power steering ($10.53). 534 rear door jamb switches ($3.16). 354 stereo tape player ($128.49). TCL 7.75 x 14 white sidewall Nylon tires on GTO ($49.51). TMC F70 x 14 red stripe Nylon tires on GTO (no cost). SVT Cordova vinyl top for two-door coupes and hardtops ($84.26). 77C three-speed manual transmission with four-barrel OHC six without Sprint package ($42.13). 77S three-speed manual transmission in GTO (no cost). 77S column-shifted three-speed manual transmission on V-8 models without a console (no cost). 778 four-speed manual transmission on GTO only ($184.31). 77X Turbo Hydra-Matic automatic transmission for GTO with 400-cid two-barrel V-8 ($226.44). 77J Turbo Hydra-Matic automatic transmission for GTO with 400-cid four-barrel V-8 ($226.44). 614 positive crankcase ventilation ($5.27). 461 Deluxe wheel discs for all models ($16.85). 454 Rally I wheels for all without 064 Décor Group ($56.87). 453 Rally II wheels for all without Décor Group 064 ($72.67). 451 aluminum hubs and drums for all without 064 Décor Group ($100.05). 061 Basic Group ($89.48). 064 Décor Group ($9.02 in GTO convertible slightly more in coupes) 071 Mirror Group ($9.05). 062 Protection Group ($22.86 on GTO convertible and slightly more on coupes).

1968 FIREBIRD 400

The Firebird return in its second year as a car that could give any muscle car on the market a run for its money when it came to looks and performance. The Firebird 400 with the 335-hp Ram Air V-8 option was capable of 0-to-60 mph in 4.8 seconds and the quarter-mile in 15.0 seconds at 110 mph. The 1968 Firebird 400 H.O. with the 335-hp option was capable of 0-to-60 mph in 5.3 seconds and the quarter-mile in 14.2 seconds.

The Firebird 400's standard equipment included a three-speed manual transmission with floor-mounted gear shifter. The engine was a 400-cid V-8 with 10.75:1 compression ratio, a Rochester four-barrel carburetor and 335 hp at 5000 rpm. It had a special high-lift camshaft, forged aluminum pistons, an Armasteel crankshaft, new push rods and guides, tulip-head valves and dual high-rate valve springs.

Model Number	Body/Style Number	Body Type & Seating	Factory Price	Shipping Weight	Production Total
FIREBIRD 400 — SERIES 223 — V-8:					
223	37	2d HT-5P	$3,216	3,076 lbs.	74,074
223	67	2d Conv-5P	$3,177	3,855 lbs.	14,544

NOTE 1: Production is for all Firebird V-8s; no breakout for "400" model available.

NOTE 2: About 21,000 cars with the 400 option were built and about 3,500 were convertibles.

NOTE 3: The Ram Air I option was used in 413 cars (321 with four-speed manual transmission).

NOTE 4: The Ram Air II option was used in 110 cars (98 with four-speed manual transmission).

ENGINES

OPTIONAL V-8: Overhead valve. Cast-iron block. Bore and stroke: 4.12 x 3.75. Displacement: 400 cid. Compression ratio: 10.75:1. Brake hp: 330 at 4800 rpm. Taxable hp: 54.3. Torque: 430 at 3300 rpm. Five main bearings. Hydraulic valve lifters. Carburetor: Four-barrel. Engine code: WZ and YT.

OPTIONAL V-8: Overhead valve. Cast-iron block. Bore and stroke: 4.12 x 3.75. Displacement: 400 cid. Compression ratio: 10.75:1. Brake hp: 335 at 5000 rpm. Taxable hp: 54.3. Torque: 430 at 3400 rpm. Five main bearings. Hydraulic valve lifters. Carburetor: Four-barrel. Engine code: WQ, WI, YW and XN.

OPTIONAL V-8: Overhead valve. Cast-iron block. Bore and stroke: 4.12 x 3.75. Displacement: 400 cid. Compression ratio: 10.75:1. Brake hp: 335 at 5300 rpm. Taxable hp: 54.3. Torque: 430 at 3600 rpm. Five main bearings. Hydraulic valve lifters. Carburetor: Four-barrel. Engine code: WQ, WI, YW and XN.

OPTIONS (PARTIAL LIST)

591 speedometer gear adapter ($11.59). 731 heavy-duty air cleaner ($9.48). 582 custom air conditioner ($360.20). 474 electric clock, not available with 394 ($15.80). 514 heavy-duty clutch and seven-blade fan, with V-8; without 582 ($15.80). 472 console, not available with contour bench seat ($50.55). 441 cruise control, not available with manual transmission ($52.66). 492 remote-control deck lid ($13.69). 404 rear window defogger, except convertible ($21.06). 361 Safe-T-Track differential ($42.13). 361 heavy-duty Safe-T-Track differential, with H, K, P, S axles ($63.19). 521 front disc brakes ($63.19). 347 four-barrel 400-cid Ram Air V-8, with 351, 354, 358; not available with 582 ($616.12. 348 four-barrel 400 H.O. V-8 with 351, 354, 358 ($350.72). 444 auxiliary gauge cluster ($31.60). 531 all tinted glass ($30.54). 532 tinted windshield ($21.06). 412 door edge guards ($6.24). 571 contoured head restraints ($52.66). SPS special solid paint, except code A Black ($83.20). STT special two-tone paint, coupe ($114.80). RTT two-tone paint, standard color on coupe ($31.60). SPR special paint code, code A Black only ($10.53). 502 power

PONTIAC

1968 Firebird 400

brakes ($42.13). 561 foull-width four-way power bench seat ($69.51). 501 power steering ($94.79). 564 left-hand four-way power bucket seat ($69.51). 544 power convertible top ($52.66). 551 power windows ($100.05). 381 manually operated rear antenna ($9.48). 394 stereo tape player, not available with 391 or 392 ($133.76). 382 push-button radio with antenna ($61.09). 384 push-button AM/FM radio and manual antenna ($133.76). 391 rear seat speaker ($15.80). 494 rally side stripes, not available with 344 ($14.74). 431 front and rear seat custom seat belts ($9.48). 432 rear shoulder belts with 431 or 754 ($26.33). 754 front seat shoulder belts, with 431 ($26.3); without 431 ($23.17). 568 contour bench seat ($31.60). 621 Ride & Handling package without 345 ($9.48), with 345 ($4.21). 471 custom sport steering wheel, with 554 ($30.54); without 554 ($45.29). 462 deluxe steering wheel ($14.74). 504 tilt wheel, not available with three-speed column shift or Hydra-

Matic without console; power steering required ($42.13). 434 hood-mounted tachometer ($63.19). 402 spare tire cover ($5.27). SVT Cordova vinyl top on coupe ($84.26). 351 Turbo Hydra-Matic with 345, 347, 348 ($236.97). 354 four-speed manual transmission with floor shift, without 37S axle ($184.31). 355 heavy-duty three-speed with floor shift with 343,344 ($84.26); with 345, 348 (no cost). 356 heavy-duty three-speed with floor shift, use with 472, include with 342 ($42.13). 358 close-ratio four-speed manual transmission with floor shift, mandatory with 37S axle ($184.31). 534 custom pedal trim, not available with 554 ($5.27). 458 custom wheel discs, with 554 ($20.01); without 554 ($73.72). 453 Rally II rims with 554 ($63.19); without 554 ($84.26). 321 front foam cushion ($86.37). 554 custom trim option ($114.88). 332 lamp group ($5.25). 331 mirror group, except convertible ($13.22). 322 rear window defogger-protection group ($55.25).

1968 GTO

The GTO was down to two models for 1968. Both the hardtop coupe and the convertible were built on the shorter two-door Tempest wheelbase. The true distinction of the 1968 GTO was its Endura front end. This was truly a Pontiac innovation, as no other GM car had it at the time. It was also a look into the future.

Hidden headlights were a very popular GTO option. A new hood was used on the 1968 GTO. It had twin air scoops flowing out of the cowl. The hood air scoops had bolted-on, closed ornaments. However, the Ram Air package included open ornaments that had to be paint matched. Owners were advised to use the closed ornaments in rainy weather. A large bulge ran up the center of the hood and came to a point at the ship's prow nose.

Standard in GTOs was a 350-hp/400-cid four-barrel V-8 (or two-barrel 400-cid regular fuel V-8). A 360-hp four-barrel version and two Ram Air engine setups were also available. The 360-hp GTO hardtop did 0-to-60 mph in 6.6 seconds and the quarter-mile took 15.5 seconds. The GTO gave Pontiac *Motor Trend* magazine's "Car of the Year" award.

Model Number	Body/Style Number	Body Type & Seating	Factory Price	Shipping Weight	Production Total
GTO — SERIES 242 — V-8					
22	37	2d HT-6P	$3,101	3,506 lbs.	77,704
22	67	2d Conv-6P	$2,996	3,346 lbs.	9,980

ENGINES

OPTIONAL "ECONOMY" V-8: Overhead valves. Cast-iron block. Displacement: 400 cid. Bore and stroke: 4.125 x 3.746 in. Compression ratio: 8.6:1. Brake hp: 265 at 4600 rpm. Torque: 397 at 2400 rpm. Five main bearings. Hydraulic valve lifters. Carburetor: two-barrel.

BASE V-8: Overhead valves. Cast-iron block. Displacement: 400 cid. Bore and stroke: 4.125 x 3.746 in. Compression ratio: 10.75:1. Brake hp: 350 at 5000 rpm. Torque: 445 at 3000 rpm. Five main bearings. Hydraulic valve lifters. Carburetor: Rochester model 7028266 four-barrel.

OPTIONAL HO V-8: Overhead valves. Cast-iron block. Displacement: 400 cid. Bore and stroke: 4.125 x 3.746 in. Compression ratio: 10.75:1. Brake hp: 360 at 5100 rpm. Torque: 445 at 3600 rpm. Five main bearings. Hydraulic valve lifters. Carburetor: Rochester Quadrajet four-barrel.

EARLY 1968 GTO OPTIONAL RAM AIR V-8: Overhead valves. Cast-iron block. Displacement: 400 cid. Bore and stroke: 4.125 x 3.746 in. Compression ratio: 10.75:1. Brake hp: 360 at 5400 rpm. Torque: 445 at 3600. Five main bearings. Hydraulic valve lifters. Carburetor: Rochester Quadrajet four-barrel.

1968 1/2 GTO OPTIONAL RAM AIR V-8: Overhead valves. Cast-iron block. Displacement: 400 cid. Bore and stroke: 4.125 x 3.746 in. Compression ratio:

JERRY HEASLEY

1968 GTO

10.75:1. Brake hp: 370 at 5500 rpm. Torque: 445 at 3900. Five main bearings. Hydraulic valve lifters. Carburetor: Rochester Quadrajet four-barrel.

OPTIONS (PARTIAL LIST)

591 speedometer gear adapter ($11.59). 731 heavy-duty air cleaner ($9.48). 582 custom air conditioner ($360.20). 701 heavy-duty battery for two-barrel models ($6.32). 474 electric clock ($18.96). 472 center console in GTO with Hydra-Matic ($68.46). 414 GTO retractable headlight covers ($52.66). 441 cruise control, requires V-8 and automatic transmission ($52.66). 392 remote-control deck lid release ($13.69). 404 rear window defogger, except convertible ($21.06). 361 Safe-T-Track differential ($42.13). 361 Safe-T-Track differential with H-K-P-S code axles ($63.19). 521 front disc brakes, requires option 502 power brakes on Safaris ($63.19). 342 400-cid four-barrel Ram Air V-8 in GTO only, not available with air conditioning ($342.29). 348 400-cid four-barrel HO V-8 in GTO ($76.88). 482 exhaust extension for dual exhaust V-8s ($21.06). 444 Rally Gauge cluster with tachometer ($84.26). 484 Rally Gauge cluster and clock ($50.55). 531 all windows tinted ($34.76). 532 tinted windshield ($25.28). SPS special solid paint ($83.20). STT special color two-tone paint, except convertible ($123.22). RTT standard color two-tone paint, except convertible ($40.02). 502 power brakes ($42.13). 561 4-Way full-width power front seat ($69.51). 501 power steering ($94.79). 564 left-hand 4-Way power front bucket seat ($69.51). 551 power windows ($100.05). 381 power antenna ($29.49). 388 AM/FM stereo radio with manual antenna ($239.08). 394 stereo tape player, not available with rear

seat speaker or reverb ($133.76). 382 push-button AM radio and antenna ($61.09). 384 push-button AM/FM radio with manual antenna ($133.76). 392 rear seat reverb speaker ($52.66). 494 Rally stripes on all GTOs ($10.53). 431 front and rear Custom seat belts in two-doors ($9.48). 442 Safeguard speedometer ($15.80). 621 Ride & Handling package ($4.21). 471 Custom Sports steering wheel in base Tempest with option 324 and all Tempest Custom, Le Mans and GTOs ($30.54). 504 tilt-adjustable steering column, power steering required ($42.13). 434 hood-mounted tachometer ($63.19). 402 spare tire and wheel cover, except convertible ($5.27). SVT cordova top ($94.79). 351 Turbo Hydra-Matic transmission in GTO ($236.97). 354 four-speed manual transmission with floor shift without option 341 or 37S axle ($184.31). 358 close-ratio four-speed manual transmission with floor shift, GTO with 37P axle ($184.31). 461 deluxe wheel discs ($21.06). 452 wire wheel discs with option 324 ($52.66); without option 324 ($73.72). 453 Rally wheel rims with option 324 ($63.19); without option 324 ($84.26). 321 Basic Group ($89.53). 324 Décor Group ($21-$83 depending on series and body style). 332 lamp group ($2.11-$15.80 depending on body style). 331 mirror group ($9.45-$13.65 depending on body style). 322 Protection Group ($34.10-$63.60 depending on body style). TPC G70 x 14 nylon Red Line tires (no charge GTO, $67-$82 on other models). TPD G70 x 14 nylon white sidewall tires (no charge GTO). TRC G77 x 14 nylon Red Line tires on GTO (no charge). TRD G77 x 14 nylon white sidewall tires on GTO (no charge). TSM 205R x 14 rayon white sidewall tires ($10.50 on GTO).

1969 FIREBIRD 400

Firebirds were restyled late in 1968 to incorporate revisions similar to those planned for the Chevrolet Camaro. Design changes included flatter wheel openings, front fender wind splits and a creased lower beltline. The gas filler was moved behind the rear license plate and a boxier split bumper grille was used. The Firebird 400 option package (UPC 345; engine code WS6) a dual exhaust system, a three-speed manual transmission with floor shifter, and a 400-cid V-8 with 330 hp at 4800 rpm.

A special hood is used on the Firebird 400 and incorporates non-functional air scoops. Also, a Ride & Handling package was required. The Firebird 400 option cost $275-$358 over

base model cost depending on transmission. The 400 Ram Air option (UPC 348; engine code L-74) included the same features as the Firebird 400, except for addition of de-clutching cooling fan and twin functional hood scoops with operating mechanism. The Ram Air IV option (UPC 347; engine code L-67) includes the same features as the Ram Air 400, plus special hood scoop emblems. The engine was a 400-cid V-8 with a special camshaft and valve train, a 10.75:1 compression ratio, a Rochester four-barrel carburetor and 345 hp at 5400 rpm. The price of the Ram Air IV kit was $832 over base model cost.

1969 Firebird 400

Model Number	Body/Style Number	Body Type & Seating	Factory Price	Shipping Weight	Production Total
FIREBIRD 400 — SERIES 223 — V-8:					
223	37	2d HT-5P	$3,262	—	Note 2
223	67	2d Conv-5P	$3 460	—	Note 2
FIREBIRD RAM AIR 400 — SERIES 223 — V-8:					
223	37	2d HT-5P	$3388	—	Note 3
223	67	2d Conv-5P	$3,602	—	Note 3
FIREBIRD RAM AIR IV — SERIES 223 — V-8:					
223	37	2d HT-5P	$3,662	—	Note 4
223	67	2d Conv-5P	$3,876	—	Note 4

NOTE 1: Total Firebird production included 74,673 hardtops and 11,641 convertibles (not including Trans Ams).

NOTE 2: 11,522 of these cars had the base 400-cid V-8.

NOTE 3: 867 of these cars had the Ram Air III V-8 (not including Trans Ams).

NOTE 4: 102 of these cars had the Ram Air IV V-8 (not including Trans Ams).

ENGINES

BASE V-8: Overhead valve. Cast-iron block. Bore and stroke: 4.12 x 3.75. Displacement: 400 cid. Compression ratio: 10.75:1. Brake hp: 330 at 4800 rpm. Taxable hp: 54.3. Torque: 430 at 3300 rpm. Five main bearings. Hydraulic valve lifters. Carburetor: Four-barrel. Engine code: WZ and YT.

OPTIONAL V-8 (RAM AIR III): Overhead valve. Cast-iron block. Bore and stroke: 4.12 x 3.75. Displacement: 400 cid. Compression ratio: 10.75:1. Brake hp: 335 at 5000 rpm. Taxable hp: 54.3. Torque: 430 at 3400 rpm. Five main bearings. Hydraulic valve lifters. Carburetor: Four-barrel. Engine code: WQ, WD, WE, YD, WA and WB.

OPTIONAL V-8 (RAM AIR IV): Overhead valve. Cast-iron block. Bore and stroke: 4.12 x 3.75. Displacement: 400 cid. Compression ratio: 10.75:1. Brake hp: 345 at 5400 rpm. Taxable hp: 54.3. Torque: 430 at 3700 rpm. Five main bearings. Hydraulic valve lifters. Carburetor: Four-barrel. Engine code: WH and XN.

OPTIONS (PARTIAL LIST)

582/C60 custom air conditioning, not available with Ram Air ($375.99). 472/D55 console with bucket seats ($53.71). SVT/G08 Cordova top on coupe ($89.52). 441/K30 cruise control for cars with automatic transmission and V-8 ($57.93). 492/A90 remote-control deck lid release ($14.74). 404/C50 rear window defogger, not available with convertible ($22.12). 481/N10 dual exhausts, available with 343 ($30.54). 691/KB2 heavy-duty Power Flex fan, for all without 582 ($10.53); for V-8 with 582 (no cost). 534/M09 501/N41 variable-ratio power steering ($105.32). 564/A46 left-hand power bucket seat ($73.72). 544/C06 power convertible top ($52.66). 551/A31 power windows ($105.32). 502/J50 power brakes, not available with 345, 347 or 348 ($42.13). 511/JL2 power front disc brakes ($64.25). 382/U63 AM radio with manual antenna ($61.09). 384/U69 AM/FM radio with manual antenna ($133.76). 388/U58 AM/FM stereo radio with manual antenna ($239.08). 484/W63 rally gauge cluster with clock, without 442 or 444 ($47.39). 444/U30 rally gauge cluster and tachometer, without 442, 474 or 484 ($84.26). 621/Y96 Ride & Handling springs and shocks, (with 345, 347 and 348 price was $4.21; with 341, 342, 343 and 344 price was $9.48). 461/N30 deluxe steering wheel ($15.80). 462/N34 custom sports steering wheel, with 342 ($34.76); without 342 ($50.55).394/U57 stereo tape player, not available with 391 ($133.76). 471/UB5 hood-mounted tachometer ($63.19). 554/W54 Custom trim option, for coupe with knit-vinyl bench seat ($110.99). 554/W54 Custom trim option, for coupe with bucket seats ($780.99). 554/W54 Custom trim option, for coupe with leather bucket seats ($199.05). 452/P02 Custom wheel covers ($20.01 with 324; $41.07 without 324). 451/P01 Deluxe wheel covers ($21.06). 453/N95 wire wheel covers ($52.66 with 324; $73.72 without 324). 454/N98 Rally II wheels ($63.19 with 324; $84.26 without 324). 321/Y88 Basic group ($113.75). 324/Y86 Décor group ($62.14). 331/WS6 power-assist group with 341 or 342 ($364.93); with 343 ($375.49); with 344, 345, 347 or 348 ($396.61). 332/WS5 turnpike cruise group, with Turbo Hydra-Matic, V-8 and 505 ($176.94). 334/W58 Rally group all 345, 347, 348 with 324 ($149.55). 334/W58 Rally group all 345, 347, 348 without 324 ($186.41). 334/W58 Rally group all 341, 342, 343, 344 with 324 ($154.82). 334/W58 Rally group all 341, 342, 343, 344 without 324 ($191.68). 344/W66 Firebird 400 Sport option, for coupe with 351, 354 or 358 ($347.56). 344/W66 Firebird 400 Sport option, for convertible with 351, 354 or 358 ($331.76). 344/W66 Firebird 400 Sport option, for coupe without 351, 354 or 358 ($431.81). 344/W66 Firebird 400 Sport option, for convertible without 351, 354 or 358 ($416.01). 348/L74 400-cid V-8 engine with Ram Air induction and four-barrel carburetor, with 345 ($358). 348/L74 400-cid V-8 engine with Ram Air IV induction and four-barrel carburetor, with 345 ($558.20). 361/G80 Safe-T-Track rear axle, regular ($42.13). 361/G80 Safe-T-Track rear axle, heavy-duty ($63.19). 364/G95-G97 economy axle ($2.11). 368/G90-G92 performance axle ($2.11). 362/G94-G83 special order axle ($2.11). 359/M38 Turbo Hydra-Matic transmission, with 341 or 342 ($195.36); with 343 ($205.92). 351/M40 heavy-duty Turbo Hydra-Matic transmission with 344, 345, 347 or 348 ($227.04). 352/M31 two-speed automatic transmission, with 341 ($163.68); with 343 ($174.24). 353/Std. Three-speed manual transmission with column shift, with 341, 343 or 344 (no cost). 354/M20 four-speed manual transmission with floor shift, with all except 347, V-8; with 3.90 axle ($195.36). 355/M13 heavy-duty three-speed manual transmission with floor shift, with 343 or 344 ($84.26). 356/M12 three-speed manual transmission with floor shift, with 341 ($42.13); with 342 (no cost). 358/M21 close-ratio four-speed manual transmission with floor shift, with 390 ($195.36).

1969 1/2 TRANS AM

PONTIAC

JERRY HEASLEY

1969 Trans AM

The Trans Am was introduced at the Chicago Auto Show and officially available on March 8, 1969. It was a sporty, high-performance machine designed to capitalize on the popular Trans-Am racing series. In 1968, a Firebird with a special 302-cid Camaro V-8 was campaigned in the races. Pontiac then developed a short-stroke 303-cid tunnel port V-8 with 485-hp for racing Firebirds, but built only 25 experimental engines.

The production Trans Am had the look of a sedan racer, but featured a 400-cid Ram Air V-8, which was too large an engine to meet the 5.0-litre racing formula. Pontiac had to pay a $5 per car royalty to the Sports Car Club of America (SCCA) to use the Trans Am name. The option (sales code 322; UPC WS4; engine code L74) included a heavy-duty three-speed manual gearbox with a floor-mounted gearshift, heavy-duty suspension, a 3.55:1 rear axle, power front disc brakes, variable ratio power steering, engine air exhaust louvers on sides of fender, a rear deck lid air foil, a black textured grille, full-length body stripes, white and blue finish, a leather covered steering wheel and special identification decals. The engine was the UPC L74 400 H.O. V-8 with 335 hp.

According to Firebird expert Eric J. Vicker, Jr., the price listed on the Pontiac build sheet for a standard Trans Am was $1,025 over base model cost. Apparently, the retail price of the Trans Am over the Firebird 400 was $1,163.74.

In April 1969, *Sports Car Graphic* gave the test to a Trans Am with the base Ram Air III V-8 and 3.55:1 gearing, It did the 0-to-60-mph run in 6.5 seconds and turned in a 14.3-second quarter-mile at 101.7 mph. *Hot Rod* tested the hotter Ram Air IV edition with a 3.90:1 axle. It ran 0-to-60 in 5.6 seconds and did the quarter-mile in 14.1 seconds at 100.78 mph.

Model Number	Body/Style Number	Body Type & Seating	Factory Price	Shipping Weight	Production Total
TRANS AM — SERIES 223 — V-8					
223	37	2d HT-5P	$3,556	—	689
223	67	2d Conv-5P	$3,770	—	8

ENGINES

BASE V-8: Overhead valve. Cast-iron block. Bore and stroke: 4.12 x 3.75. Displacement: 400 cid. Compression ratio: 10.75:1. Brake hp: 335 at 5000 rpm. Taxable hp: 54.3. Torque: 430 at 3400 rpm. Five main bearings. Hydraulic valve lifters. Carburetor: Four-barrel. Engine code: WQ, WD, WE, YD, WA and WB.

OPTIONAL V-8: Overhead valve. Cast-iron block. Bore and stroke: 4.12 x 3.75. Displacement: 400 cid. Compression ratio: 10.75:1. Brake hp: 345 at 5400 rpm. Taxable hp: 54.3. Torque: 430 at 3700 rpm. Five main bearings. Hydraulic valve lifters. Carburetor: Four-barrel. Engine code: WH and XN.

OPTIONS (PARTIAL LIST)

731/K45 heavy-duty dual-stage air cleaner ($9.48). 474/U35 electric clock, included with 484 and not available with 444 ($15.80). 472/D55 console with bucket seats ($53.71). SVT/G08 Cordova top on coupe ($89.52). 441/K30 cruise control for cars with automatic transmission and V-8 ($57.93). 492/A90 remote-control deck lid release ($14.74). 404/C50 rear window defogger, not available with convertible ($22.12). 534/M09 gear knob for floor-shifted manual transmission ($5.27). 501/N41 variable-ratio power steering ($105.32). 564/A46 left-hand power bucket seat ($73.72). 544/C06 power convertible top ($52.66). 551/A31 power windows ($105.32). 502/J50 power brakes, not available with 345, 347 or 348 ($42.13). 511/JL2 power front disc brakes ($64.25). 588/C57 Power-Flow ventilation, not available teamed with 582 ($42.13). 382/U63 AM radio with manual antenna ($61.09). 384/U69 AM/FM radio with manual antenna ($133.76). 388/U58 AM/FM stereo radio with manual antenna ($239.08). 484/W63 rally gauge cluster with clock, without 442 or 444 ($47.39). 621/Y96 Ride & Handling springs and shocks, (with 345, 347 and 348 price was $4.21; with 341, 342, 343 and 344 price was $9.48). 604/A67 rear folding seat ($42.13). 431/WS1 custom front seat belts, includes shoulder straps, in coupe ($12.64); in [convertible] ($36.86). 432/WS2 custom front seat belts, includes front and r[ear] straps, in coupe ($38.97); in convertible ($63.19). 438/AS1 fro[nt] straps, convertible only ($10.53). 708/N65 Space Saver spare tire, without 454 ($15.80); with 454 (no cost). 402/P17 spare tire cover, not available with 708 ($5.27). 504/N33 tilt steering, not available with manual steering or column-shifted manual transmission ($45.29). 391/U80 rear speaker, not avail-

PONTIAC

able in 388 or 394 ($15.80), 442/U15 Safeguard speedometer, not available with 484 or 444 ($11.59). 461/N30 deluxe steering wheel ($15.80). 462/N34 custom sports steering wheel, with 342 ($34.76).

(NOTE: Options list is a partial list for Firebird/Trans Am line. Some options may have been unavailable on Trans Ams.).

1969 GTO

DAN LYONS

1969 GTO

GTOs were based on the LeMans, with additional standard equipment features. For 1969, the body styling was left pretty much alone, with only minor refinements, but a lot of exciting things took place under the hood. At midyear an exciting new model-option aimed at young performance buyers was introduced. Standard GTO equipment included a 400-cid/350-hp V-8, dual exhausts, a 3.55:1 rear axle ratio, a heavy-duty clutch and a three-speed gearbox with floor shifter.

This year every GTO was built with the body-color Endura rubber bumper and a chrome bumper was no longer an option. No Pontiac arrowhead emblem was carried on the nose this year.

The 400-cid H.O. V-8 was gone, but a 366-hp Ram Air option took its place as a factory option. It utilized the H.O. camshaft, but produced six additional horsepower. This engine became known as the Ram Air III V-8.

Muscle Car Review did a "retro" test on the non-Judge '69 GTO in June 1995. The Ram Air III car pulled 0-to-60 mph in 7.4 seconds and ran the quarter-mile in 14.10 seconds at 98.2 mph.

Model Number	Body/Style Number	Body Type & Seating	Factory Price	Shipping Weight	Production Total
GTO — SERIES 242 — V-8					
22	37	2d HT-6P	$2,831	3,080 lbs.	58,126
22	67	2d Conv-6P	$3,382	3,553 lbs.	7,328

ENGINES

OPTIONAL "ECONOMY" V-8: Overhead valves. Cast-iron block. Displacement: 400 cid. Bore and stroke: 4.125 x 3.746 in. Compression ratio: 8.6:1. Brake hp: 265 at 4600 rpm. Torque: 397 at 2400 rpm. Five main bearings. Hydraulic valve lifters. Carburetor: Four-barrel.

BASE V-8: Overhead valves. Cast-iron block. Displacement: 400 cid. Bore and stroke: 4.125 x 3.746 in. Compression ratio: 10.75:1. Brake hp: 350 at 5000 rpm. Torque: 445 at 3000 rpm. Five main bearings. Hydraulic valve lifters. Carburetor: Rochester model 7028266 four-barrel.

OPTIONAL V-8: Overhead valves. Cast-iron block. Displacement: 400 cid. Bore and stroke: 4.125 x 3.746 in. Compression ratio: 10.75:1. Brake hp: 366 at 5100 rpm. Torque: 445 at 3600 rpm. Five main bearings. Hydraulic valve lifters. Special dual exhausts. Carburetor: Rochester four-barrel.

OPTIONAL V-8: Overhead valves. Cast-iron block. Displacement: 400 cid. Bore and stroke: 4.125 x 3.746 in. Compression ratio: 10.75:1. Brake hp: 370 at 5500 rpm. Torque: 445 at 3900 rpm. Five main bearings. Hydraulic valve lifters. Carburetor: Rochester four-barrel.

OPTIONS (PARTIAL LIST)

591 speedometer gear adapter ($11.59). 731 heavy-duty air cleaner, not available with H.O. or Ram Air V-8s ($9.48). 582 Custom air conditioner ($375.99). 444 auxiliary gauge panel ($36.86). 362 special order axle ($2.11) 364-368 economy or performance axles ($2.11). 492 electric clock, not available with Rally Gauge cluster and included with auxiliary gauge panel ($18.96). 472 front seat center console, all GTO without Turbo Hydra-Matic transmission ($55.82). 472 front seat center console in GTO with Turbo Hydra-Matic transmission ($71.62). 441 cruise control, with V-8 only ($57.93). 492 remote-control rear deck lid ($14.70). 404 rear window defogger, except convertible ($22.15). 361 Safe-T-Track differential ($42.13-$63.19). 345 400-cid two-barrel GTO economy V-8 (no charge). 346 400-cid regular-fuel two-barrel V-8 in GTO with Turbo Hydra-Matic transmission (no charge). 347 400-cid Ram Air IV four-barrel V-8, requires Ride & Handling package, not available with air conditioning or heavy-duty three-speed manual transmission ($558.26). 482 exhaust extensions with dual exhaust ($21.05). 694 Instant Aire, not available with Ram Air IV V-8 ($15.80). SPS special color solid paint all models except convertibles or with cordova top ($115.85). SPS special color solid paint on convertible or models with cordova top ($100.05). 381 rear power antenna ($31.60). 511 front disc brakes, includes Wonder Touch power brakes ($64.25). 541 power door locks ($45.29). 4-Way power full bench front seat ($73.72). 564 4-Way power left-hand front bucket seat ($73.72). 501 Wonder Touch power steering ($115.85). 551 power windows ($105.32). 382 push-button AM radio with manual front antenna ($61.09). 383 AM/FM radio with manual front antenna ($133.76). 391 rear speaker ($15.85). 392 reverb rear

speaker ($52.65). 444 Rally Gauge Cluster and tachometer, not available with Safeguard speedometer or Rally Gauges with clock ($84.20). 484 Rally Gauge Cluster and clock, not available with Safeguard speedometer or Rally Gauge Cluster with tachometer ($50.55). 494 Rally stripes ($13.65). 414 re-tractable headlamp covers ($52.60). 442 Safeguard speedometer, not available with Rally Gauge Clusters ($15.80). 578 right-hand reclining bucket seats ($42.15). 621 Ride & Handling package ($4.21). 504 tilt steering with power steering ($45.29). 471 hood-mounted tachometer, without Rally Gauge Cluster with tachometer ($63.19). TRC/D G78 x 14 Red Line or White Line tires no charge on GTO. TRT/RR G78 x 14 Red Line or White Line fiberglass-belted tires ($26.33). TPT/PR G70 x 14 Red Line or White Line fiberglass-belted tires ($57.93). 704 Space-Saver spare tire (no charge to $15.80 depending on model). 402 spare tire and wheel cover ($5.27). SVT cordova top, except convertible ($100.05). 355 heavy-duty three-speed manual transmission with floor-mounted gear shifter (no charge). 358 close-ratio four-speed manual transmission in all GTOs with 37P or 37S axle ($184.80). 351 Turbo Hydra-Matic transmission ($227.04). 588 power flow-thru ventilation ($42.44-$57.95 depending on model). 452 Custom wheel covers ($20.01-$51.61 depending on model and other equipment). 453 wire wheel covers ($52.66-($73.72 depending on model and other options). 454 Rally II wheels ($63.19-$84.26 depending on model and other options). 321 Basic Group ($107.43-$150.61 depending on model and other equipment). 322 lamp group ($37.91-$51.60 depending on model). 324 Décor Group ($21.06-$91.63 depending upon model and other equipment). 331 Power Assist Group ($359.66-$396.61 depending on model and other equipment). 334 Rally Group ($152.71-$194.84 depending on model and other equipment).

(NOTE: Some options may have been standard or not available on GTOs.)

1969 GTO "THE JUDGE"

JERRY HEASLEY

1969 GTO "The Judge"

A special high-performance "The Judge" option (RPO 554 UPC WT1) was released Dec. 19, 1968. It included one of two available Ram Air V-8s as standard equipment as well as many other muscle car features. Though more expensive than base GTOs, a "The Judge" was the least expensive of several cars now on the market with comparable equipment.

The "The judge" started as a project to build a no-frills muscle car similar to the Plymouth Road Runner. It was originally planned as a 1969-only model and as sort of a spoof on muscle car with all the gimmicks. It was named for the popular "Here come de Judge" skits on the Rowan & Martin "Laugh-In" television comedy show. However, in its final form, Pontiac's "The Judge" option was more expensive and more honest-to-goodness muscle car than it was first supposed to be. (In fact, the GT-37 LeMans of the early '70s was truer to the initial "The Judge" concept.). Released as a $332.07 option package for the GTO hardtop or convertible, "The Judge" included the Ram Air III V-8, special paint colors, special de-

cals and stripes, a 60-in. wide rear deck air foil, a heavy-duty suspension, Rally II wheels and G70 x 14 Wide Tread fiberglass-belted black sidewall tires.

As with other GTOs, "The Judge" models with the 366-hp V-8 had "Ram Air" decals and those with the 370-hp V-8 had "Ram Air IV" decals. The airfoil used on the rear of the cars was slightly different for hardtops and convertibles

Three different road tests were recorded on the GTO Judge with the Ram Air IV engine. *Car Life's* contemporary test, published in March 1969, used a car with a 3.55:1 rear axle. It took 6.2 seconds to get to 60 mph from standstill and ran the quarter mile in 97.8 mph. In June 1995, *Muscle Car Review* tested a similar car with the 3.9:1 gearing. It did 0-to-60 mph in 6.6 seconds but then pulled a 13.9-second quarter-mile at 101.5 mph. The same magazine tested the same combo at another time as well, and published figures of 5.7 for 0-to-60 and 13.20 seconds at 104 mph for the quarter. Take your pick! The Judge was fast however the tests went.

PONTIAC

Model Number	Body/Style Number	Body Type & Seating	Factory Price	Shipping Weight	Production Total
GTO "THE JUDGE" — SERIES 242 — V-8					
22	37	2d HT-6P	$3,161	—	6,725
22	67	2d Conv-6P	$4,212	—	108

ENGINES

BASE V-8: Overhead valves. Cast-iron block. Displacement: 400 cid. Bore and stroke: 4.125 x 3.746 in. Compression ratio: 10.75:1. Brake hp: 366 at 5100 rpm. Torque: 445 at 3600 rpm. Five main bearings. Hydraulic valve lifters. Carburetor: Rochester four-barrel.

OPTIONAL V-8: Overhead valves. Cast-iron block. Displacement: 400 cid. Bore and stroke: 4.125 x 3.746 in. Compression ratio: 10.75:1. Brake hp: 370 at 5500 rpm. Torque: 445 at 3900 rpm. Five main bearings. Hydraulic valve lifters. Carburetor: Rochester four-barrel. Mandatory options with the Ram Air IV V-8 included a Turbo Hydra-Matic automatic transmission or a four-speed manual transmission, a heavy-duty radiator and a limited-slip differential.

OPTIONS (PARTIAL LIST)

591 speedometer gear adapter ($11.59). 731 heavy-duty air cleaner, not available with H.O. or Ram Air V-8s ($9.48). 582 Custom air conditioner ($375.99). 444 auxiliary gauge panel ($36.86). 362 special order axle ($2.11) 364-368 economy or performance axles ($2.11). 492 electric clock, not available with Rally Gauge cluster and included with auxiliary gauge panel ($18.96). 472 front seat center console, all GTO without Turbo Hydra-Matic transmission ($55.82). 472 front seat center console in GTO with Turbo Hydra-Matic transmission ($71.62). 441 cruise control, with V-8 only ($57.93). 492 remote-control rear deck lid ($14.70). 404 rear window defogger, except convertible ($22.15). 361 Safe-T-Track differential ($42.13-$63.19). 345 400-cid two-barrel GTO economy V-8 (no charge). 346 400-cid regular-fuel two-barrel V-8 in GTO with Turbo Hydra-Matic transmission (no charge). 347 400-cid Ram Air IV four-barrel V-8, requires Ride & Handling package, not available with air conditioning or heavy-duty three-speed manual transmission ($558.26). 482 exhaust extensions with dual exhaust ($21.05). 694 Instant Aire, not available with Ram Air IV V-8 ($15.80). SPS special color solid paint all models except convertibles or with cordova top ($115.85). SPS special color solid paint on convertible or models with cordova top ($100.05). 381 rear power antenna ($31.60). 511 front disc brakes, includes Wonder Touch power brakes ($64.25). 541 power door locks ($45.29). 4-Way power full bench front seat ($73.72) 564 4-Way power left-hand front bucket seat ($73.72). 501 Wonder Touch power steering ($115.85). 551 power windows ($105.32). 382 push-button AM radio with manual front antenna ($61.09). 383 AM/FM radio with manual front antenna ($133.76). 391 rear speaker ($15.85). 392 reverb rear speaker ($52.65). 444 Rally Gauge Cluster and tachometer, not available with Safeguard speedometer or Rally Gauges with clock ($84.20). 484 Rally Gauge Cluster and clock, not available with Safeguard speedometer or Rally Gauge Cluster with tachometer ($50.55). 494 Rally stripes for GTO ($13.65). 414 retractable headlamp covers for GTOI ($52.60). 442 Safeguard speedometer, not available with Rally Gauge Clusters ($15.80). 578 right-hand reclining bucket seats ($42.15). 621 Ride & Handling package ($4.21). 504 tilt steering with power steering ($45.29). 471 hood-mounted tachometer, without Rally Gauge Cluster with tachometer ($63.19). TRC/D G78 x 14 Red Line or White Line tires no charge on GTO). TRT/RR G78 x 14 Red Line or White Line fiberglass-belted tires ($26.33). TPT/PR G70 x 14 Red Line or White Line fiberglass-belted tires ($57.93). 704 Space-Saver spare tire (no charge to $15.80 depending on model). 402 spare tire and wheel cover ($5.27). SVT cordova top, except convertible ($100.05). 355 heavy-duty three-speed manual transmission with floor-mounted gear shifter (no charge). 358 close-ratio four-speed manual transmission in all GTOs with 37P or 37S axle ($184.80). 351 Turbo Hydra-Matic transmission ($227.04). 588 power flow-thru ventilation ($42.44-$57.95 depending on model). 452 Custom wheel covers ($20.01-$51.61 depending on model and other equipment). 453 wire wheel covers ($52.66-$73.72) depending on model and other options). 454 Rally II wheels ($63.19-$84.26 depending on model and other options). 321 Basic Group ($107.43-$150.61 depending on model and other equipment). 322 lamp group ($37.91-$51.60 depending on model). 324 Décor Group ($21.06-$91.63 depending upon model and other equipment). 331 Power Assist Group ($359.66-$396.61 depending on model and other equipment). 334 Rally Group ($152.71-$194.84 depending on model and other equipment).

(NOTE: Some options may have been standard or not available on GTOs with "The Judge" option.)

1970 1/2 FIREBIRD FORMULA 400

In 1970, the Firebird went through a complete metamorphosis. While the first Firebirds were designed to compete against the Mustang, these "second-generation" cars were aimed at imported sports cars and the Corvette. They made their debut on Feb. 26, 1970 at the Chicago Auto Show. Styling changes included Endura rubber front ends with dual recessed grilles, single headlights, split side marker lamps, enlarged wheel openings, flush door handles and smooth, clean, curvy body panels. Firebird lettering and engine badges appeared behind front wheel cutouts. The only body type offered was a sleek-looking sports coupe.

The Formula 400 model-option was aimed at the muscle car crowd. The Firebird 400 with 330 hp did 0-to-60 mph in 6.4 seconds and covered the quarter-mile in 14.9 seconds.

Model Number	Body/Style Number	Body Type & Seating	Factory Price	Shipping Weight	Production Total
FIREBIRD FORMULA 400 — SERIES 226 — V-8					
226	87	2d HT-5P	$3,370	3,470 lbs.	7,708

NOTE 1: Production shown above is for Formulas with the WT, WS, YZ and YS engines.
NOTE 2: 2,381 cars had the WT engine (all manual).
NOTE 3: 396 cars had the WS engine (all manual).
NOTE 4: 293 cars had the YZ engine (all automatic).
NOTE 5: 4,638 cars had the YS engine (all automatic).

ENGINES

OPTIONAL V-8: Overhead valve. Cast-iron block. Bore and stroke: 4.125 x 3.75 in. Displacement: 400 cid. Compression ratio: 10.0:1. Brake hp: 330 at 4800 rpm. Taxable hp: 54.3. Torque: 445 at 2900 rpm. Five main bearings. Hydraulic valve lifters. Carburetor: Four-barrel. Engine code: YS.

OPTIONAL V-8: Overhead valve. Cast-iron block. Bore and stroke: 4.125 x 3.75 in. Displacement: 400 cid. Compression ratio: 10.25:1. Brake hp: 330 at 4800 rpm. Taxable hp: 54.3. Torque: 430 at 3000 rpm. Five main bearings. Hydraulic valve lifters. Carburetor: Four-barrel. Engine code: WT.

OPTIONAL RAM AIR III V-8: Overhead valve. Cast-iron block. Bore and stroke: 4.12 x 3.75. Displacement: 400 cid. Compression ratio: 10.75:1. Brake hp: 345 at 5000 rpm. Taxable hp: 54.3. Torque: 430 at 3400 rpm. Five main bearings. Hydraulic valve lifters. Carburetor: Four-barrel. Engine code: WS.

OPTIONAL RAM AIR III V-8: Overhead valve. Cast-iron block. Bore and stroke: 4.12 x 3.75. Displacement: 400 cid. Compression ratio: 10.75:1. Brake hp: 345 at 5400 rpm. Taxable hp: 54.3. Torque: 430 at 3700 rpm. Five main bearings. Hydraulic valve lifters. Carburetor: Four-barrel. Engine code: YZ.

OPTIONS

591 speedometer gear adapter ($11.59). 731 heavy-duty air cleaner not available with 348 ($9.48). 582 custom air conditioner ($375.99). 368 performance axle ($10.53). 692 heavy-duty battery ($4.21). 451 custom seat belts, front and rear and front shoulder type ($12.64). 452 custom seat/shoulder belts front and rear ($38.97). 492 electric clock, not available with 652 ($15.80). 488 Rally gauge cluster with clock, not available with 341, 484 or 652 ($47.39). 484 Rally gauge cluster with clock, not available with 341, 484 or 652 ($94.79). 494 front console ($58.98). 402 spare tire cover ($5.27). 481 cruise control ($57.93). 541 rear window defogger ($26.33). 534 electric rear window defog-

1970 1/2 Firebird Formula 400

ger ($52.66). 361 Safe-T-Track rear axle, requires specific axle ($42.13). 711 evaporative emissions control, required in California ($36.86). 531 Soft-Ray tinted glass, all windows ($32.65). 532 Soft-Ray tinted glass, windshield only ($26.33). 684 door edge guards ($6.32). 661 convenience lamps ($11.59). 521 front floor mats, pair ($6.85). 522 rear floor mats, pair ($6.32). 441 left-hand visor vanity mirror ($2.11). 502 Wonder Touch power brakes, ($42.13). 554 remote-control deck lid release ($14.74). 552 power door locks and seatback locks, not available with 734 ($68.46). 734 power door locks only ($45.29). 501 variable-ratio power steering ($105.32). 551 power side windows, all with 494 ($105.32). 401 AM push-button radio ($61.09). 402 AM/FM push-button radio ($133.76). 404 AM/FM stereo radio ($239.08). 412 stereo tape player, requires a radio and not available with 411 ($133.76). 411 rear speaker; not included in 404 and 412 ($15.80). SVT Cordova vinyl top for cars without 431 ($89.52). 461 deluxe steering wheel for 22387 ($15.80). 464 Formula steering wheel, with 501 only ($42.13). 504 tilt steering wheel, requires 501 and not available with column-mounted gearshift ($45.19). 351 Turbo Hydra-Matic transmission, not available with 341 or 343 ($227.04). 354 four-speed manual transmission with floor shift, requires V-8 and not available with 754 ($195.36). 355 heavy-duty three-speed manual transmission with floor shift, without 341 (standard). Close-ratio four-speed manual transmission with floor shift, in Formula with 37R axle, requires 361 ($195.36). 473 wire wheel discs ($73.72). 474 Rally II wheel rims, includes 471 ($84.26). 471 wheel trim rings, without 454 ($21.06). 432 recessed windshield wipers ($18.96). 321 basic group, includes AM radio, electric clock, visor-vanity mirror, outside rearview mirror, remote-control mirror, and heavy-duty air cleaner ($103.22). 731 Custom trim group ($77.94). 331 Power assist group ($374.49). 652 warning lamp group ($36.86). TML F70-14 raised white letter tires ($28.44 extra). TNL F60-15 raised white letter tires, includes 15-inch Rally II wheels ($146.39 extra). 704 Space Saver spare tire, standard with 474 or TNL ($15.80).

(NOTE: Some Firebird options may have been standard or not available on Formula 400s.)

1970 1/2 TRANS AM

ENGINES

BASE RAM AIR III V-8: Overhead valve. Cast-iron block. Bore and stroke: 4.12 x 3.75. Displacement: 400 cid. Compression ratio: 10.75:1. Brake hp: 345 at 5000 rpm. Taxable hp: 54.3. Torque: 430 at 3400 rpm. Five main bearings. Hydraulic valve lifters. Carburetor: Four-barrel. Engine code: WS, YZ.

OPTIONAL RAM AIR IV V-8: Overhead valve. Cast-iron block. Bore and stroke: 4.12 x 3.75. Displacement: 400 cid. Compression ratio: 10.75:1. Brake hp: 370 at 5500 rpm. Taxable hp: 54.3. Torque: 445 at 3900 rpm. Five main bearings. Hydraulic valve lifters. Carburetor: Four-barrel. Engine code: WW, XP.

OPTIONS

591 speedometer gear adapter ($11.59). 582 custom air conditioner ($375.99). 368 performance axle ($10.53). 692 heavy-duty battery ($4.21). 451 custom seat belts, front and rear and front shoulder type ($12.64). 452 custom seat/shoulder belts front and rear ($38.97). 484 Rally gauge cluster with clock (standard). 402 spare tire cover ($5.27). 481 cruise control ($57.93). 541 rear window defogger ($26.33). 534 electric rear window defogger ($52.66). 400-cid Ram Air V-8 (standard). 711 evaporative emissions control, required in California ($36.86). 531 Soft-Ray tinted glass, all windows ($32.65). 532 Soft-Ray tinted glass, windshield only ($26.33). 684 door edge guards ($6.32). 661 convenience lamps ($11.59). 521 front floor mats, pair ($6.85). 522 rear floor mats, pair ($6.32). 524 fitted trunk floor mats ($8.43). 434 dual body-colored sport-type outside rearview mirrors on base Firebird ($26.33). 441 left-hand visor vanity mirror ($2.11). 741 roof drip moldings ($31.60). 554 remote-control deck lid release ($14.74). 552 power door locks and seatback locks, not available with 734 ($68.46). 734 power door locks only ($45.29). 551 power side windows, all with 494 ($105.32). 401 AM push-button radio ($61.09). 402 AM/FM push-button radio ($133.76). 404 AM/FM stereo radio ($239.08). 412 stereo tape player, requires a radio and

The super-cool Trans Am was back this model year with a 335-hp Ram Air 400 engine standard. The factory called this the Ram Air H.O., but it is best known as the Ram Air III V-8. It had a 10.5:1 compression ratio and developed peak power at 5000 rpm. The base transmission was a wide-ratio four-speed manual gearbox with Hurst floor shift. The Trans Am came only with white or blue finish with contrasting racing stripes.

A rare factory option was the Ram Air IV V-8, which generated 370 hp. Even rarer was Ram Air V, an over-the-counter SPO (special production option) that could generate up to 500 hp.

Hot Rod magazine road tested a Cameo White 1970 Trans Am with the 400-cid Ram Air IV V-8, a four-speed manual transmission and 3.73:1 gears and recorded a 13.90-second quarter-mile at 102 mph.

Model Number	Body/Style Number	Body Type & Seating	Factory Price	Shipping Weight	Production Total
FIREBIRD TRANS AM —SERIES 228 — V-8					
228	87	2d HT-5P	$4,305	3,550 lbs.	3,196

NOTE 1: Production shown above is for Trans Ams with the WS, WW, YZ and XP engines.
NOTE 2: 1,769 cars had the WS engine (all manual)
NOTE 3: 59 cars had the WW engine (all manual)
NOTE 4: 1,339 cars had the YZ engine (all automatic)
NOTE 5: 29 cars had the XP engine (all automatic)

1970 1/2 Trans Am

not available with 411 ($133.76). 411 rear speaker; not included in 404 and 412 ($15.80). 464 Formula steering wheel (no cost). 504 tilt steering wheel, requires 501 and not available with column-mounted gearshift ($45.19). 731 Custom trim group, includes instrument panel assist strap, bright roof rail side interior mold-ings, custom front seat, door and quarter panel interior trim and molded trunk floor mat ($77.94).

(NOTE: Some options may have been standard or not available on Trans Ams.)

1970 TEMPEST T-37/GT-37 400/455 V-8

1970 Tempest GT-37

In February 1970, the cut-price Tempest T-37 hardtop coupe was introduced. According to Pontiac's Official Historian John Sawruk, the T-37 was an attempt to have a Pontiac that was less expensive than a Chevrolet. It was "de-contented" to have less standard equipment than a base Tempest.

The T-37 was, in fact, the lowest-priced General Motors hardtop at the time it was offered. John Sawruk describes the car as a "big mistake," but credits it with siring the GT-37. The "T" stood for "Tempest" and "37" was the Fisher body style designation for a two-door hardtop. The Tem-pest T-37 hardtop coupe was followed by the appearance of the GT-37 two-door hardtop and coupe. These models were "stripper" muscle cars like the GTO "The Judge" first set out to be. Standard GT-37 extras included vinyl accent stripes, Rally II wheels less trim rings, G70 x 14 white-lettered tires, dual exhausts with chrome extensions, a heavy-duty three-speed manual transmission with a floor-mounted gear shifter, body-color sport-type outside rearview mirrors (left-hand remote controlled), hood-locking pins, GT decals and GT-37 nameplates.

The V-8 engine offerings included 350- and 400-cid options. All models were equipped with glass-belted tires and side guard door beams.

Model Number	Body/Style Number	Body Type & Seating	Factory Price	Shipping Weight	Production Total
TEMPEST T-37 — SERIES 233 — V-8					
233	37	2d HT-5P	$2,683	3,250 lbs.	Note 1
TEMPEST GT-37 — SERIES 233 — V-8					
233	37	2d HT-5P	$2,920	3,360 lbs.	Note 1
233	27	2d Cpe-5P	$2,907	3,300 lbs.	Note 2

NOTE 1: Total production of Tempest, T-37and GT-37 two-door hardtops combined was 9,187.

NOTE 2: Total production of Tempest and Tempest GT-37 two-door coupes combined was 11,977.

NOTE 3: 1,419 GT-37s (hardtops and coupes) were built.

ENGINES

OPTIONAL V-8: Overhead valves. Cast-iron block. Bore and stroke: 4.125 x 3.75 in. Displacement: 400 cid. Compression ratio: 8.80:1. Brake hp: 265 at 4600 rpm. Taxable hp: 54.3. Torque: 397 at 2400 rpm. Five main bearings. Hydraulic valve lifters. Carburetor: Two-barrel. Engine code: XX and YB.

OPTIONAL V-8: Overhead valves. Cast-iron block. Bore and stroke: 4.125 x 3.75 in. Displacement: 400 cid. Compression ratio: 10.0:1. Brake hp: 330 at 4800 rpm. Taxable hp: 54.3. Torque: 445 at 2900 rpm. Five main bearings. Hydraulic valve lifters. Carburetor: Four-barrel. Engine code: YS, XV and XZ.

OPTIONAL V-8: Overhead valve. Cast-iron block. Bore and stroke: 4.12 x 3.75. Displacement: 400 cid. Compression ratio: 10.50:1. Brake hp: 366 at 5100 rpm. Taxable hp: 54.3. Torque: 445 at 3600 rpm. Five main bearings. Hydraulic valve lifters. Carburetor: Four-barrel. Engine code: WS and YZ.

OPTIONAL V-8: Overhead valve. Cast-iron block. Bore and stroke: 4.15 x 3.75. Displacement: 455 cid. Compression ratio: 10.00:1. Brake hp: 360 at 4300 rpm. Torque: 500 at 2700 rpm. Five main bearings. Hydraulic valve lifters. Carburetor: Four-barrel. Engine code: WA/YA.

OPTIONS (PARTIAL LIST)

492 electric clock, not available with Rally Gauge Cluster and included with auxiliary gauge panel ($18.96). 424 spare tire cover ($5.27). 481 cruise control, with V-8 only ($57.93). 421 front seat foam cushion ($8.43). 404 rear window defogger ($26.33). 534 electric rear window defroster ($52.66). 361 Safe-T-Track differential ($42.13-$63.19). 481 dual exhausts ($30.54). 344 400-cid HO four-barrel V-8 including three-speed manual transmission with column shift and dual exhausts for Tempests with Turbo Hydra-Matic transmission ($210.64).

347 400-cid Ram Air IV four-barrel V-8 including hood Ram Air inlet equipment, chrome rocker covers, chrome oil cap, dual exhausts, heavy-duty battery and F70-14 fiberglass-belted redline or whiteline wide-oval tires in two-door hardtop with Turbo Hydra-Matic transmission or close-ratio four-speed manual transmission without Lamp Group ($905.75). 348 400-CID HO V-8 includes chrome air cleaner, chrome rocker covers, chrome oil filler cap, dual exhausts, F70-14 fiberglass-belted redline or whiteline wide-oval tires and three-speed manual transmission with floor shift on Tempest two-door hardtop without Turbo Hydra-Matic, four-speed manual or close-ratio four-speed manual transmissions ($508.70). 34P 455-cid V-8 in Tempest except GTO with Turbo Hydra-Matic, dual exhausts required ($279.10). 711 evaporative emissions system, required on all California cars ($36.86). 534 Custom gearshift knob with three- or four-speed manual transmission ($5.27). 531 Soft-Ray tinted glass ($36.86). 532 Soft-Ray tinted windshield ($26.33). 684 door edge guards on two-door ($6.32). 672 headlight delay ($12.64). 414 dual horns on base Tempest ($4.21). 694 Instant Aire, not available with Ram Air IV V-8 ($15.80). 662 ash tray lamp ($3.16). 651 cornering lamp ($33.70). 654 dome reading lamp ($13.69). 664 glove box lamp ($3.16). 652 luggage compartment lamp ($3.16). 671 underhood lamp ($4.21). 521 pair of front floor mats ($6.85). 522 pair of rear floor mats ($6.32). 441 right- or left-hand visor-vanity mirrors ($2.11). 424 remote-control left-hand outside rearview mirror ($10.53). 694 wheel opening moldings for Tempest and Tempest Custom models ($15.80). Variable-ratio power steering ($105.32). 551 power windows ($105.32). 401 push-button AM radio with windshield antenna ($61.09). 402 AM/FM radio with windshield antenna ($133.76). 404 AM/FM stereo radio with windshield antenna ($239.08). 411 rear speaker ($15.80). 412 stereo tape player ($133.76). 482 Rally Gauge Cluster and clock, not available with Safeguard speedometer or Rally Gauge Cluster with tachometer ($50.55). 484 Rally Gauge Cluster with tachometer ($84.26). 634 rear lamp monitor ($26.33). 482 Safeguard speedometer, not available with Rally Gauge Clusters ($15.80). 571 reclining right-hand bucket seat ($42.13). 621 Ride & Handling package ($9.48). 461 deluxe steering wheel i($15.85). 462 Custom steering wheel ($50.85). 464 Formula steering wheel in Tempests without the Décor Group option ($57.93). 464 Formula steering wheel in Tempests with the Décor Group option ($42.13). 504 tilt steering with power steering ($45.29). 491 hood-mounted tachometer, not available with Rally Gauge Cluster with tachometer ($63.19). 355 heavy-duty three-speed manual transmission with floor shift ($84.24). 358 close-ratio four-speed manual transmission ($184.80). Black coated fabric trim in model 23327 with trim code 49 ($27.38). 514 brake pedal trim package ($5.27). 471 deluxe wheel covers ($21.06). 472 Custom wheel covers ($20.01-$51.61 depending on model and other equipment). 473 wire wheel covers ($52.66-$73.72) depending on model and other options. 454 Rally II wheels ($63.19-$84.26 depending on model and other options).

(NOTE: Some options may have been standard or not available on T-37/GT-37 models.)

1970 GTO

The GTO utilized Tempest sheet metal combined with a standard Endura rubber nose. The 400-cid two-barrel "economy" V-8 was dropped. The standard engine was again the 400-cid four-barrel, now rated at 350 hp. In addition to the optional Ram Air III and Ram Air IV V-8s, buyers could now order a 455-cid V-8 with 500 lbs.-ft. of torque. This engine was fast off the line, but could not match the top speed of the 400-cid V-8.

Early cars had stripes much like those used on 1970 GTOs with "The Judge" option. Later cars had "eyebrows" above the wheel openings.

The 1970 GTO with the 400-cid/366-hp V-8 was capable of 0-to-60 mph in 6 seconds flat. It did the quarter-mile in 14.6 seconds. The 455-cid/360-hp GTO hardtop registered 6.6 seconds 0-to-60 and a 14.8-second quarter-mile.

Model Number	Body/Style Number	Body Type & Seating	Factory Price	Shipping Weight	Production Total
GTO — SERIES 242 — V-8					
242	37	2d HT-6P	$3,267	3,641 lbs.	32,737
242	67	2d Conv-6P	$3,492	3,691 lbs.	3,615

NOTE 1: 40,149 GTOs and Judges were built in 1970.

NOTE 2: 16,033 GTOs and Judges had synchromesh and 24,116 had automatic transmission.

NOTE 3: 366-hp Ram Air III V-8s were installed in 4,356 GTO and GTO Judge hardtops.

NOTE 4: 366-hp Ram Air III V-8s were installed in 288 GTO and GTO Judge convertibles.

NOTE 5: 370-hp Ram Air IV V-8s were installed in 767 GTO and GTO Judge hardtops.

NOTE 6: 370-hp Ram Air IV V-8s were installed in 37 GTO and GTO Judge convertibles.

ENGINES

BASE V-8: Overhead valve. Cast-iron block. Bore and stroke: 4.12 x 3.75. Displacement: 400 cid. Compression ratio: 10.25:1. Brake hp: 350 at 5000 rpm. Taxable hp: 54.3. Torque: 445 at 3000 rpm. Five main bearings. Hydraulic valve lifters. Carburetor: Rochester four-barrel Model 7040263. Engine code: WT and YS.

PONTIAC

1970 GTO

OPTIONAL V-8: Overhead valve. Cast-iron block. Bore and stroke: 4.12 x 3.75. Displacement: 400 cid. Compression ratio: 10.50:1. Brake hp: 366 at 5100 rpm. Taxable hp: 54.3. Torque: 445 at 3600 rpm. Five main bearings. Hydraulic valve lifters. Carburetor: Four-barrel. Engine code: WS and YZ.

OPTIONAL V-8: Overhead valve. Cast-iron block. Bore and stroke: 4.12 x 3.75. Displacement: 400 cid. Compression ratio: 10.50:1. Brake hp: 370 at 5500 rpm. Taxable hp: 54.3. Torque: 445 at 3900 rpm. Five main bearings. Hydraulic valve lifters. Carburetor: Four-barrel. Engine code: WW and XP.

OPTIONAL V-8: Overhead valve. Cast-iron block. Bore and stroke: 4.15 x 4.210. Displacement: 455 cid. Compression ratio: 10.00:1. Brake hp: 360 at 4300 rpm. Torque: 500 at 2700 rpm. Five main bearings. Hydraulic valve lifters. Carburetor: Four-barrel. Engine code: WA/YA.

OPTIONS (PARTIAL LIST)

494 front seat center console, except GTOs without Turbo Hydra-Matic ($55.82). 494 front seat center console in GTO with Turbo Hydra-Matic ($71.62). 424 spare tire cover ($5.27). 481 cruise control ($57.93). 404 rear window defogger ($26.33). 534 electric rear window defroster ($52.66). 361 Safe-T-Track differential ($42.13-$63.19). 344 400-cid HO four-barrel V-8 including three-speed manual transmission with column shift and dual exhausts for GTO, not available with four-speed manual transmission and Ride & Handling package required ($57.95). 347 400-cid Ram Air IV four-barrel V-8 ($905.75). 347 400-cid Ram Air IV four-barrel V-8 ($889.95). 347 400-cid Ram Air IV four-barrel V-8 ($558.20). 349 400-cid four-barrel Ram Air III V-8 in GTO without WT-1 "The Judge" option ($168.51). 34P 455-cid V-8 in GTO ($57.93). 611 driver-controlled exhaust on GTO, not available with Ram Air V-8s ($63.19). 534 Custom gearshift knob with three- or four-speed manual transmission ($5.27). 531 Soft-Ray tinted glass ($36.86). 532 Soft-Ray tinted windshield ($26.33). 684 door edge guards on two-door ($6.32). 672 head-

light delay ($12.64). 601 air-inlet hood for GTO with 400 H.O. V-8, standard with Ram Air III and Ram Air IV V-8s ($84.26). 694 Instant Aire, not available with Ram Air IV V-8 ($15.80). 662 ash tray lamp ($3.16). 651 cornering lamp ($33.70). RTT standard two-tone paint ($40.02). STT special two-tone paint ($155.87). SPS special color solid paint all models except convertibles or with cordova top ($115.85). SPS special color solid paint on convertible or models with cordova top ($100.05). 502 front disc brakes, includes Wonder Touch power brakes ($64.25). 412 stereo tape player ($133.76). 482 Rally Gauge Cluster ($50.55). 484 Rally Gauge Cluster with tachometer ($84.26). 634 rear lamp monitor, except convertible ($26.33). 482 Safeguard speedometer, not available with Rally Gauge Clusters ($15.80). 571 reclining right-hand bucket seat ($42.13). 621 Ride & Handling package ($4.21). 464 Formula steering wheel in Tempests without the Décor Group option ($57.93). 464 Formula steering wheel in Tempests with the Décor Group option ($42.13). 504 tilt steering with power steering ($45.29). 491 hood-mounted tachometer, not available with Rally Gauge Cluster with tachometer ($63.19). SVT cordova top ($100.05). 354 four-speed manual transmission in cars without 37S or 37P axle ($184.80). 355 heavy-duty three-speed manual transmission with floor shift ($84.24). 358 close-ratio four-speed manual transmission in all GTOs with 37P or 37S axle ($184.80). 473 wire wheel covers ($52.66-$73.72) depending on model and other options. 454 Rally II wheels ($63.19-$84.26 depending on model and other options). 321 Basic Group ($107.43-$125.34 depending on model and other equipment). 324 Décor Group ($123.32-$124.28 depending upon model and other equipment). 322 lamp group ($7.37-$27.38 depending on model). 331 Power Assist Group ($364.93-$396.61 depending on model and other equipment). 334 Rally Group ($157.98-$194.84 depending on model and other equipment).

(NOTE: Some options may have been standard or not available on GTOs.)

1970 GTO "THE JUDGE"

DAN LYONS

1970 GTO "The Judge"

"The Judge" option was again available at $337 over base model price. It included the 400-cid Ram Air V-8, Rally II wheels less trim rings, G70 x 14 fiberglass black sidewall tires, rear deck air foil, side stripes, Judge stripes and decals, black textured grilles and T-handle shifters (on cars with manual gearboxes).

GTOs with the 1971 "The Judge" package were available in all regular colors as well as a special Orbit Orange hue introduced at midyear. Initial engine choices were the standard Ram Air III V-8 or the optional Ram Air IV V-8. Late in the model year the 455-cid V-8 was made available on a special-order basis.

The 1970 Pontiac GTO Judge with the Ram Air IV V-8 was tested by *Muscle Car Review* in its December 1997 issue. The test car had the 3.90:1 axle and did the quarter-mile in 13.60 seconds at 105.04 mph.

Model Number	Body/Style Number	Body Type & Seating	Factory Price	Shipping Weight	Production Total
GTO — SERIES 242 — V-8					
242	37	2d HT-6P	$3,604	—	3,629
242	67	2d Conv-6P	$,3829	—	168

NOTE 1: 40,149 GTOs and Judges were built in 1970.

NOTE 2: 16,033 GTOs and Judges had synchromesh and 24,116 had automatic transmission.

NOTE 3: 366-hp Ram Air III V-8s were installed in 4,356 GTO and GTO Judge hardtops.

NOTE 4: 366-hp Ram Air III V-8s were installed in 288 GTO and GTO Judge convertibles.

NOTE 5: 370-hp Ram Air IV V-8swere installed in 767 GTO and GTO Judge hardtops.

NOTE 6: 370-hp Ram Air IV V-8swere installed in 37 GTO and GTO Judge convertibles.

ENGINES

BASE V-8: Overhead valve. Cast-iron block. Bore and stroke: 4.12 x 3.75. Displacement: 400 cid. Compression ratio: 10.50:1. Brake hp: 366 at 5100 rpm. Taxable hp: 54.3. Torque: 445 at 3600 rpm. Five main bearings. Hydraulic valve lifters. Carburetor: Four-barrel. Engine code: WS and YZ.

OPTIONAL V-8: Overhead valve. Cast-iron block. Bore and stroke: 4.12 x 3.75. Displacement: 400 cid. Compression ratio: 10.50:1. Brake hp: 370 at 5500 rpm. Taxable hp: 54.3. Torque: 445 at 3900 rpm. Five main bearings. Hydraulic valve lifters. Carburetor: Four-barrel. Engine code: WW and XP.

OPTIONAL V-8: Overhead valve. Cast-iron block. Bore and stroke: 4.15 x 4.210. Displacement: 455 cid. Compression ratio: 10.00:1. Brake hp: 360 at 4300 rpm. Torque: 500 at 2700 rpm. Five main bearings. Hydraulic valve lifters. Carburetor: Four-barrel. Engine code: WA/YA.

OPTIONS (PARTIAL LIST)

494 front seat center console, all GTO without Turbo Hydra-Matic ($55.82). 494 front seat center console in GTO with Turbo Hydra-Matic ($71.62). 424 spare tire cover ($5.27). 481 cruise control, with V-8 only ($57.93). 404 rear window defogger ($26.33). 534 electric rear window defroster ($52.66). 361 Safe-T-Track differential ($42.13-$63.19). 347 400-cid Ram Air IV four-barrel V-8 ($389.68). 611 driver-controlled exhaust on GTO, not available with Ram Air V-8s ($63.19). 534 Custom gearshift knob with three- or four-speed manual transmission ($5.27). 531 Soft-Ray tinted glass ($36.86). 532 Soft-Ray tinted windshield ($26.33). 684 door edge guards on two-door ($6.32). 672 headlight delay ($12.64). 662 ash tray lamp ($3.16). 651 cornering lamp ($33.70). 654 dome reading lamp, except convertible ($13.69). 664 glove box lamp ($3.16). 652 luggage compartment lamp ($3.16). 671 underhood lamp ($4.21). 521 pair of front floor mats ($6.85). 522 pair of rear floor mats ($6.32). 441 right- or left-hand visor-vanity mirrors ($2.11). 424 remote-control left-hand outside rearview mirror ($10.53). RTT standard two-tone paint ($40.02). STT special two-tone paint on Tempests except Safari ($155.87). SPS special color solid paint all models except convertibles or with cordova top ($115.85). SPS special color solid paint on convertible or models with cordova top ($100.05). 502 front disc brakes, includes Wonder Touch power brakes ($64.25). 541 power door locks and seat back locks on two-door ($68.46). 554 remote-control deck lid ($14.74). 734 power door locks only in two-door models ($45.29). 4-Way power full bench front seat ($73.72). 564 4-Way power left-hand front bucket seat ($73.72). Variable-ratio power steering ($105.32). 551 power windows ($105.32). 401 push-button AM radio with windshield antenna ($61.09). 402 AM/FM radio with windshield antenna ($133.76). 404 AM/FM stereo radio with windshield antenna ($239.08). 411 rear speaker ($15.80). 412 stereo tape player ($133.76). 482 Rally Gauge Cluster and clock, not available with Safeguard speedometer or Rally Gauge Cluster with tachometer ($50.55). 484 Rally Gauge Cluster with tachometer, not available with six-cylinder engine, Rally Gauge Cluster with clock, hood-mounted tachometer or electric clock ($84.26). 634 rear lamp monitor, except convertible ($26.33). 482 Safeguard speedometer, not available with Rally Gauge Clusters ($15.80). 571

PONTIAC

reclining right-hand bucket seat ($42.13). 621 Ride & Handling package ($4.21). 504 tilt steering with power steering ($45.29). 491 hood-mounted tachometer, not available with Rally Gauge Cluster with tachometer ($63.19). SVT cordova top, except convertible ($100.05). 354 four-speed manual transmission without 37S or 37P axle ($184.80). 355 heavy-duty three-speed manual transmission with floor shift ($84.24). 454 Rally II wheels ($63.19-$84.26 depending on model and other options). TDR H78-14 white sidewall tires ($33.70). TGR F78-14 white sidewall tires ($28.44). TPR G70 x 14 white sidewall tires ($66.35). TPL G70 x 14 white-letter tires ($51.61). 704 Space-Saver spare tire ($15.80). 321 Basic Group ($107.43-$125.34 depending on model and other equipment). 324 Dé-

cor Group ($123.32-$124.28 depending upon model and other equipment). 322 lamp group includes cornering lamps, luggage lamp on passenger cars, panel courtesy lamps, except on convertible, glove box lamp, ashtray lamp and ignition switch lamp ($7.37-$27.38 depending on model). 331 Power Assist Group ($364.93-$396.61 depending on model and other equipment). 334 Rally Group ($157.98-$194.84 depending on model and other equipment). 332-WT1 GTO "The Judge" option ($337.02).

(NOTE: Some options may have been standard or not available on GTOs with The Judge option.)

1970 GRAND PRIX HURST SSJ

One thing that kept Pontiac on the highest rungs of the muscle car ladder in the '60s and early '70s was the fact that many people who worked for the company were dyed-in-the-wool car enthusiasts. These so-called "Young Turks" cruised Woodward Avenue, won drag racing titles and read all the car magazines of the day. When retrospect sections of those publications featured the fabulous Duesenberg SSJ, the story served as inspiration for a new high-performance version of the 1970 Grand Prix. As previously noted, the factory took things as far as a SJ package.

For muscle car enthusiasts, the big news for 1970 was the SSJ, which was a Grand Prix SJ with Hurst modifications. The SSJ could be ordered through Pontiac dealers. Pontiac built and painted 272 of the cars. They were then shipped to Hurst for the conversion work. They were based on the base or "J" model, since the vinyl accent stripes used on factory-issued SJs were incompatible with Hurst SSJ features. The SSJs were painted either Cameo White (code CC) or Starlight Black (code AA). Interiors were ivory, black or sandalwood in cloth or all-Morrokide. Mandatory options included body-color sport mirrors, G78 x 14 whitewalls and Rally II wheels. The space-saver spare and ride and handling package were recommended. After assembly, these cars were shipped to a Hurst plant in Southfield, Michigan, where frost gold accents were applied to the hood, side window frames, front of the roof and Rally II wheels. A landau-style half-top (antique white, white or black) was installed, as was a steel, electrically operated sunroof like those used in Cadillac Eldorados.

Engines for 1970 included the same base power plant as in 1969 or a 265-hp regular-fuel economy version of the 400-cid

V-8 at no extra charge. However, the 428-cid V-8 was replaced with a 455-cid/370-hp big block. Only 500 stick-shift models were built and just 329 of them had the four-speed manual gearbox. Instead of the 370-hp engine, a code LS5 455 HO V-8 could be had as an option. The SSJ conversion work took about 10 days. Special die-cast model SSJ emblems were featured for identification. Hurst and Pontiac also provided a special SSJ sales catalog.

Car Life magazine referred to the 1969 Grand Prix as "a stretched GTO" and named it the best-engineered car of the year. In *Popular Science*, a road-tested '70 Grand Prix proved faster than a Dodge Hemi Charger and Ford Fairlane GT around the road racing circuit at Bridgehampton. *Cars* magazine tested a Grand Prix SJ with the 455-cid V-8, four-speed manual transmission and 3.31:1 rear axle. It covered the quarter-mile in 14.19 seconds at 101.29 mph.

Model Number	Body/Style Number	Body Type & Seating	Factory Price	Shipping Weight	Production Total
GRAND PRIX SSJ — SERIES 276 — V-8					
276	276572-dr HT Cpe-5P		$5.132	3.784 lbs.	272

OPTIONS (SELECTED)

Pontiac air conditioning ($422). Auxiliary panel gauges ($21-$79). Cruise control ($63). Rear window defroster ($53). Tinted windshield ($22-$30). Tempest Instant Air ($16). Left remote-control outside mirror ($11). Power brakes ($42-$64). Remote-control deck lid ($15). Power front bucket seat for ($73). AM/FM stereo ($239). Rally gauge cluster with tachometer ($84). Safeguard speedometer ($16). Lleather seat trim ($199). Rally II wheel rims ($63-$84). Grand Prix "SJ" group ($223-$244). Three-speed manual transmissions were provided at base prices, including a heavy-duty type in Grand Prix. Turbo Hydra-Matic was $227 extra. Grand Prix had two other options, close- or wide-ratio four-speed manual gearboxes, both at $227 extra. 455-cid four-barrel high-performance V-8 with 10.25:1 compression and 370 hp @ 4600 rpm ($58).

1971 FIREBIRD FORMULA 455 H.O.

Styling changes for 1971 Firebirds were of the minor variety. High-back seats were used, new wheel covers appeared and all models, except the Trans Am, had simulated louvers behind the front wheel cutouts.

The muscular engine choices included the four-barrel 400-cid V-8, the four-barrel 455-cid V-8 and the 455 H.O. V-8

Muscle car lovers were most interested in the Formula 455 version in 1971, although not all buyers understood that there were two 455-cid engine options. Both had the same 4.15 x 4.21-inch bore and stroke, but the least-powerful version used

an 8.2:1 compression ratio. This engine, which cost $157.98 extra, produced 325 hp at 4400 rpm and 455 lbs.-ft. of torque at 3200 rpm. The option was the same 455 HO version that Trans Ams got as standard equipment. It was good for 335 hp at 4800 rpm and 480 lbs.-ft. of torque at 3600 rpm. This motor cost $236.97 extra in Formulas.

The Formula 455 with a four-speed manual gearbox and a 3.42:1 rear axle could go from 0-to-60 mph in 7.6 seconds and did the quarter-mile in 15.5 seconds at 89.5 mph.

1971 Firebird Formula

Model Number	Body/Style Number	Body Type & Seating	Factory Price	Shipping Weight	Production Total
FIREBIRD FORMULA 455 H.O. — SERIES 226 — V-8					
226	87	2d HT-5P	$3,625	3,473 lbs.	321

NOTE 1: 166 cars had manual transmission and seven were M13 cars (with a special type of manual transmission case)
NOTE 2: 155 cars had automatic transmission.
NOTE 3: 350 additional cars had the non-H.O. (L75) 455-cid engine

ENGINE
OPTIONAL V-8: Overhead valves. Cast-iron block. Displacement: 455 cu. in. Bore & stroke: 4.15 x 4.21 in. Compression ratio: 8.4:1. Brake hp: 335 at 4800 rpm. Torque: 480 at 3600 rpm. Five main bearings. Hydraulic valve lifters. Carburetor: Rochester four-barrel. Engine code: WC, WL and YE. UPC LS5.

OPTIONS
321/Y88 basic group ($205.37). 34U/LS5 455-cid H.O. four-barrel V-8 ($236.97). 35L/M40 three-speed Turbo Hydra-Matic transmission with V-8 engines ($201.48). 35C/M13 heavy-duty three-speed manual transmission with floor shift ($84.26). 35E/M20 four-speed manual transmission with floor shift ($205.97). 35G/M22 close-ratio four-speed manual transmission with floor shift ($84.26). 361/G80 Saf-T-Track rear axle ($46.34). 368/G90-2 performance axle ($10.53). 401/U63 AM push-button radio with windshield antenna ($66.35). 403/U69 AM/FM radio and windshield antenna ($139.02). 405/U58 AM/FM stereo radio and windshield antenna, not available with rear seat speaker ($238.08). 411/U80 rear speaker, not available with U58, U55 or U57 ($18.96). 412/U57 stereo eight-track tape player, requires a radio and not available with 411 or 414 ($133.76). 414/U55 cassette tape player, not available with U80 or U57 ($133.76). 421/A90 remote deck lid release ($14.74). 422/K45 dual-stage air cleaner ($9.48). 424/D58 rear console ($26.33). 431/D55 front console, with floor shift only ($58.98). 441/D34 right-hand visor vanity mirror ($3.16). 451/AK1 custom seat belts ($15.80). 461/N30 custom cushion steering wheel ($15.80). 464/Nk3 Formula steering wheel, with 501 only ($42.13). 472/P02

custom wheel covers for ($31.60). 474/N98 Rally II wheels ($89.52); on Esprit ($63.19). NL/PM7 Rally II wheel and F60-15 white letter tires ($162.19). 478/P05 honeycomb wheels ($126.38 ($36.86). NL/PM7 Honeycomb wheels and F60-15 white letter tires ($199.05). 481/B80 roof drip moldings, included with vinyl tops ($15.80). 484/B85 belt reveal moldings, ($21.06). 491/B96 front and rear wheel opening moldings ($21.06). 492/B93 door edge guards ($6.32). 494/B84 vinyl body side moldings, black ($31.60). 501/N41 variable-ratio power steering ($115.85). 502 Wonder Touch power brakes ($7.39). 504 tilt steering wheel, not available with manual steering or column-mounted gearshift ($45.29). 521/B32 front floor mats, pair ($7.37). 522/B33 rear floor mats, pair ($6.32). 524 fitted trunk floor mats ($8.43). 531/A01 Soft-Ray tinted glass, all windows ($37.92). 532/A02 Soft-Ray tinted glass, windshield only ($30.54). 543/C49 electric rear window defroster, not available with electric rear window defogger ($63.19). 551/A31 power side windows, requires D55 ($115.85). 554/AU3 power door locks and seatback locks ($45.29). 572/D80 rear deck lid spoiler ($32.65). 582/C60 custom air conditioner ($407.59). 601/WU3 hood air inlet, with 455 H.O. V-8 ($84.26). 652/W74 warning lamp group, includes warning lamps for low fuel, low washer fluid, seat belts and headlights, not available with 714, 718 and 722 ($42.13). 654/TP1 Delco X battery, with 455-cid V-8 only ($26.33). 664/Y92 convenience lamps ($11.59). 684/N65 Space Saver spare tire ($15.80). 691/WU1 self-charging flashlight ($12.64). 692/UA1 heavy-duty battery, not available with air conditioner ($10.53). 701/V01 heavy-duty radiator ($21.06). 704/WT5 mountain performance option, with C60 ($10.53); without C60 ($31.60). 714/U30 Rally gauges, clock and instrument panel tachometer, not available with 718, 722 or 652 ($94.79). 718/W63 Rally gauges and clock, not available with 652; included with U35 ($47.39). 722/U35 electric clock, included with W74, U30 and W63 ($15.80). 731 Custom trim group ($78.99). 734/V32 rear bumper guards ($15.80). SVT Cordova vinyl top ($89.52). ML/PL4 F70-14 raised white letter tires ($41.07 extra).

(NOTE: Some options may have been standard or not available on Formula 400s and Formula 455s.)

1971 TRANS AM

The European-looking Trans Am was back in 1971 and continued to lead the way in the good-looks department among the American muscle cars set.

Standard equipment included all-vinyl bucket seats, a Rally gauge cluster (with a clock and a tachometer), an Endura front bumper, a Formula steering wheel, twin body-color outside rearview mirrors (left-hand mirror remote controlled), special honeycomb wheels, functional front fender air extractors, a rear deck lid spoiler, a black textured grille insert, bright grille moldings, and front and rear wheel opening air spoilers.

The UPC LS5 455 H.O. engine with four-barrel carburetion, 8.4:1 compression and 335 hp at 4800 rpm was standard in all Trans Ams, as was a four-speed manual gearbox with floor shifter. As in the past, the Trans Am was offered only in a limited number of exterior finish colors. Cars done in Cameo White had blue stripes on a black base. Also available was Lucerne Blue body finish with white stripes on a black base. Two minor changes for the year were a smaller 17-gallon fuel tank and the absence of a chrome engine dress-up kit on the standard equipment list.

PONTIAC

JERRY HEASLEY

1971 Trans AM

According to one enthusiast magazine of the '70s, the 455-cid/335-hp Trans Am could move from 0-to-60 mph in just 5.92 seconds and did the quarter in 13.90 seconds at 103 mph.

Model Number	Body/Style Number	Body Type & Seating	Factory Price	Shipping Weight	Production Total
TRANS AM 455 H.O. — SERIES 228 — V-8					
228	87	2d HT-5P	$4,464	3,578 lbs.	2,116

NOTE 1: 885 cars had manual transmission.
NOTE 2: 1,231 cars had automatic transmission.

ENGINE

OPTIONAL V-8: Overhead valves. Cast-iron block. Displacement: 455 cu. in. Bore & stroke: 4.15 x 4.21 in. Compression ratio: 8.4:1. Brake hp: 335 at 4800 rpm. Torque: 480 ft.-lbs. at 3600 rpm. Five main bearings. Hydraulic valve lifters. Carburetor: Rochester four-barrel. Engine code: WC, WL and YE. UPC LS5.

OPTIONS

321/Y88 basic group includes AM radio with windshield antenna, Turbo Hydra-Matic transmission, standard size white sidewall tires, custom wheel trim rings and power steering (standard on Trans Am). 35G/M22 close-ratio four-speed manual transmission with floor shift (standard in Trans Am). 361/G80 Saf-T-Track rear axle (standard with Trans Am). 368/G90-2 performance axle ($10.53). 401/U63 AM push-button radio with windshield antenna ($66.35). 403/U69 AM/FM radio and windshield antenna ($139.02). 405/U58 AM/FM stereo radio and windshield antenna, not available with rear seat speaker ($238.08). 411/U80 rear speaker, not available with U58, U55 or U57 ($18.96). 412/U57 stereo eight-track tape player, requires a radio and not available with 411 or 414 ($133.76). 414/U55 cassette tape player, not available with U80 or U57 ($133.76). 421/A90 remote deck lid release ($14.74). 424/D58 rear console ($26.33). 431/D55 front console, with floor shift only ($58.98). 441/D34 right-hand visor vanity mirror ($3.16). 451/AK1 custom seat belts ($15.80). 464/Nk3 Formula steering wheel (no cost). 474/N98 Rally II wheels (no cost). NL/PM7 Rally II wheel and F60-15 white letter tires (standard on Trans Am). 478/P05 honeycomb wheels ($36.86). NL/PM7 Honeycomb wheels and F60-15 white letter tires (standard). 492/B93 door edge guards ($6.32). 501/N41 variable-ratio power steering (standard in Trans Am). 502 Wonder Touch power brakes (standard in Trans Am). 504 tilt steering wheel, not available with manual steering or column-mounted gearshift ($45.29). 521/B32 front floor mats, pair ($7.37). 522/B33 rear floor mats, pair ($6.32). 524 fitted trunk floor mats ($8.43). 531/A01 Soft-Ray tinted glass, all windows ($37.92). 532/A02 Soft-Ray tinted glass, windshield only ($30.54). 543/C49 electric rear window defroster, not available with electric rear window defogger ($63.19). 551/A31 power side windows, requires D55 ($115.85). 554/AU3 power door locks and seatback locks ($45.29). 572/D80 rear deck lid spoiler (standard Trans Am). 582/C60 custom air conditioner ($407.59). 652/W74 warning lamp group, ($42.13). 654/TP1 Delco X battery, with 455-cid V-8 only ($26.33). 664/Y92 convenience lamps ($11.59). 684/N65 Space Saver spare tire ($15.80). 691/WU1 self-charging flashlight ($12.64). 692/UA1 heavy-duty battery, not available with air conditioner ($10.53). 701/V01 heavy-duty radiator ($21.06). 704/WT5 mountain performance option, with C60 ($10.53); without C60 ($31.60). 714/U30 Rally gauges, clock and instrument panel tachometer, not available with 718, 722 or 652 ($94.79). 718/W63 Rally gauges and clock, not available with 652; included with U35 ($47.39). 722/U35 electric clock, included with W74, U30 and W63 ($15.80). 731 Custom trim group ($78.99). 734/V32 rear bumper guards ($15.80).

1971 TEMPEST T-37/GT-37 400/455 V-8

The performance-oriented GT-37 was available again and was advertised as "The GTO For Kids Under 30." This option (code 334) was offered in just hardtop versions. It included vinyl accent stripes, Rally II wheels (less trim rings), G70-14 tires (white-lettered), dual exhausts with chrome extensions, heavy-duty three-speed manual transmission with floor shift, body-colored outside mirrors (left-hand remote control), hood locking pins and GT-37 nameplates. It was designed to provide buyers with a low-cost high-performance option.

1971 Tempest GT-37

A "post coupe" version of the GT-37 could be ordered in 1970 and appeared on the order sheet again in 1971. However, no such cars were ever made due to the fact that the dual sport mirrors, which were standard on GT-37s, would have interfered with the ventipanes (vent windows) used on the coupe body.

De-contenting the GT-37 got as intense as using only one plastic coat hook in the car and removing the grille nameplate, even though the holes were not filled. This resulted in an extremely lightweight car that could be turned into a real "factory hot rod" with the right engine and drivetrain options. With its lighter weight, a T-37 or GT-37 with the 455 H.O. V-8 should have been a bit faster than the GTO, but it was still the flashier "Goat" that got the writeups and road tests.

Model Number	Body/Style Number	Body Type & Seating	Factory Price	Shipping Weight	Production Total
TEMPEST T-37 — SERIES 233 — V-8					
233	37	2d HT-5P	$2,928	3,450 lbs.	29,466
233	27	2d Cpe-5P	$2,868	3,445 lbs.	7,184
TEMPEST GT-37 —SERIES 233 — V-8					
233	37	2d HT-5P	$2,920	3360 lbs.	5,802

NOTE 1: Production totals above are for cars with all engines, no breakouts available.

ENGINES

OPTIONAL V-8: Overhead valve. Cast-iron block. Bore and stroke: 4.12 x 3.75. Displacement: 400 cid. Compression ratio: 8.2:1. Brake hp: 300 at 4800 rpm. Net hp: 255 at 4400 rpm. Taxable hp: 54.3. Torque: 400 at 3600 rpm. Five main bearings. Hydraulic valve lifters. Carburetor: Rochester four-barrel. Engine code: WT, WK and YS.

OPTIONAL V-8: Overhead valve. Cast-iron block. Bore and stroke: 4.15 x 4.21. Displacement: 455 cid. Compression ratio: 8.2:1. Brake hp: 325 at 4400 rpm. Net hp: 255 at 4000 rpm. Taxable hp: 54.5. Torque: 455 at 3200 rpm. Five main bearings. Hydraulic valve lifters. Carburetor: Rochester four-barrel. Engine code: WJ and YC.

OPTIONAL V-8: Overhead valve. Cast-iron block. Bore and stroke: 4.15 x 4.21. Displacement: 455 cid. Compression ratio: 8.4:1. Brake hp: 335 at 4800 rpm. Taxable hp: 54.5. Torque: 480 at 360 rpm. Five main bearings. Hydraulic valve lifters. Carburetor: Rochester Quadrajet four-barrel. Engine code: WL, WC, YE and YA.

OPTIONS (PARTIAL LIST)

711 cruise control with two-speed automatic or Turbo Hydra-Matic transmissions without air-inlet hood ($63.19). 534 rear window air deflector ($26.33). 541 rear window defogger ($31.60). 534 rear window defroster ($63.19). Safe-T-Track differential, except with code 37P or 37S rear axle ($46.34). 34K 400-cid four-barrel V-8, in all models with heavy-duty three-speed manual transmission with floor shifter, four-speed manual transmission, close-ratio four-speed manual transmission or Turbo Hydra-Matic transmission ($221.17). 34P 455-cid four-barrel V-8, all models with Turbo Hydra-Matic and dual exhausts required at extra cost ($279.10). 34U 455-cid H.O. four-barrel V-8 in T-37, requires dual exhausts and Ride & Handling package and not available with transmissions 35A, 35E, 35J or 35K ($358.09). 531 all tinted glass ($43.18). STT special two-tone paint on T-37 ($155.87). RTT standard two-tone paint on T-37 ($40.02). 502 power front disc brakes, includes Wonder Touch power brakes ($69.51). 511 Wonder Touch power brakes ($47.39). 421 power remote-control deck lid release ($14.74). 554 power door locks in two-door models ($45.29). 552 power door locks and seat back locks, on two-door models ($68.46). 561 Four-Way power full bench seat in T-37 with bench seat ($78.99). 564 power left front bucket seat ($78.99). 501 power steering ($115.85). 701 heavy-duty radiator, not available with air conditioning ($21.06). 401 AM push-button radio ($66.35). 403 AM/FM radio ($139.02). 405 AM/FM stereo radio ($239.08). 411 rear seat speaker with AM push-button radio or AM/FM stereo radio ($18.96). 411 rear seat speaker in LeMans Safari with AM push-button radio or AM/FM stereo radio ($21.06). 412 stereo 8-track tape player, requires 401, 403 or 405 radio ($133.76). 414 stereo cassette tape player, requires 401, 403 or 405 radio ($133.76). 714 Rally Gauge Cluster with tachometer, includes electric clock ($84.26). 718 Rally Gauge Cluster and clock, not available with Rally Gauge Cluster with tachometer or 722 electric clock ($47.39). 571 front foam cushion in ($8.43). 621 Ride & Handling package ($9.48). 461 Custom cushion steering wheel ($15.80). 462 Custom Sport steering wheel ($57.93). 464 Formula steering wheel ($57.93). 504 tilt steering, requires power steering ($45.29). 614 vinyl stripes on T-37 two-door, not available with vinyl body side moldings ($31.60). 721 hood-mounted tachometer on V-8, not available with Rally Gauge Cluster with tachometer ($63.19). SVT cordova top ($100.05). 35C heavy-duty three-speed manual transmission with floor-mounted gear shifter ($84.26). 35E four-speed manual transmission ($195.36). 35G heavy-duty close-ratio four-speed manual transmission in T-37 or LeMans with 455-cid H.O. V-8 ($237.60). 35G heavy-duty close-ratio four-speed manual transmission with 400-cid four-barrel V-8 or 455-cid H.O. V-8 teamed with 37P or 37S axle ($237.60). 35L Turbo Hydra-Matic, except with 250-cid six-cylinder engine or 350-cid two-barrel V-8 ($242.88). Trim-coated fabric in coupe with Trim no. 38 or 39 ($27.38). 514 pedal trim package with automatic transmission ($5.27). Custom wheel covers ($31.60). 473 wire wheel covers ($84.26). 474 Rally II wheels with trim ($89.52). 487 honeycomb wheels ($126.38). 432 concealed windshield wipers ($18.96).

(NOTE: Some options may have been standard or unavailable on GT-37).

1971 GTO

PONTIAC

1971 GTO

The biggest revisions to the 1971 GTO were under the hood. A 400-cid/300-hp V-8 was standard. Two 455-cid V-8s were optional. The first had a four-barrel carburetor and 325 hp. The second was the 455 H.O. engine with round-port exhausts, special exhaust manifolds, an aluminum intake and 335 hp. The 455 H.O. was available with a Ram Air package. The 1971 air-inlet hood was designed to keep the weather out and was not driver controlled.

According to a report in the June 1995 issue of *Muscle Car Review,* the GTO with the 455 H.O. V-8 and 3.90:1 rear axle scooted from 0-to-60 mph in 6.6 seconds and covered the quarter-mile, from standstill, in 13.97 seconds at 100 mph. A GTO with the 400-cid/300-hp V-8 took 14.4 seconds for the quarter mile at 98 mph.

Model Number	Body/Style Number & Seating	Body Type Price	Factory Weight	Shipping Total	Production
GTO — SERIES 242 — V-8					
242	37	2d HT-6P	$3,446	3,619 lbs.	9,854
242	67	2d Conv-6P	$3,676	3,664 lbs.	678

NOTE 1: The base 400-cid/300-hp V-8 was installed in 6,421 hardtops and 508 convertibles with manual transmission.
NOTE 2: The base 400-cid/300-hp V-8 was installed in 2,011 hardtops and 79 convertibles with automatic transmission.
NOTE 3: The regular 455-cid/325-hp V-8 was installed in 534 hardtops and 43 convertibles all with a four-speed gearbox.
NOTE 4: The 455-cid/335-hp 455 H.O. V-8 was installed in 412 hardtops and 21 convertibles with manual transmission.
NOTE 5: The 455-cid/335-hp 455 H.O. V-8 was installed in 476 hardtops and 27 convertibles with automatic transmission.

ENGINES

BASE V-8: Overhead valve. Cast-iron block. Bore and stroke: 4.12 x 3.75. Displacement: 400 cid. Compression ratio: 8.2:1. Brake hp: 300 at 4800 rpm. Net hp: 255 at 4400 rpm. Taxable hp: 54.3. Torque: 400 at 3600 rpm. Net torque: 340 at 3200 rpm. Five main bearings. Hydraulic valve lifters. Carburetor: Rochester four-barrel. Engine code: WT, WK and YS.

OPTIONAL V-8: Overhead valve. Cast-iron block. Bore and stroke: 4.15 x 4.21. Displacement: 455 cid. Compression ratio: 8.2:1. Brake hp: 325 at 4400 rpm. Net hp: 255 at 4000 rpm. Taxable hp: 54.5. Torque: 455 at 3200 rpm. Net torque: 360 at 2800 rpm. Five main bearings. Hydraulic valve lifters. Carburetor: Rochester four-barrel. Engine code: WJ and YC.

OPTIONAL V-8: Overhead valve. Cast-iron block. Bore and stroke: 4.15 x 4.21. Displacement: 455 cid. Compression ratio: 8.4:1. Brake hp: 335 at 4800 rpm. Taxable hp: 54.5. Torque: 480 at 360 rpm. Five main bearings. Hydraulic valve lifters. Carburetor: Rochester Quadrajet four-barrel. Engine code: WL, WC, YE and YA.

OPTIONS (PARTIAL LIST)

711 cruise control with two-speed automatic or Turbo Hydra-Matic transmissions without air-inlet hood ($63.19). 534 rear window air deflector ($26.33). 541 rear window defogger, except convertible ($31.60). 541 rear window defogger ($36.86). 534 rear window defroster, except convertible ($63.19). Safe-T-Track differential, except with code 37P or 37S rear axle ($46.34). 34L 400-cid four-barrel V-8 (standard in GTO). 34P 455-cid four-barrel V-8 in GTO ($57.93). 34U 455-cid H.O. four-barrel V-8 ($136.92). 531 all tinted glass ($43.18). 601 air-inlet hood on GTO with 455 H.O. V-8 ($84.26). 664 instrument panel courtesy lamp, except convertible ($4.21) 661 dome reading lamp ($13.69). 674 glove box lamp ($3.16). 662 luggage compartment lamp ($3.16). 691 rechargeable utility lamp ($12.64). 671 underhood lamp ($4.21). 521 front floor throw mats ($7.37). 522 rear floor throw mats ($6.32). 434 dual body-color rearview mirrors, left-hand remote control ($26.33). 444 remote-control left-hand outside rearview mirror ($12.64). 441 right- or left-hand visor-vanity mirror ($3.16). 481 roof drip scalp moldings, standard with vinyl top ($13.69). 704 Mountain Performance option with 400-cid four-barrel V-8 with Turbo Hydra-Matic transmission and without manual air conditioning ($31.60). 704 Mountain Performance option with 400-cid four-barrel V-8 with Turbo Hydra-Matic transmission and with manual air conditioning ($10.53). SPS special solid color paint on all models except convertibles without vinyl top ($115.85). SPS special solid color paint on all models except convertibles with vinyl top ($100.05). 502 power front disc brakes, includes Wonder Touch power brakes ($69.51). 511 Wonder Touch power brakes (standard on GTO). 421 power remote-control deck lid release ($14.74). 554 power door locks in two-door models ($45.29). 552 power door locks and seat back locks, on two-door models ($68.46). 561 4-Way power full bench seat with bench seat ($78.99). 564 power left front bucket seat ($78.99). 501 power steering ($115.85). 701 heavy-duty radiator, not available with air conditioning ($21.06). 401 AM push-button radio ($66.35). 403 AM/FM radio ($139.02). 405 AM/FM stereo radio ($239.08). 411 rear seat speaker with AM push-button radio

or AM/FM stereo radio ($18.96 412 stereo 8-track tape player, requires 401, 403 or 405 radio ($133.76). 414 stereo cassette tape player, requires 401, 403 or 405 radio ($133.76). 714 Rally Gauge Cluster with tachometer, includes electric clock ($84.26). 718 Rally Gauge Cluster and clock, not available with Rally Gauge Cluster with tachometer or 722 electric clock ($47.39). 571 front foam cushion ($8.43). 621 Ride & Handling package on GTO and required with 455-cid H.O. V-8 ($4.21). 461 Custom cushion steering wheel ($15.80). 462 Custom Sport steering wheel ($42.13). 464 Formula steering wheel with power steering ($42.13). 504 tilt steering, requires power steering ($45.29). 614 vinyl stripes ($31.60). 721 hood-mounted tachometer 8, not available with Rally Gauge Cluster with tachometer ($63.19). SVT cordova top, except convertible ($100.05).

35C heavy-duty three-speed manual transmission with floor-mounted gear shifter (standard). 35E four-speed manual transmission ($195.36). 35E four-speed manual transmission with 455-cid H.O. V-8 ($237.60). 35G heavy-duty close-ratio four-speed manual transmission with 400-cid four-barrel V-8 or 455-cid H.O. V-8 teamed with 37P or 37S axle ($237.60). 35L Turbo Hydra-Matic8 ($242.88). 514 pedal trim package with automatic transmission ($5.27). Custom wheel covers ($31.60). 473 wire wheel covers ($84.26). 474 Rally II wheels with trim rings ($89.52). 487 honeycomb wheels without "The Judge" option ($126.38). TPL G70-14 white-letter tires on GTO ($43.18). TPR G70-14 white sidewall tires ($32.65). TXL G60-15 white-letter tires on convertible with Rally II or Honeycomb wheels only ($74.78).

1971 GTO "THE JUDGE"

1971 GTO "The Judge"

For $395 extra "The Judge" option was available (for the last time) this year. It was discontinued in January 1971. This option (code 332) included a 455-cid four-barrel H.O. V-8, Rally II wheels less trim rings, a hood air-inlet system, a T-handle gearshift control (with manual transmission), a rear deck lid air foil, specific side stripes, "The Judge" decals, Ram Air decals and a black-textured grille. Since the option was being dropped, not all cars this year had every item in the package. If a non-critical part ran out, Pontiac built the car without it.

"The Judge" emblem appeared on the lower right-hand corner of the glove box. A large "The Judge" decal was placed behind each front wheel opening. An even larger decal was on the right end of the rear deck lid. Multi-color "eyebrow" decal stripes were placed above the wheel arches. The air foil was painted body color, but could be had in black on white cars. It carried 455 H.O. decals on its sides.

Model Number	Body/Style Number	Body Type & Seating	Factory Price	Shipping Weight	Production Total
GTO — SERIES 242 — V-8					
242	37	2d HT-6P	$3,840	3,719 lbs.	357
242	67	2d Conv-6P	$4,070	3,764 lbs.	17

NOTE 1: Prices are calculated using base option price.
NOTE 2: Weights are estimated for this model.

ENGINES

BASE V-8: Overhead valve. Cast-iron block. Bore and stroke: 4.15 x 4.21. Displacement: 455 cid. Compression ratio: 8.4:1. Brake hp: 335 at 4800 rpm. Taxable hp: 54.5. Torque: 480 at 360 rpm. Five main bearings. Hydraulic valve lifters. Carburetor: Rochester Quadrajet four-barrel. Engine code: WL, WC, YE and YA.

OPTIONS

451 Custom front and rear seat and front shoulder belts, closed passenger cars ($15.80). 451 Custom front and rear seat and front shoulder belts, convertible ($40.02). 452 Custom front and rear seat and shoulder belts, closed passenger cars ($42.13). 452 Custom front and rear seat and shoulder belts, convertible ($66.35). 722 electric clock, not available with Rally Gauge Cluster ($18.96). 431 front seat console in GTO models ($61.09). 424 spare wheel and tire cover ($5.27). 711 cruise control with two-speed automatic or Turbo Hydra-Matic transmissions without air-inlet hood ($63.19). 534 rear window air deflector ($26.33). 541 rear window defogger, except convertible ($31.60). 541 rear window defogger, convertible ($36.86). 534 rear window defroster, except convertible ($63.19). Safe-T-Track differential, except with code 37P or 37S rear axle ($46.34). 34U 455-cid H.O. four-barrel V-8 in GTO with "The Judge" option (standard). 531 all tinted glass ($43.18). 532 tinted windshield only ($30.54). 692 door edge guards, on two-door models ($6.32). 732 rear bumper guards ($15.80). 601 air-inlet hood on GTO with 455 H.O. V-8 (standard with "The Judge" option). 664 instrument panel courtesy lamp, except convertible ($4.21) 661 dome reading lamp ($13.69). 674 glove box lamp ($3.16). 662 luggage compartment lamp ($3.16). 691 rechargeable utility lamp ($12.64). 671 under-hood lamp ($4.21). 521 front floor throw mats ($7.37). 522 rear floor throw mats ($6.32). 434 dual body-color rearview mirrors, left-hand remote control ($26.33). 444 remote-control left-hand outside rearview mirror ($12.64). 441 right- or left-hand visor-vanity mirror ($3.16). 481 roof drip scalp moldings,

standard with vinyl top ($13.69). SPS special solid color paint on all models except convertibles without vinyl top ($115.85). SPS special solid color paint on all models except convertibles with vinyl top ($100.05). 502 power front disc brakes, includes Wonder Touch power brakes ($69.51). 511 Wonder Touch power brakes (standard). 421 power remote-control deck lid release ($14.74). 554 power door locks in two-door models ($45.29). 552 power door locks and seat back locks, on two-door models ($68.46). 561 4-Way power full bench seat with bench seat ($78.99). 564 power left front bucket seat ($78.99). 501 power steering ($115.85). 701 heavy-duty radiator, not available with air conditioning ($21.06). 401 AM push-button radio ($66.35). 403 AM/FM radio ($139.02). 405 AM/FM stereo radio ($239.08). 411 rear seat speaker with AM push-button radio or AM/FM stereo radio ($18.96 412 stereo 8-track tape player, requires 401, 403 or 405 radio ($133.76). 414 stereo cassette tape player, requires 401, 403 or 405 radio ($133.76). 714 Rally Gauge Cluster with tachometer, in-

cludes electric clock ($84.26). 718 Rally Gauge Cluster and clock, not available with Rally Gauge Cluster with tachometer or 722 electric clock ($47.39). 571 front foam cushion ($8.43). 621 Ride & Handling package (required with "The Judge" option at $4.21 extra). 461 Custom cushion steering wheel ($15.80). 462 Custom Sport steering wheel ($42.13). 464 Formula steering wheel with power steering ($42.13). 504 tilt steering, requires power steering ($45.29). 721 hood-mounted tachometer 8, not available with Rally Gauge Cluster with tachometer ($63.19). SVT cordova top, except convertible ($100.05). 35E four-speed manual transmission ($237.60). 514 pedal trim package with automatic transmission ($5.27). Custom wheel covers ($31.60). 473 wire wheel covers ($84.26). 474 Rally II wheels with trim rings ($89.52). 487 honeycomb wheels (standard). TPL G70-14 white-letter tires on GTO ($43.18). TPR G70-14 white sidewall tires ($32.65). TXL G60-15 white-letter tires on convertible with Rally II or Honeycomb wheels only ($74.78).

1971 GRAND PRIX SSJ

1971 Grand Prix SSJ

The Hurst SSJ Grand Prix was back in the lineup for 1971, which made sense. With the longest hood in the entire automobile industry, the Grand Prix had lots of room to stuff massive cubic inches into the engine bay, so Pontiac farmed out a limited number of cars to Hurst Performance Products for the heated up SSJ treatment. For 1971, the regular Grand Prix received a beauty treatment that enhanced it both up front and at the rear. Hurst marketed the SSJ option package through Pontiac dealers.

The basic package was about the same as it had been in 1970, although gold honeycomb wheels or American mag wheels could now be substituted for the factory-type Rally II rims. The Hurst sunroof was now described as "the same German type used in Mercedes-Benz." SSJ nameplates were located on the car's front fender tips. Hurst Fire Frost Gold accents highlighted the body. A number of new Hurst accessories were made available for the 1971 model. They included an Auto-Stick gear shifter (for cars with bench seats only), a roll control device and a digital computer to calculate speed and elapsed times in the quarter mile. Also

available were B.F. Goodrich radial T/A GR60-15 tires that could be installed in place of the standard G78-14 white-stripe tires. Engines were the base 400-cid 300-hp L78 V-8 (that was standard in Grand Prix Js) and the 455-cid 325-hp LS5 V-8 (which was standard in SJ models and optional in Js). Only 116 stick-shift cars were made and half of them had four-speed manual transmissions.

Sales of Hurst SSJs dwindled to about 157 units. Apparently, the base price of the conversion ($1,147.25) remained the same as in 1970. That didn't include destination charges.

Model Number	Body/Style Number	Body Type & Seating	Factory Price	Shipping Weight	Production Total
GRAND PRIX SSJ — SERIES 276 — V-8					
276	27657	2-dr HT-5P	$5,461	3,863 lbs.	157

SELECTED OPTIONS

Automatic air conditioning ($521). Electric clock ($18). Cruise control ($68). All tinted glass ($51). Tinted windshield ($36). Bumper guards ($16). Cornering lights ($37). Power bucket seats ($79). 60/40 Bench seat with six-way power adjustments ($79). AM/FM stereo and tape system ($373). Rally gauge cluster with tachometer and clock ($84). Cordova top ($142). Wire wheel discs ($58). Rally II wheels ($63-$90). "SJ" option ($195). SSJ option ($1,147).

1972 FIREBIRD FORMULA 455

PHIL KUNZ

1972 Firebird Formula 455

The one-two punch of government regulation and restrictive liability insurance rates pounded the pony car market niche pretty hard in 1972. This was the very marketplace that Pontiac had aimed the sporty Firebird at. As a result of the pounding, sales got very slow by 1972 and PMD cut the prices on all Firebird models to try to lure customers into the showrooms. With lower window stickers and increased customer traffic, dealers were hoping to increase Firebird sales, but a crippling United Auto Workers Union strike at GM's Norwood, Ohio, assembly plant (where F-cars were made) caused production lines to grind to a premature halt. As a result, only 5,249 Formula Firebirds were built for the 1972 model year.

The possibility of stopping production of the Firebird was raised for the first time this year. With the model's future in question, annual styling and equipment changes were kept to a minimum. There was a new honeycomb mesh grille insert, new interior trims, redesigned hubcaps and restyled wheel covers.

There was only one 455-cid engine option in 1972. This power plant now used an 8.4:1 compression ratio and produced 300 hp at 4000 rpm and 415 lbs.-ft. of torque at 3200 rpm. It sold for $231 over the price of the base 400-cid/250-hp engine.

The Formula 455 with a four-speed manual gearbox and a 3.42:1 rear axle could go from 0-to-60 mph in 7.6 seconds and did the quarter-mile in 15.5 seconds at 89.5 mph.

Model Number	Body/Style Number	Body Type & Seating	Factory Price	Shipping Weight	Production Total
FORMULA 455 FIREBIRD — SERIES 2U — V-8					
2U	87	2d HT-5P	$3,453	3,474 lbs.	276

NOTE 1: Production is for 455-powered Formulas.
NOTE 2: Price calculated by base option cost.
NOTE 3: Weight is an estimate for this model and engine.

ENGINE

OPTIONAL V-8: Overhead valve. Cast-iron block. Bore and stroke: 4.15 x 4.21.

Displacement: 455 cid. Compression ratio: 8.4:1. Net hp: 300 at 4000 rpm. Taxable hp: 55.20. Net torque: 415 at 3200 rpm. Five main bearings. Hydraulic valve lifters. Carburetor: Rochester four-barrel. VIN code: X.

OPTIONS

331/Y96 Handling Package, on Formula, includes P05. Package consists of honeycomb wheels, F60-15 white letter tires, heavy-duty front and rear stabilizer bars and heavy-duty front and rear springs. ($200). 34U/LS5 455-cid H.O. four-barrel V-8 in Formula, requires 601/634 with THM ($231). 35E/M20 four-speed manual transmission with floor shift, requires 34H 350-cid two-barrel V-8 or 34S 400-cid four-barrel V-8 ($200). 35G/M22 close-ratio four-speed manual transmission with floor shift in Formula Firebird, 400-cid four-barrel V-8 or 35X 455-cid four-barrel H.O. V-8 required ($231). 35K/M38 three-speed Turbo Hydra-Matic transmission ($215). 35L/M40 three-speed Turbo Hydra-Matic transmission ($236). 361/G80 Safe-T-Track rear axle ($45). 368/G92 performance axle ($10). 401/U63 AM push-button radio with windshield antenna ($65). 403/U69 AM/FM radio and windshield antenna ($135). 405/U58 AM/FM stereo radio and windshield antenna, not available with rear seat speaker ($233). 411/U80 rear speaker ($18). 412/U57 stereo eight-track tape player ($130). 414/U55 cassette tape player, not available with U80 or U57 ($130). 423/K45 heavy-duty air cleaner, except Trans Am ($9). 424/D58 rear console ($26). 431/D55 front console, with floor shift only ($57). 432 recessed windshield wipers ($18). 441/D34 right-hand visor vanity mirror ($3). 442/D31 non-glare rearview mirror, included with 734 ($6). 444/D33 left-hand outside rearview mirror, remote control type ($12). 451/AK1 custom seat belts ($15). 461/N30 custom cushion steering wheel ($15). 462/N31 custom sport steering wheel, included with 332 ($56). 464/Nk3 Formula steering wheel ($41). 471/P06 wheel trim rings, included with 474 and 332 ($26). 472/P02 custom finned wheel covers for Formula without 332, 474 and 478 ($50). 474/N98 Rally II wheels ($87). 476/P01 Deluxe wheel covers, not available with 332 ($31); on Esprit ($5). 478/P05 honeycomb wheels ($123). 481/B80 roof drip moldings ($15). 484/B85 belt reveal moldings, required with 582 and 534 ($15). 491/B96 front and rear wheel opening moldings ($21). 492/B93 door edge guards ($6). 494/B84 vinyl body side moldings, black ($31). 501/N41 variable-ratio power steering, required with 582 and 534 ($113). 502 front disc brakes, standard in Trans Am ($46). 504 tilt steering wheel, requires 501, not available with 35J, 35K or 35L without 431 ($46). 521/B32 front floor mats, pair ($7). 522/B33 rear floor mats, pair ($6). 524 fitted trunk floor mats, included in 724 ($8). 531/A01 Soft-Ray tinted glass, all windows ($37). 532/A02 Soft-Ray tinted glass, windshield only ($30). 534/C49 electric rear window defroster ($62). 541/C50 rear window defogger, not available with electric rear window defroster ($31). 551/A31 power side windows, required with 431 ($113). 554/AU3 power door locks ($44). 582/C60 manual air conditioning ($397). 591/VJ9 California emission test requirements ($15). 601/WU3 hood air inlet, requires 34X ($56). 611/D80 rear air spoiler ($32). 614/D98 vinyl tape stripes, not available with 494 ($41). 634/K65 unitized ignition, required with 34X in Formula ($77). 664/Y92 convenience lamps ($11). 684/N65 Space Saver spare tire, without 474 or 478 ($13). 692/UA1 heavy-duty battery, not available with air conditioner ($10). 701/V01 heavy-duty radiator ($21). 714/U30 Rally gauges, clock and instrument panel tachometer, not available 718 or 722 ($92). 718/W63 Rally gauges and clock, not available with 722 ($46). 722/U35 electric clock ($15). 731 Custom trim group ($77). 731/V30 rear bumper guards ($25). SPS/W51 solid special paint, with vinyl top ($97). SPS/W51 solid special paint, without vinyl top ($113). SVT Cordova vinyl top ($87). TNL/YH99 Formula handling package ($87). TML/PL4 F70-14 raised white letter tires ($40 extra).

1972 TRANS AM

1972 Trans Am

Late in model year 1971, rumors were heard circulating around the auto industry in Detroit that the Pontiac Firebird and Chevrolet Camaro were going to disappear from the General Motors product lineup. "The General" was very close to dropping both models because sales wre down and it was getting expensive to build them. In the end, this did not happen because a number of enthusiasts who worked for Pontiac Motor Division fought very hard to keep both of the models alive. As it turned out, both cars turned out to be big successes.

So in the long run, the company was just as glad as the "Young Turks" at PMD that the kill order was rescinded. Still, PMD came very close to dropping the Firebird and as a result, very few styling changes were made for the model year. The 1972 Trans Am looked virtually identical to the 1971 model — which certainly wasn't a "bad" thing. It takes a real expert to tell the cars of the two model years apart from each other. There was a new honeycomb mesh grille insert, new interior trims, redesigned hubcaps and restyled wheel covers.

If you want to collect Trans Ams and you like the 1970-72 "Maseratiacs," the '72 is definitely a vintage to seek.

Only one V-8 engine was used in 1972 Trans Ams. It was the 455-cid HO version with the 4.15 x 4.21-inch bore and stroke. It wore a single four-barrel Rochester carburetor and had an 8.4:1 compression ratio. The engine developed 300 hp at 4000 rpm and 415 lbs.-ft. of torque at 3200 rpm. Trans Am buyers who preferred an automatic transmission could again substitute a three-speed Turbo Hydra-Matic for the Hurst-shifted close-ratio four-speed manual gearbox at no charge.

High Performance Cars magazine tested the same Lucerne

Blue 455 H.O. in two different states of tune in its September and October issues. The car had a four-speed gearbox and 3.42:1 rear axle. In stock trim it turned the quarter-mile in 14.58 seconds at 98 mph. For the later test it was tuned by Nunzi's Automotive, a Brooklyn, N.Y., Pontiac specialty shop. This upgrade resulted in a 14.04-second quarter-mile at 103.22 mph.

Model Number	Body/Style Number	Body Type & Seating	Factory Price	Shipping Weight	Production Total
TRANS AM — SERIES 2V — V-8					
2V	87	2d HT-5P	$4,256	3,564 lbs.	1,286

ENGINE

BASE V-8: Overhead valve. Cast-iron block. Bore and stroke: 4.15 x 4.21. Displacement: 455 cid. Compression ratio: 8.4:1. Net hp: 300 at 4000 rpm. Taxable hp: 55.20. Net torque: 415 at 3200 rpm. Five main bearings. Hydraulic valve lifters. Carburetor: Rochester four-barrel. VIN code: X.

OPTIONS

321/Y88 basic group includes AM radio with windshield antenna, Turbo Hydra-Matic transmission, standard size white sidewall tires, custom wheel trim rings and power steering (standard). 321/Y88 basic group includes AM/FM radio with windshield antenna, Turbo Hydra-Matic transmission, standard size white sidewall tires, custom wheel trim rings and power steering, on Trans Am only ($66). 361/G80 Safe-T-Track rear axle (standard). 368/G92 performance axle ($10). 401/U63 AM push-button radio with windshield antenna ($65). 403/U69 AM/FM radio and windshield antenna ($135). 405/U58 AM/FM stereo radio and windshield antenna, not available with rear seat speaker ($233). 411/U80 rear speaker ($18). 412/U57 stereo eight-track tape player ($130). 414/U55 cassette tape player, not available with U80 or U57 ($130). 424/D58 rear console ($26). 431/D55 front console, with floor shift only ($57). 432 recessed windshield wipers on 22387 and 22687 ($18). 441/D34 right-hand visor vanity mirror ($3). 442/D31 non-glare rearview mirror, included with 734 ($6). 444/D33 left-hand outside rearview mirror, remote-control type ($12). 451/AK1 custom seat belts ($15). 461/N30 custom cushion steering wheel ($15). 462/N31 custom sport steering wheel, included with 332 ($56). 492/B93 door edge guards ($6). 501/N41 variable-ratio power steering (standard). 502

front disc brakes (standard). 504 tilt steering wheel, requires 501, not available with 35J, 35K or 35L without 431 ($46). 521/B32 front floor mats, pair ($7). 522/B33 rear floor mats, pair ($6). 524 fitted trunk floor mats, included in 724 ($8). 531/A01 Soft-Ray tinted glass, all windows ($37). 532/A02 Soft-Ray tinted glass, windshield only ($30). 534/C49 electric rear window defroster, not available with six-cylinder or electric rear window defogger ($62). 541/C50 rear window defogger, not available with electric rear window defroster ($31). 551/A31 power side windows, required with 431 ($113). 554/AU3 power door

locks ($44). 582/C60 manual air conditioning ($397). 591/VJ9 California emission test requirements ($15). 634/K65 unitized ignition ($77). 664/Y92 convenience lamps ($11). 684/N65 Space Saver spare tire, without 474 or 478 ($13). 692/UA1 heavy-duty battery, not available with air conditioner ($10). 701/V01 heavy-duty radiator ($21). 714/U30 Rally gauges, clock and instrument panel tachometer ($92). 718/W63 Rally gauges and clock($46). 722/U35 electric clock ($15). 731 Custom trim group ($77). 731/V30 rear bumper guards ($25). TNL/YH99 Formula handling package ($87).

1972 LEMANS/LEMANS SPORT GTO 455

DOUG MITCHEL

1972 LeMans GTO

The General Motors A-body cars, including the Pontiac "LeMans" models, had been scheduled for a major overhaul for the 1972 model year, but a 1970 United Auto Worker strike upset the plan and only minor changes were possible for 1972 models." The GTO reverted to option status this year. It was no longer a separate series.

"The Judge" option package was gone. Engine choices were the same as in 1971, but gross horsepower ratings were not advertised.

The new code 334 GTO option package was available for the style number 2D37 LeMans hardtop coupe and the 2D27 LeMans two-door coupe. It included a 400-cid/250-net hp four-barrel V-8 with dual exhausts. The price of the GTO option package was $344 over base model costs.

A 1972 GTO hardtop with the 455 HO V-8 carried 13 lbs. per horsepower and its performance really suffered for it. It required 7.1 seconds to scoot from 0-to-60 mph and the quarter-mile took 15.4 seconds.

ENGINES

OPTIONAL V-8: Overhead valve. Cast-iron block. Bore and stroke: 4.15 x 4.21. Displacement: 455 cid. Compression ratio: 8.2:1. Net hp: 250 at 3600 rpm. Taxable hp: 55.20. Net Torque: 370 at 2400 rpm. Five main bearings. Hydraulic valve lifters. Carburetor: Rochester four-barrel. Dual exhaust. VIN code: Y.

OPTIONAL V-8: Overhead valve. Cast-iron block. Bore and stroke: 4.15 x 4.21. Displacement: 455 cid. Compression ratio: 8.4:1. Net hp: 300 at 4000 rpm. Taxable hp: 55.20. Net torque: 415 at 3200 rpm. Five main bearings. Hydraulic valve lifters. Carburetor: Rochester four-barrel. Dual exhaust. VIN code: X.

CHASSIS

Wheelbase: 112 in. Overall Length: 207.2 in. Width: 76.7 in. Height: 52.6 in. Front headroom: 38.5 in. Rear headroom: 37.1 in. Front legroom: 42.4 in. Rear legroom: 34.9 in. Front hiproom: 59.5 in. Rear hiproom: 59.1 in. Trunk capacity: 14.6 cu. ft. Turn circle: 38.6 ft. Front tread: 61 in. Rear tread: 61 in.

OPTIONS (PARTIAL LIST)

422 heavy-duty air cleaner ($9). 582 manual air conditioning ($397). 611 rear spoiler for LeMans coupe or two-door hardtop $46 (only two GTOs are known to have been built with this option, which was cancelled before the model year began). 368 performance axle ($10). 364 economy axle ($10). 361 Safe-T-Track differential with 37K or 37W axles ($45). 361 heavy-duty Safe-T-Track differential with 37K or 37W axle ($66). 691 Delco X Maintenance-Free battery and required with 455-cid four-barrel V-8s ($26). 692 heavy-duty battery, not available with Delco Maintenance-Free battery ($10). 451 Custom front and rear seat and front shoulder belts, in closed passenger cars ($15). 522 602 Endura styling option, standard with code 334 GTO package ($41). 591 California assembly line emission test ($15). 34W 455-cid four-barrel V-8, requires 35L Turbo Hydra-Matic transmission and dual exhausts, in GTO (standard). 34W 455-cid four-barrel V-8, requires 35L Turbo Hydra-Matic transmission and dual exhausts in Luxury LeMans ($154). 34X 455-cid H.O. four-barrel V-8 in base LeMans coupe or hardtop with GTO option ($134). Note: the 34X V-8v was included with the WW5 option. 531 all tinted glass ($42). 532 tinted windshield only ($30). 492 door edge guards ($6). 732 rear bumper guards ($5). 681 dual horns on base LeMans ($4). STT special two-tone paint ($152). RTT standard two-tone paint ($39). 514 pedal trim

Model Number	Body/Style Number	Body Type & Seating	Factory Price	Shipping Weight	Production Total
LEMANS GTO 455 FOUR-BARREL — SERIES 2D + RPO 334 — V-8					
2D	27	2d CPE-5P	$3,066	—	5
2D	37	2d HT-5P	$2,851	—	235
LEMANS GTO 455 H.O. FOUR-BARREL — SERIES 2D + RPO 334 — V-8					
2D	27	2d CPE-5P	$3,200	—	10
2D	37	2d HT-5P	$2,985	—	635

NOTE 1: Prices include base cost of 455-cid V-8.

PONTIAC

package on base LeMans ($5). 502 power front disc brakes, includes Wonder Touch power brakes ($68). 554 power door locks in two-door models ($44). 552 power door locks and seat back locks ($67). 561 4-Way power full bench seat ($77). 501 power steering ($113). 701 heavy-duty radiator, standard with air conditioning ($21). 401 AM push-button radio ($65). 403 AM/FM radio ($135). 405 AM/FM stereo radio ($233). 411 rear seat speaker in LeMans group with AM push-button radio or AM/FM stereo radio ($18). 412 stereo 8-track tape player, requires 401, 403 or 405 radio ($130). 414 stereo cassette tape player, requires 401, 403 or 405 radio ($130). 714 Rally Gauge Cluster with tachometer, includes electric clock ($82). 718 Rally Gauge Cluster and clock, not available with Rally Gauge Cluster with tachometer or 722 electric clock ($49). 571 front foam cushion ($8). 621 Ride & Handling package ($9). 473 wire wheel covers ($82). 473 wire wheel covers LeMans with Décor Grouop ($56). 478 honeycomb wheels with decor package ($62). 478 honeycomb wheels with décor package ($92). 474 Rally II wheel rims with Décor Group ($56). 474 Rally II wheel rims without Décor Group ($87). 471 chrome wheel trim rings ($26). 432 recessed windshield wipers ($18). 721 Décor Group including Custom cushioned steering wheel, deluxe wheel discs, wheel opening moldings, pedal trim package and hood rear edge molding without WW4, WW5 options or Custom trim group ($66). 721 Décor Group including Custom cushioned steering wheel, deluxe wheel discs, wheel opening moldings, pedal trim package and hood rear edge molding with WW4 option or Custom trim group ($35). 721 Décor Group ($20). 334 GTO option for LeMans two-door hardtop ($344). 724 handling package for base LeMans coupe or two-door hardtop with GTO option without WW4 or WW5 option ($186). 621 Ride & Handling package for standard LeMans coupe, required with GTO option ($4). 461 Custom cushion steering wheel in base LeMans ($15). 462 Custom Sport steering wheel in base LeMans without WW5 option and

without Décor Group ($56). 462 Custom Sport steering wheel in Luxury LeMans ($41). 462 Custom Sport steering wheel in base LeMans without WW5 option, but with Décor Group ($41). 464 Formula steering wheel in base LeMans without WW5 option and without Décor Group ($56). 464 Formula steering wheel in base LeMans without WW5 option and with Décor Group ($41). 464 Formula steering wheel in Luxury LeMans ($41). 504 tilt steering, requires power steering ($44). 614 vinyl stripes on LeMans two-door, not available with GT option or vinyl body side moldings ($31). SVT cordova top on LeMans group except convertible and Safari ($97). 35C heavy-duty three-speed manual transmission with floor shift in LeMans except with 350-cid two-barrel V-8 or 34S 400-cid four-barrel V-8 ($82). 35E four-speed manual transmission in LeMans with 350-cid two-barrel V-8 or 34S 400-cid four-barrel V-8 ($190). 35G heavy-duty close-ratio four-speed manual transmission in LeMans with 455-cid or 455-cid H.O. V-8 without WW4 ($231). 35G heavy-duty close-ratio four-speed manual transmission in LeMans with 455-cid or 455-cid H.O. V-8 with WW4 ($41). 35L Turbo Hydra-Matic in LeMans group, except with WW4, not available with 250-cid six-cylinder engine or 350-cid two-barrel V-8 ($236). 35L Turbo Hydra-Matic in LeMans group, with WW4, not available with 250-cid six-cylinder engine or 350-cid two-barrel V-8 ($46). Vinyl interior trim in LeMans two-door models ($27). 654 Custom Trim bucket seats in GTO ($160). 634 Unitized ignition system in LeMans two-door models with 455-cid H.O. V-8 ($77). 476 deluxe wheel covers for LeMans group, except with Custom Trim Group ($31). TPL G70-14 white letter tires on LeMans with V-8 ($77). TPL G70-14 white letter tires on LeMans and LeMans Sport with V-8 without air conditioning ($77). TPL G70-14 white letter tires on LeMans and LeMans Sport with V-8 and air conditioning ($63). TPL G70-14 white letter tires on GTO ($42). TRF G78-14 black sidewall tires on LeMans or LeMans Sport with V-8 engine and air conditioning ($14).

1972 GRAND PRIX SSJ 455

TOM GLATCH

1972 Grand Prix SSJ

It was the last year for the Hurst-made Grand Prix SSJ and only a few dozen cars got the special conversion. All Grand Prixs had Turbo Hydra-Matic transmissions and more than 90 percent of them had front bucket seats. The 1972 Hurst SSJ is very hard — in fact, near impossible — to find today. Hurst Performance Products Company had no record of producing any such cars, but some are claimed to exist. In their book *The Hurst Heritage*, Bob Lichty and Terry Boyce estimated that 60 examples of the 1972 Hurst SSJ were built. This estimate was based on an interview with a former company employee who recalled delivering about that many cars to Pontiac Motor Division for shipping. During the last year of production the cars were apparently built only with a dual-gate automatic transmission.

ENGINE

BASE V-8: Overhead valve. Cast-iron block. Bore and stroke: 4.15 x 4.21. Displacement: 455 cid. Compression ratio: 8.4:1. Net hp: 300 at 4000 rpm. Taxable hp: 55.20. Net torque: 415 at 3200 rpm. Five main bearings. Hydraulic valve lifters. Carburetor: Rochester four-barrel. VIN code:

SELECTED OPTIONS

Air conditioning ($397). Front seat console ($57). LeMans two-door hardtop and Sport convertible console ($59). Cruise Control ($62-$67). Deck lid remote control ($14). Electric rear window defroster ($62). All-windows Soft-Ray glass ($39-$49). Soft-Ray windshield ($30-$35). Auxiliary gauge panel for Catalina ($38). Bumper guards ($5-$15). Warning lamps ($21). Auxiliary lamp group ($18). Convenience lamp group ($11). Front disc brakes ($46-$68). Wonder Touch brakes ($44-$46). Power bench seats ($67-$77-$103). Power left bucket seat ($77). AM/FM Stereo and 8-Track ($363). Rally gauge cluster with clock and tachometer ($92). Honeycomb wheels ($62-$123). Rally II wheel rims ($56-$87). Dual exhaust ($40). Performance or economy ratio rear axles ($10). Safe-T-Track differential was $45 extra and heavy-duty Safe-T-Track was $66 extra. Heavy-duty batteries were $10-$15 extra and a Delco X battery was $26 extra.

Model Number	Body/Style Number	Body Type & Seating	Factory Price	Shipping Weight	Production Total
GRAND PRIX SSJ — SERIES K — V-8					
K	57	2-dr HT-5P	$5,617	3,898 lbs.	60